THE
GENTLEMAN
USHER

THE GENTLEMAN USHER

The Life and Times of

GEORGE DEMPSTER

(1732–1818)

Member of Parliament
and
Laird of Dunnichen and Skibo

by

JOHN EVANS

Pen & Sword
MILITARY

First published in Great Britain in 2005 by
Pen & Sword Military
an imprint of
Pen & Sword Books Ltd
47 Church Street
Barnsley
South Yorkshire
S70 2AS

ISBN 1 84415 151 4

A CIP catalogue record for this book is
available from the British Library

Typeset in Plantin by
Phoenix Typesetting, Auldgirth, Dumfriesshire

Printed and bound in England by
CPI UK

Pen & Sword Books Ltd incorporates the imprints of Pen & Sword
Aviation, Pen & Sword Maritime, Pen & Sword Military,
Wharncliffe Local History, Pen & Sword Select,
Pen & Sword Military Classics and Leo Cooper.

For a complete list of Pen & Sword titles please contact
PEN & SWORD BOOKS LIMITED
47 Church Street, Barnsley, South Yorkshire, S70 2AS, England
E-mail: enquiries@pen-and-sword.co.uk
Website: www.pen-and-sword.co.uk

For Gillie

CONTENTS

ILLUSTRATIONS

George Dempster by George Willison (1741–1797)
(McManus Galleries, Dundee City Council)

Adam Fergusson by Pompeo Battoni (1708–1787)
(Scottish National Portrait Gallery)

Grimur Jonsson Thorkelin by an unknown artist
(National Museum of Iceland)

James Boswell (1741–1797) by George Willison
(Scottish National Portrait Gallery)

Paste medallion of George Willison by James Tassie (1735–1799)
(Scottish National Portrait Gallery)

David Hume by Allan Ramsay (1713–1784)
(Scottish National Portrait Gallery)

The Rev John Jamieson by William Yellowlees (1796–1859)
(Scottish National Portrait Gallery)

Plaster bust of Professor Dr James Gregory by Samuel Joseph
(Scottish National Portrait Gallery)

Professor Joseph Black (1728–1799) by David Martin (1737–1798)
(In the collection of the Royal Medical Society, Edinburgh)

Engraving of Sir John Sinclair by William Skelton (1763–1848)
(National Portrait Gallery, London)

Rough sketches of George Dempster and (possibly) Sir John Sinclair
(University of Toronto, Thomas Fisher Rare Book Library)

John, 4th Duke of Atholl by John Hoppner (1758–1810)
(From the collection at Blair Castle, Perthshire)

William Smith (1756–1835) by Henry Thomson (1773–1843)
(Norwich Castle Museum and Art Gallery)

Three miniatures of Mrs Raffles, Mrs Dempster and (possibly) William
Soper Dempster by Nathaniel Plimer (1757– c.1822)
(Sotheby's Picture Library)

Engraving of the House of Commons in session by B.Cole *(floruit*
1720–1754)
(Parliamentary Estates Directorate)

Engraving of Lindley Hall, Leicestershire
(The Record Office for Leicestershire and Rutland)

A print of the Pont Royale at Orléans by Bougeard
(cl.R.Malnoury – Inventaire Général Centre, 1976, ADAGP)

Photograph of the Cotton Mill at Stanley
(Louis Flood Photographers)

A drawing of Caldecote Hall by Henry Jeayes *(floruit 1790–1800)*
(Birmingham City Archives, Aylesford Country Seats and Castles)

Engraving of Skibo Castle 1890
(W.A.Macdonald)

Plan and photograph of Spinningdale Mill, Dornoch Firth
(Royal Commission on the Ancient and Historical Monuments of Scotland)

Drawing of Dunnichen House in 1848
(Royal Commission on the Ancient and Historical Monuments of Scotland)

Photograph of Dunnichen House in 1925
(Whiteholme (Publishers) Ltd.)

Floor Plans of Dunnichen House
(Royal Commission on the Ancient and Historical Monuments of Scotland)

The interior of Dunnichen House in 1966
(Royal Commission on the Ancient and Historical Monuments of Scotland)

Engraving of the Sale Room at East India House by Pugin and Rowlandson
(Guildhall Library, Corporation of London)

Shipping off St Helena, an oil painting by Adam Callander (1750–1815)
(National Maritime Museum Greenwich)

A print of Alexander Dalrymple by George Dance (1741–1825)
(National Maritime Museum Greenwich)

A memorial to Jean Fergusson in Dunnichen Church
(Author's photograph)

The Excise cutter *Greyhound* under the command of Captain Wm.Watson
(Merseyside Maritime Museum)

Perry's Yard at Blackwall painted by Francis Holman (c.1729–1784)
(National Maritime Museum Greenwich)

The *Essex* East Indiaman in Bombay harbour
(National Maritime Museum Greenwich)

A fleet of East Indiamen at sea by Nicholas Pocock (1740–1821) in 1803
(National Maritime Museum Greenwich)

A print by Tomkins *(floruit* 1790–1799) of the Mast House on the Thames
(National Maritime Museum Greenwich)

An oil painting of the Mast House in Brunswick Dock by Wm.Daniell
(1769–1837)
(National Maritime Museum Greenwich – Green and Blackwall Collections)

An aquatint of Broughty Castle by William Daniell
(McManus Galleries, Dundee City Council)

A photograph of Telford's bridge over Dornoch Firth
(National Gallery of Scotland)

Professor Adam Ferguson by an unknown artist
after Sir Henry Raeburn
(Scottish National Portrait Gallery)

George Dempster in old age by J.T.Nairn
(Scottish National Portrait Gallery)

ACKNOWLEDGEMENTS

As someone who set fire to the bulk of his political correspondence, and many of his personal letters as well, so as to avoid an inexpert biographer's attention, George Dempster would have been surprised by the volume that still remains. He might have expected collections in Scotland and England to be cared for by their white-gloved keepers, but not perhaps for so many letters to find their resting place in the New World. Having taken part in debates at Westminster during the Seven Years War, and more frequently throughout the struggle for American independence, it would have seemed to him a little ironical that one library in Canada and two in the USA now acted as host to a large proportion of the total so far discovered. When it emerged that these collections contained fulsome correspondence with family, friends and employees in the case of the Thomas Fisher Rare Book Library (University of Toronto), and with such old friends as James Boswell and Sir William Pulteney in the case of the Beinecke Library (Yale University) and the Huntington Library, San Marino, California, Dempster would have been amazed. I am sure that he, like me, would have wanted to acknowledge the care and assistance given during the five years of my research as well as their kind permission to publish extracts from the collections. In the case of Yale, additional thanks would have been forthcoming for permission from the Editorial Committee of the Yale Editions of the Private Papers of James Boswell to dip into their cornucopia. The gift from Toronto of a microfilm of his letters (and those of George Soper Dempster) to Inverness Reference Library would also have been warmly applauded on behalf of Scotland. But these ironies continue. Even India, second only to America among his global attentions, was home to archival material relative to his half-brother's affairs, and the assistance of the Director of Archives (Government of Maharashtra) helped unlock some of the actions of the Honourable East India Company in Mumbai.

So far as British collections are concerned I would particularly like to thank the staffs of the British Library for material from the Oriental & India Office and Western manuscript collections, the National Archives (Kew), the National Archives of Scotland, the National Library of Scotland, the university libraries of Aberdeen, Edinburgh, Glasgow and St Andrews, together with city archives and libraries in Birmingham, Dundee, Perth, and Sheffield for copies of manuscripts and their permission to publish extracts. Other owners who also kindly consented to publication include the Viscount Thurso (for the Thurso Papers), Major John J.Graham (the Graham of Fintry papers), Mr Richard D.S.Head (Bland Burges papers), the Head of Leisure Services Sheffield City Council (2nd Marquis of Rockingham and Edmund Burke's papers), the Governors of Dulwich College, the History of Parliament Trust (Dempster's parliamentary biography written by Edith, Lady Haden-Guest), Mrs Elizabeth Boyle (the late Dr Iain Boyle's archive), and the Blair Charitable Trust, Blair Castle. A special word of appreciation is due to Sir Charles Fergusson of Kilkerran. The republication in 2004 of the *Letters of George Dempster to Sir Adam Fergusson 1756–1813* edited in 1934 by his father Sir James, 8th Bart., is particularly welcome.

Archivists and others whose assistance was especially appreciated include Mrs Jane Anderson at Blair Castle and Mr I.V.Wright of H.M.Customs & Excise, along with dedicated officers working for local authorities in Devon, Dundee, Angus, Perth & Kinross, Birmingham, Warwickshire and Westminster, together with the Royal Bank of Scotland. Advice from the Scottish Agricultural College, Cosar Limited, Thomasina Mackay (Mackay & Co) and the Courtauld Institute of Art was invaluable. Others whose careful research was greatly valued, not least in helping to minimize errors of fact or interpretation, include Mrs Prue Stokes, a descendant of the Dempster family, Mr Amol Divkar in Mumbai, Charles Rowland in Canada, Gordon Turnbull in the USA, Russell Malloch and Dr Andrea Duncan.

Those galleries, organizations and individuals kindly permitting their illustrations to appear in the book include Archives Départementales du Loiret, France, Birmingham City Archives, Blair Castle, Perthshire, Sir Charles Fergusson, Guildhall Library the Corporation of London, Record Office for Leicestershire, Leicester and Rutland County Council, Louis Flood Photographers, Merseyside Maritime Museum, National Maritime Museum, Greenwich, National Portrait Gallery, London, National Museum of Iceland, Norwich Castle Museum and Art Gallery, Parliamentary Estates Directorate, Royal Commission on the Ancient and Historical Monuments of Scotland, Royal Medical Society Edinburgh, Sotheby's London, Scottish National Portrait Gallery, Whiteholme Publishers Ltd.

Every attempt has been made to obtain the permission of copyright holders for the inclusion of extracts from works, illustrations and manuscripts used in the book. It has required lengthy effort and if, by any chance, I have failed to obtain and record my appreciation to any copyright holder, I can only offer my sincerest apologies. Some small extracts have been deemed not to be an infringement of copyright law but it is hoped that all others have been acknowledged.

Very special thanks are due to Norman Newton and his colleagues in the Reference Library of the Highland Council and its Library Support Unit in Inverness. Their diligence and quiet determination was inimitable and Norman, an author himself, never gave up, nor accepted the occasional excuse that material could not be released from vaults in the south or elsewhere, or despatched to the wilds of the Highlands. To Jim Henderson, the erstwhile editor of the *The Northern Times*, goes the honour of inadvertantly introducing me to my publisher whose team, including Brigadier Henry Wilson, Barbara Bramall and Tom Hartman, have had an enormous influence for good – on me and the book. Finally, I want to acknowledge the debt I owe, firstly, to Jim Bell, President of Dornoch Heritage Society until his death in June 2004, who was the inspirational source for my work and who so much wanted there to be a record of Dempster's achievements. Margaret Christie deserves a mention in despatches for her work transcribing several hundreds of photo-copied manuscripts, and last but not least, Gill, my wife and senior amanuensis, who added several bars to her existing medals for patience and support well beyond the call of duty.

INTRODUCTION

George Dempster – the Man

Robert Burns described Dempster as a 'true blue Scot' – a man warmly applauded in his day for his patriotism as well as a deep humanity, integrity and benevolence. He sat at the feet of philosophers and great leaders of thought during Scotland's golden 'Age of Enlightenment' and spent half his life in the cockpit of politics at a time when wars across the continents of America, India and Europe were the backdrop to great scientific, literary and artistic achievement, as well as marked social and economic change. Instead of achieving the high political office he had hoped for, or the recognition gained by his more illustrious compatriots, Dempster became a remarkable reformer and innovator who played a significant part in expanding agricultural and manufacturing industry for the benefit of his tenants and constituents – never losing the common touch for which he was universally known. His exertions in parliament between 1761 and 1790 were followed by what he called, a 'Highland pilgrimage' – aptly summed up in the opening words of his *Bragadocio* (*sic*):

> 'I who erst saved the Highlanders from want
> and taught them how to plough, to build and to plant,
> attacked the feudal dragon in his den,
> and of his slaves made valiant men'

Dempster has become little more than a footnote in 18th century Scottish history. His name still crops up quite frequently among today's biographies and other texts but rarely more than as a passing reference. Rather surprisingly, he probably would not have objected to being remembered in this way. It took him many years to discover that such ambition as he had was 'a very false kind' and that he possessed 'neither the head nor heart of a truly ambitious man'.[1]* As he told Edmund Burke, fame held little attraction for him :

---

* See Notes, p 327 et seq.

'If I were a rich man I should much like to be the *maitre d'hotel* to men of learning and genius, but that not being the case, I must content myself with being their Gentleman Usher and introducing them to one another'.[2]

The firm place Dempster held in Scottish hearts stemmed from the influence he exercised in the many public offices he held, his endless and spirited correspondence, and the pleasure he gave to those who were so warmly entertained at his home in Forfar. His integrity, charm and altruism became bywords in the corridors of power and among those in the scientific and literary world. A self-appointed 'usher', he 'ventured to introduce' many modest men who were either strangers to the ways of London or who needed assistance of some sort or other. He nurtured many of the reforms that gained wider acceptance in the 19th century and his enormous energy and humanity inspired all who came into touch with him.

Born fourteen years before the Battle of Culloden, he had a happy childhood and an education befitting the eldest son of a gentleman. Schooling in Dundee was followed by studies at university in St Andrews. However, in 1753, when Dempster was in Edinburgh qualifying as a lawyer, his grandfather, who had been the dominant influence in his life, died. Then, only a year later, his father was killed in an accident. With sufficient, if not a great, income from the estates he inherited in Angus, he became the head of the family at the early age of 23 and spent much of the next five years in Edinburgh in the convivial company of friends, eminent philosophers and *literati* who collectively contributed so much to life in the capital.

Beyond the possibility of practising law as an advocate, Dempster had no pre-determined destiny. Becoming a merchant in the family tradition had evidently been ruled out and, although the abrupt loss of parental influence enabled him to widen his choice of a career, his friends concluded that he would stay in Edinburgh. Had he spoken about taking a seat in the House of Commons in the hearing of either his father or grandfather they would have 'cast their eye' towards his younger brother and put his 'estate beyond human reach'. Politics had been a world of 'Bedlam' in the Dempster household.[3] A life in and around the Scottish courts had its attractions, especially as he greatly enjoyed the vibrant Edinburgh society of the time, but it was a world from which only the most brilliant could break loose and Westminster beckoned. Law was not only 'the best school for acquiring eloquence' Dempster considered, but the 'best education for a legislator'.[4]

The family's deprecatory view of politics was not without foundation. Unlike members of parliament from English constituencies, Scottish MPs were rarely leaders in their communities with any demonstrable social status. Malleable or inconsequential figures were often selected by the aristocracy to do their bidding – lobby-fodder used to protect personal or sectional interests.

The corrupt state of the franchise eased the path of the ruthless. Intellectually well-endowed, and used to mixing with the great and the good in Scotland, Dempster was nevertheless strangely ill-equipped for the life he chose. He possessed the gregariousness and self-confidence of a young gentleman about town but hardly the wealth or connections so useful if not essential in parliament.[5] The posturing and ingratiation he encountered during his first election campaign in 1761, and the use made of bribery, seem to have come as a surprise. Half-promises of favour and any nods or winks that the price would be worth paying, soon evaporated. Those who gave them had been 'empty friends of a day'.[6] His friend James Boswell arrived in London in a 'flutter of joy' and Dempster, anticipating a continuation of Edinburgh's 'rational and honest kind of society'[7] which he so much enjoyed, soon found that it was absent in the south. For someone of his means and disposition the metropolis of London presented a daunting and rather lonely prospect.

Unlike one future Lord Chancellor (Thomas Erskine) who made a fortune at the bar, but who was crushed by his first appearance in the Commons, Dempster spoke 'with an assurance that . . . gave great entertainment' in the debate on the Address, catching the tone of the House almost immediately. He, nevertheless, used the occasion to 'condemn faction' and made it clear how much he disliked patronage.[8] It was a manifestation of much to come. He was often to exercise his strong independent spirit in a House of Commons ruled by alliances and personal favours. The first parliament saw him loosely attached to the opposition – a motley assemblage of usually disunited Whigs from the aristocracy. His 'proverbial candour' and non-confrontational, well-ordered speeches commanded a respect which led some to think he might be destined for high office. At times restive, and uncertain of where to put his weight, he became involved with the Honourable East India Company, and in his constituency he took a part in the affairs of town councils – launching his own bank to encourage local trade.

With few influential friends, aloof from party allegiances and a stranger to London society, he was unable to make the best of his promising start. He also allowed himself to be conjured into a wild life of boyish tricks. Aware of Lord Auchinleck's chilling disapproval of his son, he befriended the uncertain, raw young Boswell as a way of helping him prove he was not the weak-minded wastrel his father then feared. A riotous association with Boswell and 'Dash' Erskine, two men eight years his junior, did little to help his cause. Instead of cultivating the friendship of this lonely, extravagant scribbler, a colourful affair with a society hostess might have done Dempster's reputation more good.

Soon after his 'salad days' as a bachelor in London he came to accept that his brand of parliamentary behaviour discouraged intermittent Whig administrations from offering him any 'lucrative office'. The disastrous election campaign in 1768 not only reduced his already meagre finances and caused him to re-think his role at Westminster, but with the death of Rockingham, from whom he received one pensionable post, the door to political advancement closed.

As ten administrations came and went during a 29-year life in politics he was rarely silent. During the 1768–1774 parliament he spoke 193 times – more than most opposition members with the exception of Edmund Burke. To Dempster's credit, the House of Commons never lost patience with him, even when debates such as those on India and Lord North's American policies produced great crescendos of rhetoric, high drama and bitter controversy. Several times, however, he was forced to admit that a place in parliament could be 'a seat on thorns and rusty nails'[9] where the 'self-interested principles upon which . . . public men . . . act destroys much of the satisfaction'.[10] Only his work for other non-governmental bodies, particularly the British Fisheries Society, provided relief. He grew to measure the behaviour and policies of successive administrations by reference, first and foremost, to their legality. His careful harrying was on occasions turned to good advantage and he was always mindful of the way he presented his case at Westminster; he was in the most powerful court in the land.

Few of Dempster's opponents admitted that a case could be made out, even occasionally, for 'casuistry in politics as well as religion and morals'.[11] A lively conscience could certainly not be allowed to dominate. The difficulty lay in the 'glaring contradictions' in a system which required members of parliament to be 'independent men and men of influence' at the same time.[12] To overcome this, he seems to have set out during the 1770s to consolidate his personal power base in his constituency, becoming admired and supported in a way that few members were. A common touch and easy approachability gave him influence that cost little. 'The only way of settling the matter,' Dempster said, was 'to ask little favours for my friends of any of the group of ministers that I stand nearest to, just as I should do a pin or a pinch of snuff, and let the higher duties of my station be as little affected by the one as the other'. Although depressed about his debts for a decade before his marriage, and with his confidence at a low ebb, he became 'a thorn in the flesh of easy-going ministers and dilatory officials'.[13] Rather than 'sink his individual judgement in a party policy',[14] and protect only the interests of the handful of voters that were his electors, he became perhaps Scotland's first 'constituency MP'.

He played as full a part in the affairs of the Perth Burghs, his constituency, as his other duties allowed, and represented his constituents energetically and honestly, applying his peculiar brand of legal and humane scrutiny to the small as well as the great national and constitutional issues of the day. He was liked for being a people's representative in parliament as numerous civic presentations testified. At Kelvingrove he was feted by workers as a 'guardian of their manufactures' and even the owner of a Montrose whaler named his vessel the *George Dempster*.[15] Moreover, he easily adjusted to the contrasts of public life. Despite representing burghs with primarily industrial problems, his affinity with country life made him particularly sensitive to the needs of rural communities. Having one day witnessed the high drama at Westminster over the nation's loss of her colonies in America, the next would see him battling against unfair and damaging taxes imposed on hawkers and peddlers who were the lifeline of people in isolated communities. As Sir Nathaniel Wraxall said in his *Memoirs* 'he was one of the most conscientious men who ever sat in parliament'.

Always constrained by the 'rigid system of politics',[16] he might have retreated northwards had it not been for the effect his marriage had on his strength of purpose. Instead, withdrawal from Westminster was delayed by more than 20 years, and the middle period of Dempster's life became a personal quest to justify his beliefs. His canvas even broadened as he concentrated more of his energies in Scotland. He was an extraordinary Scot; a 'mover and shaker' of moderate means, a visionary ahead of his time, who, despite his many failings, was uniquely suited to the task of entrepreneurship. Being only too aware that without manufacturing innovation many of his constituents would lose their livelihood, he encouraged a host of ideas and inventions. He fought against rigid authority exercised not only by the nation's leaders in London but parochially in Scotland. Arguing the rightfulness of self-determination for the American colonists, or the need for Britain to consider allowing India to govern itself, were as much part of his gentle philosophy as encouraging more enlightened capitalism among the Scottish land-owning plutocracy. Better use of the land became a priority with him. The inability of landlords to realize that change could produce greater wealth only spurred him to campaign for a gradual approach to greater democracy and personal self-determination.

He was never a firebrand, revolutionary or socialist and Robert Owen's co-operative socialism would have left him cold. But, like many visionaries, he was impatient with the pace of change. He learned his sympathetic capitalist creed from reading and discussing David Hume's and Adam Smith's works with prestigious members of the Select Society and later at meetings of the Poker Club. The inspirational climate in Edinburgh provided a forum that encouraged frank and open exploration of every possible political, social and economic change. Such objectivity and everyday pragmatism were always uneasy bedfellows. His high principles were challenged during his time with the East India Company, but he rarely gave ground about the sanctity of the Company's charter or the laws that underwrote the British constitutional monarchy. On the right occasion he dared to speak the unspeakable and took part in all the major debates of the day. Like Burke, he believed that men had to be governed by laws they loved, whether they were New England colonists, Indian traders or Highland crofters.

All his life India was to be the source of untold expectation which turned to deepest despair. When he first became a shareholder and member of the Court of Proprietors in the East India Company it complemented his parliamentary role, added to his chances of preferment, and anyway seemed a rock-solid investment. The Company was integral to the nation's fiscal and investment life and had long been the subject of great pride by the general populace. Brave feats of arms and the presence of returning 'nabobs' and successful merchants captured the country's imagination. To the common man it was a magical world. It was a club where its members had the honour (as many saw it) to exercise influence over the pattern of eastern trade and the company's profit- ability. By this time, however, powerful groups of stockholders had begun to have grandiose ideas about their roles. As Chatham was to say, the 'riches of Asia . . . poured in . . . and brought with them not only Asiatic luxury but . . . Asiatic principles of government. Without connections . . . the importers of foreign gold . . . forced their way into parliament by a torrent of private corruption'.[17]

Unfortunately Dempster allowed himself to be embroiled in the defence of a shrewd and totally unscrupulous practitioner in the art of money-making who had been dismissed by the Company after amassing a fortune of around £300,000. Self-interest rather than the good of the Company had become widespread and powerful factions fought for influence. Dempster's support for those who were far from being the saints he thought they were was not to his advantage. Instead of devoting his energies to supporting Chatham and then Lord North's efforts to bring the Company to heel, Dempster's ten-year tenure of office, first as proprietor and then as a director, was a time when he was never far from all manner of discreditable actions. Until 1773 when he disqualified himself as a director so as to be able to speak more freely in the House, and left the machinations of Leadenhall Street for good, Dempster always hoped he could help resolve the constitutional differences between Calcutta and London and close the gap between the antagonists in parliament and the East India Company. In the circumstances, his efforts were dashed as much by the failure of the Company to defend its birthright as the endemic stubbornness and inept decisions taken by successive governments. He watched the loss of one empire in America and the erosion of another, power- lessly fretting over both.

From the moment he decided to go into politics, money was never far from Dempster's mind: 'The impropriety of continuing in parliament with so small a fortune as mine frequently comes across me'.[18] For thirty years, from the time of his first election campaign in 1761 when he incurred 'expenses' well above the average, the funds available to him rose and fell regularly, causing him to be without hope of ever having the wherewithal to continue in his chosen career. A dangerous overhang of debt was not uncommon and living beyond one's income tended to be brushed off by those with little principle. In Dempster's case, it was certainly neither an expensive life-style nor a penchant for gaming that led to his embarrassment. The rot set in when he sought re-election in 1767 and bribery charges were laid against him. Although 'vague and uncertain' and eventually dismissed, the sums he carelessly dispensed, and the ruinous legal fees that piled up after hearings in the court in Edinburgh and the House of Lords in London, added up to the huge sum of £30,000. By the early 1770s he was 'justly reckoned poor'[19] and it was to be a long time before he was able to recover from this nadir. Only by selling the greater part of his patrimonial inheritance – always a source of great humiliation – was order restored for a time. Subsequent 'highs', brought about by unexpected legacies and the exploitation of marl at Restenneth, and 'lows' occasioned by the failure of investments, were only slowly equalized by the profits made by his half-brother's 'private trade' as an East India Company captain. It was surprising that he was ever able to achieve what he did, his fortitude and resilience notwithstanding.

Unwise, if not reckless, spending on behalf of his friends added to the cost of barely maintaining himself in London. The 'slippery slope ever downward' of bribery and his 'generosity of spirit' coalesced. He rashly answered too many cries for help, many from grossly over-confident investors. Too simple a trust in others and a tendency to underestimate costs, which was to remain with him all his life, led him to court serious trouble. As he later admitted, he was never able to digest Bacon's advice about getting out of money troubles in a measured way, making time to avoid further risks, and acquiring 'frugal and parsimonious habits'.[20]

Had it not been for William Pulteney, whose wife succeeded to the estates of Lord Bath in 1767, making him one of the wealthiest men in the country, Dempster might have lived an obscure life as an impoverished Angus laird. A solid and 'unflashy' expert in the art of parsimony, Pulteney became his benefactor over more than 25 years.[21] He stood security for several important loans, including those associated with the purchase of Skibo in Sutherland, performing a unique role in rebuilding Dempster's life. Their close friendship and partnership in the House was amply demonstrated by the 50 or more letters he wrote to him. Dempster would have liked to have been the banker Pulteney became; he was 'a great model for emulation'.[22]

Dempster's friendships were as eclectic as his interests. There were those whom he came to know while studying law in Edinburgh and others with whom he worked during his days as a director of the British Fisheries Society. A few were his neighbours in Angus. Many became partners and managers in developments with which he became involved, and a galaxy of philosophers, scientists, clergy, poets, artists and wordsmiths were entertained at Dunnichen House. Close to the centre of political life for more than a generation, there were few great names unknown to him or he to them. He had many friends in and out of parliament, but few of the aristocracy found a place in this circle.

The contribution each made to the development of his ideas was revealed in the correspondence Dempster conducted with them. Sir Adam Fergusson stands out as his oldest friend. Despite their very different personalities, his unremitting penchant for legal niceties made him a good intellectual sparring partner and someone on whom Dempster could sometimes try out his ideas. They especially enjoyed unpicking the great political knots of the day. The warmest of personal relationships, born of the happy times they spent together in their youth, did, however, undergo subtle changes when Dempster found he could talk more freely to newer friends, and even business acquaintances. Furthermore, when the two families were brought together by marriage, it did not cement their friendship as closely as might have been expected. An enthusiasm for investments that his sober and unadventurous friend feared were nothing less than unwise indulgences and differences of opinion about the education of Dempster's nephew did not help. Both men did nevertheless continue to share much together, although Dempster's regular New Year missives and light-hearted verse his friend always found hard to bear.

Among his Angus neighbours, Robert Graham of Fintry and James Guthrie of Craigie (the son of his earliest solicitor) were two good friends, a twenty-year correspondence with the former showing him to be a particularly intimate confidant. Men like Francis Humberstone Mackenzie of Seaforth and Sir John Sinclair, whose dedication to improving their estates despite personal disabilities and lack of money in the one case and a self-imposed task of mammoth proportions in the other, attracted his great respect. Parliamentarians such as William Smith were as natural friends as James Richardson, the fish merchant whose fortune was made by Dempster's ideas and who was mentioned in his will. Business acquaintances and those whose support he needed in Sutherland – George Macintosh, a colleague of David Dale, and Kenneth Mackay – became valued friends, often being told more about his affairs than others closer to him.

Outside the House of Commons Dempster was in demand on numerous committees and boards as the result of the energy and close attention he gave to all he did. They valued the attention he gave to 'expenditure of public money which ministers (were) apt to exceed in'. His record of achievement with ideas also became common knowledge. He was for ever on the look out for details of 'good practice', constantly asking travellers how the farthest reaches of the continent responded to problems of employment and wealth creation. His devotion to practical solutions persuaded those of genius in the scientific as well as the literary world to take him seriously. Faced with an expert on space heating, the design of lighthouses, watermills for the cotton and linen industry, foreign practice of economics, statistics, land or crop management, constitutional law and legal precepts, to say nothing of Icelandic studies or etymological origins, his intellect would be immediately engaged. He could cajole and enlist the support of men like Professor Joseph Black, Rodolphe Raspe, Richard Arkwright, James Watt and Thomas Telford, entertain Grimur Thorkelin and Dr Jamieson, and learn from his acquaintance with Andrew Bell and William Wilberforce. Firm friendships emerged, and whether he questioned the size of the market for kelp or sought to know why His Majesty's navy did not copper bottom its ships his curiosity was endless.

It was as a landlord and agricultural reformer that he was most widely known. Towards the end of his first term in parliament he told Burke he was 'a farmer, and a very serious one',[23] but it was not until after his marriage that he had time to consider in any detail how better husbandry might be achieved and his own generally poor land improved. Until then his factor probably had a free hand. He was fortunate in discovering a rich course of marl and, subsequently, deep deposits of minute shells on the bed of a nearby loch. Then worth £200 a year, they were destined to contribute five times that amount to his income. He went on to show that his grasp of agricultural science was as keen as that of law, economics or social policy, learning in the process that better drainage, fencing, crop rotation, afforestation and all-round management, as well as the application of lime – that 'universal mineral' – enriched both the ground *and* the farmer. Well on in a long life he sponsored the Lunan and Vinney Farming Society and attended its meetings until he was over eighty.

Many of his forbears among 'improvers' from the 17th century onwards succeeded in altering the social conditions of the poor for the better. Dempster's contribution differed in several respects. His quest for increased wealth among farmers and their tenants was due to the belief that freedom inspired action. It produced its own reward rather than being the result of the uniform passion 'to better his condition' that Adam Smith believed every man possessed. He did, however, share the gospel that men were not put on the earth to plunder its riches and that economic progress was necessary if hope was to inspire and greater prosperity be able to drive the poor forward. With his practical help, those who lived in Dunnichen, Letham or the Highlands could control their own destiny.

Emigration, which so frequently followed poor harvests, famine and attempts at resettlement, only compounded Dempster's belief that if settlers could adjust to the difficult conditions they found in the backwoods of America, then the offer of land and increased security of tenure would have the same effect at home. He promulgated the abolition of 'personal services' to landlords by tenants, arguing that neither party benefited from such feudal anachronisms and sought the introduction of rents fixed by mutually-agreed arbitrators which could not be altered. The provision for heirs to inherit tenancies and an absence of rent where tenants reclaimed waste land, coupled with the building of good sound houses and the payment of premiums to the most progressive farmers, were all part of the novel practices he encouraged: 'Peep in upon Dunnichen, and if you find one of the evils I have enumerated . . . the barony shall be yours'.[24] Constant attention was paid to the introduction of new crops, grain, vegetables and fruit. Never one to do anything by halves, he battled incessantly for parallel improvements in the transport infrastructure – roads, bridges, ferries and jetties – as well as the provision of schools and churches.

He was in a long line of village developers, firstly working to bring the British Fisheries Society's projects into being, on and beyond the west coast, then at Stanley and finally at Letham close to his home at Dunnichen. Rising populations meant that it became increasingly difficult to find work in rural areas. The 'village' became a market-place, a localized place of employment and exchange. With towns regarded as 'sinks of iniquity', he was one of a handful of lairds who wanted to find constructive work for the unemployed, recognizing that only fisheries and the textile industry provided much scope.

As a member of parliament for burghs steeped in the long tradition of the linen industry, and whose interests he represented, it was natural that he should have admired the achievements of Richard Arkwright. The 'ingenious manufacturer of cotton yarn', as the *Glasgow Mercury* called him, was famed for his spinning frame and the mills that sprang up in Nottingham, Manchester and Derbyshire. Not for the first time was the livelihood of spinners in his constituency threatened and, never one to resist change once it had been clearly demonstrated, Dempster allied his interest with that of the Duke of Atholl and local linen producers to ensure that Scottish industry kept abreast of its competitors.

He was to remain a shareholder in the Stanley mill for fifteen years, long after he committed himself and other Glasgow investors to replicating such manufacturing in Sutherland, albeit on a smaller scale. Had he divested himself of his shares in Stanley when the first misfortunes were encountered he would have avoided what he called the 'heaviest' financial loss he ever experienced.[25] However doubtful about the wisdom of a substantial holding he was, coming at a time when there was a prospect of his acquiring a second estate in Sutherland, it was his first personal investment in a business (other than his Dundee Bank more than twenty years before) undertaken without external pressure. It was to teach him not only something about the day-to-day running of a mill but much about how easily blunders by management could occur. More significantly, he realized that his concept of an industrial 'village' differed from the more traditional approach.

At Spinningdale in Sutherland he was able to avoid superior patronage as he valiantly attempted to create employment on his own terms. Depending on another 'Highland patriot' to provide the much-needed direction, he backed George Macintosh to the hilt but never risked the amount of money he and his friend Graham of Fintry lost at Stanley. He rightly anticipated the social and economic consequences that cotton spinning would have on traditional work patterns, if not the consequences the ending of the war with Napoleon would bring, but only at Letham where the growing of flax and the spinning of yarn was in the blood did the linen industry flourish. There, the community spirit of his 'new' village where more than 350 came to be employed was maintained throughout the 19th century.

Such cohesion as the Dempster family had in the years before 1774 was transformed by George's marriage. The number of those for whom he had a filial duty after the death of his father had been reduced by the deaths of his older sister Peggy and half-brother Charles (in 1764 and 1772 respectively) whilst his other half-brother John, had gone to sea as an ordinary seaman in 1769. After twenty years of bachelorhood, two relatives of his father's generation (David Willison and Thomas Blair), his remaining brothers (Patrick and John) and three (if not four) unmarried sisters all in their thirties would have each concluded that few changes in the household were likely. Instead, with his debts paid off, the size of the estate halved, and the laird in possession of 'a cheerful country wife',[26] the family suddenly had a new sense of unity and purpose. The prospect of it falling apart faded. Dunnichen at last became a family haven for his siblings and, with no children of his own, he became the father figure to an extended family made up of nieces and nephews and their children. Poignant tragedies were to follow, but the care and affection which he and Rosie lavished on them during 36 years of married life never faltered.

Dempster's half-brother had been born to his father's second wife. 'Jack', as he was known to the family, was eighteen years his junior and, without more than a general education, he made up what he lacked in social polish with much intrinsic merit, courage and determination. Their relationship was slow to develop. They had been the product of different mothers and sometimes it seemed they did not share the same father, a man who had spent much of his life in his own father's shadow. Dempster had helped fit Jack out in his 4th mate's uniform in 1772, but his subsequent service aboard non-EIC vessels suggests that he made no call on him in the intervening years. Only when he was given his first command aboard the *Ganges* at the end of 1781 did the friendship that was to be so pivotal begin in earnest.

Captain John Hamilton Dempster's surprising marriage into the great Ayrshire family of the Fergussons in 1785, where George Fergusson (later Lord Hermand) and Sir David Dalrymple (Lord Hailes) were but two of Sir Adam Fergusson's relatives, became the turning-point in their relationship. Dempster felt it was an alliance that aptly consolidated his friendship with Sir Adam. Whatever doubts there had been about the captain's suitability as a husband for his friend's sister were swept away when Jean gave birth to a son and heir. This event and the captain's life-style had the effect of confirming his intention to leave Westminster, rebuild the family's fortunes and devote more time to his own interests. The incubus of uncertain finances would, he thought, be lifted by the wealth the captain would bring back from his journeys to India and China, and he would eventually become the enlightened laird and partner with Dempster.

As his young nephew George, the 'apple of his eye', grew up, the two men became staunch friends and it looked as if the gamble he had taken in buying a second estate at Skibo would pay off. Initially, three voyages in command of the *Rose* after 1787, and a total of three and a half years at sea, put a severe strain on his young wife and the family. Harrowing experiences were common during such journeys and the lack of news, rumours of disasters and threats of war meant that expectations waxed and waned with every tide. Dempster hoped that so long as there was the slightest chance that Jack and Jean could be at ease as the owners of the Sutherland estate he handed over to them, and that their occasional occupancy of Skibo when he was not at sea would encourage this end. It was an aim well worth pursuing. In 1793, when the Captain finally decided to give up his seafaring life, the relief was palpable. For five years the captain put his back into his new work, only being forced to return to sea when Jean died suddenly after barely a dozen years of married life. Two more deaths soon followed, leaving Dempster disconsolate and his high hopes in ruins.

As the new century opened, William Soper, who had been a civil servant with the East India Company for 20 years, married the captain's natural daughter. The warmth of affection Dempster had for Harriet was transferred with equal generosity to William and in turn to their four daughters and one son, yet another George. Their ten-year life together produced some consolation for Dempster, but by the time Harriet, and his wife Rosie, died in 1810 he was already in his seventies and unable to continue the struggle for the family's survival. His stoical-Christian belief and the good sense of his favourite Scottish philosopher, David Hume, ensured his equilibrium in these last years and he always remained cheerful, serenely 'playing golf, whist and the fool'.[27]

The picture of the women in Dempster's life, provided intermittently by the almost wholly male correspondence of the day, is one of devoted young mothers bringing up as many as eight children, and bearing, as in the case of Harriet, five in the short space of six years. Few had long lives; to survive, those who travelled out to India in search of husbands as well as wives who shared the rigours of a limited social life in pestilent conditions, had to be of hardy stock. The outlook for those who remained at home was only marginally better. Loyal, intelligent and hard-working gentlewomen easily fell prey to the rampant diseases of the period, even with the amount of childcare provided. Consumption, about which little was known, was to prove a deadly enemy to the Dempster family. Medical advice about the benefits of the good Devonian air resulted in more than one belated and fatal sojourn at Exmouth. Dempster's sister Helen, who lived until 1831, and his wife were two of the exceptions. Both were to be a stabilizing influence.

Rosie had been born of English colonial stock in the West Indies and, although her husband's claim that 'her last distemper was her first'[28] was an obvious exaggeration, her constitution, fortitude and constant good humour made her an incomparable companion throughout their long married life. She had not been the rich widow who had 'sown her wild oats in her first husband's fields'.[29] Instead she was a loving partner, sixteen years younger than Dempster, who was able to understand the younger generation in the family to whom she was devoted. Rosie continually renewed his resolve at times of great desolation. It was to her credit that he became the intensely family man for which many remembered him. Never happier than with 'babbies' around him or relishing boisterous games, he still found time away from his library, constant letter writing and intellectual pursuits to be with his closest family, and those who had become its extended members, beside the fireside at Dunnichen House.

Dempster was the subject of portraits by such artists as Willison, Copley, Opie, Nairn and possibly Gainsborough. They showed his self-evident composure in an unstylized manner but little of the humour and the natural *joie de vivre* that so possessed him. His language and manner captivated those who knew him as a handsome young man in a 'laced coat and powdered wig' or one more portly in old age who still played golf, continued to over-indulge his use of snuff, and whose appearance mattered less. As one anonymous writer said, 'The expression of his countenance and the tone of his voice announced the sincerity and sensibility of his heart'. Rarely, if ever, did he rely on a show of gravitas. In parliament he was always heard 'with singular and unrivalled attention'.[30] Burns referred to 'Dempster's zeal-inspired tongue'.[31] He could switch easily from a Westminster style of speech, with its mixture of delicate precision, to an argot of amusing and descriptive phraseology all his own. This did not prevent him from responding to the propriety of speaking an English which, if Boswell is to be believed, had 'improved much' by 1772.[32] Equally, when he saw others had the balance of right on their side he was never slow to change his mind. Reproached by Samuel Whitbread, the brewer, on one occasion, he said, 'I sit here to change my mind as often as my reason is convinced'.[33]

Good speaker as Dempster was, he allowed himself greater latitude in his letters which were warm and full of charm. He would write to his closest friends as he spoke to them: ending jolly quips with clusters of exclamation marks or, in the case of money, a frequent subject of concern, reducing the lessons he had learned to light-hearted maxims: 'None should despise it (except) those who can't get it by (the) pockets full'.[34] Hearing that Sir Adam was looking for new accommodation he hoped it would be 'within a trip in my slippers'.[35] Spontaneity, the deliberate use of exaggeration, and the oblique simile – 'frigid as the regions of Nova Zembla' – were everywhere in evidence.[36] Delicately contrived wit or the occasional reference to his beloved Epictetus only added to his armoury, but they would only be used to those *beaux esprits* who appreciated them. Calling himself 'a poetaster somewhat vain', he could sometimes catch truths about himself and his readers in the pithy verse some of them found so irritating.[37] When occupied with several futuristic enterprises Dempster was 'engaged with many rolls on my drum'. Political friends were 'like buckets in a well; one down when the other was up'[38] and Parliament was nothing but 'an engine to squeeze money from the people'.[39]

He never kept a book of anecdotes, nor was he introspective enough to write a journal. Unlike Boswell he never wrote to his friends with an eye on future publication and resisted any impulse to provide sketches of those whom he met. He relied on his memory to tell tales 'with becoming sincerity'. Having heard that the new Meikle Ferry inn had not been built after he had so carefully laid its foundation stone, he asked the mistress what had happened. By way of reply she 'brought the stone out in her lap'. He added the story to his list of 'silent jokes'.[40] Not without his share of vanity, he was prepared to show an intensely child-like pleasure in matters of detail, as when he wanted to know what initials he might be entitled to put after his name when he was made a member of the Royal Danish Society of Northern Icelandic Literature.

Dempster mustered an army of converts to his ideas for agricultural reform and, by encouraging manufacturing expansion, set in motion much that improved the lot of ordinary people. He was one of the first to address some of the root problems in the economy. But he was slow to apply to people many of the empirical tests he employed elsewhere. His judgement of their behaviour and motives could at times be seriously at fault and, unlike his successor at Skibo in the late 19th century (Andrew Carnegie), he sometimes failed to grasp the harsh realities of capitalism.

The economic logic behind some of his innovations was distrusted by many landowners and some of his own tenants were unwilling to follow his lead. A few rich lairds had noble intentions but other *feudal dragons* (as Dempster called them) were taken aback by his assertion that the provision of opportunity would itself lead all men to better themselves. Dempster took time to understand that long-established rural traditions were not easily replaced in the Highlands; neither did the imitation of town dwellers and agricultural communities further south come naturally. Like others who followed him, it was only too easy for developers to underestimate, not simply the harsh terrain, but the consequences long distances from markets and supplies had on profitability. Delicate as his diplomacy and negotiating techniques usually were, there were also times when his lawyer's training was upended. His zeal, simple altruism and a proneness to over-optimism could make him an uneasy partner. His enthusiasm, such as that shown for a 'model barony' at Stanley, could easily upset his patrons and 'when peers . . . and great ancient barons of the land get a misunderstanding one another and mount their high horses', he recognized it was time for him to 'belong . . . to the infantry'.[41]

For nearly 40 years Dempster's obsessive concern that Scotland should have its own militia demonstrated his proud nationalistic spirit. He saw this apparently small measure as a symbol not only of nationhood but as something at the heart of his economic nationalism. Initially, it had been his way of drawing attention to Scotland's second-class status in English eyes when, after the '45, even some Scots thought the 'the disarmed counties still disaffected'.[42] By demonstrating that the English distrust of the Scots had evaporated and that equal treatment had been earned, he hoped to see Britain make a united response to the external threats against her. This would, he hoped, enable Scotland to re-unite itself. Loyal and proud Highlanders who had made such sacrifices for King and country could not be expected to be 'industrious' without full participation in the nation's affairs.

Many industrialists and entrepreneurs live to see their empires crash or the corporate identities they long defended lost in successor businesses. All economic progress has an impermanence. Dempster's achievements in Scotland were no less transitory, but his name will for ever be associated with imaginative ventures such as those at Letham, Stanley and Spinningdale, to say nothing of the work of the British Fisheries Society and the part he played in agricultural and social reform. Whilst the record of other great statesmen, politicians and innovators in the 18th century may be more demonstrable, Dempster's canvas of achievement was huge and his mark still remains. He was wrong when he rebuffed a potential biographer two years before his death with Virgil's words from the *Aeneid:* 'You joke about the life of an individual to whom nothing but oblivion belongs'. His benevolence, compassion and unselfish service afford him a proud position among Scottish 'improvers' for all time, one that deserves to be better known.

1

EARLY INFLUENCES
(1732 – 1754)

'What matters it to me or you
On how obscure a bush he grew'
(Dempster to Boswell May 1764)

The Dempsters were an ancient family never straying far from Forfarshire, taking their name from the 'deemster', 'dempster' or 'doomster', an office-bearer who reiterated the judge's findings in Scottish Courts or proclaimed decrees of Parliament, an Anglo-Saxon word for 'he who cried doom'. Early records show the name of Dempster cropping up in 1200 when a Sir J. Dempster from one of the family's many branches was given the regal gift of lands at Knockleith and of Auchterless in Aberdeenshire. They subsequently migrated nearer the sea, first to Careston (Carolstoun) and Minresk, then to Brechin and later to Dundee and Dunnichen in Forfarshire. One member of the family was Thomas Dempster of Minresk, the historian of Etruria and a contemporary of the Admirable Crichton.[1]

Dempster's great-grandfather was the Rev John Dempster (1641–1708), the last Episcopal minister of Monifieth, who was descended from James, the second son of a James Dempster of Auchterless and Muiresk, communities six miles south and three miles south-west of Turriff respectively. John Dempster became preceptor of the Maisondieu of his native city of Brechin, then minister there, before being presented in 1676 to the charge of Monifieth parish by George, Earl of Panmure. He married Anna Maule who had previously been the wife of Alexander Erskine, chamberlain to the Earl of Panmure. She had three sons by her first husband, and five sons and two daughters by John Dempster. The latter was the last of the 'episcopals' of Monifieth, a minister whose integrity and ability accounted for him being left undisturbed in his parish for some considerable time. However, the peace of his ministry was upset in 1698 when the Presbytery of Dundee was provoked by the Rev John Spalding into charging him falsely with actions that led in 1701 to his being debarred from preaching on the grounds of 'contumacy to all the church judicatories, of giving the sacrament to persons who were Dundee parishioners, and of not observing all the fasts and thanksgivings enjoined by the Church'. Fortunately, the Synod's sentence was reversed the next year by the General Assembly and his 'pious exhortations and worthy example' enabled him to openly scorn the Dundee Presbyterians and he still refused to acknowledge William as king. This remarkable minister, un-remitting in his good works especially among the poor, eventually died in August 1708 when he was about 67 years old. [2]

The Rev John Dempster's son, George Dempster senior, was born in the old manse of Monifieth in 1677 and baptized there.[3] He may have been factor to the Countess of Panmure for a period after he graduated from Edinburgh University in 1700. Although his fortunes were to be greatly enhanced by marriage, his rapid progression to landowner, merchant and local banker had much to do with his natural entrepreneurial ability. Throughout his life he had a way with money, keeping careful records, making it work for him and rarely losing the opportunity of deal-making, but generous to his friends and family. He probably used his position with the Countess to trade on his own account, buying and selling grain and agricultural necessities in the neighbourhood. Just when he acquired the separate and generally small parcels of land across Forfarshire that eventually made up the Dunnichen estate is uncertain. His wife Margaret, whom he married in December 1699, was the daughter of the Rev William Rait, the minister of Monikie whose father had married the heiress of the last Guthrie of Pitforthie and through her he received the Pitforthie estate near Brechin.

The purchase of the Dunnichen and Dumbarrow estates in the early part of the 18th century, comprising about 3,200 acres in the parish of Dunnichen, provided the original core of George Dempster senior's numerous but quite small landholdings. There he was to build the first mansion house of Dunnichen which his son and grandson inherited, and which became the backdrop of so much of the forthcoming story.[4] The earliest settlement near St Causnan's Well, to which the later church just below the house was dedicated, had been the Church of Dunechtan in the 6th century under the patronage of the monks of Arbroath Abbey. Earlier it had been dedicated to St Constantine, King of Cornwall, follower of St Columba and martyr. Nechtan, the King of the Picts, who was said to have had a residence at Dunnichen, may have been baptised by St Boniface over the hill at Restenneth in the 7th century. By the middle of the 16th century the barony of Dunnichen and the lands of Ochterlony and Craichie had been bought by John Carnegie, the favourite but illegitimate son of Sir Robert Carnegie of Kinnaird. The property was then sold to his half-brother, another Sir Robert, who, in March 1595, obtained from James VI the charter of this barony, along with another at Lour, and the estate at Careston. In 1632, on the death of Sir Robert, two of his surviving brothers inherited

Dunnichen and Careston, John, who was to become the 1st Earl of Southesk, occupying the Careston estate.

By the time George Dempster senior died on 2 June 1753[5] his property portfolio had expanded to include holdings at Newbigging, Laws, Omachie, Ethiebeaton, Burnside, Restenneth, West Denhead, Galry (Gallery), Hillock and New Grange, as well as the barony of Dunnichen, all of which produced an annual rental of £769, a satisfactory enough income, but inferior to that of many other landlords in the county.[6] These lands amounted to some five or six thousand acres; estimates vary. Inevitably, various sales and purchases were being effected throughout his life; he was for ever in the market. In 1724, when acting as Chamberlain to the Earl of Panmure, he bought for the Countess of Panmure, for example, the barony of Redcastle on the right bank of the River Lunan, when David, the fourth Earl of Northesk, was forced to dispose of many of his holdings. The Priory and lands of Restenneth were acquired from William Hunter while he was at Burnside, and the Dempsters and Hunters shared the chancel as their family burial place.[7]

Held in high esteem, George Dempster senior appears to have been a successful merchant first and laird second. The condition of the estate at the time of his death suggests that it had hardly been his first priority, although the factor's ill-health may have been a contributory cause of the dereliction, at least at Dunnichen. There were also times when George's grandfather could give the impression of being oblivious to the condition of the less fortunate in Dundee. In February 1720 an angry mob took possession of two of his ships laden with barley lying alongside the Tay, believing that it was his export trade that had caused the dearth of grain locally. The rioters 'attacked and gutted the house, shops, cellars and lofts of that gentleman, carrying off everything they contained, including twelve silver spoons, a silver salver and two silver boxes, one of them containing a gold chain and twelve gold rings – some hair ones and others set with diamonds'. The merchant thereupon announced that anyone who could help him discover 'the havers of his goods' would be entitled to 'a sufficient reward and the owner's kindness . . . and no questions asked'.[8] He complained bitterly about 'the supineness of the magistrates',[9] but the perpetrators of the crime which cost him £1,000 were never caught or punished.

George Dempster senior and Margaret Rait had three children – one son, John (1700[10]–1754) and two daughters, Isabel who died in 1772 and Katharine (1714–1804). Their son has long been a shadowy figure, records about him being almost entirely confined to his death 'after falling from his horse while out riding at New Grange'. The pre-eminence of his father's position in the commercial life of Dundee may have prevented John Dempster from making his own distinctive mark on society. Certainly there is a complete absence of any reference to him by the family, and such hints that are provided about his relationship with his father, who always seems to have dealt with him fairly, suggest that he was not greatly enthused by the merits of his immediate heir. John married Isobel Ogilvie, the daughter of Patrick Ogilvie of Balfour, in 1730 when he was in his late twenties. They were not to be together very long before she died. The first of their five children was Margaret (known as Peggy), followed a year later by George Dempster.[11] John Dempster's second marriage took place on 13 November 1740 in the Old Parish Church in Dundee. His bride, Mrs Stewart Hamilton, the daughter of Philip Hamilton of Kilbrachmont, was to bear him five or six children (the record is unclear) who survived into adulthood.[12] Who the first-born was is not known but the son who was to become Captain John Hamilton Dempster was born in 1750 and christened on 9 August .

John Dempster lived in Dundee for at least part of his life and when his eldest son George Dempster was born on 8 December 1732 the family dwelt at Rankin's Court. One Andrew Rankin, a shipowner and Dundee burgess, had built this remarkable town house for George Dempster senior off the north side of High Street (Marketgait) in Gray's Close, formerly known as Alexander Kyd's Close (opposite Skirling's Wynd). One room had a ceiling 'richly embellished with scroll-work interspersed with foliage, fruit and flowers' and 'with joists decorated in *tempera* and inscribed with . . . quotations'.[13] The property was to undergo several alterations and in the 20th century be incorporated into premises where Messrs Keiller & Sons, the jam, marmalade and confectionery manufacturers, had their works for a long time.

From George Dempster senior's account book for 1736–52 it is clear that a large portion of his son's financial affairs were put through his books, suggesting that this was more than a simple matter of convenience.[14] Day Book entries were regularly transferred to a running monthly account settled annually at the end of the year. He not only received an allowance from his father but the latter appears to have paid many of his debts. The record implies that about the time he re-married, or soon afterwards (1740–45), John moved from Dunnichen House or possibly an estate house nearby, to New Grange outside Arbroath.[15] Whether this was to make a better life for himself and his new wife or as the result of strained relations within the family is not known. He probably worked in his father's business until, with George Dempster senior approaching 70 years, the domestic accommodation and the day-to-day running of the business in Dundee was handed over to separate management.

However this may be, John was ordering many of his routine supplies for his household at Dunnichen and New Grange from his father to within a year of the latter's death in 1753. These included oats, barley, meal, English flour, bread, butter, salt, cinnamon, honey and apples, as well as quantities of whisky. In 1748 six mattresses valued at £87 were called for and the freight bill and shore duties for furniture bought in Leith amounted to £14 14s, whilst a great deal of upholstery work must have been undertaken by Mr John Shaw to justify a bill of £382. In 1750 more than 1,600 flooring nails and 9,200 door nails appear to have been used in the further refurbishment of the house at New Grange, perhaps in readiness for the birth of John Hamilton Dempster. His father had also undertaken to pay him an 'aliment' since the sum of £666 13s. 4d outstanding on his account, which included a cow he had just bought for £20, was written off in January 1752. That year several items of expenditure were attributed to family members who appear only briefly in the records. One was the payment of £50 or so in respect of 'your daughter Agnes' nurse's fee', and another some £36 that John had borrowed from 'Miss Nancy Hamilton'. Other items of expenditure show something of the lifestyle at New Grange. Six dozen silver tablespoons and a screen were bought from Leith and 'the gavle of the Chaplin's room' repaired. In January 1752 George Dempster senior paid £114 5s.6d 'for (his son's) Christmas Entertainment . . . and the money borrowed from him'. During the summer several hundred pounds were handed out when his father visited New Grange, where the house was being pointed by a George Marshall. A horse was sold to John Crawford. How free he had become with other people's money was illustrated by the loans and occasional support he received from family and friends, including his maternal uncles, George and James Rait.

Young George's grandfather had a special affection for him. He was only 8 years old when his mother and grandmother died and his father remarried. For his part, Dempster always regarded his ageing grandfather as his mentor and probably lived under his care from his early school days at the grammar school in Dundee.[16] The builder of Rankin's Court also owned a piece of vacant land by the tower in St Clement's Lane adjacent to the well of the same name, and it was there that the small school house had been built. In the company of a few sons of the local gentry George would have poured over old and well-thumbed copies of Ovid and Horace and been drilled in the rudiments of mathematics. The civic privilege of free sittings in the west gallery of the East Church would hardly have interested the scholars, but the Town Council wanted to ensure that pupils received value for their parent's fees of a few shillings to the master. James Fergusson's claim that George first attended school in Leuchars must be suspect. If some tutoring took place in Fife it would more likely have been just before his university days at St Andrews. Even a weekly passage across two miles of River Tay would have been a daunting experience.[17] He was still at the grammar school in August 1744 when he was taken from his bed 'to see a comet shedding fire that filled and illuminated the whole heavens'.[18] Nearly seventy years later he remembered the 'dim light brushing out at a considerable distance from the edges of its disk'.[19]

Dempster was to describe Dundee as a 'dirty hole', which grew in his lifetime 'into a beautiful city'.[20] An anonymous letter written when he would have been in his teens speaks of 6,000 inhabitants going to bed by the sound of the bagpipe and the tolling of the curfew bell, with the dead being carried off to their graves by the tinkling of a hand-bell.[21] The Scottish Board of Manufacture had offered to provide a spinning school to encourage the embryonic linen trade in the town, but civic poverty precluded its acceptance. A local contribution to its funding could not be found. Such shipping as used the harbour was regularly unrigged and laid up for the winter with no voyages ventured after October. Two established churches were frequented, their sermons being timed by an hour-glass; a third was a hay repository for His Majesty's dragoon horses. Simple cottagers, drudging tenants and tradesmen were in a state of poverty, servility and depression, and whilst beef was one and a half pence a pound, a hen four pence and eggs three halfpence a dozen, there were few vegetables and even fewer among the population who could afford such luxuries. Whisky did not yet provide an alternative to the draught of malt beverage or a choppen of ale which was sufficient to send labourers home reeling.

Wooden buildings predominated, there being not more than a handful of stone houses in and around the High Street. The town's finances were in a poor state. Extravagant entertaining by an earlier Provost had caused one public room to be left uncompleted in the recently-built Town House. Unlit streets were in a wretched state, with Tindal's Wynd and St Clement's Lane coarsely paved with round 'bools' or beach stones providing narrow and often uncertain passage between the town and the shore. Open cellars and stairways jutting out into the path of travellers and horses were a hazard. Piped water from the Ladywell fountain was a recent improvement but a few wells met most needs. There were dirty houses called inns or ale-houses, whilst small and poorly-stocked shops occasionally selling oil, salt, candles, molasses, black soap and sugar, bread, milk and flour and other bare essentials could be rented even in the High Street for £3 or less. No houses attracted rents above £10 and some for much less. In the background were the merchants and landed gentry whose place in society was often resented by 'simple cottagers and drudging tenants in a total state of poverty'. Servants rode before their masters, and running footmen 'skipped it before their coaches . . . Ladies bound themselves up in bone stays and husks like Egyptian mummies'.

Dempster would have heard of Charles Edward Stuart's arrival in Scotland. Fifteen years after the '45 he recalled that, except for a few clans, the Pretender's army had 'consisted of men offering themselves promiscuously from all quarters . . . who engaged not so much from disaffection as of novelty; many indeed from the desperate state of their private affairs, the very dregs and refuse of mankind of which every country unloads itself annually into whatever armies levy recruits in it'.[22] Whether he witnessed the army's progress towards Edinbugh before the Battle of Prestonpans in July 1745, or had simply heard about the events, is not recorded, but he went on to speak of 'the crowds of giddy and thoughtless people, who, without inquiring into the justice of the cause, (were) ever ready to flock round a victorious standard'. He rightly distanced Dundee from 'the infamy of disaffection', a subject which family conversations could hardly have avoided.

When Dempster arrived at the oldest of Scotland's universities, St Andrews, towards the end of 1747, two of its colleges (St Salvator's and St Leonard's) had just been granted parliamentary approval to unite. A 15-year-old young gentleman, joining a fraternity of perhaps 150 students, 10 or so professors and an assortment of bursars, portioners and servers, would doubtless have been oblivious to the poor condition of the university's buildings, variously the subject of concern and some embarrassment to the authorities in the preceding 20 years. An eagerness to learn and the fascination of college life in an attractive setting would have diverted his attention away from what had been described as 'rather entirely neglected'. St Salvator's College consists of two spacious Courts, so said one traveller in 1723, and 'over the gate is a very fine stone spire; and to the right, as in the colleges at Oxford, is a handsome (Collegiate) Church or Chapel . . . a neat cloister well-paved and supported with pillars . . . on the ground floor of the other side of the other Court are the common schools . . . over these . . . a Hall, full 50 foot long and 30 foot wide and high. There are in this Court very good apartments for masters and scholars . . . but unaccountably out of repair'.[23] The restoration undertaken by Provost Skene twenty years before had lost much of its value and, although St Salvator's rather than St Leonard's college was to survive, it was in a state of 'hopeless disrepair' at the time Dempster arrived.[24] Of little consolation would have been the fact that the condition of the town itself was worse, its 4,000 inhabitants living in older and dilapidated houses with middens in front of them adjacent to the unpaved streets.

Another vivid description of the scene twenty years later conjures up the conditions George encountered. 'It was a curious, thrifty life that the students spent in the academic courts. St Salvator's common room was a damp vault with earthen floor and cob-webbed roof. There were dinner tables for the students – with fare consisting of bread, eggs, and fish three times a week; beef and cabbage with ale for the other four. Tables were set for students of different grades – for the *primers*, sons of the lords and landlords, in their fine gowns, who had paid the high fees of six guineas; the *secunders*, sons of ministers and smaller lairds, with robes less richly trimmed; and the *terners*, robed in poorer stuff, who paid their humble fee of a guinea and a half.' By this account the food included scones and bread with portions of milk or ale exactly allotted according to each grade of student, whilst a similar hierarchy of rooms, with and without fires, which were visited by the duty *Hebdomader* at nine at night and five in the morning, were nine feet square. Fines of twopence for lateness, and sixpence *(sex assibus)* for absence, were pocketed by the professor to complement his meagre salary.[25]

Students matriculated once soon after the beginning of the standard four-year arts course of the period; this built on the Latin, Greek, Rhetoric and Logic taught in the grammar schools. George was no exception and he matriculated there on 24 February 1748. The Principal or Provost, and six or so members of the staff of the two now united colleges, were adjusting to new responsibilities, retirements and vacancies. The University had decided to follow Edinburgh and Glasgow by doing away with the old system of regenting. Erstwhile masters who taught a variety of subjects now found themselves specialist professors. He was taught Greek as part of his study of the classics by Professor James Kemp until his death in April 1748 when Walter Wilson succeeded him. The fact that Dempster does not appear in the University's list of graduates cannot be taken as an indication that he failed to complete the course since few students at the time bothered with the formality of graduation. Final examinations and the disputation of theses had become a thing of the past so that few students took a Master's degree. Dempster's work during his second and third years would have qualified him for his bachelorship, and he studied logic and rhetoric in 1749 and ethics and metaphysics during 1750. His professors included Henry Rymer, John Young, David Young and David Gregory, the last teaching him mathematics. Had he progressed to a fourth and final (Magistrand) year in 1751, he would have studied Natural Philosophy.

It was the son of William Vilant, who had been the University's Professor of Civil History, who brought Dempster to the notice of the authorities during that first year. Alexander Vilant, a man 'regularly educated' but of no great academic ability, succeeded his father as a professor. A challenge to this arrangement by other masters of the United College, during which numerous bribes were offered, led to an action before the bench where Dempster stood surety for him. The outcome was a compromise whereby Vilant gave up his post and became the college factor, a post he held for some years despite continued backbiting.[26]

Among other students were William Nairne, who was to become Lord Dunsinnan and a Lord of Session, Thomas Webster, Philip Morison, John Halliburton, John Scott and Thomas Wolfe. How Dempster stood in comparison with his fellows can only be judged obliquely, by the frequency and variety of his reading matter at the time. Unlike some of his *confrères* whose borrowing from the University Library was extensive, his was more contained.[27] Between November and December 1747 he managed to read two volumes of *Belles Lettres* by the French historian Charles Rollin, along with a volume of his *Histoire Ancienne* that had not long been published. Several of Pope's works were taken out, and in the Spring of 1748 he was borrowing Monteith's *History of the Rebellion*, a *Miscellany* of Swift's works and, at the request of Professor Rymer who taught logic and rhetoric, a volume entitled *Presbyterian Eloquence* was returned, only for Dempster to take it out again in

November. On this occasion its return was 'on Mr Gregory's order', suggesting that his command of language may have been in danger of hindering his uptake of mathematical knowledge. Whilst his friend Nairne's reading included Abercrombie's *Instructions for Youth,* various divinity works and Derham's *Astrotheology,* Dempster was attracted by several volumes of Addison's works, Pope's translation of Homer's *Iliad,* Clarendon's *Survey of Leviathan* (his criticism of Hobbes), Hutcheson's *Ethicks,* Gibbs on Architecture, Langley's *Practical Geometry* (on 'Mr Young's order'), Cicero's *de Natura Deorum Davisii,* and volumes 2 and 3 of the *Female Spectator* at the request of a Mr Wilson. His grandfather, if not his father, would have had much to question Dempster about when he returned home from his studies.

'Archerie' had been a favoured sporting activity at the University since its foundation in the 15th century. With golf, it was considered a pursuit that would help reduce the time students had available for dicing and cards, both of which were prohibited. The University's archery competition at the Bow Butts on the edge of the links, and its courtly annual procession of tradition-ally attired archers parading through the town on their way to the butts, was a high point of the year for anyone involved. The victor's medal would hang on the winning Silver Arrow presented by the faculty of Arts in June each year. Dempster must have been especially delighted in 1750, not only to be selected for the contest but to have won the coveted trophy. Lively, if not riotous, celebrations in the winning student's rooms followed.[28]

It seems likely that George went on from St Andrews to study law at Edinburgh University during 1750–51. Some legal training was a desirable prerequisite for the son of a laird or a family with important commercial interests. Unlike the regime in English universities, interest in science and political economy was a feature of his academic training, and an under-standing of law complemented this practical orientation whether or not the student intended to practise it as a profession. As at St Andrews, the academic year started in October, with matriculation following during the Spring Term. Founded in 1582, Edinburgh's old university buildings to the south of the city were mean, if workmanlike, presenting little difference from those to which Dempster would have become used to in Fife. Its quadrangles, greens and bell tower continued to have architectural appeal, but the university's Principal described the courts and buildings as being 'much as a stranger might imagine alms houses for the poor . . . never the precincts of a flourishing seat of learning'.[29]

Charles Mackie, Edinburgh's first Professor of Constitutional History, tabulated an alphabetical list in July 1746 of all those who attended his lectures between 1719 and 1744. Other names were added for the period 1746–53, among whom were several of George's later acquaintances, including James Boswell's father, Lord Auchinleck, John Johnstone of Westerhall and his great friend-to-be, Adam Fergusson, as well as others of the Scottish nobility.

Dempster's name appears on the amended list of Mackie's students, along with the date of 1750, and the required fee of £3 for the privilege of sitting at the Professor's feet is marked off as having been paid.[30] His two courses of lectures drew heavily on accounts by ancient writers of 'all great historical events'. He first explained the great revolutions of the world and gave an account of the population migrations that took place after the fall of the Roman Empire, mentioning 'the rise and progress of the Papal tyranny'.[31] Using the *Grand Corps Diplomatique*, and *Rymer's Faedera*, he took his students through ancient treaties, examined alliances between sovereigns and acquainted them with 'the history of learning in all ages'. The 'college' or course of lectures on *Roman Antiquities* dealt with manners, customs, religion, civil government and military affairs. Speaking in Latin, he discussed Roman Law, and the forms of proceedings before the Praetors and other courts of law and equity. The teaching year started in November and finished in May.

Dempster's belief that law-making and the condition of society were inextricably linked would have derived from the style of legal training to which he was exposed. The old system of apprenticeship, with its long and unremitting drudgery of theoretical study, was being called into question. Those such as Lord Kames, who preferred a more historical approach, insisted that only with a fuller understanding of history could reforms to the law be rightly judged. The social and economic context slowly became ingredients of legal teaching, replacing over-reliance on logic and reason. At Edinburgh Dempster's theoretical studies would have been in the hands of Professors George Abercrombie (Public Law), Kenneth Mackenzie (Civil Law) and John Erskine (Scots Law). Study in the Advocates' Library, with its 30,000 volumes where unusually 'books could be taken out for study', would have been combined with occasional attendance at Parliament House, the home of the Court of Session, an essential practical element of the course. If Professor Mackenzie had followed the curriculum set out by his predecessor, Thomas Dundas, then Dempster's introduction to Civil Law would have included 'colleges' based on Van Muyden's *Compend*, Justinian's *Institutions* and Voet's *Compend*. Erskine's teaching of Scots or Municipal Law, on the other hand, took Sir George Mackenzie's *Institutions* as its core and for his lectures on Public Law Abercrombie used texts written in the previous century by the Dutch lawyer and theologian Hugo Grotius.

The progress of Dempster's studies during the last two years of his course had, however, been far from smooth. Although qualifying in law and being accepted as a member of the 'worthy and learned' Faculty of Advocates on 4 March 1755, he had also been forced to come to terms with the loss of both his grandfather and father. The two deaths, coming as they did in quick succession, undoubtedly caused great distress and consternation to the young student. The family had been shattered, more especially by John Dempster's demise in 1754 after an equestrian accident in the country around Arbroath when his father might reasonably have been expected to live for another 20 years. Coming so close on the heels of the more predictable death of the old laird in June 1753 at the age of 75, its effect must have been a devastating blow to a young man of 23 who quite unexpectedly found himself the head of his family.

Only the passing of the older of these two very different influences in Dempster's life attracted any comment in his letters. That he attended his grandfather during his last illness and watched 'while the pulse gave its last beat' is clear, and from memory in his old age Dempster recalled James Rait, the Bishop of Brechin[32] and his great-uncle, being called to the bedside and how 'eagerly' he looked 'to see the soul issue out of his mouth, and take its flight'. George Dempster senior's body was taken for burial at Restenneth Priory whilst his father was buried in St Vigean's Church near Arbroath. [33]

2

A YOUNG GENTLEMAN ABOUT TOWN
(1755 – 1760)

'A most agreeable well-bred man, sensible and clever,
gentle and amiable, quite a gentleman'
(Boswell's Journal)

Now 23 years old, Dempster was the eldest male member of the family and responsible for the well-being of a host of young brothers and sisters, to say nothing of his father's widow. Life at Dunnichen House and Newgrange would have been much in turmoil. The record provides no remembrance of the family's predicament and when Dempster recalled the episode in later life, he only records that while he was still 'studying law at Edinburgh the estate devolved upon me, and put an end to my studies' without mentioning those for whom he had a filial duty of care.[1] Daunting as the circumstances may have been, Dempster needed to take advice and consider how, in addition to his duties within the family, he was to begin the knotty task of managing a home and estates amounting to five or six thousand acres. They may have been worth around £769 p.a. but the 'farm buildings were ruinous hovels; the ground was overrun with broom and furz or whins, and many parts of the arable land were wet and boggy, all without trees'.[2]

His financial inheritance, though considerable, was not a huge fortune and, as he recalled more than 60 years later, 'unluckily, my grandfather . . . did not secure (the estate) by entailing it on our family'.[3] Its largesse may have persuaded him that he had greater freedom for action than proved to be the case. Certainly his youthful enthusiasm and some of the mistaken impetuosity of the next few years, when 'he dashed (into farming) without either skill, time or money', did not help. The amiable and exuberant company he kept during his law studies afforded many advantages socially but not all his friends were capable of providing the practical wisdom of which he stood in need. Instead they seem to have encouraged a certain vanity and 'I thought myself also learned'. The 'ruinous' state of affairs at Dunnichen were no doubt due in

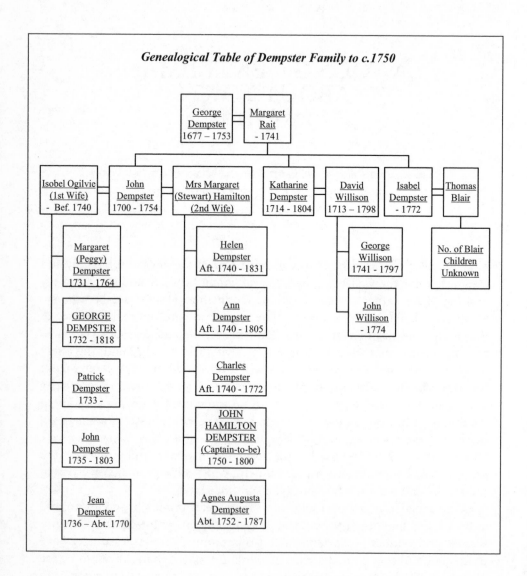

Genealogical Table of Dempster Family to c.1750

George Dempster 1677 – 1753 — Margaret Rait - 1741

Isobel Ogilvie (1st Wife) - Bef. 1740 — John Dempster 1700 - 1754 — Mrs Margaret (Stewart) Hamilton (2nd Wife) — Katharine Dempster 1714 - 1804 — David Willison 1713 – 1798 — Isabel Dempster - 1772 — Thomas Blair

Margaret (Peggy) Dempster 1731 - 1764

GEORGE DEMPSTER 1732 - 1818

Patrick Dempster 1733 -

John Dempster 1735 - 1803

Jean Dempster 1736 – Abt. 1770

Helen Dempster Aft. 1740 - 1831

Ann Dempster Aft. 1740 - 1805

Charles Dempster Aft. 1740 - 1772

JOHN HAMILTON DEMPSTER (Captain-to-be) 1750 - 1800

Agnes Augusta Dempster Abt. 1752 - 1787

George Willison 1741 - 1797

John Willison - 1774

No. of Blair Children Unknown

See Fuller Dempster Family Tree at the end of the book

28

part to the laird having been in his declining years, but, equally, they were matters in which John Dempster, his likely heir, appears to have shown little interest. When the factor died the following year it became only too clear that the estate had been mismanaged for some considerable time.

Among those to whom Dempster would have spoken about his newly-acquired stewardship was Adam Fergusson (1732–1813) who had been a fellow law student and whose own admission to the Faculty of Advocates was confirmed that year. Adam's elder brother, John, had died of consumption five years before while serving in the army and he was heir to the baronetcy of Kilkerran in Ayrshire. His father was a Lord of Session and Judiciary, and had taken the title of Lord Kilkerran. Dempster's friendship with this sober, conscientious, shrewd but unimaginative lawyer – the converse of Dempster in almost every respect – was to last for 57 years. The correspondence between the two men well illustrates the extent of their concern for each other over the period from 1756 to 1813.

It had probably been accepted that the two friends would complete their education with a Grand Tour in Europe. The expectation was that all gentlemen of means had to experience for themselves the art and culture of the ancient world before going their separate ways in their chosen careers. It would help them develop their critical faculties, acquire 'good taste' and apply their knowledge of continental languages. But in Dempster's case he now had to assure himself during the time it took to make the arrangements for such journeys that the family and estate would be properly looked after. He would not have wanted his decision to accompany his friend to be thought either impetuous or ill-considered. Such a grand tour varied in length from one to four years, or longer according to means. For Adam, his intended career at the bar was to follow his travels. In George's case, the family probably concluded that an extended absence would feed his ambition in directions other than the law, which he never greatly espoused, and enable him to pick up the reins with new confidence on his return.

In the 12 months between becoming a member of the bar and leaving for the continent with Adam in April 1756 Dempster went out of his way to maintain and cultivate many of the friendships and associations of his university days, whilst at the same time contributing to the meticulous plans which his friend was making. As a student he had been introduced into the brilliant circle of philosophers and a glittering array of talent in Edinburgh; the company of 'wits and *literati*' whose companionship he was so to enjoy after his travels. What made Edinburgh an absorbing place in which to live was what Professor Mossner rightly referred to as the essential 'clubbability' that existed in the capital city at this time.[4] Unlike London and elsewhere, where cities were larger and more dispersed, access to men of letters was greatly facilitated by the philosophical 'open market' that formed daily at the Cross, something between a Speaker's Corner and a literary 'fair'. Men of all opinions mixed in the taverns throughout the day and until the City guard's drum summoned them home at 10 p.m. There were societies for every taste, some of which ably followed the tradition established by the Rankenian Club which had done so much to enliven literary and philosophical debate 40 years earlier. Members of such societies (and clubs) were as often as not open-minded and possessed of a unique Scottish blend of bluntness, imagination, fervour and gregariousness. As Carlyle said, 'The *literati* of Edinburgh . . . were less captious and pedantic' than in London.

Edinburgh had become the focus of a unique social and artistic life. It ruled 'taste in all the arts, from epic poems to gardening' said Voltaire. Even the narrow and often filthy streets where the 'hoi polloi' rubbed shoulders with the gentry played a part in creating a vibrant centre. Good opinions of it were formed by all manner of visitors, its congeniality being so superior to Paris that Hume, who had lived in the French capital for many years, eventually chose to retire neither there nor London, but Edinburgh. Unlike other capitals it was compact and welcoming, although the Old Town's labyrinthine access on foot or sedan chair had its own hazards. Its self-confidence was born of the Scots realization that their achievements in arts and science, which the English signally failed to recognize, meant that their heads could be held high in any company in Europe. Benjamin Franklin enthused about 'six weeks of the *densest* happiness' he had 'ever met with in any part of (his) life'.[5]

The Select Society was at the height of its popularity between May 1754 and 1757. It was a club similar to those in France where debates among academics were commonplace, and a powerful forum for airing the problems of the day. In Scotland lawyers, clerics and academics, as well as other society figures became eager members, including David Hume, Sir David Dalrymple (Lord Hailes), Hugh Dalrymple, Lord James Monboddo, Henry Home (Lord Kames), William Wilkie, Robert Arbuthnot, Walter Goodall and Allan Ramsay, its originator and initial guide. Dempster was admitted on 12 June 1754. Its membership swelled from fifteen to sixty in a matter of months and rose to 150 by the end of the decade. As Hume told Ramsay a year later: 'The House of Commons was less the object of general curiosity than the Select Society at Edinburgh. The Robinhood, the Devil and all other speaking societies are ignoble in comparison. Such felicity has attended the seed which you planted.'

The subjects of the Society's debates during its relatively short heyday were selected by the chairman of a committee for questions, Sir David Dalrymple, and among the issues on which it focused were many that were to be near to Dempster's heart in later years. They included such esoteric matters as whether the number of banks in Scotland was sufficient for the country's trade, the future for the bounty on low-priced linen goods, and, of particular interest to a young lawyer, whether a man 'of ordinary parts' might become eminent in his profession.[6] Another, on the desirability of establishing a militia to aid the country's defence forces, was to become especially pertinent.[7] Among the prizes awarded by the Society was one for 'an account of the rise and progress of commerce, arts and manufactures in North Britain, and the causes which promoted or retarded them'. Not all the subjects put forward for debate were economic in character; others included the meaning of 'taste', the manners of women and the influence of climate on the Scottish character. Dempster must have found the Society's meetings a stimulating diversion for a student, a newly-admitted barrister and traveller-to-be.

Leaving behind the conviviality of the Society's Wednesday evenings in the Advocates' Library, and with farewells at Dunnichen said, the two friends eventually set out together in the spring of 1756. A week or so before, Adam Fergusson recorded in his account book that he was in Bath, suggesting that the two probably met up in London.[8] The planned itinerary included Germany, Switzerland and Italy after a short pilgrimage to the Low Countries. The last was home to many Scottish communities made up of expatriate academics, bankers, traders and, not least, soldiers, termed the 'Scots Brigade'. These formed a brigade in the Dutch army which had 'won glory as the senior regiment in the Dutch service' for nearly three hundred years and never 'lost a stand of colours'.[9] Leaving the coast the two men passed through Ghent on their way to Brussels. Given the six months meticulous planning Adam Fergusson had put into the tour, it would not be surprising if their rooms in Brussels, which they reached on 19 April, were not littered with all manner of references artistic, scientific and geographic. Furthermore, and essential for a journey of some years, there would have been a large number of trunks, some containing expensive new clothing and personal requisites purchased before they left.

In Brussels the population was 'not much more . . . than Edinburgh' or 53,000 according to 'the common computation' of Mrs Calderwood.[10] The two friends were evidently determined to combine the learning of new accomplishments, which included lessons in French and German, fencing, dancing and riding, with sightseeing and a little experience of low life. Evidence of the latter was referred to as the antics of a 'female giant'; other sights were 'the Arsenal' and 'the Prince's cabinets'. Generally, the behaviour of the *Brusselois* was 'more politer' than their counterparts in Edinburgh; they had 'the Spanish pride and the Dutch phlegm but with neither the honesty of the first or the industry of the last'. Their fencing master turned out to be a Scot named Macdonald, and, as James Fergusson said, the cameraderie at the Académie Royale 'seems to have provided them with some private jokes, and long afterwards Dempster recalled the shouts of the riding master – '*Epaule droit en avant, Monsieur Dempstair! La langue, M. le Chevalier! N'ébranlez pas M. le Baron!*'[11]

Altogether the picture was one of two energetic young gentlemen enjoying the company of new friends and acquaintants, some English and Scots, others from the Brussels bourgeoisie.[12] Good conversation and hospitality returned by dinner parties at restaurants were the order of the day, together with visits to the 'comedy' (music hall) which was very popular, despite the poor acting. The occasional concert, buying expeditions for 'cheap and charming'[13] prints and works of art, and card play, some more serious than others, added to the routine. Inconsequential flirting would have been *de rigueur*, enjoyed more among the handful of Scottish ladies who were excepted from Mrs Calderwood's conclusion that 'the British women were . . . adventuresses'. The frequent hire of masks and domino costumes recorded in Adam's account book, along with at least one 'pair of mustachoes', conjure up scenes of colourful merriment. The majority of balls and dances were in masque and 'given gratis on court days' but the mantua makers had nothing of the 'genteel style' of their equivalents in Edinburgh. After paying court 'they go home to undress and put on their masque habits, at 11 o'clock at night. At 12 they meet at the house where the plays are held, but it is floored over the pit. The whole riffraff of the town comes, and dances away, and makes a prodigious crowd. They take off their masques when it turns hot'.[14]

The natural sobriety of both Scottish gentlemen precluded the sowing of any obvious 'wild oats', but the experience was very clearly a watershed in their lives. Dempster regained the sparkle and youthful facetiousness the previous 18 months of bereavement and readjustment had done much to erode. Until this time their relationship had been that of none too compatible students. It now deepened and their 'friendship took its rise from our travelling together, knowing each other's humour, being merry, and serious, and sharing the same pleasures and the same little distresses together'.[15]

As the ceaseless questioning of Adam in subsequent correspondence bears out, the new world of the continent was the spark which ignited Dempster's curiosity about different approaches to economic and social problems. His varied friends in Edinburgh had contributed to his social 'enlightenment' but now the contrasting realities in Europe helped widen its focus. He enjoyed stays in Tournai and Namur after which the two men sailed down the Meuse to Liège, and on to Spa and Aix-la-Chapelle, Utrecht, Amsterdam, The Hague and Antwerp.

Dempster must have been bitterly disappointed when in the autumn, and after a happy and totally absorbing seven months in Belgium and the Netherlands, he was obliged to return to Dunnichen .The fact that the urgent summons he received greatly exaggerated the sickness from which his eldest sister Peggy was suffering, and that the crisis had not been life-threatening, only made his decision to return harder to bear. For a week or so he drew some comfort from the prospect of re-joining Adam somewhere along the way, but once in Angus, such a hope soon evaporated. The death of his factor which had coincided with his return only added to his problems. All his life he deeply regretted the disintegration of his plans and his premature return. He was never to see 'the glories that were Rome' and with his thoughts accompanying his friend on his journey to Italy, Adam became his proxy explorer.

In the haste to return home Adam offered to buy Dempster's share of their substantial stock of reading and reference books[16] and saw him to the packet boat at Ostend for the rough nine and a half hour crossing. There the two friends played cards on the quayside and Dempster lost four *demi-souvraines* or £3 8s. The journey turned out to be a nightmare with the ship's guns being run out at one stage in anticipation of an attack by a French privateer. He 'spent the night with the chamberpot in (his) arms' whilst others around him were being violently seasick. With the noise of the guns being loaded in the half-light of the ship's lanterns and turmoil in every quarter, it must have been daunting: 'we all expected (not with impatience, you may believe) a broadside from our foes'. However, it proved to be a false alarm and, anxious to reach home, Dempster kept enough of his faculties at the ready to deal with the inspector of Customs. He anticipated paying heavily for the import of gentleman's lace he was carrying, but perhaps not the full amount of duty. He was 'under dismal apprehensions' about the lace going into the custom house and could only hope 'to trick these watchful bloodhounds'.[17]

In November, as Dempster travelled northwards, the country was coming to terms with the possibility of a French invasion. The Seven Years War had just started and 12,000 troops were occupying all the available accommodation in Rochester, the bulk of them Hanoverians. Management of the navy was disordered, the new government administration shaky and a not disliked German king (George II), whom Dempster described as that 'good frog-eyed old man', was on the throne. Staying in London for three busy days, his fondness for the theatre took him to 'three nights of Garric' (David Garrick, the actor-manager) which included a performance of John Milton's *Comus* at Drury Lane where 'good fortune had just preserved one place in the whole house for me'. He was clearly enraptured to be back. Like many before and after him he was struck by how different everything was, while at the same time recognizing that the length of his stay outside the country disqualified him from making too many comparisons with what he found. However, the 'simplicity of dress practiced at home' when compared with the 'richness and show so universal abroad' particularly surprised him and forced him to conclude that England was 'a country without nobility'.[18]

Once back in Edinburgh, Dempster lodged with his aunt and her husband, Katharine and David Willison, in Forrester's Wynd. There, with other friends around him, he had time to pull his thoughts together before seeing his sister nearby in the country and returning to Dunnichen. 'Worthy Nairne', a lawyer friend with whom he had studied both at St Andrews and Edinburgh, had been watching his 'motions with all the vigilance of a Mentor to take care that none of them betray . . . contempt of the homely objects' around him.[19]

Evidently Dempster recognized the need to take himself 'down like an overstrained instrument to the low pitch of the rest around (him)' for appearances might impair the resolution of the new laird's problems – 'I have not entirely escaped the observation of the remarkers here, and some of 'em brand me (unjustly, God knows) with the imputation of extravagance'. He had heard of differences of opinion if not within the family then among estate staff, and foresaw 'more difficulties than I was aware of, and in unravelling them I fear attachments and passions may arise'.[20]

Once at Peggy's bedside, Dempster found her health still causing some concern. She had been 'removed to the country for the sake of the air' and, although she was not to die until November 1764, she 'was in a very weakly way much afflicted with a distress which women never name. Upon the sight of her brother who(m) she little expected, she fell into a fit of that disease in which she remained for several hours without giving any symptoms of life or sense, and on her recovery I was obliged to retire for fear of a relapse'.[21] The visit over, he could 'go over to Angus' to see what had been happening at Dunnichen. There, the immediate concern was the education and behaviour of the young, all in their teens. His 'elder brothers and sisters' had no education 'or what is worse a bad one'. Moreover, the family's anxiety, already heightened by his sister's illness, had been compounded by disarray in the estate's affairs. The accounts were 'in the greatest confusion and intricacy as (the deceased factor's) method of book keeping was singular and irregular nor intelligible to anyone but himself'. 'Not a marriage . . . nor deaths' had occurred, but he swore that 'in time to come neither my death nor that of my factor, nor both our deaths shall give much trouble to our successors'.[22] It was a promise he was to keep. Of equal consequence was the distress that had been caused by 'a great storm which had dried up the milns', forcing up the price of grain and causing famine for a period. People had been reluctant to bring their meal to market on account of the especially rigorous incursions by the Press Gang which had terrorized the population.

In the circumstances, Dempster chose to take a house in Edinburgh which, by February 1757, he was 'much busy furnishing'. After 'various ruminations' he had concluded that the 'agreeable society of both sex[es]' in the capital was preferable to that north of the Tay and that the education of his younger brothers and sisters would be better served. So far as his own future was concerned, his 'inclination (was) to do something in the Parliament House' where the law courts were held, and 'I am not so very remote from Angus as not to be able to carry on a favourite project or two there'.[23] Any hope he had of rejoining Adam on the continent had disappeared – he found that 'many parts (of his) little fortune demand the annual presence of the master'. Numerous claims on his time chained him down 'like Gulliver in Lilliput'.[24] Added to which, some of his friends, if not his aunts, had apparently been urging on him the need to 'take a wife'. But this was one step too far – 'I find, (tho' a) lover and promoter of marriage in other people, no inclination [to e]nter into that state myself'.[25]

It said much for his ability to keep matters in proportion that he could air with Adam the 'many plans and schemes in the execution of which (he was beginning) to grow much interested'. The idea of using shell marl as a fertilizer for the land had often been talked about, but he also mentioned an intention to 'build a village' – a matter that he promised to tell his friend more about later. In fact, two rural communities were to be the fulfilment of this early dream, one in Angus, the other by the Dornoch Firth in Sutherland, but not for some 50 and 36 years respectively. Foreign travel had done more than broaden his mind; it had fuelled his imagination and nurtured the first of many schemes which 'engage(d)' him 'extremely'.[26]

In the spring of 1757 the household at the newly-acquired house in Edinburgh, where his 'younger' sister Jean (22) acted as housekeeper, probably included one if not two of his brothers. The date that Dempster's aunt, Isabel, married Thomas Blair of Glasclune is unknown but she may have been the 'senior' member of the Dunnichen household at the time of the Grand Tour, if not in 1757. However, with the new arrangements in place, Dempster set about reclaiming some of the life he had enjoyed as a student. He was seen about town in 'his laced coat and powdered wig' and 'ordering his chairman (of the Sedan chair) to go to a club' with the air of a confident young laird. The irony that so many Scottish nobles who deserted their estates, hived off to London or further afield, while Edinburgh revelled in its effulgent social life would not have been lost on him.

As Dempster made his way among the 'wits and *literati*' of Edinburgh he soon found that the Select Society had languished. Its 'select' origins had been overtaken by the presence of more celebrities. There was also a host of other societies and clubs – Greig's, Walker's and Wilson's, to say nothing of Jamie Balfour's coffee house, as well as theatres or booksellers where historians, philosophers, lawyers and writers could meet. Many of this elite were older than Dempster, but their energy, wit and intelligence encouraged him to add 'his own shiney facet of high level discourse', as James Fergusson called it. Ministers from the moderate wing of the Church, such as *Jupiter* Carlyle – so-called for his god-like appearance – and William Robertson who was also a historian, were joined by John Home, Hugh Blair and Lord Hailes, David Hume and Adam Smith. Of these last two, the former had just become the Keeper of the Advocates' Library and the latter was Professor of Moral Philosophy at Glasgow University.

In his correspondence Dempster admits little influence from the works of Adam Smith, although they became good friends and were members of the subsequently-formed 'Poker Club'. In the case of David Hume – 'Dear David' on whom Dempster 'doted' – an intuitive liking for the 'Socrates of Edinburgh' was coupled with respect for the principles he espoused. Even as he passed through London the previous year he had bought the second volume of Hume's *History of England* for Adam Fergusson, recommending this 'charming pioneer' and the book's 'classical composition'.[27] Unfortunately, Dempster probably burned Hume's letters around 1816 to circumvent the attention of an unwelcome biographer so that the extent of his influence will never be known. So far as can be judged, Dempster accepted him as his guru *par excellence*, being happy to apply much of his teaching and philosophy. He recognized that he was a man whose intellect and understanding of jurisprudence and moral philosophy were unequalled, even if in his metaphysical writings he left Dempster and others of an essentially practical turn of mind well behind.

Hume's reputed atheism always prevented him from becoming an academic, and much of what he wrote was misconstrued, often deliberately. Once asked what he thought about the immortality of the soul, he answered, 'Why troth, Man, its so pretty and so comfortable a theory that I wish I could be convinced of its Truth – but I canna help doubting!' In 1751 Hume failed to obtain another university chair but by the time Dempster met him his *Political Discourses, Essays Moral and Political* and the volumes of his *History of England* were dissipating the earlier despair, so providing the setting of a glorious career. In his essay *Of Commerce*, written with something of his own brief commercial experience as a book-keeper in mind, he came closest to Dempster's pattern of thought. He drew the distinction not only between 'shallow' and abstruse' thinkers – those that fell short of the truth and those, much rarer, who went beyond it – but between the 'two divisions of mankind' with which Dempster could identify. When he stated that 'the difference between a common man and a man of genius (was) seen in the shallowness or depth of the principles upon which they proceed', he described Dempster precisely.

Hume argued that history helped to uncover human nature, that the record of wars, intrigues, factions and revolutions were collections of experiments from which politicians and moral philosophers could elicit the principles of human behaviour. This approach was nowhere better seen than in his *History of England*. This classic drew on the 30,000 books to which he had unfettered access from 1752 as the Keeper of the Advocates' Library. Although the first volume on the House of the Stuarts caused a furore among the Whigs and clerics, and Hume was vexed beyond measure – perhaps mistakenly – by Lord Chatham's strictures on the work in the House of Lords, all was not lost. In 1756 when the second volume (that Dempster purchased for his friend Adam) appeared, orders for it were good and probably contributed to the relaxing of the apparent conspiracy in the print trade which had so damaged the launch of the earlier volume.

Even while sorting out his domestic affairs in December 1756 Dempster had found time to transcribe Hume's apology for the manner in which he had dealt with religion. The philosopher had given some offence in his *Treatise* each detractor differently misrepresenting his reduction of belief to 'a lively idea'. Moreover, the first volume of his *History* had led to him being taken to task for appearing to represent Catholicism as 'superstition' and the early Protestant reformation as showing 'enthusiasm'. In the draft preface to the second edition which Dempster was digesting, he reiterated his position that it ought not to be a matter for offence if the faults of any religious sect were aired, given that 'no human institution will ever reach perfection'. Doubtless Dempster agreed that 'some more softenings' were called for; the offending passages were withdrawn from the main text.

As Dempster sought to use Hume's works to form his own judgements in the absence of Adam Fergusson, the effect of these religious polemics was predictable. His 'guru' had gone too far. Admitting the 'good sense' of much of Hume's text, he nevertheless asked his friend whether he thought 'it a sufficient justification for the liberties which Mr Hume takes at every turn with the religion of the age whose history he writes?'[28] His Christian upbringing and Episcopalian background showed through when Dempster asked how it was possible for Hume to have regard to religion 'when we consider how destitute he is of that only support of it, Faith'. Developing the theme, he added: 'Though the person devoid of faith may have some inward ideas and love of rectitude which hinder him from deviating from his moral duty, yet surely, the merit of this equitable conduct, can hardly be ascribed to any influence religion could have over him'. A disagreement this may have been, but Dempster still regretted greatly that his 'Socrates' had decided to abandon Edinburgh for London. He 'seldom differed from (Hume's) opinions without discovering soon after that education and prejudice had blinded (his own) eyes'.[29] Seven years later Dempster was to upset Dr Johnson by pressing Hume's ideas on him.

The Select Society and a group of its directors, including Dempster and William Johnstone, decided that 'it would be of great advantage to this country if a proper number of persons from England, duly qualified to instruct gentlemen in the knowledge of the English tongue, the manner of speaking it with purity, and the art of public speaking, were settled in Edinburgh'.[30] Much to Hume's chagrin they turned to the Irish actor, Thomas Sheridan, to help put their decision into practice.[31] Hume had tried to put his imprimatur on this campaign and regarded the support given to Sheridan's efforts 'vastly too enthusiastic'. The philosopher was convinced that Scots should not only write but speak standard English instead of their own vernacular. In his own case he readily admitted that, despite his mastery of the written language and idiom, his tongue 'as you will have seen (was) . . . totally desperate and unreclaimable'. Reasoned debate and the general encouragement given to the public airing of ideas, even one as potentially tendentious as this, were welcomed in this age of enlightenment. No little embarrassment had accompanied the utterances of some Scottish representatives sent to parliament in London and poor speech sometimes impaired intercourse in commerce or between the professions outside Scotland.

The performing arts always maintained their place among Dempster's priorities. He was delighted to see that another Select Society member, Lord Monboddo, an assiduous theatre-goer, and a few other lawyers had taken over the management of the Canongate Theatre which he frequently attended. In December a brilliant and controversial play by John Home was performed. It had been copied out by Carlyle, his amanuensis, since his handwriting was hardly legible. Rehearsals had taken place in Thomson's Tavern watched by Carlyle, Lord Elibank and Home after a supper of 'pork griskins'. Mrs Ward, one of the better thespians, appeared as Lady Barnet and West Digges, a bank-rupt ex-Army officer, played the part of Forman.[32] The Scottish clergyman and dramatist's earlier work had been sent down to David Garrick in London and rejected. Now *Douglas*, the new piece based on an old Scottish ballad, was not only produced at the Canongate but later performed in London. The Edinburgh performance was said to have evoked the cry of 'whaur's yer Wullie Shakespeare noo?' from some in the audience!

The blank verse tragedy was to remain in the theatrical repertoire for more than a century, but it gave great offence to the Edinburgh Presbytery and caused the Rev John Home to resign his ministry. The very existence of the theatre was to some in the Church both immoral and profane. Dempster, who had 'lost himself in ecstasy at a performance of Milton's *Comus*'[33], and who was not disposed to 'depreciate' or give it 'high rank' when it had 'given rise to a vast amount of fun', did, however, draw a fine line when commenting on the morality of *Douglas*. As a lay member of the General Assembly of the Church, he had supported a reactionary proposal 'forbidding the clergy to countenance the theatre', but, when reporting the performance to Adam Fergusson, he did not object, 'providing vice is not countenanced and the love of virtue appear to be the moral which the play would enforce'.[34] There was no doubt that *Douglas* eventually became a fine piece of theatre. The text continued to be amended in the light of constructive comments by Sir Gilbert Elliot (who became the MP for Selkirkshire in 1753) and Alexander Carlyle, and its acting won rightful acclaim, factors which Dempster may have taken into account.

Another thread in the weft of Dempster's philosophy, and hidden in the *Memorandum* written just before his death, was his reference to Montesquieu's works, where he found that 'his ideas of our constitution coincided with my own, and (he) was particularly struck by his observation that our government should end when the legislature became more corrupted than the executive'.[35] The French baron's familiarity with England, as well as the procedures of the House of Commons, made his political philosophy essential reading for law students. In this 'intellectual centre, at least the equal of Paris, London and

Vienna' (as Voltaire described Edinburgh), Dempster and his friends explored all manner of ways in which barriers to the threat of corruption at the centre of the state might be built. The characteristics of those with power to bring about reform were scrutinized. Adam Smith's *Theory of Moral Sentiments* may, consciously or not, have encouraged Dempster to put himself in the role of Smith's 'spectator' – 'someone determined to act the part of the 'good Samaritan'. In his theory, the essence of moral arguments was 'sympathy, but a specialized, conscience-stricken sympathy, like that of an impartial and well-informed spectator'.

Others of Dempster's acquaintance were well-equipped to help his understanding of the practical needs of the Scottish economy. Robert Arbuthnot, also a member of the Select Society and the second of Dempster's close friends at this time, was already a merchant by all accounts. He later became the Secretary to the Board of Trustees for Fisheries, Manufactures and Improvements in Scotland. With young William Nairne, who was to become a commissionary clerk that year, the three friends often talked long into the night about ways of achieving change or, as Dempster put it, 'Often we dissolved the unequal union of our country to England, converted it into a republic, marshalled Scotia's warlike sons, cultivated her barren fields, fortified her avenues and strong places, and re-established her long-lost independence' – all before the sun came up! [36] As James Fergusson commented later, all three friends were in their mid-twenties, putting the world to rights with all the confidence of youth, and since home rule or independence for Scotland was not a topical subject in those days, the model admired by Scottish nationalists was neither Ireland nor Denmark – but Switzerland! [37]

Dempster's overriding and constantly expressed belief in the importance of economic and social reform may also have had its origins in the debates about the role of the Commissioners appointed to administer estates forfeited after Culloden and the flight of the Pretender. In some ways surprisingly, they were not all sold by auction to the lairds and gentry who supported the administration, but rather annexed to the Crown estates. [38] Although always contentious issues, the trustees had been charged with introducing a rational system of agricultural husbandry, the establishment of manufactures, and training young people in such a way that they might be usefully employed in industry. Even eight years after the Annexation Act had been introduced, Dempster was still expatiating on the wisdom of its premise: 'Who can doubt, if this gracious and humane conduct is steadily pursued, that, in a very short time, even the name and memory of disaffection will be forgotten?' [39] – one which, in the absence of successful state intervention, he was to put into practice himself.

Whether by luck or good judgement, Dempster generally found the mood of the moment. Never unoccupied, he kept up with the activities and interests of his friends, seeking every chance to learn from them and explore their thinking. In an April letter to Adam Fergusson, which he thought might be opened by the Post Office fearing that intelligence was being passed to the French, he bewailed the war in case it prevented his friend from making his way south over the Alps to Italy. Allan Ramsay of the Select Society had been 'denied a passage through France'.[40] The searching enquiries on this occasion touched on the fertility of German agriculture, whether the populace were 'exposed to the tyranny of the great', the manners of foreigners, and 'the state of liberty' in Switzerland, all 'burning questions' in his mind.[41]

During the poor and sunless summer of 1757 Dempster was afflicted by several ailments. He had brought a fever back from the continent which lingered, and now a painful knee contributed to his being confined to his room, with his books for company and the necessity of a fire.[42] By November, with his knee still troubling him, he became depressed and went to Bath where he was 'assured by the best surgeons (there) and in London, that it (was) not of such a nature as to prove dangerous to life'.[43] All in all, things appeared to improve and when Adam returned to London in March 1758, the two friends dined together several times in April and May before Fergusson returned to Scotland to take up his career at the bar. But the fever that had accompanied the trouble with Dempster's knee may have undermined his constitution for by the middle of the year his health broke down completely. His illness was evidently serious, if short-lived, and it took its toll. From London he complained that it had 'obliterated many of my former ideas and made a strange jumble both of names and facts in my memory'. The fever had attacked him when he 'spit up an abscess form'd in (his) breast'[44] and it was some months before he was himself again, and back in Edinburgh.

Dempster seems to have practised in the courts only occasionally. This was in marked contrast to his friend Adam, who, after nearly three years abroad, was living near George's earlier home with the Willisons – the Fergusson family house was also in Forrester's Wynd and known as Kilkerran's Court – and spending all his time at the bar. That Dempster 'aspired to become a legislator'[45] rather than continue as a practising lawyer soon became evident, but the transition required a modicum of planning. The affairs of the estate at Dunnichen were in the hands of the new factor who had been kept busy with his laird's instructions, implementing basic improvement schemes on what continued to be a rundown property. Dempster would have visited Angus as often as he could, but such evidence as exists suggests that, with most if not all the immediate family ensconced in Edinburgh and with a new career in prospect, any substantial development of the estate had a low priority.[46] Some reforms may have been introduced, but he was not yet the 'improving' laird, and work that was put in hand probably anticipated his forthcoming departure to London. He would have had access to perhaps £300 p.a (out of a rent roll of £769) and probably some small investment income which would have been sufficient for his bachelor life in Edinburgh but little more.

The baton of a Scottish militia force, taken up by the Select Society in its earliest debates, was grasped with a vengeance in the summer of 1759 when Thurot, a French privateer, threatened to maraud along Scotland's eastern coasts. Amid general agitation, Montrose (a town in Dempster's future constituency) joined the pleas for arms to be distributed to its inhabitants. A national campaign to seek the extension of the English Militia Act to Scotland had its origins in a meeting attended by seventy property owners in Edinburgh on 30 November. Among those invited to join a representative committee made up of peers, law-lords, Edinburgh's provost and others, were four young lawyers, Dempster and Adam Fergusson being among them.[47] His lifelong crusade for Scotland's right to a free government, and the distinct identity such national defences helped signify and reinforce, had started. The message was taken to Westminster on this occasion by Sir Gilbert Elliot who had been armed with the notes Dempster had prepared on the subject. They were to form part of the lengthy pamphlet he published the following year and be one of the ringing themes of his maiden speech to the Commons in November 1761.[48]

Just when Dempster's aspiration to become a legislator overcame any desire he had to be a barrister is not known. It was not something that would have ever been considered in his youth: 'Had I talk'd of parliament in the hearing of my father or grandfather they would have thought of Bedlam!'.[49] Only four years before, his inclination had been to practice at the bar in Edinburgh. Furthermore, in the intervening period he had pleaded a 'few cases' and 'displayed talents that might have proved highly beneficial to himself and . . . his clients'.[50] His friends both in the profession and among the members of the Select Society (where he was now a member of some six committees) may, however, have known of his interest in having more of a hand in government than one in the courts, and expected his public-spiritedness to lead him in this direction. Good as the law was as a training for a life in politics, his decision nevertheless had many signs of being artless and ingenuous. When he offered himself as a candidate for the Perth Burghs he could only say he was determined 'to pursue such measures as (would) be most serviceable to our country and honourable to ourselves'. It was true that a seat in the House of Commons was 'the highest object of (his) ambition' and he knew that even the tacit support of the Duke of Argyll was 'the most effectual means' whereby a seat might be obtained,[51] but such patronage seems to have been lacking. It was as if he allowed his idealistic spirit to lead him, on the off-chance that he might succeed. Certainly his first campaign showed how tough and costly it was for someone with little understanding of political life not only to get into but to sustain an effective role in the House of Commons. It was to prove an invitation to penury.

The general election was to be held in April 1761 and in three letters to Sir Adam Fergusson six months or more before the event, Dempster's excitement, anticipation and fears were all too evident.[52] The first hurdle was to gain election as Provost of St Andrews, an ancient office but hardly one of great consequence. Dempster saw it as a litmus test that would show whether a young laird resident outwith the Burgh could win support in one of the constituencies that made up the Perth Burghs' seat. Opposition there certainly was, with Dempster trying unsuccessfully to enlist Sir Adam's help in swinging at least one important vote his way. His friend who was also standing for parliament at Ayr declined to approach Lord Cassels on behalf of a Mr Morrison, a bailie, whose vote he sought, and Sir Adam was himself forced to withdraw after the Duke of Argyll intervened. The incident only showed how ill-prepared Dempster was for political life when he admitted 'how impossible it (was) for people of good breeding . . . to carry on . . . in the easy genteel way' which he thought 'or at least once thought it might admit of'.[53] As it turned out, a majority of the twenty-nine members of the St Andrews 'councel' supported Dempster and he was able to turn his full attention to the main event. At the end of September he also became a member of Dundee Town Council.

The sitting member, Captain Thomas Leslie of Stenton (1701–1772), had occupied the seat since 1743, being supported by William Cavendish, the Marquis of Newcastle.[54] Apart from his long experience of electioneering, he also had the advantage of the support of his brother, John, the Earl of Rothes. Dempster described him as a 'hunter', living in 'splendour' and 'parading' in the neighbourhood; and, in contrast, himself as a 'diminutive (and) contemptible figure, not naturally ostentatious'. He was confronting not only an earl's nominee but someone who was 'the Commander-in-Chief in Ireland with all his baggage horses, coaches and footmen'. Dempster knew that he must not 'give way to modesty' and soon found he had to 'play the frog . . . puffed up to the size of this mighty court-fed ox'; accepting that for a week of the campaign at least he would have to appear what he 'never wished to be', learning just how much false posturing and ingratiation was called for and 'how impossible it was . . . to carry on (politics) . . . in an easy genteel way'.[55] This was all far from anything he had personally encountered and totally at variance with his character, behaviour which he soon learned to abhor. Those with whom he was called upon to work were, he soon found, 'the empty friends of a day'.

The juxtaposition of several events nevertheless helped Dempster's cause. The likeable old Lord President of the Court of Session died.[56] He had been respected in the burgh of Perth and his replacement was not from the Newcastle faction, thereby undermining the confidence of those who had voted for Captain Leslie for 36 years. Another ally of the ruling group was also missing from the fight to stop Dempster. Thomas, ninth Earl of Kinnoull, was out of the country, returning from Lisbon where he had been Ambassador for two years. Then in November a complication arose when, instead of there being the anticipated straight fight between Dempster and Leslie, a third candidate, Captain Haldane, whose forebears had held the seat earlier in the century, threw his hat into the ring, only to withdraw later.[57]

Dempster's nervousness about the outcome of the election was reflected in several requests he made to the Member for Selkirkshire. Sir Gilbert Elliot was Lord of the Admiralty and a minister known for his backstairs manipulation of events. However, Dempster's pleas to him were hardly those of a man expertly laying the foundation of some future personal preferment. He merely asked him to use his influence to obtain promotions for the relatives of those councillors whose votes he was canvassing. He found such importuning essential on account of his 'great desire to succeed in this attempt, upon which I consider my future fate in life to depend, and for that reason I leave no means untried to procure success'.[58] In the event he never secured a majority of the Dundee or Cupar votes, but the outcome in St Andrews, Forfar and Perth was satisfactory.

3

SALAD DAYS
(1761–1763)

*'It is expected that we Members of Parliament should be independent
men and men of influence at the same time'*
(George Dempster writing to Sir Adam Fergusson in 1783)

1761

Entry into Parliament in the 18th century was a complicated and often despicable affair. The Scottish share of the 526 seats in the united Westminster parliament, negotiated in the discussions which preceded the Treaty of Union in 1707, was 45, of which 15, including Perth,[1] were for the Royal Burghs and 30 for the Counties. By the time Dempster came into Parliament the number had increased and 558 members were returned at the general election of 1761.[2] The number of eligible voters in each constituency only totalled some hundreds and a small turnout could reduce this greatly. Only those land owners and feu-holders with an annual value of £400 Scots had the franchise. Even in 1832 there were only 3,000 Scottish voters and in 1788 county voters totalled 2,662.[3] The selection of Burgh members had been taken away from the town burgesses and rested with the magistrates (or councillors) who were a self-perpetuating oligarchy. Oaths taken by candidates were introduced to reduce bribery and the Test Oath denied the vote to any who had attended Episcopal services where the officiating priest failed to pray for the royal family.[4] The registration of fictitious voters had an effect where there was a 'needle match' between candidates.

Although Dempster was only 29 years old when he became an MP this was far from being exceptional. Eighty-four members born between 1731 and 1740 had been elected, including a young soldier under the required age who died on his way home from Germany. Charles James Fox (1749–1806) was to enter Parliament at the age of nineteen and the younger Pitt became First

Lord of the Treasury at twenty-four. The House comprised 300 or so members over forty and another 149 between 30 and 40. Dempster was among a sizeable intake of new men (some 126), the remainder having served the House under a variety of administrations; 142 had entered before Walpole resigned in 1742. A fifth of the Commons was made up by sons of peers, of which 10 were Scottish, and there were nigh on 100 who were either baronets or sons of baronets. Army officers (59), who were broadly the most aristo-cratic group, included 14 from Scottish constituencies, and naval officers (21), civil servants (7), diplomats (5) and practising lawyers (40) meant that a third of the total were engaged in the professions. Among the 50 merchants only two were not from London, one being the Lord Provost of Edinburgh and the City's member, George Lind. Dempster was one of about 300 who were not 'placemen' i.e. those who held office, contract or pension from the Government, although many in this group were not necessarily without some obligation or allegiance.

Some of the reasons why Dempster's opponent, Captain Thomas Leslie, came to lose his hold over the five burghs that made up the constituency – Perth, Dundee, St Andrews, Forfar and Cupar (Fife) – have already been touched on. Another, put forward by James Fergusson, was the fact that he was apparently near bankruptcy.[5] Dempster took courage from the support St Andrews gave him when they elected him their Provost in September. The same month also saw him elected a member of the Dundee Council and, as Dempster told Sir Gilbert Elliot in October, there was thankfully 'a total revolution in the town of Perth and a very mean servile sett who have main-tained themselves in power for 36 years were on Monday last turned down stairs'.[6] It was not until April 1761 that Dempster found he had a seat at Westminster. When the Duke of Atholl let it be known that he favoured Dempster over Leslie much of the opposition dissipated.

Needle match or not, the whole business of Dempster's first election was a costly affair. It was one thing being elected to 'the twelfth parliament of Great Britain' and quite another to be almost bankrupted in the process. He was said to have spent upwards of £10,000, an enormous sum, in what had been a keen election campaign. Lest corruption on such a scale be thought a purely Scottish propensity, in 1784 John Robinson named seventeen English boroughs where, for example, 'seats may probably be obtained with expense' mounting to £3,000 each, including Honiton, Wootton Bassett, Hindon and Arundel, and Lord Edgecumbe might require £18,000 for six of his constituencies in Cornwall. In total, sixty-eight constituencies were listed as possibly requiring the financial support of patrons or government.[7] When the second Viscount Palmerston stood for Southampton in 1768 he was invited to distribute £10,000 among 'those who could be bought'.[8] It is hard to imagine that the disbursement of sums of this magnitude came as a complete surprise to Dempster. The temptation to re-consider his position must have crossed his mind when he realized that whatever loans or other finance he had earmarked for his 'expenses' might well be insufficient to get him elected.

Such amounts stand out well beyond accepted election costs in Scotland at the time. Perth Burghs were later known to be 'venal and expensive', although this description probably derived from knowledge of the price Dempster had to pay in 1761 (and 1768).[9] It seems improbable that sizeable amounts of cash, as large as £1,000, were distributed as a 'quick fix' to secure the passage of a young lawyer without demonstrable political aptitudes or much wealth. More likely some long-lasting patronage was being bought or, of course, the amount could have been grossly exaggerated, being confused with the understandably higher legal and other costs he bore during and after the following election campaign. Then there was some cynical exaggeration of his expenses, and figures of £30,000 came to be mentioned as part of an orchestrated campaign of vilification.[10] Some scepticism is undoubtedly called for in regard to the exact 1760 figure.

Such misdemeanours and vote-purchasing as occurred in this, Dempster's first election, were all very much part of the behaviour expected of politicians at the time. Nominal and fictitious voters were a chronic scandal. Allegations of bribery were made regularly against candidates. Details of corrupt payments and straight election bribes were hard to come by, but in the case of Dempster's antagonist, Newcastle's Secret Service accounts for 19 September 1760, contained the following entry: 'To Mr T. Leslie, by Your Majesty's order, to enable him to secure his election, £500' – a sum half that which he had originally asked for. There seems a strong likelihood that Dempster had visited London the previous year in an effort to gain support for his candidacy if not overt patronage among the leading Whigs of the day. However this may be, some financial support must have come from friends and acquaintances, thereby bolstering his own funds and putting him under obligation to them not to discontinue his campaign as the cost rose. In a letter to Sir Adam which hints at this and confirms something of the expense to which he had to go, he said, 'Pray God we may answer the expectations of those who so generously support us. With regard to the means, Sir Adam, I am sorry to say they are not quite so sanctified in our corner as I could wish. For money has much influence and as it is largely administered by my opponent must not be spared by me.'[11]

Nevertheless, several of his estates had to be sold immediately to pay the debts Dempster had incurred, and a half of the 5–6,000 acres he had inherited had been disposed of by 1771, leaving only the Dunnichen properties themselves. One record suggests that it was the Monifieth estates which were sold;[12] another that the land included Newgrange where John Dempster and Mrs Hamilton had lived in the 1750s.[13] When at the end of his life and in a confessional mood, Dempster said 'he had been a bad steward of the fine estate to which (he) succeeded' and 'I wasted my fortune, sold land (and) contracted debts', he was recalling this financial albatross among other subsequent liabilities. The cost of getting into Parliament meant, however, that 'although he abandoned practical farming he did not lose either his interest in agriculture or his determination to ameliorate the poverty of the Scottish farmer'.[14]

The new Member and his sister Jean, who was to continue the housekeeping duties she had undertaken for him in Edinburgh, now had to get themselves to London and find suitable accommodation. The likely mode of transport would have been the post-chaise which was more attractive to the gentry than the stage-coach, not so much for its construction but because it permitted the one or two people aboard the freedom to select the overnight stops and the quality of the accommodation used. Not only was the accommodation out of the traveller's control when travelling by the stage-coach but their time-tables were irregular and inconvenient and offered uncertain companionship in crowded conditions. An individual aboard the post-chaise would pay £10 or £11 for the privilege of being on the road for four days, stopping to change horses several times during the hundred miles or so travelled each day, with overnight recuperation at such places as Berwick, Durham, Doncaster and Biggleswade or in favoured inns elsewhere along the route.

Once arrived in London George, who knew London, and Jean, for whom it was a wholly new and exciting experience, probably hired a hackney carriage to take them to an inn or direct to private lodgings in a fashionable area. There being few, if any, residential hotels, they may have followed the suggestion of friends who knew the owner and the standard of maid service and accommo-dation on offer. Initially the Dempsters' lodgings were in St James's Place, a favourite location between St James's Park and the street of the same name. That political firebrand, Wilkes, had lodged 'elegantly' at a Mrs Murray's in 1756 a year before taking his seat in the House, and Charles James Fox was to live there at Miss Delaney's in 1780. In the spring of 1763 the Dempsters moved to new accommodation in Westminster, moving later to Berners Street, a 'most centrical quarter'. After his marriage he was able to take the lease of a house in Knightsbridge.

St Stephen's Chapel had been the meeting place of the House of Commons since the reign of Edward VI (1547–53), a rather 'mean-looking building' where a screen divided off the chapel from the ante-chapel which served as the members' lobby. Under a gallery which was similarly equipped, and which provided accommodation for fifty members, were benches 'covered with green cloth, always one above the other, like our choirs in churches; in order that he who is speaking, may see over those who sit before him'.[15]

The Palace of Westminster itself comprised the House of Lords, the Law Courts in Westminster Hall and the Painted Chamber where both Houses could meet in conference, whilst other premises accommodated the officers of the House and were used by members as committee rooms. Like all who saw the House of Commons for the first time, Dempster must have been aghast not only at its smallness and inadequacy but by the inattentive behaviour and noise which accompanied much of the proceedings. The chamber itself was only 1,800 sq.ft in area and the lobby less than half that size. The attire of members varied from those still booted and spurred to others in threadbare coats and waistcoats or full military dress. It was not uncommon for them to stretch out along the benches; 'they could eat or sleep there' – some would 'crack nuts' or 'eat oranges'.[16] The incessant hubbub and not infrequent raucousness was only dissipated when important visitors were present to hear some of the great debates of the day.

The annual session of Parliament usually began in November or December each year and lasted into the second quarter of the next. Meeting on Mondays to Fridays for five months of the year meant that even active members spent fewer than 100 days in the House; many hardly bothered at all unless they were 'called' to do so. No sooner was the King's Speech out of the way than Dempster was making his mark, speaking 'with an assurance that for its unexampled novelty had great entertainment . . . pleaded the extension of the militia to Scotland . . . censured the German war . . . and condemned faction'.[17] Dempster had seconded the Address to the King moved by John Wilkes. Horace Walpole, who was to belabour another initiate with the words, 'He will come to an untimely beginning in the House'[18,] was content to say that 'his speech had a characteristic note of independence' and was 'less peremptory' than Wilkes who had 'passed some censures on the King's speech'. Lord George Sackville said of the new Member that 'He promises well, and though he diverted the House by a becoming ignorance of its forms, yet he proved that he neither wanted language, manner, nor matter'.[19]

When Dempster entered Parliament, William Pitt, the Earl of Chatham and *de facto* Prime Minister, had for 5 years been pursuing a vigorous and successful war policy which the King, George II, wanted to end. The King's private designs were, however, being thwarted by further victories against the French in India, and Belle Isle off Brittany had been taken along with Dominica in the Caribbean. 'Pitt Resigns' might have been the newspaper headline on the day Dempster took his seat (5 October 1761). His successor as first minister, who survived for barely 2 years, was the moderate but in-experienced Scottish peer, Lord Bute. He chose to govern 'without party', albeit supported by what Wilkes was to describe as a 'plague of (Scottish) locusts'.[20] The Cabinet became a cipher, with the king influencing the work of the Commons through his personal Tory devotees.[21] The war intensified rather than ceased, with Spain now joining in. Admirals and generals were soon reporting still more additions to the empire and, with France stripped of her colonies, a downcast Spain sued for peace.

By the end of November, and under one month in the House, Dempster was insisting on declaring his allegiance to Lord Bute in writing rather than orally so as to provide 'evidence against him(self) should (he) act contrary to his professions'. Sir Harry Erskine, the MP for Anstruther who had been the go-between, confirmed to Lord Bute that he had pointed out to Dempster 'the necessity of attaching himself to some person or body of men' and asked 'if he had made any connection with any other person'. He replied that 'he had not'.[22]

An anonymous writer was to say that 'During his public career as a Member of the House of Commons he was always heard with singular attention. This did not proceed from his delivery, although easy and fluent, or from his person and address, although the one was handsome and the other popular and seductive, but from the uprightness of his character, which impressed full conviction on all who heard him that his conduct was regulated by his heart and understanding without any personal or paltry consideration whatsoever. No man could pretend to any influence over his opinions, so that while his speeches fully illustrated the connection between eloquence and virtue his decisions were always regulated in strict subordination to his conscience.'[23] However, not all the establishment found Dempster's role acceptable. His censure of the war in Germany, where Frederick the Great had been defeated by the Russians in Pomerania and Prussia, and a request that British troops be recalled, upset Newcastle. The Duke described the utterances of Lord Shelburne, Mr Eliab Harvey and Dempster as 'the squinting speeches' of 'young hot-heads'.[24] As Professor Namier said, 'Some satisfaction was vouchsafed to Newcastle' when, in December 1761, the 'yelping young speakers' – 'those idle boys who set up to be Ministers' – gave up, at least for a time.[25]

This ignorance of political ways was soon to disappear. He quickly caught the tone of the House, but all his life Dempster was far from comfortable with the political process. During the election campaign he admitted to Adam Fergusson that he had 'already experienced how impossible it is for people even of good breeding and good temper to carry on . . . in the easy genteel way which I think or at least once thought it might admit of'.[26] Chicanery and constant 'deal-making' were not to his taste. It took him some time to realize that the solution to problems was hampered by party machinations and that it was government that was an enemy of progress. He encountered Ministers believing what they wanted to believe. They were unaware of the poor, the unemployed and social conditions not only in Scotland but throughout Britain. There was no investigative Press and TV, or reporters to bring home worrying reports.[27] Whether or not he exaggerated his ability to cope with parliament, even after long years at Westminster he insisted on calling it 'a seat on thorns and rusty nails'. As an independent member with distinctly Whiggish tendencies, he railed against the Party system, always finding the corruption which was then inseparable from the machinery of government almost intolerable. Other Members with less appreciation of his conscientious and independent approach found him a puzzle: 'We do not like him here . . . why? . . . because we are never sure what side he is to vote on.'[28]

James Boswell, who had been a member of the Select Society in Edinburgh, was to become a close friend of Dempster in London. Writing to Dempster in November about 'the bold push' Dempster seemed to have made in the House of Commons, he pleaded with him to write letters 'at least once a fortnight' so long as he was able to 'cope with so clever a correspondent' as himself.[29] Boswell had run away from home to London in 1760 after showing a temporary religious fervour for Catholicism that greatly perturbed his father, Lord Auchinleck. But, having introduced himself to the seamier side of life and received what Professor Pottle referred to as his 'sexual initiation', he was soon back in Edinburgh. There Dempster met up with him and his 'chief literary crony', Andrew Erskine, a 'poetaster with shivers of genius'.[30] Boswell was trying vainly to obtain his father's support for a commission in the Foot Guards, the only regiment (as Boswell knew) that was likely to remain in the capital in both peace and war. Considerably older than either of them, Dempster was roped in to add his contribution to some pieces of poetry written by Boswell which were to be published by a well-known Edinburgh bookseller.[31] However, when Erskine came to the conclusion that Boswell's work (his first separate publication in verse) was so inferior that it would be best printed as burlesques with 'recommendatory letters' by himself and Dempster, things began to fall apart. The publisher, not convinced that Boswell's work would sell, added to the confusion by apparently putting it about that Dempster was the author, whereupon Dempster threatened 'to have him laid by the heels for taking such liberties with a man of my rank and dignity'.[32]

Strangely, Dempster and Boswell, who were not at all alike, were to get along famously during the first three or four years of the MP's life in London, perhaps too much so. Dempster's delight in jests and a life-long penchant for all manner of amusement and nonsense certainly lent support to their relationship. The friendship understandably faded when Dempster found less time in which to indulge his friend's whims, but it only came to an end when Boswell died more than thirty years later.[33] Boswell was a thoroughly contradictory character, becoming a libertine and lover 'unable' as he said 'to contain (his) ardour'. He was for ever 'a man carried by fancy' and convinced he was 'one of the most engaging men that ever lived'. Because of his neuroses and frenetic energy, this great attention-seeker often had to draw deeply on his friends' tolerance and forgiveness. They included John Johnston[34], Erskine, Dempster and William Johnson Temple. The last, an Englishman of 'spotless purity of morals' who eventually went into the Church, became the most intimate of his friends and always a good deal closer to him than the others. Nevertheless, throughout Boswell's life Dempster filled the role of occasional father-confessor.

Little is known about Dempster's sister Jean, or 'Jeanie' as she was called. Her brother rarely refers to her leaving Boswell's record at this time to provide brief glimpses of her. The pair had 'a great deal of gentleness of manners as well as cleverness' and, when talking to Boswell of love and marriage, she 'threw out many elegant sentiments which gave (him) a more favourable opinion of her than I ever had'. A month later he was 'glad to see (her) once more', but an encounter on a wet Sunday afternoon, after he had travelled up from Salisbury, invited some far from charming remarks when Boswell said that 'I thought him (Dempster) a poor contemptible fool and (Jean) an ugly disagreeable wretch and myself the . . . most dreary of mankind'.[35] Just how short-lived Boswell's feelings could be was amply demonstrated in November 1762 when he met up with Jeanie and her brother at Paxton's New Inn in Edinburgh. Then he was considering this 'fine woman, very well-looked indeed, elegant and remarkably witty' in a very different light: 'I this night felt myself much in love with Miss Dempster.'[36]

Dempster and his sister enjoyed a convivial if rather sober life together in their lodgings and later at Berners Street, visiting new and old friends, either dining with them or at inns such as the Red Lion in Charing Cross. Taking tea at the Dempsters, as well as dinner, was a frequent reciprocal of others' hospitality. It was hardly the life enjoyed by the wealthy and although they may have enjoyed Kensington Gardens or the bright lights and music of Vauxhall, Jean clearly had much to put up with. While the business of the House occupied her brother, 'she (kept) her servants all at work'.[37] For a time her sisterly concern was directed towards discouraging the drinking bouts she feared the hyperactive Boswell encouraged, taking particular note of the fact that her brother's 'head ached like a back-gammon board' after one excursion.

1762

In January, after a motion in the House had been postponed due to the illness of its proposer, Sir Gilbert Elliot, Dempster moved to lead on the issue himself, saying that 'one ought to squeak when (one's) toes are trod on'.[38] The matter was one upon which Dempster always felt strongly – a proposition that would have encouraged the government to give Scotland its own militia. He had spoken to James Oswald at the Treasury who was thought to be 'a warm and hearty friend to (the) militia' question, and having published the notes he had given Elliot before he had been elected in the form of a threepenny, 20-page pamphlet entitled *Reasons for extending the Militia Acts to the Disarmed Counties of Scotland*, he would have been well-armed. There he had argued that 'the subject is of great importance, both to the honour and safety of the united kingdom . . . though the late rebellion [of 1745] broke out in the disarmed counties the disaffection . . . was not so general as is commonly believed. And, that arms may as safely be trusted in the hands of those living north of the Tay, as the inhabitants on the south of the Tweed, or of the Trent . . . What Scotchman would consent to a partial militia, by which those brave men who have been so successfully employed in defending us, are denied arms for their own defence? or could see without indignation, half of Scotland deprived of the benefit of this salutary law?'[39] However, by March, and on Bute's advice, the matter was dropped, much to Dempster's consternation. As he told his friend William Johnstone, and with whom he was in correspondence about the plight of his brother George, he had been led to expect that Bute would obtain a favour from the King – 'without exciting the jealousy of the people'.[40] Dempster was nearly always at variance on the militia question with his Scots colleagues in the House, and his frustration with Bute's friends and the first minister himself, to whom he was allied, led to him openly challenging the government in December of that year, speaking and voting against the peace.

In February 1762 Dempster listened to what he called 'a very grand debate in the House of Lords, upon the German war', measuring the extent of opposition that could be harnessed to that in the Commons and enjoying the eloquence and ability of the Duke of Bedford which were 'more than (he) thought he had been master of'. Lord Shelburne, who 'shone most astonishingly', was speaking for 'only the second time . . . in his life and was very elaborate'. The vote against the Administration was lost and 'sixteen peers *not the sixteen Scotch ones* stood opposed to 105 Courtiers, however this is no bad foundation of opposition, as these sixteen were weighty'.[41] Rather too optimistically, Dempster told his friend Johnstone that there was some likelihood of a visit to Edinburgh as, once the Militia issue was over, the only material business before the House would be protracted sessions devoted to private affairs.[42]

Dempster's speeches in the House of Commons showed 'shrewd common sense and a knack of (the) picturesque and homely phrase rather than any gift for the sonorous and well-rounded periods which were the contemporary ideal of public oratory'.[43] Classical allusions were disliked by many of the country gentlemen at Westminster. He was also known for his wit and repartee. On one occasion, Sir David Carnegie of Kinnaird tried to make a speech but could get no further than 'Mr Speaker, I conceive – I conceive – I conceive'. Dempster interposed: 'Mr Speaker, the Honourable Gentleman has conceived three times and brought forth nothing. I therefore conclude that we ought to be troubled no more of his abortive conceptions'. Similarly, when the same Member supported the motion aimed at taxing spinning wheels and he assured the House that the 'poorest cottar on his estate could have roast and boiled for dinner', Dempster retorted: 'Yes . . . a roasted herring and a boiled potato!'

His entry into Parliament did not prevent him from taking an active part in municipal affairs back in Scotland where he spent as much time as he could, usually during the long Parliamentary recesses. Immediately before he took his seat he had been admitted as a burgess and elected member of the Town

Council of Dundee as Councillor of the Guild, a merchant body supervising the quality of goods traded in the town, as well as building regulations within the royal burgh. One protest against his election did, however, have to be fought off. Debates in the Council were typical of others in the constituency (such as Forfar, Cupar and Perth) and exhibited the usual politicking of those anxious to make a name for themselves and some over-zealousness on the part of other bailies. Alderman Ballingall claimed that 'George Dempster of Dunnichen, advocate, should not be put upon the list for Guild Councillor for the ensuing year as he was chosen deacon to the Baxter Trade and had accepted and also was chosen Convenor of the whole Trades at the last annual election'. He was not resident in the Burgh of Dundee and a position on the Town Council of Dundee was inconsistent with being Provost of St Andrews at the same time. Furthermore, he was said to have been 'tampering and practising upon several of (its) members'. In a written submission, Ballingall requested that a vote on Dempster's appointment should be preceded by all members 'purging themselves' by taking the oath against bribery and corruption.[44] In the event no specific evidence was offered against Dempster who continued to serve as Provost of St Andrews (a post he held continuously till 1772) and as a member of the Dundee Council till 1782.

Dempster would have been greatly cheered by an invitation to become a founder member of a new Edinburgh club at the beginning of 1762 and he seems to have found time that year to attend several of its meetings. Writing to Pulteney from London, he said, 'I envy you the pleasure of the Poker Club, a society I would be fond to enjoy, to say truth . . . I have had very little of that rational and honest kind of society since ever I have been here. Good folks are shy, the distances of their abodes and the distraction of business and diversions make it difficult for them to assemble so that populous as this place is, to me it is little better than a desert'.[45] Professor Adam Ferguson, its progenitor, suggested the somewhat obscure name 'The Poker Club' to discourage non-politically-minded members of other Edinburgh societies joining.[46] At the same time, it aptly described the club's aim – of 'firing up action' on the very Militia question that Dempster so espoused. Meeting for dinner at two o'clock which was modestly priced at one shilling per head, proceedings of the Club had to finish by six. The initial limited membership of 15 'choice spirits' soon increased as their meetings at Thomas Nicholson's tavern became popular.[47]

It was more ordered but as convivial as the Select Society. Their drinking of sherry and claret restricted any excesses. The club also boasted a couple of unusual officers. 'In a laughing humour, Andrew Crosbie was chosen Assassin, in case any officer of that sort should be needed; but David Hume was added as his Assessor, without whose assent nothing should be done, so that between *plus* and *minus* there was likely to be no bloodshed.'[48] In addition to Hume, Crosbie, Alexander Carlyle, Pulteney and Dempster, its membership included William Robertson, John Home, Lord Elibank and Lord Auchinleck. It was still an active force in 1784 when it boasted 66 members.

In December Auchinleck's son, who had not yet witnessed the proceedings in St Stephen's Chapel, tried unsuccessfully to witness the great debate that followed the defeat of France and Spain. However, Boswell's curiosity 'to hear how things were carried on' soon lessened[49] and he was not in the House when Dempster and three other Scottish members ventured to divide it on the question of the peace terms. Their efforts had been encouraged by the absence of so many Whigs who 'feigned sickness'. The discussion about the preliminaries of peace was an unpopular subject and when the four members' votes became known they were called to account by their constituents – 'instructions' were drawn up and their factious conduct greatly criticized. The fact that Wilkes was one of their tellers was enough for one member to call them 'scabby sheep'.[50]

1763

In the new year Boswell's promiscuity became more manifest and, after a series of liaisons and a fanciful affair with an actress, he proposed that Dempster and 'Dash' Erskine might join him in 'damning' a play by David Mallet due to receive its first performance on 19 January.[51] Such an uproar involved intimidating the actors and was an accepted practice by those who disliked a piece. In preparation for their demonstration, the three walked from one end of London to the other and dined at Dolly's. Their physical exercise may have been encouraged by the sight of the River Thames partly frozen and with enormous shoals of floating ice often crashing against each other. Once in the theatre they 'ambushed' Mallet on the stage during the performance, and with their 'spirits high with the notion of the adventure' they hissed and shouted abuse. Boswell was only too pleased to deride Dempster's misgivings about their outrageous behaviour. A few days later they circulated an anonymous 'pamphlet' entitled *Critical Strictures on the Tragedy of Elvira*, written mainly by Dempster who thought they hardly had the right 'to abuse this tragedy: for bad as it is, how vain should either of us be to write one not near so good'. Understandably, it soon provoked the play's author to protest and the *Critical Review* to describe it as 'the crude efforts of envy, petulance, and self-conceit'.[52]

Boswell's extraordinary swings of mood were well illustrated when, in a relaxed conversation over tea at Dempster's lodgings on 2 February 1763 that 'put him into excellent spirits', he returned home to play his violin 'with unusual satisfaction'.[53] That afternoon the two men had reviewed Dempster's experiences of Westminster during the preceding 18 months and 'talked of the House of Commons, and schemes of rising in the world'. Dempster said he had a great deal of ambition, and yet much contentment. Boswell asked him what his ambition extended to. He answered: 'to be the first man in the Kingdom – a fine idea but a chimerical one. I hinted that servility to the Court might be necessary: to stoop in order to rise. But he maintained that a man who kept himself quite independent, and who showed that he resolutely acted according to his conscience, would acquire respect, and would make his way honourably. He said that a Member who sets up on that footing must be laughed at for some time, because all the patriots have at last to come in, for proper considerations; at least, the exceptions are very few. ('Members who made a parade . . . of their incorruptibility . . . swung into line with the government when the bribe got large enough'). But he declared to me upon his word that he was determined to persevere in rectitude, let the consequence be lucky or the reverse.'[54]

The next night they were together with Erskine at the first public performance of Mrs Sheridan's comedy *The Discovery*.[55] Boswell had attended a private reading of the work at the Sheridans on the last day of the old year. The whereabouts of Dempster's sister Jean are not recorded and she seems to have missed the production since Boswell had the 'troublesome occupation' of keeping two seats next to him free for his companions. Bawdy London theatres were anyway deemed unsuitable for young ladies, and, with grime, vice and gambling in abundance, there was plenty to frighten visitors and inhabitants alike. For a week or so there was a gap, probably accounted for by Boswell's resolution 'not to keep too much company with Scotch people' because he found they prevented him from 'acquiring the 'propriety of English speaking'.[56] On 16 February, Dempster and Erskine were again gratifying their 'whims', this time by forging a letter from the former's favoured philosopher, Hume, which purported to recommend a lad called Fletcher to Boswell, whom he greatly disliked. Boswell 'almost determined to break with them', but it was a relationship that neither he nor Dempster was prepared to end.

He was soon again referring to Dempster in warm terms: 'He is really a most agreeable man: has fine sense, sweet dispositions, and the true manners of a gentleman. His sceptical notions give him a freedom and ease which in a companion is very pleasing.' On 25 February Dempster and Boswell sat talking at the latter's lodgings in Crown Street, Westminster, from 10 p.m. until one o'clock in the morning. Dempster told him of his intention to write a treatise on the causes of happiness and misery, suggesting a definition of the mind of man as something 'like a room, which is either made agreeable or the reverse by the pictures with which it is adorned . . . We are apt to imagine that his gallery is hung with the most delightful paintings. But could we look into it we . . . should behold portraits of care, discontent, envy, languor, and distraction.'[57]

Soon after two unknown Scottish cousins visited the Dempsters in March, whom his friend bluntly called 'a tribe of dismal relations', Boswell's ambition to visit the House of Commons was at last realized. Dempster took him to experience 'the novelty of being in the High Court of Parliament'. Stunned by the 'tumultuous scene', he was immediately fired with the desire to become an MP and the thought of cutting a great figure as an orator in such an amphitheatre.[58] The experience was repeated later in the month when he listened to Pitt and Fox discussing the merits of a new duty on cider before returning for tea with Miss Dempster.[59] Several dinner parties followed during the summer. Guests included James Macpherson, whom Boswell called the Sublime Savage and whose comments could be as exaggerated as his own.[60]

In April 1763 Bute was replaced by a ministry headed by George Grenville which became noteworthy for the Wilkes and *North Briton* Affair upon which Dempster had much to say. It was characteristic of the period that John Wilkes, who was a man of learning, charm and ability as well as a scurrilous two-time martyr and party journalist with a scandalous private life, was able to turn an encroaching executive and the behaviour of an over-reaching House of Commons to his personal advantage. Since Boswell had struck up an acquaintance with him, Dempster told his friend what he knew of the prosecution when he returned from Scotland that summer : 'The King insisted on his ministers bringing him to punishment, which I am informed they are in some doubts about . . . However his Majesty has found the House of Commons more zealous and unanimous than any of his ministers expected. The whole House condemned the *North Briton*, No.45, and three hundred of the members voted . . . all the hard names which Lord North, Norborne Berkeley, Chace Price or Bamber Gascoyne could bestow upon it. In the course of the debate, Martin of the Treasury said that the author of that paper in which his character was traduced and in which he had received a stab in the dark was a coward and a scoundrel. Next morning Wilkes sent him that *North Briton* with his name at the bottom. Martin then challenged Wilkes. They met in Hyde Park, both parties behaved gallantly, and at the second shot Wilkes received a wound in his lower belly, of which, tho' not in danger, he is at present very ill. Proceedings have been stopped . . . till his recovery.'[61] Wilkes was illegally imprisoned in the Tower. His second self-inflicted martyrdom concerned a prosecution brought against him by Grenville. Both events gained him great popularity, despite his infamous character.

The day before Wilkes was discharged by the Court on the grounds of his Parliamentary privilege was a fine May day and a 'Thanksgiving' holiday with people at church celebrating the peace. Dempster and his two compatriots were minded to walk out to Kensington to search for 'country lodgings'. With a reduced income as the result of the forced sale of some of his estates, Dempster was probably casting around for economies. He soon moved to lodgings at No.5 Manchester Buildings, a bleak row of tenements by the River Thames. They were, however, close to parliament and as he said 'removed from noise and strife'.[62] The cost of living in London was also a problem for Boswell whose accommodation in Downing Street was paid from his small allowance of £100 p.a. Accommodation of an acceptable standard was not cheap, accounting for a quarter to a third of their budgets. Meals might be taken in the lodgings or in chop-houses where 1/6d would buy adequate sustenance, but dinners in the more convivial taverns would cost considerably more. To routine costs for such items as better class wax candles, coals and laundry had to be added the expense of clothing. This was a particularly important item for the man about town and, with the cost of hairdressing and barber's services, no mean amount. Travelling costs could be minimized in summer by walking to and from the House, but in winter the use of cabs and Sedan chairs would have been unavoidable.

Boswell's first meeting with Dr Johnson took place at the beginning of July. Their encounter had been in Tom Davies' bookshop in Russell Street and was followed by a prolonged evening at the Mitre. Dempster was quickly invited by Boswell to help him entertain 'his hero'. A fourth member of the dinner party at his Downing Street chambers was his uncle, Dr John Boswell. The evening did not pass altogether harmoniously. Dempster presumed to support the views of Rousseau and Hume in an argument with Johnson. Although Boswell 'had prodigious satisfaction to find Dempster's sophistry . . . vanquished by the solid sense and vigorous reasoning of Johnson',[63] it is probable that Dempster's quick wit punctured the 'solid sense' with some rather shrewder thrusts than Boswell cared to record.[64] Johnson complained next morning that Dempster had given him 'more general displeasure than any man he had met with for a long time'. Boswell soon told Lord Hailes the basis for Johnson's unflattering conclusion: '*Entre nous,* he saw a pupil of Hume and Rousseau totally unsettled as to principles, and endeavouring to puzzle and shake other people with childish sophistry.'[65]

A few days later, in a heavy rainstorm, Boswell sailed up the Thames with Dempster to the Navy Office and back again to the latter's dwelling with thunder still ringing in their ears. This was Dempster's remedy for Boswell's several days (and nights) of drinking and 'talking of Scotland'. Undaunted, Boswell was back the next morning to introduce his friend William Temple to the Dempsters over breakfast at Manchester Buildings. Another more amenable watery event followed in August when the two men enjoyed a day at the races on the River Thames. One race was for Doggett's coat and badge, the orange livery and badge representing Liberty which had been presented for the first time in 1716. Six watermen were required to row from London Bridge to Chelsea for the honour. The winner on this occasion was apparently a boy whom Dr Johnson had quizzed about the Argonauts two days before.[66] 'We saw excellent sport,' reported Boswell.[67]

These social encounters may have been the only chance Boswell and Dempster had to say their temporary farewells before each departed separately for the continent, the one to continue his journey towards literary enterprise and renown – via Harwich where to his utter delight Dr Johnson saw him aboard the packet boat for Holland – and Dempster to France. The reason for the latter's excursion is not recorded but he was to follow a similar pattern the following year during the Parliamentary recess when, in an inconsequential piece of verse, he spoke of 'sunshine and vacance come at last'.[68] The country was in two minds about the Peace of Paris which sealed the end of the Seven Years War. Confidence and joy there were certainly, but it was tinged with regret that, although England was supreme in America and India, so many of the hard-fought-for gains had been returned to the vanquished. Europe was nevertheless again open for trade and visitations by those able to tour and study.

In Scotland an enterprise that Dempster had 'in (his) head these last seven years' and which had been the subject of several meetings earlier in 1763 between merchants and manufacturers in his constituency came to fruition. On 1 August the Dundee Banking Company (trading initially as Messrs George Dempster & Co.) opened for business in two shops under Dundee's Town House.[69] Somewhat out of keeping with this magnificent building designed by William Adam, the bank's two shops with cellars beneath warranted a rental of barely £5 per annum. The bank's partners were broadly based, with Dundee traders in a majority, including several members of the Rankin(e) family after whom the house in which Dempster had been born was named. Only eight partners were landed gentry from the area. Their liability was unlimited and stock could be sold at public roup (auction) or by private sale with the agreement of the other partners. At that time only Edinburgh and Glasgow had recognized banks; other towns including Dundee had to depend on a few shopkeepers who would give cash for bills on London, or sell bills on London to those wanting to make remittances to other parts of the Kingdom.[70] Notes of £5, 20/-, 10/- and 5/- value were issued, reflecting the size of the bank's average dealings at the time. Dempster's bank was the first in Dundee, but its origins were not dissimilar to others that had been founded in the two main centres of Scotland's trade. Goldsmiths, grain merchants (such as Dempster's grandfather) and commission agents had traditionally been the community's exchangers of bills and money handlers. The house of John Coutts & Co, the principal root of Coutts & Co in the Strand, London, had also evolved from a business dealing in corn, buying and selling goods on commission and negotiating bills of exchange across Europe. In the absence of a local banking house, Coutts and other partnerships such as Mansfield & Co, William Cuming and a tobacco trade specialist William Alexander and Sons, handled foreign transactions across Scotland, including those in Dundee and Perth.[71]

For a generation the Dundee Banking Company remained without a rival. Its founder, George Dempster, intended it to be a bank for the town and its residents. The initial capital was £12,600, with the 36 shareholding partners paying up a tenth of their holdings. Whilst the bank flourished, playing a dominant role in the local economy, financing most of the City's industries, the company learned very quickly how dangerous it was for their notes to fall into the hands of the Edinburgh business community. This could mean that large parcels of notes might be presented suddenly and specie demanded. Edinburgh bankers had learned similar lessons from their dealings with City of London bankers who were keen to hold on to their strong position. For this reason the company resolved to redeem its notes only at its office in Dundee.[72]

Such limitations aside, Dempster was able to assist the Council 'with advances of money on easy terms, at a period when the financial department was in a critical state'[73] and the amount taken by the bank in bills grew to £133,728 in 1772, rising to £441,020 in 1792 when interest-bearing deposits were introduced for the first time, and to £1,048,607 ten years later[74] Additional competition arrived in the form of the Paisley Banking Company and the Bank of Scotland in 1791. Only after a second local bank, Dundee Commercial Bank, had been established did the partners of the Dundee Banking Company start accepting money on deposit and they agreed 'as the circulation of the bank (had) considerably diminished . . . owing to the number of branches of other banks which (had) been opened in neighbouring towns, it (was) expedient for the company to establish branches'. Offices were subsequently opened in Brechin, Arbroath, Forfar and Kirkcaldy and the bank moved to new head offices in Castle Street in Dundee. Interestingly, in 1807 both the Dundee banks were heavily criticized for being too profit-orientated and failing to provide local credit. They were accused of not being true bankers since they did not hold sufficient capital, being simply 'merchants and stock jobbers'. The directors were by then accused of policies which, if they were true, Dempster and the founding partners would have abhorred, namely only providing loans to their friends and using the proceeds to speculate in public funds. Undoubtedly, during its early years the Dundee Banking Company was little more than a local facility and the number of its cash accounts outside Dundee were severely curtailed to ensure that its notes could be redeemed at its head office in the city.

Now in his local banking role, the conscientious MP, emerging developer and local entrepreneur, was called upon to be an arbitrator between workers and management. On more than one occasion he acted as peacemaker between weavers and their employers in Glasgow, in one instance averting a serious riot. In recognition of his intervention, the city's magistrates perpetuated his memory by naming a newly-opened street in Glasgow after him.

Whatever the reasons were for Dempster's visit to France during the late summer of 1763, it was brought to an abrupt halt by the pleas of his friend Boswell. The latter had set out reluctantly to spend the coming winter at the University in Utrecht before going to Italy and subsequently to Corsica. He stayed for a short time in Rotterdam with a Scots merchant who had established himself in the town and who had a reputation in Scotland for rakishness and extravagance. Taking violently against Utrecht, Boswell soon moved on to Rotterdam where he was in despair. Dempster had warned him that 'Oxford was a joke to Utrecht'.[75] While staying at the *Hotel Moderne* in Paris Dempster received a heartfelt plea from his friend who wanted to see him in Brussels. In response Dempster dropped all he was doing and travelled the 62 leagues (186 miles) in an extremely uncomfortable post-chaise from the French to the Belgian capital. The journey took 30 hours but when he arrived there was no sign whatsoever of Boswell. A frustrated but apparently still good-tempered Dempster could not wait around or spare the time chasing Boswell in Amsterdam or wherever he had gone to. His time was circumscribed by how long he could be away from Scotland.

By October Dempster was again in Dundee from where he wrote to Boswell, pushing aside the latter's apologies for the abortive journey he had made to Brussels. For ever endeavouring to keep his friend on an even keel, Dempster referred to his having conquered the 'spleen' which Boswell regarded as the cause of all his ills. 'It is but six years since I drubbed the dog to his contentment, and he has never disturbed me since.' He went on to encourage a sceptical turn of mind, since 'by scepticism you will soon discover that some things are less insignificant and uncertain than others' and promised him 'a dish of politics' when they met again.[76]

The following month Dempster resumed his place on the back benches at Westminster and voted against Wilkes on account of his attacks on Scotland in the *North Briton*. He knew only too well the strength of public opinion against him in his constituency. Wilkes's expulsion from the House early the next year was, however, the precursor to fierce discussion about the 'general warrants' which had been used in a wholly cavalier manner to arrest those involved in the production of the weekly newspaper. Dempster was to tell Boswell that 'we have had violent debates about exemption from search warrants which empower messengers to ransack every man's papers and detain his person on bare suspicion. We have not carried the point in the house but we have made (the) Ministry confess 'em illegal and promise that they shall never be used more.'[77]

By the end of the year there was growing evidence that Dempster's salad days were over.[78] His career began to follow a more definite course and life had a harder edge. The City of London took the place of taverns and theatres and as his narrow circle of friends widened so did the number of his enemies. He was able to tell Boswell with obvious relish that every second of his time in 1764 had been occupied with the 'East India faction, private business, private pleasure, and public diversions or public dullness'.[79]

4

EAST INDIA COMPANY
AND PARLIAMENT
(1764 – 1769)

'Mr Dempster inveighed much against the Administration'
James West to Newcastle 13 March 1767

1764

Across the world the Honourable East India Company exercised all-embracing power in civil, military and maritime matters. At home, its competent executive had maintained an excellent, if always circumspect, *modus vivendi* with successive Ministries. Few parliamentarians were expert in Indian matters or well-informed about the Company's complex affairs. The two camps were on a par, similar if not comparable cockpits of influence. Occasional intrigue there was; also debate, and action overt and covert, with each governed by sets of rules and procedures that prevented only the grossest of excesses. However, change was in the air. Quiescent shareholders and a dominant executive, for so long a feature of life within the Company, were to become anachronisms. Clive's transformation of what had been an armed trading corporation into an Asiatic power sowed the seeds of dispute and excessive factionalism attracted unheard of Parliamentary intervention in the Company's affairs. A watershed in the East India Company's history had been reached.

The Company's Charter did not make allowance for intricate interplay between the Court of Proprietors and the Court of Directors. Each had evolved its own methods of doing business. The Company's power in the City of London and the pre-eminence of East India stock meant that it was an essential partner of all administrations. The often delicate and always significant relations with the Ministries were factors enough for both parties to cope with. But the influence the Company had on the nation's political, monetary and international events was nothing compared with the hegemony of its power in the East Indies. There its servants were the sole civil and military machinery of the colonial State. Oversight by a Westminster parliament, and a government pre-occupied with a multitude of other national and international matters, meant that control was far from being regular, close or expert.

Dempster was caught up in the preliminary rounds of this emerging conflict. As a 'proprietor' he acquired £2,000 of shares in November 1763, which not only entitled him to vote at the quarterly meetings of the 2,000-strong Court of Proprietors but pre-qualified him as a director – should he wish to stand for election – suggesting that 'he harboured ambitions in this direction'.[1] The General Court, as it was also called, was a mixed assembly of rich and not-so-rich men and women, although the concentration of stock into fewer hands was on the increase. Many, and certainly a majority in the early part of the decade, were not unduly concerned about Company politics. For forty years a mass of the population had taken vicarious pride in the Company's performance. It was an institution only slightly less important than the Bank of England so far as the nation's finances were concerned, providing a good return for its stockholders and loans to the government. Like many before him, Dempster must have felt his personal investment the best that could be made. He would be joining a select group of other MPs whose presence as shareholders and directors provided a convenient bridge between the government of the day and the Company. At this time about 40 parliamentarians were connected in some way with the Company.

Five years previously the proprietors had reversed a decision by the Directorate on the form of government to be adopted in Bengal. Now a new generation of proprietors joined the fray and began to flex muscles which had hitherto been relaxed. Whether Dempster anticipated that the General Court was to be used for ends for which it was not designed is rather doubtful. As Lucy Sutherland so succinctly put it: 'The first striking features of the contest of 1763 were . . . the introduction of Asiatic wealth into the electoral activities of the Company; the personal struggle between Clive and Sulivan; with the evolution of a cumbrous mechanism for the creation of votes which called into action a number of forces in no way directly concerned with the welfare of the Company and which was to prove a veritable Frankenstein's monster to its creators'.[2]

Always precarious, the standards of honesty in India came to be greatly undermined by the enormous personal gains from private trading and princely gifts. These followed Clive's victories over Siraj-ud-daula and his replacement by another Nawab, Mir Jafar, after the Black Hole affair and the Battle of Plassey in 1757. However conscientious the directors in London tried to be, India was still 10,000 miles away and letters could take a year to arrive. Furthermore, instructions to senior personnel were often unclear and the Indian *real politik*, which accounted for many actions detrimental to the Company's long-term interests allowed considerable free play. The lack of local knowledge on the part of London managers often meant they did not know what was going on. The subsequent appearance in Britain of all manner of returned Company servants flaunting Asiatic wealth, including Clive, whose own fortune amounted to £400,000, greatly bothered those such as Sulivan who could see that such riches might damage the Company and undermine its independence.[3] Their 'awful behaviour' became a 'breach of the most sacred trust one powerful nation held towards another'.[4]

Laurence Sulivan, the greatest director of the Company throughout this period, was an Irishman who did not come from one of the great Anglo-Irish families, having made a lowly way in India, and that rather inconspicuously. Although he eventually gained favour with the Governor of Bombay, his rise to power was slow. His good grasp of finance and administration was eventually recognized and, after completing a major fraud investigation, he became a member of the Council in 1751. Then, after making a fortune from private trade and official perquisites, he left the Company's service, returned to England and became MP for Taunton. In 1755, through the influence of Stephen Law, his erstwhile patron in India, he was elected to the Directorate, becoming Deputy Chairman in 1755 and Chairman on four occasions over the years till his death in 1786.

The interaction of private and public interests was never edifying. It had been tolerated so long as accepted bounds were not exceeded and the activities of ambitious fortune hunters did not get out of hand or openly embarrass their patrons and employers. The bad press the Company received throughout this period hardly helped. Even six months before Clive had returned to England the Company had been trying to find out the 'why's and wherefore's' of the *largesse* being distributed by the Nawab of Bengal. The amount individuals could import or export on Company ships was regulated, but old fears that this private trade deprived the Company of revenue also increased. It was 'contrary to all propriety' and an inquisition was called for.

The diversion of an annual sum of £27,000 to Clive by the Nawab of Bengal in exchange for a purely nominal office forced the issue. His *Jagir*[5] was always a bitter pill for the Company to swallow and something which cast a long shadow over Clive's subsequent career. Although Sulivan was willing to defend Clive at first, he recognized that there were some in the Company who wanted the question of his *Jagir* put firmly on the agenda. By 1761 the hostility of discontented servants of the Company towards Sulivan, including members of the 'Bengal Club' to which returning 'nabobs' often belonged, had erupted. The first contest in 1763 became a fight between the two men. The Sulivan party was attacked for agreeing to the terms of the East Indian settlement under the Peace of Paris that had ended the Seven Years War. Nevertheless, subsequent events owed much to Clive's damaged pride. As a victorious soldier and a newly-created Irish Lord who had been received at court and toasted in fashionable circles, he found himself unable to exercise the power and influence in the Company to which he felt he was entitled.

A special General Court on 15 March debated a technical motion to exonerate Thomas Rous, the stand-in Chairman, for the direction the negotiations had taken.[6] Vote-splitting, a gambit started five years previously, was further refined. The process involved legitimate individual holdings being 'split' and given to friends or relations, thereby enabling 'artificial' stock-holders to vote as they were directed. An investor holding £2,000 worth of stock might divide this sum into ten £200 blocks and place it with his friends, who, in return for a small fee, would vote as instructed by the patron. The elections over, the stock would find its way back to the original owner.[7] Now, a number of powerful Whig grandees took up these artificial voting quali-fications and openly joined the 'war' in Leadenhall Street. Some 657 proprietors, out of 800 present, voted. Clive attracted 220 votes against 160 for Sulivan, the remainder being for other candidates.

A battle had been won, but not the war. At the annual meeting of the General Court the following month a greater number of proprietors turned out, and with Sulivan mustering stronger Ministry support, the decision was over-turned. It would have been at about the time these two critical votes were taken, which had the effect of reinforcing government intervention in the Company's affairs, that Dempster acquired his stockholding. Almost immediately instructions were issued to stop payment of Clive's *Jagir*. As Lucy Sutherland says, Sulivan's ultimate blackmail weapon had been used.

Whether or not Dempster would have chosen to be associated with the Company's affairs at this juncture if it had not been for the pressure put upon him by his friends in the Johnstone clan will never be known. Involvement with the Company was certainly attractive to a minority of MPs, and it undoubtedly afforded a degree of useful patronage, but it would hardly have been a natural course of action for someone with no ties to India and limited resources. That the Johnstones had a hand in the timing, if not the financing of his shareholding as well, does look a strong possibility. The family was desperate for all the support it could get and Dempster might have succumbed to their blandishments. He certainly seems to have engaged in vote-splitting, and there was always the chance that he might trade his shares profitably. However this may have been, he was to spend a great deal of his time helping to defend the interests of one of the Johnstones of Westerhall, John Johnstone, whose dubious activities were a public talking point and of acute concern to the family.[8]

Sir James Johnstone, the third baronet, had seven sons. Another James (1726–94), the eldest and fourth baronet, was the head of the venerable Whig family and a close relative of the Marquis of Annandale. Dempster came to know three of the brothers – William (Pulteney) Johnstone who had been a firm friend since his days in Edinburgh, George, often referred to as 'Governor

George', already an MP and an influential proprietor during the 1760s whom Dempster thought had 'strict integrity, real worth and unsullied honour', and John (1734–95) the fifth son.[9]

When in his 'teens John Johnstone had gone to Bengal with the Company. In 1756 he was a writer in Dacca when the East India Company's settlements were overrun. After some time in prison he was released, found shelter in the French factory and the following year served as an artilleryman with Clive at the Battle of Plassey. During his temporary imprisonment he had fallen ill and been cared for by a Miss Warwick, the elderly daughter of a merchant, who had also been caught up in Dacca by the same events. Soon afterwards, and rather surprisingly, she adopted Johnstone and, believing that her nearest relation, a brother, was dead she also left him her entire estate. Johnstone's benefactress then died, leaving him the sum of £100,000. Whereupon he promptly resigned from the Company, intending to return to Scotland and become the owner of an estate. Although luck played a significant part in many of his exploits, on this occasion fate was against him. Waiting in Calcutta for a ship to England, he ran into a Captain Warwick whom he soon discovered was Miss Warwick's long-lost brother. Despite being misled initially by a cock and bull story about Johnstone being Miss Warwick's trustee until an heir was found, the Captain offered to share the inheritance with Johnstone. This he found it convenient to refuse, perhaps realizing that it was always possible someone might challenge the will or challenge his account of the earlier events. Whereupon, instead of going home he resumed his clerkship in the Company.[10]

By 1761 this 'shrewd and unscrupulous business man', as Lady Haden-Guest described John Johnstone, had become chief in the district of Burdwan and a member of the Bengal council. Two year later, and with an eye ever alert to profitable private deals, he became the natural leader of the rebels on the council when Henry Vansittart, the Governor of Bengal, sought to restrict private trade and abolish the certificates of exemption which made such trade so attractive. When Vansittart's agreement with Mir Kassim was rejected, the Nawab simply put all traders on a similar footing by abolishing internal customs duties entirely. Hostilities followed and were only halted when a coalition of Indian princes was defeated at Buxar in 1764. Once news reached London, Johnstone was dismissed from the Company's service for his part in the 'shameless proceedings' of the council. However, his luck held, if temporarily, and he was reinstated on the council. Rather inevitably, Johnstone again ignored Company regulations by securing more than £50,000 in gifts. This time he was forced to resign by Clive when he reached Calcutta in May 1765 and he finally sailed for home in October the same year. It was Clive's decision that Dempster was called upon by the family to help reverse.

William Pulteney had been endeavouring to help his other brother George when he solicited Dempster's assistance almost within days of his entering Parliament, and when he and his sister were lodging in St James's Place. George Johnstone's service during the war had not been recognized and moves were afoot to settle his further career. Dempster had then suggested that the family's connection with the Duke of Newcastle might be of more use than either his 'own poor assistance' or that of Gilbert Elliot 'whose influence at the Admiralty probably expired with his office'. Dempster had been sorry for this brother's plight and concerned that 'a man of his consummate bravery and distinguished mind should need any other aid' than that of his own character.[11] He spoke to Oswald who advised him that Lord Anson, now at the Board of Admiralty, was 'so blunt and unsatisfactory' that an approach to him would be worthless. A better solution might be a strong letter from Lord Elibank (George's uncle) to Lord Bute, whom they both knew. It was Bute's recommendation of him that finally led to his appointment as Governor of Pensacola in West Florida.

Clive had considered going to law to get the Company to resume his payments but chose instead to seek redress in Parliament. Backstairs soundings, however, showed him with little support and when Grenville offered to mediate between him and the Company he suggested that the *Jagir* might be given a limited life. Sulivan took the proposition to the Court of Directors only to see the compromise rejected. Before more could be done, John Johnstone and two other Company servants had been dismissed and the situation worsened in Bengal. A General Court in February 1764 saw nine proprietors demanding action, including two supporters of John Johnstone – his Governor brother George and Lord Elibank. They wanted Clive sent out to India in return for retaining his *Jagir*. Vote-splitting for the crucial Court meeting on 12 March this time even included employees of Customs & Excise as well as two Ministers. The Johnstones apparently had little stock for splitting. In the event Governor George read out a long defence of his brother, but failed to achieve much public support or any assurance of help. The family complained bitterly that in supporting Clive they had received nothing and had been cheated. Both sides eventually claimed victory. Clive achieved the first part of his planned deal, that he should be sent out to India as Governor and Commander-in-Chief, but, so far as his *Jagir* was concerned, he was left with the hope that 'by doing his duty' the Company might eventually be grateful. At the normal quarterly General Court on 21 March, Sulivan only narrowly survived after Clive made an attempt to link any appointment to the latter's resignation as head of the Direction.

The Court of Directors then turned to the question of Johnstone's reinstatement on the grounds of 'his services', however egregious they had been. Dempster must have been as surprised as the family were when the man's luck again held and a motion to re-employ him was passed, virtually by default. Sulivan had other important positions to defend and could not make an issue of the reinstatement without jeopardizing these. As Lucy Sutherland said, 'By this . . . manoeuvre the Johnstone group achieved an end which no responsible member of the Company could approve, and in a manner fraught with danger for the future'. As Dempster soon found out, they always seemed capable of producing *fantoccini*, or puppets made to perform by concealed strings, at the right moment. The Directorate then concluded its debate about the *Jagir*, agreeing that it should be paid for a 10-year period and Clive finally left for India. So far as John Johnstone was concerned, he behaved true to form, as has already been seen. Charged with disobedience for the second time, he resigned and came home with a £300,000 fortune! The family record claimed he spent 'about a ninth of it on the Alva, Hangingshaw and Denovan estates . . . and lived quietly on his beautiful Scottish estates till he was elected MP for the Kirkcaldy Burghs'. His own letters to Pulteney told a quite different story. This 'upright character' had lost nothing of his obsession with deal-making, stock manipulation and speculation.

At the end of the year Dempster returned north and attended several meetings of St Andrews Town Council. Will Vilant, another member of that illustrious local family, was usually in the Chair. It was during Dempster's attendance at roughly three-monthly intervals between 1765–66 that his brothers experienced something of local political life. Charles Dempster was present in September 1765 and John Dempster, who, despite his melancholic disposition, seems to have stayed the course a little longer, is recorded as having been admitted as a Councillor in September 1766. He was still there in 1768.[12] John Hamilton Dempster, on the other hand, served his apprenticeship in Dundee where he held the honourable post of Bailie and Councillor to the Guild. Like George Dempster before him, he seems to have been the shore-master for a period. So satisfied had the Town Council been with Dempster's performance at Westminster that the previous autumn they had given him a formal vote of thanks: 'Despising faction, Party measures, and other low Pursuits, the true interest of his Country has been his sole aim.'[13] His services to the burgh 'were eminently practical'. In 1766 he acquired ten acres of vacant ground belonging to the hospital which he feued out for building purposes to speculative builders to encourage development of the town westwards.[14]

Dempster's 'poor' sister Jean, who continued to care for him, had enjoyed very indifferent health. Dempster said, 'She is grown a skeleton and I've the most serious apprehensions about her'.[15] It was not until the following year that he could report '(she) is now pretty much recovered after having been very ill'. A charming postscript to Dempster's letter to Boswell, attached at 'Jeanie's request', showed her to be a woman of some humour and telling *esprit*. She asked Boswell, who was abroad, whether 'he saw the Rocks at Milleray' (sic), desiring that he would send her 'a present to the value of about £100 sterling by the very first ship'. Then, expressing her determination to stand up to Boswell, she reminded him of some of the previous gifts he had proffered: 'don't imagine that I'll be put off with a Parmazane (sic) cheese, a box of sweetmeats or a Popish relict . . . far less a story of Rousseau or Voltaire on education'.[16] But all the family was saddened in November when her eldest sister, Peggy, died at the early age of 33. Her earlier ill-health had been the reason for Dempster's premature return from the Grand Tour eight years before.

1765

With ministers becoming useful allies, destructive 'factionalism' at India House became a habit that few felt inclined to break and any thought the administration had of checking the worst excesses of vote-splitting was frustrated by more pressing matters. The constant blood-letting was to increase rather than diminish. Dempster found common ground with Sulivan and stood unsuccessfully in April as a director on the 'Proprietor's list'.[17] The usual practice before the recent conflict between proprietors and the Direction had been for the directors simply to approve and issue their nominations – the 'House List'. The advent of contested elections resulted in alternative candidates being included on the 'Proprietors' List'. 'Double-listing' occurred when both sides were content to see a name go forward or if, by including a name twice, opposition could be neutralized.

About this time Dempster moved from lodgings to a house in Delahay Street.[18] His housekeeper sister may have remained at Dunnichen for a period. From the new address he travelled by sedan chair to a House of Commons deliberating the composition of a regency council following the first attack of the King's madness. The fear was that he might die while his heir was still an infant. Speaking twice in May on the Regency Bill, Dempster eulogized the King and supported Pryce Campbell's motion against any female regent marrying a Catholic.[19] Essentially 'unconnected', Dempster was usually entered on the lists drawn up by leaders of each faction as 'doubtful' and in June Robert Nugent sought to secure him for Grenville.[20] But, as he told Boswell, 'Lord Bute, the Duke of Bedford and George Grenville quarrelled towards the end of the session . . . and the general opinion is that (the administration) will not last long'.[21] And so it proved.

Lord Rockingham's year-long Whig administration was formed in July. A common-sense politician and one of the richest noblemen of his time, Rockingham was honest, ambitious and admired for his honourable behaviour.[22] Dempster evidently had great hopes of achieving some office of state at this time, particularly since the new administrative 'team' was to be chosen personally by the new first minister and he shared his sympathy for the American colonists. Although less than he may have hoped for, the news that Rockingham intended appointing Dempster Secretary to the Order of the Thistle was undoubtedly a step in the right direction. Clearly delighted, he said, 'I really believe I have not a tithe of the pleasure in receiving this office that your Lordship has in conferring it. But if there is a man in England that would entertain a more grateful sense of the favour you have done me than myself, I wish my first year of it may be my last. I will do myself the honour to wait upon your Lordship tomorrow morning at 10 o'clock'.[23]

Dempster was only the fifth Secretary to the Order.[24] His immediate predecessor had been Lieut. General Sir Henry Erskine, the MP for Anstruther, whom he had met in the Commons.[25] Unfortunately, he died in August 1765, four months after being appointed, so precipitating Dempster's accession to the office, one that he always greatly treasured and held for 53 years. As portraits of Dempster often showed, he took every opportunity of wearing the secretary's badge with 'its thistle of gold enamelled in its proper colours upon two gold pens, in saltire, on a ground of white enamel, surrounded by the motto, in letters of gold on a green circle'. It could be worn from the neck by a gold chain or, as Dempster usually preferred, from a green riband about three inches in width.[26]

He was admitted as an officer of the 'Most Ancient and Most Noble Order' and 'slipt (his) neck into that collar' on 21 August.[27] The duties were similar to those which in the Order of the Garter belonged to its Chancellor.[28] He was required 'to transmit the Sovereign's Orders to the Knights Brethren, and attend the Royal Person to that effect'. In addition to the post of Secretary, there was a Dean (Dr Robert Hamilton), Lord Lyon King of Arms (John Hooke-Campbell) and the Usher (Robert Quarme). Fergusson described the post as 'worth at most, £500 a year' and suggested that Dempster 'did not take it seriously'.[29] This is hard to believe since the value of the office was more than the income he would have been able to deploy from his estates in Angus. It was made up of an annual salary of £300 and a fee of £100 paid by each Knight elected into the order.[30] There were 21 investitures and 23 admissions during Dempster's lifetime making a total of £2,300 in fees alone due to the Secretary.[31]

It seems, however, that he parted with the fee element of his remuneration to at least one of his ushers, Robert Quarme,[32] in recognition that they, rather than he, were present at most if not all the investitures.[33] Such puzzling behaviour is almost unbelievable in a man who always prided himself on performing even the smallest duty with diligence and energy, particularly as the office was an early token of ministerial favour and one that would have brought him into contact with many noble Scottish families. A similar and unfounded complaint against John Hooke-Campbell, the King of Arms, that he too 'never discharged the duties of his office personally' only adds to the confusion.[34] His first investiture at St James's on 23 December 1767 would have been of John Murray, 3rd Duke of Atholl.[35] The appointment seems also to have necessitated a by-election in the Perth Burghs on account of his acceptance of a paid post under the Crown which, to Dempster's relief, was uncontested.[36]

1766

Writing to Boswell, who still entertained ambitions to enter parliament, Dempster again conceded that it was 'a noble object of ambition', but added, as if to underscore his own uncertainty, that 'the roads to it were . . . thorny and so precarious' that one could 'not be too circumspect'. A seat in the Commons had to be stormed by 'people drunk and desperate'.[37] Just how short-lived political power and Dempster's own chances of preferment in a Whig administration could be were soon demonstrated. By July the 'King's Friends' who had been instrumental in Grenville's dismissal forced Rockingham out of office. An elderly Pitt, now the Earl of Chatham, quickly showed his hand, making it clear that he was minded to conduct an unprecedented parliamentary investigation into the East India Company's affairs.[38] Such a move was a serious threat not only to those like Johnstone whose future was in the balance but to the existence of the Company.

Alderman William Beckford, who had long waged his own war against returning 'nabobs' using their wealth to buy estates and votes, had argued before Rockingham's demise that it was necessary to know how the company's revenues had been 'consumed' and why the proprietors had received no increase in their dividend.[39] In this situation it was inevitable that another outbreak of factionalism at India House was looming. Exceptional profits as the result of the war brought about previously unheard of speculation in EIC stock and Clive's despatches pushed hopes of more gains ever higher. In May the directors of the Company decided to proceed against John Johnstone in the Court of Chancery. It was to be an uneasy time for Dempster as well as the Johnstone brothers. Paying off the debts that so stifled him had proved difficult and, surrounded by a family prepared to do almost anything to achieve its ends, the temptation to join their risky trading would have been great.

An unjustifiable increase in the Company dividend became the subject of popular protest. Pamphlets and strident calls in the press reinforced the 'bull' market and an organized campaign led by the Johnstones had the secondary objective of forcing the directors to abandon their legal action. Trading in futures and options flourished both at home and on the Amsterdam market, the latter by experienced brokers in London. Rising prices may have encouraged Dempster to sell much if not all of such stock as he possessed. Certainly by July he had assembled £3,000, but he was reluctant to repay what he owed to Sir Adam on account of an attractive prospect he had heard about in Holland which was, so he believed, 'made for him'. It had been a time of 'cutting and carving' and, fortunately for him, his friend was a 'less rigorous creditor'.[40] He also felt in honour bound to support the consolidation of six small banks in his constituency, having himself founded the Dundee Bank three years before. Somehow he managed to subscribe for four £100 shares in the Perth United Banking Company, retaining the investment until at least

1787 when the company became the Perth Banking Company.[41]

Like other lawyers and members in the Commons, Dempster was aware that the East India Company's independence could very well be at risk if the government was let into its affairs. Chatham seemed inclined to force a new agreement on the Company. Charters were in effect property rights giving sole and unassailable possession. 'Evil ministers' might soon think they could undermine the property rights of individuals if governments could interfere with chartered company rights.[42] Pitt's wartime extravagances, which Dempster deplored, led him to conclude that he was 'now sovereign arbiter . . . His object from the first moment of his former resignation was to attain this perch of power . . . I believe he will not pay off our debts . . . will not help the constitution and . . . will break his neck upon the backstairs.'[43]

The cautious approach of the direction at India House to the frantic speculation and the call for an increased dividend continued for much of the summer. It only changed when the directors became aware that an opposition comprising the Rockingham party at Westminster, Sulivan and the Johnstone group had coalesced and that an attempt would be made at the September General Court to defy them. Dempster, who had been a go-between, could only watch as a formidable vote-splitting campaign got under way. Any small packets of stock he may have held on to as a contribution to his friends' voting power would have been small beer. By the end of September John Johnstone showed that he had lost none of his skills in hazarding other people's money and finessing deals in a 'city of sharpers and pickpockets'.[44] He had begged, borrowed or bought £150,000 of stock. Some £37,000 of his own ill-gotten gains were used to buy this body of support,[45] and, by persuading Clive's supporters that an increased dividend was in the public interest, the vote when it came was overwhelming – a majority of 340 votes to 231. The annual dividend was increased from six to ten per cent.

An inevitable result of allowing greed to overpower prudent management was that parliament felt justified in taking a closer interest in the company. Dempster was apparently in two minds about the best way forward and at a pre-Parliament meeting in November, to which he was invited to hear the King's speech, he sought Rockingham's direction in the following terms: 'It will give me pleasure to regulate my parliamentary conduct in whatever shape is agreeable to you. Let me say even more pleasure now than when your Lordship was at the head of the Treasury. While in that situation the strongest declarations of attachment might admit of a double construction; at present your Lordship will not think I flatter when I express my very high esteem both of your public and private conduct'.[46] In December Dempster joined Rockingham in opposing Beckford's motion for a parliamentary enquiry into the company's affairs.[47] Furthermore, in the new year, his was one of the votes that surprisingly defeated the administration's proposed Land Tax.

By the spring Sulivan was ready to revive his earlier proposals for improving Company and government relations. A quarterly meeting of the General Court provided the starting point for efforts to woo the government by separating the Company's trading profits from those earned in India. By seeking an extension of the Company's Charter till 1817 and an increase in its capital to reduce its debt burden, the government stood to benefit by some £800,000 from the Company along with all the income from 'territorial sources'. In their enthusiasm, the directors offered their proposals directly to the House of Commons where, with opposition and some government support, they hoped to scupper any parliamentary enquiry. However, neither Sulivan nor Dempster could accept the terms negotiated by the directors. Both agreed with James West, another Member, that 'letting the Government into a partnership with the Company would soon end in the absolute dependency and ruin of the latter'.[48] Helped by a new intake of directors, the vote went against Sulivan in the Court and another challenge looked likely. Only an intense series of negotiations between ministers and directors diffused the situation, leaving the question of a further increase in the dividend still to be resolved.

There had been an earlier indication that a ceiling of 16% on future dividends might be acceptable, always assuming that the company's debt burden could be reduced. When it became known that any progressive increase was to be restricted to a three-year period, those speculators in Sulivan's party who had been so successful the previous year were up in arms. Their dudgeon provided yet another opportunity for John Johnstone's case to be aired and a hurried vote-splitting campaign to enforce a rise in the dividend followed. On 5 May Dempster urgently asked for clarification and the circulation of the administration's proposals among the proprietors, but the die was cast and the following day the directors' more rational policies were overwhelmingly defeated.[49] Dempster became the leader of those proprietors who, in defiance of both ministry and the direction, wanted the dividend increased to 12½%, a second rise in eight months. Engineered by Johnstone and his supporters these moves may have been, but Dempster was undoubtedly involved. They smacked of greed rather than probity and his share of 'criminality' was averred by Walpole in his *Memoirs*. Even Johnstone's *Letter to the Proprietors*, in which he had attempted to justify the methods by which he had obtained his fortune, contributed to the mood of the moment. Quite remarkably, the General Court shamefully ignored the protests of the directors and, to their despair and chagrin, decided to stop all prosecutions against former company servants. With the prosecution against him dropped, Johnstone personally thanked the General Court and walked out into Leadenhall Street.

Twelve days later, and with compromise in the air, and perhaps some sense of their earlier insane behaviour, an especially stormy General Court spent sixteen hours reviewing the situation. After the debacle of 6 May, the administration had moved to prevent the company from raising its dividend and contemplated action to prevent vote-splitting. Faced with the prospect of defeat, Sulivan softened his approach and on 26 May, to everyone's surprise, the Dividend Bill was passed in the Commons, thereby imposing less favourable conditions on the company than the opposition could have achieved had Chatham's original inquiry been accepted.[50]

The arrival of summer did nothing to bring the relief that Dempster may have hoped for. Instead, he had to face an attack on his flank that came very close to destroying his parliamentary career and impoverishing him still further. It was mounted by some of Clive's supporters who had been enraged by the actions of the Dempster, Sulivan and Johnstone alliance at India House. The purchase of the Auchintully estate in Atholl by one Robert Mackintosh went unnoticed until its new laird, a promising but long-winded lawyer who had failed to obtain a parliamentary seat at Dumfries five years before, announced his intention of standing against Dempster in his Perth Burghs constituency.[51] He was compared unfavourably with Dempster. 'All the wealth of the Indies could not give Mr Mackintosh that flexibility of temper and milkiness of nature which make a man behave with courtesy and forbearance towards those that are not of his sentiments. His talking the language of purity and patriotism availed him the less that it was well known on what foundation he stood candidate. . . . Mr Dempster (on the other hand) was exceedingly beloved by high and low, being accounted a man of honour and probity.'[52] Robert Mackintosh was already a Company proprietor when he appeared on the scene, a fact which confirmed the view in the constituency that there was more to his intervention than met the eye.[53] At India House, where he supported Clive, he had taken part in several clashes and may have been bettered by Dempster in the tempestuous debates over his leader's mission to Bengal in 1764. Common talk soon had Clive's money behind the Auchintully purchase as well as Mackintosh's election expenses.

In October, when 'the burgh elections were imminent, the town of Cupar was humming with the intrigues of Dempster's and Mackintosh's supporters; for the composition of the new Town Council would determine for which candidate the town would declare. Rumours of bribery ran among both parties'[54] and, to Dempster's surprise, John Johnstone arrived. Still hoping to win a seat in parliament himself in the south of England, the prospect of a profitable land deal in Orkney had brought him north.[55] Never given to contrition, he did at least recognize the debt he owed Dempster. Writing to Pulteney, his brother, on 3 October he said he 'thought it highly proper to make a visit to my friend here, and particularly to return my acknowledgements to Mr Dempster for his generous support which has drawn upon him so unworthy an attack'.[56] A day or so later when he was in Kirkcaldy (the seat he was to win in 1774) Johnstone had the 'happiness . . . to be witness of our worthy friend Dempster's compleat victory over Clive, Directors and the Devil at Coupar (*sic*) where all the magistrates to a man are his friends and the town by a great majority have followed the example of St Andrews, Forfar and Dundee in deciding in his favour. At Perth the magistrates are mostly his and he is gone there expecting to have their declaration also'.[57] The events of that week were, however, soon revealed in a different light.

When an ex-bailie and Cupar merchant, Robert Geddie Junior, and Robert Mackintosh later brought an action against Dempster, they claimed he had found that 'without having recourse to bribery and corruption, he would not be able to procure the voice of the said Burgh of Cupar'. He had 'resolved to have recourse to . . . unconstitutional means'. More specifically, it was maintained that Dempster and his associates 'did corrupt or attempt to corrupt' David Ritchie, a labourer, along with James Tod, surgeon; Thomas Greig, tanner; Alexander Miller, a barber and wigmaker; Primrose Rymer, a writer; James Sibbald, a shoemaker; David Duncan, Deacon of the Bakers; James Morres, Deacon of the Waulkers, all of whom were Cupar councillors or magistrates. Sibbald, who was said to have been employed by Dempster, had apparently also hosted a meeting where Morres was pressed to give him his vote and Dempster put 'three different parcels into one of the waistcoat pockets of Morres' each containing twenty one pound notes. Furthermore, at the house of the provost, Dempster 'strongly solicited' James Thomson, 'Deacon of the Fleshers', making it clear that 'he would give him anything he would ask or demand', adding that 'a trading man was always wanting money'.[58]

The indictment alleged three further instances of bribery. At the home of a tanner called John Smith he 'took out of his pocket four parcels of banknotes . . . containing eighty pounds sterling . . . saying that it would pay his debts'. An innkeeper was also offered fifty pounds and at the home of David Preston, the town's change-keeper which he visited several times, Dempster topped an offer to pay any debts he had outstanding with an additional fifty pounds if he voted for him. All in all, nearly thirty witnesses were listed in the papers sent to the Court of Justiciary after Dempster had been bailed before the Sheriff-Depute.[59]

It is hard to believe that Dempster would have been so foolish as to commit such acts in a manner beyond 'acceptable practice'. The desperate last-minute actions of Mackintosh's party did not help. They sent a town officer through the streets with 'tuck and drum' to proclaim a reward of 'one hundred pounds sterling to the discoverer of any act of corruption offered, received or refused'. If it was a trumped-up charge then it had been well done, but Dempster never denied the events under oath. When the burgh elections took place on 8 October the Dempster party found itself victorious and the officious bailie was among those who had lost their seats. A majority of the Council came out in support of Dempster, making Cupar the fourth out of the five burghs to do so. Angry protests came from the Mackintosh minority, and accusations of bribery were hurled from both sides. It was said that the election of one of Mackintosh's supporters had cost Lord Clive two hundred pounds.[60]

Three or four days before the resulting prosecution Mackintosh wrote to Grenville to solicit his 'opinion and interposition' if the case should come before the House of Commons. He had got wind of Dempster's line of defence which was to claim a Member of Parliament's privilege to be immune from appearing in court to answer the charge while Parliament was sitting. At the right time he had 'no unwillingness to stand forth in his defence against this calumnious and vexatious prosecution, brought in consequence of political spleen and disappointment'. Mackintosh and Geddie claimed that the privilege could not apply in this case, but in December the Court of Justiciary upheld Dempster's objection and adjourned the case.

A month before, Dempster too had sought advice. Writing to Burke, he explained his quandary: 'My antagonist threatens me with so many Law Suits that I am uncertain if it will be in my power to get to Town (from Dunnichen) till after the (Christmas) holidays. If he really puts these threats in execution I shall certainly complain of a Breach of Privilege. May I beg therefore you will let me know if this can be done by a Letter to the Speaker or in any other shape while I am absent. You know that I am bail'd to appear personally whenever summoned in any of our criminal courts. Can I then leave Scotland without endangering my bail? Am I not to all intents and purposes a prisoner? . . . and as such detain'd from attending my duty in Parliament? Will not my captivity be more manifest, and make a greater impression on the House when my complaint comes as it were from gaol than if I was to make it myself to the House? It is of consequence to me to be well advised as to those points, and, I apply for your advice because I know you are able to advise me and I believe you are not indifferent to my concerns'.[61]

1768

Dempster returned to Westminster from Edinburgh and voted in February with the opposition on the *Nullum Tempus* Bill.[62] Parliament was dissolved in March and a new one summoned for 10 May. With a criminal prosecution pending against him, he could not be a candidate. His friend William Pulteney stood in his place and not only won four of the five burghs – an improvement on Dempster's own performance – but his was also successful in Cromarty, the seat he elected to take up.[63] This cleared the way for Dempster's return to his old seat, although the path to it was longer than he anticipated. Thanking Rockingham in January for 'the support which (his) Lordship and friends gave (Pulteney) in his contest with Sir John Gordon', Dempster expressed his fear that the parliamentary session would end before their petitions could be heard.[64] So it proved, and although the delay was not the 'ruin' he predicted, Dempster was again invoking Rockingham's intervention almost a year later.[65] The case went first to the House of Lords and then back to the Court of Justiciary which took till August to find the charges against him to be 'vague and uncertain as to the place, mode and the circumstances of the crime libelled'. Since Mackintosh and Geddie 'had no title to bring this prosecution, which should have been at the instance of the King's Advocate', they dismissed the libel.[66] Tempers on both sides evidently took some time to calm down, with each man threatening still further legal action against the other, but commonsense eventually prevailed and the matter was dropped.

The significance of this episode went well beyond the fine line of what was and was not acceptable practice at the time. Although the charges of bribery had not been proved and the outcome of the legal process was said to have left his public reputation unstained, Dempster openly admitted that his behaviour had been severely compromised. He had endured self-seeking machinations at India House and now his own ineptitude had not only 'frayed his nerves' and taken toll of the probity he so esteemed, but left him bereft of money and self-confidence. As Fergusson said, 'The battle had been an expensive one and the only gainers by the whole affair were the lawyers who had been so busily engaged on both sides'.[67] The election campaign and litigation had cost him well over £10,000, obliging him by 1771 to sell the estates he had been so proud of just a month before the contest: 'I have been employed in (agriculture) for these last four years and hope in as many more to quadruple the values of my six thousand Patrimonial acres'.[68] Certainly the Mackintosh affair affected the life Dempster lived subsequently. He came to recognize his limitations and the need not only for frugality but a life-style which more closely matched his own ambitions. Instead of being the catspaw of others, he set out to be his own man, to be more circumspect and less ingenuous.

For the moment he had lost his peace of mind. Writing to Boswell, he admitted his affairs were 'a little embarrassed' and with 'agitating burroughs and the India Company on (his) hands' he had found wine 'a resource'. It was 'high time to take leave of it' and this he had 'done so effectually', hopefully 'for ever'. It enabled him to turn his attention to selling at least 1,200 acres of his land 'lying detached from the rest'. Clearing some of the debts that worried him so much was essential since if they were left unpaid he anticipated they would 'eat up all that now remains'.[69]

Having benefited from having his friend Pulteney stand security for him on other occasions, he now needed his help more than ever. Fortunately, he joined in 'cheerfully' and Dempster hoped, rather vainly as it happened, it would be the last time that he would have occasion to trouble him. Two surveyors were to examine the properties and an offer for the lands came to within £500 of a £17,000 estimate he had made in London, a sum which was a little more than he needed. An offer passed on by Pulteney even came from John Johnstone; he was prepared to lend him £2–3,000 should it be required. In declining it there is the ghost of a fear on Dempster's part that it would only perpetuate an obligation from which he now wished to be free. Although he maintained some affection for Pulteney's brother, he preferred to stand clear and 'preserve the liberty of speaking (his) mind and acting with independency'. Such caution never crept into Dempster's tone when he unburdened himself upon Pulteney. The latter's wealth had been the result of an exceptionally successful marriage, and their close friendship was born of a shared sense of propriety. Both enabled him to adopt a frank if sometimes frivolous tone: 'What do you propose doing with your enormous income (£20,000 per annum as it was) or what shall I do with mine when my debts are paid?'[70]

As if John Johnstone's earlier campaign wasn't enough, another arch-manipulator had been at work during this period. Lauchlin Macleane, 'one of the most interesting figures of the political underworld',[71] was an Irish adventurer who had learned his unscrupulous trade in American and West Indian land deals, becoming Under Secretary of State, and for a time his minister's 'man of business'. With extensive contacts and clients who respected his business judgement, he had 'gambled on every Bourse in Europe'. Between June and October he and Sir George Colebrooke[72] developed a plan whereby a £100,000 'bank' of Company stock could be legitimately supplied for short periods, so increasing the number of qualified voters, particularly for the 1769 election.[73] Dempster, along with Sulivan and John Johnstone,[74] seems to have become involved yet again, at least in facilitating meetings between the various groups. Several took place over breakfast at Macleane's house in Queen Anne Street. Hugh Macaulay-Boyd, a go-between for Macleane, told how on one occasion, finding himself unable to gain admittance to the Commons, Dempster was deceived into thinking he was the Member for Antrim and told the doorkeeper to let him in. The next day at breakfast Macleane had been surprised to see Boyd beat a quick retreat when Dempster was announced.[75]

1769

Dempster spent the early part of the year at Dunnichen. His spirits were still low and he was 'ashamed' to tell Boswell how 'weak' his mind had become. His sister Jean was convinced he would have neglected his sheep, 'had they not been all eaten' before he came home. Even the 'wonted pleasure' he always took in his 'ditches, hedges and dykes' had disappeared.[76] Only when he reached London the next month was he in a mood to repeat the following stanza which, 'like Fontaine's *Oraison de S'Julien*', did him 'a great deal of good'—

For me in mad ambition's tide,
In factions wild, or office high
My grief to conquer, or to hide
For what remains of life, I'll try.[77]

Battle honours in the disastrous General Election campaign that so shackled Dempster had been few and slow in coming. But two Johnstones were now MPs, Pulteney and George, the latter having been elected for Cockermouth, and Dempster's efforts to bring the clan into the Sulivan camp paid off. Now the member for Ashburton, Sulivan, was back in power at Leadenhall Street where Sir George Colebrooke was chairman and, although there had been a close battle between the Clive and Sulivan groups, Dempster had at last 'got into the India House'. Sulivan had seen to that.[78]

The proprietors' votes placed him twenty-first among the twenty-four annually-elected directors. Along with Warner, Woodhouse and William Snell, the last having served before, he was appointed to the Company's legal department, the Committee of Law Suits, where he was to serve for another year in the 1770s. Dempster could also have served on other committees at the same time, five being the maximum, but, as an untried 'poacher turned gamekeeper', it was understandable that he was not offered a place on the Correspondence Committee, in effect the Company's policy body. Its access to all foreign despatches gave it week-to-week evidence upon which to base its administrative action across the world. Control depended on directors understanding signals from their servants in India. In all there were 10 or so regular committees with other ad hoc bodies such as the Secret Committee which originally came into being when wars required the Company's shipping to be organized in convoys. The traditional committee pecking order was still in place, despite the fact that current priorities had changed somewhat. After Correspondence came Dempster's Law Suits Committee, followed by Treasury, Warehouse (imported goods), Accounts (budgets and cashflow), Buying (export trade), House (property and administration), Shipping (hiring of ships and third party exports) and Private Trade. Shipping was a good example of a committee that had grown in importance, determining as it did at what price and whose vessels were employed.[79]

In May the long boom in Company stock suddenly came to an end. With rumours of renewed French ambitions and uneasy relations with the native powers in India, those with parcels of stock were desperately selling them; as the share price tumbled a crisis developed. By the summer losses of up to £90,000 were widespread among all the main players.[80] Rockingham, with the support of Sulivan, was stirred to try and steady the ship, proposing an agreed House list for the next election and the despatch of Commissioners to India with authority to calm things down. At this point fear that the Commissioners might come across more evidence that could be used against John Johnstone,

Portrait of **George Dempster** by his first cousin, George Willison, and commissioned by Dundee Town Council in 1786. Dempster is wearing a cape of the Order of the Thistle to which he was appointed Secretary in January 1766.

(McManus Galleries, Dundee City Council)

The Pompeo Battoni portrait of young **Adam Fergusson** was painted in Rome which he reached in 1757 after George Dempster had been forced to return home to give comfort to his sister Peggy. The painting was lost in a fire during the 1900s at Kilkerran, the Fergusson family home in Ayrshire.
(Scottish National Portrait Gallery)

George Dempster had the pleasure of 'concerting' arrangements for the visit to Scotland in 1786 of the eminent antiquarian **Grimur Jonsson Thorkelin** (1752-1829). Born in Iceland, he was by then Professor Extraordinary at Copenhagen University. The two men became good friends, Thorkelin being a frequent guest at Dunnichen and Skibo. He was one of Dempster's earliest visitors to the Sutherland property. He corresponded with him until 1817. Today the Thorkelin Collection, which was acquired by the National Library of Scotland in 1819, includes 1,500 books and many early printings of the Icelandic sagas.
(National Museum of Iceland)

James Boswell's portrait was
painted in 1765 by George Willison
when both men were in Italy, one on
his Grand Tour, the other studying
painting. Although Dempster was
eight years Boswell's senior and his
opposite in almost every regard, they
remained friends until Boswell's
death in 1795.
(Scottish National Portrait Gallery)

A paste medallion of **George
Willison** (1741-79) by James Tassie,
modelled by Guilliobe.
(Scottish National Portrait Gallery)

Allan Ramsay's portrait in 1766 of **David Hume** (1711-76), the historian and philosopher. 'Dear David' was much admired by Dempster. Both were members of the 'Select Society'. *(Scottish National Portrait Gallery)*

A portrait of the **Rev John Jamieson** (1759-1838) painted by William Yellowlees. The future lexicographer arrived at Dunnichen in 1787 and was immediately befriended by the Dempster family. *(Scottish National Portrait Gallery)*

Plaster bust of **Professor Dr James Gregory** (1753-1821) by Samuel Joseph. His advice was sought about the health of both Harriet Soper Dempster and George's wife Rose in 1809/10. *(Scottish National Portrait Gallery)*

Professor Joseph Black (1728-1799) whose portrait was painted by David Martin in 1787 was described as having made chemistry a fashionable part of the accomplishment of a gentleman. His skill helped Dempster develop a profitable fertiliser from the marl on his estate.
(In the collection of the Royal Medical Society, Edinburgh)

William Skelton's line engraving of **Sir John Sinclair**, the statistician, agriculturist, politician and sparring partner of Dempster, after the portrait by Sir Thomas Lawrence, published in 1790 three years before his Board of Agriculture was set up. His arm rests on Volume 1 of his *History of the Revenue.* *(National Portrait Gallery, London)*

These rough sketches of **George Dempster** and (very possibly) **Sir John Sinclair** are included in Volume 17 of the Dempster papers held by the University of Toronto. The artist is unnamed but it could have been a member of the household at Dunnichen.
(Thomas Fisher Rare Book Library)

John, 4th Duke of Atholl (1755-1830) was the natural sponsor of the Stanley cotton mill project. In 1784 he offered to set aside a 70-acre site – part of which became the Perthshire village. *(From the collection at Blair Castle, Perthshire)*

Portrait of **William Smith** (1756-1835) by Henry Thomson (1773-1843). The
Dempsters met William Smith socially in 1783 while on holiday at Scarborough.
He was M.P. for Sudbury then Norwich, becoming first a director and then
Deputy Governor of the Fisheries Society. George Dempster was particularly
pleased to learn of his appointment as a Commissioner for Highland Roads and
Bridges in 1805.   *(Norwich Castle Museum and Art Gallery)*

Three **portrait miniatures** (more likely to be by Nathaniel rather than Andrew Plimer) included in Sotheby & Co's catalogue of an auction held at New Bond Street, London on Thursday 27 July 1933 – then being the property of Lady Mount Stephen, DBE (deceased) removed from 17 Carlton House Terrace (sold by order of the executors).

(Sotheby's Picture Library)

Possibly a portrait of **William Soper Dempster** (1763-1825). Catalogued as the portrait of a man in a dark blue coat, sallow complexion, gaze directed at spectator, crisp grey curling hair, sky and cloud background; additionally referred to as a member of the Dempster family of Skibo.

Catalogued as **Mrs Dempster** (most likely Mrs Harriet Soper Dempster) finely painted, in a low-cut white dress, with puff sleeve, nearly full face, with dark brown hair, against a cloud and sky background, in pearl bordered frame.

Catalogued as **Mrs Raffles**, a sister of that alongside (more probably Mrs Olivia Raffles née Devenish, her mother) painted at the same time, she is depicted nearly full face, with black hair, in low-cut, white spotted muslin dress, against a cloud and sky background.

the 'remarkable and ferocious Johnstone group' as Lucy Sutherland had no hesitation in calling them, opposed the idea and took umbrage at being excluded from Sulivan's coalition. Dempster could only watch uneasily, perhaps shivering more than a little when, having taken Boswell to hear part of the debate, his friend concluded that 'he was happy to hear Dempster doing very well . . . and to think that these people here in London had power over immense countries at so great a distance'.[81] Finally the Ministry wavered and, with alliances changing frequently and dissension between the Company and the administration on-going, it was not until October when the Commissioners finally sailed that a truce seemed likely.[82]

In parliament Dempster had been faithful to the Rockinghamites, voting with them in May on the issue of the Middlesex election before going north to Dunnichen.[83] John Wilkes had returned from France only to be imprisoned and subsequently prevented from taking his seat. In November, when Sulivan went over to the administration, Dempster scotched rumours that he would follow suit.[84] Writing to Rockingham, Burke spoke up strongly in his favour: 'Dempster thought as I do about Sulivan's coalition. He told me that it should make no difference in his line in India House; that there he would stand as firmly by him as he would continue to oppose his new friends in Parliament. That his political connection was with your Lordship and would always be so; but that if Mr Sulivan should find that course of conduct prejudicial to his interests in Leadenhall Street, that he would at an hour's notice disqualify for the directorship. This was what I expected from Dempster . . . not to sacrifice one duty to another; but to keep both if possible – if not, to put it out of his power to violate the principle.'[85]

One of the benefits conferred on him, now that Dempster was not only an MP but a director of the Company, were the appointments he was able to procure. A start in life as a midshipman at sea in an elite service or as a writer on land was highly regarded. Competition for places meant that someone who had the ear of the Company's chairman or his deputy was in demand. Collective decisions by the directors to support the appointment of their sons or near relatives were not unusual, especially where the emoluments of the post were good, but the process of approval could sometimes be 'a farce' if left to the clerk to the committee for passing cadets and assistant surgeons.[86]

Several of Dempster's own family already owed their start in life to him; George Willison, his first cousin, had been sent to study art in Italy in 1760. After ten years in London he had gone to India where he amassed a considerable fortune from portrait painting.[87] Other *protégés* included John Jamieson (1759–1838), the lexicographer, and Andrew Bell (1753–1832), the educational reformer, as well as numerous friends, constituents and 'some of the sons of Angus, of humble birth'.[88] As James Fergusson said, it was 'one of the most attractive traits' in his character,[89] and although as Dempster got older the begging of all favours became an irritant, it was something he did willingly.

He would not, however, have undertaken the task lightly. All those who faced the prospect of a life in India or aboard the Company's ships would have known something of the high price they could be called on to pay for making their 'fortunes'. The life expectancy of the Company's civil servants was short and the hardships only endured for the future benefits they promised. Of the 645 appointments made to Bengal between 1707 and 1775, the percentage who never returned was probably higher than 57%. During six years of peace between 1770 and 1776 six officers and cadets of the Bengal army were killed, a further nine drowned and a total of 208 died of disease.[90] Nor were work or living conditions in Bengal necessarily congenial. The Company's meagre salaries and subsistence allowances, ranging from £35 a year for a writer to £300 after many years for a senior merchant, were unattractive and made the manipulation of all monies, whether or not the Company's, a common way of life. Local trading was an essential adjunct for the majority of Europeans. Living costs were twice those in England. Clive spent £11,000 on 'table' expenses during the 20 months of his second administration and neither Verelst nor Hastings were able to live on their official earnings of £20,000.[91] Furthermore, the cost of 'suitable' accommodation could be greater than the allowances for the job when the wages of servants were taken into consideration. Living amid a people, country and climate they came quickly to dislike, the often outrageous behaviour of the Company's servants in commercial dealings was the only way they could compensate for inadequate payments by the Company.

Foremost in many minds was the prospect of subsequent good living in Britain – a lottery experience for a lottery prize. Expatriates intended using newly acquired capital for themselves, living well on the land and estates they would acquire on their return, not recirculating such gains through other commercial investments at home. Volatile market conditions across Asia and the Middle East made the whole affair uncertain and dangerous. Experience taught many bitter lessons. Profits varied with peace or war in the area, strong or weak competition, safe or disastrous voyages and surpluses or famines in such varied markets as the Gulf, Sumatra, Western India, the Coromandel, Penang, the Philippines and China. Profit margins, which could be considerably higher than in the West Indian trade or at home, nevertheless varied greatly from year to year. Those possessing little capital or access to local resources came unstuck with monotonous regularity. High on the long list of essentials for success, whether as company servant or Free Trader, was a good 'banian'. The Englishman, lacking local language skills or the knowledge of an Indian world long steeped in intricate trading deals, could achieve nothing without a reliable partner. William Bolts, the nefarious partner of John Johnstone, and whose behaviour in London is dealt with in the next chapter, was well-placed to define the role of the 'banian': 'an interpreter, head book-keeper, head secretary, head broker, the supplier of cash and cash keeper and also secret keeper'.[92] In exchange for a daily package of entrepreneurial advice and commercial experience, as well as occasionally contributing his own capital to the business, the 'banian' gained personal prestige from being associated with Europeans.

It was against this background that two members of Dempster's family came to enter the Company's service in 1769. They were not the first to do so. James Hamilton, who may have been Mrs Margaret Hamilton Dempster's son by her first husband, had gone to sea earlier.[93] Dempster's two young half-brothers had probably been living at Dunnichen where there was little outlet for their energies, and it became urgent to find them some useful occupation. John Hamilton Dempster, the more robust of the two, was the first to leave. He elected at the age of 19 to take his chance as an ordinary seaman on board the *Devonshire* under Captain Matthew Hore and in January 1769 he sailed for Madras and China.[94] Dempster's intervention had probably been un-necessary, given his lowly position, but for the other boy, Charles (then 15 or 16), he procured an appointment as a writer with the East India Company and he sailed to India later that year. These departures may have been made all the more desirable as the consequence of their mother's death* which may have occurred at about this time. John Hamilton Dempster's restlessness, which was so apparent in later years, had at least been assuaged. Unfortunately, Charles Dempster was to die in Calcutta four years later.[95]

* Since there is another Mrs Hamilton Dempster in the story she is always referred to as Mrs Margaret Hamilton

5

DOUBTS AND DUTIES
(1770 – 1774)

'I went on floundering like a blind horse in a deep road'
(Dempster to Sir Adam Fergusson, 2 August 1793)

1770

At the beginning of the new decade the Duke of Grafton, who had taken over from Chatham when the latter's health collapsed, handed power on to Lord North. His long administration not only continued the previous high-handed policies but his inept handling of affairs in the American colonies was to prove disastrous for the nation. East Indian affairs were in limbo for a period. The consequences of serious famines threatened to reduce the Company's incomes and the fear of French aggression focused the adminis-tration's attention on the sub-continent. On assuming office, North had taken 'the occasion very early to express his good wishes towards the East India Company and the Court of Directors',[1] and saw to it that the undaunted Sulivan, humbled by his defeat in the April election, was appointed a director. The latter's unequalled knowledge of Indian affairs soon enabled him to strike up an alliance with the Chairman, Sir George Colebrooke. Animosities were to continue, but the new administration was able to subdue at least some of the earlier feuding. Warren Hastings had been chosen as the new Governor of Bengal.

Dempster's profile in the Commons continued to be that of an independent opposition backbencher speaking with his usual candour, but the record suggests that his participation in debates was limited. Earlier events had taken their toll and it seemed that he found it more difficult to hold his head high. The numbers attending the House were always affected by the extent of public interest. Whilst as many as 400 members could be present for debates such as those when the Wilkes affair had been at its peak, or upwards of 300 when economic or American legislation was being scrutinized, the average attendance was around 100. It generally bore no relation to the number of

MPs in London at any one time. The social season and business affairs seem to have determined whether he attended the House or not. Dempster did vote to affirm the rights of electors in a January debate on the Wilkes case and supported criticism of the Speaker the following month over his handling of a technical motion, but he seems to have been rarely in the House until November, when war threatened.

During the summer Parliamentary recess Dempster spent two months at Abergavenny with his sister Jean, who had 'daily declined' and needed a change of air. Although resigned and cheerful, she had not responded to Sir John Pringle's ministrations which included drinking the whey of Welsh goat's milk and, troubled that her cough 'had gained so much ground', Dempster feared she was in a very bad way.[2] He was also much disconcerted by the manners and behaviour of the Welsh: 'Where we are is a very curious country . . . wild as Lochaber and as much cultivated as Middlesex. But though the people have enjoyed the benefits of the English laws since Edward the first's time, they have not yet acquired their manners. They are dirty, have the itch, and no man cares to trust his life or property to a Welsh jury. The town in which I live has no government at all. . . . Eight or ten fellows who ring a peal of bells have the chief command of the town and over-awe the inhabitants'. These his sister laughingly called 'the *ring* leaders'.[3]

The couple moved on to Bristol where they took the waters at Hotwells. Dempster's mind was apparently as much on his own finances as his sister's health. He feared he had spent the summer both 'very unpleasantly' and 'very unprofitably'.[4] Only a handful of his friends ever knew how 'bare of money' he was, and whilst indebtedness far greater than his was common, and often blatantly ignored, its undertow was no less debilitating. Litigation in the Court of Justiciary did not come cheaply and the legal costs associated with his 1768 election had been excessive, the lawyers on both sides being the only winners. Dempster had few to whom he could turn for support and all he would say to Boswell about his affairs in Leadenhall Street was that the failure of 'some friends' had made him 'more steady' in his friendships.[5] Charles Guthrie, his solicitor in Edinburgh, took a hand in finding him some interest-only loans, but 'the excessive scarcity of money to be borrowed in the Edinburgh market' forced the search to be extended to London.[6] There, Pulteney, with his greater financial acumen and immense wealth, was better placed to guide him and, as the relationship between the two men deepened, it was clear that he did more for Dempster than simply keep abreast of his affairs. Thankfully, his experience as the underwriter and 'banker' of the Johnstone family was put at his disposal.[7]

Parts of Dempster's estate had been advertised for sale in the newspapers the previous year. The fulsome correspondence he had with Boswell since his friend's return from Corsica and Ireland only revealed just how much this upset him. The battering he'd taken meant that he had hardly 'opened his mouth' in the House for two years.[8] Having rejected any idea of taking 'a feverish leave of Scotland by any means', he had contemplated giving a remnant of his estate to his sister so that 'she may take a husband and bring me a nephew'. He longed to see 'the boy for whom (he) was planting trees and building stone dykes' at Dunnichen.[9]

Such hopes that Dempster had felt confident enough to express only a year before were not to become a reality. Although there is no direct evidence available, it seems probable that Sir John Pringle's remedies for consumption proved as ineffective as others at the time and that Jean's health deteriorated sharply towards the end of the year, being followed by her death then or in 1771.

The loss of his sister and the sale of more of the estate land undermined his self-confidence. It was true that the income he received from his 'Offices' meant that he had 'more money than as a bachelor (he could) ever stand in need of,[10] but the progressive sale of his patronal inheritance was to rankle all his life. For the moment the best therapy was to respond to an urgent call from Westminster. Only on two occasions during the 1766–1774 parliament did the House find it necessary to meet in November. One was to deal with a crisis in the affairs of the East India Company in 1772. The other occurred as the year came to a close. Spanish forces had overwhelmed the small garrison on the Falkland Islands and there was a threat of full-scale war. Dempster's view was that the country's affairs in the South Atlantic were 'badly attended to . . . and will require the labour of many painful years . . . to devise plans for the good government of that vast empire.'[11]

North's response had been conciliatory, provoking the opposition into a fury. In two speeches on 7 December Dempster was at his best, combining knowledge of East Indian affairs with his support for a Scottish militia. 'God Almighty! Have we not a government that can compel every man to fight in the common cause? . . . If we have war . . . a large part of the coast of this island is destitute of defence.'[12] The recruitment of German and Irish catholic troops was no solution. It would be better to have compulsory service if necessary.[13] If it came to taking on Spain this would present France with opportunities in India and 'ships of the line' would need to be sent the East Indies: 'I am bold to say that 40,000 seamen are not sufficient'.[14] The implications for taxation and customs dues were obvious. Furthermore, without long-term plans for defending the empire and at least an increase in the strength of the navy, any response to Spain by the administration would be futile. Three days later Dempster was again to the fore when he and a number of MPs listened to an emergency motion in the Lords, only to suffer 'the indignity of being turned out of their House'.[15] Their lordships feared that information provided about the country's military unpreparedness would be helpful to the enemy. Such an 'insult' led to the Commons adjourning their proceedings in protest.

The debate continued through February and March and tempers only cooled when it was realized that immediate action was impossible. The threat of war disappeared when Lord North achieved a 'quiet settlement' with Spain.[16] This did not stop Dempster from campaigning against the use of German and Irish regiments, this time alongside the forces of the East India Company. As a director he had been told some time before about the proposal, and in arguing publicly that it would increase 'the influence of the Crown . . . creating a new standing army of foreigners', the chairman and Member of Parliament, Sir George Colebrook, took umbrage. He claimed that it was a breach of confidence, so infuriating Dempster who saw it as an outrageous way of muzzling him.[17]

A long series of debates sparked off by the actions of several London printers followed. They had disobeyed the rules of the House against reports of its proceedings being printed and sold on the streets. Lord Mayor Brass Crosby and Alderman Oliver of the City of London sought to protect them. With an eye on the freedom of the press, Dempster censured the Commons for their 'avidity for prosecution' which was below the dignity of Parliament: 'I see a new scene opened that affects the liberty of the press. . . . I do not like to see people so passionately fond of privilege'. He contended that the public had a right to 'printed reports of parliamentary proceedings' and, in the heated debates over the conduct of the Aldermen, he urged moderation, voting against their committal to the Tower.[18]

With these clashes behind him, Dempster spent the summer in England, making excursions to Surrey and Sussex where rich cultivation stretched 'as far as the eye can reach', and spending a fortnight on the Isle of Thanet. Margate had become a favourite place for both health and amusement. Unlike more fashionable watering places, it was somewhere for 'the middle ranks of people' to congregate. The profitability of Kentish agriculture continued to impress him. Riding his agricultural 'hobby horse', he was quite amazed at the richness of the 'black mold, their manure, chalk and sea weed' where farmers benefited from land values of £40–60,000. 'Thirty days' in the company of Major-General 'Bob' Clerk had 'never passed more agreeably'. His 'sound judgement' mixed with a 'share of drollery' helped to 'moderate' Dempster's envy of his companion.[19] In October Dempster returned to Berners Street to find that India stock had fallen to 7%. The only consolation was that a deal had at last been made to sell the bulk of the land earmarked to repay many, if not all, his outstanding debts. The four estates of Ethiebeaton, Laws, Omachie, and Newbigging (originally included in the barony of Downie) were sold to Sir Alexander Ramsay Irvine of Balmain.[20]

It was the end of a dreadful period that had lasted ten years. His parliamentary career could not be said to have blossomed. He had won but one public office, and that of no apparent significance. Many of his friends were frivolous and light-weight in political terms. He had allowed himself to be used by others for their own ends and to over-value the integrity he had been so determined to demonstrate in his affairs. His 'proverbial candour' had ostracized him within the opposition. Instead of carefully husbanding his limited finances, he had allowed them to be denuded. Even his search for a wife had been unsuccessful. All in all, the future depended on a serious retrenchment that allowed him to play to his strengths and avoid the mistakes that had been made. Without a new start that took account of his reduced circumstances it would not be long before he was forced to return to Scotland and admit defeat. Taking a wife might be part of the solution and provide the impetus he needed, but if his independent stance was to be the virtue he thought it could be, he would need to be more successful in his public duties and devote more time to them. He was fortunate to have retained the respect others in similar circumstances might have lost. Giving up was not something that came naturally and, as it turned out, the looming crisis in America, his election as a director at India House, coupled with the threats to the Company's position and a serious financial collapse, combined to make retreat unthinkable. So far as his personal affairs were concerned a wife with a dowry seemed essential. For a man of his age it was no mean challenge.

1772

Sir Adam Fergusson and Dempster apparently toyed with the idea of a visit to the continent, perhaps to make up for their abortive tour together 16 years before. The legal case against the two rivals to the peerage of Sutherland which had dragged on since 1767 was finally complete, thereby releasing Sir Adam who had worked closely with Lord Hailes on the Countess's behalf.[21] But in February 1772 the possibility of such a 'jaunt' was ruled out when Dempster told his friend quite bluntly, 'I don't know, my boy, where to find the cash for the expedition. And if I knew where to find it, I am certain it would be imprudence in the highest degree for me to bestow it in that way. I have a young brother to rig out for India this year which has beggar'd me.[22] My debts appear to be rather greater than I imagined. Some lands I am selling to pay 'em bring rather less than I expected'.[23] What surprised him even more when he contemplated the fact that 'the candle of his finances was lit at both ends' was his own lack of unease on the subject. Self-assurance had been a long time coming and he 'hardly ever enjoy'd better health, better spirits, or been more in a mood for leaving 'em all at sixes and sevens and exploring . . . Europe'.[24]

When he thought 'a very quiet session of Parliament' was in prospect Dempster had time to use his influence to secure a cadetship in the Company's service for the son of one of Sir Adam's friends. Cadets in the Bengal army were the equivalent of civilian Writers and the lowest rung on the ladder, with promotion at fixed intervals and strictly in accordance with seniority.[25] An earlier approach had been unsuccessful due to 'the little differences' he had with the Company's chairman and he had been rebuffed. Now all the season's appointments had been filled and it would have to wait another year.[26] His meeting with Sir George Colebrooke nevertheless enabled him to express his support for Andrew Stuart of Torrance's candidacy for a place on the Supervising Commission to India.[27] But by February he resumed his opposition and supported Rockingham on a matter of church and state politics. The administration's aim was to relieve dissenting clergy from their obligation to the Church of England's 39 Articles of Faith. Unlike Charles Fox, who was said to have only rushed into the House between gambling at White's and Almack's, Dempster quietly enjoyed 'an admirable debate . . . tho' the ministry took the side of the Established Church . . . the debate was no party one and therefore pleasant, temperate and instructive'. He considered that 'in consequence of yesterday's debate the universities will be free to relax that part of their discipline by which students of 16 years of age are at present obliged to subscribe to those articles'.[28]

Boswell, who was never greatly effective in his profession as a barrister – except when he occasionally appeared in front of his father's colleagues in Edinburgh at the Court of Session, now arrived in London to appear in an appeal from the Court of Session to the House of Lords. Boswell's marriage in 1769 to his cousin, Margaret Montgomerie, had taken place on the same day as his father had re-married at the age of 60. It had done him a lot of good but his wife's affection and loyalty were to be sorely tested over many years. 'Bozzy's' colourful letters at this time threw considerable light on Dempster's frame of mind in personal matters and romantic prospects. Fortunately his friend was resisting the temptation of further 'amorous intercourse', successfully this time, and more in a mood to think of others.

Boswell called at Dempster's lodgings in March finding that he 'had an Indian lad and an Indian boy for his servants'.[29] He 'was attended by a grave, decent-looking man whose office in the household (he at first) could not divine', but 'he turned out to be a master who came in to instruct the two Indians'. Boswell attributed Dempster's absence to 'his being abroad' but the next morning he reported having 'breakfasted with (him), whom I found as agreeable and as friendly as ever, improved much in speaking English, and appearing to be as happy as I could wish him'. Boswell's subsequent, and unusually direct, comments are quoted in full: 'Parliament and the East India Company had accustomed him to manly employment, and I could see that he was really satisfied with his situation. He is conscious of acting with honour and fidelity and spirit, and he feels himself happy in having a share in the great deliberations both as to this nation and the empire in India. He said he would not give up the enjoyment of the two sessions which he had sat (through) in Parliament for any consideration. I gave him some account of his old friends in Scotland. He said he thought with a pleasing regret of our parties with the

Ladies of Kellie in which we were so happy . . . we had taken a hearty draught of free and friendly conversation. But then I saw a specimen of his inconveniences; for in came (some) Angus lairds, speaking with a most uncouth tone, and beings of other disagreeable kinds, to all of whom he was obliged to be very courteous.'[30]

Later, when Dempster was again said to be abroad, Boswell called at Berners Street in the company of a Colonel Campbell, this time in the mood for some 'drollery'. Everything was 'in perfect Scotch confusion'. The elder of Dempster's black servants could not understand what they were up to when they began to write down an amusing inventory of Dempster's dining room furniture: 'Upon one table a stone basin with dirty water; a china "goglet" or a water bottle with water in it; a case of razors; a shaving brush, shaving box and soap-ball, a strap, and a tin jug for warming water in. Upon one chair a pair of ruffles, dirty. Upon another chair a pair of white stockings and a pair of black ditto, a stock, a clothes brush, a towel, and a shaving cloth dirty. Upon the arms of two chairs placed close together a flannel waistcoat without sleeves. Upon another chair a dirty shirt. Upon another ditto a black waistcoat and a grey frock with black buttons. Upon another ditto four combs, a pair of scissors, and a stick of pomatum. Upon the carpet a large piece of blue and white check spread out, a tea-chest, two shoes at a considerable distance from each other, a flannel powdering gown, a pair of slippers. Upon the chimney piece innumerable packets of letters and covers to be franked, a book, a pamphlet, some newspapers, and a snuff box. Hanging upon brass nails two hats, a sword and a belt, a belt without a sword. Standing in the corner a very long cane with a gold head.'[31]

That spring Dempster was elected a director of the East India Company for a second time and apparently in opposition to the usual House list. He was 'the popular choice of the proprietors'[32] and determined to 'act from my own sentiments, with the purity of which I am satisfied, than adopt those of others whose sincerity I suspect'.[33] They were important times both so far as the government's ever-expanding regulatory role in the business of the Company was concerned and for the effect they had on Dempster himself. James Fergusson was to sum up Dempster's contribution to the debates at India House cautiously: 'His ideas on what the Company's aims in India should be were unorthodox, and did not commend themselves to his colleagues. He disapproved of the power held by the Company in India, and wished it to confine itself to commerce and eschew political activity altogether.' This view, said Fergusson, was partly justified in Dempster's own time by the scandals of the Company's administration at Madras and Calcutta, and a generation later by the dangerous clumsiness of its dealings with the Siamese government and the Sultan of Kedah.[34] Other commentators in the late 19th century concluded that he was alone in the position which he took. Robert Chalmers argued that 'His mistaken notions on the subject of oriental politics must have rendered him an inefficient member of that court. Misled by the commercial origin of the corporation, he would have had the Company, after it had arrived at great political influence and had acquired extensive territorial possessions in India, resign its sovereign power and confine itself to its mercantile speculations.'[35] Today, the plethora of material that has, and continues to be published, about the Company does at least go some way to clarifying the role he played.

Unfortunately, in Britain no clear line had been drawn between what were legitimate and what were doubtful Company practices. In Bengal most servants saw themselves not only as merchants trading on their own and the Company's account but as the only 'realistic' interpreters of what was right and wrong, or allowed and disallowed. Many flabby Company edicts existed. In John Johnstone's case, the Company was slow to decide what was permissible. Local interpretations were not effectively dealt with. The faults of the system allowed him to build up many valuable perquisites and a fortune of £300,000.[36] As a Director, and a member of the Committee of Law Suits, Dempster soon came to realize that the legal loopholes so produced could not easily be closed. Defending the indefensible was a continual problem for those associated with Johnstone's defence. This most self-justifying of fortune hunters believed that his position above the law had been paid for by his years of service and the many times he had risked his life for the Company.

Dempster could only feel sadness and frustration when he heard it claimed that the Company's 'servants abroad should interfere in the election of directors and solicit votes of their friends for the nomination of men under whose orders they are to act '.[37] After the India Act had been passed, he recalled: 'The contests which have subsisted ever since among the proprietors, directors and ministry would have teized [sic] me out of my senses, and I should have died under the uneasiness of seeing so noble an object so very inadequately administer'd. By the influence of the ministry, which the several alterations in the charter has very much increased, a decent plan of governing that country has been rejected and the same unlimited and undefined powers are entrusted with the Governor-General and Council which occasioned the despotism, the anarchy and the peculations which have hitherto prevail'd in Bengal.'[38]

He would have disagreed with those who saw a deep-seated plot in what the government was doing to restore a semblance of order in London and Bengal, but the Company's independence could so easily have been lost as the result of more 'accidents' to which it was prone. Somewhat surprisingly, the Earl of Sandwich, who did little to provide the navy with the resources it needed during his second period of office at the Admiralty between 1771 and 1782, managed to initiate a more positive partnership. His administrative abilities aided the ministry in its dealings with Leadenhall Street and he exercised his personal influence with the Court of Directors with good effect, at least temporarily. The need for timber conservation had at last been recognized by the Admiralty, and now the Company's internal organisation, together with the size and number of ships to be constructed, came under scrutiny. The Company took its own action when Sulivan, after becoming Deputy Chairman, encouraged the Company's Shipping Committee to reduce abuses in the hiring of ships. But such positive steps were more than offset by those still seeking to prevent punitive action being taken against returned and existing Company servants who had engaged in doubtful behaviour. The administration's position was also strengthened by matters over which it had no control. Warlike moves by the French, the effect of news reaching London about famine in India and still more ugly stories of the Company's misrule played their part. This generated what Burke called 'the phrenzy of the people'. Such revelations were often sensationalized and any headline involving the Johnstones quickly grabbed the public's attention.

William Bolts, 'a man of bad character' and John Johnstone's partner in the firm of Johnstone, Hay & Bolts, returned to England under a deportation order after defying the Bengal government's attempts to bring him to book.[39] He brought an action against Governor Verelst and 'his case was, of course, taken up by the Johnstone party'.[40] All factions and the directors became involved. Counter-charges relating to various illegal monopolies and other offences were also made against Bolts by one John Petrie. Parliament was drawn in when the directors were slow to respond. In two editions of a publication entitled *Considerations on Indian Affairs, particularly respecting the Present State of Bengal and its Dependencies,* Johnstone's partner further alienated public and government alike by attacking those servants of the Company associated with both Clive and Verelst. The war of words had started a year or two earlier when Alexander Dow produced several volumes of his more subtle *History of Hindustan* and he was now tempted to go further in another volume, so finding himself too enmeshed with the Johnstones. Had it not been for such high profile diversions which greatly reduced the time available for dealing with fundamental Company matters, there might have been some justification for the claim that the Government was bent on a more devious course than it was.

A major crisis on 8 June 1772, 'Black Monday' as it was called, put the Company's next half-yearly dividend at risk, always a storm cone so far as the Proprietors were concerned. A cascade of financial shocks started in June when the London bank of Messrs Neale, James, Fordyce and Down stopped payment after Alexander Fordyce, a Scot and an acting partner, was found to have been a huge speculator in East India Company and other shares. He had 'dabbled deeply in Exchange alley'.[41] His failure and subsequent flight led to the collapse of other banking houses, including Douglas Heron & Co. which had branches in the Canongate in Edinburgh and at Ayr where it had been established 'not full three years'.[42] The difficulties faced by the Ayr branch were not uncommon and meant that payments due to the Company were either postponed or not made. The default was later referred to as the collapse of the 'Ayr Bank' and there were severe consequences for at least 'one hundred Scottish landowners'. Only three private banks in Edinburgh survived. The Fordyce affair led to a financial and economic recession that extended across Europe and lasted for most of 1773. It was found that 'Fordyce's name was attached to bills in circulation to the amount of four million pounds and his debts were said to amount to £300,000'.[43]

Both Sir Adam Fergusson and his brother Charles were sucked into this vortex. Several efforts were made to save the Ayr bank and it was not surprising that Dempster and Sir Adam had a hand in masterminding support lending from other banks. Writing from London, he told Pulteney that he had just met Sir Adam 'coming from the Bank after finishing . . . the *minutia* of the trans-action' (a £300,000 loan) and the 'prospect of your friends being relieved from their difficulties' and the future prospects looked good.[44] It was, however, to be a false dawn.

The Bank of England was severely criticized for not coming to the aid of the banking houses. Dempster, along with Burke and others, was concerned to encourage a system that not simply revived confidence in Scottish credit but established a better support system. Burke told him that he was 'not so unfeeling, as not to be untouched by the distresses of so many unhappy people . . . (but) . . . the plan you mention . . . would be too slow in its operation for the rapid Nature of the present Evil; as it must work slowly and insensibly . . . and ought to have the authority of some name of weight'. His idea was that the Government 'must do all' in conjunction with the larger businesses, and here he agreed with Dempster. It was important to ensure that whatever was done in England did not endanger support for credit in Scotland. Burke looked forward to dining with Dempster and his friend Andrew Stuart to go into these matters.[45]

Dempster and Pulteney decided to concert their actions to help themselves and others who had suffered. In July Dempster told him that, quite apart from various outstanding payments due from the bank (amounting to £1,500), he was likely to 'suffer more . . . than (he) could afford for (he was) one of nine solvent sureties to the (Ayr) Bank for £6,000'. Moreover, the affairs of John Fordyce of Ayton in Berwickshire, who was a relative of the crooked Alexander Fordyce, further complicated matters.[46] His effects, amounting to £14,000, had been sequestered and annuities payable by the bank amounting to an additional £4,000 were put at risk.[47] Together, Dempster and Pulteney had to wrestle with these threats to the solvency of John's guarantors. In doing so one of Dempster's debts to Pulteney came to light. 'You may remember,' said Dempster, 'the money we borrowed for a joint venture purchase eight years ago. £900 of this – in your name and mine – is still due and £400 in my own'.[48] Pulteney was ready to pay his share, but Dempster had to plead for time in the light of the Fordyce crisis.

How much Dempster was affected by the grim events of 'Black Monday' only became clear in stages. By November he told Pulteney optimistically that John Fordyce had 'finally settled all his affairs and (brought) his sureties completely out of the scrape'.[49] It had been touch and go during the summer. Furthermore, payment delays for someone in Dempster's fragile financial position were soon a matter of constant complaint. Unravelling the complex web of loans, bonds and guarantees involving investors, traders and customers, directly and sometimes very indirectly, required interminable negotiations, litigation and much heartache for the many hundreds of people affected. Dempster must have seriously questioned the wisdom of providing the bank with guarantees for sums of money he could only have paid from more land sales. But, generous to a fault, this was not to be the only time he extended sureties beyond his resources, even to John Fordyce.

Ten years later a similar affair threatened to reduce Dempster to his 'former penury, just after having emerged from it'.[50] John Fordyce got into more trouble and Dempster daily 'expected an explosion'. It appeared he had engaged in more speculative deals, this time dragging Charles Fergusson who had married Fordyce's sister and was a farming neighbour of Sir Adam's along with him.[51] Again, Dempster, Sir Adam and Pulteney backed him. The sorry tale was told in some anacreontic verses entitled *Ode to Ruin* and echoed the despair engendered in the business community at the time:

> Your wife denied a rout and coach;
> Your dress the Parliament's reproach;
> Dwell in Soho; on cowheel dine;
> Cork and recork your pint of wine –
> For see our honest Charles fail'd;
> and Ayton with him headlong trailed;
> The public cash with Ayton flown;
> And you his surety quite undone.
> Oh! would to God that this were all,
> The good Sir Adam too must fall,
> And lively Whiteford (sic), strange to say,
> Be ruin'd by another's play.[52]

This time, 'Ayton' had flown with 'public cash'. The surety risk was a sum between £10–12,000 and the matter rumbled on for a year or more. It was only in July 1784 that Dempster was able to say that 'the affair (was) in a fair way of being agreeably settled'; John Fordyce sat beside him in London as he wrote.[53]

Yet another financial crisis emerged in August when the Treasury was told by the Company that it might not be able to met its obligations. A month later the Company's Treasury Committee finally admitted to the Directors, including Dempster, that the events of the previous months were so serious that there could be a complete stoppage of payments by the Company and any relief from the Bank of England would only be temporary. The result was that the price of East India stock fell sharply. This led to the meeting of the General Court being told that a decision on the dividend due that month would have to be postponed. Parliament was to meet on 26 November and, in a search for a way forward, even the King was consulted. His Majesty supported the view that if the government was to help it would require meaningful reforms in return. At no stage was it a question of an inexperienced government machine taking over responsibility for governing Bengal. The speech from the throne merely talked of Parliament informing themselves of 'the true state of the Company's affairs'.[54]

On 7 December, the Commons debated a Bill to restrain the Company from appointing supervisors in India. Alderman Harley, a none-too-frequent speaker in the House, introduced the issues and explained the report on the Company's affairs. No sooner had he sat down than Dempster expressed his alarm, explaining that the Committee of Secrecy to which Harley had referred was 'unconstitutional, and only allowable in cases of a criminal nature'. He accepted that there was 'a deficiency of cash at present', but its affairs were 'neither in a ruinous nor deplorable situation'. Whilst not wishing to deny the power of parliament or its right to superintend the Company, Dempster maintained that, before they ventured to dispossess the Company of its privileges, the House should be first assured that they were being abused. This required an investigation in Bengal by 'a set of independent gentlemen'. Although the Honorable Alderman objected to a cost of £120,000, 'millions might be saved'. Another Member then suggested that the pledge Sulivan had given (that nothing would be done until the House of Commons had made its will known) should be accepted.[55] This provoked the Solicitor General, Wedderburn, to remind the House that it was 'not in the power of the Direction to keep their promise, should a General Court order to the contrary. Immediately after we break up, a Court may be called, the ship ordered, and the supervisors at sea many leagues before we can possibly meet'.[56]

On 18 December, the Company's counsel, Messrs Impey and Adair, came to the bar of the House and proceeded 'with great clearness and strength of argument' to present an account of affairs in London and India, calling several witnesses in support. As soon as they retired, Dempster was on his feet urging the case they had put and asking the Commons to consider how long it might be before abuses could be redressed. He asked members to recollect that the Commons was not the only branch of the legislature and that 'if this Bill passes into a law, you put it into the power of the Lords, and of the King, to prevent you from making any salutary regulations, or at least from carrying them into execution for the space of six months, or more if they are swayed by caprice or other unknown motives . . . . This parliament may be prorogued before you have time to complete the intended inquiry, and to form your great plan for the salvation of Bengal . . . . Reflect therefore, before it is too late . . . and throw out this pernicious Bill with indignation.'[57] After the Colonial Secretary, George Germain, Richard Whitworth, Governor Johnstone, Lord John Cavendish, Lord Clive and Burke had spoken, Dempster returned to the fray with a considered account of what the Directors had done to authenticate delinquency.

'As far as I know, or am capable of judging,' Dempster went on, 'the Directorate have ever since I had the honour to be an unworthy member acted with propriety'. In short 'nothing that could be done by men in Leadenhall for the salvation of the Company' had been omitted. He was at pains to separate the conscionable actions of the Company from the behaviour of those who returned home laden with iniquitous wealth. Addressing Lord George Germain, who led for the adminstration and who was a member of the Commons' Select Committee, Dempster explained that he had attended the committee on two or three days 'out of curiosity' and read the reports left on the table to be perused by Members. He accused Germain of sheltering 'exalted criminals' and made a case for his impeachment, a charge to which the Colonial Secretary pleaded not guilty since he had 'not seen anything that would fully justify (it)'. The tone of his rebuttal was nevertheless surprisingly relaxed. It reflected his regard for Dempster whom 'he always took . . . to be a man of public spirit' and it gave him 'pleasure to find' that he had no reason even after such a charge to alter his opinion.[58]

1773

There was to be no respite and the passing of North's Regulating Act later in the year presaged not the end but the beginning of another chapter of troubles. So far as Dempster was concerned, he concluded early in February that his position at India House was preventing him from performing his proper role at Westminster and he resigned his directorship.[59] A friend of Warren Hastings described the dilemma: 'The directors were much hampered in their negotiations by a party among the Proprietors headed by the Duke of Richmond, with Johnstone and Dempster who disqualified (himself) as a Director ten days ago that he might be more at liberty in Parliament. The real views of this party under the plausible pretence of being the sacred guardian of the Company's chartered rights is to get matter for forming a strong opposition in Parliament against (the) administration'.[60] The truth was that the Directors did not know what to do and were afraid to do anything in case it might be construed as challenging the Charter.

Dempster's self-disqualification probably reflected this bewilderment as much as his conviction that the House of Commons provided a better arena in which to air these issues. In the Company elections that spring Sulivan lost to a new Chairman, Crabb Boulton, when the Proprietor's list prevailed and George Johnstone used his prestige to take over leadership in the Court of

Proprietors. Later, however, and apparently with Dempster and Burke's help, the Duke of Richmond assumed that role. Rockingham now accepted that he was the 'head of a large body of Proprietors . . . men of much *natural warmth* . . . also . . . of cooler passions and yet perhaps both equally firm to the object',[61] adding that Gregory, Weir, Dempster and Adair (were) good and Honourable men, (but) I own I don't understand Mr Johnstone's politicks'.[62] Richmond was to lead a battle in the Company he was unable to fight in the House.

Between March and June Dempster frequently spoke in the House. In a 'grand debate' on 5 April Boswell, who was again in London, listened to his friend. This time he was 'less anxious' about being away from his wife; she had just given birth to a daughter. When Lord North led the debate on the Company's petition for a loan, it was Dempster who was in the vanguard of its defence, expressing surprise and horror at his assertion that the Company 'had no claim for justice for relief'. As a champion of the Company's rights he enlisted the views of 'several gentlemen, well skilled in the laws of their country, (who) have advanced it as their opinion, that the Company have an undoubted, a clear and exclusive right to the territories possessed in India, whether acquired by conquest or otherwise' and, hinting at North's duplicity, he added, 'I have now, sir, a gentleman in my eye, who formerly held the same opinion'.[63]

Debates in the House centred on the government's proposals since those originating from within the Company were getting nowhere. These included the election of Directors for four years instead of one, with a quarter of the Court retiring each year and a higher Proprietorial voting limit of £1,000. Not surprisingly, it was the appointment of a Governor-General and a Council instead of visiting supervisors that attracted the most opposition. Stormy and confused debates were the result. Dempster's role, and his point of view that the Company's future should be in its own rather than the administration's hands was summed up when he said, 'I would rather return the territory to the Mogul than suffer it to be taken by the Crown'.[64]

By the end of June 1773 the Regulating Act became law and market confidence in the Company improved. Unfortunately, it was still not the end of the affair. The devil was in the detail. Richmond tried to limit the powers to be given to Warren Hastings, the nominated Governor-General, and his Council, but these proposals, in which Dempster had a hand, failed to win support, even after long deliberation.[65] Other management issues which had been expected to attract compromise shared a similar fate and, what Walpole called the Duke of Richmond's Indian campaign only came to an end when Councillors sailed to India in April 1774. Thereafter, Dempster and the Parliamentary opposition were not to make more than occasional excursions into East Indian affairs. Humanitarian considerations which Burke and Fox had belatedly introduced into the debate would eventually bring together a new opposition.[66]

1774

In January 1774 Dempster anticipated 'a dumb session of Parliament unless the refractory Americans should fall under our consideration'. He may have wished it so, for 'I who have enjoy'd (Parliament) for 13 years am almost tired . . . .Were I to choose my walk of life again with all the experience I have it would be a private one.' The events of the previous year had obviously again taken their toll and some of his usual *joie de vivre* was missing. The 'self-interested principles upon which our public men here act destroys much of the satisfaction that would attend a seat in a less corrupted assembly of representatives.'[67] In February two issues came before the House; one related to a libel against the Speaker that appeared in *The Public Advertiser,* the other a bookseller's Copyright Bill. Speaking up for the liberty of the press he opined that it was what kept 'great men honest through fear of being exposed'.[68] Later, when the House was in Committee examining the state of the Linen Trade, he supported the granting of a bounty on printed linen, albeit 'a paltry' one, recognizing that it would not injure the manufacture of cotton or the woollen industry. In a long speech (three thousand words or so) that demonstrated how thoroughly he had read the evidence submitted and listened to the witnesses examined by the Committee, Dempster reminded North and the House that as the law stood no printed cotton, other than the manufacture of Britain, could be worn in the Kingdom, but that imports were still finding their way into the country. Illustrating two wider problems, Dempster quoted the evidence that made it clear that not only was imported dowlas (or shirting 'for the lower class of people' as Dempster said) of a better quality, but foreign diapers as wide as 60–80 inches were being brought in to circumvent a flat rate duty levied on all such material over 40 inches.[69]

As Dempster suspected, events across the Atlantic were going from bad to worse. The 'Boston Tea Party' had hardened North's resolve further and the Boston Port Bill, brought in to punish the colonists and compel ships that normally would have berthed there to dock in Salem instead, sparked a vociferous response from the Opposition. In answer to a question from Governor Johnstone, Lord North said that it was up to the Crown to decide where the Custom House should be located not the colonists. Dempster 'cavilled a little'.[70] During the committee stage of the Bill on 23 March 1774 an exceptional number of MPs were not only in attendance but spoke.[71] The opposition concentrated on the need for fair punishment of the Bostonians not the English merchants who used the port, the indemnification of the East India Company and, most of all, the vengeful step that the bill represented. Dempster, perhaps realizing that any reversal of North's policies was out of the question, used the occasion to raise the 'odious attempts to tax the Americans' by means of the Stamp Act. 'He knew of no other Act to which he gave his hearty consent in a more willing manner, than to that which was for the repeal of the Stamp Act. He said that he was very sure the destruction of America would be certain if we should offer to tax it. We should treat them as our children, nourish and protect them'.[72]

During the third reading in May of the Bill for the Administration of Justice in Massachusetts Bay, Dempster again led the opposition, claiming that it had been wrong to assume that a fair trial could not be held in the colonies: 'Surely, Sir, the bringing men over to England to be tried, is not only a direct breach of their constitution, but is a deprivation of the right of every British subject in America'. Praising Benjamin Franklin, whom he called that 'ornament of human nature . . . and highly praise-worthy', he took exception to two articles in the Bill which he could not blame the Americans for resisting. Having the Council and the judges chosen by the Crown he thought unnecessary. Instituting the office of sheriff and the taking away of the right to hold town meetings were oppressive measures.[73] During discussion of the Quebec Bill which followed, Dempster tried to introduce a clause extending *Habeas Corpus* to the province. Winning the confidence of the French settlers whose customs and outlook were different from those of the British colonists had particular merit. But war was imminent and there was no drawing back. The year was to end with riots, and the Declaration of Rights that emanated from the colonists' 'congress' in Philadelphia triggered the despatch of troops to reinforce General Gage's force already in Boston.

Having discharged his duty to America 'very conscientiously and very fruit-lessly'[74] and, with North firmly in power and a general election likely, Dempster decided the summer was a time to reconsider the subject about which he had 'a wonderful shyness'. Both before and after Boswell's own marriage, the two men had discussed women at great length, but his un-certainty about the married state persisted. As far back as 1757, when Sir Adam's father Lord Kilkerran mistakenly thought Dempster 'was soon to have another landlady' at his Edinburgh dwelling, he had expressed his reservations: 'I don't know how it is but I always change my opinion of a man upon his change of state because I think he changes his opinion of things and men from that moment. His mind contracts and his views are turned towards himself and family more strictly than before'.[75] When Boswell returned from Ireland with his wife-to-be five years previously, Dempster had written at length about his own sentiments: 'You must know that it has long been my opinion that the only field in which real honour is requisite and can be shewn is the Fair Sex. Law and manners, everything has placed them at our mercy. Exposed to passions they dare not indulge, to injuries they cannot resent, a man who applied himself seriously to the business might ruin the reputation and destroy the happiness of half the women on the Globe and escape scot-free himself. I tremble at any interferences with them, as I do to take Dresden china off its shelves. In spite of all one's care we may let it slip out of our hands, dash it against its neighbours, put it all back into its nitch (sic) and play a deal of mischief, when we mean only to gratify a baffling curiosity or have a little amusement.'[76]

Dempster's fears and inhibitions showed him to be someone almost resigned to bachelorhood who had probably been too long in male society, with few romantic or tantalising episodes that might have inspired a search for a suitable and wealthy wife. He had asked his friend: 'Why marry? This is a question I ask myself every morning, and the answer to it is not a good one. For fortune, what if she is extravagant? For beauty, what if a vixen? For conveniency, what for twelve children, a house, a coach and stables? For a companion, what (if she) has never been at school or college, has not five new ideas, no stock of knowledge, nor power of reasoning. If she's a good wife, she must think of her kitchen for which but for her you have no occasion. If a bad one of herself, of whom you are long ago tired. I think marriage is setting up a child manufactory, at which one must drudge like a horse. Children are a commodity which requires great pains in the raising, and there you are miserable till you get them disposed of.'[77]

This self-analysis at three o'clock in the morning showed how nervous Dempster was about the whole question of marriage and revealed a sense of propriety that would have been incomprehensible to Boswell. He told his friend he often felt 'an importunate fellow' who had 'often been refused a dalliance. Importuning to a woman is gallantry (but) to a woman with a fortune meanness' and, with his need for such a fortune with which to repair his finances public knowledge, Dempster felt such importuning would be 'meanness itself'. Unfortunately, the closer he came to marriage, the more convoluted his lawyer's logic became. His description of one prospect had summed up this confusion: 'As to "B" there is no doubt that it is all over. I stayed a day in Edinburgh and made two unsuccessful attempts for admittance, repeated my stanza, and set out for London at midnight. At first I thought it odd, if not cruel, not to hear me, but I now consider it as a wonderful piece of delicacy and great attention to the feelings of a lover, to contrive to give him a peremptory refusal, yet enable him to boast that he had never asked the question or talked about marriage. I shall never think more about matrimony.'[78] A month later he had 'taken Epictetus in her stead' having learned 'not to covet' what he could not obtain.[79]

When Dempster's defence of the bachelor life was swept away and he successfully wooed Miss Rose Heming is not recorded. Certainly one of his earliest intentions of 'seeking out some good widow who has sown her wild oats in her first husband's fields' had not been realized.[80] Curiously, he acknowledged a missive from Lord Rockingham five days before the wedding, thanking him for some fine venison which had arrived in good order. If this was a friendly and not unconnected gesture, it would seem that Dempster had let at least one cat out of the bag.[81] A letter to Sir Adam written just a fortnight beforehand contained no mention of the impending marriage whatsoever. Instead, he was at pains to 'be at little or no expense' in the forthcoming general election where Robinson considered his boroughs were 'very open, venal, and expensive, and very few chuse (sic) to engage with them. Government has a good interest among them, many places to be given, being ports, but no one has yet started'.[82] Telling Sir Adam that he knew enough of his 'finances to be satisfied that a contrary resolution would be madness in extreme', he admitted that 'the impropriety of continuing in Parliament with so small a fortune as mine frequently comes across me'.[83] It may be that the end of his 'independency' had been decided quickly. On the other hand, when he came to anticipate the marriage of his heir years later, he was content to leave it to chance: 'matrimony can admit of no concerted plan . . . .Providence takes that part of human life into its own hands.'[84]

His letter to Sir Adam suggests that the plans he had made earlier and which turned on withdrawing, if possible, to Scotland and not attending the first session of the new Parliament had 'economy' rather than marriage in mind. He had 'long thought . . . that unless one preserves a little freedom and independency in Parliament to act in every question and to vote agreeably to . . . one's own mind, a seat in Parliament is a seat of thorns and rusty nails. That this cannot be attained without some ease in your affairs . . . either you must be very rich or very frugal.'[85] What he seems to have failed to share with Sir Adam was the full extent of the mental turmoil and happy anticipation through which he went during the summer of 1774. Even to Pulteney he did not admit until March the next year that he had married 'a young lady (he) loved'.[86]

The announcement of the marriage, when it came in *The Scots Magazine*, was factual and no more: 'September 26th. At London, George Dempster, Esq; of Dunnichen, member for Perth, Dundee, etc. to Miss Rose Heming, sister of George Heming, Esq; of Caldecote Hall, Warwickshire'.

It was to be a long and happy marriage but without children, one in which 'providence' had clearly taken a hand. Dempster was 42, and his wife Rose, who was the younger of Richard Heming's two daughters, 26 years old. Her father had been the owner of sugar plantations in Jamaica inherited from his father and a Member of Assembly there. She had three brothers, the eldest of whom was Samuel, who inherited his father's estates in the parish of St Anne's on the colony's north coast. Leaving Francis in the Caribbean, Rose accompanied her other brother George (1733–1802) to England at the end of the 1760s.[87] At the time of the marriage, George was renting Caldecote Hall in Warwickshire, which was subsequently bought by his son in the 19th century.[88]

6

THE OCCASIONAL TRUANT
(1775 - 1781)

'I cabbaged a winter from Parliament last year'
(Dempster to Pulteney, 19 September 1775)

1775

No sooner had Dempster 'come down to Scotland' the previous October after his marriage than parliament was dissolved. At the general election he was fortunate enough to be re-elected unanimously 'without one shilling of expense'. His constituents gave him such an enthusiastic vote of confidence that he was determined to be all 'the more attached to the privileges of the people'.[1] He was, however, convinced that his attendance at Westminster would not affect the business of the House either way, and he chose to spend the first session of the new parliament in Scotland invoking the scriptural excuse that 'I've married a wife and therefore I can't come'. In fact, 'he could not budge', nor leave his 'dear wife on a bleak Scotch hill by herself'[2] in what he was prepared to admit was 'a bad house'.[3] For the first time in his life he passed a winter in the country and 'never did three months roll on with more swiftness and satisfaction'.[4]

'Rosy at the altar swore, to be my loving wife and true', and so it proved.[5] Dempster found in her 'every good thing he desired in a wife and friend'.[6] His *très chère femme*, as he called her, had 'the sense of a man (and) the manners of a gentlewoman . . . never out of humour . . . and an economical cheerful country wife'.[7] He was 'extravagantly happy in a wife who neither frowns, speaks nonsense, nor spends money'.[8] Apologizing to Charles Fergusson that they could not be *en famille* in London that winter, Dempster said she 'would have been a charming addition to our society. She is better temper'd than myself and plays whist and quadrille like an angel, and as for happiness I protest to you I did not know what it was till I was married'.[9]

Marriage called for a review of his financial position and, as he told Pulteney and Sir Adam, despite being richer than he had been when he 'lived on (his) salary in London the whole year round', as a married man this 'would be impossible'. Furthermore, 'repairs and additions' to Dunnichen were called for if the couple were to live in 'any degree of comfort'.[10] His wife's dowry of £2,000 would have been drawn from the funds George Heming brought to Warwickshire when the two young people came to England, given that the bulk of her father's estate remained in the hands of her eldest brother in Jamaica. In the circumstances, it seemed that he could 'go on without embarrassment'. When parliament met he would leave the estate 'in the hands of few friends', 'living the Session single in London'.[11]

His 'heart's ease' enabled him to concentrate for the longest period yet on improving the house and farm. Having more time to himself he discovered a field of marl, amounting to 2–300,000 bolls, which lay five and a half feet under dead sand and above which there was peat which could be sold. He anticipated that as soon as its quality had been confirmed, it would be worth at least £200 a year to the estate.[12] He also let off the last of his farms.[13] By September the property 'proved abundantly serviceable', but making Dunnichen House 'commodious enough for folks of our humble views'[14] would have been an urgent task. His grandfather's inheritance had never received much attention when other estate lands had been forcibly sold and the necessity of what he called 'several repairs and additions' was probably an understatement. For Rosie, the contrast with the warm yellow Cotswold stone of her brother's Warwickshire home could not have been greater.

Dunnichen House was a solid, square, two-storeyed property built of whinstone, sitting at the bottom of the southern slope of Dunnichen Hill, 'beautifully embosomed in trees'. A door opened up from the drawing room on the south and the garden to the west of the mansion was sheltered by a belt of trees surrounding the house and the remaining gardens to the east and south.[15] Whatever works put in hand at this juncture would not have been lavish. It was not until 1794–5 that he could afford to undertake the major reconstruction that was really called for. Dempster's residences always had a homely rather than an impressive appearance. Essential quarters such as his library, the dining room and main drawing room would have been well-appointed but not ostentatious. Comfort for his guests undoubtedly improved over the years, but apart from several medium-sized reception rooms and his library, the domestic arrangements at Dunnichen did not inspire immediate praise. He was content to describe it as his 'little farm-house'.[16]

Local gentry and his constituents were curious to see whom Dempster had chosen to be the mistress of Dunnichen. The summer's social calendar provided ample occasions for the couple to be seen together. One was a grand ball in Dundee which turned out to be a particularly hilarious affair. The sponsor of the evening was a Scottish 'nabob' called Paterson, who, having made a fortune of £40,000 in Madras, wanted to impress local society. Dempster's name was associated with the event and two or three hundred people accepted invitations. It was a warm August evening and the ballroom oppressively hot. The dancing was led off by Mrs Dempster and the 'nabob', followed by some 78 couples. After country dances and an 'elegant cold collation in an adjacent room' the ladies and some of the gentlemen returned to the ballroom and danced till three. The remaining gentlemen had, however, 'taken to the bottle . . . and continued to drink very freely'. Others would have joined them but they were refused unless they would 'drink a bottle of claret before they sat down (so) that the rest might be upon an equal footing with themselves'. The male party went on drinking till 5 am when, 'beginning to turn a little riotous, they display'd a truly British spirit by demolishing all the decanters, bottles and glasses, and, indeed, everything that was breakable in the room'. Only at six o'clock did they retire to their lodgings.[17]

Dempster's young wife would soon have come to terms with her husband's preoccupation with affairs in London and the daily stream of correspondence on all manner of subjects. This first year of their marriage was a momentous one on the American continent and Rosie's roots in that hemisphere would have made her especially sympathetic to the incoming news. The first skirmish at Lexington took place in April. Dempster was, however, only too well aware that in Scotland 'the whole body of the gentry and of the independent and enlightened class of people (were) to a man on the side of Administration' and he could not help feeling depressed by 'the insensibility of the merchants and all ranks of people'. He also had to be circumspect in his correspondence since 'every letter is opened at the post-office'.[18]

An American friend with whom Dempster shared some of his hopes and fears for the colonists at this time was Ralph Izard. He had taken a house near Dempster's lodgings with Mr Alcock when he arrived in London in 1771, choosing to live in Berners Street on account of it having become the 'home and haunt' of sculptors and painters.[19] Izard particularly enjoyed London society and 'possessed the friendship of some of the first men in (the) country' who, according to his daughter, 'were desirous that he should be presented at Court'.[20] Nevertheless, growing uneasy about 'the melancholy prospects of American politics', he left for the continent intending to return to America thereafter. From Geneva Izard wrote thanking Dempster for arranging the letting of the home he and his family had used during their stay. His personal anxiety was that two pictures, one in the parlour, the other of his wife in the 'middle drawing room', should be removed to Mr West's in Newman Street for safe keeping, but as Izard journeyed through southern France en route for Switzerland and Italy, it was the dispute between England and America that was most on his mind. He hoped that Dempster could help 'put an end to this cruel and unnatural contest'. His French contacts suggested that the loss of the two countries' mutual affection would weaken England, but the latter did not 'see things in the same light'.[21]

Dempster allowed himself to suggest to Izard that the Americans had not made proper use of an opening he considered Lord North had given them during the debates.[22] More the product of a legal mind in search of a solution than a realistic plan, he argued that 'a Ministerial declaration that it is not expedient to tax America, was a great concession from men who had talked so different a language. Had I been in town, I am afraid I should have differed from all my friends, closed in with the idea, and seconded an address to the King to instruct his Governors to apply for a subsidy by way of requisition. This would have substituted negotiation in the room of war; it would have slackened the armaments, and at last ended in leaving America just where we found her before the unlucky Stamp Act, and there she would have remained for ever. It is needless to enquire what motive this change of sentiment in Lord North is to be imputed, whether to principle or fear of losing his place. The effects of it might have been most salutary.'[23]

While awaiting news of events in America Dempster told Izard in July about the discovery of the marl pit at Dunnichen which promised to make him 'a lot of money'.[24] When it came, it was clear that Izard had been keeping a close watch on the war from his summer home in Weymouth. He told Dempster of the offer General Fraser and Sir William Erskine (two of Dempster's friends) had made to go to America and, assuming that Dempster had followed events from the *Gazette*, that more than a thousand men in General Gage's army had been killed. Having asked to be kept informed about the proceedings of the Continental Congress, and knowing Dempster's keen interest in constitutional matters, Izard told him that if America became independent of Britain 'the world would see the finest and freest Constitution . . . that any people were ever blessed with'.[25]

Having 'cabbaged ('half-inched') a winter from parliament' and in better spirits, Dempster felt his attendance at Westminster could not now be avoided. The election had been uncontested, although Perth remained a 'hostile town'. Taking new and temporary lodgings in Poland Street, he was unattended by his sister this time and without the comfort of his wife. Regretfully, he had left Rosie behind on account of 'his finances'. In time for the debate on the Address of Thanks to the sovereign, where the Commons sat to midnight,[26] Dempster commended the speech from the throne for the signal it gave that the administration was to send a Commission to America empowered to receive submissions, as well as remove restrictions and grant pardons. The administration's dilatory follow-up to this proposal nevertheless irritated him: 'would to God they were sailed, and had begun their negotiations'.[27] He picked up a suggestion made by Grenville and urged that the Commissioners should also be empowered to treat with the Congress. He was convinced that America would not listen to entreaties made through any other medium and pleaded that the Ministry would allow 'no false pride, no misplaced idea of dignity and authority' to stand in the way of 'seeking peace where alone peace may be found'. His call was for the Commissioners to be vested with discretionary powers, for, without the freedom to negotiate on the spot, peace and harmony could not be restored. It was at the conclusion of this speech that Dempster showed how strongly he felt about the American issue. In the peroration, he said, 'How ardently, Sir, this is my wish, let the trouble I have now ventured to give you this night, bear witness, if the uniformity of my conduct for 11 years that this unhappy contest has subsisted, should not be a sufficient testimony of my sincerity'.[28]

'Governor George' Johnstone was joined by his wayward brother John when the Commons came to discuss the deteriorating situation in the colony of Georgia. There, colonists had rioted in sympathy with their compatriots in Massachusetts. John Johnstone had become the Member for the Dysart Burghs, using his enormous wealth to oust James Townsend Oswald from the seat.[29] When George Johnstone drew attention to there being no evidence of open rebellion, any clash with his Majesty's troops or interference with trade, his brother readily seconded the motion. 'Most of the other colonies,' he said, 'had done something which might be construed into resistance', but not Georgia. Dempster objected to Lord North's refusal to allow witnesses in the form of West India merchants being invited to the House to give evidence of what was going on, criticizing the noble lord for not only prejudging the colonists' behaviour but 'proceeding to inflict punishment', something repugnant to 'the generally accepted ideas of justice'.[30] Fortunately Dempster appears to have been able to avoid any public representation of John Johnstone, simply treating him with the respect given to another Member of the House. He made no mention of him to Sir Adam in the surviving letters quoted by James Fergusson.

At the beginning of November, the Duke of Manchester led the Lords debate on a measure that would enable foreign troops to be employed without the consent of Parliament. A fortnight later the Commons also debated whether or not to allow the deployment of the militia at least during the present emergency. Some Members saw additional and dangerous power being put in the hands of the Crown. Dempster supported the measure but not before he had to be reminded by Alexander Carlyle of the promise he had made to introduce a Scottish Militia Bill each year until it succeeded. Predictably, he argued that those who said free Governments across Europe had been destroyed by a militia were mistaken, for history would furnish many more instances in which they had been overthrown by standing armies; and he hoped 'that a militia would be established in the north part, as well as the south part of the island, for the defence of the nation in general'.[31] The transfer of virtually all the country's readily available armed forces to the new theatre of war was under way. Additional regiments needed to be raised and the possibility of enlisting Hanoverian troops had to be considered.

Again urging conciliation, Dempster opposed the prohibition of trade with America, and supported Fox's motion for an enquiry into the 'ill success of

British arms' where he was 'sorry to see such a disposition in the Administration to stifle all enquiry'.[32] The 'olive branch petition' offered by Congress had been returned unanswered by Lord North on orders from the King. No doubt inspired by events in America, Dempster developed his ideas for the extension of democracy at home which many found too hard to bear. He favoured the extension of the Scottish franchise 'now engrossed by the great lords, the drunken laird and the drunkener bailie', and did not approve Dundas's abortive proposals for limiting the creation of county votes.[33] He wrote to Carlyle: 'Instead of curtailing the right by cutting off superiors, let it be extended to vassals and tenants . . . but I am Whig enough to think that the most beneficial law should not be crammed down the throats of any people, but their minds gradually prepared for the alteration.'[34]

1776

Travelling south after the New Year celebrations, Dempster seems to have decided to visit Edinburgh for a few days and meet up with some of the more eminent members of the Poker Club. The minutes of the club's meeting on 26 January list his attendance.

Believing that the American crisis might at last induce the Government to concede a Scottish militia, Dempster assisted in drafting Lord Mountstuart's Bill and strongly supported it in the debates of 1776. During the second reading debate, he was supported by his old friend Sir Adam Fergusson who took up the matter because he believed it would be a means of procuring 'a complete national defence'. Other speakers in favour included Sir Gilbert Elliot, Mr Thomas Townsend, Burke, Sir John Cavendish and Governor Johnstone. The last considered that the Bill was in some respects better than the English Militia Act, because it contained a clause that no man should be permitted to serve twice as a substitute, which would be the means of training a much greater number of men in the use of arms. Dempster argued that the expense of 6,000 men would not be as great as some feared, but, despite these efforts, his long-standing campaign was unsuccessful and the Bill was rejected.

Dempster was able to go home to Dunnichen a few days earlier than he had proposed and in April he reported a smooth four-day journey north, with post horses ready at every stage. He arrived home in the midst of the planting and ploughing season and found his wife 'in perfect health'. Local farmers had a good crop in 1775 and this looked like being repeated that year and, with a brisk demand for linen, prices were better.[35] Responding in June to Professor Watson's request for an introduction in London, Dempster wrote to Burke. He explained that the St Andrews University historian who was a valuable friend was about to publish a history of the Reign of Philip the Second of Spain but, being 'a modest man, and an utter stranger to London and the ways of London', he felt sure that Burke would not only put him straight but find his company stimulating.[36] Such small favours were all part of daily correspondence from Dunnichen as life at the house settled down under its 'new management'. Dempster dreamed of performing similar pleasurable duties as part of his now more relaxed lifestyle and in his role as 'Gentleman Usher'.

A good part of June and July was spent very enjoyably in the company of William Cane who invited Dempster to be one of five male guests on a cruise in the English Channel.[37] The others were Lord George Gordon, who had become an MP in 1774, Sir Charles Bingham[38], Mr Stephenson, returned from Bombay, and Mr William Hickey, an old school friend of his host, then 27 years old, who had been taken under Cane's wing on his return from the West Indies. Mr and Mrs Cane were neighbours of Dempster in Berners Street where Rosie was to join him later in the year. Their establishment was on a scale altogether more lavish than his own, Mr Cane being something of a bon viveur. Apart from six male servants indoors, there were two gardeners, a helper in the stable, and four hands who manned his boat and which had its moorings at Erith within a few yards of his second property, a small neat country house. Mrs Cane's fortune was said to be worth £30,000, whilst her husband's estates brought in rather above £2,000 per annum.

Having taken dinner together on 20 June, and drunk a toast to the 'Success (of) the Americans', the party boarded the *Henrietta*, a handsome cutter of 20 tons, and retired to their respective cots. At seven the next morning, with the vessel in the hands of a Channel pilot as well as four additional crew, and a fresh breeze from the north-west, they soon passed Gravesend. Off Sheppey a supply of vegetables and bread was sent for, and that evening they took a meal in Margate before sailing safely across to Boulogne. Finding the tide out, the cutter's yawl was launched, only for it to go aground. Cane, Dempster and the others were rescued by a bunch of French fisherwomen who came out in a flat-bottomed boat. With petticoats rolled up and their thighs bare, they lifted each member of the party bodily out of the yawl and carried them to land. The party then made for the premises of Messrs Meriton and Smith, English wine merchants in the town, where they were greeted most hospitably by Mr Smith who was well-known to Dempster as well as his host.

Lord George Gordon proposed a dash to Paris for a couple of days, which, being agreed to, three *voitures* were ordered to be at the door at daybreak the next morning. Early on the third day they reached the French capital and drove to a handsome hotel in the Rue St Sauveur. A couple of days later two banker friends of their host, the Panchaud brothers, gave a cheerful party attended by several of the *noblesse* who accompanied them to the opera in the evening. The following day Dempster and the party visited the palace and gardens at Versailles, again dining with the Panchauds.[39] Before they left to return to Boulogne on 28 June, yet another sumptuous dinner and princely entertainment was put on for them, this time by Major Baggs and Mr Taaffe, an Irish gentleman of fortune and friend of Hickey's father. Arriving in

Boulogne on 1 July, Mr Cane sent on board the *Henrietta* a plentiful supply of champagne and claret bought at Meriton and Smith's. The hampers containing the wine half- filled the cabin.

The *Henrietta* had been seven hours at sea on 2 July en route for Portsmouth, the cruise's next destination, when a Custom House cutter ranged alongside and an officer came on board to examine the vessel. The man was as civil as possible, paying the greatest respect to Dempster's ribbon and insignia of the Thistle which he insisted on wearing. Invited by Mr Cane into the cabin, the officer was obviously taken aback by what he saw: 'You've laid in a good stock of wine, sir,' to which Mr Cane replied, 'It is necessary as we mean to be out several weeks and are six in number. Besides, you know it would not do to stint ourselves.' Thankfully for all aboard the officer good-humouredly agreed: 'You are quite right to have enough. It is not to watch pleasure vessels like this that we are employed'. Whereupon, after some cold fowl and ham, and a tumbler of madeira, he returned to his cutter and stood up channel.

During a discussion over dinner the volatile and elegant Lord George Gordon suggested that their cutter should be rechristened the *Congress* as a compliment to the worthy patriots in America. Everyone concurred and drank 'Success to the *Congress*', Johnson, the master, being told that she was no longer the *Henrietta*. A bowl of punch was then ordered for the crew. On 4 July the party arrived in Weymouth, which, it had been decided, was the westerly limit of the cruise. During a ten-day stay Dempster would have particularly enjoyed the theatre where, as Hickey said, there was a set of very tolerable actors. After being feted among others by a Mr Sturt and a great Russian merchant called Mr Buxton, the party re-embarked and reached Portsmouth in the night of 16 July, finally reaching Erith in high health and spirits.

On 3 October, Dempster's half sister Helen was married at Dunnichen. Her husband, George Burrington, was then a Captain in the East India Company's forces home on leave from India. He had been married before, with a daughter Charlotte who was to become a great favourite among the family. The couple left soon after for India and spent many years away from Scotland. The pleasurable event probably helped Dempster decide that it was time for Rosie to be introduced to life in the capital as the wife of a Scottish MP and by December, she was ensconced with him at No.71 Berners Street. In a note to Pulteney, who was at 'Balls, Hertford' rather than his usual abode at Bath House, Dempster hoped that Christmas and Hogmanay would give him the opportunity to meet his wife in her new surroundings. Never missing a chance of helping his friends to secure nominations to posts in the East India Company, he added that 'the Bencoolen cadetship (was) very much at (his) service', assuring Pulteney from his experience of such matters that for £100 'it will not be difficult to get him smuggled out to that part of the world, or which is better, sent as a free mariner which secures him from being ordered home again by the rulers there'.[40]

1777

Dempster again met William Hickey, who had been aboard the *Congress* the previous summer, when the young attorney said his farewells to his friends before departing for Calcutta to practise in the Supreme Court of Judicature. Following a dinner on 15 March at Mr Cane's, where both Edmund and Richard Burke were present, a carriage made several rounds of London.[41] One circuit was to Sir George Colebrook, then to Mr Dunning and Dempster, Mr Maclean and Mr Potter, a Welsh Judge. All gave Hickey letters of introduction to friends in India, his father writing to Sir Elijah Impey, the Chief Justice, whom Dempster was to defend in the House of Commons five years later.

Throughout 1777 Dempster maintained his critical stance in respect of many of North's measures in parliament. On 18 April he demanded an enquiry into civil list debts amounting to £618,000, insisting that the King must be compelled to let the House know 'in what manner those debts were contracted'.[42] Criticizing North's financial measures outlined in the budget, and later the system of contracts that encouraged excessive profits to be made, Dempster performed his now well-established role as financial watchdog, promoting his concept of a national sinking fund at the same time. During an East India debate in May he attacked the intrigues of the Nabob of Arcot which had caused the imprisonment and death of the Governor of Madras. As James Fergusson said, the whole episode was one of the 'most disreputable in the history of the Company's administration'.[43]

Since their marriage the Dempsters had formed the habit of visiting parts of England during the early part of the summer recess before travelling to Scotland. It was to become a well-established routine and enjoyed by all. This year they spent part of June, July and August in Devonshire where they took 'Horsewell' at 'Digbury Bay' (possibly Bigbury), near Kingsbridge – 'a little retreat . . . on the brink of the ocean' – living 'quietly till we (can) taste the fruits' of a legacy he anticipated.[44] There George found a kindred spirit among one of his neighbours which helped compensate for the view he had taken of South Devonians. He found them in general 'greatly deficient in humanity' on account of their custom of plundering wrecks, something that Burke, to whom he had written, was only too well aware of since a relative of his had been a victim of wreckers on the same coast. The gentleman whose company Dempster so enjoyed had requested a copy of the Bill dealing with wrecks that Burke had moved in the session of Parliament just finished. The legal intricacies of a law passed in Queen Anne's time, giving customs officers not only power over such wrecks but the opportunity to make money themselves from such events, provided ample stimulus to his conversations with this Mr Ilbert.[45]

1778

Soon after Christmas a family party set off for what was to be an extended residence in France. The group of six was made up of his wife's brother and sister-in-law George and Amitia Heming, (who was probably carrying their second child), Charlotte Burrington, Sir Adam, and George and Rose Dempster. They were together in London on 12 December and may have spent Christmas there, but by New Year's day they were ensconced in Paris, meeting many in the expatriate and émigré community there. More than twenty years later Dempster recalled how much Mrs Dempster had enjoyed this time together.[46]

How such an adventure came to be entertained, especially at a crucial period in British relations with both France and America, is not known and, however much Dempster may have wanted to share with Rosie the pleasures he always enjoyed in France and achieve some respite from his busy parliamentary life, he may well have had other personal or political reasons for spending the first five months of 1778 there. There is no evidence to suggest that Dempster visited the Cane family who were then living none too far away at Tours. Before the family left London there had been some talk of Sir Adam and Dempster visiting Benjamin Franklin at Passy outside Paris, and Pulteney, who was preparing himself for his own mission, certainly suggested it to Lord George Germain, the Secretary of State for the Colonies.[47] Much as Dempster would have undoubtedly welcomed the opportunity to meet the leading electrical scientist of his day, a fellow of the Royal Society and an inventor in the mould of Newton or Edison, without a personal friendship to depend upon and certainly no *locus standi* with any of the three Commissioners charged by Congress to conduct discreet negotiations with the French,[48] he would have known that his position was potentially precarious. There is no evidence that the two men met. Aware that many, if not a majority, of his constituents favoured the line that had been taken by the administration in dealing with the colonists, any unofficial contact could have been politically damaging. Lord Stormont, the British Ambassador, had kept a close eye on Franklin since his arrival from America aboard the *Reprisal* in December 1776.[49] The elderly emissary's surreptitious dinner parties and meetings were closely monitored as Stormont became increasingly concerned about Franklin's efforts to forge an alliance with the French. His spies were to be spectacularly successful and, unknown to Franklin, not one of his despatches up to the spring of 1778 ever reached Congress. Just as Franklin had moved to the outskirts of Paris in an effort to frustrate observation of his many visitors, Dempster may have chosen to stay at Orléans, which *'n'est qu'un pas'* (80 miles or so) from Paris, to avoid the inference that he might be meddling in delicate affairs of state.

The family was obviously in high spirits in Paris, but unfortunate news that

Sir Adam's youngest brother James had died before Christmas on his estate in Tobago necessitated his return to Kilkerran soon after they arrived, recalling the time in 1756 when the sickness of George's sister Peggy had occasioned a similar unplanned return to Scotland. On the first day of February, and without Sir Adam, the family party travelled from Paris to Orléans with Basil, their newly-acquired servant, where they all stayed 'at a most excellent inn, *Les Empereurs*'. There they prospected for a 'country house and vineyard' to rent which 'every inhabitant of substance' possessed, and where they were to settle for the remainder of the winter. The inn was especially economical yet pleasant, and for seven *Tournois livres* per day[50] they lived 'at less expense than when we shall become house keepers', Dempster being relieved to find the cost of living in France much lower than in London.[51]

The beauty of Orléans and the surrounding district was particularly appreciated. He reported favourably on the new stone bridge over the Loire at the southern end of the Rue Royale, built only twenty years before, along with the hundred or so lighters berthed by wide quays, and the town's six impressive gates, all in his usual fulsome and enthusiastic manner. The party was captivated by the weekly performances at La Salle de la Perle, a little theatre in the Rue de Colombier.[52] Farming methods were praised; wheat and bread prices were lower than in England, horses 'in good condition' and little uncultivated land. The justice system, administered by a Lieutenant-General and twenty King's Counsel, which Dempster saw in action through his attendance at an appeal case being referred to the Parliament in Paris, also attracted his attention. After two weeks at the Inn, the party was able to move into a 'very pleasant house on the banks of the Loire' a mile or so from Orléans itself, 'with a lime tree walk, a flower plot, a green room, an orchard of dwarf fruit trees, a fish pond, a little green-house for harbouring their orange trees in winter' and an adjoining cottage for the vigneron. With greater leisure time, Dempster applied himself 'seriously to the acquiring of the French language' with which he had found difficulty in Paris and, amid all the other diversions, avidly read the daily news in the *Courier de l'Europe*. Hearing that Lord North had put forward 'propositions . . . for accommodating our unhappy dispute with America' and in desperation had repealed his earlier legislation, he presumed that it was now the 'sincere desire of the administration . . . to extricate Great Britain from the danger and expense of its present situation upon any terms'.[53]

Whether or not any contact was made with Franklin while the family was in Paris there is no doubting the quality of the intelligence that Dempster gained there during January and he would have known how quickly matters were coming to a head. News of Burgoyne's surrender at Saratoga had reached Paris the previous month, lifting spirits and enabling military and diplomatic plans to be discussed more openly with the French who had persistently made it clear to Franklin that they had no intention of supporting the colonists unless and until their break from England was likely to be successful. By February it was possible for France to move from an 'unofficial' alliance to what was to become a treaty of 'peace, amity and commerce', copies of which Stormont obtained within two days of their publication and sent to Lord North in London. Whilst Dempster was convinced that 'every effort towards reconciliation will be ineffectual' without independence being granted to the united colonies, and rightly forecast that the British commissioners[54] to be sent to America would fail in their task if all they could offer was a form of home rule, the tone of his criticisms was subdued. Intending his letter to be passed to the Lord Advocate and possibly North himself, it was as if he anticipated that it would in any case be intercepted and carefully scrutinized. He meant it to be a simple 'piece of intelligence' confirming that America would 'listen to nothing but independency at present'.

Dempster expected the commissioners would be 'as little attended to' and be rebuffed just as Lord Howe's peace mission had been two years previously. The ministry, which had been 'so deficient in point of sagacity . . . as not to have foreseen the consequences' of its misplaced actions since the beginning of the decade, was now in despair. In France there was evidence enough to convince him that any belated attempt to buy off the Americans would be scoffed at, and, although during 1777 the French government had never provided enough ships, guns or powder to do more than anger the administration in London, they were now prepared to commit themselves more openly after Congress undertook to help France reconquer the sugar islands of the Caribbean. Nevertheless, what neither London, Paris nor Dempster knew was how close a call Congress's eventual decision to ratify the treaty would be. The French were right to fear that at the last moment the Americans might be attracted to North's virtual surrender. Peace and home rule had great attraction for many Americans and a successful war was far from certain. It was Franklin's despatch in May – this time unseen by Stormont or the ministry – that saved the day. It not only set out the terms of the treaty but explained the delicate course of negotiations that had taken place in Paris over the previous eighteen months. It reached America just in time for Congress to quickly ratify the Franco-American treaty, and an alliance between the two states should war result, just two days before the commissioners arrived to argue the British proposals. In consequence, and with war now inevitable, Stormont left Paris, the first brush with France following in June off Ushant. Spain, who had been promised American help in achieving her own political ends, threw in her lot with France the following year.[55]

It is unlikely that Dempster was wholly ignorant of Pulteney's secret mission to Paris that spring. Indeed his confinement 'like a captive Jew . . . by the streams of the Loire' where he mourned the 'mischiefs' which impended, was probably a self-imposed act to maximize his friend's chances of success. The gentlemanly and habitually 'gaunt and threadbare' figure of Pulteney was certainly to be seen in Paris by early March where he registered at 'an obscure hotel in the Latin Quarter' under the name of 'Mr Williams' and sent Franklin a copy of his 'Thoughts on the Present State of Affairs with America and the Means of Conciliation'. Franklin only too easily recognized that it contained all the ideas he had himself put to Lord Howe during their talks in London four years previously.

Pulteney's first attempt in March 1777 to persuade the Colonial Secretary to let him have talks with Franklin had been discouraged. Only when rumours about a possible treaty abounded a year later was he eventually given an assignment by the First Minister to discuss the possible terms under which peace might be negotiated with the Americans. Outlining his credentials to Lord George Germain, he had explained that his agent, a Scot named William Alexander living in Dijon who was a friend of the American emissary, had cleared the way for a meeting and that Franklin 'knows that I have wished always the most perfect freedom of America with respect to taxation and charters'.[56] However, when they met he soon realized that Franklin's insistence on complete independence exceeded anything that London was prepared to grant, an insistence which was confirmed when Alexander saw Franklin alone a week or so later. After reporting to North in London about his first meeting, he returned again to Passy taking with him eighteen 'protocols of peace'. Franklin was convinced they would not be acceptable to Congress[57] and, although it was arranged that Alexander would move to Passy to keep up the pressure – and Franklin met David Hartley, another MP,[58] by the end of March he confirmed to Pulteney in writing that only a peace treaty between the two sovereign nations would suffice.[59] To Gérard, the First Secretary of the French Foreign Minister, he did however admit that the terms being offered by Britain 'would probably have been accepted if they had been made two years ago'.[60]

Pulteney had been issued with £20,000 from the Treasury's Secret and Special Service Account at this time. It was, however, an additional sum of £300 from the same source that occasioned a subsequent correspondence between himself and accountants in the Treasury when it was suggested it was for his expenses in France. Writing to John Robinson, he said, 'I wish you to understand that I neither claim nor will I accept of any expenses incurred by myself; the money is for another purpose, and the Lord North knows that to be the case'.[61] The wealthy master of Bath House, whose intention was to be his own man in affairs of state, seems nevertheless to have been prepared to succumb to 'the very tactics of bribery against which he had cautioned the Ministry'.[62] All North's secret service funds were probably ear-marked for Alexander who, once Pulteney left Paris and despite his affection for Franklin, in effect became a spy. Pulteney returned to Whitehall disappointed but still hopeful, not knowing that the King had concluded that 'I do not think much is to be built on the note from Pulteney'.[63]

Dempster's reflections at the time were written a world away from Westminster. For the family it was to be a most relaxing and absorbing holiday. They enjoyed an exceptionally fine spring: 'The transition from winter to excessive heat (had been) instantaneous. It began with this month (April) and in ten days brought out all the leaves and blossoms of our trees, but within these two days northerly winds and cold weather and rain have returned . . . not unlike English spring weather.' Dempster continued to write letters every day and would perhaps have been in touch with Ralph Izard had he known that he had accompanied Franklin when the envoys were received at Versailles by Louis XVI once the alliance had been signed; but by then contact between the two men had probably been lost. Dempster still hoped that the British commissioners might succeed in their task, but he seems to have been reconciled to the failure of all overtures to Congress and the likelihood of war: *'Aujourd'hui c'est paix; demain c'est guerre, et quelquefois toutes les deux, en vingt quatre heures'*.[64] Knowing that Pulteney had always favoured home rule, and had never been a supporter of American independence must have added to his pessimism. But the pleasures of France might have been cut short had Dempster been aware of Parliament's scrutiny of the catastrophic blunders made by Lord George Germain, General Burgoyne and General Howe. 'If I had known of General Bougoyne's (*sic*) return and examination sooner I believe those events would have shortened my stay here.'[65] As it was, he had to content himself with the knowledge that 'the two Houses would have been better employed in following poor Lord Chatham's advice, than his hearse',[66] and penning a thoughtful précis of the administration's shortcomings.

Dempster was ever mindful of how the success of the constitution for which he had 'the greatest veneration' depended on the country avoiding 'blind guides' leading a 'poor army into the ditch' as he described Germain's role in London and Burgoyne's in America. In Dempster's view, the constitution had a defect 'which will, if not always yet most frequently, prevent its being governed by its best citizens'. Although claiming that Sir Adam 'was a better metaphysician than (he) was', Dempster struggled with a concept of ministerial responsibility that meant any advice given to ministers was not necessarily the same advice offered in Parliament. He went as far as to maintain that ministers 'must offer the same advice in Parliament which has been rejected in Council, or support in Parliament what had (been) condemned in the Cabinet'. To him collective responsibility smacked of poor political morality but the dilemma lay in finding a means of avoiding 'the fall of an administration with whom you are connected'. Surprising himself, and asking Sir Adam 'to judge how far (he was) from thinking soundly', Dempster chose Henry Conway (1721–1795) as the minister 'who (had) acted the most to (his) liking in the course of almost twenty years' experience' and, like Dempster himself, a man of scrupulously honourable conduct.[67] Both were to take a leading part in attacks on Lord North in 1780–81.

On a more personal note, Dempster's letters from Orléans showed that the high hopes he had enjoyed the previous August regarding the prompt payment of an important legacy had diminished somewhat, even to the point of evaporation. Potentially damaging legal problems had emerged affecting Sir Robert Fletcher's will. His benefactor had been MP for Cricklade before joining the East India Company and was someone who apparently regarded Dempster as one of the three people 'most dear to him' through his links with the county of Angus. Dempster was a guardian and executor of his estate, as well as being a beneficiary. As Brigadier-General Sir Robert Fletcher he had commanded the Company's forces in the Coromandel and died in Mauritius of tuberculosis in May the previous year on his way home.[68] Having written to Pulteney of his complete surprise at such unlooked-for generosity, Dempster estimated his bequest to be worth between £700 and £1,000 a year for life. There was even a house in Madras which, if let, would bring in an income of £550; 'this alone is an Empire to us' he told his friend.[69] The will was ambiguous and understandably disputed by Sir Robert's next of kin and there was now the strong possibility that arbitration might fail to favour him. Furthermore, the attendant publicity of a public lawsuit would be very damaging. Dempster rightly feared that the deceased's Indian fortune would not stand up to investigation.

Sitting at his desk in M.Girard Plesson's house overlooking the Loire, Dempster set about examining those questions arising from the will that he knew would be most contentious during any hearing in open court. The extent of payments so often associated with East Indian affairs brought out the worst in beneficiaries and, knowing that few fortunes acquired in the East withstood close scrutiny, he determined to pen his own 'dissertation'. 'Will it become his executors,' asked Dempster, 'to tell the Chancellor that the Nabob had promised (Sir Robert) ten thousand pounds about the time . . . Lord Pigot . . . was deprived of his government . . . (and) his liberty . . . ? That the Nabob had authorised the remittance of £2,500 of that sum and was daily expected to pay the remaining £7,500? Would one wish to see Colonel Capper [70] giving his public testimony of the means by which Sir Robert obtained a parcel of the most valuable pearls of India from the same Nabob, which Lady Fletcher contends are hers as jewels?' The catalogue was long and the widow less straightforward in her dealings than Dempster had hoped: 'The pearls for instance, instead of being mentioned by her at meetings . . . to make an inventory of the estate . . . came only to our knowledge . . . through the captain of the ship who brought them home'.[71] She threatened an application to the Chancellor if Dempster did not give his permission for the remittances to be paid to her nominees rather than Messrs.Websters, his agents who had been specified (and who stood to receive the commission on the transfer). Then, to Dempster's amazement, he learned from Sir Adam, who was keeping his legal eye on things in England, that three eminent attorneys and counsel had decided the suit in six weeks, in 'violation of all the laws not only of nature but of art'. It was a quite unprecedented occurrence, which Dempster called 'a miracle'. The arbitrators considered he was 'entitled to what Lady Fletcher must resign on her marriage' to which, typically, Dempster's reaction was: 'to be enriched on the wedding of a bucksome (sic) widow is quite un-embarrassing . . . we must generally wait for the death of those by whom we expect to benefit'. In the event, the widow died in 1791 without re-marrying and Dempster eventually received his due, which included £1,000 a year.

With the British and French ambassadors now withdrawn, it was time for the Dempster and Heming families to return to Scotland. As the stay beside the Loire came to an end George could not resist contemplating the greater security his legacy would provide. Light-heartedly he concluded that 'if Epictetus were alive I would . . . attend his school and put some questions to him on this very subject'. Only at the end of his life did he explain that he had learned to despise wealth from that philosopher's doctrines and 'to pity those whose sole pursuit it was'.[72]

Just how much the family knew about an event that had taken place on the island of Madeira while they were in France can only be surmised. It was left to the 'Monthly Chronologer' in an autumn edition of *The London Magazine* to alert his readers to the 'lately' celebrated marriage of Dempster's half-sister, Agnes Augusta in Funchal. James Fergusson made no mention of her exist-ence in his 1934 work, only correcting his omission some years later (see p.392, Note 20). Our last knowledge of her had been as a baby being cared for by a nurse in Chapter 1. Her husband was Thomas Gordon, 42 years old, the son of William Gordon of Campbelton and described as 'a merchant' of Madeira. He became a much trusted and good friend of George, joining him in several excursions, but, so far as Agnes is concerned, she remains an unknown, unmentioned, shadowy figure living in London where her five sons were born, one of whom was to become an admiral and another a colonel in the guards, dying in France as a prisoner.

1779

Dempster came down to London in the spring, having been away since December 1777, only to become embroiled again in sundry parliamentary duties. The distressed trade of Ireland came under scrutiny when Lord Newhaven moved for an enquiry, but Dempster, along with Sir Adam Fergusson and others who accepted that the situation was serious, contested any further investigation so long as the Government persisted in ruling out a programme of relief. Dempster illustrated the lack of agreement thus: as one noble lord said, Dempster argued, 'Ireland has a broken leg; another lord says, she has a cancer; a third says, she has broken her arm; the facts are believed by all; but what relief ensues?'.[73] Then, in April, he vainly endeavoured to defer Lord North's Bill which sought to regulate the publication of almanacs and grant the Universities of Oxford and Cambridge a monopoly of such works. Arguing that the 'general liberty given in Scotland for any person to publish almanacs, (had) made the booksellers studious to be correct', Dempster sought unsuccessfully to have the matter reconsidered. In addition to dealing with administrative matters affecting the East India Company's bounty for ship-building, he supported Burke's plan for reform of the government machine, convinced that 'the influence of the Crown (was) the true cause . . . of this accursed American War'.[74]

With the long Franco-Spanish siege of Gibraltar just beginning, continuous pressure had been exerted on the administration by Burke and others to reform the country's financial affairs and strengthen its defences. Invasion was expected daily. By the end of the year Dempster was drawing attention to the fact that, although 'England was armed; Ireland was armed; North Britain was defenceless, and had, very improperly, been denied a militia for their immediate protection,'[75] but once again support for a Scottish militia was lacking.

1780

What had become Dempster's 'annual cold' forced him to 'retire from the smoke of London' at the beginning of the year to a small house at Petersham in Surrey lent him by a friend.[76] His wife Rose went with him. No sooner had they arrived than he received an invitation from Pulteney who wanted to take him down to the City to make an investment. Declining the invitation, Dempster added that it probably would not be successful as 'most of (his) City friends (had) West India(n) engagements which drain them of their cash'.[77] What had become 'a bad cold' made him irritable and, since he thought it might prevent his attendance at the House, he asked Burke on which day he was planning to move his bill curtailing the King's privy purse.[78] By 21 March, however, he was well enough to be at Westminster where the House, sitting in Committee, dealt with that part of Burke's bill relating to the household. The debate went on till well after one o'clock in the morning, Dempster arguing that it was only dealing with Ministerial edicts, those relating to peace with America and another for renewing the war. He said, 'They were reproached with wanting to take away the revenue they had given to the King, but all was a bargain, and either side might complain if the bargain was too hard'.[79] It was, nevertheless, Dempster's support in April for Dunning's famous resolution, that 'the influence of the Crown has increased, was increasing, and ought to be diminished', which was to provide ammunition for his opponents in the forthcoming general election.[80]

The summer of 1780 was marked, firstly, by anti-Catholic civil disorder led by Lord George Gordon whom Hickey, like Dempster, had regarded as a reasonable man at the time of the excursion to France in 1776, but whom he now described as insane.[81] James Macpherson, an arch 'spin doctor' of the time, and creator of the myth of *Ossian*, described how the extensive riots in June that followed Lord George's petition to the House from the Protestant Association had been extinguished.[82] Giving a succinct picture of the scene, but omitting any reference to the death of nearly 300 rioters, he reported that 'everything is quiet; the same military appearances are still kept up. A camp in Hyde Park, one in St James's Park. The bridges occupied with troops; the principal streets secured; a detachment in St Paul's and one in the Exchange etc. and patrols passing and repassing to every post. The people who had great reason to be terrified are full of gratitude to the military; and, under their protection, are arming themselves in every district of the town. Lord George was conveyed last night to the Tower and new discoveries are hourly made. A proclamation is issued, with pardons and rewards, for discoveries; a special commission is issuing and the trials will come on early in the week.'[83]

Secondly, there was a determined effort by both the King and the administration to reinforce the Tory vote at the forthcoming election, the planning for which was largely in the hands of John Robinson at the Treasury. His intrigues were to threaten Dempster's position as MP for the Perth Burghs. As the terror of the London mob subsided, Macpherson met Robinson in Whitehall to hear that he wished 'to have Perth (Burghs) out of Dempster's hands'. Rescuing seats 'out of disagreeable hands' was one of Robinson's tasks at election time.[84] The plan conjured between them was 'to let a clever fellow, a man of business go to the spot, or take some method of sounding them'. Robinson thought that a friend they had met several days before was 'the fittest man possible', one Lt.Col. John Fletcher-Campbell.[85] He saw the prospect of becoming a member of the House something that would improve his chances of military promotion, and readily fell in with Robinson's view that £1,500 divided between three of the Burghs would be sufficient to wrench the constituency out of Dempster's hands. Both Robinson and Macpherson were convinced that 'an exertion in this business will be highly pleasing here', a reference to the King who was taking an active personal part in the election, but preparations had to be put in hand immediately, certainly before 'Dempster (turned) his face to the North Pole' (his constituency).[86]

A complicated sequence of events followed. Several forces were at work for and against Dempster, about which he made no comment until after the result of the election had been declared, and then only to feign surprise at the outcome.[87] Adam Ferguson, John Home and Macpherson, all 'moderates' in the campaign for a Scottish militia, 'were to be found exploiting every resource of the existing, corrupt Scottish electoral system to win the constituency . . . for their friend John Fletcher-Campbell'.[88] Likely as not Dempster would have heard from Graham of Fintry that the Duke of Atholl was, as Fletcher-Campbell complained, 'using all his influence' against him.[89] Meanwhile, all opponents, including a third candidate, one Colonel Colin Campbell,[90] labelled Dempster a 'traitor to Scotland' for his vote on Dunning's motion.[91] Rockingham had written to Sir Lawrence Dundas about Dempster during the campaign: 'I shall not condole with you that you are becoming an object of malice . . . I have heard that my friend Dempster and you have been deemed *traitors in Scotland*.'[92] Dundas, who was the Member for Edinburgh and whose extravagance and ambition had long been much in the public eye, had, to everyone's surprise, supported Dempster's amendment to the Malt Tax Bill in May. It was the only time he is recorded to have made a speech, after twenty years in Parliament.[93]

Armed with Robinson's knowledge of 'the real sources of power . . . and whom to approach',[94] Macpherson did all he could to turn the colonel into an effective politician whilst at the same time using £8,000 of the King's largesse to secure a hold on a seat for himself at Camelford.[95] Fletcher-Campbell undoubtedly underestimated what was required of him and soon found that the support he had been promised fell far short of what was needed. The Lord Advocate (Henry Dundas) failed to come out in his favour and, canvassing hither and thither in the five towns, he was forced to accept that he had neither 'temper, health and fortune' for the task. Dempster's constituency was as volatile and contradictory as ever. The decision by the St Andrews councillors to switch their vote in Campbell's favour, at the same time retaining 'the most cordial and sincere regard and attachment' for Dempster, must have puzzled them both.[96] For Dempster it must have been a matter of some satisfaction to have thwarted, not only his opponent but Macpherson, whose so-called *Ossian* manuscripts he likened to 'Gaelic leases from Macleod of Skye's charter chest'![97]

The parliamentary session ended at the beginning of July and the next month the Dempsters stopped off at Harrogate for a week on their way north before reaching an ever-greening Dunnichen. He 'loitered' there, determined only to put in an appearance in the constituency because he 'owed it to (his) friends'. The summer at Dunnichen had been dry with everything 'parched up . . . with an unmerciful drought'. But to his surprise the larch, spruce, birch and ash trees had grown fast and he concluded that his gardener had 'given them a good education'.[98] Mercifully for Dempster, he knew at the end of August that Perth, Dundee and Forfar were firmly for him. Even his antagonists had to admit he was 'exceedingly popular',[99] and although capricious St Andrews and Cupar, with its bitter memories of the disastrous 1767 campaign, threw in their lot with Fletcher-Campbell, by October his re-election was confirmed. Pleasantly surprised 'by the successful issue of his short campaign' he was also able to congratulate Pulteney for his re-election: 'If all our constituents were like ours!'[100] But he made no mention of the fact that another member who had lost his seat was John Johnstone (Pulteney's brother). Out of the limelight at last, the unscrupulous adventurer withdrew to his estates immensely rich but as unpopular as ever. Although his death in

1795 finally brought an end to his turbulent life, he was yet to appear for one last time in Dempster's affairs.

Typically, Dempster spent Christmas drafting a letter to Lord Stormont (now in the administration) drawing his attention to the petition his constituents were about to send to the Privy Council. Concern had increased locally among Dundee linen manufacturers about a shortage of flax. A layoff of workers clearly threatened and he was determined to press their case strongly, confirming 'that our people here are in the greatest distress . . . and, without the indulgence pray'd for, must be thrown idle for a long time and in great numbers'. Earlier that year Dempster had twice asked the Right Honourable Lord to help stop hides being imported illegally through the Port of Dundee.[101]

1781

In the new parliament Dempster took the lead in opposing concessions to Irish trade at the expense of Scotland, was prominent in the East India debates in support of the Company's rights, and maintained to the end his objections to the Bengal Judicature bill. His 'proverbial candour' continued occasionally to disconcert his colleagues.[102]

A letter in April, sent round to Boswell in South Audley Street where he and General Paoli were living[103] was one of the now rarer contacts Dempster had with his old friend.[104] The two had occasionally met or corresponded. In 1779, for example, Boswell had wanted Dempster's advice about the sale of land at Lainshaw in Ayrshire, his wife's family estate.[105] They had also met briefly at a legal meeting in a committee room at 'the Shaftesbury'. Fortunately, the erstwhile 'rampages' that they had jokingly promised to repeat were missing. When Boswell returned from Richmond, Dempster had to suggest a breakfast meeting with him and General Paoli at South Audley Street on account of there being little room in Dempster's house. His 'inventory' of the household was nine people, including himself:

1 Wife
3 Nieces (Burringtons or Hemings)
1 Brother (Captain John Hamilton Dempster)
1 Brother-in-law (probably Thomas Gordon)
1 Cadet for India (unknown)
1 Lieutenant of Marines (unknown)

Then, with some feeling, Dempster added that there were a further ten people calling at the house about business 'every 20 minutes'.[106] No mention was made of the servants, but by this time his wife would have had a maid and he reported the presence of a valet who had not long been among the domestic menage and who was to be in 'his employment for forty years'.[107]

On 26 May 1781 Dempster wrote to Burke about a hitch in the progress of the Isle of Man Bill. The annexation of the island by the Crown had been before the House as far back as 1765 following the presentation of a petition by the Duke and Duchess of Atholl.[108] The Chancellor of the Exchequer had wanted powers to prevent smuggling and the clandestine trade to and from the island. Now, after the Bill's third reading, the matter had stalled and the Duke, through Colonel Murray,[109] asked Dempster to see what could be done to expedite it – Burke and Dempster having done much to promote the Bill in its early stages.[110] Meanwhile, during the debate on the causes of the war in the Carnatic, Dempster 'rejoiced at the approaching inquiry', but he begged Lord North not to make a bargain with the Company for the renewal of its charter at a time of crisis. In reply, the Prime Minister thought it more important to settle the matters in a more permanent manner than Dempster's approach of a year-to-year renewal would allow.[111]

The month of May produced a fine mixture of high-profile parliamentary activity as the affairs of the Company were exposed to searching and detailed debates, typical of those in which Dempster and others of the opposition took a full, if usually frustrating, part. He was favourably disposed towards a Bill for the better regulation of the Company's affairs, the administration of justice in Bengal and the relief of those imprisoned at Calcutta but against the establishment of English laws over the Indians, desiring that 'all the appeals that lay from the Indian courts to the Governor and council, might, in future, be determined by the judges'. North, in a careful and convincing speech, regretted that, although he had held talks with the Company's Chairman and Deputy Chairman, no acceptable solutions for the renewal of the charter had come from Leadenhall Street. The next day the Directorate of the Company proposed to pass resolutions that would 'virtually put an end to the claim of the public to the Company's territorial possessions'. Dempster was stirred to defend the Company, which 'had fought to acquire those territories under the faith of their charters and (at) great expense in the conquests'. He reminded the Prime Minister of the consequences that had followed the violation of the charter of Massachusetts Bay and that any action 'to tear from the Company by force what was not stipulated in any act of parliament', would be a breach of public faith that would 'damp(en) the spirit of enterprise and adventure, which had been productive of such happy effects'.[112] Here was Dempster entreating the Noble Lord not to quarrel with the Company on matters on which the two sides were so nearly agreed, or so he believed.

Picking up a statement by the Lord Advocate to the effect that the Company had been forced by its charter not only to have factories but to defend them, Dempster concurred readily with the learned member 'in the blue ribbon', but took him to task about the case of the land around Madras, conquered by Sir Eyre Coote in concert with the troops of the Company. In that case the Crown had not thought the Company entitled to the territory or the revenues as chartered rights. There was, he said, as one constitutional lawyer to another an issue which might be tried in a court of law, particularly since neither could adjudicate properly, both being parties to the cause.[113]

In June the work done by the Secret Committee of the Commons, appointed to enquire into the causes of the war in the Carnatic and welcomed by Dempster, was outlined by the Lord Advocate during discussion on the Bengal Judicature Bill. He explained that when it met for the first time it called for all the despatches received at India House and from this evidence the Committee had identified a number of people who were implicated. In the last despatch from Bengal it appeared that the Governor and Council had detached Sir Eyre Coote to Madras with a number of troops as soon as news arrived of Hyder Ali's invasion, that they had sent a large sum of money to the Madras presidency, that the money was to be at the command of the general of the forces, but that the civil government of the presidency was not to touch any part of it or have any sort of power over it.[114] The Commons Committee decided to set up three separate heads of enquiry – into the political, military and financial affairs in the Carnatic – only to discover that some of the people whose alleged misconduct caused them concern were in India.

In the important debate which followed, Dempster admitted 'other avocations' had prevented his being present when the Bill had originally come before the House. Examining various clauses in the Bill, he objected in particular to the Governor-General and the Council of Bengal being given 'a supreme, arbitrary, and uncontrollable power over the lives, property, and reputations of the natives of Hindostan'. In seeking to modify a clause 'so inimical to freedom', he was supported by Sir Richard Sutton, and later by Burke when he argued that 'the free system of Great Britain was considered by Britons, and justly, as the best and most beautiful fabric of government in Europe; but would the Indians think and speak of it in the same terms? No; their habits were contrary. They were familiarized to a system of rule more despotic. But must we abandon the government of the country rather than agree to rule over them by laws inimical to ourselves? Surely not: men must be governed by those laws which they loved. Where 30 millions were to be governed by a few thousand men, the government must be . . . congenial to the feelings and habits of the people.'[115] Dempster would never have agreed with another member's description of what he had just heard as 'eloquence pleading the cause of despotism'.

When George Johnstone came under fire later in the month from Fox for incompetence and suggesting that his naval command was a reward for going over to the administration, Dempster readily defended his ability and integrity, declaring that 'he never framed his friendship on such sandy ground as party consideration'.[116] Earlier that year Governor George had been given command of an expedition to the Cape of Good Hope, only to fail in reaching his destination before the arrival of French reinforcements, making the task impracticable.

During August and September Mr and Mrs Dempster were 'away on a peregrination of eight weeks' about which there is no record.[117] He appears not to have attended the winter session of parliament, nor did he vote in any of the divisions leading to North's fall. Instead, he turned his attention to his half-brother's affairs.

Several years before, Sulivan had written to Warren Hastings asking him to befriend 'the brother of my valuable friend Mr Dempster'.[118] Whether or not this plea had contributed to John Hamilton Dempster's rise in the Company's service, he had recently been promoted and Dempster was pleased to make use of his new title. He instructed the well-known publisher Mr Cadell 'to send . . . the usual Periodical Papers directed for Captain Burrington (at) Madras . . . (to be) sent by the very first Portsmouth diligence or coach for Captain Dempster of the *Ganges* East Indiaman, my brother, who will take charge of the parcel. Please accompany it with a line by the Post to the Captain'. The footnote adds that 'the speedy sailing of the East India fleet makes despatch essential'.[119]

After he had sailed as an ordinary seaman in the *Devonshire* at the end of the previous decade,[120] John Hamilton Dempster's journeys had taken him to Jamaica aboard the *Cranbrook,* (not a Company vessel), and he had signed on for a second voyage during the sailing season of 1771/2 aboard the *Devonshire,* this time as 4th mate under Captain Robert Morgan. There followed at least three other voyages aboard non-Company ships: the *Harriet,* where he was 1st mate for two journeys to Jamaica over a period of 18 months (and where he may have met the Heming family) and as Master of a transport ship called the *Blue Mountain Valley* for a four-month voyage to America. By 1776/7 he appears to have returned to life aboard Company vessels where his experience qualified him as a 2nd mate, first on the *Stormont* and then aboard the *Walpole,* under Captain Burnet Abercromby. Company records suggest that George's half-brother then spent the following two years on land before receiving notice of his first major command, the *Ganges,* to which Dempster's instructions had been sent. The principal managing owner of this three-decked 784-ton ship was William Moffat. It had been built by Wells and launched in 1778 and was one of three important Company vessels which Captain John was to command.[121] The voyage which was about to commence in 1782 was one of the longest undertaken and took three and a quarter years to complete: down to Rio de Janeiro, across to the Cape of Good Hope and into the India Ocean for Bombay and Madras, down to Sumatra and Java and on to Whampoa; the return took in a call to Simon's Bay in the Cape.

Such a Captaincy brought with it considerable opportunity for personal profit; Commanders could sell passenger places aboard their vessels for anything from £100 to £1,000, or even more. Orders for traded goods or personal luxuries, and the chance to pick up cargoes in addition to those being transported for the Company, provided scope for the Commander to add

£4–5,000 per voyage to his fortune. The Company's greatest monopoly was its shipping interest and all concerned had to take account of this fact. From the end of the seventeenth century the Company's directors had decided to hire ships rather than build them for themselves. They were hired for individual journeys and required to be vessels able to cope with the vast distances travelled and the volume of goods carried. Larger ships tended to be built as the years went by and the need for such specialized shipping led to the Directors taking on the same vessels for a number of voyages so that 'permanent bottoms' became more and more the order of the day. During the troubled sixties the Company had been over-burdened with unnecessary vessels due partly to a shipping enclave among owners. Sulivan and Sir George Colebrook, who were in alliance in the early 1770s, were accused of hiring eleven ships for goods which 'might have been conveniently carried by five' and in doing so won the friendship of eleven managers of such ships on behalf of their owners i.e. 'ship husbands'. By the time John Hamilton Dempster became a captain there were as many as 70 or 80 ships in the fleet, the number having risen greatly in the 1770s as the result of promises made to the shipping interest by those seeking support at Company elections. Commanders of 'permanent bottoms' had to be approved by the Company and were in effect its servants.[122] As Lucy Sutherland said, 'In time it became the general practice for a commander to get both a permanent bottom – or the right to have a ship in the Company's service – for himself and the other owners and also the permanent command of the ship for himself. This command became a marketable quantity to be bought and sold like a commission in the army.'[123]

7

IN THE LIONS' DEN
(1782 – 1784)

'One of the most conscientious men who ever sat in Parliament'
(Wraxall Memoirs, iv. p.339)

1782

The next two years were even more unstable than usual, both at the highest levels of government and at India House. Four ministries were to be headed by four different prime ministers. Lord North had virtually given up addressing the relationship between the Company and Government two years before. His resignation in 1782 was a belated end to the string of disastrous policies he had pursued for twelve years. Rockingham's administration followed and was able to present peace terms to the Americans who were tired of the war, but when he suddenly died in July 1782 the inter-factional rivalries of the Whigs resumed. The new chief minister, Shelburne, brought in the twenty-three-year-old Pitt as Chancellor, but within nine months this administration fell. Between May and December 1783 the Duke of Portland's oddly composed 'coalition' of Fox, with North and some of his old supporters, tried to hold the fort, but Fox's India Bill, which greatly occupied Parliament, and the subsequent un-constitutional conduct of the King, led directly to Pitt becoming Prime Minister in December.

For Dempster this was to be a time of increasing hard work both in the House and among his constituents, bringing him some unexpected but short-lived prominence. In February he was three times in Dundee and once in Montrose and Forfar on constituency business.[1] He expressed not 'the least remorse' about his truancy from parliament and was determined to put off his departure for London on account of a commitment he had given to his constituents, especially those in Perth, 'relative to . . . linen manufacture'.[2] Duties on linen were becoming a serious problem. There were always fears that continental and Irish producers would gain unfair advantage as the result of ill-considered government action. Describing Parliament as 'an engine to squeeze money from the people whose property they are appointed to protect',[3] he clearly had kept abreast of the debates on government finance pertaining to the war.

After the fall of Lord North and the return of the Whig administration, Dempster generally supported Rockingham, but he seems not to have been in the House till 24 April.[4] He probably reached London from Dunnichen that month just before Admiral Rodney's crushing defeat of the French fleet off St Lucia took place, thereby settling the ultimate course of the war.[5] There is no record of Dempster participating in the passage of Burke's Economic Reform Bill which reduced royal patronage and further curtailed the number of super-numerary court appointments. Nor does he appear to have spoken on the proposal to form a volunteer corps to protect Ireland from a French invasion or the Irish Home Rule Bill which finally became law in May, so making the Irish legislature independent of London.

A letter to Rockingham the day before the debate on the Bengal judicature resumed at Westminster (23 April) illustrated the member's almost daily role as a facilitator. Dempster enclosed a note from Lord Kinnoull asking when the eldest son of the Earl of Leven, Lord Balgonie, might wait upon his lord-ship. A similar appeal from an Edinburgh minister named Mr Kemp, 'a man of great abilities', was passed on later. The minister was concerned with 'some pretty serious (unspecified religious) grievances' which had come to light in Fife. Dempster apologized to Rockingham for being somewhat prolix in the matter, a hazard for any MP dealing with constituent's intricate concerns.[6] The next day Dempster spoke in defence of his friend Sir Elijah Impey, the Chief Justice in Calcutta, pleading that the King might agree to his recall from India so that he might speak for himself about charges of corruption laid against him.[7]

Having supported Pitt's motion earlier in the month aimed at reforming parliamentary representation in England, Dempster retained the hope that 'abuses in the part of the country to which he had the honour to belong' might also be addressed.[8] Thankfully, he found that a plan tabled in the Lords by Shelburne on 7 May had a Scottish dimension. It addressed members' long-standing concerns about civil order and gained his 'hearty assent', especially when he heard that the Marquis of Graham intended using the debate to raise the issue of a Scottish militia. In suggesting that people should be armed, Shelburne was responding to the Gordon Riots which had so 'disgraced the capital two years previously'. Seeing that an additional 1,500 men might be raised in England, the Marquis of Graham hoped that similar numbers might be forthcoming in Scotland.

At Percy Street the Dempsters heard on 3 June that Mrs Pulteney had died after what must have been a short illness, and that his old friend and Miss Pulteney had gone to the country.[9] In the Commons Dempster spoke on a Bill designed to reduce the amount of gambling. In two Westminster parishes alone there were 296 'odds and evens' tables and every country town had its share of 'an evil that required a speedy cure'.[10] Surprisingly, there is no evidence that he participated in the debate on the Highland Dress Bill, perhaps leaving it to Mr Fraser of Lovat to see that the wearing of the kilt was legalized. The law produced, he said, a double penalty: prevention of their domestic manufacture and a compulsion to wear more expensive and unfit garments.[11]

In July Rockingham's sudden death brought to an end what had been a 20-year political friendship which had started when Dempster first came into the House. He had received the post of Secretary to the Order of the Thistle from him and always acknowledged his leadership of the Whig party whenever his conscience would allow, regarding him as a wholly honourable man if a somewhat diffident leader. Dempster must have known that his further political preferment had long been ruled out, not so much because of his own uneven support of Rockingham over the years but on account of his independent disposition. The price attached to Dempster's determination to avoid being in the pocket of powerful manipulative friends had been high.

In the autumn Dempster went to Brussels with his brother-in-law Thomas Gordon for whom he always had a warm affection. Also in the party was another gentleman friend of the Gordons and a Mr Shaw from St Andrews. The four men had apparently been in Margate with their ladies. Dempster decided to leave them behind and set off for a fortnight's sentimental journey through the Low Countries which he and Sir Adam had so much enjoyed twenty-six years previously. He found Mr Weijder (which he now spelt as Weyder) dead and the Académie Royale which had provided such excellent camaraderie now in different premises but directed by the son of his old fencing master, Macdonald. The earlier buildings had been demolished and the site developed for housing. Wistfully, Dempster wrote that there were no signs of the Tosbaer family or their charming daughters. His *valet de place* was able to tell him that two of the three daughters had married and were living at Ghent. It was a visit which 'awakened a thousand strange reflections' and the erstwhile 'vigour of his youth and the full blow of his folly and ignorance'.[12] Not one to lose any opportunity of continuing his 'political researches', Dempster reported that taxation in the Low Countries was light, the land well cultivated, new building going on apace and development of the new port at Ostend had converted 'that dull hovel into the most commercial town . . . in Europe'.

It would seem that the Dempsters stayed in London on their return and avoided the worst of a quite exceptional winter across the country.[13] Unprecedented storms caused widespread damage and loss of life and were said to be worse than those that had swept away the Spanish armada two hundred years before. It was a particularly hard time for Scotland, with cattle starving and diseased, rent arrears rocketing and the poor near enough to the sea trying to stay alive on such fish, cockles or mussels as they could find.

Conditions that winter were still being talked about when the reports that made up the Old Statistical Account (OSA) came to be written almost ten years later.

1783

A committee of the House enquiring into the shortage of grain sat every day at the beginning of the year. 'I am never a minute absent from this Committee,' said Dempster, 'as I think it is the first duty of the legislature to provide food for the people'. Scottish MPs met at the British Coffee House on 10 February in response to 'the present alarming scarcity of grain' expressed by Provosts across Scotland and at the Convention of Royal Burghs.[14] The need for humanitarian aid was finally accepted in June when Dempster presented a petition to Parliament which prayed the King should 'give such relief as his wisdom should seem meet' and the administration permitted corn to be imported into Scotland – its cost being borne by payments from the land tax.[15]

Writing to Fintry about events in America, Dempster said, 'We are looking sharp for peace and it is not yet come . . . but I believe peace to be at hand',[16] but, unlike his friend Pulteney, he voted to ratify the moderate terms which Rockingham had originally produced before subsequent negotiations with America and her allies. Viewing them 'as a thing absolutely necessary for the country',[17] he misjudged the feeling of the House. When Fox put down a factious censure motion it had the effect of uniting Tories as well as discontented Whigs and Shelburne was defeated. The debate, which had started at 4 pm on 17 February, only concluded the next day at 7.30 am, the single longest parliamentary debate of the century.

Pitt's proposals for electoral reform put pressure on the democratic credentials of the Fox-North coalition which followed Shelburne's defeat. They were debated in May 1783. This time they did not gain Dempster's support. He found he could not 'as a representative of a borough . . . give a vote that would lessen the influence of his constituents'. Addressing a packed House of Commons, he said he 'did not know the sentiments of his constituents on the subject'; moreover, he had voted the previous year for a committee to examine the issues and he remained similarly minded.[18] The proposals before the House had derived from the Constitutional Society and included one that would have shortened the duration of parliaments but, in general, there was objection to piecemeal reform. The abolition of burgage tenures and the disenfranchisement of rotten boroughs were not included. Pitt was defeated on this and another bill in the House of Lords on 17 June dealing with the need for economy in government, but, as Fox said, 'If Pitt could be persuaded (to take office) . . . he would do more real service to the country than any man ever did'.

Dempster returned to a new London address conscious of the 'coolness and courage of a high order' shown by the Tory member for Appleby, even if he distrusted Pitt's youthful ambition.[19] He probably realized that he had witnessed the next Prime Minister in action. News about the Dempsters' circumstances came in correspondence with Pulteney. Not only did Dempster now propose to ride out to stay for a week in the good country air with him, his first recorded equestrian sally, but they were now living at 2, Lower Brompton Road (temporarily as it seems) where the stables were in the charge of his 'very honest coachman'. In all probability Dempster had used his own carriage since his marriage, although the imposition of a tax on post-horses that year had made long journeys by this form of transport more expensive.[20] His riding in London may have been for health reasons, the 'blister and physic (had) worked like a charm' so that he was now 'tolerably free of the pain in (his) chest and the cough and hoarseness'. Pulteney was for ever sending gifts to the Dempster household – venison and hare – but on this occasion a horse, saddle and bridle had been generously despatched from Bath House.[21] In December 1783 he was thanking him for 'the long list of game and a haunch of venison which (his) servants brought' in the absence of their master and which 'proved excellent'.[22]

With the American war over and the Treaty of Versailles signed, a chapter closed, making it a good time to break away from duties at the Commons. That autumn the Dempsters stayed in Scarborough at The Cliff where he, at least, enjoyed 'a kind of Elysian life'. The visit was to be recalled with pleasure several times in later life. A small town of 6,000 people, Scarborough was an in-shore fishing port that catered for a few affluent visitors who came to take the waters of a spa inconveniently situated down a long cliff path. Riding along the sandy beach in the morning, whether on their horses or in carriages, parties sallied 'forth with their gay and lively trains, in pursuit of health or amuse- ment . . . returning impatient only for their hair-dresser, and dinner!' Others bathed from the 26 commodious machines, at 1s. per time. Shopping was 'a very usual amusement among the ladies', followed by attendance at the theatre, where the actors performed their 'respective parts with taste', or balls at the Assembly Rooms where 'all gentlemen who dance(d) pay 2s. for music'.[23] The day was generally finished off with a rubber (of whist) in the company of the MP for Kent, Charles Marsham and his wife. Other fashion- able company included the Duke and Duchess of Rutland, Lord and Lady Chesterfield, Lord and Lady Stourton, Lord and Lady Digby, Lord Rochford and the Yorkshire MP, Henry Duncombe. Scarborough had become the watering place for the Scots as well as the English, with considerable numbers of 'hail and farewells' being made weekly as the guests of The Cliff (a 'great inn') came and went.[24] He would have bridled at the fact that there had not been a contested election in Yorkshire since 1760 and that the zeal of local politicians was 'cold to mere public questions', the county gentry being pre- occupied with manipulating the 44 voters' support for the administration.[25]

In such company Dempster soon fell to mulling over how much the exercise of power and influence in society put the individual's service to the community at risk. The matter had been sparked off by Sir Adam asking him to arrange yet another cadetship for a friend. Dempster told him how difficult it had become to achieve such placements; even Ministers, let alone the Chairman or deputy Chairman of the Company, could do little.[26] Six years later he had to admit finally that he had 'hardly any East Indian connection left' and even a berth for a surgeon's mate 'was beyond his reach'.[27] Always irritated by the way the most trifling favour often 'stamp(ed) a great value on it', and created a bias in the mind of someone who ought to be cool and indifferent in their political assessment, Dempster was soon having to apologize to his friend for what was in danger of becoming a 'Treatise on Political Morality'.[28] Nevertheless, the warmth of the company in which the Dempsters found themselves, and the congeniality of nobility 'at ease', appear to have won him over.

The exact date of Dempster's first meeting with Richard Arkwright is uncertain, but the probability is that the two men met a week or so before the family arrived in Scarborough.[29] Dempster was in error when he later recalled the event, but it had not happened by accident.[30] 'To amuse my wife and myself, and to rest my horses I generally halted a few days at the differing watering places by the way; and in that year . . . and being particularly captivated with the romantic scenery of Matlock, we staid (sic) a week or ten days there. In the course of a forenoon's ride, I discovered, in a romantic valley, a palace of a most enormous size, having, at least, a score of windows of a row, and five or six stories in height'. This was one of Arkwright's cotton mills. Dempster's curiosity was sufficiently aroused for him to ride up to Arkwright's house 'to see the head from whence the mill had sprung' and they had a brief but, as it turned out, absorbing conversation about the business there.

When the crucial debate on Fox's India Bill got under way in November dealing, as Dempster said, 'with one of the greatest and most important questions that ever came before the House'[31] the Attorney General said 'he was only gently laying his hands on (the Company's) charter for their cure'.[32] What Fox proposed was to give the Government the responsibility for the territories, confine the Company solely to its commercial activity and have the appointment of all English officials in India, from governors and service personnel down to clerks, made by a council of seven Commissioners in London. Three different grounds were laid, on three different days, for this enormous design. One was Hastings' conduct, another 'the supposed bankruptcy of the Company' and the third the radical defects in the present system of administration. As Members were aware, there were dangers in giving the administration what were for the most part negative powers such as the recall of servants they had appointed. The only exception was the provision of a £300,000 patronage fund which unscrupulous administrations were bound to misuse. For Dempster the issue did not turn on whether the Company (or the Government) could be trusted to avoid the inconsistencies of the past, but on the violation of its charter. On this occasion he changed his mind. Speaking on the second reading of Fox's India Bill (27 November 1783), he showed he was prepared to make an exception about the 'inviolable' chartered rights for which he had spoken up so forcefully in 1765. He now accepted that the Company's only role was as a commercial trading body. As Debrett recorded, 'He conjured ministers to abandon all idea of sovereignty in that quarter of the globe. It would be much wiser . . . to make some one of the native princes King . . . and to leave India to itself'. His plea was that the charter of the Company 'ought to be destroyed for the sake of (the) country . . . of India . . . and of humanity'. Dempster apparently thought the Bill would not be supported in the House and, after counselling the House against running down the Court of Proprietors, he left before the division.[33]

Sir Henry Fletcher had felt so strongly on this subject that the previous day he had resigned 'the high position he held in another place, that his mind might be free and open to judge . . . a question of such great importance'.[34] Supporting Dempster's statement that 'it would have been better . . . if the navigation to the East Indies had never been discovered', what now needed to be done was not to 'evacuate' from India since this would leave the way open for the French. Henry Dundas, now in opposition and against the proposals, believed his speech on this occasion was the best he ever made, and there were many of a high calibre during the lengthy and memorable proceedings. He argued that the Bill created 'a new, inordinate, and unexampled influence . . . when placed in the hands of the minister'.[35] The debate influenced the administration in a number of ways and not only did the Bill pass through the House of Commons but, probably to his surprise and pleasure, Dempster's name had been included as one of the seven Parliamentary Commissioners.[36] Unfortunately, the prospect of governmental responsibility in an area of long personal interest was to be short-lived.

He would have overseen the Company's affairs on behalf of the Government had the Lords voted freely and not succumbed in December to the blackmail of the King who feared the Whigs might rule India. The monarch's blatantly unconstitutional behaviour – sending to Parliament a hand-written note which Lord Temple was asked to show any waverers against the Bill on pain of 'being considered the King's enemy' – must have infuriated Dempster beyond measure. With time to consider these momentous events, he was to say that 'perhaps the constitution (had) less to fear from its representatives . . . than the smiles of (the) monarch. I amuse myself sometimes in contrasting our present situation with that which might have been, had the Court known the value of Charles Fox and Lord North (both of whom the King had peremptorily dismissed) with Mr Pitt assumed to their party, and a young and amiable heir apparent (the Prince of Wales) throwing his weight . . . into the same scale. What law could we have opposed? . . . What charter preserved . . . What economy introduced?'[37]

Dempster was in London when the coalition fell on 18 December and Pitt was appointed Prime Minister. Earlier in the month he had told Pulteney, whom he had tried unsuccessfully to meet after his absence from London, that he had been occupied for a couple of mornings with the affairs of the Smuggling Committee that was meeting under the chairmanship of William Eden.[38] Adam Smith had been invited to table some ideas on ways of preventing smuggling and Dempster enjoined his support for the work of the committee in a letter which he had received from 'a good man and deserving (Customs) officer'. Although anticipating the dissolution of the House and 'the existence of . . . all its committees', he was concerned about the 'alarming' evidence that had been collected 'threatening the destruction of the Revenue (Service), the fair trader, the health and morals of the People'.[39] Shortly afterwards he left for Scotland, reaching Dunnichen on 23 December and spending Christmas and the first weeks of the New Year amid 'frost and falling snow'.[40]

1784

On his return to London, where the weather was milder, Dempster found himself entangled in the affairs of an erstwhile member of Boswell's coterie of the 1760s and who until 1774 had represented Edinburghshire in parliament, being a Whig and a steady supporter of Rockingham. When Sir Alexander Gilmour, third baronet of Craigmillar, emerged as a rival to Boswell in 1768 for the hand in marriage of Miss Catherine Blair, an heiress and ward of Lord Auchinleck, he was described as a young man about thirty who had £1600 a year of estate, formerly an officer in the Guards, and one of the Clerks of the Board of Green Cloth.[41] Boswell had been forced to accept that all was over between himself and Miss Blair, but she was also to refuse Sir Alexander's proposals, prompting Boswell to quote Dempster's saying that 'all Miss Blair's connections were in an absolute confederacy to lay hold of every man who has a £1,000 a year'.[42] How much Dempster had seen of Gilmour in the years following his departure from parliament is not clear. His reputation as a professional debtor seems not to have diminished. Partial payment of the wages of his estate servants was one method in 1775 of temporarily coping with their 'clamour'. Also that year, Thomas Dundas of Carron Hall reminded Sir Alex how understandable it was that his offer of one year's payment of interest on a loan made by Lord Hopetoun some twenty-four years previously had been refused.[43] Now, however, the baronet was in prison and about to be driven abroad by his creditors.

Writing to Henry Dundas from Percy Street on the evening of 16 March 1784, Dempster reported that 'everything is now arranged for Sir AG's release'.[44] He was minded to attend the release in person to ensure that

Gilmour got to Dover and 'be sailed before Sunday expires'. As elsewhere, and on other occasions, Dempster's role had been not simply to make travel arrangements but, in the preceding weeks, to request, cajole and collect, quite large sums of cash to be paid to the Deputy Marshall so as to procure Sir Alexander Gilmour's freedom. Lords North, Eglinton and Cornwallis each contributed £150, with the last having promised only a month previously 'not easily' to engage again in paying others' debts.[45] For his part, Dundas put up £200 in his own name and another £250 on behalf of Dempster, it being 'the best part of the week' before Dempster could have collected such a sum himself.[46] What had brought Gilmour's troubles to a head remains a mystery but this rescue was the last anyone attempted. Several months later, Dempster 'was sorry to say (that) the very generous exertion of his friends to extricate him from difficulties in this island have only served to involve him in new ones on the continent'. By then he was convinced that Sir Alexander had all the noble virtues, but they were worthless 'unless accompanied by that dirty one economy'.[47] He died in France at Boulogne-sur-Mer two days after Christmas 1792.

At Westminster Dempster was listed by one of the whips as an opponent of Pitt and towards the end of January he had protested about the First Minister's proposed dissolution of Parliament which eventually took place at the end of March. Regarding Pitt as generally over-ambitious at a time when so much needed to be done to put straight the nation's affairs, Dempster supported Fox in his attempts to undermine him. Moreover, when Fox saw an opportunity to re-introduce his earlier India Bill, and modify it 'in respect of patronage and . . . make it generally palatable', Dempster hoped that 'a government of national unity' might be formed at the same time. This had been one of the aims of the St Albans Tavern Group which Dempster joined that month; it favoured a union of parties and preached moderation in order that something 'decisive' might be done for India'.[48] However, Fox's narrow success in the House only heralded the General Election and a dissolution which came upon Dempster 'like a thief in the night'.[49]

He learned of the election result before he knew how well he had done himself in Scotland and was greatly depressed to see how great a victory Pitt had achieved. What Dempster called the 'immense vortex', made up of the monarch and his ministers, had swallowed up the opposition. Even allowing for how much the Coalition had been disliked throughout the country, the 160 Whig losses ('Fox's Martyrs') were catastrophic; virtually every county and borough not in the pocket of a landowner had fallen. It was not surprising that he was in a melancholic mood of resignation, leaving his fate to his constituents: – 'I play upon velvet. If I am chosen – well. If thrown out – better still. More health, than in London, more amusements and better suited to my taste than in the factious brawlings of St Stephen's Chapel. More command of my time and place – better proportion between my fortune and my station'.[50] But by early April he had not only been returned unopposed in each of his five burghs but it had not even been necessary for him to show himself in Scotland. Knowing how fickle voters could be, Dempster had apparently sought the approval of the constituency for his personal attendance to be dispensed with during the campaign. Writing to each in turn, he had pleaded 'reasons of health', not mentioning whether it was he or his wife who suffered. In the event, not all the replies were received before the date of the election and Fintry was left to use his 'good offices' and ensure that all went well.[51]

Greatly relieved and duly honoured by his constituents, Dempster could only ready himself to continue doing 'more good to (them) . . . than to (himself)' and hold in check those instincts which pointed in the direction of retirement and a quieter life. He had dreamed of going to Italy which he had never seen, and enjoying 'the genial heat of a warm climate', but such thoughts were obviously more to re-equip his spirit than anything else. An element of anticipation about the new parliament existed and there were, he mused, 'a few years of life perhaps left to complete (his) business as a spectator of this earth'.[52] However, he was still in a sombre mood and clearly disappointed that the plans made by his moderate colleagues at the St Albans tavern had been so frustrated. He 'thought (himself) better calculated for a member of the Royal Society held at Somerset House than that of the *Royal Society* at Westminster – for such must our House of Commons become if kings shall take it in(to) their heads to dissolve (Parliament) when they cannot persuade us.'[53]

With London basking in warm May sunshine that was to continue for a couple of months, he hoped that things were on the mend, although a challenge by Sir Cecil Wray to the election results in the Westminster constituency, where the other two candidates had been Lord Hood and Fox, put the latter's position in doubt for a long period. It was not until February 1785, when the returning officer's report was published, that Fox knew that he had lost, albeit that in the meantime he had been returned for Kirkwall in the Orkneys. Amid the wrangling which characterized the House at this time, with some 170 new Members trying to find their feet, Dempster felt 'like Daniel in the lions' den'.[54] The prospect of a new and improved India Bill, and the fact that attention was being paid to reducing the National Debt which had spiralled during the war[55], went some way to cheer him up and the next month he had the satisfaction of seeing the House's East India Committee revived.

Although conciliatory to Pitt on matters of trade and finance, Dempster maintained a critical stance over India and continued to plead for the Court of Directors to maintain their power, since 'it was impracticable to govern India from England'. He was convinced that it would be better to have Indian affairs 'egregiously mismanaged' by the Company than 'well-managed by the Crown'. The debates on the Government of India Bill thrust Dempster into the limelight and had the effect of softening many of his earlier ideas on India.[56] Pitt had welcomed the general approval given in the House but his hope that its 'minute and component parts' would not be the subject of opposition was forlorn. Dempster said he would state his objections without arguing them. To the first, which gave the crown rights of appointment over the Company, Pitt was heard to say across the House in a low voice, 'I will give that up'. A similar concession seemed likely when Dempster raised the appointment of three commanders-in-chief and Pitt again whispered, 'I will give that up also', but when it came to the Court of Proprietors being deprived of their franchises Pitt's response was 'no'. Objecting to the proposed selection of judges from 'out of the House of Commons', Dempster insisted that they already had enough legislative, superintending and controlling power without acting in a judicial capacity for which they were not equipped. He accepted that the alternative of restoring India 'to the natives' was unacceptable, admitting that 'probably they would not govern them (the territories) better than we did', going on to propose 'that his Majesty should be requested to send over one of his sons and make him king of that country; we might then make an alliance or federal union with him and then we could enjoy all the advantage that could be derived from the possession of the East Indies by Europeans, the benefit of commerce.'[57]

A total of 271 Members voted against Dempster's unlikely, if imaginative, motion. Dempster gained the usual 60 or so votes that he had come to accept as the limit of his support, and by the summer of 1784 Pitt's India Bill had become law. The demise of the East India Company as Dempster found it in 1763 was complete. State intervention had eroded much of its purpose, most of its powers and no small amount of its prestige.

The young Pitt had risen quickly from a junior post with Rockingham at the age of 22 to Chancellor of the Exchequer and leader of the House under Shelburne and now, at the age of 24, he set out to stabilize the economy and tackle important issues that had been the subject of half-hearted action by previous administrations. He took inspiration from a variety of works, including Adam Smith's *Wealth of Nations*, which had been published in 1776. Dempster's friend Pulteney now attracted the attention of the House when more mundane but nonetheless important governmental issues came up for discussion. In August he supported a Bill dealing with the tax on letters sent through the post. Postage had long been viewed as simply a source of revenue with the cost rising each year; little consideration being given to it as a public service.[58]The franking of letters by businesses had been a way of saving costs and Pulteney was at pains to warn the administration that 'they would be deceived with regard to the degree of revenue likely to arise from the abolition of franking'. Perhaps an additional £40,000 might find its way into the exchequer and franking 'often produced gain to the post office revenue by calling forth answers to letters (that) would never have been written'.[59]

The April election necessitated the House meeting in August. Dempster was fighting to defend his constituents on the issue of a reverse tax provision affecting the price of tea and the cost of having windows in their houses. The Commutation Bill provided for the repeal of duties on tea and additional duties on houses, windows and lights, upon which subjects 'his constituents had not been silent'. The Window Tax had long been a contentious issue for the General Assembly of the Church of Scotland. In the 1760s it had despatched Alexander Carlyle (the founder of the Poker Club) to Westminster as their commissioner against the tax's application to churches. Dempster maintained that his constituents wanted a fairer system. It was no wonder that the City praised the new provisions since they took off a heavy tax on London and 'distributed it to the furthermost parts of the Kingdom'. In London, where most of the high-priced tea was drunk, it was easy to obtain from the East India Company. Producing a report which calculated what a street in Scotland consisting of sixty houses and a comparable one in Lombard Street would pay, Dempster made his point.[60] With an income in Scotland of £50 and rents of £10 per house, each with twenty windows, they would pay £2 15 per house or one seventeenth part of their income, whereas in Lombard Street with a similar number of windows, bankers and those with incomes of £2,000 a year and rents of £100 would pay less than one seven-hundredth of their income. His remedy was a 10% land tax in lieu of the intended tax on windows. Moreover, on the question of tea, he pointed to the necessity of allowing country, as well as town dealers to return their unsold stocks of tea, observing that the latter were nearer the warehouses and could take out their teas by the single chest whereas country dealers were obliged to keep much larger stocks, a familiar agenda item of rural Scottish representatives in all ages.

Dempster continued to stave off attacks on Warren Hastings, 'to whom alone he imputed the salvation of India', but that summer Pitt's India Act finally produced joint Crown and Company control of India. As had been anticipated, it contained much that had been in Fox's Bill. The Governor-General and the Board of Control in London became government nominees and the Company kept its trade monopoly.

Some of the ideas that were to be implemented on Dempster's own estates had their first airing in Parliament around this time. Rural as well as industrial development, planned villages, landlord and tenant relations, more meaningful property leases as well as rents for life and changes in the judicial system were among the subjects being examined by the new administration. The fact that Scotland, and the Highlands in particular, became the focus of attention by an English government, to say nothing of it being the target for developmental funding and bounties, was due to an exceptional set of circumstances.

Post-Union economic expansion in Scotland had been slow to reach the Highlands. Now at least two influences began to work in its favour. Scotland's contribution to the national war effort in both the Seven Years War and the War of American Independence, where Highland regiments had borne the brunt of important battles and gained for themselves an almost mystical following, meant that parliaments in Westminster were able to take public opinion with them in not simply speeding up national reconciliation after the rebellion of the '45 but by giving the Highlands a modicum of assistance and attention. Growing emigration had also to be addressed. 'Ministers know that Highlanders can fight the battles of the state. They seem, however, not to know that a Highlander can be trained to useful labour in times of peace. Nootka Sound and Oczakow have cost Britain millions; Botany Bay costs, it is said, £200 for each colonist; and yet a great part of the united kingdom perishes for the lack of bread'.[61] The defeat in America was incidental to a second trend. Losing one set of colonies in the New World helped shape a view that there might be other places nearer to home where 'charity' might begin. The urge to colonize was never wholly lost and it was thought that experiments that had taken place in New England might be applicable to the Highlands where the largely unknown land mass was considered potentially viable for increased settlement. This might discourage emigration to the very places which had caused such a loss of national prestige.

One person had done much to set the agenda for at least part of the Highland economy. John Knox, a wealthy retired bookseller and author, had made no less than sixteen tours of the Highlands in eleven years, examining development prospects associated with the fisheries industry. Despite its long-winded title, Knox's 1784 report[62] was influential in raising the profile of the Highlands and Islands and built on earlier work done from 1720 by a partner-ship of the burgesses of royal burghs.[63] The grant-making Board of Manufactures had provided for inspectors on the ground at the ports and made rules about the curing and packing of fish. Next, along with the intro-duction of the bounty to encourage the building of busses,[64] came the government-sponsored 'Society of Free British Fishery' which failed as the result of gross mismanagement and financial impropriety on the part of its members. Its Charter was not renewed in 1771.

In Knox's wake came Dr James Anderson, a Glasgow University professor employed by the Treasury in London,[65] who, having visited the Scottish coast-line, saw what he believed to be the promised land. His brief had been to report on how governmental assistance might be provided to match the numerous successful fishing ventures developed by the English, the Irish, the Swedes and the Dutch. The Scottish fisheries were generally under-capitalized and less prosperous. The west coast was better served than the east, but fishing was too often limited to domestic consumption.

Writing to Dr Anderson from Loch Hourn on 3 August 1784, Mr Macdonell of Barrisdale, Justiciary Bailie of the Southern Fishing District, wished that Anderson and a few of the Commissioners of the different boards could be 'but for a night or two in this loch, they would see what otherwise they could hardly be brought to believe. Badly as the country nets are , if the fishing continues for some time, as it has all the appearance it will, if I had 2,000 barrels, salt in proportion, and a few experienced coopers, I could engage to fill them in twenty days, at 3s. per barrel, and 4d. additional for gutting and salting. Yesternight I went into the loch, and carrying with me some nets, some small and some larger in the meshes; and I have the pleasure to tell you, that although I had but four of our small country nets in the yawl, not exceeding the fifth part of a buss train, in less than twenty minutes I hauled 12 barrels of fish . . . I leave to you to judge what a large fleet of Bounty Fishers might have landed.'[66]

What James Anderson had seen for himself drove him to draw others to his vision. Writing to Sir Adam Fergusson, who had shown some interest in his journey, Anderson talked briefly about his diagnosis: 'The natives are placed in such circumstances as puts it out of their power to exercise a spirited agriculture, or to make their fields yield half the crops they are naturally capable of being made to produce. The fisheries are nearly in the same state. In consequence of absurd laws that tie up the hands of the natives, the fish they now catch are few in number in comparison with what they might be, and the cost perhaps double the price to those who have them to sell, that they might be afforded for, in other circumstances . . . . The laws which particularly oppress them are the salt laws: and if it is ever expected to make the fisheries flourish, these must undergo a radical change.'[67] 'The imbecilities of the salt laws' were described by Dr Anderson in his account[68] and demonstrated that any campaign for simple English was as relevant then as now. Treasury 'officialese' required 'all importers of foreign salt to first land it at a custom-house (of which there were few anyway), where it was carefully weighed by the proper officers, and the importer either to pay the duty, or to enter it for the purpose of curing fish; and in that case to give bond, with two sufficient securities, either to pay the excise duty of ten shillings per bushel, or to account for the salt, under a penalty of twenty shillings per bushel. In consequence of this bond, he must either produce the salt itself at that custom-house on or before the fifth of April thereafter, or cured fish in such quantities as are sufficient to exhaust the whole of that salt, which fish he is obliged to declare upon oath, were cured with the salt for which he had granted bond.'[69] 'The wretched fisherman was further galled by the knowledge that an unlimited export of rock-salt was permitted from Liverpool to Ireland, while not a grain of it was allowed to come to Scotland', except what could be smuggled in.[70]

In October Dempster went to Glasgow during a tour through Scotland to see how manufacturing industry was faring. The previous year he had received the freedom of that city, an honour which was now to be bestowed on his new business associate, Richard Arkwright, who was there on a similar errand. The two men had apparently met again in London 'soon after' their previous encounter and, since Arkwright had offered to 'assist . . . in establishing a cotton mill in Scotland', it was opportune that they should confer about this prospect.[71] Both were royally entertained by Glasgow's Lord Provost and magistrates at the Town Hall and the following day they dined with the Lord Provost at his country seat. On the way to Kelvingrove Dempster was feted by the workforce of several manufacturing plants at Anderston who evidently held him in high esteem: 'The populace wanted to unyoke the horses from Dempster's carriage, in order to draw him to Kelvingrove (themselves)'. He tactfully declined the offer saying that 'it had been his uniform wish and practice to lead his countrymen to freedom, rather than put them under the yoke'. Arkwright, however, was required to accept their offer and the cavalcade made off amid great acclamation. On the return journey to the Saracen's Head, where they were staying, five carriages with the Lord Provost in the first and Dempster the second passed triumphantly through the crowds of people following a processional lantern on a pole decorated with the words 'The Patriot of his Country' and 'The Guardians of our Manufactures'.[72]

Having reached Angus after this excursion he had to admit he 'would give a hundred guineas for leave to remain all winter at Dunnichen'.[73] A host of other calls on his time were, however, pressing, not least those of the fishing industry (as will be seen in the next Chapter). He had thoroughly digested James Anderson's lucid report and had become a ready convert to his proselytising, urging Henry Dundas to seek help for the fisheries and to listen to what Dr Anderson had discovered about them. He himself reported that 3000 people had emigrated the previous year and that a further 150 families from Lochaber had sold up but been unable to obtain passages.[74] These were trends that needed to be reversed. At his Dunnichen fireside on Boxing Day 1784 he wrote to Sir Adam that he had 'formed a few clear ideas' about the fisheries: 'The seas abound with fish, the Highlands with industrious and good people'. Nevertheless, that winter's day Dempster had more reservations than usual about the magnitude of the task. The doubts in his mind were to be prophetic: 'I fear it would in that country be an easier task for mountains to meet, at least they are at present much nearer one another'. Then, as if allowing himself a little hope, if not expectation, he added, 'Should however the proper encouragement be given to the fisheries, it would produce still more important consequences to the nation'.

He knew from public and private meetings of farming associations up and down the mainland that there was scope for economic development on and off the western coast. In Lewis, at least, it was well overdue. Always the 'rational projector', Dempster's later report concluded that 'It is no easy matter to suggest any solid means of improving such an island as . . . Lewis yet it is ridiculous to assert that an island of such extent, bearing corn, grass, potatoes, placed in the centre of the best herring and white fishing, contains 12,000 inhabitants, and abounding in excellent lakes, creeks, harbours, cannot be made to produce more than £2,500 a year to its sole proprietor. . . . If I have not grossly misconceived the state of the Highlands, its whole valuable inhabitants are meditating a flight across the Atlantic. If an asylum nearer home were opened to them many would prefer it to a distant voyage and a hostile country. They know the Scotch are not welcome to America. It is probable the bulk of them would carry their little all to their own Hebrides could they find there a permanent settlement and juries of their friends and neighbours to decide on their lives and properties.'[75]

Such matters would come before parliament in the new year but not before other events intervened. Back in London on 23 January, Dempster was soon telling his friend Fintry that 'what with visits to pay and receive, House of Commons, City, Jack's affairs and my own, I have been in a continual hurry'.[76]

8

HIGH HOPES
(1785)

'While we are spinning cotton we may play on velvet'
(Dempster to Graham of Fintry 26 May 1785)

Captain John's first command, the *Ganges*, left the Cape of Good Hope in September 1784 on its way home from China and was off Cape Clear in Ireland by January 1785. After almost a week of strong gales, 'dirty weather and a large sea', the decision was taken to put into Cork rather than sail direct to the Downs and home. The log shows water to have been in short supply and all the lascars and Chinese aboard were suffering from scurvy and confined to sick quarters. Repairs to the ship were becoming essential and clearly going to take time. Rotted pumps were sent ashore as patterns for replacements; sails and spars needed urgent attention.

All seems to have been under control until the morning of 8 February when a Mr Dixon, Surveyor of the Revenue, and Lieutenant Lynn, commander of the pilot cutter, appeared unannounced aboard the *Ganges* and seized the ship in His Majesty's name, the cutter being placed nearby as a guard ship. This action was followed on 1 March by the seizure of the *Ganges'* cargo.[1] The longed-for happy reunion with wives and sweethearts at Deptford after a three-and-a-half-year voyage had to wait even longer, and, if smuggling could be proved, financial penalties would result. The evasion of customs duties was almost *de rigueur* for officers and crews of East Indiamen. As Dempster was to say to Fintry, such small trade had 'been done with impunity by every East India ship before and since'.[2] The *Hibernian Chronicle* reported that there were three types of tea aboard the vessel – 730,000lb of bohea, 58,000lb of congoe and 59,000lb of singlo – along with 4 full and 166 half-chests of chinaware, also, 6,800lb of raw silk. In this case, however, it appears that the seizures had resulted from Captain John's ignorance of a piece of Irish legislation which had been enacted while he had been at sea. They had been caught out by the wretched revenue and the Captain was far from being alone in his fury. Mr Savage French, a member of a well-known Cork family, shared his annoyance.

Returning from a visit to the *Ganges*, he claimed that three Revenue Officers from Cove assaulted him and trespassed on board his barge. A month later at the Assizes one was found guilty and imprisoned, and the other two were 'brought in not guilty, through the lenity of the prosecutors'.[3]

The Captain may have anticipated serious trouble since he reported what had been going on to Dempster before the actual seizures, prompting his half-brother to act on his behalf, busy as he was with other matters. On 5 February the *Daily Universal Register* reported representations which Dempster had made at Westminster against duties on printed linen on behalf of the Glasgow weavers. Then, two days before leaving for Ireland, Dempster was rather ironically contesting Pitt's Bill to regulate commercial relations between Britain and Ireland. Accompanied by Thomas Gordon, his brother-in-law, the two men set off for Ireland from London on 25 February. In Dublin they found that the ship had been released and its officers fined £2,000. Dempster concluded that there was 'no prospect of getting the fine remitted' and had to be satisfied that 'things were no worse, for by a damned Irish Law of last year (the) ship's cargo and everything on board might have been confiscated for the fault of smuggling 10lbs of tea out of a China ship by any common mariner in her'.[4] However, resolution of the affair was to be protracted and contrary to Dempster's expectation. In May it was reported that 'the whole Teas of the Ganges are burnt', presumably by the Excise.[5] Only later that year did Dempster give Sir Adam Fergusson a hint about what had been going on when, he was able to say that 'we have accomplished one point, the payment of the freight of the *Ganges* which some violent people thought forfeited by the Irish seizures'.[6]

Dempster, who was an admirer of Irish gentry, had been delighted to have an opportunity to visit Dublin – 'a noble city' with 'fields around it more verdant than those around London'.[7] The two men managed to hear debates in both Houses of the Irish Parliament, attend a play and a farce, and 'passed an hour' with Mr Henry Grattan (1746–1820), the Irish statesman who three years previously had gained independence for the Irish legislature and who also sat at Westminster. 'You never saw so wizzand (sic) a little body . . . a man who has done the greatest good to his country that was ever done without bloodshed.'[8] Dempster and Gordon's return journey from Ireland took in a visit to Anglesey in North Wales where, staying at an inn on 7 March, they reviewed what had been achieved. All in all, they had packed 'many transactions ' into a short space of time and 'been but thrice shaved and shifted since (they) had left Percy Street', a reference to what must have been for Dempster a hectic, and uncomfortable seaborne adventure in winter.[9]

Underlying Pitt's proposals to remove all trade restrictions between England and Ireland – matters which were to occupy parliament for the whole of the summer – was a concern that the actions of the American colonists might have shown Irishmen a similar way forward. In April Dempster pleaded for 'reasonable concessions being timely made',[10] reflecting something of a *real politik* that had not occurred during the previous decade. Low Irish labour costs which were said to give their trade an unfair advantage, became the issue – the very point, Dempster reminded the House, that had been made about Scotland at the time of the Union, 'yet Scotland had not grown richer, nor England poorer'. He supported free trade between the two countries which Pitt had proposed, citing the free import of beef and butter which originally had been for a trial period and now was made permanent with no ill-effects. A similar outcome for English manufacturers would mean that they could export without restriction and it would be 'a system which promised to reconcile the affections of our sister kingdom'.[11]

Dempster must have been a little uneasy about supporting unrestricted trade with Ireland, knowing as he did that Scottish linen producers and fishermen were unlikely to share his fraternal regard for the Irish. There was also the threat that the West Indian trade, so important to Glasgow and London, might be diverted to Ireland. When the debate resumed in May, after what Dundas described as 'the clamour of . . . manufacturers (expressing) their fears and exaggerations while they were at the bar (of the House)',[12] he was still undismayed and an admirer of the proposed treaty, considering it 'one of the wisest and most prudent measures'.[13] Dempster had not been swayed by North's and Sheridan's speeches, nor Fox's claim that the proposals were 'by no means reciprocal . . . just the reverse'. Instead, he stressed the necessity of taking care of the lawns and linen gauze trade of Scotland, including protective duties in Ireland. Furthermore, with his recent experiences in Ireland very much in mind, Dempster suggested a law that would allow the British and Irish reciprocal rights to fish on each other's coasts. He knew only too well the friction that existed between 'Irish sailors spoiling the nets and otherwise ill-treating . . . English fishermen, and the latter retorting in their turn'.[14] Dempster apparently anticipated the eventual refusal of Pitt's terms by a faction-ridden Irish parliament and its failure to recognize the honest attempt that had been made to redress trade injustices. He told Sir Adam in July that he thought they would have 'a horrid pelting . . . in Ireland, and by August, it was 'Adieu . . . (to) Irish propositions' and a month later, 'I am as indifferent about (the Irish) . . . as you can be'.[15]

On 14 March, soon after he returned from Anglesey, Dempster would have been especially pleased to be able to second a motion that 'a Committee be appointed to inquire into the state of British Fisheries', which was agreed. Dundas successfully asked the House to accede to his motion: 'certain regulations were necessary, and without which, that national source of British wealth . . . might run totally to decay.'[16] Dempster had decided that fish and the Highlanders must be brought together and, although he feared that it might be an 'easier task for mountains to meet', it was 'the business of the legislature to bring these two' together.[17]

Within days a House of Commons Fisheries Committee was at work producing a series of comprehensive and far-reaching reports. Dempster was probably a member of the Committee; he certainly played an important role in its deliberations. Its chairman, Henry Beaufoy, MP for the premier English fishing port of Yarmouth, became a visitor to the West Coast, travelling 'in that country fifty miles a day . . . and not (seeing) a single face, or traced the print of a human footstep'. Witnesses called before the committee from across the country included Anderson and Knox as well as fish curers, merchants, fishermen and customs officials. On 4 July 1785 Beaufoy spoke at length of the difficulties facing the fisheries and introduced a Bill designed to tackle the array of restraints and outdated laws. He made a particular point of responding to the onerous rendezvous restrictions, pleading that fishermen should have the liberty 'when they found it convenient, between the first day of June and the first day of September, to allow them to begin fishing before they reached a distant . . . rendezvous; also, that when they had been at sea three months . . . (they) could purchase fish to complete their freight . . . (and) use salt for the purpose of salting their fish, duty-free'.[18]

With only thirty or forty members present, mainly from fishing constituencies, one member urged delay to enable others to participate. This only invoked Dempster's gentle scorn: 'There could be no reason for postponing the business to another session if gentlemen did not attend their duty . . . it was of such a nature that if it could be done . . . (by) . . . two members, it ought to be so, rather than . . . (be) . . . left undone'.[19] Pulteney's defence of the Bill, which Jean Dunlop described as rather 'half-hearted', probably reflected his confidence that it would be passed.[20] It was 'harmless . . . and likely to prove extremely beneficial'. The speed with which the Committee's recommendations had been translated into a Bill had been quite remarkable. Pitt's administration saw the proposal and the growing pressure as a revenue loser, but, after some hesitation (and by excluding the recommended increase in bounty payments), he gave way to the general tenor of the House which favoured action. In the event, the Bill took only 12 days to pass from its first reading to approval by the House of Lords, whereupon the Fishery Act of July 1785 became law.

The Parliamentary Committee had also recommended the establishment of a joint stock company to implement the industry's development on land as well as at sea. The British Fisheries Society was to have powers to buy land for lease to fishermen and curers so that not only houses and sheds could be built but completely new fishing villages in the Highlands, Islands and West Coast. The task of this state-supported development agency, for that is what was envisaged, 'required the joint labour of many individuals aided by the skill of several classes of manufacturers'.[21] Never far away was another train of thought in the minds of those anxious to promote more coherent development. 'An alternative to emigration must be provided,' insisted Dempster.

'Every hint for improving the Highlands by finding employment for the inhabitants, is precious at all times, but more particularly so at the present alarming crisis of *emigration*'.[22] The Society's activities were viewed as one way of discouraging the loss of local populations.

By the middle of March Dempster was not only attending the debates in the House but engrossed 'five precious hours of every forenoon' as a member of the committee considering irregularities that had occurred in the Bedford constituency during the general election.[23] The next month he became embroiled in a government measure for which he had high expectations. Albeit that Pitt did not expect to implement his proposals for a sinking fund to pay off the national debt until 1786, Dempster was anxious to see the country follow the lead given by France, where Jacques Necker, the Swiss-French statesman and financier, had remedied many of the problems faced by their exchequer.[24] Included in his reading had been a treatise by William Playfair on the role interest had in balancing the nation's accounts. When relaxing at Scarborough Dempster had found the eldest son of the second Lord Romney, Charles Marsham, 'equally impressed with the necessity of a vigorous measure' for discharging the public debt.[25] He now concluded, using John Playfair's 'tables of trade', that 'the money to be raised (in taxes) would be no more than £50,000 to pay the interest; and one million a year dedicated to the sole service of paying off the national debt, would, in 54 years, pay off near 200 millions'.[26]

In May and June Dempster was 'battling . . . to save the poor peddlers from extermination'.[27] A £4 a year duty, over and above any existing duties, on 'all hawkers and peddlers not travelling with a horse, ass or mule' had been introduced, double that amount if they were mounted and a further £8 for each subsequent horse. Trade within towns and burghs was already largely regulated by corporations or charters and Dempster, mindful of the dependence many Scottish constituencies had on such traders, saw in this substantial tax 'a fatal stab' given to 'a useful body of men'.[28] He reminded the House that 'in the north, many persons (were) so situated that the shop must come to them, as it was utterly impossible for them to go to the shop', but, despite the opposition from the rural lobby in England and Scotland, Pitt carried the day. Other proposals in the budget debates which Dempster found equally futile and irritating included a tax on maid-servants which he felt might with equal justification 'be laid on all persons wearing watches',[29] along with another on horses which gave him the opportunity to recall his having given up using the post-chaise. The threat to farmers' livelihoods was obvious, given charges equal to the rent they paid and if they 'had but one horse, which did everything' about the farm, and only rode out on to the highway 'once in twelve months', they were still obliged to pay.[30] In committee several motions affecting Scotland induced Sir Adam to join Dempster, not least one in June that sought to remit the duty on Scottish coal. In a land where many parts were barren and 'in many parts . . . the plough was absolutely a novelty', as

Beaufoy had said, and coal might be better employed than peat or turf, there was a case for at least reducing the tax. There is no record, however, of Kilkerran supporting another plea, that the duties applicable to 'fermented wash' be remitted.[31]

A chance encounter at India House the following month amply demonstrated Dempster's ready eye for innovation and the delight he always took in broking commercial deals that might benefit Scottish industry and agriculture. At Leadenhall Street, where he had probably come to talk over Dr Anderson's recommendations to the Commons Committee on Fisheries and the possibility of a new hydrographical survey of the west coast of Scotland, he ran into Alexander Dalrymple. He was the East India Company's hydrographer of six years standing and the brother of Lord Hailes.[32] Initially the conversation may have touched on the consequences of the great storms of 1782 and the almost daily loss of shipping off dangerous headlands and on uncharted rocks. These did much to focus attention on the urgent need for warning beacons and lighthouses. As they stood talking in the hall of this cockpit of Indian trade, opposite the two lofty Court Rooms, Dalrymple fell to telling Dempster something of his experiences during his many foreign voyages.

Dempster heard that 'the coasts of China abounded with snow houses' and how 'the fishers of China carried snow in their boats, and by means thereof were able, in the heat of the summer, to convey fresh sea fish into the very interior parts of China'. Ready to take a leaf out of anybody's book and curious to know whether such a practice could replace the traditional Scottish method of packing fish in salt, Dempster 'took pen and ink, and on the spot wrote an account of the conversation to . . . Mr Richardson' – a constituent of his from Pitfour and a fish merchant with whom he was acquainted.[33] He had received 'many acts of kindness from him during his political career'.[34] However, finding that Dalrymple had not seen the Chinese method for himself, Dempster again wrote to him, this time invoking the proofs of a professor he turned to on more than one occasion. The eminent 'Dr Black,' he explained, 'has proved that a heated body communicates its heat to the surrounding bodies till they become of an equal heat. The same principle holds as to cold. . . . It might be expedient to bury the salmon when fresh caught in a large mass of snow or ice till they are quite frozen and then a very small portion of snow or ice might serve to pack them in the vessel and to preserve them in a cool state without much encumbrance.' Determined that Richardson should 'soon surpass the Chinese in that as much as we have done in many other arts', Dempster suggested that 'the place in which (the salmon) are stored . . . ought to be quite dry. Perhaps it were best lined with flag stones that retain cold better than wood. Or if one were in a hurry to embark the salmon they might be frozen very speedily first in the Ice House by splitting them or cutting them in small pieces.'

Dempster was happy to forecast the conveyance of other chilled foods 'to this dear Metropolis' such as poultry, eggs, game and other fish such as skate and both small and large smelts, all of which he was convinced would sell for double their local price. Caught up in his own enthusiasm, he concluded that 'a new kind of coasting trade might be struck out between the northern and southern provinces of this Island to the great advantage of both', albeit that it should 'be tried at first on a very small scale'.[35] The following January he 'accidentally stumbled' on an article about 'the Cold of Russia' and a piece in the February 1780 edition of *Town and Country Magazine* which he wanted Richardson to consider. The Consul-General in Russia spoke of packing eels, veal and poultry in ice before transporting them from St Petersburg to Moscow. The tubs packed with iced fish should, he said, be thawed out slowly and only done with cold water. If it was done by dry heat 'it occasions a violent fermentation and almost a sudden putrefaction. When done with (cold) water the ice seems attracted out of the bodies and forms an encrustation round them'. Reiterating this advice, Dempster urged Richardson to experiment and send salmon to London 'rammed hard in a cask with snow' and make certain he had 'some faithful friend . . . see to their thawing . . . properly when they arrive'. He had no doubt that 'were the frost to continue during the voyage the experiment is certain, but considering how slowly snow dissolves I hope it will be found a valuable pickle even in mild weather'.[36]

Recognizing that the passage times of vessels between Scotland and London would play an important part in any experiment, Dempster could not help drawing on another innovation he would have heard about from his sea-faring half-brother. Although captains of coastal vessels operating in shallow waters where grounding was a common occurrence were generally against the practice, Dempster asked Richardson whether he had ever 'thought of coppering one of (his) fishing smacks', expertly stating that 'it adds a third to their velocity, and doubles their powers of weathering a lee shore; our heaviest gales are from the south east and the whole of the East Coast of England is destitute of shelter'. Not content with 'these hints for (his) consideration', he added that smelts might be sent to London live: 'They live very well in well-boats as do salmon. As to salmon, I find they now bring them in well-boats also'.[37]

Convinced that 'commerce ever afforded . . . (a) . . . valuable premium for ingenuity', Dempster now awaited the results of Richardson's first experiments. They were not long coming. In February 1786, at a large dinner party given by Sir Adam Fergusson in London, 'all declared the salmon to be equal if not superior to their salmon' and Dempster felt confident enough to 'foretell (that) this experiment will prove a source of real wealth to any person who has perseverance enough to see it out'.[38] The following month saw another shipment which was 'never fresher nor finer' and he congratulated Richardson on 'a scheme that bids fair to double the value of your fish on this market'.[39]

146

By September *The Times* reported that the price of Scottish fish was likely to be very considerably reduced and on 23 October quantities of salmon sent from Perth 'answered beyond expectation'.[40]

Just how successful the freezing of fish became, and Dempster's role in promoting the idea, was contained in a letter Richardson later wrote to *The Scots Magazine*. He readily admitted that 'he had made the experiment rather in consequence of Mr Dempster's earnest manner of writing, than in the expectation of any good . . . (but it) answered beyond expectation . . . (and if) . . . any benefit result therefrom, either to the public or individuals, to that patriotic gentleman Mr Dempster it owes its beginning in this country and to none else'.[41] A little later, Richardson 'in the name of his own company . . . requested Mrs Dempster's and my acceptance of a bit of paper to be laid out in the purchase of such a piece of plate as we ourselves liked best'. On examining 'this bit of paper' Dempster found a bank bill for two hundred pounds Sterling![42] So delighted was he with the outcome that even 20 years later he was recalling the event in verse:

'I who acquir'd some small renown,
For sending salmon fresh to London town,'

and in his will John Richardson's name was among those to whom he wanted to leave a memento.

In July 1785, on his way to wait upon His Majesty at St James's Palace, Dempster's high hopes for the fisheries would have helped him to relax a little. Both the Irish and Fishery Bills that had been before the House were to receive the royal assent and, no longer plagued with the cold he had acquired in Ireland, Dempster processed in 'half full dress' with 'the Lord Chancellor, a great number of peers, and the Speaker and Members of the House of Commons'. Whether he managed to forget the continuing 'crisis' in his half-brother's affairs is another matter. On the morning of 29 July Dempster had written to Sir Adam in Harrogate where he was being treated for his gout, explaining little of the detail save to say that he expected to be in London for some time. 'Rosie', who had apparently been in Angus when he left for Westminster and Ireland, was by then with him at Percy Street. Tactfully he masked much that was on his mind by an oblique reference 'to a new river' (the *Ganges*, Captain John's ship) which was likely to be his 'beverage for some time'.[43]

What he omitted to tell his friend was anything about the events between January and April 1785 when the *Ganges* had been at Cork or, more importantly, the extent to which he had become personally involved in a project to establish the manufacture of cotton goods in his constituency outside Perth. At that time the English press had carried news of how additional large-scale cotton spinning investment was being contemplated in various parts of Scotland. The *Manchester Mercury* warned its readers that 'very great preparations (were being made) in Scotland by Mr Arkwright, joined by several of the most conspicuous in the landed and commercial interests of that kingdom'. The *Nottingham Journal* was like-minded in its report.[44] In fact, it had taken the best part of six months for the news of proposed new mills at Lanark, in which Dempster then had an investment as well as similar facilities on the Tay at Stanley, to be taken seriously by the spinners of Lancashire.[45]

So far as Sir Adam was concerned, he only knew what George had intended to do. A letter addressed to him at Harrogate written on Boxing Day 1784 told of Dempster's plan to leave Dundee after attending one meeting of the Town Council there, followed by another in Perth, going first to Dunkeld on 5 January and Glasgow on the seventh. But he also mentioned that his route was 'thro the islands', thereby causing his friend (and biographers) some mystification. Despite the years 'impairing (his) locomotive facility', he may have hoped to fit in a brief visit to the Hebrides and flesh out the 'few clear ideas' he had formed about the fisheries. Such a mid-winter excursion, if it did take place, would have carried its own uncertainties and been of very short duration. George had himself been uncertain how much time he had on the road to London, once he 'was beyond the vortex of (his) burroughs', and admitted that he 'could not calculate (his) course with any exactness'.[46] As he told Fintry, if not Sir Adam, he 'reached Town safely' on Sunday 23 January.

The business prospect that added to his other interests at this time was to be established on a site seven miles north of Perth. It was in the news due to the entrepreneurial spirit of the town's merchants and the close interest being shown in cotton spinning by John, 4th Duke of Atholl (1755–1830) as the result of Arkwright's phenomenal inventions. The previous year had seen the parties contributing their ideas about such a development well before the town itself had honoured Arkwright, following similar civic celebrations in Glasgow attended by Dempster. During the summer of 1784 the Duke had digested a lengthy anonymous paper which had been sent to him, with reports of Arkwright's profits 'in some years being in excess of £40,000' that could not fail to catch his eye. It was as good an investment prospectus as he was likely to receive. The author, who obviously knew the industry intimately and wrote lucidly and without exaggeration, maintained that the future for existing linen production depended on mechanization and the inclusion of cotton manufacture. Until 'water engines' had been invented by Arkwright, the cotton spun in Manchester was 'of too delicate a texture to serve as warp'. It became 'many times cheaper than it had been and the cotton yarn was so even and hard-twisted as to be peculiarly fit for the warp of that fabric'. Furthermore, since it was said that Mr Arkwright was 'too old and too rich to prosecute an uncertain and laborious discovery',[47] it was up to the industry, with the implied assistance of the Duke, to take a lead.

The 'Intelligent People belonging to the Linnen Branch' duly met on 14 July 1784 with the Duke in attendance, a meeting which was probably characterized as much by fear of Pitt's new duties and the threat cotton posed to local linen production as any great enthusiasm for new ventures. Whether Dempster's presence, and his intimate knowledge of some of Arkwright's achievements, would have had an even greater salutary effect on their motivation is doubtful; he was anyway otherwise engaged at Westminster in the midst of the India Bill debates and could not attend. An immediate outcome of the meeting was the Duke's offer to set aside a 70-acre site at Stanley for the newly-formed company's cotton mill.[48] This, coupled with his apparent readiness to support the company to the tune of £2,000, pointed not only to much detailed preparation work having been done behind the scenes but a growing optimistic spirit.

With Dempster often unable to be in Perth due to his commitments in London, Robert Graham of Fintry's role became pivotal. In 1771 he had been appointed gamekeeper to the Earl of Strathclyde, and owned the estate at Linlathen as well as the mains at Fintry just north of Dundee. The two men may have first become political associates during the election of 1780. Certainly when General James Murray (1734–1794), the MP for Perthshire with whom Dempster was quite friendly, enlisted Burke and Dempster's help in 1781 to expedite the passage of the Isle of Man Bill (set in motion by a petition from the Duke of Atholl) Dempster was obliged to Fintry 'for the communication of his Grace's letter'.[49] He was certainly the Duke's man and he was soon in correspondence with Dempster on all county and constituency affairs in which the Duke had a perennial interest.

Initially, he became a loyal political manager for Dempster in the constituency, becoming a useful go-between, an organizer of meetings for the benefit of local industry, and even politico-social gatherings such as Charity balls which Mr and Mrs Dempster were required to grace with their presence. In his first extant letter of September 1780 Dempster acknowledged the friendly part Fintry had taken in political matters. By 1782 his views had been solicited on the wisdom of launching a public subscription to build 'a handsome Town House and County Hall' for the 'Forfar folks', something Dempster preferred to see financed from 'a small county rate'. He had also had a hand in the four-county discussions called to explore the building of a turnpike from Perth to Aberdeen.[50] Their friendship for a time was more businesslike than personally cordial, with Dempster appearing to keep him at arm's length and then giving him encouragement by inviting him to avail himself, if he was so inclined, of five or six hundred elm tree saplings that could not be persuaded to grow at Dunnichen, or the gift of a pig 'bought at Glammes Market' which had been 'well fed on old pease'.[51] After Dempster left politics their friendship was to deepen, Fintry being someone always ready to assist wherever he could, and Dempster for ever keeping an eagle eye on his affairs.

Not unexpectedly, things did not always go to plan in the finical world of county politics where much was 'expressly reserved for the (Duke's) family'. Dempster's relations with Fintry had nearly been upset the previous year when he made a rare gaffe that had the effect of ruffling a few ducal feathers. Archibald Douglas, the idol of the Edinburgh mob and eventual winner in the long-drawn-out 'Douglas Case', had been the cause of the episode. He had come to prominence in Angus politics when William Maule, the sitting MP for the county, died in 1782, Douglas being returned as the new member after beating off a challenge from Sir David Carnegie. Before the 1784 General Election Dempster was telling Graham that nothing could prevent him from obeying 'Mr Douglas's summons' if he needed his support in winning the county of Forfarshire.[52]

While he did win the seat, and would 'taste the fruits of a unanimous election', as Dempster put it, the run-up to the election had produced a difference of opinion which involved the Duke of Atholl, Alexander Ogilvie-Fotheringham, himself a Colonel in the Scots Fusilier Guards and son of Thomas Fotheringham (– 1790) and the laird of Pourie, and Douglas.[53] 'There never was an election,' wrote Dempster, with his own experiences of twenty years before much in mind, 'that did not produce some mis-understandings.' Unfortunately, he had carelessly let it be known that Colonel Fotheringham was considering contesting the seat and had in-cautiously implied that Douglas was indifferent to which side the Fotheringham family took in the election, a small breach of trust that became magnified out of all proportion. He saw 'how the mistake had happened' during a meeting at the Duke's house in London where his gaffe came to be discussed and he had to blame himself for it: 'I am a blockhead . . . . Half a word of Confidential at the top of (the) letter would have rendered this mistake impossible'.[54]

Although a good start had been made in respect of the Stanley mill, Dempster appears to have had his doubts about the role his Grace had chosen to play, suspecting that he saw the venture as one way of achieving higher income and the utilization of the poorer land on his estate rather than a step towards substantial new employment and all that industrialization brought with it. He had some difficulty, if not in maintaining the Duke's interest, then in helping him comprehend how the cotton trade was already beginning to erode the traditional pattern of the textile industry in Scotland, away from silk and linen production. Not until December 1784, and after several pleas, did he agree to travel to Edinburgh to see with his 'own eyes the wonder of art' that had been going on at Penicuik and where 'Bertram & Co would wait on his Grace'.[55] The start of the cotton era had been seen at Rothesay as well as Penicuik ten years previously. It was an obvious place to begin his re-education. Penicuik had been designed and built by one of Arkwright's former workmen and his sight of the mill there may well have reinforced his Grace's belief that the Lancastrian inventor was the man to be his agent in affairs at

Stanley. By May 1785 he had appointed him his sole arbitrator on all affairs affecting the company.[56]

Dempster had been present at several meetings of the Perth 'adventurers' who came to be associated with the project. William Sandeman who owned a large bleachfield at Luncarty,[57] Peter Stewart (to whom he soon gave his power of attorney), Andrew Keay and Thomas Marshall met at Dunnichen House just before Christmas 1784, soon after the Duke had returned from Penicuik. By Boxing Day they were satisfied that the plan that had been drawn up could be submitted to his Grace for approval. There were to be eight shares in the Stanley Company, four for 'the Perth folks', one each for the Duke, Arkwright and Dempster, with the eighth at the disposal of his Grace for Fintry. The last, Dempster thought, 'would prefer being introduced into the partnership by the Duke . . . (as) a proper compliment to him'. The advance required of each shareholder was to be no greater than £1,000.[58]

For much of this period Dempster had to depend on Fintry for news from Perth. By February 1785 some of the details of the cotton-spinning project were beginning to be examined, not least the terms of the lease from the Duke, along with Dempster's own concept of developing Taycliffe, as he wanted the model barony at Stanley to be called. The latter idea, like so much associated with an investment of this size, particularly one of such importance to the local community and with the participation of such differing interests, was never to find much support, rumbling on into the 1790s by which time Dempster had realized he was fighting a losing battle.[59] His determination to pursue such ideas would have to wait until he could implement them on his own land without having to take into account ducal preferences.

The Duke upset all the Perth partners by restricting the feu of his land to a period of 21 years instead of the 99 years they had the right to expect. Dempster had urged 'every argument to induce him to agree with us . . . . The scheme will not be half so satisfactory to me'.[60] Fintry, who obviously saw another confrontation with his patron looming, had to be placated. Enlisting Arkwright's support for a longer lease, Dempster assured Fintry that 'the Duke will be in the wrong not to agree with us', which he was persuaded to do by May.[61] In the same month letters from Peter Stewart, his representative on the management committee of the partnership, showed him more sanguine generally, although both he and Fintry now had to find their share of the £1,000 advance called for. Pulling his leg about the style of his living at Dunnichen, where his wife's ears were 'overstretched with the weight of diamond pendant ear rings', his dining table 'constantly open to *Beaux Esprits*' and all 'such a blaze of beauty at Mrs Dempster's routs', Dempster said he could hardly find the cash: 'God knows, but providence will send some good body to lend it me!'[62] In the event, Fintry managed his share and received another half share as a present from Dempster when the latter agreed to acquire Arkwright's holding 'how soon ever the undertaking becomes profitable'. It was an apt reward for his mediation with the Duke and the 'infused harmony' that had resulted. Knowing that the laird of Linlathen was always short of money and had a 'numerous family', Dempster had been greatly satisfied in being able to help him 'rid himself of encumbrances' which prevented him educating and 'placing out his children suitably in the world'.[63]

With the construction of a six-storey, stone and brick-built mill apparently well under way at Stanley, and 40 or 50 workers safely arrived in Derbyshire for training, amid 'the sound of bagpipes and other music',[64] Dempster decided to take his half-brother and the ladies of the family to see a cotton mill for themselves. The Captain's affairs in Ireland were still being examined at India House, where 'the forgiveness of the captain and officers' was expected, although it still had to be to be formally approved by a meeting of the Court in October.[65] Accompanied by Arkwright who had been paid £2,000 for the use of his patent, they visited what turned out to be a struggling mill on the River Colne at Rickmansworth, north of London, where about 1100 spindles were the most that the fall of water would turn. The women employees were paid 7d a day and Arkwright thought it made a little money, but Dempster concluded that it 'was conducted with little vigour – things dirty and the machinery in bad order'.[66] Meanwhile back in Perth, Dempster's ideas about a free barony were being questioned by Andrew Keay as well as the Duke. Soon, even his interest in leases with low rents had to be switched to 'the North and North Eastern parts of Scotland' where, it seemed to the Fisheries Committee, there was 'a fund of wealth buried in poverty' and where 'a few Taycliffs . . . would go far to call forth this latent mine'.[67]

As we already know, the events surrounding the investment in Perth and early news of the worrisome affair in Ireland had probably been kept from Sir Adam. He knew less than half the story. Dempster's half-brother, 'Jack' as he was known to the family, was not without an adventurous and carefree nature which often worried Dempster. Sufficiently wealthy from his various voyages, Captain John had probably led an impetuous bachelor life when ashore. Now aged 35[68] and with few responsibilities, it was not altogether surprising that the birth of Harriet, his illegitimate daughter, became known.[69] Two of the Captain's voyages aboard a ship called *Harriet* in the 1770s may have suggested her name. After numerous amorous attachments and, being at sea for more than three years, further dalliance, if not the possession of a wife, was to be expected.

Who Harriet's mother was, and where in Ireland the Captain had met her earlier that year, have inevitably been matters of some speculation. It was, however, Charlotte Louisa Hawkins Dempster, Harriet's granddaughter, who threw the clearest light on her parentage, unfortunately provoking James Fergusson to dismiss the story out of hand. He asserted that her version of events was 'a baseless scandal', and argued, not altogether convincingly, that it was 'confuted by dates'.[70] In *The Manners of My Time* Charlotte Dempster maintained that Harriet's mother was Olivia Mariamne Devenish of Castle Dana (Casteltauna), Co. Roscommon, Ireland, whose 'extraction was partly Irish and partly Circassian'. Devenish family records suggest that Olivia's father was Christopher Devenish who died when she was about twelve years old.[71] No record of her mother exists. Olivia was to marry Jacob Cassivelaun Fancourt at Madras in 1793 and became Sir Stamford Raffles's first wife in 1805.[72] Charlotte's record may not be without its mistakes but what possible motive she could have had in making up a story about Olivia being Harriet's mother is hard to conceive. Born at Dunnichen in 1835, Charlotte spent her youth at Skibo with her brother and sisters, whom she described as a bunch of 'masterful half-Irish children'. During a long life, the latter part of which was spent on the French Riviera, she corresponded with many of the family and evidently made copious notes. Her reference to Plimer's miniature showing Harriet as 'a very pretty girl' would have been even more pronounced had she recalled the complementary water-colour of Olivia in the possession of her sister, Lady Metcalfe, and whom Lord Minto described as 'a great lady with dark eyes, lively manner, accomplished and clever'.[73] The appearance of the two women certainly showed a marked similarity.

When the *Ganges* eventually reached London the Captain seems to have divided his time between living with the Dempsters at Percy Street in London and in Scotland where one report suggests Harriet was born.[74] Writing to him from Banff on 1 October, Sir George Ramsay, a distant relative, touched briefly on the Captain's affairs.[75] Jack had apparently asked him in August 'what sum in Sterling' he had been charged for the bills he had drawn on Sir George from Batavia. Agreeing to show him his account books in London 'next month' (when he would be there) Sir George had, rather surprisingly, to remind him that the coin of all their accounts in Madras was 'star pagodas' not sterling, and that Captain John's repayment of the bills was also expected in local currency. He congratulated him on securing 'a good voyage for next season' (as Captain of the *Rose*), thereby avoiding what Ramsay thought was the next scheduled voyage of the *Ganges* to the unattractive East Sumatra station of Bencoolen.[76] Curiously, Captain John seems to have contemplated a 'jaunt to France' with Ramsay that autumn. In the event, Ramsay found it inconvenient and asked him to defer it until the following spring when he would be able to accompany him. Such goings on hardly suggest that news of Harriet's birth or, more particularly, Captain John's pending marriage to Jean Fergusson, was widespread. Dempster himself had proposed 'looking north-ward' in August, anticipating that the prorogation of Parliament would be about then. As it was, it took place in September, with the date for the recall being eventually fixed for January 1786.

Both the Fergusson and Dempster families found this a difficult period and were at pains to avoid scandal and to arrange matters with as much discretion as could be mustered. As the months of 1785 passed by, any opprobrium the

Captain's affair attracted would have been swept aside, and hushing up the birth probably took priority. Harriet's expected arrival in September or a little later and plans for her care must have been discussed in the family circle in London – made up as it was of the Dempsters, the Gordons and Ann, George's unmarried sister. Sir Adam may not have immediately grasped the significance of Dempster's two visits to Dulwich to see not only Charles Fergusson, the bride's father with whom Captain John was particularly friendly, but his daughter and Dempster's godchild, who had become 'a most beautiful and excellent young woman'.[77] What was curious in the extreme was that the four letters from George to Sir Adam were bland in their content and all referred to the continued winding up the affairs of the *Ganges*.[78] Not even the last of them written on 24 September contained a whisper of the marriage. On 25 October Jean, Charles Fergusson's eldest daughter and Sir Adam's 19-year-old niece, simply married Captain John in London.

Of all his hopes, that closest to George's heart after the events earlier in the year was that his half-brother might fall in love with such a woman, settle down, preferably on land, and produce the heir that he and Rosie had been unable to have.[79] The marriage was said to have particularly delighted the Fergussons who felt that it fitly consolidated the alliance between the two families and Sir Adam's long friendship with Dempster. Jean was handsome and attractive, and quickly established herself as a much-loved member of the Dunnichen family. Her only child, a son named George after his uncle, was born a year later.[80] The Captain's marriage 'engrossed' the family for the following ten days. Dempster had hoped to go to Derbyshire 'and pass a free day with Mr Arkwright' and the journey had been delayed by the extended coming and going at Percy Street and presumably in the Fergusson house in the country south of London. Greatly pleased at the thought of spending more time in London, he was 'relieved from the necessity' of travelling north to Scotland, even promising the family that they would be 'all together at Dunnichen next May (1786) and spending the summer in Scotland'.[81]

Just three days after the Captain's wedding Dempster immersed himself in what was to be an unsuccessful two-year rearguard action to prevent his friend Fintry from being forced to sell his estates to meet mounting debts. He had received the news more than three weeks before, but arrangements for the betrothal and the family's subsequent celebrations had prevented an earlier reply. In the light of Dempster's own controversial expenditure the following year, (see Chapter 10) the lengthy and explicit advice he gave his friend was particularly poignant and rather characteristic of Dempster's ability to often see the better course for others than himself. As usual, he could not resist a temptation to pass on extracts from his current reading and, although in other circumstances Andean husbandry methods might have been of interest to someone who had spent considerable sums improving his own estates, his friend's reactions to *The Travels of Peter de Cretza* are not recorded.

Dempster's string of legal friends and occasional financial advisers – he never put all his eggs into one basket – made him only too well aware that the City of London was at that time brimming over with cash looking for a home and interest rates at four and a half per cent were considerably lower than they had been. Accordingly, his first thought was that Fintry would be wise to spend six months advertising the property as an investment. It was excellent land: 'Remember your lands are . . . next to Guthrie . . . and see the sums he feus at!' With freely available mortgages, Dempster thought he might be able to hold on to at least parts of the estate. Quoting Lord Bacon's advice that men who extricated themselves too hastily from money difficulties generally ended up selling their property too cheaply, he begged Fintry to lessen his debts 'by well-timed sales . . . and frugal and parsimonious habits'. A family trust was not out of the question if a few of his family friends 'should interpose their credit', especially since his generosity and conduct towards them had caused much of his plight. Recalling a speech of his in the House that year, Dempster explained: 'A little sinking fund could be created', although 'some pinching and scrubbing' might be unavoidable. He remembered how his own anxiety had made him 'sell some excellent property at an undervalue' in the 1770s.[82]

It appears that another reason why the Dempsters remained in the south that winter was the move they made about the time of Captain John's wedding from the house in Percy Street to more salubrious accommodation at 18, Queen's Row in Knightsbridge. Telling Pulteney about it in November, he expressed the hope that the 'better air' of what was then open country would help him 'parry' his usual winter colds. Probably anticipating the resumption of work by the Fisheries Society, Dempster took up with Pulteney the payment of some expenses Dr Anderson had incurred during his visit to the Hebrides. He had apparently been given £100 by the Treasury for his attendance the previous winter at meetings of the Commons Committee, but no more. Troubled that the government had done so little for someone to whom they were all greatly indebted, Dempster reminded Pulteney that 'the Doctor ha(d) eleven or twelve children and cannot well afford to have the government long in his debt', and hoped that Pulteney would take up the matter urgently with Dundas.[83]

Ten days or so before Christmas the Dempsters went down to Hotwells in Bristol to see one of his wife's nieces (possibly Catherine Bryden née Heming) who was dying.[84] On the way they stayed briefly at Bath where he had given Fintry a *poste restante* address, before returning home via Chippenham in time to help Arkwright who was to be knighted. It seems that his mentor from the textile industry lacked some of the essential clothing required for his investiture. At Sir Joseph Banks's house in Soho Square those entertaining Arkwright 'were not a little surprised to see little fatty appear as a beau with a smart powdered *bag* wig so tight that coming over his ears it made him deaf; a

155

handsome striped satin waistcoat and proper coat with a sword, which he held in his hand, all provided it is supposed by Mr Dempster'.[85]

Looking back over the year now coming to an end, Dempster must have had very mixed feelings about its highs and lows, a combination of some satisfaction that his half-brother was at last married and free of threats to his career, the prospect of a new industry being introduced in his constituency and the heavy parliamentary programme. The fact was, however, that he already knew 1786 would bring additional responsibilities as the focus moved to more piscatory matters.

9

BUILDING FISHING VILLAGES
(1786 – 1787 PART 1)

'The Directors of the Company must for many years make
a point of holding one end of the rein'
(John Gray's 'Reflections' 1789)

1786

The British Fisheries Society came into being at the end of July. Sir Adam Fergusson was one of the founding promoters of the Society but Dempster, Henry Beaufoy and the Duke of Argyll deserved the greatest credit for the work they did to implement its ideals.[1] Beaufoy feared that emigration would further decimate the Highlands and Islands where, as he told the House, no less than 30,000 had exiled themselves to America between 1763 and 1775, and another 600 were about to embark that year. Fishing villages were to be developed at Tobermory, Ullapool, Loch Bay in Skye and Wick in Caithness, Dempster becoming a stalwart of the Society until 1797 when he resigned from the board. The Society was to last until 1893, passing through many changes of fortune, one being the panic caused by the temporary collapse of the industry during the Napoleonic wars. Apathy and inept management played their part and it became a much emasculated creature, greatly affected by the famine of the 1840s and the vicissitudes of the market.

The first twelve years of the Society's existence were nevertheless years of triumphal construction in the west of Scotland. Dempster and others among the Society's members were soon confirming Anderson's and Knox's recommendations about where best to locate new towns and villages and the development for which they were now responsible: 'The nation must never forget that it is to the writings and journeys of Mr Pennant, Dr Anderson and Mr Knox, it is indebted'.[2] Not surprisingly, the maxim that 'the Company should not attempt too much at once' was soon under pressure and, in trying to identify the best way to spend the money available to it, the Society chased several 'hares' before settling down, including the possibility of building a

Crinan Canal. Dempster was not without some blame in this respect.

There were to be thirteen directors, of whom eight were Members of Parliament, two being from English constituencies. The Governor was the Duke of Argyll (who held a similar position with the Highland Society) and the Earl of Breadalbane his deputy. Records differ regarding the other members. In addition to Beaufoy and Dempster, Jean Dunlop includes Adam Fergusson, Dundas, William Wilberforce, Francis Humberstone Mackenzie of Seaforth, Lord Gower, the Earl of Moray and the Marquis of Graham, leaving out from James Fergusson's list Ilay Campbell, Isaac Hawkins Browne, MP for Bridgnorth, Walter Campbell of Shawfield and George Dempster's half-brother, Captain John Dempster. The Society's secretary was John Mackenzie of Arcan near Dingwall. Subscribers were not limited to Scotland and the Deputy Governor achieved something of a coup in 1789 when he persuaded Lord Cornwallis, now Governor-General in India, to raise a £6,000 subscription with the help of the Governors of Madras and Bombay.

The Society was fortunate in having the support of the Highland Society of London and its secretary undertook work on behalf of both bodies. Eight years before, a group of Scots had met in a London Coffee House to form 'a society that might prove beneficial to the Highlands'. Their work had attracted substantial financial support, enabling them, among other projects, to fund studies on better fishing practice. Fortunately, they had the wisdom to link their work closely with the actions of the Commons Fisheries Committee from which many of the Fisheries Society members were drawn. Keen to build on its earlier research, in March 1786 the Society despatched John Knox on another northern visit and, with sufficient funds coming in, they were able to turn their attention to a handful of geographical targets where their first investments might be made. In a lecture to the Fisheries Society that year, organized by the Highland Society, Knox raised the prospect of building about 40 villages between Dornoch and Arran, each containing 30 to 40 houses, curing sheds and stores at a cost of £2,000 each.[3] The wide distribution of the lecture, including a copy sent to the King, as well as the usefulness of his ideas and reports, had contributed to a speedy tabling of the Bill to establish the Fisheries Society. With so many Parliamentarians in membership, the Society's working year now followed that of the House and with Knox away, and the Secretary, John Mackenzie, busy gaining new subscribers, it was not until December that they met again.

In 1786 the Commons anticipated the principal business of the first session of parliament would be the preliminary examination of Warren Hastings' behaviour in India. The Commons did debate the Benares charge against him, but it was to be the following year before his lengthy inquisition made the headlines.[4] In February Dempster spoke and voted against Richmond's plans for the fortification of Portsmouth and Plymouth dockyards, describing them as 'unnecessary and extravagant',[5] a rare occasion on which Pitt was defeated, and it was other fish-related business that was called. Customs and Excise and merchants in the fish trade hotly disputed clauses in the Greenland Whale Fishery Bill. The administration was against the award of further bounties to what it regarded as a flourishing and profitable business, whilst fishermen and dealers were adamant that the 40/- per ton subsidy was vital to their interests. Dempster remonstrated about what he called this ill-timed measure 'just after the war, when so many . . . brave seamen were turned ashore from the navy' and insisted that the idea of proceeding without first instituting an enquiry was 'criminal'. An examination of witnesses before the Privy Council was not in his opinion a 'sufficient ground' on which to proceed.[6]

Dempster's difference of opinion with the Revenue extended to measures that widened the jurisdiction of the Excise Courts. The matter cropped up when the House debated the Wine Excise Bill and, taking strong exception to the proposals, Dempster expressed his preference for the jury system which excisemen only used when they thought they had a hard and fast case. The full rigour of the law was more likely to be softened in court than in such proceedings. Fox also condemned summary proceedings under such excise laws and wanted them to be used with greater discretion. Pitt, on the other hand, argued that trial by jury produced inconsistent results and, if the powers of the Excise courts were limited to dealing with the non-payment of wine duties, the door would be open to every other branch of the Excise service. Dempster was convinced that the more the spirit of freedom was introduced into the operation of the excise laws the better 'they would be relished'. He had opposed the bill at every stage, because he thought it 'severely oppressive on the body of men . . . affected by it' and because it would also do nothing to prevent smuggling.[7]

Dempster's interest in the affairs of the Excise were given a boost with the news in April that his friend Graham of Fintry (and John Cochrane of Roughsoils whom he knew as a 'lively honourable man') had been appointed to the Board of Excise.[8] Fintry's appointment as a Commissioner was to give him an excellent *entrée* into a bureaucracy which wielded so much influence over the livelihood, particularly of the poor, who most felt the often punitive taxes they collected.

During the debate on the East India Company Relief Bill in June Dempster questioned whether allowance ought to be made for the difference between the customs of the East and Europe. He eulogized the ex-Governor-General, vehemently maintaining that Warren Hastings had 'established his character as a good general economist, an able financier, a discreet manager of the revenue, an acute statesman . . . and a zealous friend to the interests of his employer'. Dempster took the view that Hastings 'though in some few particulars he might not have acted precisely as the rigid rules of right directed' had been a good governor.[9]

During a busy six months Dempster received two letters from someone with whom he rarely corresponded except when he had to, John Johnstone, his old turbulent East India Company 'client', now living in retirement. In January 1786 Dempster had canvassed the wealthy renegade's support on behalf of Captain John with whom he had been discussing a possible new investment. Such an approach was probably driven more by the certainty that he had the wherewithal to help 'Jack' than any desire to re-open contact after a gap of five years or so. The letter had unfortunately been wrongly addressed, going first to Pulteney who sent it on to Alva, Johnstone's estate, where he enjoyed 'too large a farm', a distillery and the usual problems of 'ill-paid rents . . . and an immense loss during so bad a harvest'. But Johnstone had apparently agreed to purchase a one-sixteenth share in a new East Indiaman, whose 'ship's husband' was to be a William Stafford whom he had been pleased to recommend as a fit person for the job. There is no evidence that such a vessel came to be built, certainly not 'the good ship *Dempster*' as he referred to it, and in making the investment requested of him, he begged 'some months notice of the calls'. It was, he said, as if he heard Dempster's 'voice calling', encouraging the taking of a 'share in the bottom'. Referring, if briefly, to all that had been done on his behalf, he did at least acknowledge that it had been due to Dempster's 'friendly assistance' that he 'had weathered the storm that threatened to overwhelm' him and which had brought his 'barque safe into port'.[10]

A second letter in June showed that Johnstone's way with money had not deserted him. Having failed to send Dempster on time the remittance he had promised, he was full of excuses, blaming his brother Pulteney rather than himself for failing to make the contribution expected of him for his shareholding in the *Dempster*. 'I hope you will believe,' he pleaded, 'that I never lost sight of the matter, though from accidents it has not been acquitted with the dispatch it ought to have been'. With his whisky distilling on the estate more to the fore than other concerns, he added that it was 'mortifying to think that not one of our Members' (including Dempster) had said 'a word on the subject of . . . Scotch ale' in parliament. Dempster was invited to visit Alva that summer, 'where you will find me as deep in farming as you have been in fisheries', but there was little between the two men and no evidence that the visit took place. Johnstone died in 1795.[11]

In May another matter Dalrymple and Dempster had talked about at India House the previous year was pushed forward in parliament, the latter moving 'several resolutions for placing lighthouses on certain parts of the coasts in the north seas'. For Dempster, the safety of navigation in many places on the coast of Scotland was of the utmost importance; vessels were frequently lost for the want of such lights.[12] Unlike England, where there were at least a few lighthouses, the shores of Scotland were identified to shipping by the occasional coal-brazier or nothing at all. Two years before, Dempster had attended a meeting of the Convention of Scottish Burghs where a concerted effort had been made to raise awareness of the problem, pressing Parliament to take action. There were then less than 150 lighthouses in the world, and although the Swedes had invented an elementary flashing light in 1738 and the French had experimented with reflectors, there was everything to be learned about how they worked. That year in Geneva a lamp with a cylindrical wick which was to revolutionize oil lighting had been constructed by Aimé Argand.

A Commons Committee considering the proposed legislation benefited greatly from work done by the Convention's clerk, John Gray. He had been Secretary to the Duke of Newcastle and his thorough work on the legislation was to lead to him being appointed the first Secretary to the Northern Lighthouse Board. He drafted much of the Bill that Dempster was able to bring to the House in a matter of weeks. The resolutions were passed *nem con* and the Act for Erecting Certain Lighthouses in the Northern Parts of Great Britain became law. The Northern Lighthouse Board, made up of nineteen sheriffs from ten maritime counties as trustees, was empowered to make loans of up to £1,200 under the Act. Vessels benefiting from the lights were to be charged once the first four lighthouses were built: on the Mull of Kintyre, the point of Scalpay in Harris, on North Ronaldsay in the Orkneys, and Kinnaird's Head in Aberdeenshire. Pressure for a light to be installed on the Isle of May, commanding the anchorage at St Margaret's Hope on the Firth of Forth, was resisted but a start had been made. By 1789 Thomas Smith and Robert Stevenson were able to begin their work of building lighthouses throughout the kingdom.[13]

At the end of June Dempster's attention turned elsewhere, with lighthouses, salmon, investments in an East Indiaman, fisheries business and the gamut of Parliamentary affairs all temporarily pushed from his mind. Firstly, there was another civic lap of honour to be undertaken and, secondly, he had in mind the purchase of a Highland estate. (See next chapter). Tokens of his constituents' favour towards him were especially welcome. *The Scots Magazine* reported the annual convention of the Royal Burghs on 13 July in Edinburgh where he was voted a 'piece of plate, value one hundred guineas . . . for his unremitting attention to the trade and manufactures, and fisheries of this country, and for his patriotic exertions for its welfare and prosperity'. Soon afterwards he received notice that Dundee Town Council had commissioned a portrait of him by his first cousin, George Willison. Then, a few days after waiting in Perth for an opportunity to present the Duke of Atholl with more of his 'propositions' about the Stanley mill, there was another celebration, this time with 'the cotton folks' at Dunnichen House. He had seen how construction of the workers' houses was progressing and, although it was soon to be a contentious issue, Dempster's mood was euphoric.[14]

Among the 'propositions' had been one for some fifty weavers to occupy as many houses at a reasonable rent. Writing to Fintry during a visit in September to Sir Adam, Dempster could see that 'the speedy peopling' of Stanley could be jeopardized if, having found the spinners – a task that was not proving as easy as they thought – the proprietors could not make them offers of 15-year leases.[15] There was much competition for labour from other trades in and around Perth. He wanted to see shoemakers, tailors, bakers, brewers, blacksmiths, a weekly market and Church schools 'tumbling into the Burrough'.[16] Knowing that he was to call on Arkwright on his way back to London, he let the matter rest, travelling instead along a 'very fine' local turnpike between Ayr and Kilmarnock to see an impoverished coal mine. On a 12-mile journey he paid three 6d tolls and one shilling to cross a bridge. Asked whether the local populace begrudged the heavy expense, their answer 'was uniformly in praise of the turnpike roads and of the money they saved'.[17]

Once at Cromford, Dempster gave Arkwright the judgement he had been asked to make in his friend's dispute with David Dale. The Glasgow cotton-cloth producer, who had also accompanied Dempster and Arkwright during their colourful visit to Anderston two years before, had become involved with Arkwright in the construction of the New Lanark mills. An inconsequential argument between the two men, probably exacerbated by Arkwright's loss of his patent advantage, had got out of hand and was to end their partnership. Dempster had been happy to put his own share in the Lanark mill on the table with those of Arkwright and Dale. To him they had little value. Dale, on the other hand, thought that Dempster had made him a valuable gift, and offered him £1,000 for his share. As Dempster said, 'I was too glad to be rid of the extensive concern to accept . . . compensation for it'. In his arbitration, he had to tell Arkwright that he had come down in favour of Dale: 'I awarded the whole to Mr Dale, as being most convenient for him to manage'.[18]

Returning to Knightsbridge in November, before setting out northwards yet again for the New Year, Dempster's travels had brought on another cold and an 'inflammation (of the) breast and lungs'. Laid up in bed, he feared that without 'enthusiasm, confidence and . . . cooperation between his Grace and the Company, Stanley must be *belle manquée* which is the more pity'.[19] His desire to see the construction of a coal yard there led to him bewailing the outcome of Pitt's new taxes on fuel. The disparity between the cost of living north and south of the Tweed was so distressing to 'our people in Angus and Perthshire'. Whereas the inhabitants of London were warmed by coal at 1/6d a hundredweight, in Perth the price was 6/-. This, the last of his letters to Fintry for a period, had been written knowing that he would not be able to give much more attention to the mill in Stanley.

When members of the Fisheries Society foregathered that December it became clear that they would have to meet several times a week if they were to get through their work. Subscriptions had been coming in from all parts of the country as well as India. The first task was to confirm the locations of the proposed fishing villages. Anderson's broad specification had to be translated into fully-fledged, self-supporting settlements of sufficient size to accommodate shops, stores, custom houses, post offices, as well as housing and some basic social facilities. Lord Breadalbane sent out more than 200 signed letters to fishery bailies, captains of revenue cutters and estate factors on the north-west coast, asking them to find land, and ascertain the 'terms on which (owners) might be inclined to transfer in perpetuity, any parcel of land on (their) estate, bordering upon any bay, harbour or navigable loch, which may be thought a proper situation for one of the Society's villages'.[20] The names and addresses were provided by William Macdonald of the Highland Society who received a box of letters in Edinburgh by mail coach for him to despatch. By April next year forty replies had been received, although many landlords had put forward land they wished to dispose of and which was not necessarily much use to the Society. A few, including Colonel Alexander Maclean of Coll, recognized that suitable land would be less of a problem than 'inducing the people to inhabit the proposed 'villages' since, and this was to become a real concern, 'if the inhabitants . . . can procure the bare necessities of life by their labour from the grounds they possess, their ambition leads them to no further effort'.[21] However, there were obviously enough possibilities to justify a tour of the more likely sites.

1787

By the turn of the year Dempster was back at Dunnichen where in the January cold he could concentrate on his correspondence, attend to his half-brother's affairs, prepare for the Parliamentary session ahead and assess the work to be put in hand on behalf of the Fisheries Society, all in addition to the pressing new responsibilities he had acquired in Sutherland. The household was used to the feverish activity his always full agenda created, but whether its new canine members had settled down is not recorded. A month before, Dempster's neighbour at Craigie, James Guthrie, had wanted to know whether Mrs Dempster 'had admitted (Dempster's) two Highland terriers ('Fox' and his lady, 'Brisky') to her drawing room'. He feared they would give Rose 'an aversion to all Highlanders'.[22]

The birth of a son to Jean and Captain John in the previous November had been greeted with great joy. At the christening ceremony in London on 4 November, George Heming, Rose's brother, had 'officiated' in the absence of Sir Adam Fergusson, the child's godfather. 'Little George' was welcomed by the whole family and soon became 'the apple of Dempster's eye', promising to be 'everything fond parents could wish'. The only cloud over the occasion was the knowledge that Captain John would soon depart for Madras and China, leaving his young wife and child alone in London. Jean would have been only too well aware that the probable date of her confinement and that of the *Rose's* departure would be close. She had to watch as her husband and the new vessel's managing owner, William Moffat, delighted in the second ship of this name as she was being built along the Thames. Their pride in its size was obvious, large by the standards of the Company's fleet at 144 feet long and 810 tons weight, but smaller than his first command, the *Ganges*. The

Captain's visits to Well's shipyard in Rotherhithe opposite the Isle of Dogs conveyed their own message. Dempster, for his part, would have been sensitive to the distress and hardship the plan admitted, however much he may have thought the financial gains of the voyage might wipe out at least some of the expense he had incurred in buying the Highland estate at Skibo the previous summer.

With the knowledge that Jack would be unlikely to return from the East until the spring of 1788, it had been decided that Dempster would become his child's unofficial guardian. By February all was ready and the departure only awaited favourable weather. At Gravesend the last-minute personal affairs of the Captain were being tidied up as they waited for the wind to abate. He had hoped to leave at noon on 18 February, but the ship's log showed the *Rose* still waiting in the safe haven of the Downs between the dangerous Goodwin Sands and the Kent coast on the 21st of the month. Among the several debts the Captain had forgotten to pay was one from his tailors, Blackmores of Henrietta Street in Covent Garden, and he asked Dempster to pay £99 16s. 0d for work done, less £7 16s.0d for the nankeen or cotton fabric he had himself supplied.

On the *Rose* a relative of a General Maclean, whom the Captain was taking to India, had been 'perfectly worthless and . . . so drunk ever since his coming aboard that he has dirtied his small cloths (sic) and his messmates' berth so that they have turned him out'. The General had to be informed, but Captain John assured his half-brother that he felt he would be able to 'set him on his feet'. Later that evening, in an addition to his letter, the Captain belatedly got round to the always serious business for those going to sea, his personal life insurance during the voyage, asking Dempster to arrange £3,000 cover for him in all the ports and places they would call at en route to China. Anticipating that the ship might be lost on the Goodwins, he asked Dempster to 'see with (his) own eyes' that the insurance had been effected properly by his servant and that a copy had been passed to Websters, his agents, who already held two other of his insurance policies in similar sums.[23]

Dempster now turned to parliamentary affairs in London where the Commons was to continue its examination of the evidence against Hastings. All indications were that the charge relating to the Begums of Oude, and the repeal of the East India Judicature Bill, would provide much ado during February and March. After taking evidence from several witnesses during the first days of February, a Committee of the whole House turned to the fourth charge against Hastings, with Mr St John in the chair. But before debate could commence, (on 7 February) Dempster sought leave to correct some of the evidence he had given in defence of his friend Sir Elijah Impey the day before. Discovering that 'it had been less explicit and decisive' than he had intended and, to save time, he presented a paper in explanation, the gist of which was 'to authenticate the dispositions taken by Sir Elijah at Lucknow, by declaring that the translator had been sworn, and had deposed that the translation was authentic and correct'. When one member thought this unsatisfactory and that Sir Elijah should be recalled to the bar for another examination, Pitt supported him, saying that 'a *viva voce* statement was indispensably requisite'. The defendant could not be found, and Sheridan[24] rose to command the 'attention and admiration of the House by an oration lasting five hours and forty minutes'. The next day Dempster tried again unsuccessfully, asking the House to permit Sir Elijah, who was then 'waiting without the door', with his corrected evidence, hoping to speak. This time Dundas, the Solicitor-General, argued that 'if every witness could come one day and contradict what he had said the day preceding, the confusion would be endless' and Dempster's motion was denied.[25]

As the days went by, the House was influenced by the view that since Hastings had given orders for the plunder of the Begums' personal property, he was responsible for all the consequences. Dempster was forced to explain how his ideas about Hasting's defence were 'so different from those of the other gentlemen that they were likely to injure the person he meant to serve'. Although he could see that he was again in a minority, he was still anxious to explain why he thought Hastings should not be impeached. When the country granted powers to the Company to conduct the government of their territories, in his view they authorized the sending of governors to act with discretion and, unless they acted from motives of personal corruption, they ought not to be held 'amenable'. Such governors could not be called to account like British ministers at home, given the great distances involved. He justified the treatment of the Begum's eunuchs by saying that the custom of the East sanctioned such severities, that in India money was 'collected with the whip' and that 'stripes were the usual means of enforcing payment'.[26] Some members agreed that Hastings should not be judged by the constitutional maxims applicable in England and that he was deserving of applause rather than censure, but the vote again showed those in support of action against Hastings were broadly the same. Dempster was allied with 60 to 70 members out of the 240 or so present.

On 27 February the Prime Minister agreed to Dempster's request for an open day debate on his proposal for a Bill to explain and amend the East India Judicature Act that he had so long disliked. Burke and Dempster contended that 'it gave . . . great concern to find that British subjects in India were not to be permitted to enjoy the same privileges which British subjects in England enjoyed'.[27] Three weeks later, in a long and considered speech which showed much foresight and understandable diplomacy, Dempster introduced his measure. It not only contained proposals to establish a Court of Judicature for the more speedy and effectual trial of those accused of offences committed in India but new regulations to improve the management of the Company, and postulated a whole new system of government, echoing that eventually introduced in Queen Victoria's reign. The Commons had not heard such novel thoughts before.

Before turning to his main theme, Dempster 'begged leave to fix the attention of the House' on defects in the East India Acts of the previous year, insisting that 'trials by jury were the birthright of every British subject (and) no assembly had any right to take away such privilege', saying that only two cases had been decided by jury in recent years; those involved Governor Verelst and Lord Pigot. Another shortcoming was the need to extend the judicature instituted in Bengal and Calcutta, where it had been of benefit, to Madras. A third regulation would have allowed the speedy filling of vacancies in the Supreme Court. When Sir Elijah Impey was recalled the whole weight of that court's work had fallen on the shoulders of a single judge. He asked for the repeal of the authority held by the Governor-General which allowed him to seize people 'merely suspected' of holding any correspondence with princes, rajahs, zemindars or governors of factories, or *any* correspondence 'detrimental to the general interest of the Company'. There was also the need for the Habeas Corpus Act to apply to India. So long as the government of India was left in the hands of even a well-conducted Council concerned with the affairs of a trading company, it was inevitable, in Dempster's view, that the liberty of British subjects could not be guaranteed. It might, he mused presciently, be better to change the form of government altogether: 'Suppose, for instance, a government in the nature of a vice-royalty were instituted, and a viceroy was to be appointed, with a privy council to advise . . . in matters of government; he might also have a legislative council, and something like representation be given to India . . . (with) capital towns and districts . . . empowered to elect and send deputies. Such a house of representation might be empowered to receive petitions from the natives, and to grant redress'. In another of the many pointers to democratic campaigns that would be fought across the sub-continent, he pleaded that the natives should be given a degree of confidence in the British government 'hitherto unknown in India'. In also proposing the abolition of all monopolies, particularly that of opium, Dempster declared he had ample proof of the 'injurious tendency of that monopoly'.[28]

The Bill having been read, he moved that it be enacted. Opening for the government, the Solicitor General claimed that in the two cases of Verelst and Pigot there were special circumstances and the defendants had suffered unduly since the jury were quite exhausted by the time they had poured over the voluminous evidence. Juries could not be expected to understand and adjudicate on matters not within their everyday knowledge. It was left to Burke to re-inforce Dempster's arguments. He insisted that the new judicature had members nominated by ministers that exposed them to external influence, unlike juries whose members were unknown until the day and thereby less likely to be swayed. But, as Dempster would have known, his elegant scheme of things involved constitutional change and the government's only concern was with peaceable administration. The defeat when it came was crushing;

only 21 members out of 149 voted with him. Soon after these clashes the death of George Johnstone was announced. He had been a great campaigner on behalf of Hastings and it was a sad event for Dempster as he looked back over his apprenticeship in East Indian affairs and the heady days of 'vote-splitting' and rancour around the table in Leadenhall Street.

Dempster's approach to reforming the franchise in his own country had been seen as something of a puzzle among his friends. When the matter came before the House in May he was again ambivalent and declined to support the reform of Scottish burghs. It was Sheridan who presented petitions from Glasgow and Dundee, not Dempster. He 'had disappointed his admirers', after being chosen by delegates of the Convention of Royal Burghs to present their case against 'the evil' of self-election and for the popular election of town councils.[29] Dempster maintained that his first loyalty was towards those who had elected him and, although the system had obvious flaws, they were not ones that he was prepared to put at the top of his list for reform. He believed that increased prosperity would produce an inflow of new, more independently-minded voters among those able to claim the vote through being new feuholders and possessing land worth in excess of 40/- an acre.

The 26th of March was an important day for the Fisheries Society. The sum of £22,000 had been raised towards the share subscription target of £150,000. Francis Humberstone Mackenzie (referred to subsequently as Seaforth; he was created a peer in 1797)) had been re-elected through the efforts of 'one of the Proprietors in particular', as Dempster put it. Seaforth had not been present for the meeting or at the 'most respectable dinner' which followed. The only upset was caused by Knox and the manner in which he had taken Dempster and Sir Adam to task about a matter of no real consequence. They accepted that 'men embark in any public undertaking' with the right 'to say everything good and bad that comes into their heads'. They well understood how much he had done to point the Society in the right direction, but he was far from diplomatic in many of his utterances. His 'petulance' had come at a time when he had been soliciting a salaried Government post. There had also been 'some little symptoms of jealousy and misunderstanding' among the directors which Dempster wanted Seaforth to appreciate and help Henry Beaufoy, the chairman, resolve.[30] This aside, the board proceeded with some alacrity, deciding to begin with 'two stations only' – Tobermory and Ullapool. Their plans were soon in train, due in part to the 'advantage of despatch', the fact that they only had the period in the spring and early summer when the House was sitting to make their decisions.

Two months later Dempster wrote a 12-page 'address' from Knightsbridge to Charles Jenkinson, now Lord Liverpool. Having become President of the Board of Trade the previous year he was a particular target for Dempster's growing appeals on behalf of the Scottish linen industry. He had used the good offices of this expert but politically timid minister several times before. His constituents had 'instructed him to obtain the earliest information . . . about the propriety of renewing the bounties on coarse linen'.[31] They feared the administration might lower the duties on foreign imports to the prejudice of home manufacture. Dempster requested a hearing by 'his lordship's board' and support for his constituents to make their case at the bar of the House. Writing to Liverpool in May, he asked him to 'cast his eye over the map of Scotland'. He referred to the third report of the Committee on Fisheries which recalled the success achieved in the 'southern counties' (of Scotland) and the precarious state of linen manufacture in the Highlands where it was only just starting. Even the high duties imposed on foreign linens did not prevent the industry from being under-sold by the Irish, particularly in respect of 'finer species of linen used for shirting for our nobility and gentry'. Emphasizing that his 'address' was prompted only by the duty he owed his constituents, Dempster added that it was not a 'manifesto for a newspaper'; such publicity was not his style.[32] His representations were sympathetically received[33,] but the offer of a meeting at the Office of Trade had to be postponed due to his having 'to attend Mrs Dempster at the Abbey' (Westminster Abbey) on the date chosen.[34]

Yet another appeal to Lord Liverpool was sent on the same day. No sooner had his earlier letter of 26 May been closed than Dempster received a visit from a Mr Thomas B. Bryant. Given what Dempster referred to as 'the present state of our Russian Treaty', and his view that the country should be 'rather less dependant on that power for some of our naval resources', he was convinced that the ideas he had listened to from this Dunbar manufacturer of sail cloth could also be of interest to His Lordship. One step might be extending the bounty to the growing of hemp, another increased Scottish production of cordage. In typical Dempster manner, he did not think His Lordship 'would find half an hour mis-employed in hearing this Gentleman'. Furthermore, if Lord Liverpool 'should incline to send for him', Dempster explained that he was 'to be heard of at the 'George and Vulture' tavern in Cheapside'.[35]

The next day Dempster invited Grimur Jonsson Thorkelin to his home for breakfast at 9 o'clock.[36] He had met this Icelandic antiquarian and historian towards the end of 1786 soon after his arrival from Denmark and when Thorkelin was in lodgings with a Mrs Wood in Brownlow Street near Drury Lane. Their friendship was to continue until Dempster's death. Having received the title of Professor Extraordinary at Copenhagen University, Thorkelin had successfully applied to the Danish king for a grant to visit England in search of documents about the early history of the Norsemen. As a scholar, and likely to be appointed head of the Danish State Archives, his reputation was sufficient for him to be enthusiastically welcomed in London where, having made contact through John Pinkerton with the Hon John Cochrane (the 5th son of the 8th Earl of Dundonald), he was soon received by George III and Queen Charlotte at Windsor. The King later opened his private library to him at Buckingham Palace.[37] His visit had been sponsored by both Sir John Sinclair, about whom more will be heard later and who had met him in Denmark, and Lord Buchan, the founder of the Society of Antiquaries of Scotland. He soon had many friends in London and was to be much lauded for his first transcription of the *Beowulf* manuscript which he found in the British Museum.

Warm as Thorkelin's welcome among antiquarians became, Dempster would have been anxious to see that his friend's earliest encounter with officialdom was not repeated. The tale of his brush with Customs at Gravesend when he arrived the previous August aboard the *Nestor* would have reminded him of his half-brother's own difficulties with government servants in Cork in 1785. It summed up much that foreign visitors suffered at that time. Thorkelin told the story that 'at Gravesend, there came aboard two customs officers, and again below Greenwich the ship was searched by the General Inspector. They (the customs officers) remained unmovable in the ship until it was entirely unloaded, and watched closely that nothing was carried to land from cases, barrels and the like, except to the royal customs house. I and my baggage also had to go there, where everything is called <u>Germanic</u> or <u>French</u>. I was closely examined, clothes, books and each separate paper taken up and shaken and laid down, according to the nature of the circumstances, in the greatest disorder. Now I thought at last to receive them: but was mistaken and was kept waiting no less a time than till the 25th. Then I was told I must pay £5 8s.6d, the half being the duty on the books and manuscripts, the remainder being simply perquisites for a vast number of officers. The hand-written books and things are and ought to be free, and yet I had to pay duty on them which is done in a peculiar way. They have to be valued by the owner, and the valuations confirmed by oath according to the English fashion which is that, while the oaths are recited in the so-called <u>Council,</u> the swearer holds a Bible, and kisses it at the conclusion. Strange, I thought, that these people should curse the catholics, and yet follow their habits.' Having endured all the hardships at sea and believing that all was now over he had then encountered 'the worst of all'.[38]

As a result, Dempster now wanted to carefully 'concert' the arrangements made for the Professor's visit to Scotland. He was to join the tour starting on 25 June by the Fisheries Committee who were visiting possible development sites on the West Coast. Dempster was to be a member of the Society's team and, as he told Thorkelin, 'he had undertaken to witness the laying of the foundation stone of a New Town or two'.[39] Both Knox and Anderson favoured the neighbourhood of Dunvegan on Skye, Stornaway in Lewis, Loch Boisdale in South Uist, Tobermory on Mull and Bowmore in Islay, but more detailed appraisals had to be made on the spot. The absence of any roads or possible road access to many of the sites, and the fact that excessively high building costs would rule out others, meant that close inspection was vital. A week later Dempster told Thorkelin that the party would be leaving London on the evening of 7 June and that he had arranged for him to be accompanied in the post-chaise to Scotland by another member of the team, his MP friend Mr Isaac Hawkins Browne. So that the two men could become acquainted beforehand, Dempster suggested that they met at Waghorn's Coffee House in Old Palace Yard and then the three of them could walk together to Browne's house in Abingdon Street. Thereafter, he hoped Thorkelin would join him for dinner.[40]

Just before the Society's seven top men[41] set out with Thorkelin for what was to be an important tour the Duke of Argyll received via Lord Breadalbane 'a collection of extracts, amounting to four score pages, from every paper and letter given to the Society . . . in the words of the different correspondents themselves'.[42] The team's secretary was determined that they should each have proper information. Sharing Hawkins Browne's post-chaise, Thorkelin left London on 7 June, stopping off at Birmingham, Bolton, Halifax, Leeds, Manchester, Sheffield, Edinburgh, Linlithgow, Stirling and Dunkeld, before joining the remainder of the party at the Duke's castle in Inveraray nearly three weeks later. Then, duly refreshed, the full party travelled to Mull where several hundred acres were to be acquired, going on to Staffa, Coll, Islay, Canna and Dunvegan at Loch Bay on the west of Skye. After crossing to Harris, they explored sites in Stornaway in Lewis, returning to the mainland at what was to be Ullapool; then on to Lochinver and south to Gruinard and Loch Torridon before reaching Oban via Skye on 10 August. Dempster's friend, Sir Adam, was at least one of the party to feel the effects of such a gruelling journey; his gout meant that he took another 10 days to reach his home at Kilkerran. Dempster, who had planned to withdraw two weeks before the tour was concluded, also probably suffered as much. He never claimed to be at home on even the calmest of water.

Fortunately for the party the sturdy revenue vessel *Prince of Wales*, under the command of John Campbell, had been put at their disposal. Referred to by the party as a cutter, she was more probably a sloop of 144 tons with a complement of 52 and 16 guns, including two long six-pounders.[43] If the vessel followed the design used in England it would have had an exceptionally long bowsprit; one more than two-thirds the length of the hull gave them the extra speed needed to chase smugglers. They encountered no rough weather even in the Minch; instead, the captain complained about the lack of wind and a calm sea.

Beaufoy had been unable to join the original party. Instead he had gone separately to Ullapool where he pushed forward with the preliminaries for the purchase of a farm, being joined there by Dempster and Browne when the party returned from the Outer Hebrides. The farm was to form the greater part of the 1,500-acre site of the Society's fishing station; laying out the new town started in 1788.

Dempster provided a friend 'with whom he had shaken hands at Inveraray Castle' with a report on how the team had got on: 'I could have wished you had been with us on our rich expedition, which for good weather, good humour, good entertainment and accommodation could not be overpraised. I don't know whether most to commend the Peers or Commoners of the Committee'. But there was no such richness so far as the Highlanders were concerned. Their industry was that of 'a squirrel in a cage' and their perpetual efforts to 'keep body and soul together' left him disconsolate; they were living in 'huts not hovels . . . without any of those things we call comforts. A pot for potatoes and a few blankets (were) literally the whole furniture of the house where the animals and the people got out at the same hole'. The Committee had, however, been offered 'many spots of 1,500 and 2,000 acres for our new town where, when planted, they will thrive quicker than mushrooms'.[44]

Two decisions had been reached about suitable sites: Ullapool, with which Dempster was to become closely involved, and Tobermory on Mull. Robert Mylne (1733–1818) was appointed as the architect for the second location, where the Duke of Argyll had already put matters in hand. Whilst he was at pains to ensure that 'any person going there (was) not to consider himself absolutely confined to the plan', the new public buildings were to be limited to a custom house which Beaufoy said 'would be instantly established . . . whenever trade should appear there', a storehouse, an inn, and necessary breastworks along the front of the harbour.[45] House plots were lotted out on the hill behind and subsequently occupied by the families of forty-one tradesmen and labourers. As the landowner, the Duke kept a paternal eye on the work and was prepared to be flexible about the land required, even being prepared to buy back the Society's warehouses at 60% of their cost if they were unprofitable, such was the Governor's commitment to the Society's work.

It would seem that for a moment or two, while in the Inner Hebrides, Dempster had fallen out with Sir Adam, more especially about the selection of Tobermory. He had to explain to his friend that he 'would never intentionally make mischief', acknowledging that the reason for their 'frequent diversity of opinions' was that they liked 'one another so much'. Sir Adam's dour, if public-spirited, disposition had its virtues, even when it came to the dreams Dempster may have entertained at this time: 'You never appear to me more amiable than when I see your grave face and sound head prepared to blow all my speculations into the air from whence they came'.[46]

Of all the places visited by the team at this time the island of Canna always exercised a special fascination for Dempster, its magic being responsible for his pressing its claims for development attention well beyond the Society's 'intended plan'. The directors reached Canna 'at four o'clock p.m' (on 5 July 1787) where they were joined by Captain Macleod of Herries in his brig. 'A ling (was) brought on board five and a half feet long, weight 44lbs. (and) three shillings were asked for it, because we were strangers to the price of fish there.'[47]

For several years thereafter it seemed that Canna might become 'a fit station' for one of the Society's villages, not least because of its excellent harbour. The fifty-five tenants there were fisherfolk, if somewhat preoccupied with kelp-making[48] but a suitable site was available and the threat that 'an engrossing tenant' might provoke unnecessary emigration were all good reasons for Dempster's defence of it. There had been time for Dempster to be rowed out round Compass Hill in the company of Sir Adam, Lord Breadalbane and Hawkins Browne, to see a 'singular circumstance' that had been noted by Hector McNeil, a local tacksman. There, 'immediately under the rock . . . the north point of (their) compass veered about, and settled at due south and remained there. At a little distance on either side, the needle recovered its usual position. His Lordship then directed the boat to row with great quickness past the rock when . . . it was again affected'. A vein of iron ore and tuff with a high iron content on Dempster's 'magnetic mountain' provoked the party to conclude that it 'was the largest loadstone as yet discovered in the world'.[49]

While Dempster was on the west coast Mrs Gordon died in London on 18 July. Agnes Augusta had given birth prematurely to yet another child after having borne Thomas five sons in little more than a half a dozen years. Dempster was stunned; it was 'a purely unalloy'd loss and misfortune to me, to her husband, her five boys, her sister Miss Dempster (Ann) and to all her friends, for she was a very good woman and happy in a good husband'.[50] The news did not reach him until 5 August when, having left their companions at Loch Broom, Dempster and Hawkins Browne 'crossed Ross-shire at the wildest and most mountainous part' and reached Tain, where Browne went south to Perth and he across the firth to Skibo.

Skibo was hardly in a state to be welcoming either to Dempster or Thorkelin, who had also arrived after his visit to Thurso, and who, probably exhausted by his five or six weeks travelling, was now confined with a leg ailment and being looked after by Mrs Houston.[51] Since there was much that the new laird and Lord and Lady Gower[52] had to discuss as adjacent landlords, Dempster spent some considerable time at Dunrobin on this visit. In a note to Thorkelin from the Castle he explained his absence and told him how much the Sutherland family was looking forward to meeting him and that all the manuscripts he wanted to see would be available to him once he was fit enough to inspect them. That day Dempster was to see Mr Fraser, his factor, about 'the whitening of the house' (white-washing) which he hoped to see 'shining like silver before (his) return', but a plan had apparently been devised for him to go 'with Lord Gower to make a little expedition to Loch Shin in the interior of the County which may last a few days'.[53] Also to have been included may have been Hugh Rose of Aitnoch, whom Dempster soon came to respect – he 'knows the way to set this country on its legs and does all the good he can'.[54] However, it seemed that he had his doubts about his neighbour's future intentions, 'for noble personages . . . can not enter into the spirit of improvement or see its importance, unless it were by inspiration. The dispositions of both however seems very good'.[55]

Lord Gower was a co-director of the Fisheries Society whom Dempster may not have met outside their formal meetings in London, and certainly not at either of his two principal homes (the other being Trentham in Staffordshire). At Dunrobin Castle he found Leveson-Gower 'a man of taste, virtù, reserved and very well bred', adding, more colourfully for Sir Adam's benefit, that 'he (did) not like the bag-pipe . . . and (had) converted the piper into the porter' at Dunrobin. The Countess, on the other hand, then only 22 years old, occasioned in Dempster a flow of simpler and more direct adjectives when he reported that 'she (was) sensible and engaging and pretty and a good wife'. His obvious admiration would have been influenced by the fact that he, along with Sir Adam and Lord Hailes, had been one of her 'tutors' in 1766 when the Earl and Countess of Sutherland had died, leaving Elizabeth, then barely one year old.[56] She had lived in Edinburgh during her minority and married Earl Gower only two years before.

Rosie, and various members of the family, at last arrived at Skibo in September, having probably been warned not to expect the comfort and attention she enjoyed at Dunnichen and, curious if not anxious, to see what had so preoccupied her husband's attention in the Highlands for well over a year. It was to be a stay of six weeks or so. Dempster had been delighted with the news that they were 'to pay me and this beautiful place a visit' and, despite his fear that 'the season (might be) too far advanced' to show it off properly, a large part of the Dunnichen entourage duly arrived.[57] In addition to his wife, Sir Adam's eldest sister, Jean Fergusson (1728–1804) and niece Betsy (Elizabeth, 1768–1804), they were joined soon after by Captain John's wife Jean, and young George who 'begrudged coming so far and returning'.[58] Another in the party was Dempster's unmarried sister Ann, who was soon asking the last member of the party, Charlotte Burrington, 'whether she sang'. They were to remain there till October when they returned to Angus. Professor Thorkelin probably left a little earlier.

Inevitably Dempster had much to do on the estate and the ladies would have been left largely to their own devices, to say nothing of the professor who may have paid another visit to Sir John Sinclair in Caithness which, to Dempster's disgust, he represented 'as finer than Sutherland'. At Skibo it had been a good year for potatoes and it was to Dugald Gilchrist, who had originally brought 20 bolls of seed potatoes into the county during his time as factor on the Dunrobin estate (1737–1757), that Dempster ascribed the quality of the 'blessed root' the family was then enjoying. Among the agricultural prospects probably not shared with them was the possibility of 'boiling instead of watering flax', gleaned from an article in Donaldson's *Edinburgh Advertiser*. Notwithstanding such diversions, it was clear that the party enjoyed Skibo's aspect, the view of the Dornoch Firth being compared to Dundee at the mouth of the Tay and (what became) Bonar Bridge to Perth, the extreme of its navigation. On the Firth 'if you find two houses within gunshot of each other – I'll eat 'em', said Dempster.[59]

Only towards the end of their stay did the family dare to entertain in their new, and far from yet well-ordered surroundings. On 30 September 'Seaforth and his Lady' dined with them, being served 'a dish of greengages, Orléans plums and French rennet (and) apples as ripe and delicious as . . . could be got in St James's Street'. Rosie greatly enjoyed the occasional ride across the estate and travelled 'like a boatman' across the firth on one of the nearby ferries. Dempster was convinced she would return south 'tolerably broken in for a Highland laird's wife!' Jean's nineteen-year-old sister, Betsy, stayed on when Mrs Hamilton Dempster and young George, who had a persistent sore throat, left early.

'Tearing himself away from the most delightful spot and best climate (he had) ever owned in Scotland'[60], Dempster returned to Dunnichen determined to introduce Thorkelin to someone who had become another frequent guest. It was to be the start of a process that eventually reversed the commonly held opinion that the Scots language was nothing more than a corrupt English dialect.

The Rev John Jamieson (1759–1838), the future lexicographer, had settled in Forfar six years previously when he became the minister of the newly formed seceder congregation in the town.[61] Although he soon proved that he 'had the happy art of making friends of the wise and worthy', it was a period when seceder ministers experienced a good deal of petty persecution and his friendship with the Dempsters was an obvious blessing. The young man was able to borrow from Dempster's library, receive and send letters free of charge (while his friend sat as an MP) and be included in the social circle at Dunnichen House. As Jamieson himself said, 'I would have been blind indeed had I not seen the beneficent operation of Providence in opening up my way to external respectability'.[62] This was to be a lifelong friendship and both men spent many a happy day walking and riding together, returning to Dempster's library for 'intellectual employment' when the weather was bad, often tracing the origins of Scottish vernacular words in continental languages.

The professor soon had Jamieson giving him examples of Highland speech, which he called 'this contemptuous language . . . more ancient than the English', adding with some emphasis, that 'I have now spent four months in Angus and Sutherland, and I have met with between three and four hundred words purely Gothic, that were never used in Anglo-Saxon . . . . All or most of these words that I have noted down, are familiar to me in my native land'. To oblige him, Jamieson wrote down some of the 'remarkable and uncouth words of the district' in a two-penny note book and from this conversation his dictionary of 'two volumes quarto' was to emerge twenty years later.[63] The

A View of the House of Commons about 1725

A line engraving by B. Cole of the **House of Commons in session** in the first half of the 18th century. St Stephen's Chapel, which was 'a rather mean-looking building', had been used since the reign of Edward VI. Visitors may have been impressed by proceedings in the House, particularly during major debates, but the gallery was small and inadequate. The chamber itself was only 1,800 sq. feet in area and the lobby less than half that size.

(Parliamentary Estates Directorate)

During the first decade of the 19th century Rose Dempster's nephew, the Rev. Samuel Bracebridge Heming lived at **Lindley Hall** between Hinkley and Atherstone in Leicestershire. 'Sam', who was always a welcome guest at Dunnichen, was Rector of Drayton and an honorary fellow of Caius College, Cambridge.

(The Record Office for Leicestershire & Rutland)

The print by Bougeard shows the **Pont Royale** at Orléans from le quai de Prague. Built between 1750 and 1760 it was much admired by all. The Dempster family rented a house with a vineyard a little to the south of the city during their stay in 1778.

(cl R. Malnoury – Inventaire Général Centre, 1976, ADAGP)

Although this photograph of the **Cotton Mill** at **Stanley** alongside the River Tay includes many later additions it still gives an idea of what Dempster, the Duke of Atholl and the Perth 'adventurers' were about when they started the business around 1785. Unfortunately, a fire in 1799 resulted in Dempster losing a huge sum of money which he could only hope to make up from the profits of another voyage to India by his half-brother, Captain John. *(Louis Flood Photographers)*

Caldecote Hall in Warwickshire, a drawing by Henry Jeayes (c. 1790-1800). Part of the house 're-edified' at the start of the 17th century is shown, but it and the parish church to the right were altered out of all recognition in the 19th century. The Hall was the home of Rose Heming at the time of her marriage to George Dempster in 1774 when it was rented by her brother George.
(Birmingham City Archives, Aylesford Country Seats and Castles)

The engraving above shows **Skibo Castle** as it looked in 1890, some seven years before Andrew Carnegie, the Scottish-born American steel magnate, purchased the estate. The smaller house to the left may have been used by the Dempsters, but it was demolished with other parts of the property to make way for the construction of Carnegie's mansion. When George Dempster and his half-brother Captain John Hamilton acquired Skibo in 1785 it comprised some 4,000 acres and was in much need of improvement. The estate increased in size to 22,000 acres and, although both men made valiant efforts to provide housing and employment locally, the property was only lived in for short periods by its first Dempster owners, despite being for George 'the only habitable spot in Scotland he ever was possessed of'. *(W.A. Macdonald)*

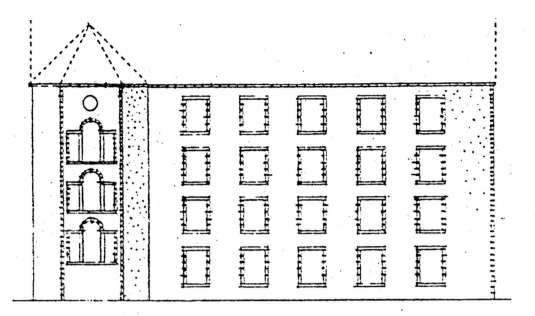

East Elevation – partly re-constructed

Plan of **Spinningdale Mill** based on a site survey by the *Royal Commission on the Ancient and Historical Monuments of Scotland in 1966.*

A photograph of the now ruined **Spinningdale Mill** on Dornoch Firth. Constructed in 1792/3 the mill had in part been funded by 'tobacco lords and Virginia planters', Glasgow merchants whom Dempster persuaded to risk a hundred pounds or so each. It was to produce shawls and handkerchiefs, and in providing local employment Dempster hoped it would reduce emigration. Sold in 1805, it was lost to fire a year later. *(Royal Commission on the Ancient and Historical Monuments of Scotland)*

A delightful drawing of **Dunnichen House** *the property of George Dempster Esq.,* taken from *Forfarshire Illustrated*, published by Gershom Cumming, engraver, 1848.
(Royal Commission on the Ancient and Historical Monuments of Scotland)

A photograph of **Dunnichen House** taken by J.B. White of Dundee in 1925. The house is surrounded by many of the trees grown by Dempster in his nursery.

(RCAHMS and Whiteholme [Publishers] Ltd.)

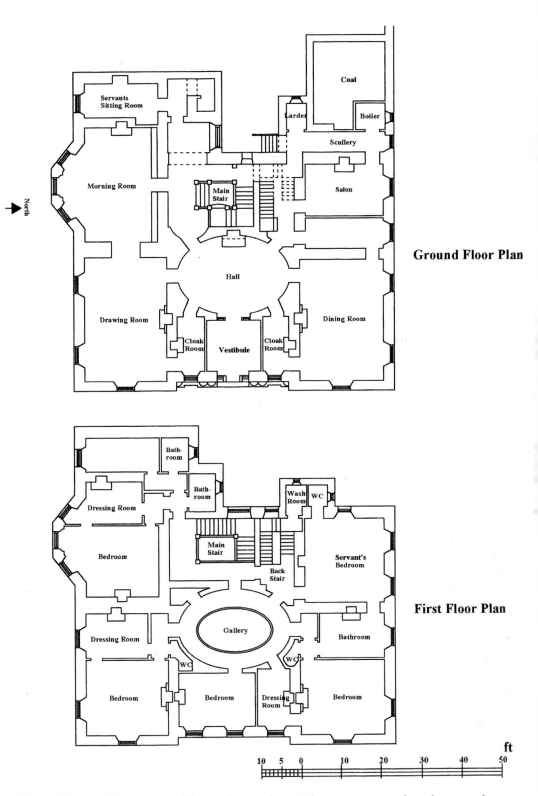

Ground Floor Plan

First Floor Plan

Floor Plans of **Dunnichen House** from a late 19th century record as they may have been after the extensive redevelopment of the mid-1790s and redrawn by Trevor Black, Architects, Invergordon.

(Royal Commission on the Ancient and Historical Monuments of Scotland)

The interior of **Dunnichen House** following the redevelopment set in train by Dempster between 1794-95. Photographs of the Hall and Gallery were taken in 1966 when the property was for sale. The house was demolished in 1970. *(RCAHMS)*

support Thorkelin provided, however, was not to be acknowledged in the dictionary itself.

Thorkelin left soon afterwards to receive an honorary law degree at the University of St Andrews (26 October 1787), some three years after Dempster had been granted his own Hon.LL.D.[64] He then rode south via Edinburgh and Dunbar and Dempster soon wanted to know of his safe arrival at his lodgings in Brownlow Street, off London's Drury Lane, and how much he had sold his horse for. Like the good host he was, he arranged for the shirt the professor had left behind at Dunnichen to be available for collection at the London Coffee House in Ludgate Street.[65]

Writing to the Duke of Argyll with an account of the costs likely to be involved in building wharves, warehouses, houses and inns at the Fisheries Society settlements, Dempster feared that his long report would 'tire his Grace's patience to read it'. A similar account, when '*his* fingers were tired', had been sent to Sir Adam, along with the warning that his theories about what might be achieved in the Highlands 'had been nearly overset' by what he had found in Dornoch, the neighbouring village to Skibo. It was 'the most miserable of places altho' anybody who likes to set up a trade in it (was) free to do so, as I was told – but my mind was agreeably relieved when I learnt that much of the property of that town belongs to the Countess of Sutherland whose guardians had not authority to feu the lotts for building houses in the room of the present hutts and ruinous pig-stys.'[66]

Dempster became more closely associated with the Society's development on Loch Broom in 1788. Mull, on the other hand, was in safe hands, even if it became more of a commercial and less of a fisheries success. The Loch Bay project went ahead later, only to be frustrated by a long-drawn-out land deal, uneven local support, unwelcome emigration to America and environmental and administrative problems which were never fully resolved. Dempster's pleading for Loch Bay as 'one of the finest situations for a seaport town in Europe'[67] and his personal negotiations with Macleod of Macleod eventually pushed the project forward, enabling 1,000 acres to be purchased, but the heart of the local population was never won.

As for Canna, Dempster's 'private rhapsody', which 'was so well placed . . . that it would be almost inexcusable in the Society to suffer it to slip through their fingers',[68] it was not to be. He had gone out on a limb only to find himself forced to agree with the Society that the island's lessee had demanded an exorbitant price for the land they wanted. By June 1790 he concluded that 'I fear it is over with Cannay (sic). We have a perfect right to refuse . . . so farewell Bonny Cannay . . . farewell poor inhabitants'.[69]

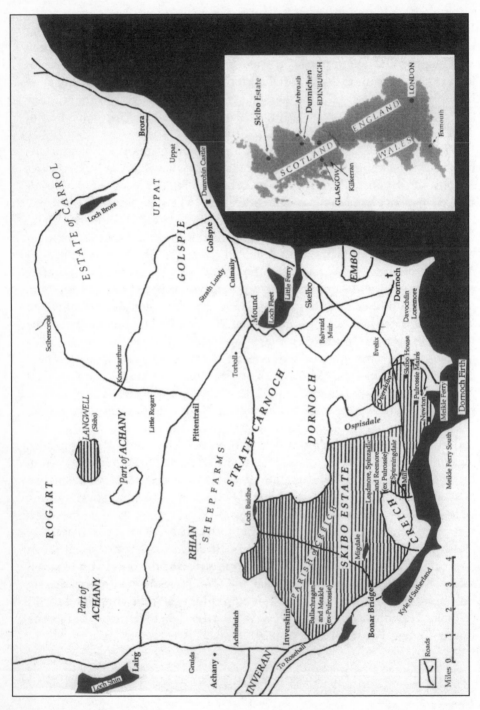

Sketch Plan of Skibo Estate at the end of the 18th Century (*incorporating ex-Pulrossie and Overskibo land*)

10

SKIBO IS ACQUIRED
(1786 – 1787 PART 2)

'The only habitable spot in Scotland I ever was possessed of'.
(Dempster to Sir Adam Fergusson, 10 November 1786)

1786

In the spring of 1786 Dempster persuaded himself of the wisdom of acquiring a second country estate. It was a surprising decision from almost every point of view and one that soon had many of his friends reeling, if not the family too. It looked as if he had lost all good sense, and for someone who was no stranger to the consequences of rash decisions about money, and whose close financial shaves had nearly put an end to his political ambitions once before, it looked like an aberration. With his finances always in a precarious state such a purchase could only be made by added indebtedness and when it became clear that the interest payments were unlikely to be offset by income from the estate, at least for many years, the prospect must have looked bleak.

It was not as if it was an acquisition in Angus, a part of the country with which he was familiar, but one in the Highlands, 150 miles to the north and on the east coast about which he knew little.[1] His ignorance about Skibo, the extent of the property and the lie of the land, which was 'much greater than I imagined' was admitted a year later when he 'rode round it' and found for the first time Lochs Buie and Laggan, as well as Migdale.[2] Furthermore, bidding as he did for both a Sutherland and a Caithness estate at the same auction only illustrated how speculative the decision had been. Among the reasons subsequently put forward to explain it was his wish 'to put into practice on a larger scale his views on the duties of a landlord, and to assist thereby a far more wretched part of the agricultural population of Scotland than the farmers of Angus'.[3] He may have been stirred by Knox and Anderson's portrayal of the Highlander's plight, but this alone hardly accounted for his actions. Much more likely would have been a chance tip about the estates' disposal from one of his lawyer friends in Edinburgh. For the announcement to have had this effect, he must have been trying to fit together the pieces of what became an

177

intricate jigsaw. One can only surmise what went through Dempster's mind when William Ramsay, the Edinburgh solicitor, sent him the articles of roup.[4]

The *Caledonian Mercury* of 26 April 1786 carried the first of more than a dozen advertisements which appeared in the Scottish press announcing a 'Judicial Sale of Lands in the Counties of Sutherland and Caithness', either together or separately.[5] Hugh Inglis, one of the previous owner's creditors, a Bengal merchant and later Chairman of the East India Company, had set the process in motion.[6] The auction at New Session House in Edinburgh was scheduled for 5 July. In addition to the rents in money and kind, the notice provided a general description of the two estates. As surveyed, Skibo itself then contained 3,946 acres (excluding three sheilings for pasture) and 'the greatest part of the lands' were 'one entire free barony, called the *Barony of Skibo*'. The gardens, 'which were of remarkable good lands', and mains [home farm] of Skibo consisted of 319 acres, with the farm enclosed and neatly subdivided in small enclosures, surrounded with belts of planting, hedges and hedgerows. A 'convenient' mansion house had a large pigeon house and 'proper' office houses. Langwell, the second property scheduled to come under the hammer, was a separate item above Berridale Braes on the Caithness coast and evidently more attractive, with its mansion house in 'beautiful and romantic' surroundings, and 'no cattle more acceptable to drovers than from this estate'.[7]

Dempster had obviously devised a plan that he could justify to himself and which he hoped eventually would overcome the anxiety shown by family and friends and mollify the inevitable opposition to what they feared could be an investment too far. Humanitarian motives played some part in his thinking, but he relished devising schemes for the benefit of his family just as much as for the common weal. There is little doubt that Captain John and Dempster had spoken generally about the desirability of his half-brother giving up his life at sea – his wife was carrying their first child – and settling down in Scotland, and that the auction of Skibo in July became a possible way of bringing this about. Dempster certainly did not act alone. Both men were well aware that unusually good fortune would be needed if Jack was to pay for the estate's purchase 'in a voyage or two', given the constant risks and growing doubts about the profitability of long Eastern voyages. Moreover, even if its capital indebtedness could be wiped out, the estate's renovation and development would be a serious drain on their resources for many years to come.

Dempster could never keep his plans completely to himself, but his closest friends were often the last to know what he intended. The Pitfour fish merchant was probably one of the first to learn what 'My brother Capt Dempster and I have decided'. Writing to James Richardson in June, Dempster begged him not to say anything about it until he gave him the all clear. They had 'sent (an) offer as high as 30 years purchase for both or either

178

estate' expecting that by the time his letter reached Pitfour from London 'it will have changed Masters'. Although convinced that Skibo was worth 'at least £5 per acre', Dempster was far from certain which estate he wanted. As to Langwell, 'by my information here it runs six or eight miles into the country and seven miles along the coast. This makes about 40 square poles or nearly 20,000 acres, at present in a state of nature. Of the two I am not sure but this would be the most desirable purchase'.[8]

Life was wretched on what would eventually become a 22,000 acre estate[9], 'from the point of Ardnacalk on the north bank of Dornock (sic) westward to Port Leak . . . an extent of 12 or 14 miles'.[10] As Dempster concluded when he came to write the annex to the OSA, there may have been 200 or so families living on these estates, with the exception of the mains of each place. 'The farms are of small extent in regard to arable land. They produce some corn and potatoes, hardly sufficient to maintain the families of the tenants. They pay their rents by the sale of cattle, which are fed in their houses, on straw, through the winter, and pick up a miserable subsistence on the waste and common ground of the estate, during the summer. The whole of the present rent is from £700 to £800 a year, of which more than a fourth part is paid by the two large farms belonging to the mains, or mansion house. The estates furnish some wood, with which, and the swarded surface of the ground, cut into the form of large bricks, they make houses and offices for themselves, covering them with the same swarded turfs, cut thinner, and resembling slates in their form. Once in three years, all the earthy part of these houses is thrown on the dunghill, and new houses built again of the same materials. The cattle commonly occupy one end of the house during the winter season. Some holes in the walls and roofs serve for windows and chimneys. An iron pot for boiling their food constitutes their principal furniture. Nothing can exceed the wretched appearance of these habitations'.[11]

Such a prospect would have daunted even the most optimistic and wealthy developer; little wonder that the proposed purchase attracted the opprobrium and concern of his friends. The great famines of 1783 and 1784 had made their mark on the 1700 souls in the parish of Creich which stretched from Invershin in the west to the boundary with Dornoch in the east. The number of the population was broadly the same as at the start of the century, despite some emigration to the Americas and a drift of more people away from the parish's western fringes towards the coast. Able to understand some English, but generally Gaelic-speaking, they were 'inoffensive', law-abiding folk, all without exception belonging to the established Church, the source of pitiful poor relief, cut off from other similar Highland communities whose young migrated each spring and summer to the south in search of better-paid work. Their parents scratched out a living on thin soil and land owned for the most part by those rarely in residence. Survival depended on neighbour helping neighbour, coping as best they could with irregular harvests which produced a plenty and then a scarcity of fodder, food and subsistence crops, and management practices that were unchanging rather than improving.

Skibo had been a Viking stronghold till the 10th century. By the 13th century it was in ecclesiastical ownership and a bishop's palace until Dornoch Castle took over this role in the 16th century. The estate's fortunes had been tied up with those of the Gray family for two hundred years. However, around 1744 the lands fell into the hands of Sir Patrick Dowall, the Gray's Edinburgh lawyer, and by 1751 the Hon George Mackay, his nephew, the Member for Sutherland and younger son of Lord Reay, had succeeded him.[12] He at least restored the farms, undertook a little afforestation and built two houses to the south and west of the castle which itself remained uninhabitable. Nevertheless, after 5 years his debts outstripped him and the property was sold to William Gray, himself a remote member of the Gray family. He was a retired sugar planter who had made his fortune on the Herboreal estate in Jamaica where he had become Provost Marshal. Like his predecessors, he too set improvements in train and, with his greater financial resources, was able to develop Skibo (and apparently the Langwell Estate in Caithness), putting some life into the erstwhile deserted farms and crofts. After four years of endeavour he died at Skibo in 1760, having found the upkeep of the estate a losing battle, much as each of the previous owners had done. Initially his widow, Janet (Sutherland) Gray,[13] tried to continue her husband's re-development, hoping that it would once again become an echo of the palatial residence it had been in the 13th century during Gilbert of Moravia's time. She was at least able to give the castle a slate roof, a rare benefit in those days and the first of two in the county (the other being the cathedral in Dornoch). Then, finding the life too unsophisticated for her taste, she withdrew to London, leaving Skibo to be a worrying nightmare for another 20 years and without the affection it needed. She had only recently died, aged 90.

Most records indicate that Dempster purchased the estate without much ado. In the event, it was a far from straightforward acquisition with legal processes and Dempster's search for the funds with which to close the purchase persisting from 1786 to 1790. It was to cause him much consternation. The sasine [deed] states that he 'was seised (sic) in the lands of Skibo Castle, called the mains of Skiboll, on 22 January 1787', much understating the saga.[14] What seems to have happened was that William Gray's not inconsiderable debts had never been paid off, either during his own or his wife's lifetime and an appeal to the High Court in Edinburgh in 1780 led to the properties being regarded as those of a bankrupt, hence the sequestration order and their ownership passing to the Court of Session.[15] The Court in turn appointed a 'judical' factor to manage the properties until such time as a sale could reimburse the creditors.

William Ramsay had been authorized to bid on Dempster's behalf. Three days after the auction he reported that 'the estates were exposed separately,

Langwell first, which was purchased by Sir James Hunter Blair[16] for £7,350, which was about £175 above my Commission' (the limit he had been given by Dempster). 'Skibo, I purchased for £11,500'.[17] The 'upset' or reserve prices had been £8,866 and £4,195 respectively. A recapitulation of the proceedings included in the papers given to the High Court in 1790 explained that 'in consequence of a process of Ranking and Sale,[18] brought at the instance of Hugh Inglis, late of Calcutta and now of London, against William Gray and his creditors, the lands of Skibo and others were . . . exposed to sale before Lord Eshgrove'. There, they 'were purchased on behalf of (Dempster) at the price of £11,500 Sterling'.[19]

Dempster had, however, 'granted (a) Bond for the price with a Cautioner' and a 'Decreet of Sale was pronounced in his favour'. In fact, his old and ever-generous friend Pulteney had provided the bridging finance. The estate was so encumbered with secured debts and fixed charges that it took some considerable time to resolve the ranking of creditors on the proceeds of the sale, a process not helped by the Court's slow administration of Gray's affairs. Dempster sought to acquire the superiority of what he had purchased, i.e the *dominium utile*, with a view among other things of acquiring the fishing! This called for lengthy interpretation of mediaeval documents couched in language no longer in use.[20] As the result, it was not until 1790 that the 'Ranking of the Creditors' was finally pronounced and 'a remit obtained from (the) Lordships to Lord Alva . . . to authorise a scheme of division'. When this was prepared and an Act approving the scheme pronounced on 22 December 1789 the judge found 'the same was to be the rule for the purchaser paying the price'. This meant that only by 1790 had Dempster 'made payment to the different creditors . . . according as they (were) allocated (within) the sum of £11,500'.

During the two-day hearing before the Court of Session at the beginning of June 1790 Dempster was at last able to state that he had 'fulfilled what was incumbent upon him by the . . . Articles of Sale' and consequently an application was made on his behalf for 'a Warrant to get the Bond he granted with a Cautioner for the price . . . delivered up'. Lord Alva appointed a writer to examine and report on the petition and the matter was finally concluded at the end of the month. How Dempster was to achieve his subsequent mortgage became clear slowly.

The creditors who had been discharged included Hugh Inglis, from London and 'late of Calcutta', who received £4,052; John Cartier, of Westminster and late Governor of Bengal, the sum of £3,939, and Sir William Forbes of the bankers James Hunter Blair & Co. a further £3,309.[21] Together with some £200 paid to Isaac Grant, the sum of £11,500 finally 'exhausted' Dempster's purchase price. Others, including Captain Charles Gordon from whom the nearby Pulrossie estate was also to be bought, had originally made claims[22,] but Inglis and Cartier were the preferential creditors, each having loaned Gray the sum of £7,500 in 1777, secured on the lands at Skibo and Langwell. Their separate petitions had been heard in 1788, only for them to be remitted for examination until Inglis forced the issue in 1790.

Writing from Edinburgh, William Ramsay told Dempster that the agent who had conducted the sale of Skibo 'had informed him that the note of the admeasurement had been taken from the information given him by . . . the former proprietor'. He also enclosed a copy of the Judicial Rental, that set by the Court of Session. Belatedly, and unaware of the temporary financial support Dempster had from Pulteney, Ramsay suggested that Sir Hector Munro, the MP for Inverness, might be the best person to help him.[23] A later letter from Ramsay to the factor clearly showed that there had been a dispute about the price and whether or not the mains was included in the sale.[24]

It was not until the end of 1788 that the purchase of the Pulrossie estate from Charles Gordon could be made. Bought by Captain John 'with his own cash', it was made up of several separate stretches of land along the Dornoch Firth. Those at Ballachragan and Meakle (now Maikle) to the north-west of Bonar Bridge were farthest from the mains; nearer was the land around Spinningdale which included the old Leadmore oak plantation and the burn down from Loch Migdale. The Murrays of Pulrossie had earlier styled them-selves 'of Spanziedale'.[25] Both estates abutted parts of Earl Gower's land together with that of other owners such as Gilchrist of Ospisdale who, in turn, farmed the land at Airdens above Bonar.

When in the possession of Mr J.Salt around 1765 the mains, Newton (Point) and part of Fload amounted to some 500 acres, but the Pulrossie estate as a whole was considerably larger. Writing to Graham of Fintry, Dempster explained that it had a proportionately better rent role and that a deal had been done at £7,500. The rental of £300 compared favourably with Skibo's net income of £400. The arrangement meant that he could 'mortgage it with Skibo for the price of Skibo (£11,500). I think there can hardly be better security than that . . . in the world, especially corroborated with (the) Captain's and my personal bonds'.[26]

Dempster was by then seeking the long-term funding he needed and 'Willie' Ramsay had 'only been able to hear of £10,000 to be lent on this security at 5%'. It seemed for a time that Mr D. Erskine, a business friend of Robert Graham, might be prepared to lend at a half per cent cheaper: 'I cannot tell you how much this would conduce to the happy arrangement of my affairs for a few years till the Captain be able to pay for both'.[27] To avoid giving offence to Ramsay, Dempster asked Fintry to apply for it in his own name. It turned out, however, that Erskine was only prepared to offer £5,000 at the lower rate and he had to contemplate 'getting the payment of Skibo postponed till Martinmas', to make certain that all the funds were in place.[28]

These problems were only resolved in July 1789 when, in a particularly adroit move, the much-sought-after 10-year mortgage was at last secured at four and a half per cent. With relief, Dempster told Fintry that William Young

(– 1824), the natural son of Patrick, Lord Elibank, had agreed to provide him with £12,000. Thirty years before, Elibank had been one of the lawyers who had assumed the management of the Canongate Theatre. His son, now a fine gentleman – though evidently not known personally to Dempster, had gone out to India as a Writer in 1765 and, after being appointed Collector of Tirhoot, rose to be third in the Council at Patna. He returned to England in the summer of 1786 with a fortune and a share in an Indiaman.[29] This time Young was to employ Erskine 'as his man of business' in a deal which William Ramsay and John Johnstone, Dempster's *bete noire* from his days at India House, had agreed to facilitate. Its terms were so good that Dempster fearfully recalled an earlier deal that had fallen through when the lender then had 'eaten his fingers with vexation'.[30] It had obviously been touch and go whether he could fund the deal.

During the settlement period, consideration had been given to acquiring the small estate at Overskibo to the north-east of Pulrossie. The Overskibo lands had been held by another branch of the Gray family from 1642. When George Ross of Pitkerrie, who had carried on a business in London as an army agent under the name Ross & Ogilvy, died in 1786[31] his estate came on to the market. Mr A. Ross, writing from Argyll [Street or shire] in September 1787, apologized for not being able to accommodate Dempster personally, as Overskibo was in the hands of the trustees of his marriage. It was nevertheless their intention (Mr Oswald and Sir Thomas Dundas, – the MP for Stirlingshire) to dispose of it and Ross 'was in great hopes that Dempster would be the purchaser'.[32] A Mr Andrew Davidson seems to have been in occupation at the end of 1788,[33] and it was not until 1795 that a deal was finally struck at £2,100, a little more than its value.[34]

Unlike Dempster's other home in Forfarshire, built by his grandfather, little is known about what the mansion house at Skibo looked like and which Dempster and his heirs occupied until 1866.[35] It was largely obliterated by Andrew Carnegie and intervening owners a little more than a century later, being transformed into a baronial palace. The small handful of other habitable properties on the estate, including Pulrossie House, avoided such a fate, but at the time Dempster acquired them none were in a wholly satisfactory condition. Such brief references as had been made about the elderly Mrs Gray's roofing or to the terraces below the castle being firmed up and the gardens being improved add little to the picture of the property at this time. It seems that the mansion had received some attention in 1782 and, although generally water-tight, rain got into several of the adjacent houses which Mackay had built (including an apartment for a housekeeper and the servants hall) since the roof and gutter leadwork had not been properly overlapped.[36]

On 10 November 1786 Dempster was impatiently awaiting a delivery of the deeds of Skibo at the family's new London home in Knightsbridge: 'the moment they do I shall sign them and wait on Pulteney to do the same'.

Having had time to digest Sir Adam's lengthy advice to him about the purchase, Dempster was in a mood to be frank with his friend. Ten days previously the ever-cautious solicitor had written him a long gloomy epistle about the wisdom of proceeding as he intended, probably echoing the thoughts of the family at that time.[37] He had not been privy to Dempster's plans and, although pleased that the money for the purchase had been found 'so as to avoid any embarrassment about the price of Skibo', Sir Adam now argued at length about the futility of improving land that was unlikely to produce enough income to justify the expense and feared that the cost of borrowing, which he assumed Dempster had to make, would not be recovered by income from the property. He envisaged Dempster having to find a tenant for Skibo since the alternative of keeping it himself, even during his lifetime, was 'not a choice' in his opinion. In the event of his death, it would be undesirable for his heir, perhaps abroad or living between 200 or 600 miles away – to find himself burdened with a farm in Sutherland which, even if it could be sold, would probably not fetch its original price. To these not unreasonable warnings Sir Adam added his 'clear conviction' that if Dempster wanted to purchase an estate it should be in the lowlands. In his friend's opinion, Skibo was an inconvenient and remote location where 'the excessive poverty of the people' meant that it would be the duty of anyone settling among them to improve their lot and 'assiduously by every means . . . rendering their situation easier'.

In a dozen or so lines Dempster answered what Sir Adam's 'unimaginative common sense' had taken six pages to express.[38] His five 'justifications' were:

- 'I agree with you if the money were always to be borrowed; but if (the property is) worth keeping, Jack will pay for it in a voyage or two'
- 'If the difference between the rent and interest is pay'd out of my savings, which I am certain I am able to do . . . there is no great harm'
- 'I am anxious my brother should have a farther inducement than even a wife and children to save money'
- 'If it shall be deemed expedient to part with this estate it will not sell the worse that we are not obliged to sell it' – and finally,
- 'It is actually the only habitable spot in Scotland I ever was possessed of'.[39]

A few days before, Dempster's solicitor neighbour James Guthrie of Craigie, a partner in Guthrie and Storie in Edinburgh,[40] had written welcoming the fact that he had 'found in London funds to answer the term of payment of Skibo, for had you left it to your friends here we could not have borrowed so large a sum under £5%'. Nonetheless, he too took Dempster to task for his decision to buy Skibo and revealed that he had not only a very close understanding of how his friend's financial affairs were likely to be adversely affected but an intimate knowledge of the area around the property and how desperately poor many in Sutherland were. Guthrie considered that, whilst 'the distant advantages' his friend expected appeared very uncertain, the 'inconveniences' were 'inevitable'. Outliving his client, and becoming one of Dempster's executors, he was someone in whose 'abilities and integrity' he had 'implicit confidence'.[41] When Guthrie concluded that 'I have examined the state of your last year's expenses, which I imagine are much the same with former years, and I protest I know not wherein you can expect to retrench a great deal', Dempster must have known how potentially undermining of his affairs the deal was. Having long wished to see Dempster's income increased, 'because I think you could enjoy it', Guthrie now feared that it would be difficult for him to live in London on less than he had done and anticipated that even without the costs associated with improvements at Skibo, Dempster's income would fall by £300 a year.

Guthrie was careful to distinguish between the potential of the estate for someone with the time and money to develop it and a man such as Dempster whom he feared had placed too much weight on the contribution Captain John's future voyages might make to the family's available capital. Dempster had probably used the same words to Guthrie as those written to Sir Adam Fergusson, that 'Jack will pay for it in a voyage or two'. But Guthrie knew only too well that borrowing money at 5% and achieving a land yield of only 3% could spell trouble for someone with limited funds. He was himself in process of buying part of Fintry's land next to his own at Craigie on similar terms, and, as he said of Skibo, 'Nobody can be more sensible than I am of the uncommon beauties and many advantages of that estate; I have admired its fine exposure, its excellent soil, its great extent, its rich shelly banks, its quarries of free stone,[42] its fine navigable basin, its dry walks, its trouting river, the populessness (sic) of the country, the cheapness of labour, the adjoining estates just now on the market etc., etc., etc.' In short, it was 'a most desirable purchase . . . for a man from beyond Inverness who would reside (there)', but nothing short of a 'mill stone' for Dempster, especially when account was taken of the exhausted state of the land, 'beggared' tenants, their ruined houses and 'everything about it daily growing worse'. Guthrie's final fling was to conclude that it was an 'immense' distance away from Dunnichen,[43] 'so impracticable to yourself in winter' and without someone 'whose fidelity' could be trusted, the estate would be impossible to manage.[44]

1787

With his half-brother's departure aboard the *Rose* and his attendance at Westminster commanded earlier than usual in February, Dempster had little time that first winter after Skibo's purchase to come to grips with his additional responsibilities. Depending heavily on the advice of the local gentry regarding appointments and sources of supplies needed for the estate, he had to familiarize himself with a largely unknown assembly of people and put together a team that could be trusted to carry on during his absences. The first priority had been the appointment of a factor. With Dempster away for long periods, a good pair of eyes and ears were called for. Such a management linchpin would determine what might be achieved and the working relationship between the two men would be crucial. A factor had considerable discretionary powers and the boundaries of their responsibilities in the 18th century were often ill-defined. The keeping of basic records and the collection of rents, preferably in an unobtrusive manner, was as essential as being a good organizer. John Fraser was a natural choice and came recommended by Colonel Sutherland and Dugald Gilchrist, neighbouring landowners at Uppat and Ospisdale. Dempster appears not to have met him before making his appointment, and Fraser to have cheerfully accepted 'any allowance' Dempster was pleased to give him. The son of an Inverness vintner, he had worked his way up from being a confidential clerk to the important position of factor to Earl Gower on the Sutherland estate. He had been the judicial manager for Skibo during the period the estate was in sequestration and therefore came to the job knowing a good deal about the property and its tenants, but it was not surprising that Dempster was concerned to test his competence as well as his local knowledge during their initial correspondence in 1786–7. Skibo was a rundown estate with little prospect of supporting many employees. The task ahead required more than the usual diverse range of duties and hard work that he would have been used to. It would have been understandable therefore if, behind the flurry of instructions he issued, Dempster was not also questioning his new factor's motives in accepting what would have been a demotion. He needed to assure himself about the wisdom of Fraser's appointment.

The new factor was soon writing at length about the condition of the estate and wanting Dempster's instructions about the rent roll.[45] Fortunately, Dempster had created a good impression among those whose co-operation he needed, despite having to deal with several at arm's length rather than face to face. His extensive research over the years and growing competence in agricultural matters, particularly on the question of soil fertility, stood him in good stead. The 'Scotch method of improving land by means of lime' which he set out for Thorkelin's benefit a year or so later demonstrated some of the lessons he had learned. Hugh Rose from Nigg also quickly recognized that Skibo's new owner was 'a friend and patron of the deserving industrious'.[46] This was a good start and, after commending a Mr James Roy,[47] Rose undertook to write to him about local 'fisheries, manufactures and shells – and perhaps some political hints'. Dempster let it be known that he wanted to hear all such ideas and, having toyed with shipping shells up the Dornoch Firth to Skibo, Rose was able to tell him that Fraser had already been in touch with someone who had been thwarted by tides and currents in similar experiments. There was, however, 'a good bank of shells mixed with sand near to the ferry' which might be mixed with compost material.[48]

The picture that emerged from six letters sent to Dempster by John Fraser was of an estate 'in quiet desuetude'.[49] It had been much neglected but, to the laird's relief, the conscientious factor had most tasks well in hand. Nevertheless, some tenants had grown accustomed to having the run of the estate and had cut down both planted and natural trees for their own use. Fraser thought that the young ash and birch trees in the nursery, as well as those around the mains which had been 'cut with a knife about a foot above the ground', might have been used by people in the neighbourhood to thresh their corn. He was firmly of the opinion that the 'whole tenantry . . . and others nearest to Skibo . . . ought to be brought before the Justices' to stamp out any repetition of such practices. Rents were to be collected from January 1787, but the value of services previously rendered by the tenants at Clashmugach could not be included in the rent till 'Whitsun Day', the day on which the 'present possessor of Skibo' (unknown) would also be removed. Fraser was able to send Dempster the rents for Newtown,[50] Meikle, Pulrossie and Creich, although they were 'not exact to a pound or a shilling'.

By the middle of February red and white clover seed was being delivered by a small boat from Cromarty to Port Creich through the good offices of John Davidson at Overskibo,[51] although the quantity of rye seed required still depended on a decision being taken about the number of acres to be planted. In Cromarty William Forsyth (and his father James before him) were pioneers of the wholesale trade in grain and farm goods who had launched 'boldly into the speculation at a time when the whole country seemed asleep around him . . . and purchased a freighting boat . . . and hired a large sloop for trading with Holland'.[52] On the question of a prosecution for the earlier damage of trees, Dempster decided not to take precipitate action; that would send the wrong message. Despite some initial opposition, his ideas worked well and Fraser was appreciative of his showing 'so much charity' to his tenants.[53] He only hoped that 'he had not been too indulgent'. The new individual leases were probably to be introduced more slowly than Dempster had originally intended.[54]

With good tenant relations restored and his factor expecting orders in respect of the mains and the gardens at Skibo, several money matters needed settling. Fraser had spent £132 14s. 5d which was rather more than he had collected from the tenants. The stipends of the ministers at Lairg, Creich and Dornoch[55] had to be paid, and Thomas Mackay of Lairg now sought an increase. His stipend had not been augmented since 1718. Fraser was soon able to tell Dempster that a gardener, Robert Ross, had been appointed on trial for a year, albeit that any instructions for him would have to be sent to himself since the man could neither read nor write.[56] Beehives were to be bought, the 'Rheinberg' was not to be touched and he was asked to find out whether there were any fish in Loch Migdale on the estate. Temporary arrangements for both the occupancy of the mains by a Mr Houston and

Overskibo by Davidson required firming up so as to bring order to 'the farm, plantings and enclosures', but, in the event, these had to be put off until Dempster was 'on the spot' and could 'come to a bargain'. Fraser knew how 'much engaged' Dempster was at Westminster, but this did not prevent him from hoping he might be able to return to Sutherland at the end of May or early June.

The first of Dempster's long-mooted agricultural and land tenure reforms, some of which had been tried by others elsewhere in Scotland,[57] were soon to be implemented at Skibo, at a pace which had already made at least one group of tenants uneasy at the idea of change. Determined as he was to ensure that those directly employed, as well as those farming their land, should have 'nothing to divert their attention from their own businesses', he elected to package up his proposals rather than introduce them piecemeal. Writing to Sir Adam Fergusson later that year, he said, 'What I am about is this. You know some part of this purchase is a Highland estate. There are upon it about 40 families. The whole rent, but well paid, is £170. . . . My project is to give this estate what I call a *constitution*. I fix all the present tenants for their lives at the present rent in their houses, gardens and cultivated ground. At their deaths I give the refusal to the person they name for their successor at a rent to be fixed by two arbitrators. . . . I give leave to anybody to settle on the waste ground, paying one shilling a year for their lives. . . . I abolish all personal services'.[58] Whilst other landlords were clearing their tenants off their land Dempster wanted to give his tenants at Dunnichen and Skibo long leases at low rents, thereby encouraging them to cultivate waste ground by abolishing what he called feudal 'personal services', including binding them to cut their landlord's corn, spreading his manure and carrying his coal and peat. Most Scottish tenants resented these obligations.

Calling his new rights the *Constitution of Criech* (*sic*), this being the parish in which Skibo was situated, Dempster hoped that one day they would become more widely accepted as the Constitution of the Highlands. He warned Sir Adam, recalling his earlier experiences with the Duke of Atholl, 'For God's sake don't say a word against it. One word of your mouth will blow away as many happy visions of the future prosperity of the Creichs as ever illumined the dying moments of a saint'. The terms to be offered were, that:

1. Every settler will have given him a stone of iron, for making hammers, and other instruments
2. Also seed, whether potatoes or corn, for what ground shall be culti-vated in the first two years
3. The new settlers will be free from all services whatsoever, and from thirlage[59] to the mill
4. They will only have to pay one shilling a year of rent, during the life-time of the first settler
5. Their heirs or children will have a preferable right to their possessions,

188

of cultivated and enclosed, at such a rent as shall be fixed at the time of their succeeding to the possession, by arbitrators mutually chosen

6. No addition will be made to this rent during the lifetime of the said heir or children

7. The same rule or preference will be observed in favour of all future heirs of the settler; so that possession may belong for ever to the family of the man who made the first settlement: provided always that the heirs and children of the first settler shall build stone houses upon the possession; and that the houses in time coming, be roofed with straw, slate, or heather, and not with divots

8. The new settlers will have a right to take peat from the nearest mosses upon the estate for their own use

The formal phraseology must have bemused many of his tenants but he was aiming to produce a novel two-way deal with them whereby they gained a charter of rights that spelled out fairness and security in exchange for additional income for himself as landlord, based on their expected and increased productivity. 'Part of my project is to contribute my mite towards rendering the Highlands of Scotland the Norway and Sweden of Great Britain by enclosing and planting only such parts of it as has been tirred [denuded] to the bones . . . and at present is certainly not worth one farthing the 100 acres'.[60] Ever employing comparisons with other countries whose rural economies he had either heard about from his friends or seen for himself, he looked forward to the day when 'this country, though mountainous and at present barren, will assume the appearance of North Wales and Switzerland, where liberty (will have) rendered barren mountains fertile and populous.'[61]

For Dempster reform was not, as sometimes suggested, a moral crusade or simply a humanitarian response to those in need. At the heart of all his agricultural and other improvements was the desire to affect the prosperity of communities, industrial as well as rural. A system that could arbitrarily remove a man and his family from his farm, place him at the beck and call of a tacksman and reduce him to beggary or even emigration did nothing for the country. He saw the prevailing feudal system as the single greatest factor preventing incomes from rising, putting more money into local circulation and enabling employment to be generated. Abysmally low incomes and meagre commerce resulted in a continuously faltering economy. It was so counterproductive that the 'lower classes . . . do not yield nett into the Exchequer above 1/72 part of a penny per head from their consumption of . . . articles subject to Excise and Customs'.[62] In Parliament Dempster had demonstrated that his understanding of elementary 'oeconomics' matched his grasp of law. As laird and improver he became convinced that the prosperity achievable by secure and independent tenants, with 'freedom as to their persons and security as to their possessions', would be the bedrock of such financial prosperity as he might achieve. Like others before (and after) him he saw his own self-interest directly determined by what the communities around him could achieve. Poor tenants and employees meant low income for *him*; prosperity meant wealth for *him*.

It is interesting to surmise that, in the midst of so much venal and un-scrupulous behaviour during his days as a director at India House, Dempster may have learned something of the occasionally farsighted and sympathetic administrations in rural areas controlled by 'residents' of the Company over-seas. Although never a member of the Correspondence Committee with its direct access to the huge number of reports, analyses and speculations sent to London from the Company's settlements on the sub-continent and elsewhere, it is hard to believe he did not occasionally delve into this mine of prolific thought. The Committee of Law Suits, of which he was a member, would itself have been concerned to advise and give guidance to far-flung civil administrations. Sitting in the Court of Directors, he certainly considered major despatches requiring comment. That there were those in India who devoted their energies to improving husbandry, inaugurating freer trade, trial by jury in civil cases, or dealing effectively with the complaints of an unhappy peasantry is well documented.

In Sutherland Dempster believed 'he had laid the foundation of a system of improvement to the property which exposed him to no expense, and which might prove highly profitable to (his) heirs'. In a long essay to Thorkelin, but written in the third person, he spoke conservatively about the estate where the rent was only £160 per year and consisted of 5–6,000 acres (a figure nearer that mentioned in the roup) made up of 'hills, dales, marshes, lakes and rivulets' and where only 4–500 acres was cultivated. Fifty or sixty poorly lodged families had been 'harassed a good deal by (having to provide) personal services to the former proprietors and what little money they had was taken from them by the payment of a Septennial Sasine *[sic]* or fine for a lease of seven years'. In August he anticipated that twenty new settlers would be 'on the barren hills' by 1789 and 'the following year will produce, I hope, twice the number'. For the benefit of Thorkelin and 'his Danish friends', Dempster compared Skibo's potential with what he had achieved at his 'paternal inheritance' in Angus where he had spent twenty out of twenty-seven years '400 miles distant from my estate in consequence of my public duty'. He was confident that Skibo could be turned around in the same manner.

It was true that the Dunnichen tenants had been similarly poor, without leases and obliged to provide services to the laird, albeit that these were more moderate and defined. There he had taken charge of most of the farms, enclosed and improved them and planted all the barren and waste land with fir and other trees. He let the properties at three to five times the old rent and the leases, for 19 or 30 years, always including the lifetime of the tenant, who was excluded from all services. The only obligation on them had been to enforce good agriculture. If the tenant built any new houses or stone walls at his own expense, his heirs paid for them according to their value when the lease expired. Planting rows of large trees grown in his nursery on each side of stone walls, his tenants had been allowed to cut down a third of them at the end of their lease, this being the only method he had found of preventing trees from being destroyed by the carelessness of the farmer and some reasonable indemnification for the injury done to their land by their shade and roots.

As the result the value of the land had risen to two-thirds of the rent and £90 rent had recently been achieved for a 75-acre farm. Overall, properties in the parish were making ten times what they achieved 120 years before and rents were paid in money not kind. Estate income had risen from £300 when he started to £800; his tenants, instead of being 'extremely poor', were now more wealthy. Their houses, horses, carts and equipment were all said to be four or five times more valuable than they were. The people were well-clothed and fed. Some were now able 'to lend money and entertain their proprietor . . . and a general emulation prevails (about) who shall have the best ploughed fields and produce the best crops'. Dempster believed that tenants and farmers were the most industrious and sober part of any county's population, especially if they had security. At Dunnichen they were 'more enlightened, intelligent and civilized than they were, and though exempted from obligations to perform any services' they would help the family without charge. 'I have never been able, with all my rhetoric, to persuade one of my tenants to accept payment or hire for their labours!'[63]

Now Dempster had to set to and prove his critics wrong about Skibo. It had been a struggle to obtain the finance for its purchase and one that convinced him he could hardly succeed in Sutherland and at the same time remain an MP in London. His resources, if not his strength of purpose, were simply too limited.

11

LEAVING WESTMINSTER
(1788–1790)

'I am done with politics'
(Dempster to Sir Adam Fergusson 2 November 1791 from Dunnichen)

1788

If the serendipity of Skibo's acquisition was not soon to disappear, Dempster had to match the financial contribution anticipated from his half-brother's voyages with an increase in his own income. In January, and 'enjoying supreme health', he turned his attention to two projects on the Dunnichen estate, both of which were to be highly successful.

Nearly thirty years before, he had drained 'Dunnichen Moss', the marsh below the house, 'dragging the shell marl from the bottom with boats and machinery'. This had helped improve the arable land and, with good crops of cereals, turnips and clover being regularly harvested by his tenants, he decided to exploit Loch Restenneth on his Angus estate. Similar works had been done by Captain Strachan, a neighbour, when marl had been taken from the loch of Balgavies, a wetland along the Lunan, on his estate, in much the same way as ballast was dragged from rivers such as the Thames in England. The Earl of Strathmore had lowered the level of Forfar Loch to gain access to profitable shell marl. Chemical analysis showed it to be similar to lime but, being already in a pulverised state unlike lime, it required no calcination before being put on the land.

Writing to Thorkelin, Dempster said he was 'taking measures for draining a lake here about a mile long and half as broad, filled with . . . two of the most vendible commodities in this country'.[1] What was to be pioneering work on the application of lime in agricultural land improvement depended on expert advice. The eminent Professor Joseph Black (1728–1799) and Mr Rodolphe Eric Raspe (1734–1794), a German mineralogist who was then touring Scotland, were called in to provide it. The former's work on limestone was to help him make a remarkable leap in chemical analysis and prove the Law of Constant Proportions (that the chemical composition of any pure substance is constant). Black was always able to demonstrate his experiments at both Glasgow and Edinburgh universities 'with unparalleled fastidiousness and elegance'. He had made chemistry 'a fashionable part of the accomplishment of a gentleman'.[2] Having obtained his neighbour's consent, Dempster then placed an order with a contractor for 'the great work'.[3] The extraction of clay with a calcareous content was something about which 'people (were) not very sanguine'. Some were unaware that, under favourable conditions, freshwater molluscs flourished in lakes, where their dead shells accumulated on the bottom to form the whitish friable calcareous deposit known as marl.[4]

The plan involved the construction of a kiln, unlike the 'reverbatory' or draw-kiln, some 20–30 feet high and 8–9 feet in diameter, which allowed a free passage of air and the insertion of previously beaten and dried strips of peat before the fire was lit. It was important to ensure slow and uniform burning. The burnt material and resulting lime was then slaked with water and tested to see whether it dissolved in spirits of salt 'without effervescence'.[5] Despite the doubts that had been expressed about the project, Dempster was convinced that it would be much used as a valuable fertilizer and bring in an income of £900-£1,000 per annum. How correct his forecast that the marl would be successfully 'calcined into lime' was demonstrated over the next decade when sales in excess of £14,000 were generated.

Dempster also had in mind the creation of a new village, sited on the 66-acre farm of Letham just to the east of Dunnichen, much of which was unproductive moorland. New amenities and what in Angus was to be called a *Deed of Privilege* were to be given to the villagers. It had many of the features of the *Constitution of Creich*, but in Letham his tenants and newcomers were to learn additional skills, grow flax, spin yarn, weave and finish cloth, and turn their community into a centre for the manufacture of specialized linen goods. The deed offered the inhabitants common land on the meadows either side of the River Vinney below the farm and provided for them to have stone and clay for buildings.[6] The division of the estate into farms of a more economical size and the enclosure of their run-rig land meant that a measure of readjustment would be called for. Dempster offered feus of £2 per acre after an initial period when the land would be free. A novel feature at Letham was to be its housing plots, each 30 ft from the street with a small garden behind, reflecting the laird's conviction that the citizens of the village 'should not have more land than a house and garden'. Dempster's dream of a new village at Stanley, which had been thwarted by the Duke of Atholl, was to be realized in Angus.

Not surprisingly, Dempster's constituency affairs continued to be centred on the problems of the linen industry, some sectors of which required the continuation of import duties and an export bounty to survive. In January he sent a lengthy petition from manufacturers in Forfar, Montrose, Dundee, Arbroath and Brechin to Henry Dundas, arguing that 'Ireland has beaten us out of the manufacture of the linen she makes and sends here. This is of the finer kind principally used for shirting'. In general, with government support, the industry was able to compete with Germany, but there were now legitimate fears that this trade could soon be at risk and 'our industry will be found instantly to decline, and at last to vanish'. He hoped that Dundas could be made into 'a friend to the bounty on linen, and to the whole wise system of laws for encouraging the linen manufacture of Scotland'.[7]

In March Robert Melville, a would-be settler at Ullapool, approached the Fisheries Society in the expectation that they might be in need of someone to construct and manage the development. He was the young nephew of a Robert Fall who owned a fishery and general commercial business in Dunbar. The two had been in business together, but it had failed and, rather than emigrate, he wanted 'to be serviceable both to the publick and myself in Scotland'. This led to him being invited to prepare plans for Ullapool's infrastructure and a contract being given to him for the construction of houses including one for himself along with sheds, storehouses and a smokehouse which he could lease on condition that he undertook their repair and maintenance. His appointment was 'a fortunate circumstance for the Society', as Dempster described it to Sir Adam Fergusson who, unlike Dempster, was in London attending meetings of the Fisheries board. It seems that Dempster had met Melville at Dunnichen some time in April and, although he had some reservations about the appointment, he was convinced that the Society would 'have a settler of great skill in the fisheries and one who will be supported with a considerable capital by his friends'.[8] Dempster set to at Dunnichen to draw up the regulations under which the land at Ullapool was to be lotted out.

Since the three directors of the Fisheries Society who lived closest to Ullapool, Lord Gower, Seaforth and Dempster, were usually otherwise engaged in London, particularly during the early part of the summer when construction could proceed, it was decided that a private member of the Society would carry out regular inspections of the progress being made. They considered themselves fortunate in finding Donald Macleod of Geanies, a lawyer and Sheriff of Rosshire with a farm at Rhidorroch some miles outside Ullapool, to undertake the supervision until such time as a resident agent could be appointed.[9] He was able to report in June that 'Mr Melville had proceeded much further than he could have expected from the sixteenth day of his arrival'.[10] The fact was, however, that Melville was to become wholly unpopular with the local community, greatly disliked by the settlers for his overbearing manner and rightly blamed for his poor supervision of later construction work.[11]

Now with two estates, and for reasons 'amounting like Spaniards to one hundred', Dempster found it 'very inconvenient' to be at Westminster and he chose to spend all but a month or so of 1788 in Scotland.[12] This did not prevent him from keeping a close ear to what was going on in the House, but, perhaps not surprisingly, he made little reference in his letter to Sir Adam about Skibo. In March the debate on the India Declaratory Bill, in which Sheridan 'spoke with great animation for two hours and a half' and Dundas was 'on his legs above three hours', was referred to as the 'hot work' his friend had been forced to endure in the House. More to his satisfaction was the news that an attempt had at least been made by Sir G.Page and Fox to repeal the much-resented tax on shop rents.

During the early part of the year various documents and essays were exchanged between Dempster and Thorkelin on subjects ranging from fishing for salmon, based on the practices adopted by the Bornholm fishery, the genealogy of the Macleods, the state of Scottish peasantry and a 'little essay' on the problem of slavery. This last Dempster described as 'the best, the most sensible, the most learned and the wisest and most moderate (he) had ever read on the subject'. It was 'highly amusing' and apparently traced the history of slavery in Europe from the Middle Ages.[13] Also among Dempster's voluminous reading had been John Pinkerton's *Preface to Scottish Poetry* which had given him new ideas about the Picts, an account of Tartar koumiss (served in Mongolia instead of wine or spirits) and Dr Hutton's 'Theory of the Earth'.[14] He also hoped that Thorkelin would publish something that people could afford (less than two guineas) about the ancient constitution of Iceland and the present state of that country; after that a 'new Icelandic grammar and dictionary 'would have a good sale', a matter about which Thorkelin's London printer would be able to advise.

To his great surprise and gratification Dempster learned that Thorkelin had put his name forward for membership to the Royal Society of Northern Icelandic Literature of Denmark.[15] The honour and his subsequent enrolment inspired a wholly typical Dempster response. He immediately wanted to know 'the initials of this Society that I might subjoin them to my name like the fellows of the Royal Society and other Societies do on certain occasions'. Stepping up still further his stream of thoughts on Highland development which had become his 'home-bred Hobby Horse', he had the wit to add that Iceland was 'the foreign steed' he rode 'with as much pleasure'. Thorkelin, who had been sent a copy of the *Constitution of Creich,* was given news about how this reform was proceeding. In common with many of Dempster's friends, the professor had been a convinced sceptic of the Sutherland purchase and Dempster was delighted to demonstrate 'how ill-founded some of (his) apprehensions were'. The newly-introduced 'conditions' which were probably only applicable to new settlers at this stage and which he hoped were 'sufficiently liberal', had apparently not stopped 'sober, steady, active young men with keen wives and cattle . . . flocking in'. Davidson had assured him that there would be 'twenty new settlers next year . . . and if so, the following year will produce I hope twice the number'.[16] Dempster was convinced that the *Constitution* was 'very advantageous for the proprietor, whose fortune every generation (would) receive, (based on) the value of the industry of the former generation'.[17]

During the summer there had been a simple ceremony in Angus and another opportunity to measure reaction to the improved security Dempster was providing for his tenants.[18] The streets and plots of Letham had been marked out by plough and work had begun on building the new village there. Some had not found it easy to accept the offer of the *Deed of Privilege*, preferring the old way of life to the new. The waiving of payments for the first year, and feus of £2 per acre subsequently, were attractive benefits but such new privileges caused a degree of bafflement in the community. The experience in Sutherland was being repeated.

Dempster's letters to his relations at this period made up for a dearth of information about the family's life both in London and at Dunnichen. Two in April and June to Captain John's wife Jean, Sir Adam's niece, show the deep affection and minute concern he had for all those close to him.[19] Since the Captain's departure in February the previous year he had himself received two letters but neither said 'one word about (the Captain's) health or (that) of the ship's company' and he could only assume, gloomy as he was, that the voyage was going well. To his wife he seemed to have been even less generous, and this peeved Dempster. He hoped that Jean's father would collect her from Newhailes at Musselburgh, five miles outside Edinburgh, where she was staying, but, if not, he wanted to send one of his servants from Dunnichen (Seth) to be her 'conductor'. When it later emerged that Charles Fergusson had taken her south, Dempster at once wanted to pay the cost.[20]

In passing on another invitation for her to visit Thomas Gordon, now a widower after his wife's death the previous year, and living at Balmaghie House, he obviously thought that there would be plenty of room for little George. The healthy country house aspect of the fine mansion would be good for them both. Dempster's unmarried sister, Ann, may have been living there at the time and 'she would have something more to do'.[21] The alternative of staying in London at the Captain's home in Red Lion Square was something he would have discouraged. With money never far from his mind, Dempster kept his 'strongest argument for last. It would be a prudent and economical measure', adding that he did not 'scruple to feel economy at the head of all virtues'.

When Captain John took to sending his wife a bunch of letters addressed to various members of the family, Dempster was understanding of the fact that Jean had opened those addressed to him: 'I give you full powers over all of them'. He read news about little George as if he 'were his mother'; he was growing apace and showing 'a wonderful prematurity'. Such was his anticipation of news about the child's father that in June he had 'a messenger waiting (the arrival of) every post night in Forfar'.[22] But Dempster became increasingly irritated that his half-brother was not getting the most profitable voyages to India, suspecting that he had insufficiently influential friends in the

Company and at Westminster. 'The truth is (that) the whole profits of the trade are now confined to the Bengal voyages. A man may sail till he is grey-headed between Europe and the other parts of India making only bare bread, but a voyage or two to Bengal is still a fortune'. The captain may have complained in his letters about the poor amount of business done during the *Rose's* voyage. On its first voyage the vessel had called at Madras and Whampoa in China rather than Calcutta. It was enough of an issue for Dempster to invoke Sir Adam's help since he was convinced that 'no captain ever was worse appointed than Jack in Parliamentary friends'.[23] Reluctant as he was to solicit favours, he asked his friend to see what could be done, whilst at the same time writing himself to Dundas[24,] since it would cost him little 'to mention the matter to any of the Directors of the Committee of Correspondence or to the Chairman or Deputy'.

Dempster's decision to leave Parliament was no sudden aberration and hardly due to the 'bad state of health which disabled him from performing his duty agreeable to his own satisfaction', the official reason given to the Town Councils of each of the Burghs in his constituency.[25] 'Thwarted ambition' and the knowledge that 'it was now twenty years since (he) found (his) opposition to any measure one of the necessary accompaniments of its success' certainly played their part. As he told Fintry, a 'little independence (was) now the sole object of (his) ambition'.[26] The compound force of three threads of reasoning had its effect: those spun from his long exposure to parliamentary procedure, the duties he owed his family, and what can only be called Dempster's innate and irrepressible sympathy for those in need.

As James Fergusson said, Dempster did 'nothing by halves' and with his increased commitments in Angus and the Highlands he decided he could not afford 'his public duty': 'I would advise no man to go into Parliament with a fortune less than £6000 a year'.[27] His contemporaries were soon to discover that he had the ability to become an increasingly innovative farmer, landlord, reformer and 'improver' during a strenuous second career that was to peak during a dozen or so of his nearly thirty remaining years. Having fought a long uphill battle to recover only slowly from the extraordinary costs associated with his early elections to Parliament, and now again burdened with new debts and responsibilities at Skibo, he had to reconcile himself to the fact that 'his favourite projects, could be pursued as well or better outside Parliament as in it'.[28]

Knowing that he and his wife Rose could not produce children, or the heir he always wanted, it was understandable that Dempster's ambition centred more and more on his half-brother's child. A secure and definite path forward for little George now took priority. A scheme whereby Captain John and his family would have the wherewithal to do what he had not done for himself had particular attraction. If he was not to fail in this endeavour, other commitments would have to be surrendered. The influential laird of

Dunnichen could, he hoped, supervise and watch developments in Sutherland and Angus, whilst continuing or expanding his public work and private interests, but not at the cost of remaining an MP. That was too high a price to guarantee a beneficial outcome to these plans.

By all accounts Dempster's peregrinations and his work on behalf of the Fisheries Society contributed to his love of the Highlands and Islands, but the appalling conditions he encountered compared so unfavourably to life in more southerly Scotland that he felt compelled to see if the improvements there could be transferred northwards. Periodic forays could do little of themselves to address such problems, whereas the risky, if timely, purchase of Skibo enabled him to have the base from which to set his own agenda for Highland regeneration and complement the work of others in the field of fisheries. He had 'something of the vision, the altruism, and the good sense which were behind the Fisheries Society'.[29]

The Society's directors had been re-appointed in April and Dempster felt it was his duty to visit Ullapool in the autumn 'to inspect the progress . . . where, if it does not rise to the sound of the lyre, it springs very fast to that of the bagpipe'. He humorously thought that, although he did not want to force the pace unduly, 'a gentle application of heat might be applied with great success to the walls, especially when the plant is only beginning to sprout in a cold climate and bleak country'.[30] Accompanying him on this occasion were Major Baillie of Rosehall (by Lairg),[31] Captain John Gordon (late of Pulrossie) and his half-brother whose ship the *Rose* had reached the Downs on 22 June 1788. All three were shareholders in the Ullapool project.[32] Dempster's original plan had been for Seaforth and Lord Gower to join him, but neither was available.

Reaching Ullapool, he found that the town had been marked out and Morrison[33] and Melville were well ahead with some of the house construction and the inn; only the warehouse had not been started. 'We had the satisfaction of finding the several works of the Society carrying on with vigour and spirit by the several contractors. Three vessels were riding at anchor in the roadstead, boats were constructing for the approaching season of the fisheries, hemp was spinning for nets and tackle, coopers were busy preparing calks'.[34] Writing to Seaforth, his co-director, he reported that the houses seemed to have been built 'according to contract', but he doubted the wisdom of using tiled roofs 'in that wet and windy spot'. The Inn 'was far advanced, well-built but not then roofed and most beautifully situated' and, inspired by finding that the people were buying and spinning flax which Melville had imported, Dempster hoped this would 'prove a great resource and indeed . . . a necessary one where the livelihood of the people (depended) on anything so precarious as the herring fishery'.[35] Unfortunately Morrison was to become ill early the next year and be replaced by William Cowie, a builder from Tain recommended by Donald Macleod.

Having spent the year in North Britain, Dempster resumed his duties in Parliament in December. He had heard from the Provost of St Andrews that Captain George Murray RN, the uncle of the Duke of Atholl, would contest his seat at the 1790 election, a decision 'they knew . . . was not contrary to the wishes of Mr Dempster'.[36] George III had been ill for some time and at the beginning of November, with the King's mind in turmoil, his doctors were of the opinion that he would not recover his sanity. The Whigs saw an opportunity to regain office and overturn Pitt if Fox could redeem a promise made by the wayward Prince of Wales to offer him the government if ever he was able. The choice of a temporary Regency with an Advisory Council, or the formal appointment of the Prince Regent, became matters of long and fractious debate stretching well into 1789 and meant that the Dempsters felt obliged to spend Christmas at Knightsbridge, dining with Thorkelin and a 'noble Danish friend' in Hampstead.

Two days before Christmas Viscount Palmerston, the Member for Boroughbridge, reported that 'we had a late sitting last night on the amendment proposed by Mr Dempster to address the Prince to take the administration of the government on himself instead of proceeding in Mr Pitt's mode. C(harles) Fox, who had been much out of order two or three days ago, was however down and made an excellent speech, as did Lord North. The speaking on the other side was very indifferent and Pitt made no figure till we came to divide, when contrary to my expectation, as well as that of most people, we were beat by 73. . . . Pitt's resolutions now being passed are to be communicated to the Lords today and we are to do nothing more till they have agreed them, which with the intervening of Christmas Day cannot be till the end of next week.'[37]

1789

As the New Year came in Dempster was in his study at Knightsbridge mulling over new ideas as had been his wont at this season for many years at Dunnichen. Writing to Seaforth, he enclosed a card with his belated greetings and tried out on him 'the idea of a Society or Association of Highland Proprietors for encouraging the highlanders to remain at home'. Conscious of the need to publicize his plans at Skibo, which had been left largely in the hands of Fraser, his factor, he had drafted a 'Notice' over the Christmas period to be pinned up across the parishes of Creich and Dornoch to encourage new settlers to come forward. He sent a few of the 'hand bills' to Seaforth for information.[38]

The 'Notice' talked of the waste lands on the Skibo estate which had been surveyed and found to contain a great deal of land 'fit for being fettled'. Encouragements included the gift of a stone of iron for making hammers and other instruments. New settlers would be free from all 'services' and from thirlage at the mill. Rent was to amount not just to one shilling a year during the life of the first settler but it was fixed for the life of his heirs and children. Peat for their own use could be extracted from 'mosses' near the houses they would be encouraged to build. Enquiries could be made to the factor Mr John Fraser or Mr Andrew Davidson of Overskibo. In all, not a bad offer.

From Fintry came news that Forfar and Dundee had declared their support for his successor, Captain Murray, and that St Andrews and Cupar were likely to do the same despite the poverty of many of the tradesmen and some of the guildry. Extreme caution, reminiscent of his own election in 1767, was still called for: 'their necessity and not their will might consent to what could not be called corruption, but remuneration'. Dempster seems to have learned his lesson: 'a scrimp free election is better in case of a Petition than a unanimous one with any well-grounded charge of corruption'. The declaration of the Perth voters did not take place until February. Dempster had some 'misgiving about Lord Kinnoull's interest there', and when the Provost and those with whom he had worked to create the cotton mill at Stanley showed themselves in favour of Captain Murray he was much relieved: 'The declaration . . . afforded me inexpressible satisfaction'.[39]

All manner of constitutional proprieties were threatened by the King's incapacity and the appointment of a regent. They provided Dempster with ample opportunity to delve into the way authority was to be given to various commissioners to open parliament, give royal assent to the Bill appointing the Regent and determine the limit of his powers. He had been 'more disposed to retire' until he witnessed 'a new scene of more imbecility' than hitherto.[40] Interpreting the precedents established in the reign of Henry VI called for considerable research and, at pains to remind the House that the commission then given to the Duke of Gloucester was strictly limited to giving the royal assent, Dempster was in his element. He was offended by the idea of a commissioner appointed by the two Houses of Parliament giving royal assent since, 'if the necessity for giving such power on one occasion was established,' it might be extended to many more; thus the two Houses might go on, trampling upon the royal prerogative and making their own creature give the royal assent to every bill'. He saw the whole proposal as 'an un-Whig, un-Tory, odd, awkward, anomalous monster' to be resisted at all costs. However, the Master of the Rolls considered the limited proposals put forward by the Lords a reasonable compromise and to do what Dempster asked would allow the Regent 'to exercise the whole of royal power without any restrictions whatever'.[41] In February all was resolved at least temporarily when the King was declared 'convalescent' and able to open parliament as usual.

Very severe weather after Christmas delayed Captain John's departure for Madras and Bengal, his second voyage in the *Rose*. Fresh breezes from the north-east, snow and a great quantity of ice in the Thames marooned the crew and many of the passengers aboard the ship. Jobs had to be found in the hold for the crew. Only the orlop deck was free of ice and could be cleaned. Some officers and passengers were able to return to the shore for short periods. Eventually the *Rose* sailed in April and Dempster turned his attention to the Navy Estimates which contained proposals for '20,000 seamen to be employed for the service of the year 1789'. He wanted economy rather than even an extra 2000 sailors when the country was at peace and people required relief from 'the heavy load of taxes with which they were burdened'. After the Chancellor of the Exchequer agreed to the repeal of the tax on shops during a debate in April, Dempster saw an opportunity to achieve similar action in respect of the duties and restrictions that had been placed on hawkers and peddlers in 1785. The reports laid before the House indicated that the revenue had fallen since their imposition and he wished to see an end of the present arrangements. With the support of Pulteney and Hawkins Browne, he demonstrated to the Chancellor's satisfaction that there was a fairly general desire for such action and as a result a compromise 'to explain and amend' the Act was agreed, effectively undermining the tax.[42] Outside the House, London was 'in ferment with Hastings' trial, Brooks's Gate, the Grand Procession . . . and brilliant illuminations'.[43]

The previous year William Wilberforce, an old Fisheries Society colleague of Dempsters and the Member for Yorkshire, had founded an association for the reformation of manners and was now about to begin his long struggle for the abolition of the slave trade.[44] The set of propositions he brought to the House that spring inspired Speaker Grenville to praise his speech as one of the 'most masterly and eloquent' he had ever heard, but the City of London (in the form of Alderman Newman) pleaded against such a 'rash and precipitate' proposal as abolition would be, 'producing in the City a sense of bankruptcy and ruin'. Dempster's view was obviously cautious; 'undoubtedly they owed humanity to all mankind', but he was reluctant to interfere with the interests of those who were planters. Perhaps with the two closest members of his own family in mind, Rosie his wife, who was the daughter of a slave-owning planter, and Jack his seafaring half-brother, Dempster reminded the House that the slave trade had even been 'deemed an essential nursery of our seamen and had cherished it in consequence'. He was to call it one of the 'hidden rocks, a snare' that Parliament faced at that time,[45] and although he had no objection to preventing British subjects from becoming slaves, he 'could not with any pretence of right, prescribe to the gentlemen of the West Indies by what hands their plantations should be cultivated'.[46]

During the subsequent Budget debate Dempster again pleaded for cuts rather than increases in taxes in time of peace, censuring Ministers' 'general extravagance' and urging foreign alliances as a means of reducing the size of the army and navy. So far as the separate provisions for India were concerned he was even more forceful. Many of the points he made would have cropped up in conversations with old India hands or from the stories told him by Captain John over dinner. He argued that only the removal of 'despotic obstacles to commerce and manufactures would operate advantageously in favour of the revenue'. India, which was 'a country without a constitution', groaned under 'the internal oppression of government customs, having toll-bars and offices erected over every river, and across the entrance of every road, so that the miserable natives were obliged to pay repeated duties'. Landowners were the opium trade's contractors, whom Dempster saw as obliged to 'give poppies the preference over every other product of cultivation'.[47] Then, thinking of his own constituents and the problems they anticipated with the import of finished cotton goods from the sub-continent, he stressed the need for only raw cotton to be exported to Britain.

While in London Dempster was almost wholly reliant on Robert Graham to give him news of progress at the Stanley mill. He may have visited the site once that year. An occasional meeting with the Duke of Atholl at his London home did little more than provide him gossip and social news. By June he had convinced himself that the new manager to replace Andrew Keay at the mill had not been for the good. He had duly responded to another expected call for capital from the partners, sending David McVicar a 'large sum' at Whitsun, but 'as usual (it had not been accompanied) by a single line' from him in return. Only when Arkwright agreed to 'receive and instruct' McVicar did Dempster feel more comfortable.[48] Cotton cloth was selling so cheaply in London that he was now 'really afraid that (the) mill (was) a losing concern, and if so, the losses (would) not be on a small scale'.[49]

Dempster introduced a Fishery Bill that year 'to correct the shocking alter-ations of Beaufoy, (which) unknown to any of us, had made in the old one'.[50] Unfortunately for him, he appears to have jumped ahead of his colleagues in the Society and acted without their authority. A year or so later Dempster explained that he had been 'wrong-headed' and the clauses were withdrawn to avoid further embarrassment. Other proposals for improved roads in the Highlands were received favourably and efforts to abolish the iniquitous tax on salt for curing cod, ling and herring continued. Dempster concluded that, unless the government could be helped off the hook it had impaled itself on, the prospects for change were poor. All the Treasury could see was the substantial tax income it derived from the import of salt.

Having written much of his *Discourse* to the Fisheries Society at Dunnichen the previous year, Dempster now added the finishing touches to this substan-tive piece of work at Knightsbridge. His research had unearthed Dr Swediaur, 'an ingenious physician and chemist' who had followed the design of the great Dutch refineries of salt and erected a works at Port Seton on the Firth of Forth. As Dempster said, 'He has actually made a great quantity of very fine salt and has no doubt of reducing the price of this commodity greatly, were he enabled to make the savings in time, labour and fuel, which the use of rock salt would infallibly admit of.' To avoid the idea being tossed out, he tempted officials in the Treasury with the prospect of Great Britain achieving (almost) a monopoly of such supplies in Europe: 'Difficulties arising from revenue considerations, as well as from a mistaken policy of the actual salt-makers in both parts of the island, form strong obstacles to the completion of a system of salt laws which might give Great Britain, now dependent on other nations for salt, almost the monopoly of this article in Europe.' Finally, to gently rub in his argument further, he added that 'No other nation possesses, in like plenty, the two necessary articles for a trade in salt, *viz.* coal and rock-salt.'[51]

When the Fishery Society's auditors met in a private room at Waghorn's Coffee House in Old Palace Yard, Westminster, hired out at the very reasonable cost of nine shillings, they had before them 'the General Account of Monies' received and paid out between January 1787 and March of that year. The accounts showed that £4,594 had been spent on revenue and capital works and that all was well financially, given that only 30% of the proprietors' capital had been subscribed and bank borrowings made up roughly half the expenditure. An important consideration for the spring meeting of the Society was the length of leases to be given to tenants. Dempster and Neill Malcolm, who had been asked to consider lotting out the land, tabled two not dissimilar sets of regulations for Tobermory and Ullapool. The appointment of a permanent agent in each place was also needed and Seaforth's nominee, approved by Donald Macleod of Geanies, who had temporarily stood in as agent – was accepted as 'the best qualified person' for the latter town. William Mackenzie, who had been a clerk at the Gairloch fishery, was appointed. Other more disturbing items on the agenda included the design of the pier which had proved unsatisfactory, the lack of a road to access Ullapool from the east, the erection of custom houses, the limited amount of order being kept by the bailies and the 'overbearing' behaviour of Melville.

Dempster's correspondence with Francis Humberstone Mackenzie of Seaforth was open and frank. It reflected what Dempster called their 'congeniality of sentiment respecting the sources of prosperity of the Highlands (which) renders your letters peculiarly acceptable to me'.[52] Their friendship blossomed still further that summer and, since neither were to contest the 1790 election, both men were content to contemplate life after Westminster. Seaforth, always lacking the resources with which to carry out the improvements he wished for his own estates and determined to restore his finances a little by living for a few years in Lewis, had decided to give his interest in his Ross constituency to his friend William Adam. Seaforth was a likeable and generous 35-year-old who had been denigrated by some who spoke of him as 'being deaf and dumb',[53] but his disabilities, which were the result of scarlet fever when serving as a midshipman in the Navy, did not impair his effectiveness either socially or in the House. He had learned to 'talk with his fingers' and only part of his speech suffered. It is beyond doubt that Dempster knew at least something about the doom-laden utterances of the unfortunate Coinneach Odhar (Kenneth Mackenzie) and the two men must have discussed the likelihood of the Seer of Brahan's predictions being fulfilled. Such uncertain 16th and 17th century spells and witchcraft may have been of little general interest to the pragmatic Dempster, but any effect they had on his friend would have been a genuine concern.

The story was told that when Lady Seaforth had been left alone at Brahan Castle by the third Earl of Seaforth, she called in 'dun-coloured' Kenneth, the Brahan Seer, in an effort to establish her husband's whereabouts. Rather indelicately, he told her that he was having a 'merry' time in Paris, an answer which, according to tradition, led to the Seer being brought to trial and subsequently burned to death in a barrel at Chanonry near Fortrose. Nevertheless, before his death, he had pronounced that the Seaforth family would die out 'in sorrow', that the last chief would be deaf and dumb, that his four sons would pre-decease him, that after his death no Mackenzie would rule in Brahan and his estates would be inherited by a 'white-hooded lassie from the east'. Seaforth's deafness had not been seriously alarming to his clansmen, but when one of his four sons died he became dumb with grief and was said never to have spoken again. On his death in 1815, and with his other three sons also dead, the estates went to his eldest daughter. She had lived in the West Indies from whence she arrived at Brahan as the widow of Admiral Sir Samuel Hood who had died in 1816. The prophesy was thereby complete. She had come from the east to enjoy her melancholy inheritance, hooded in two senses, by name and in the coif of a widow.

Seaforth had married the Dean of Lichfield's daughter and both couples enjoyed each other's company, always sharing news of Captain John's voyages. He was for ever sending presents to the family. The previous year Dempster had occasion to thank him for some well-cured herrings and dried cod which were the 'admiration of all who tried them' at Dunnichen.[54] That summer a letter sent 'from sea' by Seaforth soon after the Dempsters had entertained them did not stop a further invitation being extended, with Dempster wishing that the easterly wind might 'force him into Arbroath' so that they could 'repay some of the civilities' they owed them.[55] Both men had some concerns about one or two of the Fisheries Society's directors 'interfering directly or indirectly with the commerce of the country', a reference to those who considered the Company should trade in its own right. This would have meant competing with those whom it was endeavouring to help and Seaforth hoped 'a little expense (would soon) open their eyes'.

The Society's affairs necessitated a great deal of hard work which weighed heavily on the Duke of Argyll, Hawkins Browne and Dempster. The three stuck 'to the business from one till four (o'clock) three times a week' in the absence of other directors 'whose attendance (was) precarious'.[56] He would have liked the support of Seaforth, but by then the family, which included the Seaforths' son and heir who had been born the year before, had left Castle Brahan en route for Lewis. There Dempster hoped his friend would establish another settlement even if the Society might be reluctant to support it. A township on land, which Seaforth had already earmarked, could be 'lotted out and then divided into 400 equal parts . . . capital (from) the Company would furnish (the buildings) and (Seaforth's) protection, influence and assistance in other respects would prevent abuses, procure inhabitants (and) attend to their wants and wishes'. Envious of the opportunity and sanguine as ever, Dempster recalled the delegated powers given to the Duke of Argyll, Lord Breadalbane and two other directors to sanction such a 'triffling expense'. At the end of what was a long letter, his apology said it all: 'I never end about a new town!'[57]

In July Dempster wrote to James Bland Burges, Under Secretary for Foreign Affairs, regarding changes in the English (and potentially Scottish) County Court system. The matter between them was academic in its outcome, but within three months Dempster was able to use the contact he had made to help three Scottish seamen who were being held in Spanish jails without money to buy their freedom. Burges obviously used his influence to assist in their release; it did 'honour both to the spirit and the temper of our Ministries'.[58] Two days before his final speech in the House of Commons Dempster spotted 'a new opening afforded by the Tobacco Act' and wrote 'very fully to Mr Dundas on the subject'.[59] Then on 22 July he spoke in favour of supplying corn to revolutionary France. Questioning the administration's response, Pulteney referred to the fact that 'Mr Dempster was for relieving France in this hour of her distress; 20,000 sacks of flour could not injure this country, but might materially serve the other'.[60]

After what had been his concluding and a 'tedious' session at Westminster, the Dempsters, along with sister Ann, left London for Scotland on Monday night of 27 July, staying, as had become their practice, for a few days en route at Buxton.[61] 'Rosie' and George were to travel northward via Liverpool, 'which I must see before I die', leaving Ann, whose health was poor, behind to receive 'the best care we own'.[62] Dempster may have also wanted to see something of the Cheshire salt mines to further the studies he had made of salt production. From Buxton he proposed to 'take the western road, being desirous of seeing a mineral salt pit'. Writing to Sir Adam with an account of his travels, Dempster gave his first reaction to the revolutionary fervour in France which was much in the news. Louis XVI had summoned the States General to address the country's near bankruptcy in May and the Bastille had just been stormed. He judged, rightly as events proved, that 'the proud noblesse (would) not submit and that the licentious populace will drive many people back again to the nobles' standard, and that the fair kingdom you and I visited will be deluged with the blood of its best citizens'.[63]

Dempster's *Discourse* contained several attractively-argued proposals. One would be implemented at Spinningdale on the Skibo estate and another, though never brought to fruition, must have been the subject of some speculation between himself and Captain Jack when the two men were on the tideway, viewing the docks and shipyards down the river to Gravesend. 'If shipbuilding be a very lucrative business in the River Thames,' he argued, 'where the price of materials, and the rent of ground, are very high, it ought to be much more lucrative at the (Fishery) Company's settlement, where the price of materials . . . labour . . . and the rent of the ground are very low'. Accordingly he at least wanted to see 'in the heart of every settlement . . . a dock-yard walled in, with a basin or canal running through the middle of it'. Thames-side shipbuilders 'have not the economy of a saw mill'[64] and 'the rate of wages' given to ship-carpenters and common carpenters on the west coast of Scotland 'does not amount to a shilling a day, whilst on the River Thames it is three shillings and six pence'. Timber, iron, hemp and other materials could be brought from Scandinavia, paid for in cash or 'purchased in exchange for fish'. But Dempster knew then, if not when musing with his half-brother, that both ideas, cogent as they were, would be deemed ancillary to the Society's aims.

His eighty-six-page 'book', as he called the *Discourse*, was a 'lively and very readable production'.[65] It may not have had a large sale, but it was not for the sake of trying. Dempster even sent a copy with an inscription to His Royal Highness, William, Duke of Clarence, later William IV.[66] Some paragraphs had been set in italics, including those relating to ship-building. These Dempster thought were 'a little visionary'.[67] The review of what had been achieved in Mull, Ullapool, Skye and Canna was comprehensive enough, but it omitted any reference to Seaforth's plans for the Outer Hebrides. This lack of 'common justice' done to his friend prompted Dempster to recall a more frivolous omission of his own when he had given 'a ball at St Andrews and . . . neglected inviting to it so many of (his) best friends; an incident (he said) that nearly lost him his standing in the town'. This probably occurred when he was first elected Provost in the 1760s. Now penitent, he promised to include more examples in any second edition. He encouraged his friend to take to heart the lessons he had learned exploring the English Lake District where 'customary rents' could not be 'removed or racked . . . and the hills were commons and the inhabitants . . . at liberty to enclose or improve them'. The 'perfect transition from deformity to beauty' and the entitlement to vote for County members (of parliament) once they had improved the land to 40/- a year and become a freeholder were obvious examples of his aims for the tenants on his estates.

Looking up the hill from his study window at Dunnichen, Dempster mused contentedly that 'the last spot of the heathy mountain behind my house is put this summer under tillage and the tenant is buying marl to the value of £4 per acre on it, having reaped a rich crop off a neighbouring field treated last year in the same manner. A farm at the foot of the hill which yielded but 6/- per acre last year, the people are feuing from me eagerly just now at 40/-.'[68] The weather had, however, not been good and a third of his crop of oats and a fifth of barley had been lost at Dunnichen, prompting him to worry a little about Skibo where he had set a surveyor the task of 'finding lime rocks and a mineral well', hoping that the profitable ingredient that had made all the difference to his finances in Angus would perform similarly in Sutherland.

1790

The new decade was said by James Fergusson to have been some of Dempster's busiest years, hard as it is to imagine any time when he was not energetically committed to his work, home and family. Writing to Thorkelin, who had been forced to cancel an expedition to Iceland due to bad health, it is clear that Captain John's wife had taken up residence at the Dempster's house in Knightsbridge – for comfort's sake or economy is not disclosed. Later that year the Captain stayed with Thomas Gordon at Balmaghie by Kirkcudbright.[69]

Dempster, who had been kept abreast of the progress being made by the Fisheries Society, would have been delighted to hear on 25 March that Pulteney had been appointed a director. He was to be one of the Society's new leaders and the two men were to work together successfully inside and outside the Commons. Had Dempster been aware of the casual attendance being put in by some of the directors at the Society's meetings he would have noted with satisfaction a letter to the Duke of Argyll which spoke of Pulteney being 'very diligent and attentive . . . so that really unless he had been amongst us I don't know what would have become of matters. Mr Browne attended next best', although it seems he was not well acquainted with Scottish affairs.[70] Seaforth, on the other hand, had been in two minds about resigning his directorship and Dempster had to remind him that his 'presence near the scene of our activity has more effect than you are aware of, and you are beloved and esteemed by every one of our colleagues'.[71]

There were no roads worthy of the name north of the Tay except those constructed for military purposes and, with travel between the west and east coasts a wretched horseback ride through mountainous terrain, the viability of the new settlement at Ullapool was gravely disadvantaged. Dempster had endeavoured to start a rolling programme of road construction the previous year when he reminded the House about the long-standing recommendations made by the Common's own Fisheries Committee on the subject. He also moved an Address to His Majesty suggesting that the Commander-in-Chief in Scotland be allowed to carry out a survey of possible routes.[72] The Address brought word from Lord Adam Gordon who, at the request of the Secretary of State, asked Dempster, the mover in the Commons, for his opinion and explained that the Sheriffs Depute in Inverness, Ross, Sutherland and Caithness had been requested to 'procure previous information'. Admitting that he 'did not pretend to such a knowledge of the interior of that country as to be able either to point out a line of roads or to suggest to which of them a preference . . . should be given', Dempster recommended Macleod of Geanies as the better source of such wisdom so far as Ross was concerned. He undertook to obtain additional information 'from other quarters'. Eight essential routes were eventually formulated by George Brown of Elgin during the autumn of 1789 and considered by the Society's directors after Pulteney had studied them in the Secretary of State's office.[73]

It was to be 'grave work to make good roads'. The cost of repairs in Lewis, put by Seaforth at 10/- per mile, greatly amused Dempster, who had been used to construction in towns costing £200 per mile and at least £95 per mile 'in plain country'. A contract for 'turnpiking' the road between Forfar and Arbroath had just been let at such figures; 'the traffic . . . will afford it now and be doubled by it'. He expected expenditure of more than £10,000 over the next two years in Angus alone.[74]

Worried that the new civic figures on the Forfar and Dundee town councils would not be resourceful enough, Dempster himself addressed some of the problems associated with expanding the turnpikes. How to persuade landowners to pay survey fees, establishing the best width of pavé and lining up toll-keeper's wages with the anticipated income from tolls, were questions on which he offered his opinion.

At meetings of the Stanley company, where Fintry and he had been asked to provide between them another bond for £800, Dempster feared that it would be 'a miracle if some blunder was not committed' with David MacVicar in charge and 'conducting the whole himself'. It was hard for the company 'to be borrowing when all the cotton spinners in GB are making fortunes',[75] and he vainly hoped that a proportion of MacVicar's salary should be converted 'into a percentage on the profits'.[76] Quite apart from the low level of water in the Tay that summer, which was having an effect on production, Dempster's concern was growing that newer machinery had not been installed and the absence of any dividend, to say nothing of the constant calls for cash, was becoming a burden.

Dempster probably knew in advance that Lord Gower, his close neighbour in Sutherland and co-director in the Fisheries Society, had been chosen to replace the Duke of Dorset as the British Ambassador to France. He would have followed his appointment with more than just a political eye. His admiration and concern for Lady Gower, the Countess of Sutherland, probably equalled his interest in how well her husband would handle the country's affairs at this critical juncture. Lord Gower, who had been mentioned as a possible Prime Minister in 1783, and subsequently appointed President of the Council, was now in Paris. The couple's performance there was enough for one Whig member to suggest that 'his spirited conduct . . . merited a reward and Lady Sutherland is formed for representation. She has all the grace and manner to make her admired in public and every domestic and elegant talent to render her equally captivating in private'.[77] Soon after the flight of the French king and queen to Varennes Gower was to conclude, perhaps a little harshly, that 'if this country ceases to be a monarchy, it will be entirely the fault of Louis XVI. Blunder upon blunder, inconsequence upon inconsequence, a total want of energy of mind accompanied with personal cowardice, have been the destruction of his reign'.[78]

As President of the Dundee Whig Club Dempster sent a congratulatory address on behalf of the Club to Jean-Baptiste Treihard, the President of the National Assembly in Paris on 4 June 1790.[79] Its message reflected the early and misplaced reactions of many to the Revolution, that it was 'the triumph of liberty and reason over despotism, ignorance, and superstition'. Then, as if suspecting that events might take a more sinister turn, (and with Dempster's style very apparent) the Club re-affirmed the value it attached to the monarchy and British institutions: 'Our Sovereign, the guardian of our constitution and father of his people, is almost an object of our adoration; and our nobility and clergy form useful and illustrious members of a state where all are subject to the laws'.[80] There were, nevertheless, only two Scottish expressions of support despatched to France at the time, and there were those who saw Dempster's action as anti-monarchist. The Dundee Whigs followed the example set by the Reform Burgesses of Aberdeen and the Revolution Society of London.[81]

The summer saw no reduction in the number of guests coming and going at Dunnichen. A talented German nobleman, Count D'Erval, who had been in the King of France's bodyguard, had arrived in Scotland along with a friend on a walking tour but lacking the necessary social introductions. His mistake had been noticed by Sir William Murray of Ochtertyre when they reached Auchterarder or Crieff. He had commended them to the Provost of Dundee which led on to their being received at Dunnichen for three days. Finding that the German was an accomplished musician, the family enjoyed his playing of the 'cello and harpsichord. Dempster encouraged them to follow the (700 mile) route on foot that retraced his own journey to Staffa and back. On their return, and after they had spent a few more days in Forfarshire, presumably recovering, he sent them on their way with an introduction to Pulteney at Bath House and others of his friends in London. Recollection of the French hospitality Sir Adam and he had experienced 'excited a great desire in (him) to be of some use to this meritorious and suffering foreigner'.[82]

At the Court of Session in June the bond Dempster had given in respect of the Skibo purchase was finally 'delivered up' and the 10-year mortgage put in place. With the safe return of the *Rose* only two months before, George and the Captain could together contemplate the future with a degree of confidence. However, it was not until the next year that he was able to say with some relief that 'all idea of a sale of our property is vanished'.[83] The pressure exerted on him by his friends and advisers to reconsider his decision had not abated since 1786, but his usual sanguine outlook and effervescence now returned.

Progress on the production of lime from Restenneth had gone well under the watchful eye of Dr Black, and Letham had doubled its inhabitants as the new village emerged. The advertisement for weavers and tradesmen he had circulated the previous year had produced good results.

When Dempster took the decision to be 'done with politics', he was, as James Fergusson said, 'at the height of his reputation' and only 56 years old. He would have drawn some satisfaction from knowing that 'his exertions both in and out of Parliament to encourage Scottish trade, agriculture, manufactures and fisheries' were recognized, and, even more, that his colleagues in the House respected him for 'his efforts to curb taxation and reduce the national debt, and for his championship of the distressed, whether famine-stricken Highlanders, poor hawkers, or American loyalists'.[84]

Three years after his withdrawal from politics the *European Magazine* published an engraved portrait of Dempster 'showing a head and shoulders in profile, set off by a neat tie-wig, a good forehead, a strong nose, a firm if rather heavy chin and a mouth and eyes full of humour', [85] Its unexceptional eulogy was typical of many that were written at the time, simply regretting the 'retreat from public business of an eminent and respected man . . . at a time . . . when the united force of talents and integrity is particularly wanted'. As James Fergusson said, the writer of the eulogistic paragraph 'probably considered that Mr Dempster's public career was now over, and that, however much he might be liked and esteemed, a man who retired from Parliament with nothing more to show for it than the nickname of "Honest George", and a record of having opposed nearly every Government in power, had rather wasted those twenty-nine years'.[86] Few of his friends left any record of his departure but Pulteney would have been one of the first to deny any ungenerous comments when he spoke for many at Westminster: 'I wish that he was still in Parliament'.[87]

Such regrets as Dempster may have had probably stemmed from the way a parliamentary career had constrained his natural commercial instincts. With his good measure of business foresight he may have done more to exploit the application of science. Many of his generation among the landed gentry were as perspicacious but few had the breadth of interest or the entrepreneurialism he was capable of showing. Dempster's roots lay deep in the merchant class; wealth creation from trade had been the watchword. As a lawyer who decided not to practice, he chose politics as the more fashionable route to achieving change. He had enjoyed life in Parliament but probably always believed he possessed enough commercial acumen and business sense to have become a merchant like his grandfather, building his reputation as a reforming laird and agriculturalist on the back of a successful business, perhaps as a grain dealer or importer. Indeed, he had concluded after only a dozen years in the House of Commons that 'Were I to choose my walk of life again with all the experience I have had, it would be a private one'.[88]

Dempster would have known many men whose philanthropy had been built on the acquisition of wealth, men with such qualities even in the neighbourhood of Skibo. The Forsyth family and George Ross of Cromarty who had been highly successful traders, promoters of improved farming methods and creators of sizeable industrial employment were remarkable benefactors to their local community. William Forsyth, whose father had started the business supplying teas, wines, spices, cloth, glass, Delftware, furniture, iron, timber and flax seed from Holland, developed the entrepot status of the port at the entrance of the Firth. Ross, who had acquired Cromarty in 1772, and who died the year Dempster bought Skibo, had built houses, a chapel, a nail and spade manufactory and established a hemp and rope factory employing 200 people. They were men who with beneficial zeal had already exploited what Hugh Miller called the *terra incognita* of economic opportunity.

As the year came to its close the Duke of Atholl, whose imprimatur had been so much on the Stanley project, lost his wife – an 'inestimable woman . . . so exemplary a creature, such a wife (and) such a mother'. Dempster was wholly genuine in the condolences he asked Fintry to convey to his Grace and his regret was that of a man 'very sincerely and affectionately attached to the family'.[89] The Perth venture, however, had never been much more than a substantial investment for Dempster and 'with no suitors to receive, no hopes to disappoint and always something more agreeable to do' he now looked forward to seeing what sort of fist he could make of being his own master.[90]

12

INVESTMENTS AT SKIBO
(1791–1792)

'Our cotton mill goes on charmingly'
(Dempster to Sir Adam Fergusson 9 September 1792)

1791

Dempster best summed up his new and extraordinarily varied life when he wrote to Sir Adam a year later. Just how much he omitted from this happy litany will soon be apparent, but there was ample evidence that he was not going to be idle either at Dunnichen or Skibo: 'I am full of occupation from morning to night, what with selling marl and peat, what with enclosing 130 acres of land round Lochfiethie, what with attending to all the concerns of the new village and villagers of Letham, and to the execution of our new road bill and turnpikes, visiting and receiving visits from a few kind neighbours – not to mention a new study, the Gothic language, that is the Norwegian and Icelandic, which I now read pretty near as well as Chaucer and find it to be clearly the language of our great great great . . . grandfather's own language'.[1]

An old parliamentary colleague, twenty years his junior and who had recently married for the second time, was among the first to add his interests to those that Dempster listed. Sir John Sinclair of Ulbster and Thurso Castle shared Dempster's passion for agricultural and industrial expansion and had taken part in many of the important debates of the 1780s as well as being a member of the St Albans Tavern Group. Initially, he supported Pitt's economic policy, only to become disillusioned. What had looked like a promising relationship with the first minister deteriorated both for reasons of policy and Pitt's irritation with Sinclair's manoeuvres. He had angled successfully for a baronetcy, but by the time Pitt agreed to give him the nominal title of 'commercial negotiator' to facilitate Sir John's seven-month journey of 7,500 miles across Europe in 1786/7 his conceit and boring pre-occupation with the minutiae of foreign political and economic progress had become too much to bear. Sinclair collected all manner of information from the courts of Russia, Poland, Austria, Hanover, Denmark, Sweden, the Low countries and France. Believing that the systematic investigation of 'great opportunities' was an important element of any government's work, he subsequently suggested the adoption of a unified approach to agricultural, fisheries and transport matters. The administration brushed this aside, fearing that it smacked of a 'descent into particulars' – a phrase of Sinclair's that usually described lifeless detail.[2] As a result, and with Scotland's needs paramount in his mind, Sinclair turned to Henry Dundas for support. The latter became Secretary at the Home Office that year just as Sinclair was starting work on the research he felt so necessary for effective action, work that was to lead to his *Statistical Account of Scotland*. Unlike the information collected by governments in other countries, and which usually focused on the existing state of affairs, Sinclair's intent was to see it used for the future betterment of the country.

Two more different men would be hard to imagine. Sir John Sinclair had little, if any, sense of humour, whilst Dempster bubbled over at the slightest provocation and rarely resisted a chance to tease him. Dempster was modest and Sir John pompous, quite convinced of his own importance. Both were enthusiasts in their different ways and very capable of hard work. They became good friends as well as being bedfellows in the cause of economic development. Dempster, who could also descend into particulars, recognized the deep sincerity and remarkable contribution Sir John was capable of making to Scottish agriculture. As James Fergusson said, he was 'perhaps the only one of (Dempster's) contemporaries who surpassed him in versatility of interests. Politics, economics, philology, agriculture, stock-breeding, naval and military science, the collection of statistics and the judging of pipe music – he was an expert in all these and many more.'[3]

When Dempster heard of the impending publication in 1791 of the first volume of Sir John's account of parish life, he immediately enthused about it, saying that 'This is a most valuable and useful work. It is a real Dooms-Day Book, and promises to be more read and quoted than any book printed since Dooms-Day Book. The older it grows, the more valuable it will prove' – and so it became.[4] Dempster was correct in forecasting that it would 'be resorted to by every future Statesman, Philosopher, and Divine'. Uniquely, every Parish minister in Scotland had been asked to provide information about the geography, natural history, population and employment of his parish. 166 specific and precisely-worded questions formed the basis of Sir John's request, many of which would be highly contentious today. The number of artists, jews, negroes, gypsies and persons born in England were sought. The alacrity with which many of the clergy supplied answers did them 'infinite credit'. Eventually, 21 volumes of replies were published over a period of nine years (covering 938 parishes). The first appeared in May 1791 and that written by the Rev George Rainy[5] for the parish of Creich about 1793 included Skibo. A small part of the estate was in Dornoch, about which the Rev John Bethune reported separately.

The *Statistical Account* was Scotland's first national census. Its bleak recital of rural life along the Dornoch Firth was in stark contrast to the urban development which had followed the 'Age of Enlightenment' and the growing prosperity of Scotland's principal centres of population. The blossoming of creative activity that had spread from European centres encouraged the great strides being made in architecture, art and music, but such developments had wholly bypassed communities in the Highlands. The picture given of the parish of Creich in a dozen or so pages was of some 1,700 people, with few childless couples, eking out a harsh and uncertain existence. The crops were mainly barley, white oats, small black oats, potatoes and a 'small quantity of peat'; 'small and white' salmon caught in baskets under the cascade of the River Shin, other 'larger and good' from elsewhere; trout from Loch Migdale; little seaweed for manuring the land but 'wholesome short seaweed' being used as winter cattlefeed; small hardy black cattle everywhere; perhaps 1,500 horses and, towards the west end of the parish, 4,000 sheep pushing out people, cattle and horses; with smallpox inoculation for a few. In tolerably good years the area was self-sufficient in food, but poor crops in the summers of 1783 and 1784 had produced 'great distress' and, although none died from want, distributions of food had been supplemented by a 'gentleman in Glasgow, of uncommon benevolence, who had lived in the parish when a boy, and who sent money, and five bolls of white pease, which were distributed among upwards of 80 persons'. There were no bridges in the parish but 5 or 6 cobbles or yawls, capable of carrying 2 horses each, ferried people across the firth; the prospect of a government-funded bridge at Culrain 'amused the populace', however convenient it would have been for drovers and inhabitants alike; people foretold good cattle prices if the cattle were willing to swim the Kyle; hard and gravelly roads were common; the character of the people was described as 'regular and orderly' and many behaved in 'an exemplary manner'; all spoke Gaelic and many English too; what they wanted in point of industry they made up by frugality. There had been one capital crime in 20 years and that had been for theft and house-breaking.

As if the catalogue was not long enough, there was constant flooding of arable lands and meadows along the Kyle, particularly in the west of the parish, a lack of manufacturing employment and seasonal work migration. Of the last it was said that 'young lads, in spring and summer, usually went in great numbers to the south in search of employment. There, they were got high wages, and returned in winter to their parents or relations, somewhat in the style of "gentlemen", and were a burden on their friends the whole winter until they set out again in spring. Some of them married in the south; others died, or were picked up by recruiting parties. Unmarried girls went to the south also for service, especially before harvest.'[6]

The importance of an adequate road system in the Highlands and elsewhere had been a priority in Sinclair's scheme of things and in April Dempster was adding his plea that 'I shall also have the pleasure of seeing good spacious roads connect every town in the county, and convenient parish roads form communications for every gentleman and farmer with the great turnpike roads'.[7] He was firmly of the opinion that 'roads are the first work the nation should undertake, long at least before it goes to war with France'[8] also echoing the cry ever since, 'Do not forget our Highland roads. In the happy state of our finances the judicious application of a few thousands in piercing the north and west Highlands with good roads would be a most patriotic application of public money, and quickly repay the bountiful treasury for its expenditure.'[9] As Dempster said, it was 'just sixteen years since I moved this measure in our county and stood alone'.[10]

With possible new roads in the Highlands beginning to be surveyed, Dempster continued to press for action. The efforts of Sir William Pulteney, who championed the cause inside Parliament and Dempster outside it, were rewarded in 1792 by the passing of the Turnpike Act. The system which required proprietors of land on either side of poorly kept tracks to provide six days of 'statute labour' each year for maintenance was replaced by one of equivalent grants. The construction of the road halfway from Dingwall to Ullapool was one of the first results, justifying the use of another of Dempster's favourite verbs. 'Expatiate', he said to Sir Adam 'on the intersections of the country by the arms of the sea, on their being in a rude state mere en-cumbrances to travellers, but when improved by roads along their sides and bridges at their tops, they become natural inland canals carrying trade and intercourse to every corner of the interior country – O, that I had a gold mine!'[11] By 1799 he was able to exclaim with obvious satisfaction that 'the mail coach has reached Inverness, and the turnpike roads the extreme of Aberdeenshire'.

Spring brought news of two of Dempster's old friends. Thorkelin was returning to his duties in Copenhagen after what had been a long leave of absence. Dempster responded in a warm farewell letter. He amused himself with the thought that Thorkelin might one day be appointed Governor of Iceland, admitting that it is odd that (his) 'hobby horse' should have become Iceland. He wished that 'all who liked one another were obliged to settle in the same Parish'. Telling of his wife's interest in building a cottage at Lochfiethie, Dempster toyed with there being a corner reserved in it for the professor. The two men were never to meet again although they did occasion-ally correspond. Dempster's farewell summed up their relationship: 'your temper, your manners, your honourable character, & your vast learning were delightful to me, and to all your friends'.[12]

The second contact was with Boswell from whom Dempster had not heard for some while. The first sentence of his letter dated 30 April 1791 showed

Boswell in a sober mood: 'My Dear Dempster. We must not entirely lose sight of one another rather we must not suffer out of sight, out of mind to be applicable to two such old friends, who have always lived pleasantly together, though of principles directly opposite'. He had been stirred to write what may have been his last letter to Dunnichen by the rumour that Dempster was to accept 'one of Pulteney's seats' and return to Parliament. Learning that it was false, he was greatly relieved, 'for it would have been a sad degradation; but though not in Parliament you can be mischievous enough as a "Whig Dog", as Johnson would say; or rather as something ever beyond that.' Boswell had resigned the Recordership of Carlisle and 'the melancholy event' of his wife's death now 'hung' on his spirits. Nevertheless, he took great satisfaction from his *magnum opus,* a copy of which he could not promise to send Dempster because 'it is too great a work to be given in presents as I gave my Tour (of the Hebrides). So you must not expect one, though you yourself form part of its multifarious contents'.[13] He had a 'good house in Great Portland Street' where his two eldest daughters lived with him while his sons were at Eton and Westminster – 'daughters to clothe!, sons to educate!' Dempster guffawed. Recalling the 'tissue of pleasant occurrences' during their 31-year acquaintance, Dempster congratulated him on his *Life of Dr Johnson*, musing that he had begun 'to think (he) would take as much time in writing this life as (his) hero did in living it'. An order would nevertheless be placed with his Edinburgh bookseller.

In what for Dempster was an unusually pensive reply to his old friend, written in a clear hand, he was sufficiently inspired by Boswell's 'moderation and wisdom as to money affairs' to recall his own circumstances. 'Were I to begin life again,' he wrote, 'I would spend the first twenty years of it in getting a great deal of money. I would try to be a Banker, or Corn Factor, a manufacturer, to marry a rich widow. Instead of endeavouring to fortify myself with a Stoical indifference above money, I would apply my Stoical principles to the expenditure of it.' He then chose their mutual friend, Pulteney, as 'the great model for emulation. Independent in his principles, simple in his manners, diet (and) dress, yet able without rummaging to the bottom of all his pockets and fob, to pay £80,000 for seats in Parliament to bestow upon his friends and relations,' which enabled him to respond to the rumour about his own return to Westminster.

'There is no truth,' Dempster wrote, 'in (Pulteney) having offered me a seat, as there could have been no probability of my accepting it. My own seat did not cost me Five Pounds a year for my constituents always treated me except to the Election dinner.' He was like a leech sucked full of the political life and 'the tide of (his) own ambition (had) turned', Dempster explained. In his 'rusticated situation' he had never to 'forget the resource of all politicians in retirement – trees. Like Sir Robert Walpole I talk to my larches and find them very conversible.' Metaphor followed metaphor, as if reminding Boswell that he wasn't alone in his literary skills – 'calculating chances, the living to 60 years of age is one of the best prizes in the lottery of life, and to have done so without knowing much the want of health, or at all the real want of money, is such an additional bonus to my lottery ticket as few adventurers can boast of.'[14]

Growing ever more concerned for his wife's health, Captain John had taken Jean and young George to Cadiz and Lisbon at the beginning of the year, hoping that the 'balsamic' air of the voyage and a stay in Portugal would help her consumption.[15] On New Year's Eve a letter written in early December and surprisingly signed 'Your ever affectionate brother *and his wife*' reached Dunnichen where George Blair, George Heming, Charlotte Burrington,[16] Rose and a few more friends, including 'Jack' Guthrie, were 'ending the year' in merry mood: 'We are all made happy by the agreeable accounts of our dear sister's happy recovery.' For his part, Guthrie was 'very thankful for the berth (Captain John) had procured him on Captain Hardinge's ship', a likely reference to the despatch of his second son who was christened after Dempster (as George Dempster Guthrie) and who served in India till his death in 1816.[17] In the absence of any specific mention of young George by his father, Dempster's reply 'infers the best' about him and assumes 'it will all be fun' for the five-year-old – 'how he will pick up the Portuguese language!' He was particularly concerned that the British Minister in Lisbon should be made aware of the Dempster presence in that city, asking Walpole to alert the Minister there and ensure their welcome was more than the 'bare civilities of a British Consul'.[18] The family had hoped that their stay in Portugal would be extended into the summer.

By March the Captain was expected back: 'Perhaps you are all safely arrived by this time in England' and Dempster awaited news of how he meant to pass the summer, forbearing to outline his own plans for being at Skibo. Readying him for his return to rural life, their correspondence turned on appropriate clothing for him and the condition of the Captain's horses.[19] In fact, the family seems to have returned without Captain John who journeyed separately via Marseilles, from which port he travelled across revolutionary France, arriving in Paris at the end of May, 'where no wise strangers should be and no good Frenchman out of it'.[20] While waiting her husband's return, Jean Hamilton Dempster, who was now eating 'like a dragon' and in improved health, stayed with her father in Dulwich before travelling north in May to Newhailes in the company of Allan Fergusson,[21] Kitty Burrington and Stratton, her new maid.[22] The party had delayed its departure because her coachman had been dismissed at Dempster's 'earnest request' and alternative arrangements had to be made. Eventually they travelled with Sir Adam Fergusson who had been suffering the ill-effects of various medicines prescribed for his gout and who was to take the waters at Buxton. Charles Fergusson, however, had another reason to write to Captain John.

Sir John Sinclair had written to tell him that he had a friend who wished to purchase some property in Scotland. He had heard that 'Captain Dempster intends to dispose of the estates of Skibo and Pulrossie and indeed, unless he resides on the spot, he will not find them very profitable bargains. If that is Captain Dempster's intention, my friend would go as far as eighteen thousand pounds, payable at Martinmas.'[23] Having been shown the letter to his brother, Sir Adam thought it important enough to go straight to the House of Commons where he found Sir John 'very much uninformed about the matter'. What happened next was that the usually unimaginative Sir Adam overstepped the caution of his profession – 'a little below the bounds which I generally prescribe to myself' – perhaps thinking he saw the chance to confirm the advice he had given Dempster against the purchase of Skibo in 1787. The Captain's pardon for raising the matter was invited, but he sought to 'prepare (him) for the offer that may be made'. Sir Adam evidently knew little of the Captain's affairs in Sutherland, admitting to only occasionally seeing his handwriting 'on the outside of a letter (to Jean) . . . (but) . . . I have never seen within it'.[24]

Dempster was unaware of what had passed in London at the time. That May he was still longing for his sister-in-law and her son to pay him a visit in Forfar: 'Don't mind the expense. . . . I'll wager you have spent less money than you would have done living *en famille* at Knightsbridge.' The barley fields below the house at Dunnichen were a good sight and the fruit trees coming into bloom. He was a little worried about his wife, Rose, who had caught a cold early in the winter and not shaken off the cough and asthma 'it brought along with it'. He contemplated a productive year; the more so 'when the drain shall have produced its full effect' and there was better access to the marl and peat from Restenneth. The 'pleasantest of all the projects (he had) ever tried', the development of Letham, was well under way, an investment which 'if it (were) followed up by Captain John and little George (would) make Dunnichen *alone* worth a least a couple of thousand a year'. He had feued out all but ten acres, and masons, carpenters and quarriers were all hard at work 'at the expense of the feuers'. A church was in prospect and he had offered to build it a steeple 'for till we have got a steeple and a clock, to strike the hours, we'll not discover the time nor wear the appearance of a town'.[25]

With Captain John back from France, Dempster caught up with the events that had been sparked off by Sir John Sinclair's letter. He was ready to share his thoughts with his half-brother, frankly and objectively. Referring to the £18,000 offer for both Skibo and Pulrossie, he maintained that since 'these purchases having been made solely with a view to your benefit and particularly to furnish you with an ever inexhaustible, useful employment when you gave up the sea life', he had wanted to say nothing till his return. Dempster asked him to turn the matter over in his mind until such time as they could meet, anticipating that a sale would 'indemnify us and give you £1,000 in your pocket'.[26] As he could see the possibility of living within his income 'by saving, retrenching and pinching', he did not want to dictate to the Captain even about his own share of the purchase, insisting that he had 'gone on since (he) left . . . without borrowing any money or neglecting any interests', correctly interpreting the replacement of the bond guaranteed by Pulteney with the mortgage. Ramsay, the lawyer (now Sir William[27]), had apparently heard again from the unknown prospective buyer who appeared to be in earnest and 'would wish to enter at Martinmas'. He left Captain John to judge for himself, adding only that 'had the East Indian Trade gone as we had reason to hope my answer would have been <u>no</u> , very flat. You will judge how far the falling off of that trade may make it advisable to listen to these proposals. If you had had £50,000 in your pocket and Pulrossie paid, I think you would have been a king, almost a God.'

The matter was not pressed further. He knew Jack well enough to let him decide, but the tenor of his advice was against acceptance. He spoke from 'the experience of these last two years . . . (when) . . . the time (had) gone most interestingly and amusingly' and he was confident that a success could be made of the venture. Instead, he asked the Captain, who was to sail again in April 1792 for Madras, to secure a berth for George Heming on the *Rose*: 'a charming lad and modest'. He had been staying with the family at Dunnichen and was someone whom Dempster felt he 'must endeavour to serve'[28]. In the event by October all idea of a sale had 'vanished' and, as if to make a point, Dempster told Sir Adam that he 'would be charmed to see how much the value of both estates is increased by their union. Like husband and wife they lie in one another's arms. . . . They form an extent of 14 or 15 miles along the north bank of the Firth of Dornoch which is on the point of becoming one of the most beautiful of our firths.'[29]

At Skibo Dempster's factor, who had been asked to investigate a market for seaweed, had found that Mr Houston was the only person who dealt in kelp and his prices were paltry. Previously purchased timber lying unused at Pulrossie had to be sold off and a potential clash with Colonel James Sutherland of Kinnauld had to be resolved. By 'some means or other' he had 'got himself into possession' of Dempster's principal seat, No. 27, in the church at Rogart which 'ought to have been possessed' by Dempster's tenants on the Langwell estate. Polite letters had not done the trick and Fraser brought an action before the Sheriff who fined Sutherland £5 and ordered him to give up the seat 'at his peril'. Such 'disagreeable work' was all part of his duties and when the defendant appealed the decision to the Circuit Court in Inverness he asked his laird to ensure that Sir William Ramsay, the estate's solicitor, had instructed an advocate to put Captain Dempster's side of the question. Turning to the condition that the tenants found themselves in, Fraser asked Dempster whether the punitive prices for meal (18/- a boll) and small quantities of barley (16/-) also prevailed in Angus; food was short and not 'a single drover' had been seen in the county, affecting the prospect of his collecting the Martinmas rents.[30]

Dempster knew that the Captain's party would be unlikely to link up with his own and reach Sutherland before the first or second week in August. Having spent three weeks in Paris and a fortnight in London at Red Lion Square, there was an obligatory family stay at Newhailes to follow. The visit to Edinburgh started in July, but he learned from Guthrie that Jean Dempster had a slight malady and was being cared for by Mr and Mrs Blair,[31] and for some reason young George had been left behind at Newhailes. Just how the child responded to Lord Hailes who was 'a short, stout person with a thick, short neck, of apoplectic appearance, fat cheeks, and pursy mouth,' and very much at home 'presiding' at dinner parties, is not recorded.[32] He would nevertheless have been aware of the awesome size of the library built by the eminent judge's grandfather – dubbed by Dr Johnson 'the most learned room in Europe' – which, by this date, doubled as a drawing room as well as being the remarkable sanctuary where so much of Lord Hailes' scholarly work had been penned.[33]

At Dunnichen it seems the house was in turmoil and repair work to unstable walls had necessitated the shifting and temporary storing of furniture; some rebuilding was also contemplated. Writing to the Captain, he explained that 'some part of my house is like to fall which will make a repair, and consequently some enlargement, a necessity'. This phase of betterment followed works done in 1775 and more significant developments were to follow in 1794–5. Outside, life was more normal with the Captain's horses, about which he continually enquired, in good shape. Dempster had promised that 'one week before you reach us your horses shall be brought over to our stable at Panmure; they run out in rich grass and have their corn daily so that they will be in prime order'.[34] They were 'fat, hearty and quite sound' and awaited the care to be given them by the new coachman Dempster hoped he had found for the family.[35] Master George's prize pony, 'Toby', was 'impatient' for his young rider's return, but a small saddle, bridle, cropper and whip needed to be included in the baggage from Edinburgh. Dempster always wanted the best for the pony and its dam, sending them both for their winter pasture to Glamis Castle.

The Dunnichen party set off for Skibo, anticipating that the Hamilton Dempsters would follow once 'his dear sister' was fit to travel. Although when she eventually arrived her spirits and appetite were good, her consumptive cough and irregular pulse rate were among the 'alarms on her account' which Dempster watched 'assiduously'. He had previously told her something of the family's recreation together, including walks and climbing expeditions during a fortnight of 'uninterruptedly fine weather'. Several times they picnicked by Loch Migdale and roamed over the nearby hills. One occasion after dinner, his wife, with Betsy and several 'country guides' took it into their heads to 'retire into the woods'. Soon afterwards those at the house heard the voices of their guides 'calling from the top of Loch Migdale . . . . The truth was that they had no idea of the height till they tried it and then they found hill after hill that led them on till they were unable to go on and (were) ashamed to return'. When they did reach home, out of breath after scrambling down to reach more level ground, Dempster had been forced to scold 'Mrs Dempster for being the ringleader of this expedition'.[36]

With the whole family eventually re-united at Skibo, and the ladies often out riding and making social calls on the neighbouring gentry, Dempster and his half-brother were able to give attention to the affairs of their estates. The Captain appears to have come north determined to fulfil his responsibilities, even being prepared to toy with the 'notion that if he were in Parliament he could do good to the Highlands', at least to please Dempster. 'He would not,' Dempster said, 'be afraid of rising up in Parliament and telling them they ought to make roads and bridges . . . that they ought to lower the rate of licences on many of our infant trades such as tanning and candle making, and that they should really contrive something of a constitution, whereby the people might have some hold of their possessions than their present tenures'.[37] But many details of the Captain's plans were little more than repetitions of Dempster's own mantra and he had already told his half-brother that he had secured a third voyage for the *Rose* with all its risks and potential benefits, about which Dempster, probably with some reluctance, was forced to congratulate him.[38]

As the two men discussed Dempster's stewardship of the Pulrossie estate on behalf of his half-brother, a discrepancy in the Captain's title came to light. Establishing an accurate terrier of estate land often proved an almost impossible task for many landowners, but this threat to his title was sufficiently serious for Sir William Ramsay to advise them to seek counsel's opinion. In October George Fergusson (later Lord Hermand) writing from Kilkerran opined that there was a risk that the title could be challenged and he recommended, 'no doubt . . . attended with some expense', that a [Crown Charter] be sought since 'there is no other way as the law is now understood by which he can obtain it'.[39]

The idea of building a cotton mill at Spinningdale, to the west of Skibo, was without doubt first mooted at this time.[40] Dempster knew that the presence at long last of his half-brother in Sutherland provided a quite exceptional opportunity for the two of them to dream together about what might be achieved over the next 10–15 years along the Dornoch Firth. Any means of replicating the fourfold increases in ground rents being achieved in Lancashire and the tripling of them elsewhere in Scotland where industrialization had occurred would be worth attempting. These encouraging trends were not lost on either man. Pleased as he was to be able to tell Sir Adam in October that the Captain had 'lotted out a sea port town that will adorn the coast of Sutherland and enrich its fields', he had to admit that they had done little more than peg out a few possibilities.[41]

Each approached the prospect of a mill from very different standpoints. The use of the firth may have attracted the seafarer, whilst the other had long pondered how the Highlands could share in the nationwide development of the cotton industry. What someone eighteen years younger than Dempster, who had been at sea for more than twenty years and used to the sole command of a hundred men or so at sea, made of the placid rural scene around him can only be guessed. It could not have been further from the gregarious bustling life in such ports as Whampoa, the Canton anchorage or Madras, with its shops stocked with European millinery, haberdashery, madeira, claret, cutlery, perfumery and glassware.[42] From being an exporter and importer in his own right, and used to all manner of profitable 'indulgences', he was expected to become a small-time entrepreneur. Anticipating his half-brother's questions about the vagaries of journey times by coastal vessels, or the intricacies of getting in and out of the Firth, he had raised these matters in his correspondence with John Fraser. But even a new port for the despatch of estate timber by sea or the import of goods and raw materials would, on the face of it, have had little prospect of paralleling the success achieved by the Forsyths at Cromarty. Spinning cotton would have had little intrinsic attraction for the Captain.

Dempster's plan to see a small cotton mill and its associated housing built at Spinningdale was part of his new approach to investment. Asking Fintry to see what he could do to encourage the other shareholders in the Stanley mill to let him sell his share at par, he explained his thinking. His money was not needed at Stanley now that they 'were prosperous' and he really wished 'to constrain (his) worldly concerns within as narrow a compass as possible'.[43] Though critical elements of the project such as a reliable source of waterpower to drive the mill, cheap labour and access (through the Captain's proposed port) would have been debated, there was certainly no detailed plan at this stage. Further research was required and, with neither man in possession of the large sums of capital any creation of manufacturing employment would demand, considerable financial support and competent management would be essential if anything was to be achieved.

What they contemplated 'was no easy matter . . . and cannot be easily ascertained', but, as Dempster wrote later, 'the understanding, industry and ingenuity of man are superior to . . . brute creation . . . (just as) . . . the value of an estate inhabited by mankind (is superior) to one occupied by sheep'.[44] Such accord as existed between George and the Captain was sufficient for an invitation being sent to George Macintosh, a colleague of David Dale, to come up from Glasgow and see for himself what was being contemplated. His credentials for the task were better than might have been expected. He had spent thirty years in the textile industry, founded a dyestuffs company 'with a Gaelic-speaking workforce to help preserve trade secrets' and seven years previously had established Scotland's first Turkey Red Dyeworks with financial help from David Dale.[45] The latter, who never saw Spinningdale, was to express his pleasure in encountering several examples of 'landed gentlemen interesting themselves in what must not only promote their own interests but the interest of the nation in general'.[46] By 26 November Dempster felt confident enough to write that 'the plan for establishing a branch of the cotton industry . . . is now finally settled'.[47]

Macintosh probably viewed the land along the Dornoch Firth just before the family's return to Dunnichen in the last week of November. He apparently saw enough of what was planned to agree his interest in the project, but his assurance was 'more from patriotic motives than profit'[48] and reflected understandable scepticism. The Dempsters left Skibo 'with sorrowful hearts for we are going to a colder climate and an uglier place'. By 11 December severe wintry weather had set in at Dunnichen; the thermometer showed 12 degrees below freezing at nine in the morning. On the estate Craichie Mill Farm needed some improvement but rent rises had been agreed, Cunninghame House had been let to 'Lindsey, the butcher' who intended to open a Public House and the 'marsh account' (marl from Restenneth) showed a clear £600 profit which would be 'touchable, spendable, towards Balnoe and other purposes'.[49] Quite apart from felicitations to all members of the family, Dempster had time to correspond with Dundas about the circumstances that Colonel Burrington found himself in at the Cape; an 'appointment' was being mooted. Moreover, a request had been made for his wife, Helen, whose financial position caused the family some concern, to go out to join him.

Just before the end of the year Dempster appealed to his friend Graham of Fintry, who had been appointed a Commissioner of Excise in 1787, on behalf of an exciseman's destitute widow whom he had heard about from the factor at Skibo. It was 'a most compassionate case – the old woman, a decent one . . . in absolute poverty. The poorest woman in short in the poorest town in the whole universe – Dornoch'.[50]

The Captain's party had taken longer to return south, with stops in Edinburgh and Newcastle, and once in London on 20 December the Captain rented accommodation in Gower Street for a short period – a location Dempster was quick to remark that would have been better had it been in Gower's County (i.e.Sutherland). Those horses that had gone lame on the journey south had been taken for examination to Tattersalls who had a veterinary stable behind St George's Hospital. His wife and son were both suffering from coughs which were still causing him some concern. Writing to his half-brother, Dempster told him that he had asked David Dale to write to him from Glasgow about Spinningdale. He also enclosed an offer by one of the Captain's tenants to buy his property on terms that Fraser, the factor, had recommended.

1792

No sooner had Dempster reached Angus the previous November than he left again, this time to visit Glasgow to talk to Macintosh about Spinningdale and meet others that might be interested in the project. The Captain may have come from Edinburgh to join the party.[51] Earlier correspondence with likely financial backers must have confirmed some support for the inaugural meeting of the Balnoe Company which took place in the second week of January. The company's name had been taken from the Gaelic *baile nuadh* – Newton being the most southerly point of Captain John's Pulrossie estate and aptly describing what the company aimed to achieve. There had been talk of measures being taken in the spring for 'building two weaving houses for twelve looms each',[52] and in his enthusiasm Dempster spoke to Sir Adam of 15 or 16 lots having already been taken, which would give 'the Captain's new seaport . . . the appearance of a town by next year'.[53] All in all, even such hyperbole could not hide the fact that an energetic start had been made.

In Glasgow Macintosh had been busy since Dempster's visit despite the death of a clerk which had delayed work on the company's Memorandum of Association. His 'chief attention' had been to find 'a proper person to manage and conduct (the) spinning branch' of the project, in the hope that it could begin similarly at Easter 'as we do the weaving'. He had 'set upon one that, could he be prevailed (upon) to go . . . would ensure our scheme', a Mr Urquhart from Ross-shire who had 20 spinning jennies and 40 looms, but it was not to be. He also wanted a check made on the likely head of water available. Davidson of Overskibo was asked 'to examine the falls of water near and nearest to Balnoe for our carding and roving machines – a moderate fall of water (would) do'.[54]

The possibility that a group of Glasgow gentlemen, tobacco lords and Virginia planters, might put up a proportion of the capital had obviously featured heavily in Dempster's plans. Such merchants were typically sleeping investors in such industries as glass, textiles, pig iron, sugar and collieries, relying almost entirely on management to deliver agreed returns. If they elected to join a venture located in the Highlands Dempster knew just how unusual it would be. They belonged to 'a tightly-knit' and 'established kinship group' that rarely invested in manufacturing projects outside the West of Scotland.[55] Much was made later of their 'patriotism' and 'public spirit', but it is hard to imagine that non-pecuniary motives or philanthropic support for a 'social experiment' were much to the fore. They had, however, been impressed by the experienced leadership Dempster had recruited and, knowing his record, an experimental project even in far-off Sutherland might just produce acceptable results. At least four of the Glasgow shareholders had family connections with the County of Ross (if not Sutherland), including Macintosh. They were hard-headed and unsentimental businessmen and the venture must have been viewed by them much as a 'flyer'. They would have known that the risks were high, given the nature of the trade as well as its distant location, but, at the end of the day, their wealth would hardly be threatened by an investment of £100.

In addition to four members who initially held two £100 shares – David Dale, George Macintosh, Captain John and Dempster himself – there were fifteen other shareholders with a single £100 share. The tobacco merchants included three members of the Robertson family in Glasgow, William and James, who were brothers of John Robertson who owned extensive estates in the West Indies and managed the Glasgow Arms Bank, along with Andrew Robertson. Also from Glasgow were Robert Dunmore who was 'esteemed the very chief of the old tobacco lords'; Robert Bogle of Baldowie, the son of a Virginia merchant and an industrialist in his own right; Robert Mackie, a West Indies merchant and a William Gillespie. Others among the original members were John Mackenzie who was expected to become the company's representative in London; Dugald Gilchrist of Ospisdale, and, at his suggestion, William Munro of Achany, landowners adjoining the Dempster property. Benjamin Ross, a merchant and agent of the Linen Bank in Tain, David Scott of Dunninald near Montrose and Captain James Rattray of Arthurstone were also included. Dempster's factor at Skibo, John Fraser, became a shareholder, being listed along with John Ramsay who was soon to be appointed as acting manager for the project.[56]

The capitalization of the company proved more difficult than had been anticipated and would be a continual problem; seven shares remained unallocated for some time. The shortage of subscribers, even to raise the total of £3,000 they had set themselves, must have made the five-member standing committee of management in Glasgow question the wisdom of going ahead with construction and the purchase of plant, to say nothing of the working capital that would be needed. The partners from the tobacco trade must have been aware of the threat this posed, but what they had done had been 'chiefly to oblige Mr Dempster and myself'.[57] Whatever the situation, it seems that Dempster, Dale and Macintosh had allowed their enthusiasm to get the better of them, especially in going ahead without fully understanding the project's likely capital requirements.

A decision not to enrol any more partners and seeking funds only when desperately needed was to be short-sighted. Although nobody expected to make a profit on their money, Macintosh admitted that they had become 'a little more sanguine'. Dempster may have anticipated that those involved would increase their stake if and when it became necessary, which the other two were forced to later as pressures mounted. He had taken account of other likely risks and was aware of the need for a gradualist approach, which may or may not have been recognized by the tobacco merchants, but this only emphasized the importance of making sure the equity in the business was sufficient. In the OSA Dempster noted that 'it is one thing to build a village, to which people may resort if they choose it, and another to drive them from the country into villages'. He anticipated that increased wealth would be the nub of eventual success, 'the latter will augment the quantity of the production of the soil, both for the maintenance of people and cattle'. What had not been foreseen was how a Highland community would respond to industrialization. The weight that Macintosh (and Dempster) put on 'common people in the county (acting) with rationality and moderation in their charge for labour' was to be misplaced.[58]

In February Dempster asked his half-brother, who was a shareholder in the Balnoe Company, to sign the Contract of Co-Partnery and return it to John Fraser. Then, a few days before the *Rose* was due to set sail for Bengal, the Captain reported from Dulwich (where he was staying with Charles Fergusson) on the state of his financial affairs and the location of all his papers 'of consequence'. He had borrowed £2,500 on their joint bond from Robert Steel in London and was awaiting Dempster's bill for £5,000 at 'Mr Davidson's counting house'. His assets included £10,000 in goods (for sale in Madras) and £4,500 in dollars 'all insured', with the policies lodged with Steel and John Ferguson & Co., except one for £4,000 that was in the care of Mr Mavors. Other items scheduled for the ship's hold, either making up the twenty-five tons of 'privileged' goods a captain was entitled to carry on the outward journey for sale in the east or, more likely for consumption during the voyage, were, however, missing. Arrangements made the previous autumn for some sheep from Dunnichen to be delivered to the quayside in London had gone awry, along with the arrival of two passengers – 'no sheep, no William, no Jamie Mason . . . no help for it!'[59]

The *Rose* had been prepared for sea at Deptford between the end of January and mid-April. When she finally sailed there were 121 crew, 39 passengers and 105 army recruits bound for Bengal.[60] At the top of the passenger list were three of the Burrington family who were to leave the ship at Cape Town and join Colonel Burrington there in July 1792.[61] Before he left the Downs the Captain mentioned the financial plight of Mrs Helen Burrington, telling Dempster who was Colonel Burrington's attorney that he had sent him 'all the receipts for cash' he had disbursed on 'account of our sister Mrs Burrington' and that his assistance had included 'taking the lease of Mrs Burrington's house and buying her furniture'. He obviously wanted to be able to report to the Colonel that all was well when the ship reached Cape Town.

Having 'a good Purser this time' aboard the *Rose* enabled the Captain to put on record more about his finances.[62] Clearly the laird of Pulrossie's affairs were in a confused state, to say the least. Keeping account of expenditure and managing the Captain's estate, along with his own at Skibo, must have been a constant problem for Dempster. The analysis, which 'for a sailor I hope you will find . . . tolerably accurate', showed additional debts attracting 5% interest well in excess of £5,000 and, despite an over-drawn position with John Ferguson & Co., his last action had been to pay £50 on Macintosh's draft for Balnoe.[63] The Captain had come to respect Macintosh and trusted Dempster 'to make a good bargain' for him. Although he had some doubts about 'the land to be settled by Rose of Nigg' (whom he obviously liked less than Mr Macleod of Geanies) he looked forward to hearing more about developments at Spinningdale while he was away.

The intention at Spinningdale was to produce shawls, simple coarse fabrics and handkerchiefs, an 'article at present reckoned most advisable to make', made from raw material imported into Glasgow and shipped monthly from Leith or Grangemouth. Finished goods were to be sent back to the Clyde and London for sale. Twenty to forty acres of land were to be feued from Dempster's estate. In April estimates for a four-storeyed mill, stores, weaving house for 22 looms, smithy, wash house and 'barracks' for work-people began to arrive on Macintosh's desk. Left more to his own devices than he antici-pated, and without the day-to-day support of any of the managing partners, he complained to Dugald Gilchrist at Ospisdale. Reconciling excessively high quotations from Glasgow tradesmen took up time and 'the whole burden of setting matters on foot here lies most completely on my shoulders who had enough to do before'.[64] James Boag, a Dornoch bailie and carpenter-turned-general builder, who had built several churches and one or two of the few large buildings in the area, was apparently asked to design and construct the project.[65] John Ramsay, whom Macintosh had been 'uncommonly fortunate' in recruiting as manager, and Dale, under whose supervision Boag was to work, would have melded their complementary experience. A young man with 'honour, integrity, attention and sobriety', Ramsay had not only been an 'excellent' cotton spinner but possessed 'a very useful mechanical genius . . . and (was) good at manufacturing', as well as being said to be a more than adequate book-keeper and administrator.[66] Publicity was given to the venture by the *Glasgow Advertiser and Evening Intelligence* when it reported that the foundation stone had been laid by John Barclay Esq., on 17 May but building work was to take far longer than the partners expected. It was not until 1794 that the contractor's bills started to arrive in earnest.

The spring report from Fraser on the state of the estate confirmed what Dempster had rather expected. The factor had found his duties for the Sutherland family, as well as those for Dempster and Captain John, too much for him. He was forced to give notice of his resignation, effective when the Dempsters came up to Skibo later that year. He was rightly sure that 'none of the tenantry (would) complain of any injustice or bad usage at (his) hands'. In sharp contrast to the year before, living conditions were a little better and advertisements for drovers had been successful. Fraser hoped improvements to Pulrossie Mains, the Captain's domain, would be 'to his liking' but in his absence, Dempster would have to take a personal interest in obtaining much in the way of rents on the Skibo estate when he arrived and, in the case of the farm at Prontinach, the boundaries needed establishing before a lease was offered.[67]

At Dunnichen Dempster's attention had been drawn to other problems. Major Scottish banks were lobbying ministers to give them 'the exclusive circulation of paper money' throughout the country. This threatened private banks at a time when there was a need for better credit facilities in remoter parts and new branches such as those in Stornaway, Thurso and near his Skibo estate at Tain.[68] He had also asked Pulteney to clarify the Turnpike Acts since he 'hoped to have seen a little money voted towards their *completion*'. The 'horrors of France' still occupied his thoughts, and, writing expansively to Edmund Burke in February (who had put forward yet another *protégé* for a berth on the *Rose)*, he had sought to minimize their earlier differences about the French Revolution and Hastings' prosecution. Dempster considered the country had fallen into 'the hands of those who appear to an old man, rash and presumptuous boys', and implored Burke 'not to withdraw from the great stage on which these twenty and seven years (he had) acted so conspicuous a part'.[69]

He was also grateful to Sir Adam Fergusson, who was going to Buxton to have more treatment for his gout, for seeing that his copy of the House of Commons *Journals* were bound by Websters, the publishers. He had changed his mind about making 'some of the spoils' of his public life available, at least to 'his heirs'.[70] Doubtless under pressure from constituents and friends, he had come to accept that 'their value rises in proportion as we recede from their area' and he could not 'be out of fashion altogether'[71], a very different view from that taken when the subject of a biography about him was broached in later life. Not having explained anything to his friend about the establishment of the Balnoe Company (in which Sir Adam seems not to have been invited to invest) and only briefly mentioning the developments at Newton and Spinningdale the previous year, he added his oft-repeated motive for this work, saying that his 'receipt for preventing emigration is to give the tenure by which they may improve waste land, and manufactures by which their industry may enrich them'.[72]

By the start of June the Captain's wife and Master George were expected in Edinburgh. Accompanied by Miss Allan Fergusson, they planned to spend a month or so with Lord and Lady Hailes before going on to Angus en route for a family holiday at Skibo. However, Jean warned Dempster that the judge had 'of late been ailing and that his eyes (were) so weakened as not to admit of his reading and writing as usual'.[73] No one was surprised to hear of the great man's death when it came in November. Jean's arrival coincided with the start of the social calendar in Forfar and Dempster sought to give her news of the subscription balls being planned, the last of which, on 5 August, being the signal for the family's departure to Sutherland. He hoped that 'such powdering and flouncing' would compensate a little for the absence of her husband who had a 'good ship' and was a 'skilful conductor'. The Dempsters' own ball at Dunnichen had been 'very brilliant with between 80–90 well-dressed and well-pleased folks (who) stayed together till 4 in the morning'.[74] The state of the house, described a week later in a letter to Sir Adam as 'like to fall about (his) ears' to the 'terror' of his wife and the 'wonder' of his neighbours, must have at least been adequate for the occasion after the improvements done the previous year.[75]

'Rosie' Dempster would have been well-used to her husband's generally frugal and sometimes disordered domestic lifestyle: 'You know how I live and what a shabby fellow I am'.[76] Unlike the display of wealth and the more usual trappings of prosperity exhibited by some of his neighbours, his homes, if not in the state Boswell had found his lodgings in Berners Street exactly twenty years before, had never received the attention they warranted. He had spoken of 'building a house here' (at Dunnichen) as well as another by Lochfiethie the previous year, although the latter had been initially conceived as a replacement for a cottage there that the family used infrequently. A good voyage by his half-brother might enable him 'to make some arrangement with (him) in building a joint house at Loch Fiethie'. Dempster had earmarked several hundred acres for the venture and mused about the pleasure it would give him 'if our joint riches could lay the foundation of a house there worthy of the estate and the place'. Such was the 'prize of (his) heart'. Even in his will he recommended that a portion of the Barony of Restenneth be 'converted into a most beautiful residence elevated and on a drier soil . . . than Dunnichen'.[77]

Not unexpectedly, Jean had been given news of Spinningdale where in addition to 'weaving houses and other works', her husband's own venture at Newton on the Pulrossie Estate had attracted the support of a Dundee gentleman who had 'promised to erect a linen manufacture'.[78] But by August, when the two families reached Skibo, the 'tradesmen's houses (were) not yet built'. Only in his imagination could Dempster see the trees and forest yet to 'bestud' the area, and 'supplying the Navy with timber and their owners with gold'. Notwithstanding these dreams, his tenants on the Skibo estate 'were building so many stone houses, garden walls and stone enclosures, that stone itself grows scarce and valuable',[79] and by October he had 'forwarded a herd' of calves to market and taken in a good corn harvest.[80] Along the Cromarty Firth he had seen one end of 'the fine road now carried half thro' between Dingwall and Ullapool'. With Dempster's spirit lifted by regular exercise, life was 'a feast' to him every morning and 'our cotton mill goes on charmingly'. The banks of the Kyle appeared to him already a paradise, 'highly improved and ornamented'.[81] Whether or not it was so, Fintry had been told that both the warehouse built at Newton and the beginnings of the mill at Spinningdale had been supplied from vessels unloading from the Firth.[82]

All in all, Dempster was in his element and wrote to Macintosh at the end of October in tones of great optimism and gratitude: 'I rejoice at two things – one that you don't call for any more money, for I have none; the other that you and Mr Dale take the business (at Spinningdale) into your own hands, and mean carrying it on like men of business. You are both inimitable, and I must still insist on contributing my prayers and best wishes for your ultimate success, *on which* the prosperity of Sutherland in a *great measure depends*'.[83]

Lord Hailes' failing health had necessitated Jean staying on at Newhailes after the visit to Skibo and when he finally died on 23 November she was able to comfort her aunt from her lodgings with Mr and Mrs Grant at their home in Hanover Street, Edinburgh. Dempster wanted to invite her and Master George to Dunnichen but he feared life would be too dull for them in Angus. Despite another ball in Forfar which had been a 'very merry dance', the 'cribbage and brag for the oldies and fatties' may have had less appeal.[84] In any case Dempster was busying himself in the profitable disposal of Restenneth's marl. His *'mea menia'* made him not simply 'the only marl and peat merchant to any amount in the county'[85] but a regular client of Dr Black who, even at Christmas, had sent him the results of a comparative test of Sutherland and Lord Elgin's limestone, the latter's being better by half.[86] More pertinently, Dempster, who had 'never more inclination to write', had spent as much time as he could preparing an index of references to himself in seven volumes of the House of Commons Journals.[87]

13

THE CAPTAIN AND THE
FAMILY AT SKIBO
(1793–1795)

*'A little beginning is actually made
towards converting Sutherland into a Lancashire'*
(Dempster to Sir Adam Fergusson 27 November 1794 from Skibo)

1793

At Dunnichen a long winter had been followed by a late spring with hard frosts preventing the growth of new grass for the cattle. Indoors for much of the time, Dempster kept abreast of events in London and Paris through regular reading of the *Courier de l'Europe* and the English and Scots newspapers. Still 'pretty near as bare of money' as he used to be, he had plenty to occupy his mind and 'prevent languor and indolence'.[1] Most of the year he spent in Angus dealing with county affairs, the building of the new village at Letham and the Captain's business. At the same time he kept a close eye on the reports he received about construction work on the Skibo estate in Sutherland. Also never far from his mind was the mill at Stanley where there had been changes. He continued to retain a substantial financial interest, although virtually no involvement in its day-to-day running. Replacement partners had been appointed following the death of William Sandeman in 1790, along with William Marshall and Andrew Keay whose places were taken by other members of their families.

It was around this time that Dempster had occasion to visit his friend whom Boswell had called 'Worthy' Nairne in their days together at Edinburgh in the 1750s. William Nairne had been raised to the Bench in 1786, taking the title Lord Dunsinnan after the family seat to the north-east of Perth.[2] From 1790 he spent law vacations there, rarely receiving visitors and living very simply on his own with a few servants. Dempster had intended his visit to be short but after a violent storm he dropped a hint to his host that he might have to remain at Dunsinnan overnight, a suggestion that only made him agitated, even to the point of his ordering Dempster's carriage to the door. When the coachman, who knew how bad the roads were, even to Perth six miles away, flatly refused to harness the horses in such weather, preferring to lie on straw in the stable if he could not get any better lodging, Nairne saw that there was nothing for it; Dempster would have to stay the night.[3] Explaining the difficulties in his household to him, Dempster's host turned to him in despair, saying, 'George, if you stay, you will go to bed at ten and rise at three; and then I shall get the bed after you'. Although the two friends corresponded, whether they ever met again is not recorded. When there was a possibility in 1811 that Dempster might entertain him at Broughty Ferry and draw the 'hermit from his cell',[4] the gathering (which was to have included Sir Adam and Adam Ferguson) had to be cancelled due to his lordship's death in March that year.

January saw the usual round of pleas for Dempster's help, several of which concerned the well-being of Excisemen and their families on whose behalf he asked Graham of Fintry to intervene. Correspondence about possible 'proper' tutors for Master George also began in earnest. It was an object he 'had vastly at heart' since his nephew had discovered 'a turn for reading and thinking'.[5] One tutor suggested by Dr James Anderson was the son of Mr Duncan, a minister in Dumfriesshire,[6] but it was his brother-in-law at Balmaghie in Galloway who proposed a better solution. Dempster's sister and her husband Thomas Gordon had employed James Henderson to tutor their sons Thomas and James and, since they were of an age to go to school, he was persuaded to undertake similar duties at Dunnichen.[7] With this decided, Dempster wrote to Master George's mother who was still in Edinburgh and far from well, about the boy's small black Arabian pony who had become a companion for 'Toby', comforting her with news that her husband's ship was expected to come from St Helena 'under a good convoy'.[8]

Out of patience with the French from whom he had 'expected a pattern of true freedom', Dempster could now only 'wish them a sound drubbing'. The war with France began on 8 February and was to last, with two short intervals, until 1815. With the greater part of British forces mistakenly destined for the West Indies and the country's defences abysmally unprepared for the conflict ahead, the administration was forced to mobilize its traditional 'home guard'. In Scotland they were the 'fencible regiments', made up of local gentry and their retainers, from which depleted regiments of the line were often repaired. In a scribbled and obviously hasty note to Dempster the day after he had an audience with the King, Lord Gower invited him to accept the command of one of the battalions in the regiment of fencibles for the county of Sutherland. Colonel Wemyss had been 'prevailed upon' to accept the command of 6 battalion companies, one of grenadiers and one of light infantry, each with one captain, one lieutenant, one ensign, three sergeants, three corporals, two drummers, two pipers and sixty men.[9] Not surprisingly, since he was in his sixty-first year, Dempster declined any command and put Captain Kenneth Mackay of Torboll's name forward in his place, adding that he should find no difficulty in raising his company, 'being known to the tenants (and) liked by them'.[10] By August similar arrangements had been put in hand in Angus where Dempster was able to return the hospitality given him in 1786 by Alexander Maclean, the Laird of Coll who had become the commander of a division of Lord Breadalbane's fencibles.

In Sutherland Dempster also charged Mackay of Torboll with responsibility for his and Captain John's estates following Fraser's move to full-time duties with the Sutherland family. A new factor at this time of great construction works, when the tenants would have been particularly uncertain about how changes would affect their lives, presented its own problems, especially as it was seen as a temporary appointment. Just how Mackay had adjusted to his factory was apparent from a long letter written at the beginning of January.[11] Rent payments had been slow and disputes due to poor cattle prices the previous autumn had caused a good deal of grumbling. How this affected recruitment into the fencibles is not recorded. Donald Sutherland of Ferrytown had 'returned the rent and arrears of his house amounting to £16 17s. 6d', George Gordon 'had a charge of damages by comprisement' and a debt which Captain John had hoped would have been discharged as the result of his building works was still outstanding.[12] Dempster had handled a request from a Miss Gray sympathetically but the lady had subsequently sought the return of her written agreement, hoping to be able to persuade him to offer better terms. Getting to grips with the intricacies of agreements made by Fraser, and for which the paperwork was sometimes missing, led Davidson (of Overskibo) to intervene on behalf of one of Miss Gray's sub-tenants. He believed Dempster had given permission for their land to be enclosed.

Davidson, with whom Captain Mackay thought Dempster should be more forcible – it would 'have a good effect at his time of life' – had nevertheless kept quite a good weather eye on the estates. The different plantations at Pulrossie were 'tolerably well-cared for, and would thrive rapidly if allowed' and the factor had offered him additional labour to heel in plants sent from Dundee; less to his liking was the absence of any sheep at Pulrossie or Newton. On the other hand, William Munro of Achany, Dempster's co-partner in the Balnoe Co., had taken up residence at Skibo House, a move that the two men must have agreed previously. Probably anticipating further absences by its seafaring owner, he had also made an offer of the existing rent of Pulrossie mains, promising to seed grass areas and preserve its plantations once they were enclosed, at his own expense. The Dempsters seem to have taken to Mackay during their stay in 1792 and, for his part, his remembrances to 'my' young Master George showed who had captivated whom. Since his laird would not be present at Whit Sunday when the yearly report was presented to the tenants, he contented himself with looking forward to Dempster's visit in the summer.

With the country at war, some of Dempster's old worries about his half-brother's safety resurfaced and the Captain's absence had an effect on the health and composure of Jeannie. George's own strength of purpose and determination was being tested by the expensive and largely experimental works on his two estates. With the Captain away, there were few in the immediate family with whom he could share his plans for Master George, now seven years old. Not surprisingly, he became unwell and suffered 'a month's confinement', but, as he wrote to Richardson, his fishmerchant friend from whom he continued each month to receive 'one of the finest Tay salmon',[13] he was fortunate 'to have three complaints and not a mortal one among them'.[14] His usual *joie de vivre* only returned slowly. Before it became apparent that the *Rose* had been required to wait in St Helena for a convoy, the comfort he gave his sister-in-law was as fulsome and humorous as ever: 'I have no uneasiness at not hearing by the *Ganges* . . . these monkeys (the crew) had not been able to write from Madras and must have had their letters ready to pop into the *Ganges* as she passed'. At the time navigation required 'the Captain's utmost attention' and the transfer had apparently not been made.[15] Concern also mounted for young George Heming in India when Dempster's neighbours at Burnside, over the hill from Dunnichen, reported the murder of their son William there and the 'dreadful mistreatment' of the second mate at the hands of pirates. The family and guests, which included the Misses Guthrie and Mr & Mrs Blair, had reason to fear that George Heming might have been involved in this affair, although they were 'in hopes that George had quitted the ship in Bengal'.[16] Fears about the *Rose* were only laid to rest in July when news came that another ship in the same convoy, the *Winterton*, was known to be safe.[17]

By May it became clear that Macintosh had serious reservations about the disarray into which the cotton trade had fallen following the outbreak of war. Firms across the country were short of orders and lost business could not be made up. This did not immediately affect the prospects for the Balnoe Co. in Sutherland since the commercial world had yet to realize how long the hostilities would last, but Macintosh's words that a 'good peace (was) the only thing that would make a rapid improvement' in the situation were prophetic. Reports he had received from John Ramsay pointed to additional problems, the first of which was an overspend on the construction of the workers' cottages which, although it had strained the company's fragile capital resources, he was still reluctant to relieve by obtaining additional partners. What nearly changed his mind was Ramsay's insistence that 'another weaving shop' with twenty looms at a cost of £100 was required. Furthermore, he told Dempster that he would make his 'own share up to £400 if a few of the rest' of the members would contribute another £600. He anticipated that there would be no difficulty in getting Captain John and Mr Scott (of Dunninald) to do the same.[18] Nevertheless, it was clear by July that Dempster was reconciled to the fact that more capital had become a necessity and, writing to Jean, he could only hope that 'the Captain will bring home a shipload' of money.[19] Just how much responsibility at Spinningdale rested on young John Ramsay's shoulders was demonstrated by the fact that Macintosh, his immediate supervisor, was himself unable to leave Glasgow on account of other business engagements, although he hoped to be able to make a short visit to Spinningdale either late in June or August.

Throughout the summer Dempster was unavoidably involved with family affairs and unable to give Sutherland much attention. Near the top of the list of his preoccupations was the advice and guidance he felt obliged to give his sister-in-law about Master George's education, particularly as his father's letters demonstrated a similar concern. 'Let me send up a young man to attend him,' Dempster offered, 'he can board with you'; and Mr Blacklock's nephew (the tutor he had in mind) could give him 'instruction as to prevent any inconveniency for want of school(ing) till the Captain's return'. According to Dempster's 'notion', and his father's too, 'he should have been attending school with a private tutor to attend him wherever he was'. He feared that without a public school he would not acquire 'that degree of manliness that (was) necessary in this scrambling world'.[20]

Work on the new village at Letham had gone on apace. Regular meetings of the Board of Trustees, which Dempster attended when he could, had ironed out many of the development problems, including expansion into the manufacture of Osnaburgh thread and a beetling mill for the use of 'the weavers of our coarse linen'. All in all, Dempster felt that Letham 'was succeeding to (his) utmost wish'. There was not three acres 'undisposed'. His only disappointment had been the lack of any offers to build a church – nor had anybody applied to him to construct a steeple so that the village could have 'a clock, a bell and a sundial, for the use of the town and the ornament of the country'.[21] By March 1793 Dempster was telling Fintry that he had sent a petition to the trustees on behalf of 'the best flax dresser' in that part of Angus. A Robert Jamieson built a flax mill and a house for himself in Letham, partly on credit, and was highly regarded in the community. His brother-in-law and two relations worked as weavers and builders at the mill. Continuing his encomium at the progress that had been made, Dempster invited his friend 'to take a peep (at) the industry and exertions of this little knot of friends'.[22] What Fintry was to make of the miniature Bengal cattle to be landed from the captain's ship, the 'size of good English sheep' and kept to give milk to his Letham tenants, was not recorded.[23]

Albeit that 'all the fleet were in company', as the *Rose's* journal recorded with obvious relief, the homeward journey from Calcutta had been slow, and when she eventually reached London in August the vessel was well overdue. The last lap from the South Atlantic outpost of St Helena had been in the company of a large convoy of East Indiamen escorted by naval ships, in total some fourteen vessels.[24] The only threat now before the ship was that it might be boarded and members of its crew 'impressed', a hazard faced by all mariners in the Channel. Unfortunately, 21 August turned out to be a most unwelcome day for some 34 aboard. Those impressed included a gunner's mate, quartermaster, a boat's mate, the poulterer and 31 seamen.[25] Care also had to be taken to avoid the temptation of selling off any of the cargo of tea to smugglers who operated just outside territorial waters. On this occasion, and after taking on a pilot in the Downs and off-loading the cargo into lighters which shuttled up-river from Gravesend, the passage up the Thames towards the Blackwall yard went smoothly. The Captain's journal reports that the unloading took from 26 August to 23 September when 'His Majesty's Inspector' came aboard, 'examined and cleared the ship'.[26] The release of tension must have been evident for all to see, none more so than Captain John who had concluded 'that this (was) the moment for quitting the India Service'.[27] As they caught sight of the recently built five-storey masthouse, now a prominent landmark on the river for all returning seafarers, and the docks where kintledge, or iron ballast, and sailing gear would be removed once the vessel was tied up, the Captain could only hope that he had the strength of purpose to persevere in his decision. No one knew better than he how much of a difficult turning point it was to be.

After 'as successful a voyage the present times admit of', the reconciliation of his finances and the question of a future career on land were now important matters to be discussed.[28] The first was the conventional if always complicated outcome of any voyage. In hoping that Jack would have 'better voyages', Dempster would have known just how dependant the success of any private trade was on the marketability of outward and inward cargoes purchased for sale. Clothing of all types, leather goods, glassware, wines and spirits and personal perquisites, tended to make good prices in the East, but a glut of anything could upset the best calculations. Some captains had a flair for anticipating demand, whilst others seemed doomed to select goods without appeal.[29] It was, of course, equally important that vessels reached their destinations at the right time and before markets became over-subscribed or saturated. However, until the income from private trade and moneys received from the sale of passenger places on both outward and homeward legs of the voyage had been netted off against the loans incurred to finance it, the results of the voyage could not be established. Passengers could be required to pay the captain between £50 and £1,000 each depending on the status of those carried, an especially profitable perquisite in times of war.[30] Imponderables such as custom-dues, duty, sale discounts and warehousing costs added to the uncertainty and all private trade had to be auctioned 'by inch of candle' in the General Court Room at Leadenhall Street which doubled as the company's saleroom when necessary.[31]

Captain John's reasons for choosing this moment to leave his seafaring life behind were never specified, but the owner's plans for an unwelcome and speedy turn-round of the *Rose* to take advantage of the increased demand for shipping in wartime certainly closed any loophole of doubt he may have had. Ships had been taken up 'three months sooner than necessary'. There was talk of a voyage 'to Barbados with troops', and a family acquaintance, George Elphinstone, Captain of HMS *Robust,* had been appointed to lead an expedition against the French at Toulon.[32] Against this background the Captain was looking for further financial security for his new life. The value attached to the command of an East Indiaman was considerable and the Captain asked William Moffat, the *Rose's* principal managing owner, for £8,000 to surrender it. He had, however, made the proposal to Moffat conditional on another old colleague and one of his best friends being given the command. Wemyss Orrok had been the *Rose's* first mate for each of the vessel's three voyages and was well overdue for promotion. Unfortunately, Moffat had earmarked the captaincy for a nominee of his own, and his offer to Captain John of 'only £6,000' was 'a great disappointment'. Jeanie, his wife, was 'enraged at the little man'. Fearing that a worthy price would not be achieved and that her husband might change his mind about leaving the sea, she insisted that he immediately 'take the coach after dinner' from Dulwich (where they were staying with Charles Fergusson) and re-open negotiations with Moffat. Moreover, his wife urged him to seek arbitration, should it be necessary. Her heart was 'set on (his) being off the sea', but the 'little man was deaf' and remained intransigent.[33]

The outcome of this disagreement only became apparent when the *Rose*, having 'hardly put her head into the Thames . . . was taken up again for another voyage'.[34] Her commander was to be Captain Alexander Gray who left Portsmouth the following year, again bound for Madras confirming that Captain John had made the break with Moffat. An unknown but amicable financial settlement had obviously been agreed since a little more than six years later the two men who had a high regard for each other were together again. The Captain may even have had Moffat's help to become a Ship's Husband.[35] However, for a time at least, he was to lose something of his social standing as an active captain of the 'John Company' and be seen less frequently in his blue coat and blue lapels, yellow metal buttons, buff waistcoat and breeches.[36]

The financial reconciliation of the *Rose's* voyage took some time to achieve. Calculations of his net income included the total achieved from 'primage', a percentage of the ship's earnings shared proportionally among all on board – together with his captain's pay, perquisites and private trade. By October some details of the Captain's financial position emerged. An extract from the accounts he sent to Dempster showed that to an opening balance of £21,132 had been added £28,498 as the result of the *Rose's* voyage. Contra expenditure, made up of outstanding debt liabilities, amounted to £32,625, making the 'Captain's fortune' at this time £17,005. Of the 13 items that made up the income of £28,498, six accounted for over 90% of the total and five were entered in round figures, suggesting that the Captain's principal deals had been on a grand scale and, for once, well in excess of the average gain of £4–5000 he and other middle-ranking captains achieved. The more precise sum of £1,725 was the Company's payment of his bills as Captain and a similar smaller sum (£1,200) would appear to have been his official share of the Rose's cargoes.[37]

Dempster was 'well pleased . . . (with) . . . the moderate bounds' to which the Captain had limited 'his ambition respecting money' and his apparent contentment with '£800 a year', a sum which indicated that he had committed all the capital he had to what he hoped was his last voyage. He also showed his appreciation of two gifts that had been part of the Rose's cargo, one an Arabian horse 'of the most beautiful kind' which was a gift from an Indian friend, but which 'enriched and beggar'd him'[38], and the 'little bull and cow from Bengal' referred to earlier. At Dunnichen he began to 'entertain a higher opinion of the cultivability of Scotland' and a good barley crop had been safely gathered in. The results of better husbandry meant that crops were being grown across the hills at heights not previously thought possible. In the excellent weather Dempster spent much of his time on estate affairs, hoping greatly that Jack and Jean would come northwards. He mulled over at great length how Master George was to be brought up now that he had determined to make him his heir to the estates in Angus and Sutherland. What had been happening at Spinningdale and elsewhere was for once far from his mind.

When the Rose was at the Cape the Captain had written saying how much he wanted young George to go to school. Now that he was home and able to resume his care, the matter was taken up in earnest. Dempster had not been impressed by the 'academies round London'. They were 'seats of idleness and nurseries of vice', places used by 'parents who know little about education, and mean their children for active life'. Recalling that from the time his nephew had been born, his 'mind (had) been employed in thinking how he should be educated'. Dempster now characteristically wrote down his advice, albeit in a pedantic manner. He even thought it wise to send a copy to Sir Adam Fergusson for amendment and comment. Whether the child's father ever saw it is doubtful. Dempster nevertheless asked the captain to remove young George from Mr Shaw's soi-disant academy at Enfield which he and young Charles Fergusson attended.[39] In December, uncertainty about the form of young George's education took on a new significance. Captain John was apparently 'still balancing about sailing again' and Dempster had to admit that 'till that point be decided' he expected 'him and his wife to forget there is such a thing as education or . . . a son to educate'. Disturbing as this was, it also meant that there was little likelihood of the boy being taught in the country of his origins – 'to combat the idea of a London academy'. Much as he knew 'what castles in the air we uncles build for our young folks!', Dempster dearly wanted to make him 'a pattern Scotch laird'.[40]

1794

Having spent Christmas at Dunnichen, Dempster took advantage of an especially mild winter that year. The 'most distant and elevated hills (were) destitute of snow' and the good weather encouraged a brief visit by George and Rosie to Skibo.[41] He was obviously anxious to know how much construction had been completed at Spinningdale and to view the estate which his constant engagements the previous year had prevented him from seeing. The contractor, James Boag, had been hard at work on the mill as his accounts were to show. Ten new houses for workers and the renovation of older houses for the manager and his servants were well under way, along with two slate-roofed weaving sheds and, a barrack for the employees, and the impressive mill building itself was being progressively equipped. The machinery to be installed included 'two large carding engines, one picking engine, one billie engine, one drawing frame, one roving frame, ten common jennies of 96 spindles, two slabbing jennies, three large mules for fine twist, of 144 spindles, and one 64 stretching frame'.[42] A large water wheel and associated drive works were also in construction. Together these works were to cost considerably more than the capital that had been subscribed, but Dempster was probably unaware of this at the time. Even much later in the year he was pleased to be able to tell Sir Adam that 'our Glasgow friends' had 'adorned' the banks of the Firth 'with a palace cotton mill round which a little town is rising tolerably fast'.[43]

Although the weather was mild enough for the planting of fir and larch trees, other activity on the estates was altogether less pleasing and Dempster had to ask Kenneth Mackay to give urgent attention to several important matters. The factor was to spend five days trying to sort out rent arrears and offers being made of cattle in lieu. A second meeting with the tenants had to be scheduled for March when Mackay proposed to enlist the assistance of 'Mr Davidson and three of the most intelligent men on the estate of Pulrossie' to listen to their difficulties and any instructions Dempster had about the issuing of summonses. The dismissal of the gardener was contemplated; despite having a 'strong family' to support him he had not paid his rent for two years. At Newton 'the enclosing of the hill (was) going on', but it was not planted; neither had the storage building associated with Captain John's weaving sheds been started; only rudimentary masonry work was in place. The roofing was not expected to be completed before the summer. To the long list of uncertainties was added Captain Mackay's imminent return to the colours for a period: 'I must have all settled before the end of next month when my leave expires and I have no sort of confidence in the people that must be employed'.[44]

At Dunnichen Dempster found the experimental heating system to be used at Spinningdale keeping the saloon, dining room, drawing room and principal bedrooms warm. It circulated hot air 'by means of an oven that bakes the air and diffuses it in tubes'.[45] The 'contrivance' was probably similar to that devised by William Kelly for the mills at New Lanark – 'perfectly simple and the expense nothing'.[46] Dempster confidently foretold that 'in the houses of the next generation there (would be) but two fires, one in the kitchen and one in the air oven'. It seems to have survived the major works that were soon to be undertaken at the house but it never worked wholly as intended. (see 1808)

Christian Dalrymple records Jean and Captain John arriving at Dunnichen 'in the Spring'.[47] Their presence, and confirmation of the success of the *Rose's* voyage, probably gave Dempster the confidence to spend a considerable sum of money on improving the family home. Rarely did any windfall Dempster received during his lifetime stay long in the bank and the structural works carried out at Dunnichen three years before had done little for the family's living conditions. It seems that his wife and half-brother had persuaded him to 'build a house' since the 'old one . . . would have fallen of its own accord'.[48] In April, with the first moves being taken, he wrote to Graham of Fintry asking whether he could use his influence as a Commissioner of Excise to obtain suitable transport to move to Skibo what they needed there while the work went on in Angus: 'I am going to make some addition to my house here' and 'we are all going – wife, brother (and) his wife *bag and baggage* to remain at Skibo till it be done – about September 1795'. What he wanted from Fintry was 'one of (his excise) yachts to carry a crowd of people and a great quantity of goods!' Suspecting that it might be an unreasonable request, he added, 'I know you wont let (it) test you in any misapplication of the Excise's navy'. The proposal involved the Excise cutter sailing from Arbroath to Cromarty Firth in early June with Mrs Dempster and Rose, an unknown niece, aboard. Both had been 'complaining of their lungs'.[49] George had hoped to get leave from his wife to be in 'the sailing party' rather than be left at Dunnichen as he told Fintry.

No immediate reply from Fintry was forthcoming and a fortnight later Dempster repeated his request, this time giving more detail about what the move entailed: 'Do you think we could get a cast of one of your yachts about three weeks hence to convey a great parcel of our folks and a few tons of furniture to the Firth of Cromatie?'[50] Fear that his friend, or one of the captains involved, had found the whole matter 'improper or even inconvenient' was fortunately for Dempster soon dissipated and at the end of June the arrangements were in place. Fintry had 'done our transport business neatly like a good friend'. Everything was 'prepared (so as) to detain Captain Elder off Arbroath (for) as short (a) while as possible'.[51]

While the house was being made ready for the family's move, news of Miss Allan Fergusson (Jean Hamilton Dempster's sister) came from her father.

Writing to the Captain, who had shown much concern for the family, Charles Fergusson told of her failing health and the care she was receiving from her sister, Betsy.[52] Also enclosed was a belated official receipt for 4 chests of port wine delivered to the *Rose*.[53] Other correspondence kept the Captain abreast of the movements, promotions and fate of many of his ex-colleagues and demonstrated the warmth and esteem in which he was held. The families whose relatives he had known or taken to India as passengers over the years often kept in touch. Among the officers whose friendship he especially valued were Innes, Baigrie, Orrok and Kyd, and a letter from Kyd's sister following the death of her brother particularly demonstrated the affection the family had for him. Apparently there had been the possibility of one of Colonel Kyd's two sons by an Indian mother being sent to school with the Captain's young George. She wrote: 'I shall always feel myself highly obliged for the great care you have taken of my sister's boy . . . and the affection you show for him, and the great interest that the ladies of your family have been so good as to allow themselves to have for him'.[54]

Fintry's good offices were obviously successful and Dempster was to use the excise cutter on several other occasions; nothing exceeded 'the courtesy and attention' the family received from Captain Gillespie.[55] But he had left Dunnichen with evident reluctance. The house was in the hands of 'the under-taker – an ominous word' who had promised to 'have it ready for us by the middle of next September if I shall then be alive. In the meantime we have all taken up our habitation here and are so well pleased with our situation that it shan't be for want of punctuality that I shall be disposed to go to law with the contractor'. Much to Dempster's relief and satisfaction, the Captain had 'taken as kindly to the plough shaft as if it were his ship's tiller or main sheet'. On the other hand his wife Jean's health, about which he had learned not to prognosticate for fear that her condition would quickly change, was a perpetual worry to them all: 'She, the Captain and I have observed, that we no sooner announce her perfect recovery . . . than her cough and spitting of blood return'. For the moment she was 'stout and hearty' and Master George who was coming on 'in all parts of his education very well' had apparently at last got a good tutor.[56]

Riding along the banks of the Kyle of Sutherland regularly each day in November, Dempster had time to consider 'some additions' he wanted to make to the report on the state of agriculture in Forfarshire for Sir John Sinclair. Its writing had been largely in the hands of the Rev James Roger who, as a 'young clever probationer' and ministerial assistant at Monifieth, had contributed to the earlier *Statistical Account* for the parish of Dunnichen.[57] Dempster's interest in Sinclair's doings, hitherto largely the result of the original 'doomsday' project, increased when, after some opposition in Parliament, Sinclair's Board of Agriculture was finally launched in the autumn of 1793 and those 'persons who *gratuitously* devoted their services' met under his 'presidency' to promote the cultivation and 'pasturage of the soil'.[58]

The King appreciated the establishment of the Board of Agriculture, saying through a secretary (who answered on his behalf a letter sent him by Sinclair) that 'His Majesty . . . considers the success (of it) . . . a concern which very essentially interests the general good of the community at large . . . and contributing importantly to the good of his country'.[59] Dempster had pulled the baronet's leg about the Board's remit and thought it might also be used to relieve 'the commercial and manufacturing distresses of the Empire . . . your publications would thus be infinitely more entertaining'[60], but he was only too well aware that, despite his friend's over-reliance on 'facts' and a manner that won him respect if not affection, his work for reform in agriculture could be beneficial to Scotland and particularly to the Highlands. Their subsequent correspondence during Sinclair's two periods of presidency of the board (and an 8-year gap from 1798 when he lost control of 'his' board) amply demonstrated a close if not altogether whole-hearted friendship. Dempster watched the younger man's strenuous efforts to achieve the better use of agricultural resources and the effect that running the gauntlet of changing ministerial favours had on him, much as he had done during his own period in the House. As Mitchison said, 'Sinclair was to spend much of his life discovering that ministers do not really love independents, however much they may appear to respect them.'[61]

Sinclair's work in 1793 on the House of Commons Committee set up to address the shortage of specie in the banking system had so indebted Pitt to him that he had been able to gain the Prime Minister's support for the formation of the Board.[62] It was to be a voluntary organization-cum-government agency with no executive power, a small budget of £3,000, a Secretary (Arthur Young) who was paid £400 a year, and a mixed bag of trustees drawn from the great and the good.[63] Being naively 'flattered' at being made an honorary member of the Board, although probably unaware that he would be required to pay a fee of ten guineas for the privilege, Dempster wanted to do what he could to help. Sinclair had been forced to carry out surveys that were at the heart of the Board's early work at county level due to the Archbishop of Canterbury's opposition to more research at the level of the parish and, under Dempster's eye, the Rev James Roger was soon 'working and travelling like a trooper'. Regretfully he was unable to accept an invitation to dine in London with both the Board of Agriculture and the Fisheries Society. Sinclair had not given him sufficient notice of the event.[64]

1795

At Skibo the year opened with Dempster being asked by a nephew of Thomas Gordon of Balmaghie to support his brother-in-law as the parliamentary candidate for the Stewartry of Kirkcudbright.[65] Writing to Sir Adam,

Dempster expressed his surprise that so modest a man was contemplating such a step. He was well-liked and had undertaken his laird's duties with diligence, presenting the new church on the estate with Communion vessels (which are still in use) the previous year.[66] He felt such public duties would redress his otherwise quiet rural life as a widower. Unfortunately, for some unknown reason, Robert Burns, the Ayrshire bard, took against him, saying in one of several election ballads:

> 'And there was Balmagie, I ween,
> In front rank he wad shine;
> But Balmaghie had better been
> Drinking Madeira wine'

Sir Adam reminded Dempster that he was already committed to Patrick Heron of Heron, Tom Gordon's opponent, who eventually won the seat. How much Burns's verse influenced the electorate is not recorded.

Plans were being made for Charlotte to join her father, Colonel Burrington, and his wife Helen in India where he had been transferred. The idea was that she should travel there aboard Captain Ralph Dundas's ship, the *Prince William Henry*. What the family did not know until May was that the Colonel had been killed the previous October during a battle between East India Company forces and the Rohilla Chiefs. Charlotte Burrington had long been Dempster's ward and, having spent much of her life at Dunnichen, she was hoping to see her father 'for the first time in her life'.[67] Mrs Dempster had 'acted a parent's part . . . all along' and was looking forward 'to crown the whole by attending her to London and seeing her safely embarked'.[68] Fortunately the ship's departure was delayed and the much belated news of her father's death reached her as she was about to embark. Writing in July to Sir Adam, Dempster reported that 'My wife attended Charlotte to Portsmouth, where she learnt the afflicting and disconcerting news'. Despite her loss, Charlotte decided to sail for Calcutta 'having a sister well married there'. The following year she met and married Charles Boddam, a collector of revenue. [69]

Writing to Captain John from Bengal in February, a friend gave him news of his sister Helen, Burrington's widow, and enclosed a copy of the will since he was one of the Colonel's executors. The estate in India was 'very desperate', but the Nabob intended making Mrs Burrington a gift of Rs.40,000 which would supplement her pension. 'She was extremely disturbed but I am happy to inform you that being with her daughter (Mrs Francis Hawkins) who has lately made her a grandmother she has recovered the shock more than you could have expected . . . her grand-son amuses and employs Mrs Burrington sometimes so much that she seems to bear her loss undoubtedly well.'[70] By the end of the year it became clear that Mrs Burrington had decided to return to England and that the Governor had recommended her pension to the Court of Directors in London. She was to sail on the *Anna*, commanded by Captain Mungo Gilmour.[71]

With the Captain assuming responsibility for the mains at both Skibo and Pulrossie, and promising to make 'a pretty vigorous farmer', Dempster could turn his attention to the business affairs of the two cotton mills and a host of matters being put before him by Sir John Sinclair albeit after spending two weeks at the Strathpeffer Spa in the company of Sandy Duncan. There he 'plied the waters assiduously' and, quoting Psalm 103, renewed his age 'like the eagle'.[72] Such refreshment was probably only too necessary.

Dempster would have been aware of how the Stanley mills had progressed since the new partners had been recruited in 1792. Profits had been made, if not the dividends he had hoped might be agreed, and by 1795 more than a hundred families were living in the village atop Sheil Hill overlooking the River Tay. The large six-storey water-driven mill stretched out two hundred yards below. Despite an always fragile balance between costs and uncertain markets in what was by then a highly competitive industry with a good deal of over-capacity, plans were afoot to build other mills. The OSA for Perth referred to a linen mill coming on stream in 1796 bringing the asset value of the two facil-ities to £10,500, second only to New Lanark at £24,400.[73]

Neither Dempster nor the Captain were much involved with the day-to-day running of the mill at Spinningdale, but they would have known about its fitting out, Ramsay's recruitment of foremen and the twenty-eight apprentices to be employed. George Macintosh, who had borne 'the whole burden, trouble and correspondence of the business', appears to have taken to confiding in Dugald Gilchrist of Ospisdale rather than Dempster – probably believing him to be more objective. However, it was Macintosh's report and accounts in March 1795 that not only brought home what had been going on but focused the attention of both the Glasgow and Sutherland partners on several questions affecting the viability of the investment. Both parties knew that 'the dullness of the trade' in time of war had not helped, but the time it had taken to establish the business had also contributed to few goods being produced in 1794–5. More critically, the Glasgow partners put no small blame on the 'indolence' of the local populace who did not 'seem ready . . . to learn the weaving and spinning trades, and thereby earn money by labour and industry',[74] whilst Gilchrist, speaking for the Sutherland partners, had to admit that the company's balance sheet had 'a very unpromising appearance'.[75]

The local partners' conviction that a shortage of capital rather than the productivity of the mill's labour was at the heart of the problem did not endear them to their Glasgow colleagues. As Gilchrist said, both sides recognized that 'money must be got in one shape or another or the business given up'[76,] and a loan of £2,500 was to be approved – but Dempster must have shared the common concern that the mill then contained less than half of the machinery for which it had been designed. About 30 looms were making pullicates (cotton handkerchiefs) – 'equal in quality to any done (in Glasgow)' – and 10 common jennies and 3 mule jennies were spinning cotton yarn. Although the buildings and machinery were 'substantial, convenient and well-executed', the higher than expected cost of 'the water trink (lade or mill-race), miln wheel and ark (wheel housing)' compounded their problems. Labour rates at 8d per day in summer and 6d in winter meant that spinning and weaving costs were considerably cheaper than in Glasgow and freight charges did not exceed 3%, but the imbalance of capital spending, limited capacity and market opportunities very different from those originally conceived had put the affairs of the company in jeopardy.

Meetings of the partners took place at Dornoch in April and Glasgow in July. That in Sutherland was attended by Gilchrist, Monro of Achany, Fraser (Dempster's erstwhile factor), Ross from Tain and the two Dempsters. They recognized the changed circumstances, supported the request for additional loan capital, and with so much at stake considered Macintosh should employ an assistant so as to make the management of the company easier. Surprisingly, none of the Sutherland and Ross partners appear to have attended the Glasgow standing committee which had overall responsibility for the company's management. Instead, letters from Gilchrist and Dempster recommending the continuation of the business and the proposed loan were tabled. In agreeing to empower a sub-committee made up of David Dale, Macintosh and William Gillespie (replacing Andrew Robertson, who had died) to procure the £2,500 loan, the only condition they made was that no more should be spent on houses or buildings at Spinningdale. There obviously had been much discussion about the wisdom of continuing with the business and some reluctance to support the Sutherland plea. The resolution was to 'continue a little further'.[77]

Of a total expenditure of £2,778, £1,514 had been spent on what Dempster rightly called 'the palace cotton mill'. Small as it was by the standard of Stanley, the slate-roofed 73 feet by 37 feet four-storey building was not only impressive against a background of the blue waters of the Firth and the oakwoods of Leadmore but its architecture was less monotonous than that often associated with industrial buildings. Inside there may have been all the signs of the squalor and 'noisy, evil-smelling machinery' which those accustomed to an outdoor life found abhorrent, but the passer-by would have had to admit its simple dignity.[78] Its 'full-height canted stair-tower lit by Venetian windows in the front elevation and a semi-circular latrine tower at the north gable',[79] and the harled walls of the mill with sandstone dressings, adjacent to the two well-roofed weaving sheds and warehouse and housing, stood as a testimony to what was a courageous venture.

The overspend of the initial capital and the subsequent need for an advance of £728 from the bank in Tain must have disturbed Dempster. Such attraction as local industrial employment had for Highlanders was also beginning to wear thin. Their inclination was still for the unrestricted open-air life and alternative employment being provided by wartime army recruitment did not help. As the result, 'the manager (found) difficulty in getting apprentices for the weaving and spinning'.[80]

In July there was news of Mrs Dempster's nephew, George Heming, the 'young lad' who had gone out to India three years before. Returning safely to 'Old England' after what would have been an especially speedy ten-month round voyage had it not been for his unscheduled five month detention in St Helena, Wemyss Orrok was able to reassure the family of his whereabouts. He had evidently not found life in India to his liking and Captain John's compatriot commander found him 'near dead at St Helena till (he) took him on board the *Phoenix* where there was good eating and drinking that he is now fat and well'. The Captain had passed on the news that there was the possibility that the Nabob of Oudh had settled £5,000 a year on 'poor' Mrs Burrington. His letter demonstrated the close friendship of the two men; loans were frequently made between East India captains. It seems that 'had it not been for (his) success in (obtaining) passengers home' Orrok would not have been able to repay monies put out by Captain John to increase his private trading on the voyage.[81]

Captain John's reply soon brought another letter from Orrok full of welcome gossip about the appointments and promotions of various shipmates and his reaction to changes in Company regulations that had been introduced. Two years previously the directors had decided that only ships over 1,000 tons would conduct the China trade and those of 800 tons would be confined to the India trade. This had Orrok's support, but greater control over the appointment of commanders and the ending of the system of 'hereditary bottoms', whereby they determined the next commander, would have worried both captains. However much Captain John enjoyed these reminiscences, and clearly, despite his protestations to the contrary, he still longed for the fraternity of the sea, he would not have relished Orrok's next voyage. Apparently William Moffat, Jeanie's *bête noire*, had been given the management of all the 15 ships contracted by the government to carry soldiers to the West Indies and, knowing the better-than-average financial reward of such work, he had put his own three vessels at the top of the list.[82] The Company expected each vessel's commander to accept such duty, but several, including Captain Gray, pleaded sickness, so that his Chief Mate, Mr Smith, had to take charge of what Orrok warmly referred to in writing to Captain John as 'our favourite *Rose*'. He much regretted that Halliburton, the *Rose's* second mate, had not made enough from his last voyage to repay a loan the Captain had made him, adding that he had told him that he must borrow the sum since money was short on account of the 'great expense in improving so large a farm'. Such was Orrok's regard for Captain John that it was his 'utmost wish to have some small place near you all' when he had enough money. So far as the voyage to the West Indies was concerned, it was to be 'most unpleasant' for both Orrok, and his wife who was to be on board. The *Phoenix* would be carrying 510 Irishmen and their Officers to the West Indies, 'who regularly got drunk every night', at least while waiting at Portsmouth for the ship to sail. He could only hope to be back 'in time to save our season to India'.[83]

In the autumn, and in the middle of its consideration of an Enclosure Bill, the Board of Agriculture had written to its members and circulated its concern, unnecessarily as it turned out, to more than fifty newspapers across the country that the year would produce another poor wheat crop.[84] This action and his pre-occupation with a survey of roads in Caithness being made at the time probably prompted Dempster to put pen to paper about the need for 'a New Board or Commission for improving the Highlands'. He was not going to be outdone by Sinclair. To make the proposition easier to accept 'he hoped to see (him) president' of such a board with 'a suitable reward for (his) zeal and assiduity'. The plan (of which only an outline was produced) contained elements of improved land use and the construction of roads, bridges and ferry piers which were not to be addressed in any co-ordinated way until the middle of the 20th century with the formation of the Highland & Islands Development Board. Administratively, he obviously wanted to avoid Sinclair's superfluity of trustees and the panoply of power he had assembled, figuring that a small board of five members and a secretary meeting either in London or Edinburgh would suffice. With such a lean administration reporting annually to parliament and concentration on specific infrastructure works, he hoped to avoid public funds being 'squandered on jobs . . . or injudiciously managed'.[85]

With the exception of a few short excursions south with his wife, including his attendance at the Michaelmas Headcourt in Angus – Dempster had spent the whole year at Skibo.[86]

14

CALM BEFORE THE STORM
(1796 – 1799)

'This year has turn'd with nothing but misfortunes'
(Dempster to Robert Graham of Fintry, 20 September 1799)

1796

The contractor at Dunnichen House did not achieve his promised target of completing the rebuilding works by the previous September and Dempster was to spend considerably longer at Skibo than he anticipated. Some records refer to Dunnichen House as having been 'built in 1794'. Whether or not the earlier property was completely demolished is not recorded. Certainly the east frontage was of considerable merit with a very fine fanlight of late Adam pattern and coupled Doric columns.[1]

Dempster's life was made up of 'planting, enclosing and farming as keenly as if I were personally to reap the fruits of them, join'd to a game of cards in the evening, attending to my little financial and economical concerns, with the writing and deciphering they occasion'. Apart from visits in the summer season to Kilkerran and Newhailes when Master George was left in the care of his uncle at Skibo, the Hamilton Dempsters continued to live at Pulrossie House for much of the time.[2] The Captain carried out his role as laird with energy and enthusiasm and it was presumed that he had settled in the country for life. He had accepted responsibility the previous year for the mains at Skibo as well as the home farm on his own estate, and Dempster had been happy to conclude that 'if he pursues this system steadily, he will have no reason to regret the exchange of professions, health and security amply compensating the difference of profit'.[3] Now, a year later, Sir Adam Fergusson was about to retire from Parliament and it was his turn to be encouraged to do his bit to improve the 14 million acres of waste land in Scotland 'of which a good half is capable of being ploughed or planted'. Dempster was sure that he would not 'regret exchanging the pavement of London for the meadows of Kilkerran'.[4] He particularly drew Sir Adam's attention to the humanity and benevolence of a Yorkshire improver by the name of Thomas Parker who had raised £300 for the relief of Shetland islanders in 1783 when their crops failed – 'I shall bid him call on you'.[5]

Not without some secret satisfaction Dempster received a legacy of £500 during the second week of the New Year from the executors of John Johnstone whose affairs had caused him so much heartache in the 1770s. He had died the previous December. Another quite different gift sent to Skibo had been a copy of Snorri Sturluson's History of Norway (the Heimskringla) from Professor Thorkelin which had encouraged his further study of Norwegian. Reading another treatise on the diseases of Iceland, he found its prosody complicated and unintelligible, despite discovering the similarity of some Danish words amusing – *dampar* for perspiration, *sweaty holes* for pores, *mawless* for want of appetite, and *speakingers* for philosophers. Dempster was not beyond heaping praise on his worthy Romans, and even the 'illustrious Grecians', but his nephew, busy studying the classics and English grammar in the schoolroom at Skibo, appears not to have shared such enthusiasms.[6]

James Henderson, who had become Master George's tutor, rarely chastised him and when the 10-year-old got into trouble it was usually because the lesson 'was too long'. On one occasion, while sitting outside the house 'to take my afternoon nap', Dempster overheard his tearful frustration through the schoolroom window and cries of 'I need not try. I am sure I can't get it this afternoon, or tomorrow afternoon, or ever!' This time he was sent to his bedroom and forfeited the ride on 'Toby' that usually followed his studies. Asked the next day as he was getting dressed what the rumpus had been about, he replied, 'Only lessons, Uncle, I do assure you. I do hope you don't think me capable of anything else that would get me such a punishment'.[7] The fact that Dempster was 'almost as much pleased with this answer as if (he) had been his father and mother' spoke well of the kind but firm regime James Henderson had introduced. A valued member of the household, Henderson was 'destined for the Church'[8] and someone about whom Dempster was to say when he had been six years in his service 'neither our ladies nor I have one single impropriety even either in word or deed to lay to his charge'.[9] Young George had 'grown a considerable favourite and confidant' with a gentle nature and 'a turn for reasoning'. 'There cannot be a finer boy,' his uncle added.[10]

The pastoral scene on the Sutherland estate was idyllic that year. Christian Dalrymple gave a similar report on life at Newhailes where it was 'the happiest season we had passed for long. . . . No dear friend was taken from us this year by death'. It was all a far cry from the bustle further south where the threat of a French invasion persisted. The weather had been especially good and the husbandry generally successful after difficulties across the country the previous year. Dempster was relishing having let one 50-acre farm for 30 shillings an acre and prices for cattle and cereals were to be good.[11] All around 'the turnip are sowing very fast. The cows yielding torrents of milk. The calves grow elephants and the geese are all turning swans.' On the table were 'fine grilse and some trout in quantity . . . (and) game abounds – particularly grouse and hares'. Several West Country horses were purchased from England and working oxen were selling at eighteen guineas in Birichen market. Cattle prices were rising all over the Highlands, but the Indian bull had died, being left out one cold winter night; it was to be stuffed by a dresser in Forfar. Tups were being bought for £3 3s to £3 10s from Macleod of Geanies, who had over-seen the start of construction at Ullapool for the Fisheries Society eight years before, and the possibility of a land swap with the Achany estate was expected to save 'half a shepherd'. The shepherd was of the opinion that 'the fine land and much espoused pasture of winter on Achormorly (sic) will save . . . many a sheep'.[12]

Dr James Anderson, an old friend from his days with the Fisheries Society who was giving up his well-cared-for estate at Cotfield, wrote to Dempster warning him that he had shipped some 150 kinds of his best gooseberry plants to Skibo. Knowing that he was 'now planting and ornamenting the place', he also included several cuttings of a 'magnificent' weeping willow which had come from a 60-ft-high tree 'never known to lose a twig by the severity of the weather' and 'quite different from those sorts that have been hitherto culti-vated in Scotland'. Among 'promiscuously tied up' bundles of sacks Dempster found several fine apple trees: a 'winter Maurice', 'a Redstreak of Maurice' and a 'Wallidraggle'. Anderson's prolific family who had caused Dempster so much concern in the 1780s when he found the Treasury had not paid him more than £100 for the cost of his West Coast explorations were well. The drawings of one son, an engraver, were sent as a present for Master George.[13]

The extent of the estate was being increased through the sale and purchase of parcels of land; 'bargains' were struck about the 'sixpenny' lands at Migdale and Little Creich, together with land at 'Cuthil, Cuthildale and those parts (around) Skibo Castle called . . . Hilltown and (the) Height of Skibo'. Towards Bonar 'Tulloch, Middle Swordale and Sleastany' were acquired, whilst 'Gavary and Barracks' were alternative parcels being considered.[14] A good deal of hard bargaining was called for, since few of the names of such areas appeared in their respective charters. Boundary disputes were common and 'to settle (the) marches' between the Captain and George's land, and that of Dugald Gilchrist and Mr Houston, called for arbitration by Mr Trail, the Sheriff of Caithness, always assuming that Lord Gower approved.[15]

Taking everything into account, the two estates had been slowly but steadily transformed. Ten years of work was paying off. The hedges began 'to peep through the banks of the ditches' at Pulrossie; extensive liming had improved many of the fields and, although only twelve inches high, the 206,000 fir and larch saplings that had been introduced already seemed 'forests to their planters'. New houses included a row of servant's houses at Skibo where those 'below stairs' included a new cook as well as the old kitchen maids.[16] Tenants had been won over and both Dempster and his half-brother's standing in the community had risen as their commitment to improved agricultural profitability, and the generosity and indulgence they often showed, became known. Nonetheless, unlike Angus where there was a lively public social life to be enjoyed, there were few such occasions in Sutherland when neighbouring lairds and their ladies came together. One exception that year had been the 'very good election dinner' which followed the renomination of General James Grant, the Sutherland MP. There were 'salmon by way of smelts and a sow for a side dish' and, except for the Dean of Guild, John Barclay, who had laid the Spinningdale foundation stone, 'it did not produce a single drunken guest'.[17] Private social life relied a great deal on family visits, although Skibo also became something of a staging post for travellers, if, that is, they could reach it. That month Sir John Sinclair had spent several days kicking his heels on the other side of the firth 'the wind not admitting of a passage for his chaise and horses. When he does cross it is to drive on to the Orkneys to offer himself as candidate for that County'.[18]

Some problems were less easily resolved. The minister at Creich 'had exercised much patience' about his claim for a stipend increase and, unable to settle the matter with the factor, he appealed to Captain John. The Rev George Rainy had even taken the opportunity a year or two earlier to use the text of the OSA to set out his case. The stipend had been fixed at £25 per annum in 1708, but it was withdrawn 'by the Committee for managing the royal bounty' in 1789. Thereafter Lady Ross Baillie 'out of her own liberality' had paid the salary and added benefits in kind, but this too had apparently come to a halt. He hoped, since the 'living being now more than doubled, even in this corner (of the country)', that more could be done.[19] Writing to the Captain, Rainy accepted that he was 'considered officious', but 'the situation of my family at this time renders it necessary for me to get payment of the Augmentation by every legal method in my power'.[20] This was understandable for someone who had at least seven children in addition to those who died young.[21] Whether the augmentation resulted is not recorded.

At Spinningdale Mill output was barely credible and a Mrs McIntyre wrote to tell Dempster that 'if pullicates keep at their present price we shall clear 6 to 800 (handkerchiefs) . . . this year'.[22] The operation of the Balnoe Company and life in the spinning and weaving community at Spinningdale and Newton were, however, not matters over which Dempster or his half-brother could exercise much direct control. When the company that year elected to withdraw from such linen weaving as had been attempted at his 'seaport' of Newton due to the lack of waterpower, the Captain only consented (as a partner) under duress and was 'much mortified' at the change, a view that Dempster probably shared. 'I have received a long letter from our worthy partner Macintosh with Aitken's report.[23] The Company are clear for changing (their operations) from Balnoe to Spinningdale and retaining the name Balnoe for the sake of not altering the contract. I sent my consent to both proposals at the same time. I think they are wrong and that it would ultimately have been more the interest of the Company to have retained the seaport town even if they had worked their machinery with horses.'[24] The latter suggestion was hardly feasible and, although he thought they 'ought to go on with the town of Balnoe as if nothing had happened', little more was to happen. By April the following year announcements appeared in the *Edinburgh Advertiser* confirming that the company was to be dissolved and was offering its few assets, including the bleachfield, for sale. Local concern centred on the state of the road at Spinningdale, where 'a bridge will be absolutely necessary over the brook and if our statute labour would give a carriage broad . . . it would be a great improvement'.[25]

In the autumn Dempster reported two mineral discoveries. One he thought would certainly be of interest to Sir Adam, who had inspected the quarries of Carrara in Italy during his grand tour, and the other, a new attempt to mine coal at Brora, would remind him of the duties they both had shared when they were appointed curators of the Sutherland estate and tutors to the infant Countess thirty years before. With Jean and Captain John safely home from Newhailes, Dempster rode westward beyond the bounds of the estate and discovered (as if for the first time) a 'lake called in the map Loch Shin, about 25 miles long' where he had been shown a rock which had been 'burnt for limestone'. Two specimens had been sent to the Highland Society where they had been polished and put on display, one of 'a most beautiful blue and white marble . . . the other a spotted white marble'.[26] For once Dempster's keen prospecting gaze had failed to alight on something that could be exploited commercially. There was 'however' a chance that the story might be different in Brora. Coal that 'wore a promising appearance' had been discovered at Strathsteven on the estate at Uppat belonging to George Sackville Sutherland. His father, who had been 'setting down a drain well in his garden, (had come) upon the same seams of coal at a considerable distance from the place where it (had) been lately discovered'. There was 'every reason to hope that other seams (might) be discovered below the present one and that those lower seams (might) be richer and a superior quality'.[27]

The invitation to subscribe funds 'for ascertaining the extent and value of the coal', and circulated among 'the nobility, gentry and corporate bodies', accepted the general perception that the county abounded 'in coal and other minerals', recalling how 'coal was dug and salt made at Brora' before the Union. Subsequent efforts in the 1760s and 1770s had been encouraged by the Annexed Estates Commissioners and the curators of the Sutherland estate, but, as the latest prospectus recalled, these had been frustrated by numerous impediments, including uncertain funding and the variable quality of the coal extracted under difficult and often dangerous conditions. For a time in 1765 a Customs duty on coal carried coastwise along the Moray Firth also prejudiced sales. The endeavours of John Williams, a Welshman with mining experience in Midlothian, ended finally in 1769 and Robertson & Co., to whom the rights had been assigned, continued intermittent production of coal and salt at the behest of the tutors before abandoning their efforts in 1778.[28]

The prospective funders of the new feasibility study were reminded of the continued 'great demand (for) lime, coal and salt, the ability of obtaining which (had) contributed so much to encourage the Commerce and improve the Agriculture'. The venture needed 'three or four hundred pounds' and 'men of skill must be brought in to inspect the coal . . . and fine utensils purchased'. As a curator of the estate until 1786 when the Countess came of age, Dempster would have been familiar with the previous mining attempts, but whether he attended the meeting in Dornoch during December at which the draft prospectus was drawn up (and a sample of the coal put on display) is not recorded. Whilst its text suggests that he had a hand in the authorship and, as he told Sir Adam that month, he was certainly one of the group involved, it is unlikely that he wanted any involvement closer than being prepared to use his friend's help in identifying those men in the mines of the south of Scotland who might agree to become 'faithful coaliers (sic) for our experiment'.[29] It was more a matter for Lord Gower and the Sutherland estate to exploit. The absence of experienced management had contributed to previous failures and, although sufficient coal was eventually mined to enable 20,000 tons of salt to be produced between 1814 and 1828, (and the mine operated with varying degrees of success between 1874 and 1968) Dempster had more than enough to do encouraging those responsible for his own spinning interests elsewhere in Sutherland, to say nothing of Stanley at Perth.

1797

In February Boswell's executor, solicitor and partner in one of the three Edinburgh banks that had survived 'Black Monday' wrote to Dempster explaining that 'our poor friend Mr Boswell' had directed that mourning rings were to be given to several of his friends. Boswell had died in 1795 and Sir William Forbes had been looking for an opportunity to send one to Dempster. He now proposed to use the good offices of Donald Macleod of Geanies (who was at the time of his writing in his office) to pass on this memento of 'Bozzy'. He also knew how much pleasure it would give Dempster to hear that the sons of his old sparring partner 'show every appearance of turning out well . . . and that the oldest, who is now of age and studying law here, has behaved in the kindest and handsomest manner to his younger brothers and sisters'.[30]

Sir William had been prompted to write after reading Sinclair's *Statistical Account* for the Parish of Creich, 'being highly flattered to find' that he 'entertained the same sentiments' as Dempster 'in regard to the improvement of the country'. He enclosed an advertisement distributed to every kirk and manse in the county that showed how similar his own efforts in Aberdeenshire had been to those of Dempster in Angus and Sutherland. He had formed the idea of establishing a village after succeeding to the estate of Pitsligo, making roads through the estate to connect it with Buchan and 'prevailing on . . . two or three manufacturers . . . to come and settle in the village'. It must have been music to Dempster's ears to hear that its success 'far exceeded (his) most sanguine expectations; for since the publication of the advertisement last Spring about 120 lots (had) been taken'. The parcelling out of land had doubled rents and, with local facilities already including a school house and inn, he had appealed to the Society for Propagating Christian Knowledge for a missionary to be established there – the 'expense of erecting the church and a house for the minister' he would bear 'very willingly'. What Dempster thought of silver medals being awarded as 'the reward of industry at New Pitsligo' only became clear later. There Forbes had found one way of giving his tenants an incentive through his 'premiums' and medals.[31]

The need for a militia 'in the disarmed counties' was finally recognized by Parliament in June. With the country in dire financial straits, the threat of imminent invasion and mutiny among the Channel and North Sea fleets, it was all hands to the pump. To Dempster's delight and surprise, since he had doubted Dundas's intentions for some time, a Scottish militia was introduced by the new Secretary of State for War. With the long-fought battle now over, he was prepared to hold Dundas in increasing esteem. Dempster had protested about its absence at the start of the war with France in 1793 when there was an increased demand for manpower in the army and navy, and French designs on Scotland were confirmed by the privateers seen off her coasts. Press gangs had been out in the Highlands and 6,000 men were to be called up from Scotland. The schoolmaster or constable in each parish was required to make up a list of all those men eligible to serve, but, with a long list of exemptions, the brunt of this service fell on a limited section of the popu-lation and riots ensued in many parts of the country.[32] Dundas, who thought that very few people 'would exert themselves . . . if it were really granted' and always had misgivings about trusting arms 'in the hands of the lower classes', was eventually forced to give in. In the absence of Lord Gower, Captain John, now a Deputy Lieutenant of the County, had the duty of reading out the text of the Militia Act at Dornoch on 1 August.[33]

Also that month there was the possibility of a visit to Skibo by Andrew Bell and his wife. He had been known to the family for a long time, Dempster being a friend of his father, a man with an inventive turn of mind. Bell returned from Virginia in 1781 and took orders in the Church of England soon afterwards. Whereupon in 1787 he went to India at Dempster's instigation. Unfortunately he had been forced to return home in 1796 for the sake of his health and, perhaps stirred by the publication that year of Bell's pamphlet entitled *An*

Experiment in Education, Dempster appears to have written to him in Edinburgh about Master George's education. His reply was warm in his regard for both Dempster and his half-brother, who he referred to as 'My Captain', perhaps recalling his voyage aboard the *Rose* when he was deposited at Madras. His name does not however appear in the ship's log.[34]

With reconstruction work at Dunnichen apparently finished at last, the Dempsters returned there from Skibo in early November after what had been a stay of more than three years. It was to be the longest period he ever spent in Sutherland. Just as the outgoing baggage train had been substantial, so with the return; it included cattle shipped south for market 'where the proceeds (of £160) would pay some rents', a satisfactory outcome given 'the great falls in the cattle market to the northward'. Both George and the Captain appear to have got on well with their factor, Captain Mackay of Torboll. It was a partnership that was to stand the Captain in good stead in the months to come. Dempster also heard that Mackay had been given the task of collecting Lord Reay's rents. As a neighbouring landlord this made eminent good sense. Already busy filling some of the gaps in the Sutherland establishment, Dempster told Torboll that there was 'an admirable gardener on his way to Skibo' and he hoped 'a very good grieve (would) soon follow' as soon as he had been hired.[35]

The Hamilton Dempsters had gone to Newhailes, probably reconciled to the fact that their life together was coming to an end and that the happy times spent at Pulrossie and Skibo with George, Rosie and young George, would never be repeated. Jean's state of health, always precarious, had not greatly changed and she enjoyed brief periods when her consumptive cough and frequent debility was absent, but her growing weakness must have been evident for all to see. The couple's farewell to the firth and the estate where the Captain had worked so hard must have been especially poignant. Sometime towards the end of their stay more pressure came from another quarter. Moffat, the managing agent and effective owner of his beloved ship the *Rose* (now under the command of Captain Gray), wanted to know what it would take for the Captain to accept another command after four years ashore. News of such an invitation had to be kept from his wife. He probably also recalled events in 1793 when, in better health, Jean had become so 'enraged' at the sight of that 'little man'. Captain John does, however, appear to have discussed the proposition with Dempster.[36]

1798

Although Jean Dempster's health gave way in November and she was 'visibly worse', the family at Newhailes was cheered for a time by a temporary improvement, and Christian Dalrymple (who had inherited the house on Lord Hailes's death in 1792) was able to say that they had begun 'the year merrily with our dear Mrs Dempster'. In the spring, accompanied by her husband and

Jean Dalrymple,[37] she returned to Dunnichen where she was cared for by Rosie, Catherine Heming, the elder of her two Heming nieces, and Sir Adam's niece Betsy.

Arriving very weak and emaciated, 'her distemper assumed a still more alarming appearance' and Dempster was forced to conclude on 23 April that she was dying. Several local doctors attended her and written advice was sent from Edinburgh by a Dr Spens but their efforts provided 'but . . . short and triffling (sic) relief'.[38] Surrounded by the family she struggled on until 5 May. She was 32 years old when she died and had been married barely thirteen years. For many of these she had endured the ever-present worry about her beloved husband's long and dangerous voyages and brought up her only son in a series of family homes. Buried in the Dempster family burial-ground within Restenneth Priory, the plaque to the memory of 'Jane' (a name by which she was known within the family) conveyed nothing of her qualities. So ended the short life of a 'beautiful' and brave woman.

Within days of the melancholy scene of Jean's demise, Dempster turned his mind to its many consequences. It was as if the family had anticipated exactly what would happen when the tight spring of their short life together was broken. Moffat's offer to give his half-brother 'command of one of the Company's finest ships' was quickly accepted and a broken-hearted Captain resolved to resume 'his profession for a voyage or two'. Young George and Mr Henderson, his tutor, were to remain at Dunnichen[39] while he went to London to settle the terms of his appointment, the plan being for him to return north again in the autumn. He wrote to Lord Gower resigning his command of the volunteers, leaving Dempster to tell those in charge on both Sutherland estates what had occurred and to issue the 'several directions which he meant to have done on the spot'.[40]

Dempster's sadness of the past weeks could only be drowned by work. He attended to 'a drove made up of the cows . . . unfit for the dairy' that the Captain wanted to catch the market and arranged for a surplus of coal which lay at Newton to be sold off. He immersed himself in his old interest of soil fertility, insisting that the grieve 'set vigorously about drawing shells and shelly sand from the sands between Dornoch and Ardnacalk' once the barley season was over. Having himself frequently searched for shell deposits which, when mixed with heavy soil produced a slow-acting fertilizer, he urged the work forward, hoping that more extraction would be possible. 'There is,' he said, 'a stratum of 'em of about a foot under the sand everywhere', but, being well to the east of the northerly ferry landing, they were probably just beyond the Skibo estate boundary.[41] Writing in July when the drove had been assembled, corn sent to Leith, rotation plans agreed and he had received a worthless order for his rent from the tenant of the small Langwell estate above Rogart, Dempster pressed the subject further.[42] Now that he had a free hand he was determined to prove himself right and that the 'shells will answer as well as any lime'. If, as he said, 'Captain Dempster had taken my advice, he never would have bought one boll of (lime) while shelly sand could have been found'.[43] Elsewhere on the estate, the road to Spinningdale was being built under the supervision of Captain Mackay, the factor now on half pay from the army. Action was threatened against those felling some of the oaks in the plantation west of the mill and in Migdale wood. He also fought off a Window and Commutation tax assessment 'since due notice was not given'. With his mind alert as usual, Dempster was pleased to be able to point out that the property had been unoccupied as well as unfurnished at the time of the assessment.

1799

Dempster's ambition 'to have seen Captain D change his life' and remarry never stood much chance against the call of the sea.[44] With his fragile hold on the life of a countryman broken, the question now arose as to how the two Sutherland estates were to be managed. Each was not only individually owned with its separate identity, but the chain of command, accounting practices and tenant-landlord relations differed. Although Dempster had kept a close eye on his half-brother's affairs, and during previous absences had his power of attorney, the suddenness of his departure south meant that there were arrangements about which Dempster knew little. His own factor at Skibo was to say with some frustration that 'the intromissions of both estates are so involved in one another that it is totally out of my power to keep the payment from each distinct'.[45] Coming to grips with the situation, he found that most rents had been received, but several had been paid with cattle that was passed on to Ramsay.[46] A cattle and horse sale raised £220 for the Captain with five cows sold by roup and the others by private bargain. All the steers and a few of the young cattle were unsold. With Lord Reay away, and having 'little to do in that quarter but collecting rent', Mackay was prepared to give some thought to the command of the Captain's Volunteer Company. However, with Ramsay threatening to leave the Captain's service, he had to contemplate spending more time at Skibo. [47]

As the year rolled on the effect of the Captain's absence was felt more keenly. Fearing that his laird would be displeased about some changes in the agreed rotation of crops at Pulrossie, Torboll wrote to Dempster to explain how they had come about. The Captain's forthright and often blunt manner could be fearsome. Without a copy of the lease in front of him Mackay thought the forfeit would be 30/- per acre or 10 guineas on his rent. Having raised the possibility of taking over the management of Pulrossie farm himself, he wanted to make it clear that he had less time available than Ramsay and that 'a decent servant that understood the management of the young plantations and oversee the farm with (his) directions' might be better. With any change of occupancy he wanted to inspect hedges and enclosures to avoid later recriminations, and he thought some of the Pulrossie sheep and cattle might be better sent to Dunnichen for eventual roup there. Whether because of building work he had done at Pulrossie or at Spinningdale Mill, Mackay passed on to Dempster news of James Boag, the latter's contractor, whom he had met: 'I saw (him) and mentioned his credit with you for the whisky'.[48]

Mackay was annoyed that Ramsay had chosen to leave just at the beginning of the corn harvest and begged Dempster to speak to the Captain about it. 'I think this a very improper period for leaving the farm as he is well paid for his attendance and as he is acquainted with the servants employed and has open accounts for the operations in this crop I think he ought to see it put into the store yards, and I beg you say so to Captain Dempster without delay.' If a new appointment was not to be made, Mackay could see his own 'intromissions' proving detrimental, especially on account of the distances involved, and his not being able to attend personally to many matters. He hoped therefore that 'a man of character . . . who can write and cypher a little could be found'.[49] However, when it became clear that he could not himself take on both Pulrossie farm and plantations and look after Skibo for the 'two years you think necessary', Mackay wrote to Captain John accordingly.

As well as immersing himself in estate affairs, Dempster looked for the greatest comfort in his 'beloved son and heir'. In six letters to Sir Adam between June and August Dempster picked up all the themes of their earlier correspondence about Master George's education, insisting that his views were 'to prevent his being good for nothing' and hoping that his first visit to the family at Kilkerran could soon be arranged. Without his mother, it was all the more important for George 'to be known to his maternal relations'. Fortunately the boy was 'happy at the prospect' and soon 'tailors, shoemakers, bootmakers (were) all at work to equip our young hero for his first campaign'. Accompanied only by his tutor, the visit south in July coincided with the summer stay of several of his aunts and uncles (including Lady Hailes, her step-daughter, Charles Fergusson, his grandfather, his daughters and James his son, just returned from India 'after a very tedious passage')[50]. It must have been a daunting social baptism for a motherless thirteen-year-old. Unfortunately, neither Dempster's sister Helen (Colonel Burrington's widow) who was paying her first visit to Dunnichen since returning from India, and whom the family hoped would stay the whole summer, nor Rosie, could join the party. Using a figure of speech that could irritate his friend, George explained the problem Sir Adam's invitation created: 'The ropes of Lilliput' pinned them all to Angus. Known to be a favourite at Kilkerran Dempster too was 'moored by a cable for the rest of the season'. He could not leave Dunnichen since, despite his 'dislike to the benches of justice', he had agreed to act as a Commissioner of Appeal and would be 'executing the Assessment on the Revenue Act'.[51]

After young George and Mr Henderson returned from Ayrshire, Sir Adam gave Dempster his report. He had found a 'boy of quick parts, sound under-standing for his years, capable of much application when led to it, of an excellent natural temper and compliant disposition' but his friend 'trembled' at any mention by his uncle of the value of the estate to which he was to succeed (a thought he erroneously attributed to Dempster) and any prospect that so 'active (and) spirited' a person might spend his life as 'a young laird in the country. If I mistake him not, he will not do it'.[52] Although Sir Adam was conscious that he may have spoken out of turn, he added his support for Master George 'being tried with the study of Greek', only to receive Dempster's refusal to contemplate what had been his own 'horrid and barren task'. All in all, however, it had been a beneficial visit, and despite any mis-conceived ideas he had about his nephew's education, he still looked forward to him becoming 'a judge and an improver of land and a planter of trees, a good father of a family, an agreeable companion (and) an honourable gentleman', all his own qualities in fact.[53]

Somehow Dempster had been 'long prepared for the blow' that occurred one night in September when the sky over Stanley and the River Tay was 'enlightened with . . . flames'. The new flax mill built alongside the original cotton mill only three years earlier burnt down.[54] Coming as it did when high production costs had already jeopardized the mill's operations and the switch to spinning flax had proved abortive, the disaster triggered the immediate winding up of the partnership. After a partners' meeting, Dempster 'huzza'd' the decision on behalf of Graham of Fintry and himself, assuming that the building insurance would cover their losses. But no sooner had David MacVicar taken on the task of disposing of the business, and James Keay reported the extent of the company's indebtedness, than a more miserable story emerged. The fire had been the last straw and, although Dempster initially thought MacVicar was 'mismanaging' the company's affairs and intended 'to have a personal interview' with him, the position was hopeless.[55] There was no doubt that the partners would have to meet considerable liabil-ities and it was to take until 1802 to find purchasers for the business – and then the sale only made £4,600, well below the asking price.[56]

Dempster bitterly regretted the lack of determination he had showed in 1791 when he had tried to withdraw as a partner. He had 'weakly suffered (himself) to be over-ruled' and it rankled. Not being 'able to extricate'[57] himself from the company, all he could do was to bemoan the successful exit of those shareholders who had escaped 'by their strength, others by our weak-ness,' leaving 'a few of us poor mice to be crushed under this immense ruin'. 'Where now,' he asked, 'were the Duke of Atholls, our Arkwrights and Sandemans?' The old incubus he had for so long managed to avoid had caught up with him and brought him to 'the heaviest in point of finance that ever (he) experienced'.[58] This was not strictly true, but he certainly lost more than he expected, some £6,000, perhaps as much as £8,000.[59] Coming at a time of so much turmoil in the family's affairs, he must have been tempted to hope that the pending voyage of his half-brother might at least make up some of the loss. He still had 'the wherewithal to supply (his) few wants', but it was a substantial sum and one which kept him for a time 'as poor as a church mouse'.[60]

Where Captain John spent the 18 months before he sailed is a matter of some speculation. The original plan for him to return north in 1798 was probably not adhered to and, whilst he may have stayed for a time with his father-in-law in Dulwich, he was not among the party that assembled at Kilkerran in the summer.[61] He does, however, appear to have stayed at 29 Percy Street in London for at least the last three months of 1799, travelling from there in September for a last visit to Dunnichen. Other addresses which his Sutherland factor used in writing to him during this period included Grafton Street and Rathbone Place. When he heard about the fire at Stanley and his half-brother's £6,000 liability, his immediate and generous offer of help showed how much he was aware of the burdens Dempster now bore. 'While I am away,' he pleaded, 'for God's sake let me take upon me to pay the interest of your loss. I would not on any consideration have you fret yourself about money matters or deny yourself any comfort. I have a few thousand with Scott if you are pressed for cash. They are at your service as my investment can be had very well on credit. Besides I can borrow what I want in London.'[62]

He would have had much to do catching up with modifications to Company rules and regulations which were constantly being reviewed, preparing himself and the ship for the forthcoming voyage and exchanging information and plans with those of his old ship-mates who were in England at the time. His good friend Wemyss Orrok had finally been given the command Captain John knew he richly deserved, replacing Gray as commander of the *Rose*, and was in London until April 1799 when the vessel left for Madras and China. Jeremiah Dawkins, whose place Captain John was to take aboard the *Earl Talbot*, had brought his ship back from her maiden voyage to Whampoa in October the previous year and the two men (along with John Dale who had been Dawkins' Chief mate) would have undoubtedly met and discussed the finer points of the vessel's performance. Built by Perry at Blackwall and launched in 1796, the *Earl Talbot*, was the second vessel of that name and a rugged 1200-ton, three-deck East Indiaman designed for the China trade.[63]

It was especially important for any commander to optimize the number of wealthy passengers he might take on a voyage, particularly in wartime. Their contribution to his income, and the standing in which he was held as their ship-borne host, could be significant. On this occasion Captain John knew that he had at least one place spoken for in the vessel's roundhouse, his own preserve. His natural daughter Harriet was to accompany him to India. The mystery surrounding her birth in 1785 and what sort of life she had enjoyed in the fifteen intervening years remains, save for the fact that she may have stayed with the Dempsters at Dunnichen around this time. Recalling the event to her eventual husband, Dempster was to say that 'she was my guest and darling some years before (he) saw her'. It had been a happy occasion, maybe one that had helped lift the veil over a very personal episode in his half-brother's life. Her uncle had obviously been delighted to meet her at long last, later describing her warmly as 'a virtuous girl with a tender and feeling heart and no small share of good sense'.[64]

It would have been only natural for Captain John to have sought out Harriet after his wife's death and he may have seen the forthcoming voyage to India as a way of keeping her close to him. A suspicion even exists that he may have taken her to see his Sutherland properties around this time.[65] Additionally, and quite fortuitously, there was to be another member of the family on the vessel. Sir James Dalrymple, a nephew of Alexander Dalrymple, the East India Company's hydrographer and brother of the now deceased Lord Hailes, was one of the very few baronets ever to figure on the roll of the Company's officers. He had sailed as 4th officer on the last voyage of the *Dublin*,[66] and by the time he reached home in December 1797 he had done well enough to be recruited by Captain John and be promoted to 2nd officer. Such an advancement would have particularly pleased his father, a Lord Provost of Edinburgh, ironic as it would prove, given the work his uncle and Dempster had put in trying to reduce the loss of shipping as the result of uncharted hazards, albeit off Scottish coasts.

15

MISERY LOVES COMPANY
(1800 – 1804)

'In a state of agony and despair'
(Dempster to William Soper Dempster, 3 February 1802)

1800

Dempster appears to have reserved his celebrations of the new century to the end of its first year rather than its beginning. Offering his congratulations to Sir Adam two days before the start of 1801 on 'our having lived to see a second century', Dempster prayed that the future might be 'as free from pain' as 1800 had been, so allowing it to be accompanied with 'as much vigour . . . (and) as many hearty laughs'.[1] Unfortunately, and totally unknown to him, heart-breaking events a world away in the South China Sea had already taken place and, nearer to home, signals were misread about illness that was destined to shatter many of the family's hopes and aspirations.

On 4 January 1800, three days before Captain John's ship and the rest of the East India fleet sailed from Portsmouth, Dempster entertained James Headrick who had come down from Caithness on an errand from Sir John Sinclair.[2] Winter had a firm grip on the Angus countryside and Headrick, a versatile assistant of 'Agricultural John', and who was to become minister of Dunnichen in 1807, was stormbound at the house along with another (unnamed) 'sensible philosophical friend'. Dempster's concern was to ensure that he had more copies of Sinclair's discourses and to know whether there was a chance he might 'waylay' his friend on one of his journeys southward from Thurso.[3]

The *Earl Talbot* sailed from Portsmouth on 7 January along with other 1200-ton Chinamen the *Cirencester, Canton*, and *Ganges*, reaching Bombay safely on 26 May.[4] Being among the first ships of the season to dock usually brought better profits and this feat may have been achieved on this occasion. On board were 28 tons of cotton worth £22,540 and £1,200 of pig lead which were part of Captain John's private trade. He calculated that 'in the event of an accident happening to the *Earl Talbot*' his liability was £5,533, a sum adequately covered by insurance taken out before he left England. The calculations took into account £6,206 worth of respondentia bonds in his favour – payable 'at 60 days after the ship's safe arrival in China'.[5] Accordingly, his 'declared risk' was recorded in Bombay and a copy passed to his lawyers in London.[6] Among the cargoes was one of cochineal and other merchandise worth £5,477 17s. owned by Augustus Moses Cleland, the vessel's chief mate, which was sold leaving some 'camblets and pig-lead valued at £884 9s. 3d.' in the hold. With the proceeds Mr Cleland acquired 'a quantity of cotton and other merchandise' and, being in a position to help his captain with his own local purchases, he claimed to have lent him the sum of £3,746. The significance of this not uncommon practice between officers only became clear a dozen or so years later when Cleland's brother brought an action against Captain John's heirs in the Court of Session to recover what he claimed was an unpaid debt.[7]

The vessels were moored in Bombay harbour for ten weeks while their cargoes were unloaded and others put aboard for Canton. A letter dated 15 June advised the Court of Directors in London that 16,000 bales of cotton for shipment to China were to be divided between the four ships. In addition 3000 candies of much sought-after sandalwood were to be loaded.[8] These arrangements were said to have 'accommodated the just expectations of the captains of your China ships'.[9] In the event, satisfaction was only achieved after the strongest representations had been made about the heavy extra charge each captain was required to bear for overseeing the compression of the cotton by 'Mr Henshaw's lately invented presses' and their want of funds to meet such an expense. The amount Captain John was eventually liable to refund, with interest, was £623 7s. 6d.[10]

The Governor's directions to Captain Dempster and his three colleagues well illustrated what was involved. The cotton 'will be embaled and sufficiently pressed to be commodiously stowed in the holds . . . so as to leave sufficient room both for the ship's stores, and the Privilege Tonnage of yourselves and officers.' Furthermore 'you are to cause the ships to be sufficiently and properly ballasted for the purpose. You are to apprise the Company's warehousekeeper as soon as they are ready to begin to take in the cotton, and the warehousekeeper is ordered to concert with you relative to the number of bales to be sent off to the ships daily which must be so arranged as to enable (the) Government to despatch you all in company by the 10th of August . . . and excepting the lead which you have on board on your own accounts with the Company's licence, you are not to lade anything on your own or any other account without leave previously obtained from the Governor in Council.'[11] The precision of such orders was commonplace within the Company and nobody would have been surprised when Mr Robert Kitson, the warehousekeeper involved, formally requested additional temporary labour to do the job.

In Bombay Captain John and Harriet were well looked after by Captain Philip Dundas, a nephew of Henry Dundas and brother of Ralph Dundas, the captain who had taken Charlotte Burrington out to India in 1795. His uncle had procured for him the post of Master Attendant with the Bombay Marine Board and 'he had £10,000 a year and (had) accumulated £70–80,000'.[12] According to Dempster, Captain John, who was 'reckoned the best of modern navigators and, in whose conduct the owner of the ship placed such confidence as to leave the bulk of the ship uninsured', had so impressed Dundas that he had an additional passenger for him on the journey to China and thence back to England. He chose 'sending his amiable wife home by the *Earl Talbot* (mistakenly referred to as the *Earl Spencer*) though by a circuitous voyage, to every other ship of the season'.[13] However, Captain John seems to have had some premonition on this occasion that 'the melancholy event' of his death might be about to occur. He had made several wills, but in a Deed of Entail drawn up by Guthrie in Edinburgh just before he left England the 'lands and estates of Skibo, Over Skibo (and) Pulrossie' were left to young George and his heirs.[14] So far as his daughter was concerned he may have thought that, like many women before her, she would find a husband among the Company's civil or military personnel and make a new life for herself in India. Any fears Harriet had about her father would have been allayed by the confidence all his friends had in his ability.

The *Earl Talbot* and her three companions were about 'to proceed on their voyage on the 13th August, when, in moving down the harbour, the *Ganges* stranded, but luckily got off the next morning without damage, and the four Indiamen commenced their voyage on the 17th August'.[15] Sailing by the eastern passage, they would have been scheduled to travel north of New Guinea and west of the Philippines. All appears to have gone well until the fleet was overtaken by a 'dreadful typhoon' in October 1800 and the *Earl Talbot* was lost: 'all the ships were shattered, some lost masts, all lost sails' and 'the captain, cargo, ship's company and passengers were swallowed up, and not a vestige of the ship ever heard of again'.[16]

What happened to Captain John's ship is only partially explained by such records as are available. Some thought she had foundered on the dreaded Pratas Islands in the South China Sea, others that the many shoals in the Paracel Islands were responsible.[17] She had been seen by Captain Thomas Robertson of the *Cirencester* when the two ships were together 'in the tempest' and he reported the vessel as having 'put back to Malacca to refit' after being dismasted, a possibility which gave rise to the expectation that it would be at least 9 months before she reached home.[18] One commentator writing in the *Bombay Courier* told a not dissimilar story, taking account of the wind during the 'gale' and the bearings of the *Talbot* from these rocks before it came on.[19]

It seems that Captain John's ship outsailed and parted company with another East Indiaman, the *Walthamstow*, on 20 October. The *Marquis of*

Wellesley nevertheless kept company with her until 8 p.m. on 22 October at which time she bore east by south from the *Wellesley* and was considerably to the southward and eastward of the Pratas. The situation of the *Wellesley* and the *Earl Talbot*, and their distance from each other about 12 hours before the gale came on meant, in the commentator's view, that Captain John would no doubt have 'taken the same measures for the safety of the *Talbot* which succeeded so well in placing the former so far from all danger, she would have been at noon on the 24th in nearly the same situation as the *Wellesley*, had she not met with some serious loss to her masts during the gale'. The inference was that 'being disabled from making her way to the northward against the heavy swell which continued to the time the other ships anchored at Macao, the *Talbot* had bore up for some port on the coast of China, or perhaps Hainan for the purpose of securing jury masts.' As to the Pratas, 'she seems to have been in no danger from them during the gale . . . an accident could not have happened except by such neglect as cannot be supposed'. There was therefore every reason for hope, it was argued, since the idea of the *Earl Talbot* being lost was 'almost absurd'. She was 'as good as any, and better than some of the fleet, all of which except her had arrived'.

When some of the fleet returned to London in June 1801 (including *Cirencester*, *Canton* and *Arniston*) it was clear that other vessels would be late. The *Ganges*, for example, had suffered badly from the typhoon and, although she delivered her cargo to Canton safely, the Company's supercargoes had ordered her back to Bombay for extensive repairs in April 1801. With calls at Penang, Columbo and Calicut, the voyage from China had taken three months and five days. She finally reached London on 17 September 1802.

One of the duties of the Company's marine surveyors in Bombay was to keep charts up to date, particularly in waters where ships had been lost. The Marine Board and the Indian Navy had trained a number of highly competent officers for this purpose as captains needed to be aware of where they might shelter to protect their valuable cargoes, ships and crews during the severe storms so prevalent in the South China Sea. Lieutenant McCluer, the surveyor who had been sent to look for such shelter as vessels might find in the event of these hazards after the loss of the *Antelope* packet in 1783 and a man much respected by James Dalrymple's uncle (Alexander Dalrymple), probably influenced the decision by Dundas and the Marine Board of which he was a member, to despatch two survey ships, *Comet* and *Intrepid*, to search for survivors on this occasion.[20] An earlier search by the *Viper*, authorized by the supercargoes in Canton, had failed to throw any light on the loss. The survey ships eventually departed from Bombay on 24 May 1801 and a report from Penang where the vessels docked a month later indicated that they were preparing to examine some of the shoals in the China Sea.[21]

Early next year notice of the Marine Board's intention to reduce its expenses by 'laying up some of the larger cruisers' was met with considerable consternation. A letter of protest by some of the Board's captains contained pleas that nothing be resolved since there was 'much room for serious apprehension respecting the safety of the *Intrepid* and *Comet*'.[22] News that the hunters themselves were missing caused despair and disbelief throughout the Company. All hope faded when HMS *Arrogant* returned from the search area 'without having received any tidings of either of these Cruisers'.[23] In total 124 officers, seamen, lascars and sepoys had lost their lives. As Dempster said, 'What was more extraordinary' than even the loss of the Captain's ship was that 'the same fate attended two well-appointed vessels despatched by Captain Dundas in search of his wife and friend'.[24] It was not until 1803 that the Court of Directors in London was forced to accept that 'no intelligence whatever has been received of any person who was on board' and that the circumstances of the *Earl Talbot*'s loss were 'wholly unknown'.

Back in Scotland Dempster was dealing with a matter of concern to local farmers, unaware of the forthcoming events in India. In March he wrote to Lord Liverpool about an Order in Council that prohibited the export of Scottish barley to England. His correspondent, with whom he had dealings in respect of the linen trade 13 years before, was 'happy to hear from a person of whom I always entertained an high opinion, and the sincerest regard'. But in a four-hundred-word reply, and couched in the language of a defensive civil servant of any age, he explained that Dempster was wholly mistaken. The King had no powers to prohibit by Order in Council the carrying of any corn from any part of the Kingdom to another and none had been issued. To Dempster's delight, four days later he received another letter from the same meticulous minister.This time it admitted that an error had been made. Furthermore, the Lords of the Treasury now meant to apply for an Act of Indemnity for what they had done. With one victory gained, Dempster pressed home his advantage, asking to know what exactly had happened in the Privy Council. This his lordship meekly explained would be improper for him to disclose. Dempster again used his advantage in June on the issue of taxes associated with property transfers. On this occasion a 'once bitten, twice shy' Lord Liverpool referred him to 'the person sprung from his loins', his son, Robert Jenkinson, and a future prime minister, who took 'a very active part in this and every other sort of business' in order that he might consider whether it could be dealt with in the next session of parliament.[25]

In May Dempster made plans for young George to have some respite during the summer from the Latin and arithmetic lessons he had been receiving from Mr Henderson. The tutor had taken over the house in South Street, St Andrews, which Dempster rented and where the company included Dempster Heming who was now twenty-two years old.[26] He had matriculated at the University the previous year, carrying off 'the prize of £10 10s . . . for the best translation of an oration of Cicero's'. For George, Dempster proposed a stay at Newhailes with his Fergusson relatives, where the young folk could 'inhale by the absorbent and lymphatic vessels of their mind . . . many useful facts and valuable principles'. He was convinced he required the 'stimulus of good example' and 'a learned atmosphere' which would be provided at his uncle and aunt's table.[27]

The stay at Newhailes duly took place, but by November, when news of his father's safe arrival in Bombay filtered through, young George was kept with the family at Dunnichen instead of returning to St Andrews. At the end of the summer he had 'a very smart touch of a fever' and a tell-tale 'little short cough' which remained with him and necessitated his being 'perpetually under the nursing eye of Mrs Dempster' and the three doctors called in to advise the family.[28] Perhaps unduly impressed by Sir Alexander Douglas's optimism, 'our most skilful Angus physician', and despite the absence of the 'healthy rosy cheeks that marked a confirmed state of health before the fever robbed him of those symptoms', Dempster thought the 'continuance of our careful regimen (would) soon restore him to perfect health'.[29]

1801

In the spring Dempster was beside himself with fear for the life of his young nephew who was now suffering from a 'severe visitation' of the consumption that had carried off his mother. Weakened by the fever and bronchial cough of the previous summer, his condition steadily worsened. A nourishing diet and his aunt Rose's continual care achieved little. In the absence of his 'poor' half-brother who knew nothing about the crisis (and whose death, although feared, was unconfirmed) Dempster felt acutely aware of the need to do all he could to save him. In desperation, he turned to Captain Elder of the Excise for help in transporting 'the only fruit of a happy marriage' to Devon where it was thought the milder climate might still save his life. It is 'for Exmouth I propose to steer', adding a prayer that 'would to God this place (might afford him) a ray or even a spark of hope'. 'Ready to obey (Captain Elder's) summons whether to Arbroath or Dundee' their route was to be first to Portsmouth where the excise cutter occasionally 'brushed' the East India Company's ware-house in its 'going and coming'. Armed with a letter of authorization from Fintry and the Excise in Edinburgh, the vessel sailed on to Exmouth with its sad cargo, reaching South Devon at the end of the month.[30] There it became apparent that the boy's disease had become virulent and Dempster 'closed his innocent eyelids on the 17th of April'. He brought the fourteen-and-a-half-year-old boy's body home to Dunnichen 'after a passage of 18 days' aboard the excise vessel and buried him in Restenneth Priory 'at his most excellent mother's feet in our chapel there'.[31]

Dempster's mind was 'smashed and broken to pieces' by the loss: 'What a moment was that . . . when I received his last breath and saw his innocent expressive eyes shut for ever!' In what James Fergusson described as 'a pathetic letter' which painted 'what must have been the sharpest sorrow of

Dempster's life', he expressed the grief that both the Dempster and Fergusson families shared, 'the link which connected our families by blood as well as affection'. He admitted 'but little consolation from (his) wife, for she loved and mourns for George as if he had been her own and only child'. Only the probability that his father would never learn of his death seemed to offer a glimmer of relief. Writing to Sir Adam he said, 'I . . . have some degree of horror superadded to my grief every time I think on his loss having happen'd during the absence of his father and on the sorrow which this loss will occasion him. A friend . . . observed I had got a cure, tho' a bad one, for the loss of my nephew, in the danger to which . . . his father has been exposed.'[32]

Meanwhile, in India Harriet had met, fallen in love with and married William John Soper on 17 January 1801, just seven months after disembarking at Bombay and totally unaware of her father's death the previous October. William Soper had been a friend of Philip Dundas in Bombay, where, for a few months at least, Harriet would have enjoyed a colourful social life among the expatriate community. Born in 1763, he was the son of John, a clothier, and Agnes Soper of Ashburton in Devon. The town was one of several in the county engaged in the production and sale of long-ell serge, a durable worsted fabric for rough wear. Clothiers were usually men of means, as well as being parliamentary electors, who resided in the town's East or West Street and attended the regular serge market in Exeter. When 18 years old, his parents successfully petitioned the Court of Directors in Leadenhall Street on his behalf for a position as Writer and a certificate submitted by a local writing master and teacher of mathematics spoke of him as 'well qualified to act as a clerk or writer'.[33] He reached Bombay in 1782, being successively assistant accountant, custom master and junior merchant with the Company until 1790. Progression to general and military storekeeper at Surat followed and by the time he left Bombay he was a senior merchant and marine paymaster there.[34] As Dempster was to discover when they finally met, he was 'an elegant, good temper'd, sensible, wise and frugal man, self-educated as far as our English classics, our poets and essayists can convey the title of being educated'.[35]

At Dunnichen the family spent the rest of the year slowly coming to grips with what looked like a double tragedy, drawing increasing comfort from the fact that the Captain may have been spared the news that would have awaited him and that Harriet was at least safe in India. Life had gone on more or less as usual, with Dempster in July again using his influence to find employment for a young Dundonian. A David Hackney, who 'had been regularly bred to business'[36] and whose ambition was to work for a company controlled by an old MP colleague of Dempster's, required his assistance. Introducing him to William Smith, the member for Sudbury who had become a director of the Fisheries Society a dozen years before, about the time that Pulteney had joined the Board, Dempster used the opportunity to renew their friendship. He recalled the 'two young and amiable persons' whom Rosie and he had met during the memorable holiday at Scarborough.[37] As the year turned, his 'gamekeeper went . . . in pursuit of seventy head of deer' only to return with moorfowl, whilst two of his best neighbours, Major Gardyne, who was Graham of Fintry's cousin, and one of the Guthries were on their death beds.[38]

During the second week in December the 'greatest fall of snow ever remembered' fell along the Dornoch Firth with drifts that lasted for three days.

1802

News from Philip Dundas that when they married the couple had been unaware of the Captain's tragic death much relieved the family who at first feared she had been the target of a fortune hunter.[39] As a consequence, a letter from William Soper which reached Dunnichen at the beginning of February, and posted seven months previously from Bombay, was responded to as warmly as circumstances allowed. Dempster congratulated Soper on his marriage to his 'dearest niece', wishing the couple 'all the happiness . . . from a virtuous union of hearts and affections' and that 'they be blessed with a numerous and prosperous progeny'. Assuming by then that Harriet knew about her father's death and that she would have 'shed many tears already for this dismal piece of news', he welcomed Soper's intention to return home as soon as prudence allowed so that he could 'enjoy the society of (his) relations and friends and the benefit of (the) mild wholesome British air'. Telling Soper that he had refused to look at Captain Dempster's settlements 'until the last minute of our hopes that he (might) see them himself', Dempster could now refer to his finding 'a treasure in Harriet little looked for at the time of (his) marriage'.[40] What had happened was that 'Mrs Dempster's love marriage became a mercenary one. He who had married my niece in her petticoat found himself in the arms of the heiress of all her father's and brother's fortune – and that fortune, Skibo'.[41]

In April the solicitors dealing with the Captain's estate 'opened a small red trunk of a chaise seat . . . which he had left . . . together with a large chest' containing papers and memorandum books, one parcel of which had been marked 'to be burnt in case of my death'.[42] A month later the trustees broke the seals on the settlements and Dempster was able to write to Soper confirming that 'you well may find your wife heiress to the bulk of her father's fortune – his landed property in Sutherland. In his absence the estates have been managed by his land steward, Captain Kenneth McKay' (*sic*). He explained that 'the first duty that falls to Harriet to perform (was her) signature of a deed . . . by which she will be enabled to make some return to you in case of her leaving the world before you (and) for the generous provision you made for the recourse of that event'.[43] This was a reference to the Rs.50,000 (£6,000) Soper had put in trust for her and the children of the marriage. It was to remain in Company bonds until 1813.[44]

Writing to Fintry the previous month, Dempster spoke of the harrowing experiences he had endured and the toll the death of the Captain and his son had taken of his spirit and constitution, coming as it did after the financial pressures resulting from the closure of Stanley. 'These last 14 or 15 months have been very fatiguing ones' and, although given to exaggerating his ailments, he said, 'I have already lost the sight of one of my eyes, and I hear very indifferently with both my ears and my memory has failed me to a degree that surprises myself'.[45]

Obviously with his Stanley indebtedness much on his mind, Dempster took the opportunity of telling Soper about 'a present Captain D made (him) before his departure – of £300 a year for himself'. There was no corroboration for this gift save in one of the minutes of a trustee's meeting, and, realizing that it might have to be squeezed from any residue of the Captain's estate, he felt his claim to such an annuity had to be backed up by reference to a letter he had received from his half-brother in 1799. Much to his relief it was willingly 'ratified' by Soper in due course and, although he 'suspended (his) acceptance of it', it formed 'an army of reserve' relieving Dempster's mind from 'uneasiness about money matters'.[46] The way the matter had been settled increased the esteem in which he held his new nephew.

In three short years his half-brother's family, with the exception of his 'natural' daughter, had been wiped out and the household at Dunnichen inevitably took time to return to some semblance of normality. It was only the thought that Soper and his wife might soon return to England that enabled Dempster to put the tragedy aside and turn his attention again to matters agricultural.[47] In the meantime the solicitors and trustees faced the time-consuming task of copying minutes and sending documents for signature to India, a procedure that would hold up any settlement. Dempster could not help being bothered by all manner of estate problems since he had been asked by the trustees to 'act under (his) former commission until Mr & Mrs Soper authorise(d) some other person to act for him'. Such duties brought their own problems. In May a General Baillie from Peterhead who had been on the lookout for a farm and winter residence (with Rosehall as a summer retreat) wanted 'to step into (Mr Rose's[48]) shoes' at Skibo Mains.

Sir John Sinclair evidently saw no reason in April to hold back sending Dempster a copy of his plans for improving his estates in Caithness. Dempster was equally in no mood to brush away his friend's request and with contact between them temporarily in abeyance – 'you being in parliament and (me) being out of it', he settled down to write a considered commentary on the document.[49] He noticed both Sir John's continued refusal to abolish the requirement of his own tenants to provide him with 'personal services', a long-standing disagreement between them, and how the layout of a projected farmhouse was 'very faulty'. With his usual candour he explained that 'the vicinity of the dung court will render it unhealthy and the position of the house

This engraving by Pugin and Rowlandson shows the interior of the **sale room** in East India House during an auction. Prior to its rebuilding in the late 1790s it also served as the General Court room where the directors and proprietors met, including Dempster. A new sale room came into use in 1800 which was almost identical in design and proportion. Both had a gallery, were lighted from the top and surrounded by niches for statues. *(Guildhall Library, Corporation of London)*

Shipping off St Helena, an oil painting by Adam Callander. Situated 1200 miles from the west coast of Africa and 1800 miles from Brazil, the island of St Helena was an important supply station and convoy rendezvous for vessels bound to and from India and China. *(National Maritime Museum)*

A print of **Alexander Dalrymple** (1737-1808) by George Dance dated 1794. He was the brother of Lord Hailes and born at Newhailes. After a period as a member of the Madras Council he was appointed hydrographer first to the East India Company and then to the Admiralty in 1795. Neither body had made such an appointment before. He produced a quite remarkable number of nautical charts, mapping many of the routes taken by East India Company ships – so contributing greatly to their safety.

(National Maritime Museum, Greenwich)

A memorial in Dunnichen Church to **Jean Fergusson,** daughter of Sir Adam Fergusson's brother Charles, and wife of Captain John Hamilton Dempster. She died aged 32 leaving her son George aged 12 in the care of George and Rosie Dempster.   *(Author's photograph)*

JANE FERGUSSON Wife to JOHN HAMILTON DEMPSTER of Polrofsie, and eldest Daughter of CHARLES FERGUSSON, second Son of the late Sir JAMES FERGUSSON of Kilkerran Bar.t. died on the 5th and was interred at Restennet 14th day of May 1798. I. H.D.

The **Excise cutter** *Greyhound* under the command of Captain Wm. Watson 'on a wind chasing...' Although generally working from English home ports, vessels of this design were similar to those used in Scottish waters. The revenue cutter *Prince of Wales* was put at the disposal of the Fisheries Committee for its visit to the Hebrides in 1787.

(Merseyside Maritime Museum)

Holman's painting of **Perry's Yard at Blackwall** c. 1774-1784. Captain Dempster's ship the *Rose* was built at Well's Yard a mile or so upstream from the Blackwall slipways on the north side of the River Thames.   *(National Maritime Museum, Greenwich)*

The *Essex* East Indiaman refitted and at anchor in Bombay harbour.
(National Maritime Museum, Greenwich)

A **fleet of East Indiamen at sea** was painted by Nicholas Pocock in 1803. It is believed to represent the *Hindostan* of 1248 tons under Captain George Millett leading a convoy during its return voyage from China. Such a vessel would not be dissimilar to Captain John's command in 1800, the *Earl Talbot*.

(National Maritime Museum, Greenwich)

The print by Tomkins (above) and the oil painting by William Daniell (below) show the remarkable **Mast House** along the River Thames which formed part of Perry's Blackwall dock and shipyard. The 5-storey structure, in what was called the Brunswick Dock until 1806 when it was bought by the East India Dock Co., was a prominent landmark for seafarers. The river and shipbuilding always fascinated Dempster, even to the point of his asking how Scottish ship carpenters might be better employed: Thames-side crafts-men 'have not the economy of a sawmill'.   *(National Maritime Museum, Greenwich)*

(National Maritime Museum, Greenwich – Green and Blackwall Collection)

William Daniell's fine aquatint of **Broughty Castle**, Forfarshire (now Angus) was published in 1822 and catches something of the attraction the newly created seaside resort had for visitors. Although Dempster lived in St Andrews for some years following the death of his wife, the wandering 'desert nomad' (as he called himself) never lost his affection for Broughty Ferry, even riding on the sands when nearly 80.

(McManus Galleries, Dundee City Council)

Telford's iron bridge over Dornoch Firth, at what today is the village of Bonar Bridge, opened in 1812 and was to stand until 1892. Southey described it as 'spider's web in the air'. Dempster had long encouraged its construction, but the Meikle Ferry disaster of 1809 accelerated the work. He was only completely satisfied when it was painted and new milestones properly installed in 1817. *(National Gallery of Scotland)*

Although painted towards the latter part of his long life of 93 years, **Professor Adam Ferguson's** portrait (by an unknown artist after Sir Henry Raeburn) conveys something of the philosopher's quiet charm and contentment. The founder of the Poker Club whom Dempster regarded as the 'modern Epictetus' was then living in St Andrews and being cared for by his two unmarried daughters.   *(National Gallery of Scotland)*

A portrait of **George Dempster** in old age by J.T. Nairn. He wore the green ribbon and badge of the Secretary to the Order of the Thistle on all manner of occasions even aboard ship in 1776 with his friends William Hickey and William Cane where it obviously impressed customs officers. In retirement it was still his constant companion, a reminder of days at Westminster. *(Scottish National Portrait Gallery)*

directly between the yard and the sun will render it a Greenland quite unoccupiable' for the wintering of animals. It needed to be south-facing with the cattlesheds on the north side as had been the practice in Angus. To reinforce the point he sent Sir John a rough sketch of a farm layout at Dunnichen which he said was typical of arrangements in Angus.

Dempster then used the text of a speech given to a meeting of landowners, and with which he had been only too pleased to agree, to list some of the questions facing farming for Sinclair's benefit. The undisclosed speaker, an Englishman with an estate in Caithness, who had tactfully apologized for his 'impertinence' in speaking to a Scottish audience, went on to address many of the fundamental issues in a forthright manner. He first asked who was best fitted to improve agriculture: 'Is it the Country Gentleman?' Had they been 'bred to that profession' and did the 'industry' have the 'rigid economy' and strict control over their stores and produce? Were they 'early risers in the morning?' Equally pertinent were the questions that followed: 'Do our ladies understand calves, cheese and butter? Do we ourselves understand buying and selling cattle? Do we attend all the fairs and markets in the county? And if we did, are there not sharp hands there who <u>would sell us in one end of the market and buy us in another</u> as the common phrase is? Are we residents the year round? Does not the education of our children carry us to towns? Our military and naval employment causes frequent absence from homes? Are we prepared to renounce all the amusements of ambition and hopes of preferment . . . and devote our lives to the unintermitting labours of agriculture and also to train our children to the same humble line of life?' Seeing the answer '<u>No</u> in the faces of (his) hearers', he reminded them that 'overseers will perform all these duties', but 'Gentlemen, your overseers will cheat you and you will spoil them – not that they are rogues and you fools'.[50]

Such straightforward and practical speaking warmed Dempster's heart when he first read the speech. The 'first law of nature and (the) great maxim of life' that 'no business can be so well attended to as by (an owner) himself' was a message he had endeavoured to preach constantly over the years. The English landowner echoed his doctrine in Angus and Sutherland: 'Let your own farmers improve your land and their own farms'. The message that 'gentlemen can and ought, and are able and could be great gainers by giving them (capital and skill)' was exact. Securing the ability of tenants to pay their rents was expressed in a language he had himself used: 'Don't take his rent in kind for in a cheap year and plentiful he pays you too little rent (and) in a dear year when nature has spoilt his crop, you take it all leaving nothing for the maintenance of his wife and family.'[51]

Amid the uncertainty and upheaval facing the family Dempster may not have been able to pay much attention to a visit paid by Robert Owen to the '*palace cotton mill*' in Sutherland. There, despite the continuing difficulties, Macintosh's commitment (and to a lesser extent Dale's) was still evident. He had persuaded the successful developer of the mills at New Lanark, which by then were making sizeable profits on expanding home and export business, to come and advise him on ways of achieving improved working at Spinningdale. However, Owen was not impressed: 'the works were not extensive and were in ordinary condition; and we remained only long enough for me to discover what improvements to recommend without going to great expense, for the locality was unfavourable for extension or for a permanent establishment'.[52] There were some hundred people employed there at the time and, whilst Dempster was to make two further visits the following year when 'a busier or more enchanting scene (he) never beheld', he had come to accept that the abandonment of the business loomed.[53]

He had given up all hope of Captain John's survival. However, it was not until October, after Philip Dundas had paid two visits to Dunnichen on his return from India and delivered William Soper's present of a beautiful 'Cornelian snuff box set in gold',[54] that Dempster finally took the decision to insert news of the *Earl Talbot*'s loss in the newspapers. A formal period of mourning for the family could then begin.[55]

1803

With the lint mill in Vinney Den at Letham causing trouble, Dempster felt obliged to approach James Watt in January in the hope that the great engineer could advise him what to do.[56] Having only met him on one occasion many years before, he asked Sinclair, who was setting out for London from his house at Charlotte Square in Edinburgh, to pass on a letter. In this he explained the fairly 'crude' process being used whereby the imported flax was hung vertically so that the 'scutchers' could strike it at right angles 'with great force and rapidity', and questioned whether a machine would not be better. With more than 100 such mills in Angus at the time he concluded that they presented an ideal commercial opportunity. Replying from Heathfield Hall, Watt enclosed a sketch of a possible solution which those at Letham might try. Watt, now retired, and an 'ex-engineer' who had endured 7 years of a 'most malevolent law suit', also suggested various experiments. He concluded that the problem arose from over-zealous scutching, for though the operatives first struck the flax at right angles, 'they immediately bend the flax into something of a horizontal position and consequently the following scutchers strike it obliquely'. The fibres of Dutch flax which had been finely combed 'as a horse's tail' were very prone to damage. Watt promised to speak to 'better experts than himself' (probably meaning either his son or members of the Boulton family) and, as an expression of his esteem, he hoped he would 'never forget Mr Dempster nor the service he has done his country'.[57]

In February, concerned about his partial blindness and increasing deafness, he wrote to George Chalmers, FRS, FSA, complaining that 'Time . . . with its inexorable scythe has put out one of my eyes and that my very best. He has almost sealed up one of my ears and is very busy about the other'.[58] Although also bothered by the amount of weight he was putting on, and his general frailty, Dempster had to admit that he was free 'of all bodily pain' and enjoyed 'very good spirits'.[59]

A letter from the Sopers written the previous November reached Dunnichen on 20 April. It brought the news that the couple were coming home, not so much by choice but on account of the Indian climate and the effect it was having on the health of both of them. Dempster wrote the following day welcoming the decision and telling them that 'their worthy friend' Philip Dundas, who had so ably represented their interests 'with zeal and attention' and helped the trustees sort out the Captain's affairs, had obtained a seat at Westminster. He was also about to re-marry.[60] However, Dempster's principal concern was with their health. The Indian climate had produced its usual crop of 'ailments' which George could only hope would dissipate once they left London and reached Sutherland with its 'no finer air in the universe'. He hoped they would use the opportunity to visit Harriet's aunt Mrs Helen Burrington at Fitzroy Place (or Square) as well as Kitty her daughter who was about to sail for Bengal aboard the *Preston*. In asking Harriet not to forget her uncle Thomas Gordon, who was then living at Percy Street, Dempster was at pains to tell his new nephew that he was 'the worthiest man on earth'.[61]

The family at Dunnichen included Kitty Burrington and Dempster Heming, together with Charlotte (Mrs Boddam) and her four-and-a-half-year- old son who were overjoyed at the prospect of the couple's arrival; 'open arms and open hearts' awaited them. In a rare and especially warm postscript, Rosie added her own welcome to 'dear Harriet': 'I make no doubt your uncle has told you how happy the thoughts of seeing you and Mr Soper makes us, and that we hope you will consider Dunnichen as your home. As soon as you land I hope you will write to us and (I) flatter myself you will have it in your power to inform us your voyage entirely freed you of all complaints, and in our fine Northern climate you will be reinstated in good health. With kind compliments to Mr Soper and love to yourself, hoping to embrace you soon, I remain my dear Harriet, your affectionate aunt.'[62] For Harriet it must have been a time of some relief and great joy. Having spent her youth outside the Dempster family circle, to say nothing of the Fergusson family into which her father had married, she now had George and Rosie to herself. Although 71 and 55 years old respectively, the Dempsters were only too anxious to do all they could to provide both of the newly-weds with the supportive family which neither had. William Soper's parents had died while he was in India.[63] He was also to visit friends in Devon and his only brother, Walter, who was married to his cousin Elizabeth. His sister Eleanor had died in 1800.

Dempster's confidence in the eventual profitability of the new village at Letham had been borne out by the turn of the century when the rents reached £125, some twenty times what the original farm had been worth. On 26 April he felt able to put his proposals for governing the village before the residents, having told a friend he would 'apply to the King to give the people leave to choose a magistracy for their police and government'. 'Six of the wisest and discreetest' of the householders and tenants assembled in the Society Hall, which was to become the Feuars' Hall, and were invited 'to serve for one year as assessors to the Baron Bailiff of the Barony of Dunnichen'.[64] They were to meet as often as the town's affairs required and administer justice as well as manage the school and the mill. In order to overcome the natural reluctance of tenants to participate freely in the democratic process at the heart of Dempster's design, and since ballots were rarely, if ever 'secret', given the power and influence of the local laird, his inventiveness was invoked to produce what came to be called a 'voting stick'. Several examples subsequently came into use, but that at Letham was a rectangular block of wood, two inches by three-quarters of an inch and half an inch deep with a central slide which could be pushed out in either direction – somewhat similar to a slide rule. It was possible to determine which end to push out by touch and the voters' choice, their 'yeas' or 'nays', were only revealed when the sticks were turned over by the person counting the votes.[65]

A less promising prospect was nevertheless developing in Sutherland. The situation at Spinningdale had reached crisis proportions and news from Macintosh prompted Dempster to repeat his gratitude to him in a last-ditch effort to keep up his spirits. In May he wrote that 'among ourselves, I may say, there are only myself and George Macintosh, fit to improve the highlands and protect their inhabitants. . . . I must say, without arrogance, had there been more George Macintoshes and George Dempsters, in every parish in the highlands, the wisdom of the legislature would not now have the painful task of contriving inefficacious means of preventing . . . the depopulation of a vast tract of our kingdom.'[66] The last was a reference to money voted by the government 'for Scotch improvements' and which Dale and Macintosh solicited through the good offices of Thomas Telford.[67]

A request for a grant was put before Dempster's old benefactor, Sir William Pulteney at Telford's home in Shropshire, but he was 'perfectly convinced that government will not interfere in this business'. He thought that if there was 'any prospect of continuing the manufactory by means of the people in the country, and . . . the sum for the machinery (was) not very great . . . some mode of subscription . . . might be found'.[68] Macintosh was to learn that a bureaucratic interpretation of the grant scheme meant that the government could not interfere. The money was only '*for specific purposes of a general nature!!!*' – the italics spoke for themselves – and, although he sent Pulteney more details of what was required, 'the government (would not) attend to any application respecting the manufactory in Sutherland'.[69] With another share offer out of the question, the sale of the mill became the only option, if it could be achieved.

Dempster's concern for his constituents never deserted him. Now, more than a dozen years after he had left Westminster and even longer since his discussions with Dalrymple about the need for lighthouses, Dundee's Town Clerk received a letter from him in May which one local historian described as 'a specimen of the value of a vigilant Parliamentary representative'. Asking William Chalmers to raise the issue with his magistrates 'without loss of time', Dempster explained that a motion was to be put down in Parliament 'for the lighting of Bell Rock or Cape Rock' at sea to the east of Dundee. It was thought that 'a petition from the maritime towns' would secure the measure. Content that the seriousness of the subject excused forthright language (and instructions) to a fellow lawyer, Dempster concluded with a plea that he should 'state (the Rock's) dangerousness strongly and briefly, and pray the House to take measures for erecting a lighthouse on it. There is not a day to be lost!' Instructions to whom the petition was to be sent and apologies for writing in haste and probably illegibly – 'to save a post' – concluded the missive.[70]

That summer Dempster turned his attention to yet another venture at Dunnichen. The previous year he had rebuilt the church and restored the old well of St. Causnan, renaming it Camperdown Well in memory of Admiral Lord Duncan and his victory over the Dutch in 1797.[71] This time he aimed to spread the gospel of improved agricultural management on his own doorstep. 'The Lunan and Vinney Farming Society' was formed on the 4th of the month with the Rev James Roger as its first secretary and Dempster its 'Perpetual Preses'.[72] Named after two Angus rivers, it had been launched in April at a meeting in the Dunnichen Inn when thirty-four people assembled, of whom eleven were landowners. They had been invited to 'a farmers' feast to be held annually where dinner would be on the table at three o'clock'.[73] It was to be one of the first such clubs and met annually to provide an opportunity for discussion of all manner of agricultural affairs. The first five meetings saw debates on the importance of maintaining superior breeds of cattle and horses, the rotation of crops, the rearing of poultry and hogs, the cultivation of wheat and the possible use of gypsum as a manure. At the 1807 meeting, and obviously at Dempster's instigation, the 'question as to whether carcasses of meat might be transmitted to distances packed in ice' was mooted.[74]

On their arrival in Scotland during the summer the Sopers took possession of the estates at Skibo and Pulrossie, and added the name Dempster to their own.[75] They were mutual guests of each other – the Dempsters with the young couple at Skibo for three months in the autumn and the Soper Dempsters at Dunnichen both before and afterwards.[76] Settling down quickly, they 'lived with us as our children', considering 'my wife as a mother and me as a father'. Harriet expected her first child in March 1804 but it appears to have arrived a month early.[77] Writing to Macintosh in the middle of September from Skibo, Dempster was so at ease with his new family around him that he had to ask him the name of the inventor of the mule jenny used in the mills (Samuel Crompton). He was full of nostalgia about the many times he had spent there along the Kyle which was 'not inferior in beauty to any navigable Firth in the world'.[78] Life had regained its attraction for him and, finding that Soper played 'most wind instruments with great taste', he was able to enjoy family gatherings, never without his much-loved game of whist. [79]

By October Dempster's worries about Spinningdale resurfaced. He twice visited the mill where he never beheld 'a busier and more enchanting scene', but there was little prospect of saving it and he was reluctant to bother his nephew, the 'proprietor', given his own plans. 'So well conducted an undertaking' could not compete and he had to content himself with carrying away 'some of the yarn, finer than the spider's web', as a memento. However, there was some better news. A John McIntosh, recently returned from Bengal, was in negotiation with William Soper about renting the farm at Swordale. This would be 'the first attempt towards improvement beyond Spinningdale' and his nephew 'looked forward to the prospect'.[80]

In the middle of November Dempster told Sir Adam of the death six weeks previously of the only one of his brothers to die at Dunnichen. Other than the brief description of John Dempster he gave at this time, nothing is known about his life. Aged 68, Dempster admitted that 'death was a deliverance for him', and few men 'ever had less enjoyment of life, for melancholy, as the poet says, had marked him for her own. Altho' blest with a fine taste and considerable poetic genius, yet his diffidence and timidity made him shun all society'.[81] The fact that he is never mentioned with the family either at Dunnichen or Skibo suggests that for most of his life he lived outwith Angus.

A second unhappy occurrence happened about this time, a few details of which were revealed in Dempster's will. His good friend Robert Graham of Fintry, who had become a Commissioner of Excise in 1787, had been peremptorily dismissed 'after 16 years of faithful service'. Having 'borrowed a few hundred pounds from a friend in the Excise to purchase a commission for his son (and whilst) . . . educating his family of 12 children[82] and increasing the public revenue, he wasted his own, for (by) trying to stop some gross peculations he was himself dismissed as a peculator'.[83] He had probably stumbled on some bribery in the Excise and in trying to expose it had become a casualty himself. The circumstances which Dempster described as a 'horrid injustice' were so unfair as to prompt him to invite the executors to insert the text of his settlement 'in the public newspapers'. Fintry, who was to live until 1812, was 'only rescued from want by his generous friends, particularly General Sir Thomas Graham of Balgowan'.[84]

1804

Dempster's usual New Year letter to Sir Adam, as well as another in November (the only two to survive that year), duly reported the Soper

Dempsters' progress since their return from India. Though aware through a visit to Dunnichen at the end of the previous year that his friend's nephew, James Fergusson, had lost his 'young, beautiful, sensible and amiable wife' Jean Dalrymple, it seems Dempster was a little out of touch with events that made it a sad year for the Fergussons. Charles Fergusson's sister Jean died in the June 'after a tedious illness' and Betsy, his daughter, died of consumption at Exmouth after being accompanied there by Kitty, whose own illness had prompted the journey south. Then in December Charles Fergusson himself died four days after seeing his son James married for the second time, to Miss Henrietta Duncan, the second daughter of Admiral Duncan.[85]

On 10 May Dempster told Macintosh that he had been prepared 'for the unpleasant tidings' about Spinningdale Mill. David Dale had apparently at long last persuaded Macintosh to sell it, having himself handed the management of New Lanark over to Robert Owen at the beginning of the century. He had sold Catrine in Ayrshire in 1801 prior to retiring to his estate near Cambuslang.[86] Dempster regretted that the work was to be abandoned, and still more so that it has been attended with so much loss to Macintosh: 'Alas! bonnie Spinningdale! Alas, poor Sutherland!'. And, in a timely reference to Earl Gower's fortuitous change of fortune the previous year when both the 3rd Duke of Bridgwater[87]and the Earl's father died, he added: 'Oh, were you or I, either of us, or both together, Marquis of Stafford, this patriotic beginning of industry, riches and comfort, should not die of a consumption and want of sustenance'.[88] The double inheritance made him one of the richest men in Europe and, with real money to hand at last, the family was able to shape the future of Sutherland for the rest of the century.[89]

It was not until the end of the following year that Macintosh was able finally to tell Dempster the outcome of the sale of Spinningdale Mill. He then put down his thoughts about the reasons for 'the want of success (of their) well-intended scheme of establishing a manufacture in the North' in which both Dale and he had lost 'a very great and heavy sum'. The letter summed up the whole affair.[90] A Mr McFarlane, who was 'a bred spinner' with another cotton mill in the Glasgow area and someone who had 'made some money', had agreed to pay £2,000 for the mill over a ten-year period. The works were sold 'for a mere trifle to a fortunate individual who used the precaution of insuring them; and lucky it was that he did so'.[91] Dempster was called on to renounce and assign his rights in the Balnoe Co. to McFarlane who had chosen to alter the plan of work at the mill and employ more women than hitherto. Macintosh wished him well. He hoped that the present proprietor would do better than they had done, arguing that 'had we prosecuted the weaving alone, without the spinning, we could not have suffered much'.

The two-fold cause of Spinningdale's failure was expressed succinctly. The first was 'a want of industry' by those who became spinners and an absence of 'regular and close application to the manufacture'. 'I mean,' wrote

Macintosh, 'due and proper attention to work, for although the machinery was unexceptionally good, we never did get such attendance given by the workpeople . . . (they) produced never more than a half or two-thirds per spindle' when compared with labour in and around Glasgow. 'It is now a fact well-known and ascertained that a cotton mill never will yield profit unless it gives a certain quantity of yarn per spindle.' The second and evidently more significant cause lay with the management. Apparently this had passed to a Mr Snodgrass, 'a man of very superior abilities as a mechanic experienced in the . . . business' but who lacked 'judgement and experience to manage workpeople and (he) became too indulgent (and) aimed too much at popular humanity, and lent much money to workpeople without even knowledge, (till too late)'. This had 'occasioned loss, idleness and dissipation', despite Dale and Macintosh having sent him support in the form of 'an excellent clerk, and solid spinner and mechanic, to manage these two different (functions)'. Unfortunately, Snodgrass and the new clerk 'quarrelled and fought'.

16

A NEW LEASE OF LIFE
(1805–1809)

'I am fostering my second infancy with all the
attention of a fond parent'
Dempster to Sir John Sinclair, 6 August 1809 from Skibo

1805

Dempster's description of himself as 'an old swan' belied the very active and generally happy years he enjoyed at this time. The nightmare at the start of the decade was behind him and he was generally in 'excellent health' in spite of having put on a good deal of weight.[1] He renewed his efforts on behalf of the Highlanders, keeping constant pressure on all those who might use their influence favourably, or those who seemed to be dodging their responsibilities. In Angus he was busy forming part of a brigade of Volunteers, enlisting Rosie's help – for 'she followed the camp'. The flow of ideas, plans and projects never lessened, and his mind and imagination were still extraordinarily sharp. It was as if he had a new lease of life. Legal loopholes or the minutiae of taxation continued to be given the closest scrutiny and his pursuit of all inventions or recondite scientific discoveries was unremitting. Far from allowing old age to dull his colourful written language, he found ever more aphorisms with which to entertain his correspondents. His capacity for looking at issues from oblique angles persisted and his flights of fancy increased, neither of which attracted ridicule among those friends who knew him well. All things considered, Dempster was as ebullient as ever and had a firm grasp on life.

Rather surprisingly, it was Sir John Sinclair who probably best summed up Dempster's qualities, despite having received more than a fair share of his protestations over the years. Writing at the end of his life, with a warmth of which Dempster would have thought him incapable, he said: '(Dempster) was an excellent scholar, well acquainted with several foreign languages, conversant in all the principal branches of modern science, and, to crown the whole, he was justly entitled to be considered both an accomplished gentleman, and a benevolent man. He had a peculiar felicity in expressing his thoughts in writing; and when speaking on any interesting subject, his manner, tone of voice, fervour, sincerity, and the candour with which he seemed to be animated, operated like a charm, and gained on every heart. He spoke without the least premeditation, and was always listened to with attention and delight.'[2]

Relieved of the responsibility for the Sutherland property, Dempster still had plenty to do in Angus, but he knew how much Soper Dempster had to learn if the erstwhile Indian civil servant was to become a successful farmer. His enthusiasm 'for improving his estates . . . and particularly for the improvement of them by roads and bridges' was welcome, but he was 'a stranger in that country'.[3] Consequently Dempster used every occasion to improve his nephew's understanding of the task he had so readily taken on, suggesting that he involve himself with the activities of the Fisheries Society and attend meetings of the Lunan and Vinney Farming Society whenever he was in Angus. Evidence of Soper's often over-zealous approach and a less tolerant regime at Skibo was, however, not long coming. His wrangling over the extent of the estate occasioned a regular correspondence and Dempster would not have been slow to pick up any signs of what he regarded as inequitable practice.

Mrs Soper Dempster, 'with a pretty boy on her knee', as Dempster described young George Soper Dempster, her first child, born the previous year, was staying at Dunnichen along with Charlotte Boddam's two youngsters. The house had 'a cheerful appearance' with both George and Rosie thoroughly enjoying the 'feelings and amusements of grand-fathers and grand-mothers'.[4] Harriet would give birth to Eleanor, the second of her children in August and was obviously happy and enjoying family life. Although the news she received early that year probably came as a great surprise, it could not have come at a better time. The events which unfolded in London must have held a very special importance for her.

Her mother's first husband (Jacob Fancourt) died in Madras in May 1800 and four years later Olivia Devenish was in London petitioning the East India Company for a pension from the compassionate fund. Life had not been easy for Olivia. She possessed no wealth, having in all likelihood been an illegitimate child herself, and someone who lost her father before reaching her teens. She had few friends with any influence and was greatly in debt. Nevertheless, it seems that this 'tall, distinguished-looking lady, with flashing black Italian eyes', ten years his senior, had captured the heart of a 23-year-old administrative assistant who had perhaps processed an award of twenty-five guineas for her from the Company and a pension at a daily rate of one shilling and three pence. After a brief romance of six months or so, Olivia and Sir Stamford Raffles, as he became, were married on 14 March 1805 in the Parish Church of St George, Bloomsbury. Accompanying the bride appear to have been just two friends, a Mariamne Etherington and Maria

Walthew. Just six days before the wedding Raffles had received confirmation of his appointment as an Assistant Secretary on the staff of the new governor of Penang, Philip Dundas; he who had lost his first wife aboard the *Earl Talbot*. Raffles's salary rose overnight from £70 per annum to £1,500 and carried with it the rank of Junior Merchant.[5] Accompanied by his eldest sister Mary Ann, the couple left for the Malay peninsula almost immediately aboard the *Ganges* to begin a marriage that brought Raffles 'domestic enjoyment . . . (and) . . . a companion who would soothe the adverse blasts of misfortune and gladden the sunshine of prosperity'.[6] Later, as the Governor's wife, Olivia's task was rarely easy, but her grace, dignity and friendliness inspired genuine affection from the people of Java. In his reminiscences, the Malay secretary, Abdulla, wrote that 'she was not an ordinary woman but . . . in every respect co-equal with her husband's position and responsibilities . . . always at work with diligence as day follows day'.[7]

Realizing that her husband's new responsibilities precluded any early return to England, and that Olivia and Harriet might never see each other again, arrangements seem to have been made for them to sit for Nathaniel Plimer, the miniaturist, who lived in New Bond Street.[8] Harriet's death only five years later at the age of 25, and that of her mother in Java in 1814 when she was 43 years old, only served to demonstrate the wisdom of such a decision. Harriet had probably travelled south from Dunnichen with her husband, who may not have met his wife's mother. Another miniature painted around this time and described as a portrait of 'Dempster of Skibo and Dunnichen' may have been that of William Soper. The sitter certainly looks as handsome as Mary Campbell, a friend of Harriet's, described him, if somewhat younger than his 42 years.[9]

Dempster was greatly cheered when he heard of Sir John Sinclair's proposal in February for a Society for the Improvement of Edinburgh and 'the possibility of a new professorship or two at the university'.[10] Recalling that during his lifetime the population of 'the town in which I was born – Dundee' had increased from 8 to 24,000 inhabitants, and not less than 3,000 houses had been built without such a society, he saw greater prospects for Edinburgh where its streets were 'little better than a rabbit warn' (warren). Its elevated position would enable sewerage to be carried down every slope and 'an immense reservoir at the extremity of the common sewer' could contain 'a precious manure that would sell for millions'! So far as the new professorships were concerned, he wrongly assumed that Pulteney (who had funded Edinburgh University's first ever Chair of Agriculture 15 years before) rather than Sinclair was behind the project. He soon saw how support might be given to a novel professorship close to his own heart. Dempster asked his friend whether he had read 'John Leslie on the nature and propagation of heat', since a subdivision of 'the vast field of natural philosophy' might be appropriate. He had in mind an 'igneous professorship', a post which John Leslie (of Largo in

Fife) might fill. In the event, the latter was awarded the chair of mathematics that year.[11]

Five days later Dempster had the delicate task of explaining to Sir Adam that he had unearthed an unpaid debt owed to Captain John's estate. Apparently Charles Fergusson, the wine merchant, had died without settling a loan made to him in 1799 when the Captain was staying with the family in Dulwich and at a time when the seafarer had 'a few thousand with Scott' (see Chapter 14). Sir Adam replied saying that it was 'an additional proof to the too many which I already had of the total unfitness of my unhappy brother for the profession which he had adopted'.[12] a reference to the financial mis-adventures that had caused him so much worry over the years.[13]

On 30 May a link with the past was broken when Sir William Pulteney died aged 76 and Dempster lost his most generous and influential friend. Together they had attended meetings of the Select Society and the Poker Club and been closely involved with the events at Leadenhall Street and Westminster after he had become a proprietor in the East India Company. In his last years Pulteney had continued to represent Shrewsbury in the House of Commons and had been Governor of the Fisheries Society. In the circumstances Dempster was more than delighted soon afterwards to hear from William Smith after a gap of several years, a communication which may have conveyed his parliamentary friend's condolences at Pulteney's death. Smith had added the direction of the Fisheries Society to his earlier appointment as a Commissioner for Highland Roads and Bridges.[14] Recalling his own service with the Society, Dempster assured him that he would not only find such work an 'agreeable occupation' but, as he clearly did, a source of pleasant 'recollections for Old Age'. Regretting that 'Alas, poor Sir Wm. Pulteney has not lived to partake of his reward', he could only console himself with the thought that 'he is gone to receive a much greater – a suitable recompense for a life spent . . . a long life devoted I may say, to being useful to his country and friends and family'.[15]

For someone such as William Smith, whose only connection with the Highlands had been a father who had sent 'presents of tea and other luxuries to Flora Macdonald when she was in the Tower',[16] it was not surprising that Dempster wanted to take the occasion of the death of his predecessor in the Fisheries Society to 'prepare (his) shoulders to sustain the greatest share of its burthen'. He could not resist putting in a plea for the Society to re-examine fishery development in the Western Isles, assuring him that his 'great object was not to catch fish, but people', but he also felt compelled to address the 'subject on which I never enter without tiring my hearers and correspondents' – his own work. 'I did not begin my share' in providing for the Highlanders, he wrote, 'till my hairs were grey and my hams feeble. The strength of my body and vigour of my mind (if it ever had any) were on the decline before the emigration of the Highlanders called my attention to the state of the

Highlands.' Listing the action he had taken in Parliament to obtain £15,000 to buy corn to save them from starvation,[17] the work of the Fisheries Society and 'the lighting of their sea coasts', he willingly acknowledged the work of 'bolder politicians' in the building of the Caledonian canal and roads and bridges.[18]

Thomas Telford wrote to Dempster in November from his home in Shropshire recalling reports he had received from Hawkins Brown and Pulteney about how Dempster's 'early zeal was displayed in all that related to the improvement of your native county' and that he had had 'more than one opportunity of tracing in (his) footsteps the dawnings of the improvements in the North'. The two men had corresponded during the summer and now the continued improvement of Sutherland roads, the prospect of the 'direct and perfectly safe channel' provided by the Caledonian Canal between Inverness and Loch Eil, and the possible locations for a bridge over the Dornoch Firth, were much on his mind. Having passed up the Firth from Tain to Culrain, it occurred to Telford that a 'good wooden bridge at the ferry at Bonar' might suffice, but local word had it that 'such quantities of ice accumulate at this place that a bridge there would be liable to be destroyed'. There was also a need for a road through the hills towards the south to 'avoid returning down the Dornoch Firth to Tain', that over Struie.[19]

During the winter Dempster's unmarried sister Ann, who had enjoyed many holidays with the family, died at Bath.[20] George himself, now aged 73, suffered a sufficiently severe illness to invite to Dunnichen his wife's nephew, the Rev Samuel Bracebridge Heming, the Rector of Drayton in Leicestershire.[21] Recalling the incident the following year, Dempster invited Sam 'to see the robust health of the dying man, whose bedside (he had) attended so dutifully'. Sam Heming was always welcome at Dunnichen and someone for whom the family had much affection. His father, who had accompanied Rose to England and married into the wealthy Bracebridge family, died in 1802 and, after his mother re-married, it seems his son felt more able to travel, despite his parochial responsibilities. Surrounded so often by many mothers and children, Dempster was pleased to admit how much he stood 'in need of an additional confessor-companion at least to this nunnery', a role the rector filled admirably.[22]

1806

The great fire which gutted Spinningdale Mill in 1806 brought to an end the valiant efforts that had been made since 1791 to create employment in Sutherland.[23] This disaster had yet to happen when Dempster wrote to George Macintosh in February to console him about the death of Pitt. The demise of their mutual hero had followed hard on the heels of Lord Nelson at Trafalgar and Dempster was less than sanguine about the new administration's interest in Scotland, fearing that 'the Gaels (were) expiring like a candle in the socket'. With some premonition that both David Dale and Macintosh might also be near the end of their lives,[24] he reiterated the hope, long-shared between them, that the provision of 'canals, roads and bridges, may still preserve this ancient and valuable race of people, to whom I am as much attached as if I had been born on the banks of the Kyll (sic), and bred like you, at the school of Creech (sic)'.[25] It was a typically warm farewell and demonstrated the sentimental mood that had gripped him for much of February. Writing to Sir John Sinclair soon after, he put in a plea for 'a little more zeal for preserving the known Highland heroes, instead of a suspicious Highland Heroic poem, (James Macpherson's *Ossian*) the credit of which, even supposing it to be genuine, is by the confession of all the sensible Highlanders, to be transferred to the Irish Gaels'.[26]

Dempster's main aim in writing to Sir John had been to seek his help in lessening the growing bureaucracy of the Customs and Excise: 'a Macedonial phalanx of armed men hundreds deep'.[27] Ever increasing stamp duties were making the provision of new leases for his tenants an expensive affair: 'My Letham is stampt (sic) to atoms!' He pleaded for his friend the President of the Board of Agriculture to intervene with the Prime Minister so that duties as much as £1, £2, and £3 on land leases of a quarter, half or three-quarters an acre, might be moderated. Such taxation was becoming 'an insurmountable obstruction' to newcomers beginning to build similar villages to Letham.[28]

Happily watching Harriet's two-year-old son grow up prompted his uncle to reply to a letter he had received from Thorkelin in April. Dempster's friend had married in 1793 and christened one of his three sons Georg Dempster Thorkelin.[29] He prayed that his own George, who was 'a hopeful youth', might 'resemble his namesake'. Their renewed correspondence led to Thorkelin introducing him to a Count Ravenstow and the despatch of more Icelandic literature for him to study. Dempster's reply (and his last recorded letter) included a typically effusive plea for Iceland to be allowed to trade freely with the rest of the world and so 'increase the revenue . . . of its sovereign the King of Denmark'.[30]

During the summer the family spent a 'few weeks' at Broughty Ferry 'for seabathing',[31] but Dempster was homesick for Skibo, hoping that Soper Dempster, Harriet, their young son and Eleanor (known as Helen, who had been born the previous year) would long 'enjoy all the comforts of that delightful estate'.[32]

1807

Dempster's interest in politics, intellectual pursuits and agricultural development flourished. Able to continue reading at least some of his favourite authors, he browsed each day among his eighteen volumes of Cicero, Pliny's *Natural History* and an encyclopaedia of antiquity.[33] He particularly enjoyed being kept abreast of Sir John Sinclair's work at the Board of Agriculture by the frequent 'rich and entertaining' reports and memoranda he sent him. Such 'chit chat' was 'precious'.[34] He also made an attempt to develop a small circle of mainly retired political and literary characters from his past, but, quite naturally, it was the family and those on the estate who were at the heart of Dempster's life in his old age. They provided some comfort for the future.

A count of those spending the New Year at Dunnichen revealed just how full the house could still become. In addition to his wife and an unmarried 'very accomplished niece', Margaret Heming, there were Helen Burrington (now Mrs Francis Hawkins) and Charlotte Burrington, the wife of Charles Boddam, who had returned from Bengal the previous year for health reasons with her son and three daughters in the care of a governess.[35] To these seven or eight guests were added the Soper Dempsters with young George and Helen, both under three years old, and the baby daughter Harriet who had been born at the end of the previous year. Such a 'baker's dozen' must have put a good deal of pressure on the accommodation provided by the five or six rooms around the rebuilt first floor gallery and in the attics.

With Dempster's correspondence 'now neither amorous nor treasonable', he could afford to speak of the death of 'Jacky', a green linnet, so beloved by Dempster's nephew and who had survived 'his master six years'. It was mentioned in letters to both Sir Adam and Sir John, although only the former was treated to a verse account of its long life, 'inspired by Melpomene' (the Muse of Tragedy). Such a poem, if not lost on Sinclair, would, he hoped, be permitted 'like the birds (to) cheer (his) labours with a song' while he was engaged in more serious and useful matters.[36] Throughout May Dempster was very ill with dysentery and considered himself 'bound for that dreary habitation' the grave. He had been 'reduced to a shadow', but a month later he began putting back the weight about which he so often complained. The remedy had comprised a 'farinaceous' diet relieved by 'a bit of chicken at dinner', milk and water to drink, and a daily excursion in his chaise.[37] By July his strength had returned sufficiently for him to deal with other concerns. He had spotted the possibility of 'an Alpine wheat that may be sown as late as our barley'[38] and was 'moving heaven and earth to get people in power to attend to a clause in the Whisky Bill' which had been 'artfully worded'. Distilling had been made 'penal'. Both were items where Sinclair's view was urgently wanted and, in good parliamentary fashion, he included the number of the relevant statute:- Stat.46 Geo.3 Cap.102 Sect.38.[39]

No doubt at Dempster's suggestion, his nephew at Skibo was spending time and effort attempting to change the law on entailed estates. The draft of a Parliamentary Bill to permit the heirs of entail to grant leases longer than their own lives was to result. Death nullified such tacks (leases) and, since tenants were being discouraged from improving their land, William proposed that tacks of up to 14 years should be allowed. Although Lord Reay, whom Soper

Dempster had consulted previously about the high contributions called for in building new roads, was lukewarm about its benefits, his lawyers in Edinburgh managed to get a commission appointed. A meeting of proprietors with similarly entailed estates followed, only for the proposition to die when a majority decided that security of tenure and the amount of betterment undertaken by tenants were not linked.[40]

Soper Dempster had his fair share of disputes about pasturing rights, threats to plantations and rents, to say nothing of unexpected claims against Captain John's estate well after the three years allowed for their proper submission. Even so, it was the manner in which he dealt with these that did little to win him friends and may, as a consequence, have constrained the social life the family enjoyed at Skibo. Dempster was prompted on one occasion to hope that he and Harriet 'were sustained at the Tain Races and Northern Meeting and encouraged thereby to resort to both annually'.[41] His nephew found difficulty in coming to terms with the fact that the boundaries of large estates were hardly, if ever, specified in their charters. His lawyer had to remind him that land was conveyed as described and boundaries settled by long possession, rather than the far from credible stipulations in a few old charters.[42] It was not until 1810 that some resolution of his differences of opinion with neighbouring landlords was achieved.

An occasional visitor to Skibo at this time was Richard Dunning, Lord Ashburton, who had become the laird of Rosehall in 1805.[43] Like Soper Dempster, who had been born in Ashburton, he was an Englishman whose family had long been associated with the Devon town and who was also the owner of a Highland estate in need of improvement.[44] Unlike Soper Dempster, who found his estate responsibilities a full-time job, Lord Ashburton had a relaxed manner and humorous disposition which helped him in the task he had set himself. Although he was infrequently at Rosehall, he was sailor enough to use the firth occasionally on his visits to Skibo, sailing down the firth in his boat.[45]

The Soper Dempsters' health suffered from a climate to which they were unaccustomed and rarely, if ever, it seems, were the family able to travel far together. The laird had been in correspondence with William Dick, a well-known London surgeon, about a liver disorder which he believed would greatly benefit from his return to India. Dick could not agree with such a remedy, much to Harriet's relief, and suggested the waters and salts of Cheltenham would be just as good. A plan for the two men to meet in Mayfair had to be scrapped when Dick was appointed unexpectedly as Chief Surgeon to Prince of Wales Island.[46] Suggestions by friends that they might spend the winter this year at Cheltenham were not taken up and contact with Dempster appears to have been limited with gifts of fruit occasionally sent to Dunnichen from the garden at Skibo.[47] A depressed market for cattle led to Dempster suggesting a drove from Skibo to Angus. Some 198 head of cattle, along with several horses, came under the hammer in October. A number of tenants had apparently used this route to auction their animals when Dempster had been in charge at the castle.

1808

Unable to contemplate travelling to a softer climate that winter, and with William Kelly's convection-heating system at Dunnichen proving inadequate, Dempster was forced to purchase three 'Franklyn' stoves from a firm in Newcastle to keep the drawing room, little dining room and his study warm. 'Not breathing one mouthful of air colder than 52 on the Fahrenheit thermometer,' he sat down to compose another 'batch of epigrams'.[48] Among the verses was a *Familiar Epistle* written to Sir John Sinclair, part of which is quoted below. Its message about the inadequacy of ferry boats was prophetic:

> I who acquir'd some small renown,
> For sending salmon to London Town,
> Now in Fame's temple claim a higher place,
> For planning safety to the travelling race.
> And O Sir John! I ask thy powerful aid,
> (For publication is thy joy and trade)
> Proclaim my plan in all our towns and counties,
> Promote subscriptions; move for royal bounties.
> The clergy too my zealous Muse invokes,
> to preach my project to their drowsy flocks.
> The plan itself prepare, my friend, to hear.
> 'Tis not quite new, nor difficult, nor dear'.
> How many lives are on our ferries lost?
> How oft have you on all of them been tost?
> Sitting for Cornwall, or for Johnny Groats,
> Your life is spent in open ferry boats:
> How oft we've heard your tragical remarks,
> On drunken boatmen, and their crazy barks:
> How oft when hurrying you have been delay'd!
> How often drench'd! and oftener still afraid!
> For all those ills a certain cure I've found:
> Ferries! Get life boats – who shall then be drown'd?
> No more sad tales our Papers shall relate
> Of husbands lost, and wives disconsolate:
> As safe convey'd to Pettycur we are,
> As o'er a bridge, or in some man of war . . . ..

The previous December Dempster had remonstrated with Sinclair about what he believed had been a recent and substantial emigration from Caithness. This he did not attribute to any ineptitude on the part of the 'President of the Board of Agriculture', although he reminded him somewhat abruptly that 'his cousin, the Countess of Sutherland' had also been responsible in 1807 for 'dismissing at least 600 families, man, woman and child, in the Parishes of Lairg and Rogart for the paltry consideration of a little increase of rent'. He was in no mood for excuses from Sinclair, declaring that he continued to 'act the Inquisition', always sending him queries about such matters as the state of Angus cattle, 'and never the respondent'.[49]

Now, with a copy of *The Star* dated 5 January in front of him, Dempster had evidence not only of the emigration he feared but news of what had happened to the unfortunate passengers and crew of the *Rambler*.[50] The vessel, under the command of James Norris, left Stromness on 1 October, only to be wrecked near the Bay of Bulls in Newfoundland, where 138 out of 144 passengers and crew lost their lives. Dempster felt that the real loss had occurred when the emigrants were forced to 'set their feet into the *Rambler*'. What had caused them to contemplate emigration was as important as any enquiry about the 'accommodation and safety' aboard such ships.[51] In February, and somewhat unfairly, he questioned Sinclair further: 'Should not you have known if the vessel was fitted out & mann'd & victualled as our human law directs? Should not you have known from whence they came, & who and where they were going?'[52] As it turned out, Sinclair, who would usually have known about such ship movements, had been in London.[53]

Of equal concern was the scarcity of meal and corn across the north and the near famine conditions that prevailed. It seems that Soper Dempster at Skibo had been prevailed upon by Dempster to write about his experiences. 'Poor Highlanders' were coming down from the hills in dozens and 'on their knees' to bless those who could supply food and seed corn. The laird of Skibo had secured some supplies, but it was 'far short of what they will need'.[54] Dempster was concerned to keep up his nephew's spirits in such circumstances. Living a rather lonely existence at Skibo and, so far as Dempster was aware, just two servants, 'G. Forbes and Mary Donaldson', he did it in the way he knew best. The 'thirty lines' he wrote may have been 'as soporific as so many opium pipes', but they were a gentle means of encouraging him to keep in touch, especially as the anticipated ice and snow might bring its own depression. However, Dempster could not help telling his nephew that he had brought on the 'thirty lines' himself. It was always 'dangerous to tell a poet that his composition made you laugh!'[55]

In March he continued to hope that Sinclair would follow his example and free his tenants from their 'feudal fetters and disgrace' an issue between them that dated back to at least the summer at Skibo in 1791 when Dempster had wanted to show him 'the first fruits of the abolition'.[56] The 'degraded state of agriculture', particularly in Caithness, was solely due in his opinion to 'a want of security in the tenure of its farmers'.[57] Relief continued to be called for in the Highlands where two poor seasons probably meant that meal, potatoes and seed would be in short supply. He proposed that vessels carrying stocks of potatoes and corn should be moored at strategic points and contractors be given credits to support a 'fair price' and avoid a black market.[58]

But it was soon clear that the loss of the *Rambler* had not been forgotten. Although he considered Sinclair to be 'the great reservoir into which all new discoveries flow(ed)', Dempster wanted to see more action on his friend's part, giving him two suggestions in July. The first of these included a drawing of a method of preventing frost damage to fruit trees. The use of a 'woollen net of twofold untwisted yarn' worked 'most successfully', excluding the frost, admitting the sunshine and allowing the fruit to set as in a peach or cherry house.[59] One of the threads of every mesh was cut. Sinclair accepted this as 'an excellent idea', but, with his hands 'already more than full', he only had time to ask Dempster to arrange for some practical trials of his second and more urgent idea.

This had been referred to in his *Familiar Epistle* and addressed the constant loss of life at sea. Dempster proposed the introduction of 'Life Passage Boats' which, although conceived as vessels 'widely different' from lifeboats, can only be assumed to have been a class of well-built vessels capable of 'keeping passengers not only safe but dry'.[60] They were to be fit for use on crossings of the Irish Sea, the Minch and Pentland Firth. Citing Denmark, where 'sailing life boats that defy the surges of the ocean, cross the most dangerous surfs (and) encounter the most violent storms in all seasons of the year', he was convinced of their value; he had apparently tried 'to raise a subscription for a pilot boat at Dundee, albeit unsuccessfully.[61] Forced by Sinclair 'to knock at other doors for the admission of this project', Dempster then took up the baronet's suggestion of an approach to Francis Freeling. Whether or not his ideas were 'laid before the Post Masters General' is not known.[62]

Having done what he could to stem the famine in Sutherland and with the winter behind him, Soper Dempster set out to visit Dunnichen in May, bringing with him his own 'address' composed in honour of Skibo. He well knew Dempster's predilection for such verse in his old age, as well as the beauty of the Firth:

> Oh Skibo Thou'st a charming Place:
> Assist me, Muse, its charms to trace.
> Of Dornoch's Firth the boast and pride;
> And she a comely strapping lass.
> Thy Poolyheurich smooth as Glass,
> Bringing Sea Trout twice a day,
> And various fishes, from the sea.
> Surrounded too with fertile lands,

Cordalies's Woods, and Dornoch's Sands,
Sweet are the walks in Ev'lick's Vale;
Sweeter thy rides to Spinningdale.
Thy ample Bounds extending reach,
To Rogart, Dornoch, Lairg, and Creech;
Abound with Game of every kind,
Hare, Partridge, Grouse, Roebuck, & Hind.
Your early Garden likewise bears,
The choicest Fruits, Plumbs, Apples, Pears,
Thy Climate's hot, (be 't understood,)
Hot for such a latitude.
Immortal Gods Oh! grant my Prayer,
To live – die or be buried There.[63]

Henry Dundas, 1st Viscount Melville, and Dempster corresponded for several years after each had retired from politics.[64] Although sometimes disappointed by Dundas's decisions, Dempster never altered the view he expressed to William Carlyle more than 40 years earlier that he had been a great acquisition in parliament and a man with 'an exceeding good capacity and a very good heart'.[65] There is little evidence that their relationship was ever close, but his name had been a natural inclusion on Dempster's 'roll-call' of those whose friendship he wanted to cultivate and several frivolous, if friendly, letters and 'epistles' passed between them. He had told Sir Adam in 1800 how, when asleep, he dreamed about assisting 'at several cabinet councils' at which 'Hary'(sic) had been present.[66] On this occasion Dempster had apparently been considering ways of lessening the harm done by the Corn Laws and in his reply Dundas warned him that any 'juggling' would 'meet with more difficulty' than he thought.[67] Dundas went on to explain that, after a few months at his son's house in London, he was equally determined, not unlike Dempster, to 'indulge himself without reserve' in farming on his estate at Dunira near Comrie. There he could renew the acquaintance of such Edinburgh friends as were alive whenever he chose.[68] Later in the year Dempster suggested that he might like to buy some of the Shetland cattle at Dunnichen, but Dundas had already 'been provided from the West Highlands with (his) annual stock' which was as much as he 'could carry comfortably through the winter'.[69] He died in May 1811.

In July Dempster was irate; his attention had been drawn to a specious publication by Lord Selkirk who had been instrumental five years before in settling 800 emigrants in Canada.[70] Drafting a long letter to the *Dundee Mercury*[71] under his favoured pseudonym *Scoto-Britannicus*, (and adding only at the end that he was 'once a small Highland proprietor'), he 'trembled' to see such deceptively pleasing theories in 'the hands of active and practical men'.[72] Selkirk had argued that Highlanders were 'necessarily idle' and a 'useless encumbrance standing in the way' of improvement. Attacking it as wholly ill-judged and a series of paradoxes, Dempster could only wonder how such conclusions had been arrived at, particularly when those who had been removed from their homes achieved success across the Atlantic. How could 'a race of happy, industrious, and brave people' be incapable of performing similar feats in their own land. It was a paradox that Lord Selkirk and other proprietors could defray the expense of conveying such people across the Atlantic, assist them with the costs of erecting 'huts', the provision of food and tools with which to fell trees, to say nothing of in effect allowing them to obtain the very perpetual leases they had been refused in Scotland. Furthermore, surely 'his Lordship' could grasp that for less expense such tenants would have been able to 'fertilise their barren spots'. Why had it been necessary for them, 'their pregnant women and aged parents (to) cross a turbulent ocean of three thousand miles broad . . . to set about (doing) what they might as well have done at home'? Selkirk omitted any account of what some 'mild treatment' in their own country might have achieved, reminding him, if not of his own efforts, then those of Lord Breadalbane and Lord Seaforth. Why not, he added, 'a description of the cultivation of the gardens at Dunkeld and Fort William'? Dempster's lamentation, and the energy with which he argued that 'ten industrious families in Britain (were) of more real value . . . than ten thousand such families on the other side of the Atlantic', showed how well able he was to defend his corner even in his seventy-sixth year.[73]

During the summer Dempster read some of Alexander Balfour's work. The Arbroath poet and novelist had received Dempster's 'encouragement and cheering counsel' several times before. On this occasion, he returned the author's manuscripts, adding that his elegiac verses were very good.[74] Such was Dempster's disposition that he willingly devoted time to those whom he was happy to regard as his protégés, and his generosity towards any friend in need could be as spontaneous as it was heartfelt. On another occasion, reacting to bad news about an old friend, Dempster had grabbed a bundle of banknotes that were on his desk, saying, 'Give them to Woodfall with my kindest regards'.[75]

Before the year ended he had the great pleasure of hearing from Francis Humberstone Mackenzie who was staying at Castle Brahan. It had been a long time since he had heard from Seaforth, who, having given up his seat in Parliament to William Adam, had left for the Caribbean to become governor of Barbados for six years. Dempster had written to him about Fraser[76] whom his friend hoped would be able to join his regiment unless another 'good man' could be found as a replacement.[77] Seaforth and his lady had enquired at the ferry whether the Dempsters were at Skibo, but they had already gone south, and he was left with writing about how much he had been struck by 'recent improvements' in the county, inspiring him to do likewise in Lewis.[78] By the time he wrote a second letter Seaforth was evidently feeling his 54 years, admiring his old friend's 'health and vigour' despite 'standing before (him) on the list of Advocates . . . making exertions superior to (his) as a lawyer', but he was delighted to 'have lived to see old Caledonia so wonderfully improved'. So far as his own prospects were concerned, he recalled a promise made to Lord Melville 'years ago' that 'the moment (he) felt the symptoms of declining health', he would resign his responsibilities. This had occurred that summer when 'a weakness in (my) eyes gave me notice that the time was come'.[79]

1809

Dempster enlisted Lord Erskine's help in a campaign to speed up the administration of justice in Scotland and reduce the delays and cost associated with so many cases.[80] His correspondence with the eminent barrister who, until 1807, had been Lord Chancellor started before the New Year. Dempster had been forced to advise a widow that her claim would cost more than she might receive. Legal aid was far off. Erskine could see no way of applying the 'excellent law of England'; there was simply no justice in cases involving ten or twenty pounds. He admitted, and Dempster concurred, that the lack of any reform was 'an awful consideration', insisting that it needed a Napoleon, who 'had already done more for France' than any government.

The same theme had been the subject of at least three other representations. In a lucubration to Sir Adam at the New Year when he was 'cooped up' in his study and snow lay on the ground around Dunnichen, Dempster had dealt with his friend's obvious criticism of a plan whereby 'Gaelic Judges' travelled the area settling disputes so as to avoid lengthy and expensive court proceedings elsewhere. Again under the name *Scoto-Britannicus*, he had written to a Dundee paper suggesting that the use made of circuit judges in rural Wales might be copied in the Highlands. Should suitable local accommodation be lacking, such 'ambulatory justice' might be dispensed, if necessary, from their 'yachts when in harbour'. Countering what Sir Adam regarded as this exaggerated solution, Dempster proposed that circuit courts in such mainland towns as Dingwall, Dornoch, Thurso and Fort William should sit 'till the rolls are clear'd'. In a few days they could do an 'immense' amount of work.[81]

Looking for reinforcement to his argument, Dempster wrote to his erstwhile companion on the board of the Fisheries Society, Sir Ilay Campbell, who was then Lord Protector of the Court of Session and 'at the heart of the Commission investigating the Administration of Justice in Scotland'. But again, whilst there was no difficulty with 'the machinery of business', and he expected to be able to say 'something pointedly' about jury trials, he did not anticipate a quick solution.[82] Pressing Lord Melville on the same point three weeks later, it was clear that he was 'a great enthusiast on the subject of juries . . . in criminal cases' but 'a sceptic' so far as their use in civil cases was concerned. Melville had compared the expense of litigation in England and

Scotland, and was convinced that Scotland had 'a tenfold advantage over our Southern neighbours especially with regard to the causes of poor people, such as widows'. Dempster was pleased to note Melville's acceptance of the fact that improvement was called for 'in our small debt courts', also that regulations, 'even in the article of expense', might be forthcoming.[83] Unfortunately for all concerned, news came in April that Ilay Campbell's review had run into the sand: the 'judges seem at present to be averse to any change'.[84]

The first of several versions of Dempster's most frequently quoted satirical poem describing some of his achievements, entitled *Bragadocio* (sic), had just appeared.[85] An explanatory note about some of the allusions contained in what he himself called a 'silly *jeu à Esprit*' were probably written after its first recipients had questioned them. It was a piece far from mere 'empty boasting'. It well summarizes what he had done specifically for the Highlanders. By implication he drew a distinction between the men of Forfar along with those who had 'immigrated' to the new community at Letham (where 350 were then at work) and those less malleable in the north whose culture and habits prevented them accepting his attempts at industrialization. Overall, the verses provided an apt context for the continuing debate he was having with Sinclair about future needs in Sutherland and Caithness.

> I who erst saved the Highlanders from want,[86]
> And taught them how to plough, to build[87] and to plant,
> Attack'd the feudal dragon in his den,[88]
> And of his slaves made valiant Highland men:
> Illum'd by night their seas, and coast, and bays,[89]
> With all the splendor of a noon-tide blaze;
> Of seaboard towns the first foundations laid:[90]
> Plann'd a canal with many a costly lock,[91]
> Surpassing far the coast of Languedock.
> Tho' old, still active in the Highland cause,
> I drew my pen to give it English laws;[92]
> In vain I tried the Highlanders to keep
> From being devour'd by flocks of lowland sheep;
> But rage for rent extinguished every thought,
> For men who bravely had our battles fought.
> How oft to all my Highland friends I've said,
> 'Oh, quit your gibb'rish, bagpipe, kilt and plaid.
> For how can union ere be found among
> Two people, strangers to each other's tongue?
> Your pipes seem groaning to our nicer ears;
> Your dress, to ladys, nakedness appears'[93]

Although he allowed himself a brief moment in April to thank Sir John Sinclair for the account he had sent him of Wellington's 'disastrous' retreat from

Corunna, Dempster now wanted to use his position as an 'honorary and zealous Member of the Board of Agriculture' to plead for the growing of two crops in England, since neither would grow well in Scotland. The southern counties could produce flax seed 'in perfection' if it was afforded a 'bounty as . . . lately granted to Ireland' and, if an account he had been reading of tobacco growing as far north as Finland was to be believed, he thought 'that ill-considered act restraining us from planting Tobacco in Great Britain' should be repealed.[94] Reminding Sinclair that some Scottish tobacco planters had been obliged 'to burn whole fields of it, worth 2/6d per lb' since the government purchased it 'by force' for only 4d per lb, he recalled having seen tobacco 'thrown into the Thames'.[95] It seems that these 'hints' were the start of a fuller paper meant for publication in the *Farmers Magazine* which Dempster wrote after the visit of his English friend William Smith.[96] It rehearsed the reasons why farmers south of the border were seldom removed from their farms, were encouraged to pass on their property to their sons, paid lower rents than their Scottish counterparts and could 'at a triffling expense' (*sic*) vote for Members of Parliament. In a telling phrase, he added that 'the plough is there represented in Parliament and cannot be oppressed. In Scotland, rents only are represented, and therefore cannot be restrained'. He owned that 'we of the Scottish Nation had indeed learned many useful lessons from our English neighbours but that our education was not completed'.[97]

Sam Heming was one of several guests at Dunnichen that spring, but once they had left, and with the prospect of an extended stay with the Soper Dempsters at Skibo in mind, George and Rosie took the opportunity of visiting numerous friends round about.[98] It was, however, the picture painted by Rosie of the 'Beefsteak' party at the end of June, and, poignantly, the last social gathering in Forfar the two of them would enjoy together, that must have remained long in Dempster's memory.[99] Writing to her nephew, she said, 'Mr Dempster assi(sted) Mrs Ogilvy in directing it, and he (Mr D) insisted that the ball should be opened by a reel danced by him and Mrs O, and Mr Ogilvie and your humble servant, both the gentlemen the same age. After the reel Mr Dempster begged to observe no excuse need be offer'd by the rest of the gentlemen for not dancing. I never saw Mr D in greater spirits and no young man could have gone thro' the task with more attention and good humour.'[100]

The Dempsters took up what was to be a long residence with William and Harriet at Skibo at the beginning of July, enjoying a gentle round of social calls and family amusement in between which George continued what Sinclair called his 'political exertions'.[101] With the latter back in Edinburgh after attending several 'Agricultural Festivals' in Bedford and Norfolk, the family was in hope that he might give them 'a <u>long</u> visit'. Having been 'scolded' by his nephew for understating the population of Skibo in a report to Sinclair, Dempster confessed that 'the tide of its prosperity (was) only beginning to flow' and that there were now 240 tenants on the estate, which had doubled its rent roll since the property 'came into the possession of our family'.[102] In a singular reference to his half-brother a few days later, Dempster assured him that 'farming (was) a surer road to wealth than the command of an Indiaman', recalling that in 1797 'the Hon. John Cochrane bid my brother to quit his ship if he wanted £50,000, and buy 50,000 acres of Highland mosses'. This was 'long before Lord Meadowbank or Mr Smith of Sevenbridge' knew how to improve their mossy land.[103]

In excellent spirits, he proposed going south into Ross to examine a 'miraculous apple tree', something no less interesting 'to us Northern gardeners . . . than Dr Jenner's discovery of the cowpocks (sic), or Dr Jenner's discovery of stilling the sea by oil'. On what seems to have been a rainy day, always a spur to his writing, Dempster elaborated amusedly on the origins of the latter discovery. He explained to Sinclair that the secret was known to the tacksmen of St Kilda a century before and how Martin Martin, a visitor there in 1697, told of a factor who, being overtaken by a storm while collecting rents on the island, 'suspended fat St Kilda puddings superstitiously from the stern of his boat into the sea'.[104] Dempster also told of an old woman who sent him as a boy to say 'certain words at a . . . well' as a cure for toothache whilst 'holding a key for some minutes between (his) teeth'. The lodestone, as he said, had 'been accidentally discovered to be a cure for the toothache'. He felt it might be worth enquiring whether other 'superstitious pranks' might have some foundation in natural causes![105]

William Smith, accompanied by his wife Frances[106] and her sister, at last came to stay in early October where 'ripe walnuts & luscious peaches, green-gages and pears are or have been the constant desserts of our . . . family dinners for these last two months'.[107] The 'whole garrison of this castle, reinforced by Lord Ashburton, all rejoiced at the prospect of (their) arrival'.[108] It had long been Dempster's ambition to get to know him better, not least because, having become Deputy Governor of the Fisheries Society after the death of Pulteney, he had responsibility for its work in the Highlands. He may also have feared that Smith's 'many rather impersonal charitable designs'[109] might be under-mining the Society's work. News of the Smiths' coming had been all the more pleasurable to 'everybody here' since Dempster feared Inverness might have been the 'prescribed bounds of (his) excursion'.

Apparently it was Mrs Smith who had 'prompted' the journey further north-wards. George stood ready, with his eyes 'open'd very wide to behold such old Friends, and (his) ears erect to learn (Smith's) adventures' and ready 'to discuss the fertile topics of conversation this neglected . . . part of our Island' afforded. What his guests made of his travelling instructions is not recorded. Hoping for a pleasant day for their crossing the Firth, Dempster added in-cautiously, 'It has usually been reckon'd a safe one. But 2 months ago, from impatience to go to a Fair, twice the number of people, at least 130, crammed themselves into a boat, more than she could carry, and all but a few perished, which has brought the Ferry very unjustly into some disrepute, for the same accident might have happened at Lambeth or Hampton Ferries, and will I trust never happen here or anywhere else again.'[110]

William Smith's visit coincided with his formal inspection as the Society's Deputy Governor to Lochbay, Tobermory and Ullapool, the last being the development in which Dempster had taken a close interest in 1788. He had been hospitably entertained by the chiefs at Castle Grant and Dunvegan. The year before, after a period when the Society had lost touch with much that was going on in Wester Ross and rents were allowed to get into serious arrears, it had been forced to supply meal to the settlers after yet another failure of the herring fishing. Smith reported to the Annual General Meeting (in 1810) that there had nevertheless been signs of the herring returning and, although little had been done since 1798, he described the town as well laid out and the houses as being 'exceedingly decent'.[111] He maintained his optimism about the employment prospects in Ullapool, but signs of the ultimate failure of fishing development at the other two centres must have been evident to Dempster.[112] He could usually recognize too sanguine a view in others, if not in himself. Only the Society's investment at Caithness provided any really new impetus and this would have been high on the list of matters the two men talked over at Skibo.

Travelling on roads that were worse than they had 'conceived', William Smith's party left towards the end of October for a short visit to Caithness.[113] What Dempster called their 'Argonautic Expedition'[114] provided the Deputy Governor with some insight into the works that the Society had in hand in Wick. Thomas Telford had originally put Portmahomack high on his list of possible new fishing ports when he surveyed the north-east coast in November 1790, but the directors had chosen the already prosperous town of Wick, buying nearly 400 acres of land from Sir Benjamin Dunbar in March 1803.[115] Smith was cared for at the latter's home at Hempriggs during his stay there.

Dempster was anxious that Smith, in his role as a Commissioner for Highland Roads and Bridges, should 'contrive measures for making Justice travel along them'. In his view the Commission had concentrated on opening 'roads through all the mountains, and (building) bridges over all the Torrents of the Highlands' without taking account of other parallel needs. Admitting that Smith was 'not engaged in the work of a day', it still seemed to Dempster that everything was taking too long to achieve. Coupling yet another plea for jury trials in civil cases with the urgency for road building, Dempster tried a little flattery, suggesting that 'it is from the hands of English Gentlemen, liberal enough to think Scotland part of their own native country, & to love it as such, that we are to look for this blessing'. Their discussions at Skibo had unearthed the fact that sections of new roads required separate petitions to the Commission. This convinced Dempster that they were tackling the work piecemeal instead of establishing a Standing Committee (or 'rather a <u>sitting</u> Commission') that could implement a rolling programme and deal with other matters such as 'the improvement of waste lands'.[116]

The Smiths left Skibo and returned south to Sandgate soon after their return from Caithness. Dempster probably hoped they would stay longer but Sir Charles Ross was expecting them at Balnagown Castle, and 'circum-stances' obliged them 'to take (their) leave . . . suddenly'.[117] Sir Charles had been in touch with Soper Dempster, telling him that they would be without Lady Mary, his wife's absence apparently being no impediment. He also hoped that George might sometime find the time to visit him, much as he feared that the laird of Dunnichen would 'scarcely recollect' him after 'so great an interval'.[118] So far as Smith was concerned he was satisfied that he had achieved 'the objects of (his) excursion' and, in Dempster's case, the visit had done nothing to dull his interest in using him as a valuable conduit for some of his own ideas.

How seriously the family at Skibo took Harriet's ill-health that autumn is not at all clear. Lord Ashburton had been aware at the end of November that something might be amiss.[119] The birth on 25 November 1809 of the Soper Dempsters' fifth child in six years (Rose) had undoubtedly precipitated a crisis and by 10 December her husband was sufficiently concerned to write 'a very full and distinct account' of it to Dr James Gregory, Professor of Physic in Edinburgh, receiving a fifteen-page commentary by way of reply, two weeks later. Calling her condition nervous 'hysteria', the only 'uncommon' aspect of her case was, in his view, that it 'should have come upon a lady . . . doing her duty to the state . . . bearing and nursing children'.[120]

Soper Dempster was to tell Sam Heming in May the next year that 'her complaint (was) . . . of a consumptive nature, brought on by taking too great freedoms with her health at Dunnichen and Broughty Ferry'.[121] By then Harriet's health had 'created the greatest uneasiness' in the minds of the family. They would have known 'not to be too sanguine as a disease of such well-known danger . . . often remits . . . but returns with unabated violence'.[122]

DARKNESS AND LIGHT
(1810 – 1812)

'We are got into the hottest battle that death wages
against us mortals'
(Dempster to Sir Adam Fergusson, 9 January 1810 from Skibo)

1810

It was an unusually mild winter at Skibo, Dempster's 'most favourite spot on this earth'. Even at the age of seventy-eight he still rode as much as he could and, despite growing worries about both the health of his niece and later his wife, neither of whom were ever far from his mind, his intellect and interests continued to match his constitution. Writing to Sir Adam Fergusson in January, he relied on news about the war against Napoleon to portray his mood, comparing the now frequent death of his friends to Wellington's costly victory the previous summer. His own 'metamorphosis' compared well with the remarkable changes in fortune suffered by the royal families of France and Spain where the King of France was 'a Chelsea pensioner' and Charles IV of Spain (together with his son Ferdinand VII) effectively 'a French prisoner'.[1]

Playing 'a bit of a shabby Scotch Lady's trick' – taking a 'peep' at a letter to be forwarded to another before re-sealing and posting it – Dempster told Sam Heming in March that he feared Walter Gray, the son of one of their 'best neighbours' at Dunnichen, had been 'seduced by drink' at Rugby School, a 'most degrading vice'. He had not succumbed to the beatings 'which few of us . . . escaped at his time of life'. What Dempster really wanted to hear was that Dempster Heming had 'something better than a mere licence to practice in court'. He had been called to the bar three years before and recently Lord Melville had written to say he had recommended Heming to his son, the Rt. Hon.Mr R. Dundas, 'which may lead to something better'.[2] The judge Dempster hoped his namesake would some day become was not to be; instead he rose to the rank of Lieutenant-Colonel in the army.

Dr Gregory had apparently received not one but two reports in Edinburgh the previous year. They came from Dempster as well as his nephew. His own wife's health had also been of great concern. As he later told William Smith, 'You had hardly found your way to Sandgate when, in answer to separate consultations, Dr Gregory of Edinburgh sent us a confidential line to prepare Soper Dempster and me for the worst'. He now concluded that Harriet was consumptive and that Rose 'had water in her pericardium which would sooner or later stop the motions of her heart': a better one 'hardly ever beat in a human breast'.[3] Her general health had always been good, with no serious illnesses during the 36 years they had been together, and Dempster was beside himself in expectation of her sudden death. Rosie's fainting fits became more frequent and Dempster took her out in the carriage from Skibo 'as often as the weather (would) permit, but even in doing so, and while she (was) getting her cloaths put on, fainting fits frequently (intervened)'. His hopes of her recovery lessened each day.[4]

In April, and with Dempster's language now bereft of much adornment and his memory of the year awry (he dated his letter to Sir John Sinclair as 1809), he was in a sombre and increasingly fearful mood. The burial cortege of a tenant who had died 'after a few days sickness' was passing the gate at Skibo when news came that the two daughters who had attended him during his sickness were 'only yesterday seized with the same fever'. Not surprisingly, he concluded that 'this house resembles the Governor's in a siege to which every hour brings reports of the death or wounds of some of the garrison'. Death was on his mind as he reported the possibility that yellow fever had broken out in Caithness after a sailor aboard a vessel from the West Indies had been landed there. The newspapers spoke of Caithness and Sutherland vessels being quarantined at Leith. 'The facts' reaching him concerning this 'calamity' were that 'in the Parish of Rogart with a population of 2,000 souls, fifty of its inhabitants (had) been buried since Christmas' and on Lord Ashburton's estate six tenants had died within three months.[5]

Although Dempster accepted that the earlier efforts he and Sinclair had made to alleviate 'the same counties from famine' had been largely ignored by the administration, he could not resist telling his friend the course of action he would have followed if he had still been at Westminster.[6] In suggesting that any resolution to the House would have included reference to a 'dangerous fever' having broken out in Caithness and Sutherland which had 'increased, is increasing, and ought to be diminished', he played on the well-known words of John Dunning (Lord Ashburton's father) when thirty years before he had drawn attention to the ever increasing powers of the Crown. Now it was his duty to act 'like a modern senator'. Accordingly, he limited his plea to Sinclair, asking him to 'turn to the Report of the Winchester Gaol Committee'. This had dealt with a similar 'distemper' that had made 'great ravages among the Spanish prisoners' at the prison there. Although the physician sent to Winchester to investigate the outbreak had now retired to Charlton House in

Surrey, he would, he was certain, 'attend your summons', should Sinclair be able to consult him.[7]

However valuable Dempster's local knowledge and legal expertise would have been to his nephew, both men could have done without being involved in the latest round of their long-standing property dispute in Sutherland which came to a head in June. The four parties disputing the marches between their estates had separately prepared their claims and sworn their testimonies in April 1809 – Harriet and William at Dunnichen in the presence of George and his steward, Alexander Loudon; the Marchioness and Marquess of Stafford at Cleveland House in London in the presence of two of their servants; Dugald Gilchrist of Ospisdale along with the Sheriff Clerk of Sutherland and Andrew Fraser an upholsterer from Cromarty; and Hugh Houston of Creich whose witnesses were Cosmo Falconer at Rhives and Lt. Col. Alexander Sutherland of Culmaily. The four landowners whose estates abutted had agreed to 'fix and ascertain the exact boundary' between them and, in effect, revise what had been an unsatisfactory agreement made in 1744. Each had agreed to be bound by an arbitration made by three arbiters – George Sackville Sutherland of Rhives in Ross-shire, Hugh Ross, the Sheriff Substitute, and William Munro of Achany. Soper Dempster appears to have set the process in motion and probably thought he was protecting the long-term interests of his young son George who was heir to the estate, the entail having been confirmed soon after the couple's return from India.[8]

In Dornoch on 18 and 19 June, after agents for the parties and the witnesses cited in the agreement had met and 'perambulated' round the land in dispute,[9] they met 'repeatedly' to consider the various claims which had long been a cause of much irritation 'maturely and deliberately'. Soper Dempster had certainly fallen out with Dugald Gilchrist, and whilst the old laird had probably been able to at least prevent open war with the owner of Ospisdale and retain stable relations with the other landlords, the same could not be said for his nephew.[10] The immediate outcome published at the end of the year included new boundary trees, and burns, reinforced with more permanent marks and march stones, to prevent future misunderstanding. Just how fragile the decret arbitral was became clear the next year.

Dr Gregory's predictions proved 'oracular' and Rose Dempster's condition suddenly worsened on 5 July and she died at Skibo five days later. Dempster was heartbroken: 'God allowed me to enjoy my sweetheart, but has taken my heart from me when stepping into my second cradle – His will be done. She was 16 years younger than me. I had in my folly allotted her at least that number of years to survive me, for her last distemper was her first'.[11]

He had been unable to write anything since the crisis of 5 July, but as soon as Dempster reached Dunnichen he felt compelled to tell Soper Dempster and Harriet something of what had happened on the journey. Making 'the first use of (his) pen' for ten days, he gave them a shortened account, recognizing that it would 'admit of a (fuller) description on a less melancholic occasion'. Apparently he and two servants intended to stay at Dalwhinnie, but on their arrival at the favoured hostelry they found 'the Marquis of Stafford & Family preoccupied every hole in the house, except a back room, the size of your bedroom in the old House'. As he said, 'it had, luckily two beds in it, where Perryman, Jessy, and I passed the night'. But scarcely had his head 'touched the pillow' than a servant in the house checking to see what accommodation might still be available, brought news that Lord Lovat and his lady had arrived 'and were sitting in their chaise till a bed in a garret should be prepared for them'. Dempster must have got up for he 'left them both fast asleep' as they were very tired but gave no clue as to where they eventually found a bed. He was evidently none the worse for his own unexpected accommodation *à trois*, being able to receive the Marquis's 'very obliging messages of condolence' in the morning. As might be expected, these tragi-comic events neither dulled his interest in the rest of the journey, nor his concern that the children at Skibo should know that all was well. The greatly improved Highland road and the 'beautiful bridge of seven arches' over the River Tay' were duly reported, and young George and 'Missey' (probably his eldest sister Helen) were assured that 'the Jay (was) alive' along with five peacocks, sixty turkeys, and a tame lamb!'[12]

Fortunately, the family rallied round quickly and by the time Dempster returned (along with his wife's body for burial) his ward, Mrs Charlotte Boddam, had arrived to take charge. In the middle of holidaying on the Norfolk coast with her children 'she had no sooner been informed of my being here, and alone, than she broke up her bathing quarters at Yarmouth, and came flying post(-haste) to Dunnichen, which she enlivens a little'.[13] The next day Dempster wrote to Sir Adam telling him of the short eulogy the Rev James Headrick had delivered the previous Sunday in the church where Rose had been 'one of his most constant attenders'. He had concluded his sermon with words that were 'elegantly expressed, and so full of beauty and truth, that they drew irresistibly tears over (his) iron cheeks, and defied the (Stoic) precept'. Familiar as he had become to death, with the loss of so many friends and relations, Dempster still found himself ill-prepared for it, unlike 'sextons and grave diggers'. He nevertheless admitted to being in a 'better state of health than (he) had known for twenty years', the gift of 'temperance and tranquillity'.[14]

Almost immediately after Rose's funeral at Restenneth Priory on 21 July news came that William and Harriet were to 'break up housekeeping at Skibo Castle' and planned to stay at Dunnichen on their way south to Devonshire in order that Harriet might 'try the effect of our mildest British climate'. The 'milk regimen, regular airings, (and) the mild summer air of Skibo' had been of no avail. The Soper Dempsters had been unable to attend the funeral, since Harriet's health was 'nearly as bad (as Rose's) and had created the greatest uneasiness'. They were to leave their three youngest daughters (Harriet, Rose and Charlotte) in Sutherland, taking only George and Helen with them to Ashburton.[15] The family's mode of travel had yet to be decided and, whilst a ship was an option at this time of year, Dempster argued that, since they were 'rich, and in no hurry – and Harriet (might) catch a cold and get a fright', that would 'defeat the whole purpose of the journey'.[16] If it had been a case of conveying Harriet to Lisbon or Madeira, Dempster said he would have been pleased 'to call weigh the anchor' himself but his rule was to 'never go by sea when you can go by land'.[17] Dr Gregory advised that the 500-mile journey should be taken 'by easy stages'. She did not seem 'to be the worse' for the journey to Dunnichen from Skibo, but 'part of the West road used to be very rugged and fatiguing' and might be 'a sad aggravation of all her suffering'.[18]

Although Harriet was to live in her husband's home town for the few months left to her, the consumption was unremitting and she died on 17 October at the age of 25.[19] Thus ended a life that had begun uncertainly and which had only been relieved by short periods of happiness in India and at Skibo. Dempster's 'dearest niece' had been a devoted mother to her five children, all of whom married successfully, and someone of whom his wife had been especially fond. The life the two women shared during the family's 12-month stay at Skibo could never have been either carefree or without its tensions as one watched the pain or weakness in the other, but the affection Rosie always showed the young mother, surrounded by all her 'babbies' as George had called them, would have been a great strength. Her untimely death came almost ten years to the day after her father, Captain John, had lost his life at sea and, just as there had been two catastrophic deaths in 1800, so now, with these two members of the family closest to Dempster's heart. He had lost all those to whom he had devoted his years since leaving Westminster, and when Sir Adam Fergusson's sister Helen (Lady Hailes) also died in October after a sudden illness he could only 'muster all (his) troop of friends'. It was 'poor consolation' for those that had been spared.[20]

The speed with which life at Dunnichen returned to some sense of normality was due to Charlotte Boddam's care of the household and Dempster's resilience in the face of adversity. Charlotte and her three daughters were in good health, but there was no news of her husband Charles.[21] It was not until the New Year that Dempster found time to write to Sir Adam about what the future might hold in store, but even by September, and with Harriet in Devon, some of his old spirit had returned. Work again became the best therapy and at the eighth annual gathering of the Lunan and Vinney Farming Society Dempster was in the chair as usual. Annual meetings, with their 'modest feast' and the consumption of only 'liquor of native manufacture', had been highly successful and membership had risen to eighty. In reminiscent mood, he used the occasion to recall that 'sixty years ago the district was covered with furze and broom, while bogs were to be found at every turn; now the fields were

302

clean and well-drained, roads were abundant, and wheat was largely culti-vated'.[22] Elsewhere local farming societies were also thriving, even if some dared to introduce negative rules and regulations wholly abhorrent to Dempster's friends. In Strathmore farms might be inspected every summer and fines imposed on those who permitted weeds to grow unchecked. By the time of the 1811 meeting Dempster was able to report the award of several gold and silver medals to encourage best practice. This more positive approach, and the use of 'premiums' as they were called, was the idea that Sir William Forbes had favoured in 1797. Correspondence with Sinclair showed that he had lost none of his concentration or appetite for debate.

On 15 September he congratulated Sinclair on his appointment as a Privy Councillor – 'one of finest feathers Royalty has to bestow' – and thanked him for 'noticing (his) domestic calamity'.[23] His friend's condolences were heart-felt and he knew it. Two weeks later, after reading part of a Sinclair report to the Rev Headrick who was visiting Dunnichen, Dempster was happy to note the rapidity with which progress was being made; it was 'astonishing'. After an absence of a 'whole year', his rents and the income from wheat and turnips 'had doubled', thereby quadrupling the value of his 'little property'. It was, however, all very different from the state in which he found Caithness on a visit there (presumably from Skibo the previous year). Trusting that Sinclair would bear his comments 'like a friend', Dempster said he had been struck with its resemblance to Forfar 'sixty years ago'. Enlisting the help of his 'rustic muse' he took Sinclair to task in the following verse:

> Be not, I pray you, Good Sir John, forgot
> The humble Inmate of the Caithness Cot
> Presst by an Iron Feudal Hand,
> To seek protection in a foreign land,
> Whilst Skibo's tenants find themselves at home
> For which, in vain, your's, cross the Atlantic mean.[24]

A week or so later it was not emigration from an unhappy Caithness that was on his mind. When he wrote what he called 'a second diatribe', dealing with the law forbidding the Bank of England to pay specie when demanded, he was fortunate in knowing that Sinclair never quarrelled 'with any one, for differing with (him) in opinion'. Dempster, who had long deprecated Pitt's Act at the height of the Napoleonic wars which relieved banks of the obligation to redeem paper money for gold and silver coin, had sought to eradicate 'the distemper of unexchangeable bank notes'.[25] In language that showed no lack of the characteristic 'charm', and which Sinclair had to admit won most hearts, he added: 'Notes . . . like their mothers laugh in your face. They deny being obliged to pay, but obligingly tell you, if you dislike their notes they will exchange them for their mother's notes.'[26] Sinclair's answer came shortly afterwards and praised both the Bank of England's bullion report which had so provoked his friend and the existing system which had worked well enough for 13 years.[27] Three days later Dempster wrote again to the new Privy Councillor, defending his views, but by then Harriet was dead and serious lucubrations were out of the question. He was to remain unconvinced about convertibility until his 82nd year when he finally conceded that he had been fighting a losing battle, much to Sinclair's satisfaction. He then changed his opinion 'as he did his shoes, and for the same reason, because change is for the better'.[28]

Giving his nephew news of the three children he had deposited with the family at Dunnichen, Dempster hoped that the events of the year would be the last time he would need to 'tear off the bandages which time wraps round our bleeding wounds'.[29] He suggested to the non–classical student that Greek mythology might help 'in the perpetual conflict we frail creatures are engaged in', perhaps thereby sending Soper Dempster to his library. He hoped he might parry death's blows and be like Antaeus 'gaining and recovering . . . strength by touching (his) native earth'.[30] Helen and George, now five and six respectively, had apparently remained at Skibo while Charlotte, Harriet and baby Rose, who had yet to reach her first birthday, were in the care of a children's maid. She had asked his advice about how long the period of mourning would last, a matter which he could only refer to their father.

Amid these and other concerns, and with Soper Dempster still in Devon, it fell to Dempster in November to use his influence regarding the appointment of a new minister in Sutherland following the death of the Rev George Rainy. The elders and 'heads of families' in the parish of Creich[31] asked him, as a man of 'distinguished rank in society', to help them avoid having to consider a late name put on the list of candidates under consideration. In addition to the Rev Neil Kennedy and the Rev Duncan McGillivray,[32] both of whom were acceptable to the petitioners, an earlier assistant to their previous minister had thrown his hat into the ring and they feared this Mr Cameron might be forced on them. Four years they had endured his inferior sermons and the parish was exerting its power to oppose him; they 'humbly expected' Dempster to do the same. Unfortunately the parishioners were to be gravely disappointed. Lord Ashburton, who called the unwelcome Murdo Cameron 'Murder-Text Cameron', reported later that his curious sermons were continuing. He too had found the decision far from his liking and much preferred the teaching of Dr Blair from Dornoch.[33]

Among the letters of condolence was one from Mr W.L.Brown, the Principal of Marischal College, Aberdeen. Another had been from James Guthrie of Craigie, who found it almost impossible to convey his feelings about the death of Harriet and, realizing that Soper Dempster now 'had sole charge' over the family, he could only advise him to take care of his own health so as to be able 'to execute the arduous, interesting duty' he now had to perform. The lawyer presumed that he would not return to Scotland before the following spring and that the mild Devonshire winter might help restore his 'pristine constitution'. He feared that Dempster, from whom he heard 'almost daily', was not as well as when he left Dunnichen; his 'spirits, appetite, and sleep (were) more variable & for the worse'. He had accompanied him on a successful week's tour to friends 'at the foot of the Grampians' and another 'jaunt' was in prospect, but not until after the regular autumn drove of Skibo cattle to Angus. He thought it essential that Dempster be encouraged to 'keep moving'. Although there was talk of him passing the winter at St Andrews or Broughty Ferry, he was anxious to let Soper Dempster know that he was unlikely to 'form or execute a permanent plan without (his nephew's) assistance'.[34]

Mrs Helen Burrington, Dempster's widowed sister, now over 70, was living in London at 23, Gloucester Place, Portman Square. Although her companion Mrs Miller had written to Ashburton and regular letters had been received from Dempster and Mrs Boddam, she had lost contact with Soper Dempster and had become alarmed about the family in Devon. This did not stop her from commenting somewhat enviously that her brother 'jaunts about astonishingly!'[35] Mrs Helen Hawkins (her daughter) and Francis, her husband, both of whom were in India and expected to return in two years time, knew nothing of the family's double tragedy. Charlotte Boddam's son, George, was at Oundle School and occasionally stayed at Gloucester Place during his vacations.

Writing to William Smith in December, Dempster took the trouble to raise the question of those 'poor females', some of whose financial affairs he looked after, and 'who think their little fortunes of £100, and £150, safe in my hands' and which yielded them a few pounds in interest yearly. Some lived 'spider's lives in solitary corners' and that 'graceless fellow called Tierney'[36] had 'charged the Fund with 10% income tax', leaving Dempster to indemnify himself by stopping 'as much from the interest' as had been formerly paid to them. He had considered paying the income tax himself, but the cost would have been 'penal'. Since the law left them with little on which to live, he wanted Smith to raise their plight in the House: their prayers would 'waft the whole Sandgate family to heaven!'. Confirming that he had kept up with news about the war, and not lost his fondness for metaphors, he compared Wellington's campaign in Portugal to a game of chess: 'Massaena (sic) will not move till he has more pieces than Lord Wellington.[37] He can then exchange piece for piece, and if he remain with a single pawn more when all ours are taken, we lose the game – Good God, what carnage my foreboding mind presents to itself!'[38]

1811

With no immediate family left or a younger generation whom he could take under his wing, Dempster accepted that he would now have to live within himself and enjoy the company of those few friends that remained. The Dempsters had taken a house in South Street, St Andrews, some time in 1799[39] one that was to be described as more attractive than the tall, grim-looking property which his Skibo nephew was to own in the 1820s.[40] This may have been the most obvious place to live, but he was caught in two minds: 'What the sequel of my life will be, how long it will last, where, and how it will be spent, none but God knows. I do not.' He may have hoped to be able to spend some time with the children at Skibo, but Harriet's death made this more difficult. However, it was clear that Broughty Ferry was a strong contender for at least part of the winter, perhaps to lighten the burden that Charlotte Boddam had assumed at Dunnichen the previous July. He was soon telling his friends that he had a little *pied à terre* at the ferry.

Dempster was in imaginative mood over the New Year. To Sir Adam he confided his dream of again staying at Kilkerran and visiting other old friends en route. Consulting old James Guthrie at Craigie, the two 'second Ulysses' plotted a summer jaunt together in the company of William Douglas of Brigton.[41] This was frustrated by the death of Lord Dunsinnan who was to have joined them and the possibility of a 90th birthday party for Dr Adam Ferguson substituted. He held on to his friendship with the old professor who, like Dempster, had moved to St Andrews for more companionship and where, also in 'grass-grown' South Street, he was looked after by his two unmarried daughters. Dreams were one thing, achieving them another. He cautioned himself 'to make no very distant engagements for parties of pleasure'[42] and humorously bewailed his self-imposed abstinence and restricted diet:

> Here Dempster –
> And before dinner catches podlies (pollack)
> Dinner! what brought that strange word up?
> Dempster can neither dine nor sup:
> Dempster can neither sup nor dine;
> He dares not touch beer, grog, nor wine.
> True disciple of Gregory's school
> He eats – I mean he starves by rule:
> 'Tween you and me – the more the fool.
> What would our jovial neighbours think
> Of life, deprived of meat and drink?

At Broughty Ferry for a few days in January where he was enjoying 'a fine frosty morning', thereby denying his earlier boast that 'she is ever green, nor frost has felt, nor snow seen',[43] he apologized to Sir Adam for his 'paltry poetastic vein'. More unwelcome verses followed; this time Dr Gregory's ministrations were evidently on his mind:

A libertine, who shan't be named,
By age and sickness quite reclaim'd,
Fond to prolong his shatter'd life,
Took to starvation, and a wife.
At school he read how Epictetus
Lived to a hundred on potatoes;
How Gregory, in times much later,
Ascribes longevity to water.
He, therefore, eat but one poor dish;
Tasting no wine, not flesh, nor fish.
His gout and gravel both march'd off,
And soon were followed by his cough;
His walk grew firm, his colour clear;
His limbs grew fine as any deer.
His wife, with joy, perceived him younger;
But in a month he died – of hunger.[44]

His 'dear little grandson' wrote to him in February. Admitting to him that he had fallen from his horse while riding on Broughty sands, Dempster promised that he would 'never mount him again'.[45] George was at Ashburton with his father and not unnaturally missed the company of his four sisters and that of the Boddam girls. Life at Skibo had become a dull affair and he could only look forward to another visit to Dunnichen.

In a letter from Dunnichen which Dempster not only wrongly dated 1810 instead of 1811 but March instead of April he revealed the continuing depth of his bereavement and the sense of loneliness that threatened to engulf him.[46] His melancholia had not been helped by a bad cold and cough and, with the occasional quiet visit to Rosie's grave in the chapel at Restenneth only serving to remind him of a happier past, he fell to debating (with himself rather than Sir Adam) those elements of his religious belief that gave him most comfort. Although 'not endow'd with faculties to perceive God', he was convinced that the creator had given his 'highest creature' the gift of 'moral' as well as physical powers sufficient to acquire 'as much happiness as he destines to be our lot'. The difficulty was that, unlike his great-uncle (the Bishop of Brechin), Dempster's 'eye of faith' had dimmed when his 'visible organs . . . worn and tatter'd, by age or sickness' had worn out and were no longer 'a fit habitation for our spiritual part'. He did not know what had become of it. Only the fact that he could not be blamed for his 'ignorance', and that it was not 'in God's plan that we should know' the future, provided comfort. He loved 'the face of the heavens, and the earth' and had amply demonstrated his 'love (of) its inhabitants' but for someone who had relied on his mind and the reasoning power he had in abundance, faith had been an odd requirement, and one about which he felt a little uneasy.[47]

He was still at Dunnichen in June, but the handful of letters that exist only provide the briefest of news about the family. Telling Sinclair in an aside that the minister's manse was being repaired and that this had 'estranged' them from one another, Dempster referred pessimistically to the effect the war was having on rents, commenting on the bankruptcy which was 'striding in its seven mile boots all over the Kingdom'.[48] Only at the end of the year did he confide to Sinclair that he had been leading 'an academic life' at his house in South Street in St Andrews during the summer and that some of this time there had been spent in the company of William Soper Dempster and his son.[49]

His nephew may have come south after an ugly incident in Sutherland one night in June. Mayhem had resulted after carefully prepared piles of cut peats – the work of a long day by some of his tenants at Skibo – had been scattered across the moss of Lochanaguish. A breakdown in the accord made between the adjoining landowners the previous year had not been long coming. This time the dispute was about a right of *commonty,* or tenants' traditional access to land to cut peats or graze cattle. By September lawyers for Dugald Gilchrist, the proprietor of Ospisdale, and Soper Dempster, who was administrator at law (guardian) for young George Dempster, were in Edinburgh beginning long hearings before the Court of Session. Both sides had their versions of the story about that night's illegal and 'oppressive' action. The men from Ospisdale had clearly had enough and, having watched what had been going on, decided to take the matter into their own hands. It was subsequently claimed that their actions were justified and Soper Dempster, who by nature appears to have been a litigious man and one who, as it was said in court, 'had yielded to his former propensities' lost his action.[50]

His nephew and young George returned with Dempster to Dunnichen in the middle of September.[51] Much as he would have liked to have visited Sir Adam at Kilkerran that summer, one or two 'obstructions' thwarted his plan, not least the fact that his 'guests' at home, Charlotte Boddam and her four children and the five Soper Dempsters – could not be left alone. He also lacked the 'bodily strength . . . (for) so long a journey'. Unexpected visitors with whom Dempster, could mull over pleasant old 'excursions' were additional, if more pleasant, impediments. Ewen Cameron of Fassieburn, a mutual friend, came '50 miles on purpose'. Meanwhile he was planning a repeat meeting of what he light-heartedly called the *Dunnichen Dune Body Club* in honour of his eightieth birthday in December.[52]

Dempster spent at least part of the winter at St Andrews. Town life had its attractions and, until he became too frail to travel far, he was content to become a 'Bedouin'.[53] He wanted to be 'near a public library and a game at whist', neither of which was possible on his visits to Dunnichen House where children made up the majority of the inhabitants.[54] Although 'balloon-like' in appearance – 'so full of inflammable air, it takes strong cords to prevent my flying up in the air' – and in spite of a cataract in one eye, he was in surprisingly good health for his age . He was soon 'playing golf, whist, and the fool' better than ever.[55]

1812

Responding to Dempster's request for help regarding one of his tenants, William Smith gave him the surprise news in March that the work of the Highland Roads and Bridges Commission was coming to an end. In a letter from his town house in Park Street, Westminster, where he had just been visited by Lord Gower, Smith explained how it had 'done much good in the Highlands', but its existence could not be prolonged: 'I think we have already spent too much upon Scotland'. Ever-increasing expenditure on the Caledonian Canal, whose usefulness was 'so much disputed', was largely to blame; it had become the Commission's 'millstone'.[56] Including Soper Dempster in his greetings, it was clear that despite his busy parliamentary life, Smith retained fond memories of his stay at Skibo.

On May Day Dempster's 'brains (became) too hot when the (plight) of the Highlands got into them' and he chose to rebuke Sinclair for insinuating that some Sutherland tenants were idle. To news of the clearances by Lord Gower, whereby sheep were made 'the rivals of man', had been added the suggestion that 'men were born, like oxen, to labour only'. Dempster would not accept this and reminded his friend that men 'were also born to fight our foes – to love their benefactors, friends (and) families'. He obviously hoped that Lord Gower would soon understand the need for men to be set piece work and be paid suitably for their labours. He did not want to see a return to 'those disgraceful days (when) the factor called 50 men from their own work in Kildonan to work in the gardens at Dunrobin (and) sent them home again, unfed and unpaid'. Much as he recognized the problem all improvers had in reconciling 'their contradictory projects', he was prepared to put the blame for the clearances on those who had advised the owner of 200,000 sheep to prefer them to men. The solution which might come about 'in time no doubt' was 'to loose human industry' on the thousands of acres that were occupied by sheep, and 'worth 3d.'; under cultivation they might be worth £1 per acre. 'But,' he concluded, 'what is time to a Noble family?[57]

Returning more 'coolly to the improvement of Sutherland', Dempster passed on to Sinclair the theory put forward by Dr Adam Ferguson that one look at the map would confirm that 'the people least favoured by climate (were) most at their ease, best fed, housed, clothed, and . . . longest lived'. Although nearly blind, deaf and confined to his chair, Dempster's neighbour at St Andrews was as charming and cultured as ever, with 'a soul like a girl(s) in a convent' and the two men happily agreed, if the theory was true, that Sutherland was a 'fitter country' for 'habitation and comfort than the New World or Indostan!'[58]

Dempster must have been greatly saddened by the death, at his home on General Graham's Balgowan estate, of his long-standing Forfarshire friend Robert Graham of Fintry. He referred to him in his will as 'a man resembling the late William Pitt in his character except that he used no popular arts to rise into office'. Never one to forget the duty he owed old friends now deceased, Dempster explained to Soper Dempster that he was to 'take up the one big, and two little daughters of Fintry & set them down at Balgowan' where Sir Thomas Graham may have cared for them temporarily.[59]

Quite apart from remembrance of the simple favours each had done the other over the years and the trauma of his dismissal as a Commissioner of Excise Fintry was probably the one link Dempster had with a man whom it appears he never met, but whose works he much enjoyed - Robert Burns. Dempster would have been well aware of the friendship and patronage his friend had extended to him in his last years and Fintry may well have brought his name to the poet's attention.[60] Burns had alluded to Dempster as 'a true blue Scot' and praised his 'zeal-inspired tongue',[61] but, when he wrote (in his *Epistle to James Smith*) 'a title, Dempster merits it' he had touched on an honour which many thought he greatly deserved, and Dempster knew that Burns did not give praise without good reason.[62]

Wandering between St Andrews and Dunnichen like the desert nomad he was content to be, Dempster reported the safe return of his nephew to Skibo in July, although he had been obliged to abandon his carriage somewhere on the way north. Among matters discussed with William before he left had been one that would have brought back the sad events in the South China Sea a dozen years before. The Court of Session's decision in the case brought by the Rev John Cleland was due to be reviewed in December 1812.[63] It concerned the repayment of the loan he claimed his son, the *Earl Talbot*'s first mate, had made to Captain John while the ship was at Bombay in 1800. Dempster had been sent the papers but could 'see nothing alarming' in them. The fact that the plaintiff could not produce any proof of the transaction ever taking place led him to conclude that 'if the case were mine I should see more cause for joy than sorrow'. It 'ought to be thrown over the Bar, as being highly vexatious', which was exactly what happened.[64]

John Pinkerton turned up rather unexpectedly at Dunnichen in July. For a few years in the 1780s, and before moving into cheaper accommodation in Kentish Town, this *enfant terrible* of the antiquarian world had been a neighbour of Dempster in Knightsbridge.[65] Both men then shared a friendship with Thorkelin and this had inspired Dempster's reading of his earlier works. Dempster had been unable to help him obtain some sinecure, advising him, as a then unmarried man, to reduce his expenses by becoming 'a lodger and boarder in London, somewhere near the (British) Museum'.[66] Subsequently Pinkerton's notoriety increased, although a large section of the literary public, including Dempster, continued to regard him as a man of letters with considerable standing. He produced an impressive number of publications on a range of very diverse subjects,[67] but remained a hypochondriac who often quarrelled with those who tried to help him and never lost the touchiness and self-assertiveness which upset others. At the time of his visit to Angus this controversial character, now divorced and 'annoyed by a variety of circumstances, but particularly by the embarrassed state of his pecuniary affairs', – had left London and taken up residence in Edinburgh.[68] The following year a disastrous one-night performance of his play *The Heiress of Strathearn* led to another retreat. He eventually died penniless in Paris during 1826.[69]

Unlike the Rev James Roger, who found Pinkerton 'self-opinionative and unamiable' and a man who 'would not tolerate that any statement or theory of his own should be impugned or questioned',[70] Dempster was content to be amused by him, believing he had 'lighted a spunk (match) to give us a faint glimpse into that dark dungeon' (of Celtic history).[71] 'Pinkie Winkie', as another of his hosts called him,[72] attended the 10th anniversary meeting of the Lunan and Vinney Farming Society as Dempster's guest, even debating the fertility of fiorin grass (or white bent-grass) with the members. Not unexpectedly, his bearing and behaviour ellicited some unease among younger members of the household who considered him obnoxious. He had the habit of quickly outwearing his welcome. A 'young miss of thirteen' asked her grandfather before the distinguished guest arrived at the breakfast table, 'When is Mr Pinkerton going away?' 'Whisht, my dear,' said Dempster with a smile.[73]

Lunch parties with Lord Duncan, James Fergusson's brother-in-law and Guthrie of Craigie were always enjoyable,[74] and another Forfar Beefsteak gathering attended by a hundred or more guests had its attraction for Dempster, but the high point of the summer was a 'picnic dinner' by the side of Loch Fiethie in honour of Wellington's victory at Salamanca. It took place on what was 'without exception the finest day in the whole season'. With fifty-five of his neighbours, family and friends around him, George was in his element. He had been 'prompted' to 'stick up' a notice on the cottage window reminding everyone that 'an epilogue would be spoken by the Laird of the Lake, in his character of Captain of the Dunnichen Company of the Militia'. After the company had walked, danced and supped beside the loch, Dempster read his piece:

> While Wellington expels those Frenchies
> Out of the Spaniard's Towns and Trenches;
> And while the tenant of the North
> In frozen Majesty comes forth;
> And while our fleets command the main,
> And seek for hostile fleets in vain
> Shall we thus idlers here remain?

No! We'll bravely act our parts.
Ladies! T'is Your's to win our hearts.
To sprightly lads by arming prove
To be worthy of the ladies' love.
Old Age itself's a poor pretence,
To shrink from War in their defence,
But till Invasion's call to arms
Subdue us, Ladies with your charms!
To Fiethie's banks devote a day
To walk, fish, dine, drink, dance and play;
To Wellington we'll charge our glasses,
Hot or not, my bonnie Lassies!
Our Army, Fleet & gallant Graham.
A second bumper, justly claim.
A third you won't refuse sweet Ladies
To him who rais'd the siege of Cadiz.
Let us in each revolving year
Eat a pic..nic Dinner here;
And to mark the occasion, Please
Be't called the Feast of Salamanca,
To make you laugh, I'll be your Sancho (Panza).[75]

As well as his nephew's descriptions of Skibo, Dempster had been delighted to hear about young George and his father's stay with 'the Marchioness' at Dunrobin Castle. He insisted that 'comprehending Dunrobin and its good inhabitants' needed to be 'gotten by heart'. Recalling his own experience, he hoped she had not 'stollen my boy long enough, to perfect him in her own art of stealing hearts'. He need not have worried about the impression either visitor had made. Writing to Dempster after their visit, the Countess expressed her pleasure at meeting George: a 'most engaging and interesting' child who, as anticipated, had tempted her 'to act the part of a gypsy . . . and to steal him'. Referring to Soper Dempster, she saw 'how truly he values his connection with you'. Furthermore, the visit enabled her to hope he would return to Dunrobin on some future occasion and be able to share their 'satisfaction in seeing a general improvement in this County' where 'at least we flatter ourselves that a greener shade is spreading'. Having lately 'seen and admired Skibo' and 'the great progress' made, congratulations were in order.[76]

News of Telford's achievement at Bonar where his bridge at last spanned the Kyle would have spread rapidly. What Southey called 'a spider's web in the air . . . the finest thing that ever was made by God or man'[77] had been built in little over a year. Although the Meikle ferry continued to be used by the inhabitants of Skibo and others on either side of the firth to the east, it must have pleased Dempster to know that one of the most important transport problems north and southward in the Highlands had been overcome. Telford's bridge was to stand until 1892.

Infirmity probably prevented Dempster from attending the unveiling of his commemorative plaque at the bridge in 1815. The stone had been sculpted in Angus some time before and delays in approving its final wording caused problems for the mason. Three additional names were carved on his 'mural monument' in a space that had probably been earmarked for the number of bridges and miles of road for which the Commissioners had been responsible. Another error, as Southey pointed out, was to fix the tablet against the Toll House instead of the bridge. It was Dempster's tribute to some of his closest friends and allies in the long battle to open up the Highlands, including Sir William Pulteney, Isaac Hawkins Brown and William Smith, and, writing to the last-named, it was apparent that he was simply content to know that his name as the stone's donor was at least associated with theirs.[78]

18

THE FINAL YEARS
(1813–1818)

'I now in fame's temple claim a higher place'
(A 'Familiar Epistle' to Sir John Sinclair in 1808)

1813

At the turn of the year, the Countess of Sutherland sent Dempster her greet-ings from Richmond.[1] His admiration for 'one of the most beautiful women' had not dimmed but 'why', he asked, 'set a high value on corresponding with a beauty you can't enjoy – and (whose) riches you don't share in?'.[2] Writing to Sir Adam in his 'annual account', he 'well remember(ed) the era' when the Countess's claim to her title had been finally upheld in 1771. Then his friend and Lord Hailes had 'gained honours and fortune to her ladyship, and fame and glory' to themselves.[3] At St Andrews Dempster had been in the company of Dr Adam Ferguson who was in his 90th year, very deaf and almost blind, but still in 'full possession of his mental faculties'. This 'modern Epictetus' never failed to inspire and, like Dempster, was 'keen for conversation'.[4]

In April the Bedouin's thoughts turned to Indian affairs for a short time. Dempster would have known something of how the character of the East India Company's administration on the sub-continent had changed out of all recog-nition in the absence of such towering figures as Sir George Colebroke or Laurence Sulivan. The successful military campaigns in the period to 1805 had been conducted by a Governor-General (the future Duke of Wellington) who had little interest in the Company's mercantile role. Patriotic fervour in the country had produced not just imperial heroes but an upsurge of religious moralizing that was to reach as far as India. Above all, the renewal of the charter in 1793 had not produced the benefits hoped for, and with divided and indecisive leadership from Leadenhall Street and poor profits from India, the Company was not only on the brink of ruin but further parliamentary constraints on its power became an inevitable consequence. Parliament had recently taken away all its trading privileges, together with its monopoly of trade with India (although not with China) and rival Lancastrian merchants and shippers were now free to reap the benefit.

The new regime meant that the East India Company's traditional policy of antipathy towards a missionary presence in India was relaxed, much to the satisfaction of evangelicals at home. Proselytizing among the native population which had become a matter of great debate was to surge forward once it became official policy. Quoting a speech made in the House where it had been argued that 'God never intended us for the Government of a Kingdom 15,000 miles off, and consisting of 50 million inhabitants', Dempster added his own contention in a letter to William Smith that 'God never intended his worship, and the belief of him, to be uniformly the same, over the whole face of the earth – but to be adored'. On the face of it, it was an unusual subject to broach with the MP for Norwich, but Smith had become involved in the debate and Dempster knew of his ardent advocacy of non-conformist denominations in Parliament. He could only invite him to 'go on, My dear Sir, in the glorious occupation of a benevolent man . . . peopling countries (and) enlightening dark and deluded ones. Heavens! what scope for genius!' His legal mind, now beginning to consider the things of eternity, could only think in terms of a *magna carta* for India that provided 'at least some privileges for the conquered provinces'. Turning to his copy of the Muslim scriptures, he quoted from the 'Alcoran': 'Cursed is the man who removes a peasant who pays his rent' and reminded Smith, before calling a halt to his 'pearls' of wisdom, that even Cornwallis and Lord Moira had insisted on idle proprietors keeping their rights.

Albeit that his analysis was lengthy, it was finely crafted, confirming Dempster's exceedingly live mind. Among the 'axioms' rehearsed in his *Lucubrations on Indostan* was the need to translate English books into local languages, including good novels which would entertain better than the bible, – the export of schoolmasters to teach English (so long as they did not mention the word 'religion' for 'the first 50 years'), and a 'sepoy corps' to boost Dr Bell's work in applying his 'Madras System' of teaching. All in all, Dempster was convinced that, since God had 'permitted (England) to conquer the Mogul Empire', she had a responsibility to 'improve their . . . government, arts, sciences and morals' to fit the population for self-government. It was the same argument that had been put in respect of America.[5] On the subject of religious rights in India, Dempster enlisted the support of his 'pious ward' Charlotte Boddam, 'now a widow of one of the principal civil servants of the Company, (and) a judge of a wide district', who sat at his side while he was writing. She assured him that 'the word of God was for nine long years unheard of there; she had a long way to go to take the sacrament, which was then but slovenly administered'. He was keen to see chaplains appointed as well as writers, a whole 'establishment' similar to the civil and military regime, whereby bishops, rectors and vicars became a common sight. It might help prevent 'the burning of widows' on funeral pyres and the 'exposure of old parents . . . to be washed in the sacred waters of the Ganges'.[6]

Dempster spent the early part of July at St Andrews where he was engaged in replacing several of the trustees who had died, and who had responsibility for administering young George Dempster's inheritance at Skibo. A decision had to be taken about the Rs.50,000 put in trust in India by Soper Dempster for Harriet on her marriage thirteen years before. The money remained there in Company bonds. His nephew's choice of William Smith from among '6 or 7 millions of Englishmen' clearly pleased Dempster and demonstrated how much the friendship started during the Smiths stay at Skibo in 1809 had deepened. Writing to Miss Smith (the eldest daughter) Dempster asked her 'to choose (a) favourable moment' to broach the matter with her father'. He assured her that the task would 'be a sinecure, and his salary, the doing of a friendly act for four delightful girls'.[7]

William Smith, who was nearly 60, considered himself too old to take on the responsibility of executor, particularly where the interests of four young girls were involved. Such trusts inevitably led to more work than was initially thought. He suggested that someone younger, whose judgement and thinking might be more akin to the needs of the younger generation, should be appointed. His decision had not been taken lightly; their friendship, and the respect he had for Dempster was obvious: 'whatever you may believe . . . never suppose for one moment that it is possible for me to think of you but with the greatest respect and regard'. Neither did Dempster's 'political lucubrations' fail to amuse him, especially when he could 'trace the same spirit of liberality and moderation' in them which had 'distinguished (him) thro' life'. The latter was a reference to Dempster's earlier thoughts on religious teaching in India which Smith had probably discussed with allies in parliament and those endeavouring to free religious observance.[8] Smith's advice was that 'all direct instruction' in religion was to be avoided in India. It would 'perhaps be most effectually introduced through our arts and sciences . . . milk for babes!'.[9]

Also that summer Dempster took on the task of producing a record of his neighbour's agricultural achievements. James Guthrie of Craigie, whose modesty was 'equal to his skill as a farmer', had been reluctant to contribute to Sir John Sinclair's account of Angus. He and Dempster had known each other for 73 years and soon after the laird of Dunnichen became an MP Guthrie had taken control of 150 acres on the Craigie estate which would 'hardly have kept 10 Highland sheep alive thro' the year' and 50 acres of 'oily and tarred muir' overgrown with whins. The whole blighted and windswept area had steadily become fertile over the years, so that his cows now gave milk in December as well as June, and it was difficult for Dempster to say 'in which month of the year, his mutton (had) most flavour or fat'. Now all around were shady groves of oak, beech and elm trees, and stone walls enclosing fields with sheep 'let to . . . Dundee butchers at £5–7 per acre'. He recalled the 'tortures of requisition' that had been endured – the trenching, liming, dunging and draining of the land – to discover 'its hidden treasures'.[10]

Their friendship, and the encouragement the one gave the other, had been inspirational. Guthrie, who did employ a foreman, although 'the very name of a grieve or overseer put him into a cold sweat', had shown what could be done. Dempster wanted his name to be 'enrolled among the earliest and best farmers' in Sinclair's county report. Its publication had been promised for 1809 and was eventually completed in 1814, the year in which he resigned from the Board of Agriculture. On top of his parliamentary duties Sir John had also been hard at work developing his own estates and the new town of Thurso. By this time, although another national survey was in his mind and George asked him to broaden the range of questions to be asked so as to throw more light on such subjects as educational progress and the eating habits of 'labouring people', Sinclair's influence was waning.[11] The Board's always strained finances restricted his work and an effort to achieve a general Enclosure Act failed. Neither would the Board of Trade consider accepting responsibility for agriculture. Few government subventions were received and, whilst the Board of Agriculture continued its programme of lectures and the dissemination of all manner of good practice advice to farmers, the contribution he had made to a better understanding of the needs of the agricultural industry had been largely completed. The small measure of the success such men as Sinclair, Guthrie and Dempster had, each in their different ways, was summed up by a French traveller who found that 'every gentleman's conversation was taken up with turnips, clover, enclosures, and drains'![12]

A property transaction which Dempster rightly called 'incredible' was another reason for writing to Sinclair at this time. In the spring of 1786 when he bid for Skibo, there had been a second estate at the auction, one which Dempster 'came within ten pounds of buying', namely Langwell at Berriedale in Caithness, which William Gray had also been forced to sell.[13] Sinclair's purchase of Langwell from Hunter Blair in 1788 for £9,000 which had been made possible by his wife's dowry would have been well-known, as were the improvements he had wrought there. But in June Dempster heard that it had been sold to James Horne, an Edinburgh lawyer and Sinclair's agent, for what he described as the enormous sum of £40,000. He was flabbergasted; it was a miracle. Dempster seems not to have known the state of Sinclair's finances or the build-up of debts that virtually bankrupted him by 1811. Even the pension of £2,000 p.a that went with the sinecure he had obtained from Spencer Perceval, the Prime Minister, did little to remedy the situation and, having decided to sell those estates which he had added to his inheritance, it was natural that Langwell should be one of the first to go.[14]

In July there had even been the prospect of Dempster paying a visit to Sutherland. The affection which Dempster had for his nephew had not diminished despite the contrast in their personalities and it was only put off 'till next year' because of his many other occupations. Not the least of these was 'the paternal charge' Dempster seems to have taken of the two Hawkins boys. Soper Dempster had also invited James Guthrie to Skibo, but he had declined the invitation, despite the 'infinite pleasure' he would have had in seeing the lands of Skibo and Pulrossie which he had admired nearly 30 years before. Surprisingly, the old lawyer, who had so feared Dempster could not sustain a home in London as well as an estate where 'the inconvenience' of its location was 'inevitable', never seems to have returned to Skibo.[15] In September another of Dempster's heartfelt interventions brought a reply, this time from Viscount Sidmouth, then Home Secretary in Lord Liverpool's administration. His plea for leniency in the case of a prisoner of war was refused, Sidmouth regretting a policy which he could only describe as 'austere and inhospitable'.[16]

Dempster had become reconciled to the loss of those dearest to him and was able to maintain his life on an even keel for several years, but the death that month of his oldest friend Sir Adam Fergusson was, without doubt, especially painful news. Despite being very ill at the end of the previous year his old friend was active almost to the last. Sir Adam had been able to visit Ulster during the summer of 1811 where he had enjoyed the company of the Fergusson and Dalrymple nieces.[17] It had been a friendship that had lasted 57 years. Dempster appears to have written few words about the event to other friends, and his own last letter to him had been in February.[18] Not unnaturally, he shared his sorrow with Sir Adam's nephew, now the 4th baronet of Kilkerran and whose legal career in Calcutta Dempster had followed with interest when Captain John travelled to and from the subcontinent.[19] Writing two letters to Sir James Fergusson, one in September the other at the end of December, he took comfort in the long life his uncle had been granted, ten years more than the prescribed three score years and ten. Recalling their adventures together in France, Staffa and the Hebrides, George added as an afterthought that they had both been flogged by the same schoolmaster. He regretted being unable to pay his respects at Kilkerran on account of his 'sand glass being nearly as low' as his friend's. In military fashion Dempster wrote 'on a drum head' and, with his 'wife, brothers, sisters and nieces all lying dead around' him, he could only expect 'to be order'd every minute' to die himself.[20]

Sir Adam had been a dry, unhumourous and often unimaginative solicitor who was 'unshakeably orthodox in all that he did',[21] someone who was not always the easiest of friends. Unlike Boswell, who disliked him from the time when he had 'evaded' contributing to his collection of funds for Corsican relief, Dempster always respected his views and found his temperament a good foil to his own. In the years up to 1798 when Jean (his niece and Captain John's wife) died, the two men had shared much together. Thereafter it would seem that their physical separation did not wholly account for an intangible undercurrent in their relationship. Letters between them continued to be warm if less frequent, and probably reflected the distrust Sir Adam may have had of Captain John Hamilton Dempster as much as the end of the close ties between the two families. The suspicion remains that the 'venerable and respectable baronet', as well as some of the Fergusson family at Kilkerran or Newhailes, had been content to see Dempster pour out his affection, first on his half-brother, in spite of his decision to go back to sea, and then on the Captain's daughter, Harriet, without interesting themselves greatly in such matters. If, as seems likely, Dempster recognized this reservation in their relationship, and he certainly knew that Sir Adam's original views on the purchase of Skibo had never changed, this would account for the disappointment apparent in his later letters and his inability to share so much of his own family news with his friend.

1814

At the start of the year 'joy in heaven over one sinner that repenteth' marked Dempster's long-coming conversion to paper money. Staying at St Andrews over the New Year, he had decided to 'renounce (his) inveterate passion for gold in (his) 82nd year'. Although now frail, he was in as good health as could be expected. Sinclair, who reported this fact to Mr Lemaisky, an old friend of Dempster's in Edinburgh, was only too ready to analyse the detailed arguments expressed by a 'Forfarshire friend' in a letter to the *Dundee Mercury* on the question of bank note convertibility. Dempster had signed it 'L.L.D. from Farmtown'.[22]

With life at Dunnichen less appealing in winter, Dempster regularly spent some of those months at St Andrews. His well-wrapped-up figure became a common sight about the town. His daily routine there was made up of reading (particularly Pliny), and exercise to and from the library and across the links, together with a round of light-hearted social calls in the afternoon when he could enjoy a favourite hand of whist. He used to send round a vehicle which he called 'the *route coach*' to collect the old ladies who helped make up his whist parties.[23]

> 'To the end of his life from his earliest nonage,
> He divided his hours into two equal parts,
> And spent one half sleeping, the other at cartes'[24]

It was a time for enjoying memories, especially those associated with his early days as the representative of the town. In his youthful impetuosity as a prospective MP and when still learning how important it was to encourage his voters, he had given his hairdresser five guineas, an exceptionally high recompense for a shave! Meeting the barber several days later Dempster expressed his disappointment that he had also been shaving the opposition and receiving a similar gratuity: 'Mr Bell, I did not expect this', he expostulated, to which the barber replied, 'Troth, I just wanted it to pleasure ye baith'. Similarly, when calling at the house of another trader, he 'made a fashion of kissing an honest matron, quietly placing five gold pieces in the hand that was modestly extended to protect her face. Contemplating her glittering prize, the delighted housewife exclaimed, "Kiss my dochter too, sir!". Dempster always revelled in such happenings and shared them with the Rev James Roger whose cure at Dunino was only four miles from St Andrews .[25]

One of the topics discussed at what was to be the final meeting of the Lunan and Vinney Farming Society in July, its twelfth anniversary, was blight in that year's barley. The suggestion was made that such damage might be prevented 'by pickling the seed'. Dempster reminded the members that the clergy were the first promoters of agriculture and they used all such measures. 'Around the monasteries,' he said, 'the best soil was a garden and the worst a grave.' Another item of business before the Society was the written resignation of the Rev James Headrick who had been a stalwart member for some years. When Charlotte Boddam stayed at Dunnichen following her return from India her children, however, soon took to calling him 'headache'.[26]

Dunnichen's minister was at the centre of a storm of 'lengthy and wearisome' correspondence that autumn. Some of the blame for Headrick's impoverished and unhappy state lay at Dempster's door and it would be surprising if George did not regret not having done more for him. Headrick had been appointed assistant and successor to Dr Thomas Mason in 1807[27] and all had gone well until the old minister died, whereupon Mason's children 'attacked' an agreement dealing with the minister's stipend, 'framed' by the Rev Dr Hill, Principal at St Andrews, and 'executed' by Dempster. It seems that it was imprecisely drawn, and after Mr Hutcheson, the Forfar writer whom Dempster employed to collect and apply the stipend, refused payment of it for two years Headrick had been forced to petition for his rights.[28] Action was taken by Mason's heirs firstly in the Sheriff Court and then before Lord Pitmilly who decided in their favour. As Dempster said later, 'a very hard bargain was driven with poor Headrick who has nothing else to subsist on'.

Apparently it was Dempster's letter to Dr Hill of 18 November 1809 that had been at the heart of the problem. It had been written a week after Dr Mason died, just as Harriet was about to give birth and when his wife Rose's health was giving great concern. Writing to Dr Hill on 17 October 1814, Dempster said 'he was then uninformed, having none of the papers with him'.[29] For the heirs, Dr John Lee of St Andrews maintained that it was only after the matter had been successfully before the court that Dempster chose to object, calling it 'most unjust, (and) that we ought not to sully our hands with illegal spoil'. He added that when the case had been considered by Dempster in 1809 before any legal proceedings took place, he 'declined giving any opinion, saying he was not lawyer enough to determine whether Mr Walter Cook's or Mr Headrick's opinion was the soundest'.[30]

By November 1814 the matter was before the Court of Session in Edinburgh where Mr Erskine had to rely heavily on Dempster's letter. It was argued that 'we must place Mr Dempster's changes of opinion to his memory which is all fair as at the distance of seven years, we are all apt to forget'. Nevertheless, Dempster seems to have criticized the court and his 'animadversions on Lord Pitmilly's judgement' meant that some of his evidence could not be given.[31] The heirs, for their part, were content to call attention to 'the singular variableness of Mr Dempster's statement and the unaccountable self-contradictions and inaccuracies in which he has involved himself by his rash interference'.[32]

The hearings of 1814 apparently achieved little. Two years later Headrick was to remind Dr Lee that he had 'no less than seven obstinate and expensive law-pleas' forced on him since he became minister and he was again summoned to appear before the Court of Session in July of 1816. Dr Lee had recently 'arrested' the whole of his stipend, leaving 'five young children exposed to all the horrors of starvation'. His pleas for a settlement, made to both Dempster and Dr Lee, had not brought a solution, and he was desperate: 'It is impossible you can get the whole stipend without blotting me and my family from existence.' He hoped that a stop to further legal proceedings could be agreed. If not, he would 'most cheerfully go to prison; or to death'.[33] What Dempster knew of the situation by then is not known. Fortunately, it appears that relief was eventually forthcoming and Headrick remained Dunnichen's minister for over 30 years.

Others knew nothing of these stresses and strains. Robert Jamieson, a ballad collector and antiquary then in his thirties, wrote to Thorkelin in September describing Dempster as being 'cheerful, amiable and respectable as ever', adding that he and his deceased friend Sir Adam 'seemed to belong to another age, and another state of society, more perfect than that we live in'.[34] A month later Dempster replied to William Smith's last recorded letter, freely admitting he was still very conscious of Sir Adam's 'immolation'. It arrived at a moment when he did not know what he had done to offend 'Time'; he was carrying off 'more friends than he (brought) him'. He had also watched the long illness of an unknown 'kinsman and friend' of fifty years who was finally buried in October and, with the passage of time much in his thoughts, he recalled how they had met at Scarborough thirty-two years before. Thankfully, like the turkeys in the yard, he was ignorant of future destiny. Smith had given him the pleasure of learning of 'the honourable place' in his house in Essex where he had hung his portrait. It would remind his family of their time together in the Highlands.[35]

1815

The country's celebrations of the victory over Napoleon at Waterloo were short-lived. The sudden fall in prices led to unemployment and ruin for farmers and traders alike. The Corn Law in 1815 which aimed to reduce the imports of cheap grain only pushed up prices, thereby reducing demand and greatly increasing unrest among both industrial employers and the poor. With one last exception, these were matters now beyond the reach of Dempster and for Sir David Wedderburn, Bart, of Ballindean, his parliamentary successor, to deal with.[36]

Dempster took it upon himself to speak up for the labourers working on the construction of roads in Sutherland who were not being paid regularly by the contractors, a matter about which he had heard from his nephew. In a clear and well-written letter to the Treasurer of the Highland Roads & Bridges Commission which belied his 83 years, he sought not only to redress this 'gross injustice' but delicately suggested a remedy that might be acceptable to the bureaucracy in Edinburgh whereby ministers of the parishes through which the roads went 'certified that the people employed had all been paid their promised wages'.[37]

In the autumn the Rev James Roger, who had earlier seen to it that Sir Walter Scott received an honorary membership of the Musomanik Club, a poetical society in Anstruther of which he was the chaplain, took it upon himself to arrange for Dempster to be honoured with a diploma.[38] Dempster's appreciation written from Dunnichen showed him in something of a reverie; accepting that 'such pieces of good fortune' were often preceded by the super-natural, he explained that he had been visited by Apollo 'though my windows were shut, he opened my door, presented me with a sprig of laurel, and most benignly said:

> "Accede! O magnos, aderit jam tempus honores,
> Care Deum".'

Albeit that he considered himself 'twice as mad' as any member of the Society, he was evidently well enough to promise its members that he would endeavour to attend their meeting the following year.

1816

The last of that great generation of convivial literary figures, Dr Adam Ferguson, finally died, exclaiming to his daughters with bright assurance that 'there is another world'.[39] His death further isolated Dempster and the loneliness he had fought off for so long now increased. Except for Mrs Boddam, her children and the Soper Dempster young who spent some time each year at Dunnichen House the rest of the family were distant.[40] Among his dearest Angus friends only James Guthrie remained.

Dempster nevertheless kept up his habit of writing to friends at the turn of each year. It seems that the late Graham of Fintry's wife had died leaving the young girls for whom Dempster had such affection alone and orphans. He included a bequest of £100 in his will to each of Fintry's unmarried daughters so long as annuities had not been paid by the Government at the time of his death in compensation for the injustice associated with their father's dismissal. He always thought they had been very shabbily treated. In a letter to Sir Thomas Graham, who had become General Lord Lynedoch after the Battle of San Sebastian, Dempster explained that he was at St Andrews for a few days only 'to pay (his) respects to the five female orphans of our late friend Fintry. They bear their . . . loss with the hereditary dignity and patience of the family'. Fortunately, marriage was eventually to come to the girls' rescue, but, as Dempster said, 'The fate of the family (had) hitherto been tragical. I hope the tragedy may end happily.'[41]

The Rev Roger's suggestion in June that 'he would be pleased to undertake his biography' put Dempster in a spin, being as it was totally at variance with his wishes. Principal James Playfair at St Andrews, an elderly relative and Roger's patron among academia in the university, may have encouraged the approach. But quite apart from his suitability as an unprejudiced and competent reporter of the intricate political life he had enjoyed at Westminster, to say nothing of dubious escapades with Boswell which might have displeased the cleric, Dempster was convinced that his was the life 'of an individual to whom nothing but oblivion belongs'. Quoting Dido's dying speech from the *Aeneid* – 'Vixi et, quem dederat cursum fortuna, perigi' – he set about destroying those of his private papers that were in the library at Dunnichen. What happened to Roger's own 'budget of letters' from his father to Dempster was not recorded.[42]

1817

By the winter of 1817 Soper Dempster's children had left Dunnichen and were in 'winter quarters' at Skibo from where William sent Dempster 'an excellent cask of cockles, well-pickled'.[43] The children's return coincided with a downturn in Dempster's health. He seems to have suffered a stroke. His appetite, bodily health and appearance had not altered since his nephew had last seen him in the summer, 'but his mental faculties (were) much impaired'. He had lost the use of his limbs and was confined to his bed and an easy chair. Being no longer able to write, Rose Guthrie (who was a beneficiary in his will) endeavoured to keep at least some of his friends informed of his condition. Unable to visit him as frequently as he wanted, James Guthrie noted that he had no desire to see anybody other than those who were in attendance on him. A second visit to Dunnichen that year which Guthrie now knew Soper Dempster would have to make gave him the opportunity of warning him about the desirability of an executors' meeting[44] to consider the 'necessary business of the estate' which 'should be no longer delayed'. The autumn sale of Skibo cattle in Angus had produced its usual clutch of accounting problems.[45]

Dempster would have been happy to have heard from his nephew all the goings on that summer in Sutherland and supported the local clamour there had been to see Telford's bridge properly finished. It was finally painted in July and milestones put in place along the roadside northward to Caithness.[46] His successor at Skibo had done his best to keep the estate in good order, but, as a widower with housekeeping help, his factor and only the occasional visit of his children for company, life there was but a pale shadow of former days.[47]

The unfortunate adventures of his neighbour and friend, Lord Ashburton, whose property at Rosehall adjoined the westerly edge of the estate, did, however, provide a useful talking point which Dempster would have enjoyed. Ashburton had written to Soper Dempster who was away when, on the night of 5/6 May, there had been a great storm over the Kyle of Sutherland, with much lightning and the wind blowing 'a perfect hurricane'. A great fire broke out and gutted his house in the course of an hour and a half. It had been in the care of a housekeeper and her sister who had been awakened by what they thought was the violent opening and shutting of doors. Thinking that someone was breaking into the property, they ran downstairs from the garret just in time to save their lives and found the drawing room in flames. By the time the gardener and gamekeeper, along with four or five masons who had been engaged in renovation work and temporarily housed in a servant's house, started over-zealously saving 'kitchen pots and pans!' it was clear all would be lost. While the gardener from the lodge called off the 'corps from their culinary attempts', a chambermaid had the presence of mind to think of rescuing Ashburton's portrait of his father (John Dunning) which Soper Dempster had seen when it was painted in 1815, but this too was consumed in the inferno.

In language of which Dempster would have much approved, Ashburton poured out his regret that 'nearer 150 than 100 dozen' bottles of Madeira, claret and whisky had been lost: 'Vulcan had entered' and was, he feared, 'too strong for Bacchus!' They had received more heat in one hour than such articles acquired 'in the course of a voyage to India!' The idea of the home-less laird of Rosehall 'bivouacking under the canopy of heaven' until he could convert a laundry 'the size of a nutshell' into alternative accommodation, and having to deal with the all-grasping 'Mr Murder-text Cameron', would have cheered anyone whether on or off their sickbed. Had it not been clearly in jest, his warning about the castles at Dunrobin and Skibo, 'for fear that their turn might be next!', might have been more worrisome.[48]

1818

Dempster died on 13 February and in accordance with his wishes was buried in Restenneth Priory Chapel beside his beloved wife Rose. Whether, as he had requested, he was carried to the church 'by the male inhabitants of Letham' attended by his surrounding neighbours whom he had wanted 'entertained at Forfar with everything good' will never be known. Among the first to send their condolences to his nephew was Principal William Brown,[49] followed by the Marchioness of Stafford,[50] Sir Robert Anstruther[51] and Dempster's 'old and most valued' friend William Smith who had been hoping to renew his friendship.

The Dunnichen estate passed to his sister Mrs Helen Burrington, who, with the trustees, had responsibility for disposals from the estate to Dempster's next of kin. Charlotte Boddam probably stayed at Dunnichen for some time. On the death of old Mrs Burrington in 1831 Mrs Helen Hawkins, her daughter, inherited the property which then remained in the hands of the Hawkins Dempster family until they died out after 1917. William Soper Dempster's life at Skibo was unrecorded, but each of his four daughters married into distinguished Scottish or Irish families and when he died in 1825 the Sutherland estate passed to George Dempster, to whom Dempster had bequeathed the gold repeating watch and seals which he had worn since 1765.

Soper Dempster's boy appears to have gone to Trinity College, Cambridge, after being called to the bar in 1826, and as an LL.D he became assessor to the Rector of the University at St Andrews. He married Joanna Dundas of Arniston in May 1827. The year before he obtained a private act of parliament enabling him to borrow money and sell the Langwell enclave and other lands to pay for improvements he had undertaken at Pulrossie.[52] Finally, with the Skibo lands heavily burdened with debt, the sale in 1861 of that part of the estate at Balblair to Sidney Hadwen presaged its total disposal five years later to Thomas Chirnside (1815–1887), one of two brothers from the Borders then living in Victoria, Australia. Having sold Skibo he passed the next winter in Rome and spent the last 20 years of his life at Ormiston Hall, near Tranent.

Dempster's will expressed a few of his hopes and fears for the local community in Angus, demonstrating how much he wanted to see others complete at least some of the projects he had initiated. A wish to see a striking clock installed on a steeple in Letham similar to that at Restenneth and a marble stone marking the foundation of Letham in 1788 were personal flourishes. He repeated the plea made 15 years earlier for neighbouring justices of the peace to be allowed to hold monthly small debt courts whilst fearing that the village might become a burgh with a corporation instead of a self-governing and independent town. His only wish, as the property developer he was, concerned the 150 acres adjacent to Loch Fiethie (the Larches) where he recommended his heirs and successors build a 'beautiful elevated residence . . . on a drier soil . . . than Dunnichen'.

House and farm servants were remembered, along with his factor and grieve, those with accommodation being given the use of their houses rent free for the rest of their lives. Books and the gifts he had received from the Convention of Royal Burghs, including civic medals and chains, were to be attached to the estate and remain with his successors. The list of those who were to receive mourning rings or small mementoes included more than thirty family and friends. All his young nieces benefited and few of his less fortunate friends and tenants were forgotten.

So ended the life of a man who had kept the respect and affection of friends and family alike for eighty-six years. As readers may well conclude for themselves, the attraction of Dempster's life lay as much in his character and personality as in his achievements. In parliament Dempster's love had been of liberty and independence of mind; in his constituency and the Highlands it was of employment, profit and improvement. Closer to home, his love was of ideas and those who shared their imagination, creativity and skill with him. None of these joys was insulated from another; his delight was as much in the nursery as in the highest court in the land. He diffused happiness and drew his greatest satisfaction from a role as the 'gentleman usher', putting those he met in touch with those he knew and exercising a deep humanity in all he did. Had George been pressed to reconsider his belief that his was a life 'to whom nothing but oblivion belongs', he might have chosen another quotation from Virgil:

'Forsan et haec olim meminisse iuvabit'
or
'Maybe one day we shall be glad to remember even these things'.

NOTES

The following abbreviations have been used:

EUL   Edinburgh University Library
FN   Footnote
GMA   Government of Maharashtra
HLC   Huntington Library Collection
NAS   National Archives of Scotland
NLS   National Library of Scotland
PBR   Perth Burgh Records
UT   University of Toronto, Thomas Fisher Rare Book Library
WWM   Wentworth Woodhouse Muniments in the Sheffield Archives
YBL   Yale University, Beinecke Library

Introduction

1   Dempster's *Memorandum* to his successors and heirs found after his death (Lowson's *Portrait Gallery of Forfar Nobles* p.14)

2   WWM, Dempster to Burke, 8 June1776 from Dunnichen

3   YBL (C937) Dempster to Boswell 10 January [1766]

4   YBL (C941) Dempster to Boswell, 13 April 1769. See also Cole, *The General Correspondence of James Boswell 1766–1769 Vol 2.*

5   In *Thoughts on the Education of George Dempster, Junior* (written to Sir Adam Fergusson on 16 October 1793) Dempster said: 'I would advise no man to go into Parliament with a less fortune than £6,000 a year'.

6   *Letters of George Dempster to Sir Adam Fergusson (1756–1813)* edited by James Fergusson using the 1934 edition published by Macmillan & Co. When quoting from individual Dempster letters between Dempster and Sir Adam, as in this case, the reference is to the number given to each by Sir James in his book e.g. GD Letter '10', 3 September 1760 from Edinburgh. Quotes from his 'commentary' are referred to as 'James Fergusson', with the appropriate page number.

7   HLC Dempster to Pulteney, 9 February 1762 from the Speaker's Chamber

8   Harris's Debates cited by Edith Haden-Guest in Namier and Brookes' *History of Parliament* Vol.2 p.314

9   GD Letter '22', 26 January 1775 from Dunnichen

10 GD Letter '20', 31 January 1774 from London

11 NLS, ADD MS 3873, ff.120–1, Dempster to Charles Jenkinson, Lord Liverpool, 19 June 1787 from Duns Hotel
12 GD Letter '32', 22 September 1783 from Scarborough
13 *The Scots Magazine*, December 1932. James Fergusson's Bicentennial Article 'Honest George' p.200
14 James Fergusson's Introduction p.xvii
15 James Fergusson's Introduction, p.xviii
16 NLS, MS. 3873, ff.120–1, Dempster to Lord Liverpool, 19 June 1787
17 Taylor and Pringle, *Chatham Correspondence* III, p.405
18 GD Letter '21', 12 September 1774 from London
19 Lowson, *Portrait Gallery of Forfar Notables,* Dempster's *Memorandum* p.14
20 NAS, Dempster's 'confidential' note to Graham of Fintry October 1785
21 Adam Smith to James Oswald, 19 January 1752 from the *Oswald Memoirs* cited by Edith Haden-Guest in Namier and Brookes' *History of Parliament.* Sir John Sinclair reported that Pulteney 'having been accustomed to live on £200 a year . . . thought it a great extravagance to spend £2000 per annum, when he might have spent £20,000'.
22 YBL (C954) Dempster to Boswell, 8 May 1791 from Dunnichen
23 WWM, Dempster to Edmund Burke, 26 September 1768 from Dundee
24 James Maclaren (Editor) *The History of Dundee* 1874 citing *The Scots Magazine*, p.367
25 NAS, Dempster to Graham of Fintry, 20 September 1799 from Dunnichen
26 HLC, Dempster to Pulteney, 15 March 1775 from Dunnichen
27 James Fergusson's Introduction p. xx
28 NLS, MS.5319 f.152, Dempster to Wm.Smith, 1 December 1810 from Dunnichen
29 YBL (C938) Dempster to Boswell, 1 July 1768 from Dundee. See also Cole, *The General Correspondence of James Boswell, 1766–1769 Vol 2*
30 *Annual Register*, 1791, pp.219–220
31 Robert Burns's *Vision;* see also Lowson, *Portrait Gallery of Forfar Notables* p. 4
32 Wimsatt & Pottle *Boswell for the Defence,* 22 March 1772
33 Egerton MS, 255 p.160 (British Library) Quoted by Thomas *The House of Commons in the 18th Century* p.200
34 NAS, Dempster to Graham of Fintry, 26 May 1785 from London
35 GD Letter '16', 1 October 1771 from Berners Street
36 The Novaya Zemlya archipelago in Russia with its extreme climate
37 *Epigram on myself – from the French* included in GD Letter '98' 6 January 1809 from Dunnichen
38 NAS, Dempster to Graham of Fintry, 28 January 1789
39 HLC, Dempster to Pulteney, 5 February 1782 from Dunnichen
40 NAS, Dempster to Graham of Fintry, 24 September 1792 from Dunnichen
41 NAS, Dempster to Graham of Fintry, 16 May 1784 from London
42 Dempster's *Reasons for Extending the Militia Acts etc.* p.7

Chapter 1 (pp. 16–26)

1 Charlotte Louisa Hawkins, *The Manners of My Time* (Edited by Alice Knox) pp.11–12
2 This and subsequent genealogy generally follows the text provided by J.Malcolm in *The Parish of Monifieth in Ancient and Modern Times* and Alex. J. Warden, *Angus or Forfarshire – The Land and People*, vol. III. Inevitably some discrepancies occur in, for instance, birth and marriage dates.

3   The WWW site of James Dempster at Elgin lists George Dempster senior's siblings as Mary (b. 1676), John (b. 1679), Charles (b. 1680), James (1682–1684), Henry (b. 1683) and Jean (b. & d. 1685)

4   The date Dunnichen House was built is uncertain but it could have been as late as 1729.

5   The inscription which formed part of a monument in Monifieth Church until 1813, to the east of the pulpit, seems to have been inaccurate. According to Kirk Session Records George Dempster senior did not die in 1752 but 1753, and his wife Margaret Rait died on 9 May 1741 not April 1740 as inscribed.

6   New Grange was commonly two words at this time, later becoming the one word which is used subsequently in this text. The estate was probably purchased in 1753 for £3,000 and the Ethiebeaton estate was disponed in 1746 to Dempster by the Duke of Douglas (Malcolm p.313). Omachie was bought from Alexander Duncan in 1726 whilst Laws stayed in the Durham family until Dempster bought it at the end of the 17th century (See Malcolm, *Parish of Monifieth*).

7   *Restenneth and Aberlemno,* Ministry of Public Building and Works,1969

8   *Chambers Domestic Annals of Scotland,* Vol.III, p.452

9   Letter dated 27 February 1720, George Dempster senior to the Hon. Harry Maule of Kelly, cited by Warden.

10   Fergusson quotes 1706 but the correct date is 1700. The Register also shows him to have been baptised in 1703 in the Meeting House.

11   Information about both the total number of children John Dempster fathered and by which of his two wives is far from clear. In a letter to Pulteney in June 1760 George referred to the family comprising 12 children but this may well have included some who died young. Mrs Hamilton Dempster's children are justified by oblique references made in correspondence. Both Jean and Helen were, for example, referred to by Dempster as 'my youngest sister' which is correct in so far as the former was a full sister and the latter his half-sister.

12   Dundee Old Parochial Register. There is no record of Mrs Hamilton's first marriage to a Mr Stewart. Her second marriage, however, to John Dempster was on 13 November 1740, 'having been three times proclaimed on the sabbath'. Whilst the register has Mrs Hamilton's father as Philip Hamilton of *Kilbrahmont* this has been taken to be Kilbrachmont or the 'Kilbrackmont' mentioned in Dempster's correspondence with Sir Adam Fergusson.

13   A.C.Lamb, *Dundee, Its Quaint and Historic Buildings*

14   Dundee City Library, Rare Books Section. In a note from Dempster dated 24 July 1799 he expresses the wish that his grandfather's account book be preserved in his library 'as the source of our family and for statistical purposes'.

15   Warden's *Angus or Forfarshire* refers to the lands at New Grange being acquired by Francis Ogilvy around 1590. They were later included in the portfolio built up by George Dempster senior and the house then became John Dempster's home. New Grange and its estate was one of several properties his son was forced to dispose of after his election to parliament. The purchaser then was William Moir of Lomay in Aberdeenshire whose son sold it to John Hay in 1822, changing its name to Letham Grange when the estate was linked to those of Letham and Peebles. The original Dempster property was long gone when in 1830 the new Letham Grange (now a hotel) was built.

16 Dempster was seven years old when he went to Dundee Grammar School (Dempster to William Adam, 9 December 1804 – cited by Lang from the Blair Adam Muniments)

17 George took a long time, if ever, to feel comfortable about sea journeys. At the end of his life, he recalled frightening crossings of the River Tay:

'An old escape comes fresh into my brain.

Have I not cause of ferries to complain?

Once I cross'd Tay to Sandy Duncan's wedding;

But, lack-a-day, I did not see the bedding:

A hugh (sic) broad letter, edg'd and seal'd with black,

To Provost Thomson's fun'ral called me back:

Tremendous winds, and tides, and foaming waves,

Exposed us twice that day to wat'ry graves'

18 GD Letter '107', 6 January 1812 from St Andrews

19 *The Scots Magazine* Vol.73, p.713

20 Dempster to Dundas, 31 January 1788 cited by James Fergusson p.175

21 This and the subsequent description of the town in 1746 is taken from James Thomson's *History of Dundee*, published in the *Dundee Magazine* for 1799

22 George Dempster, *Reasons for Extending the Militia Acts to the Disarmed Counties of Scotland*. Edinburgh, 1760

23 J. Macky, *Journey through Scotland*, 1723

24 Cant, *The University of St Andrews*, p.110

25 Graham, *Scottish Men of Letters in the 18th Century*, pp.371–2

26 In 1760 Dempster was again forced to intervene on Alexander Vilant's behalf. Frivolous complaints about his lack of deference to certain professors, which 'every important person in St Andrews called into question, provoked Dempster into a remembrance of the 'very high opinion' he had of him. The factorship was 'the only thing on earth that Mr Vilant has to depend upon for bread'. (NLS, MS. 16719, f.185)

27 St Andrews University 'Borrowings Register' 1747–48; students and professors were required to enter all books taken from and returned to the Library.

28 Cant, *The University of St Andrews* p.95

29 Principal Robertson appealed for funds for new buildings in 1768 – *The Scots Magazine* XXX p.114

30 EUL, Mackie's Class List, p.207

31 *The Scots Magazine*, August 1741, pp.371–373 *An Account of the University of Edinburgh, the professors . . . and the parts of learning taught by them.*

32 James Rait (1689–1777) was the son of the Rev William Rait, minister of Monikie and brother of Margaret, who married George Dempster senior. He had been consecrated Bishop of Brechin in 1742 and lived in Dundee. The elder Dempster's account book referred to earlier contains detail of the rent paid for the family pew in the Bishop's chapel.

33 The monument to his memory in St Vigean's Church, Arbroath, bears the date 2 November 1753, but the correct date (1754) is given in *the Scots Magazine* where the death is announced (J.Leng *Roll of Eminent Burgesses of Dundee* FN p.218).

Chapter 2 (pp. 27-43)

1 Dempster's *Memorandum* to his successors and heirs, James Fergusson pp.346–7. See also Alexander Lowson, *Portrait Gallery of Forfar Notables*

2 OSA for Dunnichen Parish, p. 428

3 Dempster's *Memorandum*, James Fergusson pp.346–7

4 Professor E.C.Mossner, *The Life of David Hume,* p.272

5 See Janet Adam Smith's *Life among the Scots*

6 NLS, Adv.MSS 23.1.1. Minutes of the Select Society

7 John Robertson, *The Scottish Enlightenment and the Militia Issue* pp.85–86

8 James Fergusson provides the only record of the two friends' tour, basing his comments (pp.5–8) partly on Adam Fergusson's account book.

9 James Fergusson *Lowland Lairds* p.19

10 *Mrs Calderwood's Journey* from *The Coltness Collections* printed for the Maitland Club of Glasgow in 1842. With her husband, Mrs Margaret Calderwood (the eldest daughter of Sir James Steuart of Goodtrees – Solicitor-General of Scotland) spent 1756 in Brussels and Spa.

11 James Fergusson p.6 and GD Letter '74', 28 February 1795 from Skibo; and *Mrs Calderwood's Journey*

12 Among the British were Turberville Needham, Houston Stewart (later Stewart-Nicholson), a Mr Townley and a recent graduate from Cambridge called Webb. Their other acquaintances included Count Callenburg, M. Weijder, and the Tosbaer family (with three daughters). The Count was Austrian, Belgium's ruling power in this period, who had a 'fine large old-world house' but 'indifferently furnished' in Brussels.

13 GD Letter '3', 5 December 1756 from Edinburgh

14 *Mrs Calderwood's Journey* p.261

15 GD Letter '8', 20 November 1757 from Bath

16 Including Nugent's *Grand Tour,* Poellnitz's *Memoirs* and Richardson's *Observations on Painting*

17 GD Letter '1', 23 November 1756 from Dover

18 GD Letter '2', 26 November 1756 from London

19 William Nairne was to become Lord Dunsinnan and a Lord of Justiciary. Called 'worthy' by Boswell, Nairne's own appearance habitually fell short of the standards Dempster set for himself.

20 GD Letter '3', 5 December 1756 from Edinburgh

21 GD Letter '3', 5 December 1756 from Edinburgh

22 GD Letter '5', 19 February 1757 from Edinburgh

23 GD Letter '4', 16 December 1756 from Edinburgh

24 GD Letter '5', 19 February 1757 from Edinburgh. Only his sister Peggy was older than Dempster; whether his use of *elder* was an error cannot be rightly established.

25 GD Letter '2', 26 November 1756 from London. According to a later letter it seems Dempster's name had been linked with Lady Elizabeth Erskine, Andrew Erskine's sister, Mary Fletcher and Catharine Maxwell who married John Fordyce of Ayton.

26 GD Letter '3', 5 December 1756 from Edinburgh

27 GD Letter '2', 26 November 1756 from London

28 GD Letter '4', 16 December 1756 from Edinburgh

29 GD Letter '4', 16 December 1756 from Edinburgh

30 From the 'Regulations' published by the Select Society

31 Thomas Sheridan was a Dublin actor and father of Richard Brinsley Sheridan, the Irish dramatist.He had published papers and given lectures on English elocution that were so popular – despite his Irish brogue – that hundreds of gentlemen and ladies enlisted for them in 1756. (See Pottle, Introduction to *Boswell's London Journal* p.9)

32 When the play transferred to London the names of these two parts were changed to Norval and Lady Randolph respectively. (See Graham, pp.64–71)

33 James Fergusson, p.25

34 GD Letter '5', 19 February 1757 from Edinburgh

35 James Fergusson, p.347

36 GD Letter '6', 30 April 1757 from Edinburgh

37 In *Lowland Lairds* p.122

38 The ambiguity of the Annexation Act of 1752, and the subsequent 'piecemeal administration' which never rose to the heights envisaged by its drafters, is discussed in Chapter 7 of *Cromartie: Highland Life 1650–1914* by Eric Richards and Monica Clough.

39 Dempster *Reasons for Extending the Militia Acts etc.* p.14

40 GD Letter '8', 20 November 1757 from Bath

41 GD Letter '6', 30 April 1757 from Edinburgh

42 GD Letter '7', 28 August 1757 from Edinburgh; Adam was then staying with a banker in Rome.

43 GD Letter '8', 20 November 1757 from Bath

44 GD Letter '9', End of September 1758 from London

45 Philips *Public Characters of 1809–10* p.248

46 No letters between Dempster and Adam Fergusson during the period September 1758 and September 1760 were available to James Fergusson in 1934. He admits the gap and partially fills it with a reference to peat extraction and land drainage work but much of this took place later.

47 See Robertson *The Scottish Enlightenment and the Militia Issue* pp. 108–110

48 *Reasons for Extending the Militia Acts to the Disarmed Counties of Scotland*, published by Dempster in Edinburgh, 1760

49 YBL (C937) Dempster to Boswell, 10 January 1766

50 Richard Philips (Editor), *Public Characters of 1809–10*, p.248

51 NLS, MS 16714, f.219 Dempster from St Andrews, 20 September 1760

52 Adam Fergusson had succeeded to the baronetcy on the death of his father in January 1759.

53 GD Letter '12', 14 October 1760 from Edinburgh

54 Newcastle also had his problems at Ayr, where the town council had become disenchanted with the antics of noble lords and 'rammed' yet another 'unpalatable' candidate down his throat. (See Bruce Lenman *Integration etc . . . Scotland 1746–1832* p.32)

55 GD Letters '10' to '12', 3 and 14 September and 14 October 1760 from Edinburgh

56 Robert Craigie of Glendoich

57 Captain Robert Haldane (1705–1767), the candidate in question, was a member of a large Scottish family that in the 18th century included James (1768–1851) the Scottish minister who with his brother Robert (1764–1842) was to found the Society for Propagating the Gospel at Home after service in India. The Haldane family at Cloan, Auchterarder have a portrait of Dempster which his descendants presented to Miss Elizabeth Haldane, C.H.

58 NLS, MS.11015 Dempster to Sir Gilbert Elliot from Perth, 19 October 1760. Two other letters were sent to him on 5 October and 13 November. A fourth letter dated 2 December 1760 was not sent to Elliot but to an unknown friend in London.

Chapter 3 (pp. 44–60)

1   There was a 'cantonment' or the rough grouping of Boroughs into a constituency. Perth was then the 'presiding' borough with others in the constituency (Dundee, St Andrews, Forfar and Cupar) taking a turn in order of precedence as determined by the Scottish Parliamentary Roll.

2   6 Members died before the session opened on 3 November 1761. See Lewis Namier *England in the Age of the American Revolution,* III, p. 217. His analysis of the composition of the 1761 Parliament is used in the next paragraph.

3   In Sutherland twenty-two of the 34 electors ('life-renters') were beholden to Earl Gower and the Countess of Sutherland.

4   They included the Oath of Allegiance, the Oath of Abjuration and the Test Oath. (See Dyer)

5   James Fergusson FN1 on p.56

6   Sir Gilbert Elliot of Minto (1722–1777) was Lord of the Admiralty, a Member of the Select Society and a friend of Dempster. He became the third baronet of Minto. See NLS, MS. 11015 and Dempster's letter to Sir Gilbert dated 5 October 1760 from St Andrews.

7   Laprade, *Parliamentary Papers of John Robinson 1774–1784* p.106–111. John Robinson (1727- 1802) was MP for Appleby and then Harwich. He was one of several secretaries to the Treasury Board, signing all letters for the issuing of money, examining warrants for the King's signature and overseeing all parliamentary business. He was the monarch's trusted counsellor – his eyes and ears in parliament, superintending the elections of 1774, 1780 and 1794. His duties made him in effect the Government's whip – seeing that members of the administration were present and that a majority was achieved at general elections.

8   Brian Connell, *Portrait of a Whig Peer*, Andre Deutsch. 1957 p.91–2

9   Laprade, *Robinson Papers*, p.7 referring to the 1774 election

10   One such accusation quoted by Warden in *Angus or Forfarshire*, Vol.III p.198 was that Dempster was 'fined the very large sum of £30,000 sterling'; another inaccurate rumour was perpetuated by Roger in *Social Life in Scotland* vol.i. p.334 where the election (of 1761) was said to have been annulled on account of bribery.

11   GD Letter '12', 14 October 1760 from Edinburgh

12   James Thomson, *The History of Dundee*, 1874, p.365

13   Warden, *Angus or Forfarshire*, Vol.III, p.198 (whose unreliability has already been referred to)

14   James Fergusson *Honest George, The Scots Magazine* December 1932 p.199

15   Carl Moritz *Travels* pp.52–53, cited by Thomas *The House of Commons in the Eighteenth Century*

16   Moritz's *Travels* p.53

17   Horace Walpole's *Memoirs of the Reign of King George III* records Dempster's maiden speech, vol i. pp71–2

18   Walpole speaking of Sir Nathaniel Wraxall in 1781

19   Lowson, *Portrait Gallery of Forfar Notables* p.4. Lord George Sackville was writing to General Irwin on 16 November 1761

20   In 1762 Mansfield was Bute's Lord Chief Justice, Kinnoull had just retired with Newcastle from the cabinet, his brother, Hay Drummond was Archbishop of York; Oswald and Elliot were Lords of the Treasury; Sir Andrew Mitchell, the MP for Elgin

was British Ambassador in Berlin; Colonel Graeme was the Queen's Private Secretary; John Douglas a Canon of Windsor and future bishop; Allan Ramsay the painter, and Robert Adam the architect, in highest favour at Court; whilst Scottish commanders were in high positions in Portugal, Canada, Florida, the Windward Islands, Dominica and Bengal. (Mathieson, pp.45–7)

21 G.M.Trevelyan *History of England,* p.547

22 Namier and Brooke (Edith Haden-Guest) p.314

23 Philip's *'Public Characters of 1809–10',* London 1809 and cited by James Fergusson in his Centennial Article in *The Scots Magazine,* pp.205–6

24 Newcastle Papers Add MS. 329, Duke of Newcastle to the Earl of Hardwicke on 15 November 1761

25 Sir Lewis Namier, *England in the Age of the American Revolution,* Macmillan, 1961, pp.306–7

26 GD Letter '12', 14 October 1760 from Edinburgh

27 An example of what could occasionally be achieved by the Press occurred in 1845 when the correspondent of the London 'Times' brought news of the tragic events at the remote Croik Church at the time of the Sutherland Clearances.

28 The comment was made by a Whig MP to John Jamieson, the future lexicographer. (Andrew Lowson *Portrait Gallery of Forfar Nobles* p.31)

29 YBL (L415) Boswell to Dempster, 19 November 1761 from Edinburgh. See also *The General Correspondence of James Boswell 1757–1763* edited by Hankins and Caudle, due to be published by EUP and Yale University Press in 2005.

30 As Professor Pottle described him in his introduction to Boswell's *London Journal 1762–1763* (p.8 in Yale Edition 1992) the Hon. Andrew Erskine was the younger son of the 5th Earl of Kellie whom Boswell met at Fort George in May 1761 when accompanying his father on a tour of the Northern Circuit. Dempster had given Boswell a letter of introduction to Erskine. Sometimes nicknamed 'Dash', he was a lieutenant in the Army. He committed suicide in 1793.

31 Alexander Donaldson, the bookseller, had published a similar collection of poems in 1760

32 GD Letter '13', 8 August 1761 (The last of Dempster's letters to Sir Adam for 5 years – the lost correspondence spans August 1761 to July 1766).

33 Boswell left Dempster a gold mourning ring at his death – a token confirming that their friendship, though interrupted, was never quite broken.

34 According to Professor Pottle, John Johnston of Grange, then in his early twenties had met Boswell when both were studying in Robert Hunter's Greek class – a bland and affectionate friend who was not much of a correspondent to Boswell's annoyance [not to be confused with the John Johnstone whose story is more fully told in Chapter 4 et al].

35 Pottle, *Boswell's London Journal 17 July 1763*

36 From 'Journal of My Jaunt, Harvest 1762' cited in Pottle's *Boswell's London Journal,* 1762–63, 1950, pp 106–7

37 YBL (C935) Dempster to Boswell, probably written around 1765. Dempster's verse reads: 'While you in distant regions roam, I guard your liberty at home. So when the husband takes the air, the House employs his spouse's care. She keeps her servants all at work, now saves a fortune, now a cook'.

38 EUL, Ms.Dc.4.41 Letter to Alexander Carlyle, 30 January 1762.

39 NLS, RB. S. 1302 (5)

40   HLC, Dempster to William Johnstone, 11 January and 9 February 1762 from St James's Place. For convenience, William Johnstone (1729–1805) is referred to subsequently as Pulteney or Sir William Pulteney. He adopted the name when he married the heiress of the first Earl of Bath in 1767. His brother George Johnstone (1730–87) had returned from the West Indies after killing a clerk in the second of three duels during his life and the Admiralty was being understandably slow in finding him a new appointment. The next year he became Governor of West Florida – duelling this time with Lord George Germain.

41   HLC, Dempster to Pulteney, 6 February 1762 from London

42   HLC, Dempster to Pulteney 9 February 1762 from the Speaker's Chamber in the House

43   This quotation and the report of Sir David Carnegie's speech are from James Fergusson's Introduction, pp. xix- xx

44   Dundee Council Minutes of 29 September and 6 October 1761

45   HLC, Dempster letter to William Pulteney, 9 February 1762

46   H.G.Graham, p.112 suggests that Ferguson was standing by the fire with a poker in his hand when he was asked what the club should be called and had urged members to 'poke up' the fire of their patriotic zeal.
Adam Ferguson (1724–1816) became Professor of Moral Philosophy at Edinburgh University in 1759 having been a chaplain to the Black Watch in the Austrian Succession War. Dempster and he were to live out part of their retirement at St Andrews.

47   Another record says a house near the Nether-Bow

48   Alexander Carlyle's *Anecdotes and Characters of the Times* p.441

49   Pottle, *Boswell's London Journal* 9 December 1762

50   See W.L.Mathieson pp.52–58. John Stuart Mackenzie used the epithet 'scabby sheep'. He had been recalled from Turin in 1761(where he had been the British Minister) to undertake the management of Scotland and became Keeper of the Privy Seal.

51   A Scottish poet who, when living in London, changed his name from 'Scots Malloch to English Mallet'. His plays were failures but he had the distinction of writing, with James Thomson, the song 'Rule Britannia' used in *Alfred* a masque he wrote in 1740.

52   Nine months later Dempster was still advising Boswell to 'make no more sallies into the streets', having earlier prescribed 'two or three brisk capers round the room' as a remedy for Boswell's spleen or melancholia.

53   A letter from Boswell on 19 November 1761 – soon after Dempster had made his debut in the House Boswell told him that he had 'lately begun to learn the violin'.

54   Pottle, *Boswell's London Journal,* 2 February 1763, and p.174

55   Mrs Frances Sheridan, mother of Richard Brinsley Sheridan, the Irish dramatist. She was a novelist and the author of one or two plays.

56   Pottle, *Boswell's London Journal,* 3 February 1763

57   Pottle, *Boswell's London Journal,* 26 February 1763

58   Pottle, *Boswell's London Journal* 11 March 1763

59   Breakfast would be taken around 10 a.m, dinner at about 4 p.m (although it was slowly getting earlier) and tea after 6 o'clock. A light supper might follow.

60   James Macpherson (1736–1796), the poet, forger and translator, had published *Fingal: An Ancient Poem* in 1762 and a dubious collection of poems attributed in their original form to Ossian, the Gaelic poet, in 1765.

61 YBL (C933) Dempster to Boswell, 19 November 1763 from Manchester Buildings. A long-delayed letter from Dempster written in Scotland earlier in the year but mis-addressed. See also Pottle, *Boswell in Holland,* 26 November 1763.

62 Pottle, *Boswell in Holland,* Dempster to Boswell, 25th May 1764 from Manchester Buildings

63 Boswell's letter to William Temple three days later

64 James Fergusson, *Honest George – Dempster of Dunnichen's Bicentenary, The Scots Magazine,* December 1932. For full report see pp.312 – 316 of Boswell's *London Journal.*

65 Boswell to Lord Hailes, 23 July 1763. Leng, *Roll of Eminent Burgesses of Dundee 1513–1886,* p.219

66 By Dr.W.S. Lewis in the *Virginia Quarterly Review,* 25 (1949) and referred to obliquely by Professor Pottle in a footnote on page 332 of *Boswell's London Journal*

67 Pottle, *Boswell's London Journal* 1 August 1763

68 Pottle, *Boswell in Holland,* 25 May 1764. Lang, *A Life of George Dempster* p.41 suggests that Dempster's visit to France may have been to assist Andrew Stuart MP, a lawyer collecting evidence on behalf of the Duchess of Argyll in 'the Douglas cause'.

69 HLC, Dempster to Pulteney, 16 March 1762 which also shows that Pulteney had sent him his own 'tract' on banking.

70 Charles Boase, *A Century of Banking in Dundee; being the Annual Balance Sheets of the Dundee Banking Company from 1764–1864,* 1867. The author was the manager of the bank at the time.

71 Sir William Forbes, *Memoirs of a Banking House*

72 The £1 bank note promises to pay 'One pound and sixpence at the end of six months, either in cash or in notes of the Royal Bank or Bank of Scotland, and for ascertaining the demand and option of the directors, the accountant is hereby ordered to mark and sign this note, on the back hereof'. The promise was made by Robert Jobson, cashier to George Dempster & Co.

73 *The Roll of Eminent Burgesses of Dundee 1513–1886,* John Leng Dundee 1887

74 S.G.Checkland, *Scottish Banking – A History*

75 YBL (C930/1) Dempster to Boswell, 23 August 1763 from Brussels. See also Pottle, *Boswell in Holland,* 23 August 1763. Dempster asked his friend to 'consider Holland as the dark watery passage which leads to an enchanted and brilliant grotto. For such is a French Academy; and above all, such will you find Paris when you understand the language'.

76 It was at the close of this letter that some clue was given to why so few letters written to Dempster over the years have survived: 'Your letters are smoke long ago'. In later life he burned all his Parliamentary correspondence, perhaps with more reason, but other material was also destroyed to frustrate the unwelcome advances of a prospective biographer. (YBL, Dempster to Boswell, 29 October 1763 from Dundee)

77 YBL (C935) Dempster to Boswell (undated) but said to have been written early in 1765.

78 *My salad days, when I was green in judgment* – Shakespeare's *Antony and Cleopatra,* I,v.

79 YBL (C934) Dempster to Boswell, 25 May 1764 from Manchester Buildings 4 June 1764. See also Pottle, *Boswell in Holland,* 4 June 1764

Chapter 4 (pp. 61–81)

1   An investment of £2,000 was recorded in the Company's Stock Ledger. This was the minimum required to become a director and compared with the £500 for a proprietor. See James Parker, *The Directors of the East India Company,* Ph.D Thesis 1977, University of Edinburgh.

2   L. Sutherland *East India Company in 18th Century Politics*

3   In 1772 a Committee of the House of Commons listed £2,169,665 taken in presents between 1757 and 1765 (Marshall *The Writings and Speeches of Edmund Burke,*p.163)

4   P.J. Marshall, p.140–1

5   A *Jagir* or *Jaghir* was the stipend paid from land-tax revenues to someone appointed to administer an area. A *Jaghirdar* was the holder of such rights (Hindi).

6   Sulivan had decided to stand aside for a year to avoid being caught by rules requiring the rotation of directors. He continued to exercise control through Rous who was in effect his puppet.

7   See Philip Lawson's *History of the East India Company* pp.79–80. Sulivan also described to Lord Shelburne how the 1763 system worked: 'There is no voting by proxy and every proprietor at a contested election swears the stock is his own. Therefore a man who has £1,000 stock and lends a second half of it for a qualification, a Note of Hand is given for the sum it amounts to and he pays it back hereafter, gaining or losing the difference of the market price'. (L.Sutherland)

8   See Parker, p.82 et al., along with Lady Haden-Guest's biographical summaries in *The House of Commons 1754–1790* vol.II (Namier & Brooke).

9   George had been Governor of West Florida in 1763. The other Johnstone brothers were Alexander (d.1787), Patrick (d.1756) and Gideon. The last married the celebrated actress (and mistress) Mrs Jordan in 1779. He was the only other brother to have gone to India where, with his wayward brother John, he too became embroiled in receiving presents from the Nawab in Calcutta. (p.173 P.J.Marshall)

10   C.L.Johnstone's *History . . .* p179 and Namier and Brooke p.687. The tale about young Johnstone follows a combination of these two sources. The fuller version written by C.L.Johnstone sets the events in Calcutta rather than Dacca.

11   HLC, Dempster's letters to William Pulteney, 17 January and 6 February 1762

12   Minutes of St Andrews Town Council 1 December 1760 to 7 August 1772

13   Minute of Dundee Town Council dated 26 September 1763

14   John Leng, *Roll of Eminent Burgesses of Dundee 1513–1886,* Dundee, 1887, p.220

15   YBL (C934) Dempster to Boswell, 25 May 1764 from Manchester Buildings. See also Pottle, *Boswell in Holland,* 4 June 1764

16   YBL (C935) Dempster to Boswell from Delahay Street, Westminster (undated but probably early 1765)

17   James Parker p.82 records that Dempster endeavoured to become a director of the EIC in 1765 and 1767 and only succeeded in 1769.

18   YBL (C936) Dempster to Boswell, 1 July 1765 from London. See also Brady and Pottle, *Boswell on the Grand Tour*

19   Pryce Campbell (1727–68) was MP for Nairnshire between 1761 and 1768, having been the Member for Inverness.

20   Namier and Brooke, *History of Parliament 1754–1790,* Vol.IIp.314. The author of pages 313 to 317 was Edith, Lady Haden-Guest. Subsequent references to her brief

but useful summary of Dempster's parliamentary career are shown as Namier and Brooke (E H-G).

21 YBL (C936) Dempster to Boswell, 1st July 1765 from London. See also Brady and Pottle, *Boswell on the Grand Tour*

22 Charles Watson-Wentworth, Marquis of Rockingham (1730–82) was leader of the Whig opposition before being called to be Prime Minister in 1765. He repealed Grenville's Stamp Act and after his resignation in 1766 opposed Lord North's ruinous American policy. He again became the First Minister in March 1782 but died four months later.

23 WWM, R1/481 Dempster to Rockingham, 15 August 1766 from London. Dempster would have known about the great developments put in hand at Wentworth Woodhouse, his Yorkshire seat where among other improvements the home farm of 2,000 acres was at the centre of agricultural experiments.

24 The Order of the Thistle had been put on a regular footing in 1687 and was modelled on the Order of the Garter. The number of Knights was 12 and the colour of the riband 'over the left shoulder across the body and tied under the right arm' green. The embroidered 'paste-board and tinsel' star sewn on the coat and an enlarged collar-badge was altered in 1715. De La Bere, *The Queen's Orders of Chivalry* is perhaps wrong to suggest that Queen Anne was responsible for developing the order.

25 GD Letter '2', 26 November 1756 from London. Dempster refers to him as Sir Harry. He was the 5th baronet of Alva and Cambuskenneth and MP for Anstruther. The earlier secretaries were Sir Andrew Forrester (appointed 1687), Sir David Nairn (1704), George Drummond (1736) and Sir Henry Erskine (1765).

26 Sir Nicholas Harris Nicholas *History of the Orders of Knighthood of the British Empire* Vol.3 p. 74.

27 YBL (C937) Dempster to Boswell, 10 January 1766

28 The duties were generally vague but at investitures the statute required the person being admitted to the order to be 'received at the door of the Chapter room by the two junior Knights Brethren present and conducted between them . . . to the Sovereign, preceded by the Secretary, bearing the Ensigns of the Order on a cushion.'

29 James Fergusson p. 62

30 This had been increased in 1720 before which time the fees paid by Knights included the sum of £55.11s.1d to the secretary. Other fees to officers, including Lyon King of Arms, the usher, heralds, pursuivants and trumpeters brought the total cost up to £297.

31 2 in 1767; 3 in 1768; 1 in 1770; 1 in 1771; 3 in 1775; 1 in 1776; 2 in 1786; 1 in 1793; 1 in 1794; 1 in 1797; 1 in 1800; 1 in 1805; 1 in 1808; 1 in 1812; 2 in 1814 and 1 in 1815 – making a total of 23.

32 Appointed in 1762, Robert Quarme had been forced to petition His Majesty for a salary 'in like manner with Ushers of the Garter and Bath' suggesting that he did not have great wealth. When the 8th Duke of Hamilton was appointed to the order in 1786, 'Mr Quarme officiated as Secretary for Mr Dempster, which he had not done for twenty years though worth three hundred a year to him and as gentleman usher. He administered oath in one capacity and brought ribbon in another, as the King observed to Lord Stormont'. (MSS of the Marquis of Ailesbury, p.275).

33 Robert Quarme held the office until 1787, being followed by Matthew Arnott (till 1800) and Quarme's son thereafter.

34 See Arnot's *History of Edinburgh* p.493 and *The Juridical Review* of December 1933, p.322

35 Correspondence on 7 January 1768 between MacKenzie of Delvine and the Duke of Atholl refers to £50 being paid to the Dean and the £100 to Dempster being distributed between the clerks and macers of judiciary. (Atholl MSS 42.II (5) 24 and 49. (7)3.)

36 In January 1766 St Andrews Town Council met 'to choose a burgess . . . in room of George Dempster Esq., lately chosen burgess who hath since accepted the Office of Secretary to the most ancient and noble Order of the Thistle'. In the chair was Alex Watson.

37 YBL (C937) Dempster to Boswell 10 January 1766

38 Once Rockingham laid down his seals of office the King sent for Pitt and created him Earl of Chatham. Giving up his seat in the Commons, he came into the administration ostensibly as Lord Privy Seal.

39 Sutherland, p.148 citing L.Scrafton to Clive, 12th April 1766. William Beckford (1709–1770) was MP for London between 1754 and 1770. Baptised in Jamaica, he was the son of the Speaker of the Jamaica House of Assembly. Educated at Westminster and Balliol he was Lord Mayor of London between 1762–3 and 1769–70.

40 GD Letter '14', 26 July 1766

41 The bank opened for business on the 6th May 1766. The Perth Banking Company was subsequently absorbed by the Union Bank of Scotland in 1857 and amalgamated with the Bank of Scotland in 1955 (see Robert S.Rait, *The History of the Union Bank*, p.131).

42 Philip Lawson *The East India Company – A History*, Longmans, 1993, p.117

43 GD Letter '14', 26 July 1766 from Battersee (sic) London

44 HLC, PU 622 John Johnstone to Pulteney, July 1767

45 Sutherland, p.145

46 WWM, Dempster to Rockingham; letter dated 5 November 1766.

47 Namier and Brooke (E H-G) p.314

48 Sutherland p.164 and cited from a report by James West MP (1703–1772) to the Duke of Newcastle dated 13 March 1767

49 Court Book 76, p.33 cited by Sutherland on p.170

50 Sutherland pp.173–176

51 The account of this episode is taken from James Fergusson's account on pages 65–67 of *Letters of George Dempster to Sir Adam Fergusson 1756–1813*. It had originally been told in the Scots Magazine, vols.29 and 30.

52 Ochtertyre MSS. vol.i. p.423 quoted on p.66 by Fergusson.

53 Edith Haden-Guest uses 'Mackintosh' and James Fergusson 'Macintosh'; the former spelling has been adopted in this text. Born in 1727 and died in 1808, he was the son of Robert Mackintosh of Dalmunzie, minister of Erroll. His hopes of the Dumfries seat had been dashed when his patrons failed to support him. Cantankerous all his life he was (according to Fergusson) his own worst enemy.

54 James Fergusson, p.66

55 Johnstone was acting for Lord Galloway and had discussed the deal in Edinburgh with Adam Fergusson and Andrew Stewart.

56 HLC, PU 615, John Johnstone to Pulteney, 3 October 1767 from Edinburgh. Johnstone stood unsuccessfully for Haslemere.

57 HLC, PU 626, John Johnstone to Pulteney, 8 October 1767 from Kirkcaldy.

58 NLS, S.274, Geddie and Mackintoshs'complaint before the Court. See also Grenville Papers, Mackintosh to Grenville, 16 November 1767

59 NLS, S.274

60 NLS, MS. 11015. In a letter to Sir Gilbert Elliot (19 October 1760) Dempster openly demonstrated his awareness of the fact that towns 'were purchasable'.

61 WWM, Dempster to Burke 11 November 1767 from Dundee

62 A defect in the Duke of Portland's title to his lands led to a demand for legislation to extend the provisions of an act of James I barring claims against any title which had been quietly enjoyed for 60 years before the passing of that act. What had been a local dispute in Cumberland became a national one due to a high-handed interpretation of the law by the Treasury. The opposition denounced what they regarded as the arbitrary use of royal power. In 1769 an act resolved the question by relaxing the limitation so that 60 years' possession would in all future times be an answer to Crown claims. (see J.Steven Watson *George III*)

63 Cromarty was an *alternating* seat; three Scottish seats were shared between the electors of Caithness, Nairn and Clackmannan each returning a member to one parliament, and those of Bute, Cromarty and Kinross to the next. (See Michael Dyer, *Men of Property and Intelligence,* SCP. 1996 p. 14)

64 WWM, R1/927 Dempster to Rockingham, 7 January 1768 from Edinburgh

65 WWM, R1/1128 Dempster to Rockingham, 12 December 1768

66 James Fergusson, p.67. Several reports which appeared subsequently suggested that Dempster was more deeply involved in illegal doings than is today accepted. However, James Fergusson takes Rogers in *Social Life in Scotland,* vol. i. p.334 to task, without doubt rightly, for referring to an annulment of Dempster's election in 1761; similarly the erroneous claim said to have been proved against him that he was fined £30,000 sterling made by Alex J. Warden, *Angus or Forfarshire, The Land & People,* Vol. III.

67 James Fergusson, p.68

68 WWM, 1/223 Dempster to Burke 26 September 1768 from Dundee

69 YBL (C938) Dempster to Boswell, 1 July [1768] from Dundee. His mention of being a director of the EIC suggests that it may have been written a year later. See also Cole, *The General Correspondence of James Boswell, 1766–1769, vol 2*

70 HLC, Dempster to Pulteney, 28th June 1769 from Dundee

71 Namier, *England in the Age of the American Revolution,* London, 1961, p.272

72 Sir George Colebrook, the MP for Gatton and a reckless banker, soon abandoned his ministerial connections and stood out at the head of the dissidents.

73 James N.M.Maclean in *Reward is Secondary* , pp.222–3.

74 Writing to Pulteney on 22 July 1768, John Johnstone, who was probably a subscriber to 'the great fund', complained that 'Macleane has never yet thought to settle the account. I have often given him broad enough hints that I wished it concluded'.(HLC PU.635)

75 Maclean, pp.224–5

76 YBL (C939) Dempster to Boswell, 7 March 1769 from Dunnichen. See also Cole, *The General Correspondence of James Boswell, 1766–1769,* vol 2

77 YBL (C941) Dempster to Boswell, 13 April 1769 from Suffolk Street. See also Cole, *The General Correspondence of James Boswell, 1766–1769,* vol 2

78 YBL (C941) Dempster to Boswell, 13 April 1769 from Suffolk Street. See also Cole, *The General Correspondence of James Boswell, 1766–1769,* vol 2

79 The account of the EIC committee system is based on James Parker's text pp.335–339.

80 Sir George Colebrooke and Vansittart were ruined, Lord Shelburne and Lauchlin Macleane lost £30,000 and £90,000 respectively and Sulivan more than £15,000.

81 Brady and Pottle *Boswell in Search of a Wife,* p.308

82 Reforms which the Company's Commissioners were to have carried through were halted at the end of 1769 when the frigate *Aurora* foundered and Vansittart, Scrafton and Forde were drowned. The task had to be restarted and progress was hampered by a long search for members of what was this time to be called a Supervising Commission. Dempster tried to persuade Sir Adam Fergusson to become one of the nine appointees – See GD Letter '17', 2 October 1772 from London.

83 Dempster's letters to Boswell from Dunnichen indicate that he was ill with 'a putrid dysentery' for most of July but he returned to London thereafter, writing to him from Greek Street in the middle of August.

84 Dempster did, however, disqualify himself when he was a Director for the second (and last time) in 1772.

85 Burke to Rockingham 6th November 1769; see Parker p.84

86 Cotton *East Indiamen,* FN p.122

87 Dempster often recommended Willison to his friends and his portrait of Dempster in the McManus Gallery in Dundee is a fine example of his work.

88 Warden, *Angus or Forfarshire, The Land and People,* p.199

89 James Fergusson FN p.47

90 P.J.Marshall, *East Indian Fortunes,* Oxford, 1976, pp.217–219

91 P.J.Marshall p.189

92 William Bolts, *Considerations on Indian Affairs, 1772–5,* i.84 (Quoted by Marshall p.45)

93 UT, Vol.2, Dempster to Jean Hamilton Dempster, 5 December 1792 from Craigie. It appears that Dempster had little contact with him and 'his little foibles'. He had been upset by the way James Hamilton had persuaded his sister (a Miss Hamilton) to part with £1,200 before his last voyage in 1792. His ship the *Adventure* cannot be confirmed.

94 *Devonshire (2)* had been launched in 1763. Leaving the Downs in January 1769 the vessel reached Madras in June 1769, Whampoa in October, St Helena in May 1770 and was back at the Downs on 23 August 1770.

95 James Fergusson, p.77

Chapter 5 (pp. 82–99)

1 Sutherland p.203–204 citing Powis MSS, Colebrook to Clive, October 1778

2 Sir John Pringle (1707–1784) a distinguished physician and reformer; physician to many of the Royal family including George III.

3 GD Letter '15', 17 July 1770 from Abergavenny.

4 HRC, Dempster from Bristol to Pulteney who was at Spa in 'Germany', 13 September 1770

5 YBL (C941) Dempster to Boswell 13 April 1769 from Suffolk Street. See also Cole, *The General Correspondence of James Boswell, 1766–1769, Vol 2*

6 HLC, Dempster to Pulteney, 13 September 1770

7 See correspondence between John Johnstone and Pulteney in 1761–86 (HLC, PU 624–667)

8   YBL (C941) Dempster to Boswell 13 April 1769 from Suffolk Street
9   YBL (C941) Dempster to Boswell, 13 April 1769 from Suffolk Street
10 YBL (C942) Dempster to Boswell 24 June 1769 from Dunnichen
11 Wright, *Cavendish Debates*, Vol.2, p.177
12 Wright, *Cavendish Debates*, Vol 2, p.190
13 Namier and Brooke (E H-G) p.315
14 Wright, *Cavendish Debates*, Vol.2, p.177
15 Hansard, 1770, col.1323
16 Watson, *George III*, p.63
17 Wright, *Cavendish Debates*, Vol 2, pp. 337–339, 352
18 Wright, *Cavendish Debates*, Vol 2, pp. 383–5, 389.
19 GD Letter '16', 1 October 1771 from Berners Street. When a Chief Engineer and a Lieutenant-Colonel, General Clerk had apparently taken part in a secret expedition under the command of Admiral Hawke to capture Rochefort in 1757. It had ended ignominiously. James Fergusson, pp. 37–38, and G D Letter '7', 28 August 1757 from Edinburgh.
20 John Thomson, *The History of Dundee* p.396; Malcolm, p. 315 refers to Irvine living at Ethiebeaton House until his death in 1806. His heir sold it in 1818 to Robert Arklay. The farms at Laws and Omachie were sold around this time to David Kerr who was the owner of Grange, and Patrick Anderson, Provost of Dundee. Omachie had been bought in 1726 and possibly sold by the Dempsters before this disposal.
21 See James Fergusson p.341. The resolution of this long-drawn out action had been largely due to Lord Hailes who drew up the 'Additional' Case which finally decided the House of Lords to give their decision in the Countess of Sutherland's favour. Sir Adam had been closely involved with the legal proceedings. He was a second cousin of Lady Sutherland's father, the 17th Earl.
22 James Fergusson suggests that this was John Hamilton Dempster. If so, the expenditure probably related to his new uniform as 4th mate aboard the *Devonshire*. Charles Dempster who had gone out to India as a writer in 1769 died in Calcutta on 13 November 1772.
23 If it is assumed that the original inheritance was some 5,000 acres (to take Dempster's own figure) producing an income of £750 or so, and that a half had been sold, his income from this source may have been reduced to around £375 p.a.The remaining 2,500 acres would be around Dunnichen and Letham. The smaller estates sold by this time included those at Monifieth in 1761 (and possibly Letham Grange). Together these may have produced £20,000 towards debts in excess of this sum. His income from part of his 'pension' from the Order of the Thistle (say £250) and investments in the EIC and elsewhere would have totalled under £1,000 p.a.
24 GD Letter '18', 8 February 1772 from London
25 P.J.Marshall, *East Indian Fortunes*, p.17
26 GD Letter '17', Postmark 25 January 1772
27 GD Letter '18', 8 February 1772 from London and Add MS 29133, f.533. Stuart was another member of the Select Society and a friend of both George and Sir Adam. Sulivan writing to Hastings on 28 April 1773 explained that they had failed to recruit any one of conspicuous character to lead the supervisory team. Those who had turned the task down included Mr Cornwall, Sir Jeffery Amherst, Burke, Colonel Barré, Sir Richard Sutton and Sulivan himself. The fact that Stuart had accepted, and was 'a Scotchman' gave Sulivan's enemies 'scope for attack'.

28   GD Letter '18', 8 February 1772 from London

29   In June Pulteney took Dempster's 'little black child' for a walk. The child's leg had not quite healed from some disorder and needed to be treated daily at hospital. This prompted Dempster to suggest if the Pulteneys were agreeable, that the child might benefit from a little country air and spend a few weeks with them at Bath House in the care of Mrs Pulteney's lady's maid. (HRC, Dempster to Pulteney, 3 July 1772)

30   Wimsatt and Pottle, *Boswell for the Defence 1769–1774,* 22 March 1772

31   Wimsatt and Pottle, *Boswell for the Defence,* 28 March 1772

32   Namier and Brooke (E H-G) p.315. James Fergusson says he was the only candidate put forward by the Proprietors. The fact that he was not included on the House list suggests that he continued to be viewed with suspicion. Although Dempster was to be unsuccessful in his candidacy as a director in both 1773 and 1774, he retained a place in the General Court by virtue of his shareholding.

33   From James Parker's account p.84 where he cites Copeland, vol.2, pp. 322–323, and Dempster's letter to Edmund Burke of 4 August 1772

34   James Fergusson p.73

35   Robert Chalmer's *Biographical Dictionary* Div.III, p.70. The text continues: 'It seems very extraordinary that Dempster . . . should have so violently opposed himself to the true interest of the country. The error into which he fell is now obvious; he wished to maintain an individual monopoly, when the great wealth of the country rendered it no longer necessary, while he proposed to destroy our sway over India, when it might be made the means of defending and extending our commerce. Finding himself unable to alter our Indian policy, he withdrew from the directory and became a violent parliamentary opponent of the company.'

36   Marshall concludes that Johnstone's fortune was probably second only in size to Clive's. He is supposed to have been worth £300,000 when he returned to Scotland, where he bought three estates and built up a parliamentary interest. See C.L.Johnstone, *History of the Johnstones,* pp.180–1

37   Sutherland p.214 citing Richard Barwell to R. Leycester, 5 November 1773, *Bengal Past and Present, The Letters of Richard Barwell*

38   GD Letter '20', 31 January 1774 from London

39   A.F.Steuart *The Last Journals of Horace Walpole,* p.72

40   L.Sutherland, p.220

41   *The Scots Magazine* June 1772, p.311

42   *The Scots Magazine* June 1772 also reported that 10 banking houses in London stopped business on 19 June; the knock-on effect in the case of Douglas Heron & Co. meant an irrepressible demand for specie in place of paper notes. Although a fund was opened by other merchants to indemnify the Bank of England, who had refused to discount their bills, the Ayr branch collapsed along with all the others.

43   James Fergusson, p.301 quoting *The Scots Magazine,* vol.34. p.304–5 and 311

44   HLC, Dempster to Pulteney, 3 July 1772 from London

45   WWM, Burke to Dempster (incomplete and in draft) around September 1772

46   John Fordyce of Ayton (1735–1809) was a friend of Sir Adam Fergusson whose brother Charles married Fordyce's sister. He was Receiver-General for land tax in Scotland before being appointed Surveyor-General of Crown Lands. He was MP for New Romney and Berwick-on-Tweed.

47   HLC, Dempster to Pulteney 28 July 1772 from London

48 Their 'joint venture' may have been related to Dempster's purchase of East India Company shares in 1764.

49 HLC, Dempster to Pulteney, 14 November 1772 from London

50 HLC, Dempster to Pulteney, 5 February 1782 from Dunnichen

51 Lang (p.135) suggests that 'lively Whiteford' was Sir John Whitefoord of Ballochmyle

52 The slightly fuller text of these verses, written as a backward look at 1772, was included in GD Letter '94'and written sometime in 1807.

53 GD Letter '39', 21 July 1784 from London

54 L.Sutherland pp.237–8 who also cites the *Correspondence of George III*, vol.2

55 Sulivan sat as the Member for Ashburton between 1768 and 1774

56 Hansard, 1772, cols. 559–562

57 Hansard, 1772, cols. 657–658

58 Hansard, 1772, cols. 659–666

59 Dempster resigned at a meeting of the Court of Proprietors on 24 February 1773 after saying he was not prepared to support propositions that surrendered some of the company's freedom in exchange for financial assistance. He would not 'have any hand in carrying them to parliament'. (*The Scots Magazine* Vol.35, p.529)

60 General Caillaud wrote to Warren Hastings on 15 March 1773 (L Sutherland, FN, p.247)

61 Rockingham to Burke, c.December 1773; 'Burke, Dempster and Lord John Cavendish seem to have helped Richmond considerably'. (L Sutherland FN p.248)

62 WWM, Rockingham to Burke – in an incomplete letter written around January 1773; *The Correspondence of Edmund Burke Vol.II July 1768-June 1774* edited by Lucy Sutherland, p.401

63 Hansard, 1773, cols. 807–808

64 Namier and Brooke (E H-G) p. 315 citing Brickdale's Debates

65 Richmond to J.Adair, December 1773 cited by Sutherland FN. p.282

66 L. Sutherland p.271

67 GD Letter '20', 31 January 1774 from London, in which he also refers to Sir Adam's candidature for Parliament at Ayr which he successfully contested.

68 Hansard, 1774, col.1015. See also Lang pp..86–7

69 Hansard, 1774, cols.1151–1158

70 Horace Walpole, vol.1, p.326; the debate took place on 14 March 1774

71 They included Messrs. Herbert, Byng, Stanley, Ward, Jenkinson, Fuller, Van, General Conway (Sec. of State in Rockingham's ministry 1765–66 and a long opponent of North's policies), Charles Fox, Captain Phipps, Colonel Barré, Lord North and Dempster. North's contribution to the long debates on American affairs included 17 speeches on the Boston Port Bill, 15 during consideration of the two Massachusetts Bills and 72 on the Quebec Bill.

72 Hansard, 1774, col.1175

73 Hansard, 1774, col.1317

74 *Correspondence of Ralph Izard*, Ann I.Deas, p.55

75 GD Letter '5', 19 February 1757 from Edinburgh

76 YBL (C942) Dempster to Boswell, 24 June 1769 from Dunnichen.

77 YBL (C942) Dempster to Boswell, 24 June 1769 from Dunnichen.

78 YBL (C941) Dempster to Boswell, 13 April 1769 from Suffolk Street
79 NLS, MS.3112, Dempster to Boswell, 23 May 1769 from Suffolk Street
80 YBL (C938) Dempster to Boswell, 1 July 1768 from Dundee. See also Cole as above
81 WWM, R1/1506 Dempster to Rockingham, 19 September 1774 from London
82 Laprade pp.5–9 for 'Minutes as to Scotland'
83 GD Letter '21', 12 September 1774 from London
84 GD Letter '69a' 16 October 1793 *Thoughts on the Education of George Dempster Jnr*
85 GD Letter '22', 26 January 1775 from Dunnichen
86 HLC, Dempster to Pulteney, 15 March 1775 from Dunnichen
87 See Heming Family Tree
88 *Warwickshire Country Houses* records that the house was sold three times during the 18th century (to Sir Nathan Wright, Robert Princep and Thomas Fisher of Raunston in Leicestershire). It was then rebuilt and subsequently passed first to the Earl of Strathmore and then to one of George Heming's sons, Dempster Heming (1778–1874). After subsequent ownership by a Henry Townsend, it was substantially rebuilt in 1879 and became 'a visually unexciting neo-Elizabethan building'.

Chapter 6 (pp. 100–123)

1   Dempster to Izard, 3 December 1774 and 5 March 1775 from Dunnichen (See *Correspondence of Ralph Izard of South Carolina*, edited by Anne I. Deas)
2   GD Letter '22', 26 January 1775 from Dunnichen
3   HLC, Dempster to Pulteney, 31 March 1775 from Dunnichen
4   YBL (C946), Dempster to Boswell, 16 February 1775 from Dunnichen
5   GD Letter '97', 7 March 1808 from Dunnichen
6   HLC, Dempster to Pulteney, 12 September 1775 from Dunnichen
7   HLC, Dempster to Pulteney, 15 March 1775 from Dunnichen
8   HLC, Dempster to Pulteney, 31 March 1775 from Dunnichen
9   Included as a 'sequel' in GD Letter '22', 26 January 1775 from Dunnichen
10 HLC, Dempster to Pulteney, 15 March 1775 and GD Letter '22', 26 January 1775. The 'salary' may have been income from his shares in the East India Company or a portion of his pension as secretary to the Order of the Thistle.
11 HLC, Dempster to Pulteney, 15 March 1775 from Dunnichen
12 HLC, Dempster to Pulteney, 19 September 1775 from Dunnichen
13 GD Letter '31', 21 September 1783 from Scarborough
14 HLC, Dempster to Pulteney, 31 March and 19 September 1775 from Dunnichen
15 *Ordnance Gazetteer of Scotland*, Vol.II and Alex J.Warden's *Angus or Forfarshire* Chap. xvii, p.201
16 Dempster to Izard, 3 December 1774 from Dunnichen
17 James Fergusson pp 87–88
18 Dempster to Izard, 7 June 1775 from Dunnichen
19 *Old and New London* compiled by Edward Walford in magazine format about 1880. John Opie who painted Dempster's portrait was said to have been a later resident of Berners Street.
20 Anne I. Deas, p.vi. Ralph Izard (c.1742–1804) was appointed by the American Congress to the Court of the Grand Duke of Tuscany in 1777 but could not be received there since the expectation was that England would soon crush the revolution.

Instead he kept up a correspondence with Abbe Niccoli, the Tuscan minister in Paris which enabled useful information to be passed to Washington. He was one of the commissioners who had an audience with Louis XVI in 1788. In his later life he came a Senator.

21 Izard to Dempster, 8 August 1774 from Geneva

22 Dempster to Izard, 5 March and 30 April 1775 from Dunnichen

23 Dempster to Izard, 30 April 1775 from Dunnichen

24 Dempster to Izard, 6 July 1775 from Dunnichen

25 Izard to Dempster, 1 August 1775 from Weymouth

26 Horace Walpole, *Journals,* vol.1 pp.486–7

27 Dempster to Izard, 23 December 1775 from Poland Street, London

28 Hansard, 1775, cols.791–795

29 James Townsend Oswald was the son of James Oswald who appeared briefly in Chapters 3 and 4, and who held the Dysart Burghs seat between 1741–1747 and 1754–1768. He was what Lady Edith Haden-Guest called a 'quasi-civil servant' who kept a place in the administration whoever was in power. His son on the other hand had nothing of his father's career and never spoke in the House. It is interesting to note that in 1769 he is said to have married Janet, daughter of Alexander Gray of Overskibo.

30 Hansard, 1775, cols. 1061–2

31 Hansard, 1775, col. 862

32 Hansard, 1776, col.1146

33 *The Scots Magazine* 1775 pp. 225, 289–91, 402–12, 566–9.

34 EUL, Carlyle Ms.Dc.4.41

35 HLC, Dempster to Pulteney, 2 April 1776 from Dunnichen

36 WWM, Dempster to Burke, 8 June 1776 from Dunnichen. Robert Watson was Principal of United College, University of St Andrews and Professor of Logic. His great interest in Spain led Dempster to call him an historian mistakenly.

37 The episode recorded here is taken directly from the *Memoirs of William Hickey* edited by Alfred Spencer Vol.2 pp.72–79.

38 Sir Charles Bingham, became 1st Earl of Lucan, Co.Mayo in July 1776

39 In the 1760s the Parisian bankers of Isaac Panchaud and Foley had been engaged in all manner of 'bullish' share dealing much of which being to the detriment of the East India Company.

40 HLC, Dempster to Pulteney, (20 or 26) December 1776 from London

41 Chapter 28 of Volume 3 of Hickey's *Memoirs* tells of Wm.Cane's move to Tours in France as the result of rising debts and a writ taken out against him by a Mr Littlekales in 1777. Vol.4 indicates that he was still in Tours in 1796 when he wrote the last letter Hickey ever received from him.

42 Hansard, 1777, col.142

43 James Fergusson p.93

44 HLC, Dempster to Pulteney, 8 August 1777 from London

45 WWM, Dempster to Burke, in June and 3 July 1777 from Devon

46 GD Letters '77' and'93', 2 March 1796 and 1 January 1807. In the earlier of these two letters Dempster gives one name of those visited in Paris. A Madam Rochard married another émigré, Monsieur Brunet Harvoin who was finding life difficult on his officer's pension. (See also UT Vol.4 , letter in 1797)

47 Huntington Library Quarterly XVII (1953), *Franklin and the Pulteney Mission* by Frederick B.Tolles pp.37 – 58

48 The other two Commissioners were Arthur Lee and Silas Deane.

49 David Stormont, 7th Viscount and 2nd Earl of Mansfield

50 Local money in circulation, originally from Tours, and worth less than the French *Livre.*

51 GD Letters '23, 24,25,' in February and '26 and 27' in April and May 1778 respectively (all from France) – from which these and subsequent extracts have been taken.

52 At the time of Dempster's visit the theatre was in an old indoor tennis court (jeu de paume). A new building replaced what was in effect a 'salle de spectacle' some 15 years later. (Archives Départementales du Loiret)

53 GD Letter '24', 4 February 1778 from Orléans

54 Carlyle, Eden and Governor George Johnstone (Pulteney's brother). In search of employment George Johnstone had restored his position with North and was appointed to the Peace Commission, thereby incurring ridicule as a result of his earlier criticism of the Commission's leader. Dempster says in Letter '26' that Governor George had replaced Richard Jackson who was to have been a member of the Commission. The Secretary to the Commissioners was Dr Adam Ferguson whom Dempster was to get to know more closely in his old age at St Andrews where both men spent some of their retirement.

55 See Schoenbrun, *Triumph in Paris – The Exploits of Benjamin Franklin,* Chapter 13

56 William Alexander, Pulteney's business agent, came to know Franklin in Edinburgh in 1771. His daughter Mariamne married Franklin's grandnephew (Jonathan Williams) in Paris in September 1779. Alexander's close relationship with the American Commissioner led to him being used by Pulteney on North's behalf but as soon as the peace was signed in 1783 he left France and settled down as a tobacco merchant in Richmond, Virginia.

57 The talks eventually conducted by the government's conciliatory mission reflected ideas put forward by Pulteney in some pamphlets and several memoranda written by him and studied by the three Commissioners aboard the *Trident* as it carried them to America.

58 David Hartley (1730 – 1813) was a friend of Franklin and a fellow experimental scientist. He helped to negotiate the Treaty of Paris in 1783.

59 David Schoenbrun, *Triumph in Paris – The Exploits of Benjamin Franklin,*pp.203–7

60 Franklin to Gerard, 30 March 1778 (See Huntington Library Quarterly XVII (1953) p.49)

61 Laprade *Parliamentary Papers of John Robinson* pp.143–146 and 186–7. A packet of 'curious and unexplained' correspondence dated June and July 1778 is the foundation of this episode. It contained 'Some Papers on a Secret Service with Lord North, Mr Wedderburn, Attorney-General, Mr Pulteney, and Mr Whateley transacted by me by Lord North's Special orders. Purpose most secret and confidential'.

62 Huntington Library Quarterly XVII (1953) p.51

63 Huntington Library Quarterly XVII (1953) FN p.50 – quoting Wedderburn to Eden, 7 April 1778, Stevens, *Facsimiles* No.428

64 GD Letter '25', 19 February 1778 from Orléans

65 GD Letter '27', 29 May 1778 from Orléans

66 Lord Chatham had died on 5 May

67 GD Letter '27', 29 May 1778 from Orléans. After a distinguished military career,

Conway had entered Parliament, becoming Secretary of State in Rockingham's 1761–2 administration. Dempster and he were of like mind about the American War.

68 Fergusson explains (pp.92–93) that Sir Robert Fletcher (c.1728–1776) 'had been one of the faction on the Council at Madras led by George Stratton which, in 1776, quarrelled with Lord Pigot, the Governor, and actually imprisoned him on account of his attempts to reverse the policy favouring the Nabob of Arcot which they were pursuing. The Nabob . . . had paid large sums of money to the members of the Council with whom he intrigued. Lord Pigot died in prison on May 11 1777, just after the East India Company voted his restoration.'

69 HLC, Dempster to Pulteney, 5 and 8 August 1777 from 71, Berners Street

70 James Capper had been Commissary-General at Madras in 1773

71 GD Letter '26', 16 April 1778, from Orléans. The *Greenwich* under the command of Captain Arthur Gore had arrived at the Downs – the sea between the Goodwin Sands and the town of Deal on the Kent coast – in July 1777. (Hardy's *Register of Ships*)

72 James Fergusson, p347. The Stoic philosopher, Epictetus (c.50 – c.130) – so beloved by Dempster – had a conception of God as the father of men. This was more in keeping with belief in a personal and transcendent God than with the Stoic pantheism he in-herited. Whether he was influenced by Christian ideas has been hotly debated. (Cross's *Oxford Dictionary of the Christian Church*)

73 Hansard, 1779, col.250

74 Hansard, 1779, col.1302

75 Hansard, 1779, col.1179

76 George had told Boswell a year earlier that he had moved out to Putney 'near London because my lungs won't let me live in it'. (YBL (C 947) 12 February 1779)

77 HLC, Dempster to Pulteney, 18 January 1780 from Surrey

78 WWM, Dempster to Burke, 18 January 1780 from Surrey. Dempster feared that Burke's efforts to curtail His Majesty's privy purse would be viewed as a 'trifling' proposal and hardly the object of a serious plan.

79 Horace Walpole *Journals* vol.2 p.290

80 John Dunning (1731–1783) had been Solicitor-General in 1768 under Grafton. He adhered to Pitt in later life, and became 1st Baron Ashburton. His motion in the April 1780 debate included the much-quoted phrase about the power of the Crown. The vote against the government on Dunning's motion was carried by 233 to 215.

81 *Memoirs of William Hickey* Vol.2 p.266

82 By 1780 this 'indomitable Scot' was 'ready with his pen to back up any Ministerial policy'. For a salary of £600, 'the Government found in him a useful mercenary who could tune newspapers to dance to party measures, and with truculent advocacy fill columns, which Walpole called 'columns of lies'. He became the member for Camelford as the result of the 1780 election. (Graham, *Scottish Men of Letters*, p.236)

83 NLS, MS. 16736, f10, to 'J. Home Esq.'. The recipient suggested by Lang was Prof. Adam Ferguson but it could just as simply be the John Home to whom it seems to have been addressed. Ferguson, Home and James Macpherson were supporters of Col. Fletcher-Campbell in the campaign. Writing to Macpherson on 6 August Ferguson says that he was reluctant to find himself against his old friend on this occasion since 'every man of us (was) disposed to wish him personally well'.

84 Laprade, pp.24–5

85 John Fletcher-Campbell of Boquhan was the second son of Andrew, Lord Milton (1692–1766). His father had spent his life managing all the patronage of Scotland as

the henchman of the politically all-powerful Lord Islay (See Graham, *Scottish Men of Letters*, p.177

86 Laprade, p.vii
87 GD Letter '28', 26 August 1780 from Dunnichen
88 Robertson, *The Scottish Enlightenment and the Militia Issue*, p.175
89 NAS, Dempster to Graham of Fintry, 10 September 1780 – Dempster acknowledges 'the friendly part you have taken in my political matters'. Dempster's correspondence with Robert Graham of Fintry – whom he was to describe in his will as 'a man of exemplary public virtue and loyal attachment' spans the period from 1780 to 1811 and well illustrates how valuable an aide and friend he was to become.
90 GD Letter '28', (FN) 26 August 1780 from Dunnichen.
91 Namier and Brooke (Edith Haden-Guest) p.316
92 Namier and Brooke (Edith Haden-Guest) p.361
93 Namier and Brooke (Edith Haden-Guest) p.360
94 Laprade, p.vii
95 Laprade, p.58
96 Minutes of St Andrew's Town Council 1780
97 Rev.Charles Rogers, *Century of Scottish Life*, p.60. Dempster had been in a minority of Scots in his scepticism about Macpherson's claims – the majority of the country wanting to believe their veracity at all costs. He would have delighted in Dr Johnson's aphorism that 'a man might write such stuff for ever if he would abandon his mind to it'.
98 GD Letter '28', 26 August 1780 from Dunnichen
99 NLS, MS. 16736, f.271, Adam Ferguson to Macpherson, 6 August 1780.
100 HLC, Dempster to Pulteney, 12 October 1780 from Dundee
101 National Archives SP54/48/18 & 97 Dempster to Secretary Stormont 21 April and 27 December 1780
102 Namier and Brooke (Edith Haden-Guest) p.316
103 Pasquale de Paoli (1725–1807) was a Corsican patriot who became a friend of Boswell during his travels there in the 1760s. On the outbreak of the French Revolution he became Governor of Corsica but returned to England in 1796.
104 YBL (C949) Dempster to Boswell, 24 April 1781 from London
105 YBL (C948) Dempster to Boswell, 11/14 July 1779 from London
106 YBL (C949) Dempster to Boswell, 24 April 1781
107 Rogers, *Century of Scottish Life*, pp.61–2.
108 The Atholl family had acquired the Isle of Man in 1736. It had subsequently become the base for a great deal of smuggling into Wales and North-west England, reaching a point in 1764 when the Customs Commissioners estimated more than three quarters of a million pounds worth of illicit commerce was being done. They had concluded that the only solution was for the Crown to buy the fiscal rights of the island. The Duke of Atholl sold the rights for £70,000 together with an annuity of £2,000. (See Graham Smith, *Something to Declare*)
109 James Fergusson p.194 refers to Captain George Murray of Pitkeathly who was the uncle of the Duke of Atholl and who offered himself as a parliamentary candidate for Dempster's seat after he decided to retire from Westminster.
110 WWM, Dempster to Burke, 26 May 1781 from London.
111 Hansard, 1781, cols.134–136
112 Hansard, 1781, cols.311–314

113 Hansard, 1781, cols.320–321

114 In 1778, Raghonath Rao was to be lent troops in return for a large subsidy to the Company but other Maharatta chiefs refused to accept him and they utterly defeated the Bombay army. Only when Hastings marched an army across India from Bengal to Gujarat where he defeated the Maharattas was a semblance of peace restored. The French had in the meantime induced Hyder Ali, the ruler of Mysore, to interfere in the struggle and his armies swept across India to the gates of Madras. Sir Eyre Coote's victory at Porto Novo in July 1781 eventually settled matters but there had been all manner of financial manipulation by Hastings and the native rulers to save the Empire. These were matters to be investigated during his impeachment proceedings in 1785.

115 Hansard, 1781 col.554

116 Namier and Brooke (Edith Haden-Guest) p.316; Dempster had voted with North.

117 NAS, Dempster to Graham of Fintry, 6 October 1781 from Perth

118 British Library Add MS. 29143, f.247 and quoted by James Fergusson on page 77

119 Bodleian Library MS.Montagu d.7 Fol.36r., Dempster to Mr T. Cadell, 6 December 1781

120 See Chapter 4

121 British Library The *Catalogue of East India Ships' Journals and Logs 1600–1834* pp.621 and 684

122 James Parker, Chapter 4 pp.395–397

123 Lucy Sutherland, pp.92–93. 'Hereditary' or 'permanent bottoms' described the system whereby a vessel's commander 'could use his command for his own private purposes and hand it on to whom he pleased, when it suited him, with little interference from either owners or (the) company'. See also Jean Sutton, p.72

Chapter 7 (pp. 124–139)

1 NAS, Dempster to Graham of Fintry, 2 February 1782 from Dunnichen

2 HLC, Dempster to Pulteney, 5 February 1782 from Dunnichen

3 HLC, Dempster to Pulteney, 5 February 1782 from Dunnichen

4 Laprade, *Robinson Papers* pp.40–41 record that Dempster's vote 'could not be got' for the debate and division on Sir John Rous's motion of no confidence in Lord North's administration on 15 March 1782. North resigned on 27 March.

5 NAS, Dempster to Graham of Fintry, 2 April 1782 – 'I am about to leave the country' (Scotland); Rodney's victory had occurred on 12 April 1782.

6 WWM, R1/2056 and R117/4/9 Dempster to Rockingham, 23 April and 5 June 1782 from Percy Street

7 Hansard, 1782, col.197

8 Hansard, 1782 col. 1435

9 HLC, Dempster to Pulteney, 3 June 1782. However, by the following January good wishes were being sent from the Dempsters to the second Mrs Pulteney, Margaret Stirling.

10 Hansard, 1782, cols.111–113; the game was usually referred to as 'EO' – a form of roulette.

11 Hansard, 1782, cols.113–114

12 GD Letter '29', 27 September 1782 from Brussels

13 On 2 January 1783 Dempster had hoped to call on Pulteney at Bath House.

14 Perth Burgh Records B59 34/66 and 67

15 *The Scots Magazine*, 1783, p.416; Speaking in the fisheries debate the next year, Henry Beaufoy referred to £14,000 having been voted for relief in Scotland – *The Scots Magazine*, 1785, p.484.

16 NAS, Dempster to Graham of Fintry, 4 January 1783 from London

17 Namier and Brooke (Edith Haden-Guest) p.316 – quoting Debrett, ix.206

18 Hansard, 1783, col.874; Cannon, pp.91–4

19 Namier and Brooke, vol.iii, p.301

20 It was not until May 1785 that he was able to tell Graham of Fintry that he had exchanged his two black horses for 'four bays and a pair of postillions'.

21 HLC, Dempster to Pulteney, 26 February 1783 from Lower Brompton Road

22 HLC, Dempster to Pulteney, 3 December 1783 from Percy Street

23 Schofield's Guide, 1787, pp.31–7

24 Visitors at this period stayed at coaching inns such as the *Bell*, the *Bull* and the *George* or in lodging houses, including those newly built on the Cliff. There was no *Cliff* Inn according to the Information Librarian of Yorkshire County Council.

25 Laprade, *Robinson Papers*, pp.121–3

26 By the 1780s efforts were being made to reduce the number of offices and posts which had so much increased in Hastings' time. Pensions were introduced for men who had no opportunity for higher office and many servants were forced to come home to a very limited 'subsistence'. Army officers found few promotion openings and bankruptcies, the result of uncertain conditions, began to rise. (Marshall p.246)

27 NAS, Dempster to Graham of Fintry, 29 June 1789 from Knightsbridge

28 James Fergusson, FN p.118 and GD Letters '31' and '32', 21 and 22 September 1783 from Scarborough

29 Richard Arkwright (1732–1792) of Cromford in Derbyshire was the inventor of the water-powered spinning frame which was used at the first of his many mills. By 1767 the frame could produce cotton thread of sufficient tenuity and strength to be used as warp. James Hargreaves (1720–1778) had just invented his spinning jenny at this time and some reports date the erection of Arkwright's water frame spinning mill as 1769. He was knighted in 1785 and became High Sheriff of Derbyshire in 1787.

30 Writing to Sir John Sinclair in January 1800 Dempster 'thought' his first meeting had been in 1796

31 Hansard, 1783, col.1301

32 Hansard, 1783, col.1300 – said to be a quote from Howell's State Trials, vol.8, p.1213

33 Although Colin Gibson in his article *Honest George* (*The Scots Magazine*, August 1965) is hardly justified in describing this speech as 'seriously advocating self-government for India', at least in any modern sense, Dempster's argument did reflect some of the imagination that had been so sorely lacking in attempts to resolve the Company's position.

34 Hansard, 1783, col.1302

35 Henry Dundas (1742–1811). That December, Pitt, Robinson and Richard Atkinson met at his house to plan the overthrow of the Coalition and when Pitt took office Dundas resumed his post as Treasurer of the Navy. During the spring of 1784 he shared with Pitt the brunt of the Opposition's attack, maintaining that the King had undoubted right to choose his ministers. When the election came, he was in charge of the Government's arrangements for Scotland. He was only second to Pitt once the administration was confirmed, becoming virtually minister for Scotland and wholly in charge of Indian affairs. He was to hold high office for the next twenty years. (Namier and Brook, vol.ii., p.357)

36 Fergusson, p.122; another Commissioner was Gilbert Elliot, M.P. for Roxburghshire; see Namier and Brooke (EH-G), p.394

37 GD Letter '34', 5 April 1784 from London

38 HLC, Dempster to Pulteney, 3 December 1783 from Percy Street; William Eden was then Joint Vice-Treasurer of Ireland.

39 Glasgow University Library, MS Gen. 1035/165, Dempster to Adam Smith, 18 December 1783. Smith had become Commissioner of Customs.

40 GD Letter '33', 23 December 1783 from Dunnichen

41 The Board of Green Cloth was a department of the Royal Household controlled by the Lord Steward. Originally its business of legal, financial and judicial control within the palace had been conducted from a green-covered table. According to Vol.55 of *The Scots Magazine* 1793, Sir Alexander Gilmour was appointed one of the Clerks in place of Mr Verson and in 1778 was succeeded by Sir William Cunninghame.

42 John Wain, *Boswell's Journals* p.193; Boswell to Temple 8 February 1768

43 NLS, MS. 10787 p.353; Thos. Dundas to Sir Alex Gilmour November 1776

44 NLS, Melville Papers MS.1055 ff, 169 to 172 Dempster to Henry Dundas on 16 and 17 March 1784

45 Charles Cornwallis (1738–1805) had been forced to surrender to the American armies at Yorktown in 1781. He was in England in the interval before becoming Governor-General in India in 1786. He attended the meetings at the St Albans Tavern in 1784. See Earl Cornwallis's letter to Lt. Col. Ross of 7 February 1784 from Mansfield Street. *Correspondence of Charles, first Marquis Cornwallis*, edited by C. Ross.

46 Writing to Fintry at the end of March Dempster tells him that he was 'in a sad state of pecuniary preparation' so far as either the journey to London or the election itself was concerned. A lack of ready money may have carried more weight with him than the state of his health which was put forward to explain his absence from the constituency. Being one of the sureties in the Fordyce case, which still had not been settled – was another cause of Dempster's financial worries.

47 GD Letter '38', 28 June 1784 from London

48 Namier and Brooke (Edith Haden-Guest) p.316 and Cannon, *The Fox-North Coalition*, pp.176–196

49 NAS, Dempster to Graham of Fintry, 25 March 1784 from London

50 Among the casualties that Dempster reported to Sir Adam (GD Letter '34', 5 April 1784 from London) were Lord J. Cavendish who had lost at York and Jack Baker in Hertford. He anticipated that Bing (Middlesex) and Fox himself (Westminster) would also prove to have lost.

51 NAS, Dempster to Graham of Fintry, 25 March 1784 from London

52 Dempster echoing Adam Smith in Chapter 2

53 GD Letter '34', 5 April 1784 from London

54 GD Letter '36', 26 May 1784 from London

55 Although put considerably higher by Dempster, the National Debt was probably in the region of £200 million, an enormous sum by any standard. Pitt's subsequent management of the economy, particularly in regard to increased revenues, meant that five years later it had been extinguished and Consols which started the period at 60% had fallen to 3% at par.

56 Hansard, 1784, cols.1147 et al. The motion was debated on 16 July and the Committee Stage on 19 July 1784. In all, however, many days were spent on the Bill.

57 What the consequences would have been had the Prince of Wales been so dispatched

does not bear thinking about, hence Dempster's reference to the Monarch's other sons. His dissolute habits and thriftlessness were already a by-word. Although Dempster urged parliament to appoint the future George IV as regent, it is clear from subsequent letters to Thorkelin that he 'did not greatly approve of the Prince of Wales'. Fergusson p.127

58 In 1782 the postage rate between London and Edinburgh was 7d, rising to 11d in 1801 and one shilling and a penny half penny by the Napoleonic Wars. Mail coaches had been introduced in England in 1782, thereby speeding delivery somewhat.

59 Hansard,1784, col,1331

60 Hansard, 1784, cols.1332–1338

61 A writer to the *Caledonian Mercury* in Inverness published on 20 and 24 October 1791. (Nootka Sound is in Canada whilst Oczakow is in Poland)

62 Written in 1784, Knox's *View of the British Empire, more especially Scotland,with some Proposals for the improvement of that Country, the Extension of its Fisheries, and the Relief of the People'* was an influential document.

63 *'The Co-Partnery of the Freemen Burgesses of the Royal Burrows (sic) of Scotland for carrying on a Fishing Trade'*

64 Decked, not open, tough Dutch-style fishing boats which gained favour after 1750. The bounty had been withdrawn by the time the British Fisheries Society came into being. Dutch profitability was helped greatly by using busses as 'feeders' to fast vessels ('Jaguars') to get fish to market.

65 In 1777 Dr Anderson had written his *Observations on the means of exciting a National Industry*. This was followed by *Essays on Trade* by David Loch in 1778.

66 An extract from *M'Donell of Barrisdale's* letter quoted by Jean Dunlop (p.19)

67 Anderson to Sir Adam Fergusson, 18 November 1784, James Fergusson p.148

68 Anderson, *Account of the Present State of the Hebrides*, pp.35–36

69 Anderson, *Account of the Present State of the Hebrides*, p.38 'The penalties are so high as infallibly to ruin any of those who, thro' forgetfulness, casual accidents, or ignorance, omit in any case to comply with the letter of the Law with the most scrupulous punctuality'.

70 James Fergusson, p.149

71 NAS, RH4/49/2/266–270 Dempster to Sinclair, 21 January 1800

72 The account of Dempster's visit to Glasgow appeared in the *Glasgow Mercury* on 7 October 1784 and is quoted by R.S.Fitton in *The Arkwrights, Spinners of Fortune*.

73 GD Letter '40', 26 December 1784 from Dunnichen

74 Ian Adams and Meredyth Somerville, *Cargoes of Despair and Hope* p.167

75 Seaton of Mounie Papers, Aberdeen University Library MS.2787/4/2/9

76 NAS, Dempster to Graham of Fintry, Friday 28 January 1785 in which he said, 'We reached Town safely on Sunday evening yet {this) is the first evening I have been able to spare a few minutes to write to Scotland'.

Chapter 8 (pp. 140–156)

1 British Library L/MAR/B/86B.The *Catalogue of East India Ships' Journals and Logs 1600–1834* p.259 shows that the *Ganges (1)* eventually arrived at Deptford on the Thames on 9 April 1785, three months after reaching Cork.

2 Writing to Fintry on 27 July 1795 Dempster recalled the ship 'putting in there in

distress and (its crew) disposing of their little commodities with the savages which has been done with impunity by every East India ship before and since'.

3   *Hibernian Chronicle* 31 March 1785

4   NAS, Dempster to Graham of Fintry, 7 March 1785 from Aberconway

5   NAS, Dempster to Graham of Fintry, 26 May 1785 from London

6   GD Letter '42', 22 August 1785 from London

7   NLS, MS. 3112, f.22 Dempster to Boswell 23 May 1769 from Suffolk Street – 'They are honourable and the most *dégagée* people in the three kingdoms'.

8   Louis Simond, a French traveller in Britain between 1810 and 1811, described Grattan at Westminster as 'old and toothless, and speaking like a Jew, uncouthly and carelessly, but ardently, and with that seemingly self-conviction which is among the very first requisites for eloquence'. Simond's Journal Vol.1 p.55

9   NAS, Dempster to Graham of Fintry, 7 March 1785 from Aberconway. The reference to the house in Percy Street suggests that when the Dempsters moved to Knightsbridge it might have been kept on as Captain John and Jean's London home.

10 *The Scots Magazine* April 1785 vol.47 p.180

11 Hansard, 1785, cols.330–331

12 James Fergusson's commentary, based on the *Scots Magazine* (op.cit.) speaks of 'petition after petition . . . being hurled at the House of Commons during March and April by various groups of manufacturers in Liverpool, Bristol, Nottingham, Glasgow and many other places, above all Manchester'.

13 Hansard, 1785, cols.671–674

14 Hansard, 1785, col.626

15 GD Letters '41','42' and '43', 29 July and 22 August and 8 September 1785 from Percy Street

16 *The Scots Magazine*, May 1785 vol.47 p.219

17 GD Letter '40', 26 December 1784 from Dunnichen

18 *The Scots Magazine*, October 1785 vol.47 p.484

19 Hansard, 1785, col.930

20 Jean Dunlop, her excellent history, *The British Fisheries Society 1786–1893*, p.22

21 Dunlop, p.23

22 Dempster's report to the directors of the British Fisheries Society in 1789

23 Laprade, *Robinson Papers* p.71. In 1784 Robinson had listed Sir Robert Bernard as the candidate at Bedford who might win in what was 'an open seat'. If he did he said that he would be 'pro' the administration.

24 *The Scots Magazine* (vols. 47 and 48, pps.386–390 and 475 respectively) contained numerous articles at the time, providing its readers with population statistics, together with detailed sources and size of government revenue and expenditure.

25 GD Letter '31', 21 September 1783 from Scarborough

26 Hansard, 1785, cols.429–430. John Playfair (1748–1819) was the eminent Professor of Mathematics at Edinburgh University.

27 NAS, Dempster to Graham of Fintry, 10 May 1785 from London

28 Hansard, 1785, col.886

29 Hansard, 1785, col.574

30 Hansard, 1785, col.561

31 *The Scots Magazine*, vol.48, pp.483–484

32 Alexander Dalrymple (1737–1808) had been a member of the Madras Council between 1775 and 1777 and was appointed the Company's hydrographer at India

House in 1779. He took up a similar position with the Admiralty in 1795, dying as Christian Dalrymple said in *Private Annals of My Time* p.28 of 'vexation' after 'being unjustly deprived of his office in the Admiralty, a blow from which he never recovered.

33 *Correspondence of Sir John Sinclair,* vol.i, xiv, p.216. Dempster's note of the conversation is contained in a letter to Richardson dated 18 July 1784 (PBR).

34 NAS, RH4/49/2, Dempster to Sinclair, 21 January 1800

35 PBR, MS101, Dempster to James Richardson, 5 October 1785 from London

36 PBR, MS101, Dempster to James Richardson, 16 January 1786 from Knightsbridge

37 The Navy had by then sheathed the bottom of all its ships with copper sheets as a deterrent to infestation, discovering in the process that it helped increase their speed. During the 1780s the East India Company had followed suit. See Sutton, p.56 and Morse, p.180

38 PBR, MS101, Dempster to Richardson, 12 February 1786. By 'seeing it out' he meant 'building large ice houses on the banks of some rivers from which they can be annually supplied with ice (and) by improving a sort of smaller ice house in the vessels destined to transport the fish to the London market'.

39 PBR, MS101, Dempster to Richardson, 25 March 1786 from Knightsbridge. This time Dempster was at pains to suggest the erection of stone partitions in the hold of the fishing smack so that a mass of ice could be put round the fish – 'ice in such a mass would stand 14 days or 3 week's thaw'.

40 The 27 September report (p.2 col.3) contained the suggestion that the Hon. Captain Cochrane, brother to Lord Dundonald, rather than Richardson or Dempster was behind the promotional efforts that had been made.

41 *The Scots Magazine,,* 3 October 1786

42 NAS, Dempster to Graham of Fintry, 5 December 1791 from Dunnichen

43 GD Letter '41', 29 July 1785 from Percy Street

44 Fitton, *The Arkwrights: Spinners of Fortune* p.75

45 NAS, Dempster to Graham of Fintry, 28 October 1785 from London where he refers to 'being done' with Lanark.

46 GD Letter '40', 26 December 1784 from Dunnichen. Lang states that 'Dempster made his own tour of the Hebrides in the winter of 1784–1785'. p.173

47 Atholl MSS, Blair Castle 25/9/1 p.4 refers to an anonymous memorandum entitled *Considerations on the Cotton Manufacture.* The content and style suggests that Dempster had a hand in its writing perhaps assuming that it would carry greater weight without his signature.

48 Stanley had originally housed a grain mill, cotton goods being produced there between 1729 and 1745 when Lord Nairn sold his forfeited lands to the Duke of Atholl. ('Where there's a Mill . . . ' by Geoffrey Borwick; *The Scots Magazine,* Nov.1998 p.491) The new company was variously described but to all intents and purposes it was 'The Stanley Cotton Co.' The possibility of calling it after Dempster was only mooted to avoid confusion with similar small operations locally.

49 NAS, Dempster to Graham of Fintry, 10 September 1780 from Adamstown

50 NAS, Dempster to Graham of Fintry, 2 February 1782 from Dunnichen

51 NAS, Dempster to Graham of Fintry, 23 February 1781 from London

52 Laprade, *Robinson Papers* (p.101) had marked Douglas down as a member who would be re-elected and 'steadily for' the administration similarly with General Murray, the Perth County MP.

53 NAS, Dempster to Graham of Fintry, 25 March, 6 and 12 April 1784 from London

54 NAS, Dempster to Graham of Fintry, 16 May 1784 from London

55 NAS, Dempster to Graham of Fintry, 13 December 1784 from Dunnichen. Bertram Gardner & Co were Edinburgh bankers who, with Peter Brotherston, had formed a partnership in 1776 to develop the Penicuik mill on 5 acres of land.

56 NAS, Perthshire Sheriff Court deeds; see also Fitton, *The Arkwright Empire*, p.69 et al

57 Fitton p.77 says that Sandeman brought in George Penny who had started making cotton muslins in Perth some three years before.

58 NAS, Dempster to Graham of Fintry, 26 December 1784 from Fotheringham where he and Mrs Dempster who had been spending Christmas there were expected back at Dunnichen the next day. It seems, however, from GD Letter '40' and that to Graham of Fintry (both written on the same day) that the Dempsters returned a little earlier than had been planned.

59 The Duke was at first amenable to the idea but conventional legal opinion was suspicious of the loss of control he as landowner would risk. (See Lang p.224)

60 NAS, Dempster to Graham of Fintry, February 1785 from London

61 NAS, Dempster to Graham of Fintry, July 1785 from London

62 NAS, Dempster to Graham of Fintry, 26 May 1785 from London

63 NAS, Dempster to Graham of Fintry, 1 July 1785 from London

64 *Derby Mercury* 12 May 1785

65 GD Letter '42', 22 August 1785 from London

66 NAS, Dempster to Graham of Fintry, 5 July 1785 from London

67 NAS, Dempster to Graham of Fintry, 25 July 1785 from London

68 Lang refers to him as being 27 in 1781 when commanding the *Ganges* (or 31 years old in 1785).
    It seems more likely that he was born in 1750 and would have been 35 at this time.

69 Harriet Soper Dempster (1785–1810) was known as Harriet Milton before her marriage. Doubt has been expressed about her date of birth with the earliest being c.1783 or 1784. However, a tablet to Harriet's memory in Ashburton Church (now removed) recorded that she was 25 when she died in October 1810 – hence the 1785 date of birth. Furthermore, her father, Captain John, was at sea for three years between 1782 and January 1785.

70 James Fergusson p.290. It is now clear that Harriet married William Soper in January 1801. In the case of Olivia, the record on the tombstone in Java indicates her birth was 1771 and that she died 43 years later, in November 1814. Lang on Dempster (p.270) has nothing to add, accepting Fergusson's rebuttal of Charlotte Hawkins Dempster.

71 See *Historical & Genealogical Records of the Devenish Families of England and Ireland* by Robert Devenish and Charles McLaughlin, pp.285–9 and the Devenish Family Tree.

72 Jacob Cassivelaun Fancourt was an assistant surgeon in Madras. He died at Ryacotta in May 1800. On 14 March 1805 Olivia married Thomas Raffles, Esq., of the Parish of St George, Bloomsbury.

73 Lord Minto's letter of 31 May 1811, referring to Mrs Raffles, is quoted from Boulger's *Life of Sir Stamford Raffles* p.11.

74 Included in Notes sent by Andrew Lang to Mrs Prue Stokes of Biddenden, Kent

75 UT, Vol.1, 1 October 1785, Sir George Ramsay to Captain Dempster. George and Rosie occasionally stayed with Sir George (6th baronet) and Lady Ramsay at Banff.
76 Ramsay had evidently been mistaken since the next voyage of *Ganges (1)* between 1786 and 1787 was direct to Madras and Bengal.
77 NAS, Dempster to Graham of Fintry, 4 November 1785 from London
78 GD Letters '41' to '44' from Percy Street, London
79 GD Letter '89', 18 June 1801 from Dunnichen
80 James Fergusson p.155
81 NAS, Dempster to Graham of Fintry, 4 November 1785 from London
82 NAS, Dempster to Graham of Fintry, 28 October 1785 and a 'confidential' note from London around the same date
83 HLC, Dempster to Pulteney, 14 November (1786)
84 NAS, Dempster to Graham of Fintry, 22 December 1785 from Chippenham, Wiltshire. It seems that George and Amitia may have had two daughters in addition to Catherine. Margaret was living at Dunnichen in 1807 and an Amitia married the brother of Lord Summerville that year.
85 Atholl MSS, Blair Castle 65/5/171, Wilhelmina Murray to Captain George Murray (her husband), 25 December 1786

Chapter 9 (pp. 157–175)

1   Jean Dunlop, *The British Fisheries Society* Chapter 3.
2   Dempster's *Discourse*, p.33
3   Knox's lecture was published subsequently under the title: *A Discourse on the expediency of establishing fishing stations or small towns in the Highlands and Hebride Islands*
4   Hansard, 1786, col.114
5   Hansard, 1786, col.1096
6   Hansard, 1786, col,1378
7   Hansard, 1786, col.122
8   NAS, Dempster to Graham of Fintry, 7 April 1786 from Knightsbridge
9   Hansard, 1786, col.168
10 UT, Vol.1, 24 January 1786, John Johnstone to Dempster from Alva
11 UT, Vol.1, 21 June 1786, John Johnstone to Dempster from Alva
12 *The Scots Magazine*, vol. 48. p.385
13 See James Fergusson, p.151 and W.H.Davenport Adams, *The Story of our Lighthouses and Lightships*. Dempster may have known Thomas Smith (1752–1815) who had been born at Broughty Ferry, although at this time his lamp-making expertise was confined to improving Edinburgh's street lighting.
14 NAS, Dempster to Graham of Fintry (who was at Stanley), 22 July 1786 from Perth
15 NAS, Dempster to Graham of Fintry, 22 September 1786 from Kilkerran
16 NAS, Dempster to Graham of Fintry, 15 November 1786 from Knightsbridge
17 NAS, Dempster to Graham of Fintry, 22 September 1786 from Kilkerran
18 NAS, Thurso MSS, Dempster to Sir John Sinclair, 21 January 1800
19 NAS, Dempster to Graham of Fintry, 15 November 1786 from Knightsbridge
20 This lengthy circular letter dated February 1787 appeared in *The Scots Magazine* (see vol.XLIX pp.96–97)
21 Answers to the Fisheries Society questionnaire. NLS, MSS 2619, p.28
22 UT, Vol.1, 13 November 1786, Guthrie to Dempster. Dempster seems to have had

a special liking for dogs. When in Anglesey the previous year visiting the Parys copper mine of Roman origin, he had heard dogs barking. Concerned about their welfare his guide explained that 40 pair of terriers were kennelled there and used for the occasional amusement and sport of the mine's owners. (Dempster to Graham of Fintry, 7 March 1785)

23 UT, Vol.1 Captain John Hamilton Dempster to Dempster, 18 February 1787

24 Richard Brinsley Sheridan (1751–1816), dramatist and Under Secretary of Foreign Affairs under Rockingham. A friend of Fox, he gained his reputation in Parliament from the great speeches he made during the Hastings impeachment proceedings.

25 Hansard, 1787 col. 274

26 Hansard, 1787 col. 339

27 Hansard, 1787 col. 637

28 Hansard, 1787.cols. 740–1

29 William Law Mathieson, *The Awakening of Scotland: A History from 1747 to 1797* p.106

30 UT, Vol.16, Dempster to Seaforth, 23 April 1787; the proprietor referred to was most likely Dempster himself.

31 British Library Add MS 38221 f.227 Dempster to Lord Hawkesbury 21 February 1787

32 Dempster added that Ireland exported up to 20 million yards and other countries a similar amount, whilst Scotland did not supply more than 15–16 million yards. Broadening the argument, he asked for the northern part of Britain not to be 'sacrificed at the shrine of our richer neighbouring manufacturers in England. For the Manchester cottons and the cutlery of Sheffield (would) gain more than we lost'. If Liverpool were to visit Scotland, he would have 'the testimony of his own senses'. Taxation imposed over a 40-year period was also another impediment especially on a land whose agriculture had none of the inherent advantages possessed by England. (Add MS. 38222 ff.31–36 Dempster to Lord Liverpool, 26 May 1787).

33 British Library Add MS. 3873 ff.120–1, Dempster to Lord Liverpool, 19 June from Duns Hotel

34 British Library Add MS. 38222 f.47, Dempster to Lord Liverpool, 31 May 1787. The reason for Rose Dempster's visit to Westminster Abbey is unknown.

35 British Library Add MS. 38222 f.36, Dempster to Lord Liverpool, 31 May 1787

36 Grimur Jonsson Thorkelin was born on 8 October 1752 in the Hrutafjord region of Northern Iceland. His parents, who never married, came from a family 'of some importance'. The island was then a dependency of Denmark where the population was ill-fed, ill-housed and subject to the ravages of earthquakes and volcanic eruptions, to say nothing of the oppressive and restrictive government in Copenhagen. His early education owed much to his foster parents and in 1770 he was sent to school in Denmark. Passing his first examination in philosophy at the University of Copenhagen in 1774, he spent a short holiday in Iceland, his last contact with his birthplace. In April 1791, after his visit to Britain, he returned to Copenhagen, marrying the widow of a wealthy brewer nearly ten years his junior in 1792. He died in 1829.

37 Elizabeth H. Harvey Wood, *Letters to an Antiquary – the Literary Correspondence of G.J. Thorkelin (1752–1829)* Vol.1 p.40

38 Thorkelin wrote to Johan Bülow (1751–1828) in Denmark the day after he had been released from the clutches of the Customs Officers at Gravesend. (Harvey Wood, Vol.1 p.38–39)

39 EUL, Dempster to Thorkelin, 27 May 1787

40 EUL, Dempster to Thorkelin, 3 June 1787

41 The Duke of Argyll, Lord Breadalbane, Sir Adam Fergusson, George Dempster, Isaac Hawkins Browne MP, Seaforth, and Lachlan MacTavish who acted for the Board of Trustees for Manufactures and Fisheries. Professor Thorkelin appears to have stayed with the party as far as Stornaway, going on alone to Thurso to meet Sir John Sinclair before returning to Sutherland to be Dempster's guest at Skibo.

42 British Fisheries Society Letters vol.1., and quoted by Jean Dunlop, p.30

43 HM Customs & Excise records show that the *Prince of Wales* (one of several vessels with this name) had been built at Cowes in 1777 and at this time she was stationed on the west coast. When converted to a brig in 1789 her patrol area appears to have been between Islay and Port Patrick and her station Oban.

44 Dempster to (unknown friend) 30 September 1787 from Skibo; included in EUL papers but not from Thorkelin.

45 Dunlop, p.82

46 GD Letter '48', 15 October 1787 from Dunnichen

47 *The Bee* Magazine, March, April and May editions in 1792

48 J.L.Campbell, *Canna*, Chapter 13

49 *An Account of the Magnetic Mountain of Cannay*, written by Dempster in *Archaeologia Scotica*, Vol,1, 1792, pp.183–4

50 GD Letter '46', 23 August 1787 from Skibo

51 She was probably the housekeeper whose recommendation of a local doctor was to be used 'should (Thorkelin's leg) still give him pain'. Her husband was interested in running the mains. Fraser's letter of 24 March 1787.

52 George Granville Leveson-Gower (1758–1833), later Marquis of Stafford, Lord Trentham and 1st Duke of Sutherland. Lady Gower was the Countess of Sutherland in her own right

53 EUL, Dempster to Thorkelin, 17 August 1787 from Dunrobin

54 Hugh Rose died at Nigg in 1791. According to James Fergusson (p.167) Sir John Sinclair considered him 'one of the most intelligent and sagacious farmers that the North could boast of'. (See note 46, Chapter 10)

55 GD Letter '46', 23 August 1787 from Skibo

56 A legal expression for the guardian to a minor. The duties of the guardians or 'curators' included oversight of the Sutherland estate.

57 GD Letter '46', 23 August 1787 from Skibo

58 UT, Vol 1, Dempster to Jean Hamilton Dempster, 30 September 1787 from Skibo

59 EUL, Dempster to Thorkelin, 30 September 1787 from Skibo

60 GD Letter '46', 23 August 1787 from Skibo

61 Born in Glasgow, the son of a minister, John Jamieson entered the humanity class at Glasgow University at the early age of eight. Three years later his precocity enabled him to graduate to the logic class and at 14 years old he started his theological studies at the Associate Presbytery of Glasgow. After 16 years in Forfar he became the minister of the Nicolson congregation in Edinburgh, publishing the first edition of his dictionary in 1808. He married Charlotte Watson by whom he had 14 children. He died at his house in George Square in July 1838 (from Elizabeth Harvey Wood's delightful profile of him).

62 A biographical memoir published in Tait's *Edinburgh Magazine*, August 1941 p.523 and recalled by Harvey Wood

63 From the 'Memoir of Dr Jamieson' in the abridged edition of Jamieson's Dictionary published in 1867.
64 St Andrews University Library, Senate Minutes
65 EUL, Dempster to Thorkelin, 19 December 1787 from Dunnichen
66 GD Letter '48', 15 October 1787 from Dunnichen
67 GD Letter '50', 20 March 1788 from Dunnichen
68 British Fisheries Society Letters, I, p.184, John Mackenzie to Pulteney, August 1790
69 *An Account of the Magnetic Mountain of Cannay*, written by Dempster in *Archaeologia Scotica*, Vol,1, 1792, p.1

Chaper 10 (pp. 177–191)

1 Writing to James Richardson in June 1786 Dempster said that a 'Mr MacAlpin was the first man who opened my eyes fully to the superior advantages of the East Coast. The many advantages of a coast situation in general I was always persuaded of'. Who he was, or when such a revelation occurred is not known.

2 GD Letter '46', 23 August 1787 from Skibo

3 James Fergusson p.155.

4 It might be surmised that Sir George Ramsay, his brother, encouraged Captain John (to whom he was always 'Jack'), and through him George Dempster, to think about buying an estate. It is hardly likely that William Ramsay would have sent only one set of auction details at this time, however fortuitous the choice of Skibo was. Writing to Soper Dempster in May 1802 Dempster refers to Sir William as an old schoolfellow and near relation of Captain John.

5 University of Glasgow Library (Special Collections), *Caledonian Mercury* No.10083. Other editions on May 3, 10 and 24, and June 14, 21 and 28, as well as 3 July, carried the advertisement.

6 A director of the EIC (and Chairman in 1797 and 1800), Hugh Inglis was a firm friend of Dundas and Sulivan until the latter's death in 1786.As Sir Hugh Inglis he was said variously to be residing at Beckham or Buckam in Devonshire at the time of the Court of Session hearings in 1790. He sat as MP for Ashburton in the 1802–1806 Parliament.

7 This Langwell in Caithness should not be confused with the much smaller and separate estate made up of East and West Langwell, an enclave in Sutherland to the north of Rogart which was later purchased by Dempster. Correspondence with John Fraser in June 1792 refers to his Church seat at Rogart 'which ought to have been possessed by . . . tenants of Langwell'. The Church of St Callan in Rogart had been rebuilt in 1777.

8 PBR, MS101, Dempster to Richardson, 20 June 1786 from Knightsbridge

9 It has to be said that the total acreage of the Dempsters' estate remains in doubt both initially after the auction and in later years. To the OSA figure of 18,000 acres in 1793 was added other parcels, possibly making 22,000 acres and a block of land amounting to some 35 sq miles in due course. Additional purchases were offset by sales from time to time and all landowners were for ever trying to clarify what they owned and what they did not.

10 The western boundary of Dempster's Skibo estate described here as Port Leak was also referred to as Port Leek, Port Leik, Portenleick or Port an Lec. It was the point on the Kyle of Sutherland at Invershin opposite Culrain. There was an inn near the

present Invershin Hotel which served those (including the drovers and their cattle) crossing the Kyle.

11 The subsequent account was written by Dempster around 1793–4 as an annex to Sir John Sinclair's Old Statistical Account under the title of *A Plan for improving the estates of Skibo and Pulrossie*. It contained some progress that Dempster would have been proud to report, more especially the security of tenure given to the tenants, but the picture was still much as it was 6 or 7 years before.

12 Hon. George Mackay of Skibo (c.1715–82) was the member for Sutherland between 1747 and 1761. He became Master of the Scottish Mint in 1756. His brother, Alexander Mackay of Strathtongue, took over the seat between 1761 and 1768 before becoming the MP for Tain between 1768 and 1773. He is buried in the Church of Scotland in Tongue.

13 Janet Sutherland was the eldest daughter of Major George Sutherland of Midgarty.

14 NAS, RS3/441, ff201v–207r

15 The date of sequestration, 6 years before its sale and during the lifetime of Janet Gray, suggests that she had tried unsuccessfully to sell the property or pay off her husband's creditors, only to find that she was bankrupt and this had forced the Court to step in.

16 After the 1784 General Election a scheme had been devised whereby Sir Adam Fergusson became MP for Edinburgh after he had lost his seat in Ayrshire. James Hunter Blair of Dunskey, the sitting member, merchant and banker, was ousted, with Dundas arranging his retirement. He became Lord Provost after applying for the Stewardship of the Manor of East Hendred, although Dempster thought that he was to be made Receiver-General. (Fergusson p.128 and p.137, GD Letter '35' and Namier and Brooke p.420)

17 UT, Vol.17. William Ramsay to Dempster, Edinburgh 8 July 1786

18 Ranking was having a place on the list of claims on a bankrupt's estate

19 NAS, CS112/34. Petition by Dempster before the Lords of Council and Session in Edinburgh on 3 and 4 June 1790 from which the subsequent extracts are taken.

20 Based on Counsel's opinion of the Court of Session Papers which was kindly arranged by Thomasina Mackay, Lib N.P. of Inverness in 1999.

21 Sir William Forbes (1739–1806), 6th baronet of Pitsligo, had been a partner in Coutts Brothers & Co in 1761 where he met Sir James Hunter Blair. Fergusson, p.171, reports that Thorkelin on his journey south in 1788 stayed with him in Edinburgh.

22 The documents refer to other probably smaller creditors who 'had produced interests in the said Ranking and Sale'. They included agents for William Campbell, Captain Walter Gray (brother german to the deceased Wm. Gray); Robert Johnstone, an Edinburgh merchant; Mrs Ann Sinclair of Brabster and Mrs Janet Sutherland (Lady Brabster).

23 UT, Vol.1, Letter from Wm. Ramsay to Dempster, 26 July 1786

24 UT, Vol.1., Letter from Fraser to Dempster, 24 March 1787 from Dunrobin: 'If your dispute is ended by arbitration or by a proof, you'll find my opinion of the Mains and Fishing (rights) to be pretty just'.

25 Malcolm Bangor-Jones in letter to author, 15 March 1999

26 NAS, Dempster to Graham of Fintry, 4 February 1789 from Knightsbridge

27 NAS, Dempster to Graham of Fintry, 4 February 1789 from Knightsbridge

28 NAS, Dempster to Graham of Fintry, 18 February 1789 from Knightsbridge

29 See Murray, *The Five Sons of Bare Betty*, pp.159–204. The correspondence between William Young and the fifth Lord Elibank, his 'old and infirm' father, is an endearing

story of deep affection between the two men 'at so dreadful a distance'. His 'beloved and adored son' had gone out to India without a 'solicitation' of the Court of Directors whom he regarded as 'a parcel of rascals'. Just before he died he explained 'why your name is Young and mine is Murray. Young was the surname of Lady Elibank my wife, she was of a very noble family, I loved her dearly, and owed my all to her. She took you under her protection, and begged you might take her name. This I thought too flattering for me, and for you, to be rejected. It is for that reason your name is Young, and that perhaps is an additional reason why I love you with more than paternal affection before you was old enough to discover how worthy you are of it'. A lengthy letter to General the Hon. James Murray, his uncle, in April 1779 spoke of there being no letter from his father. He had died exactly 8 months previously, and the news had not reached him!

30 NAS, Dempster to Graham of Fintry, July 1789 (undated)
31 See Peter Gray, *Skibo, Its Lairds and History*, Edinburgh 1906, p.63
32 UT, Vol.1, Letter from A.Ross to Dempster 14 September 1787
33 Andrew Davidson's name, along with that of John Fraser, appeared on the public 'Notice' inviting settlers to Creich.
34 UT, Vol.17, Captain Mackay to Dempster, 10 July 1795
35 Illustrations provide some idea of Dempster's two houses and doubtless drawings of Skibo exist but few, if any, show what it looked like in the mid 18th century.
36 UT, Vol.17, Fraser to Dempster, 6 November and 14 December 1786
37 UT, Vol.1, Sir Adam Fergusson to Dempster, 31 October 1786 from Kilkerran
38 James Fergusson, p.23, refers to Sir Adam's character.
39 GD Letter '45', 10 November 1786 from Knightsbridge. The two friends had almost certainly discussed the purchase, albeit after it happened.
40 Sir James Guthrie of Craigie (1740–1830) was a large landholder in Forfarshire. James Fergusson notes that his second son, who was with the East India Company, had been christened after Dempster, George Dempster Guthrie.
41 George Dempster's will, entered at Edinburgh 6 March 1818
42 Apologizing for the delay in his reply to Dempster, James Guthrie explained that he had sprained his thumb while assisting his quarrier in extraction works on his own estate.
43 Dempster had already discounted this. Writing to Sir Adam, with some economy of the truth, he said 'the distance I think nothing of, the roads being good'.
44 UT, Vol.1, James Guthrie to Dempster, 13 November 1786
45 UT, Vol.17, Fraser to Dempster, 9 December 1786 from Dunrobin Castle
46 Hugh Rose was a Sutherlander born in 1767 in the parish of Creich, the son of the Rev Hugh Rose who later became a minister at Tain. Using profits made from supplying the navy in the West Indies, Rose developed an estate at Calrossie and Tarlogie, becoming a well-known improver. Several references show him to have been very knowledgable about fisheries. His first letter to Dempster is dated 2 December 1786; UT Vol.1
47 Roy had originally worked as a clerk in a factory in Inverness and in 'Forsyth's' agricultural business at Cromarty; he now wanted a lighter job.
48 UT, Vol.1, Fraser to Dempster 14 December 1786 from Dunrobin. The north side of the Meikle to Tain Ferry across the Firth was immediately adjacent to the Skibo estate.
49 Frazier Wall, p.22 and UT Vol.1 – 6 letters from Fraser to Dempster dated 14 and 20

December 1786; 9 January, 15 February, 27 February and 24 March 1787 from Dunrobin.

50 Present day Newton Point is thought by some to have got its name from the 'new town' that Dempster set out to build near the old Meikle Ferry but the name is older.

51 UT, Vol.1, Letter from Andrew Davidson of Overskibo to Dempster, 9 March 1787. The seed supplier in Cromarty was Mr Forsyth who shipped it up from Leith and he was requested to mark Dempster's bags for 'Skibo' and Davidson's 'Overskibo'. John and Andrew Davidson appear to have lived at Overskibo.

52 Hugh Miller, *A Scotch Merchant* from *Tales and Sketches*, pp.303–4

53 Dempster upset his tenants when he only offered 'county prices' for goods from their farms that they did not pay in kind. With a Mr McCulloch at their head, they organized a petition. In January Fraser urged Dempster to give them no answer until the question of changing the 'methods of paying (rents) on this estate during the sequestration' had been resolved. UT Vol.1, Fraser to Dempster 9 January 1787

54 Writing to Dempster from Nigg on 12 April 1787, Hugh Rose advised him to 'wean his tenants slowly from every improper biass (sic) or habit'.

55 £9. 14s. 5d, £4. 7s. 6d and £4. 5s. 4d respectively (quarterly). The Parish of Lairg included the northern fringe of the Pulrossie Estate and the enclave of Langwell above Rogart.

56 The gardener's wage was to be £3 per annum with accommodation and benefits in kind, the lowest rate paid to gardeners at Dunrobin Castle.

57 The long tradition included Sir Archibald Grant of Monymusk, Robert Maxwell of Arkland, John Cockburn of Ormiston, Barclay of Urie, William Fullarton of Fullarton, John Orr of Barrowfield, Lord Kames, Lord Gardenstone, Sir John Sinclair of Ulbster and 'Turnip' Townsend et al. Writing to Thorkelin in December 1787 Dempster acknowledged that many of his neighbours had improved their estates 'to much better purpose', for during 'these 27 years that I have been an improver, I presume, I have spent 20 of them 400 miles distant from my Estate, in consequence of my public duty'.

58 GD Letter '46', 23 August 1787 from Skibo

59 The practice whereby grain produced on certain lands had to be ground at a stipulated mill and a proportion paid to the miller.

60 GD Letter '46', 23 August 1787 from Skibo

61 EUL, Dempster to Thorkelin on 29 December 1787 which includes a paper on *The State of the Northern Parts of Scotland*

62 As above, Dempster to Thorkelin on 29 December 1787

63 As above, Dempster to Thorkelin on 29 December 1787

Chapter 11 (pp. 192–211)

1 EUL, Dempster to Thorkelin, 10 January 1788 from Dunnichen. The two commodities were 'turff and marle' (sic).

2 Donaldson, p.48–9

3 GD Letter '49', 5 March 1788 from Dunnichen

4 *Restenneth and Aberlemno*, Ministry of Public Buildings and Works, HMSO,1969

5 Dr Black to Dempster, 28 November 1789 from OSA for the Parish of Dunnichen pp.426–7

6 See Ishbel Kidd and Peter Gill *The Feuars of Letham*. Dempster may have been inspired

to build Letham as the result of talks he had with Lord Gardenstone after a visit in 1783 to his village.

7   NLS, Melville Papers, MS 1030 f1–4 Dempster to Dundas 31 January 1788

8   GD Letter '54', 9 April 1788 from Dunnichen

9   Donald Macleod was the eldest son of Hugh Macleod and a great-nephew of Duncan Forbes of Culloden

10   Argyll I, p.218, quoted by Dunlop on p.50

11   Dunlop, p.57

12   GD Letter '50', 20 March 1788 from Dunnichen

13   EUL, Dempster to Thorkelin, 27 March 1788 from Dunnichen

14   James Hutton (1726–97), the Edinburgh doctor who founded modern geological theory.

15   EUL, Dempster to Thorkelin, 22 November 1788. This letter confirmed the Patent he had received.

16   Dempster to Sir Adam Fergusson, 3 August 1788. James Fergusson suggests on p. 193 that this was Duncan Davidson of Tulloch who was to be elected MP for Cromarty in 1790, but it may more likely have been one of the Davidsons of Overskibo.

17   EUL, Dempster to Thorkelin, 27 October 1788 from Dunnichen

18   Dempster recalled it as 'last week' in his letter to Thorkelin of 3 August 1788

19   UT, Vol.1, Dempster to Jean Hamilton Dempster, 16 April and 2 June 1788 from Dunnichen

20   Lord and Lady Hailes – Sir David Dalrymple (1726–1792) and Sir Adam Fergusson's sister Helen (1741–1810). She had become his wife in 1770. Sir Adam's brother Charles and Ann Fordyce whom he had married in 1764 had a daughter Jean (1777–1803) known as 'Jane', who married Captain John Hamilton Dempster. Sir Adam's other nieces were his brother Charles's unmarried daughters, Betsy, Allan, Nelly and Kitty. (See Fergusson Family Tree)

21   UT, Vol.1, 16 April 1788, Dempster to Mrs Jean Hamilton Dempster from Dunnichen

22   UT, Vol.1, 2 June 1788, Dempster to Mrs Jean Hamilton Dempster from Dunnichen

23   GD Letter '52', 27 March 1788 from Dunnichen

24   Henry Dundas had been elected President of the Board of Control in September 1784, becoming Home Secretary in June 1791 and Secretary for War in July 1794.

25   A Minute of the meeting of Dundee Town Council on 22 November 1788 refers to the Provost, Alex Riddoch, producing a letter from Dempster and the Council's resolution in appreciation of his services.

26   NAS, Dempster to Graham of Fintry, 17 January 1789 from Knightsbridge

27   See Dempster's 'Thoughts on Master George's Education', GD Letter '69a' 16 October 1793.

28   EUL, Laing MSS, Dempster to Dr Alexander Carlyle, 10 July 1788 and James Fergusson's conclusion on p.193

29   James Fergusson, p.201

30   GD Letter '55', 12 April 1788 from Dunnichen

31   In March 1788 (GD Letter '51') Dempster mentioned that R.Baillie was to come down to Dunnichen 'to supply George's place as an escort to the ladies'.

32   Dempster's *Discourse to the Society for extending the Fisheries and improving the Sea Coasts of Great Britain*, London, 1789, p.25

33 Roderick Morrison had been the factor at Coigach from 1784 and he owned a farm at the Laigh of Loch Broom. He had already himself made a start on developing an infrastructure for the fisheries when the Society arrived.

34 Unfortunately 'the summer and autumn fishing that year failed entirely. Nor did the herrings make their appearance in any great quantity during the winter'.

35 UT, Vol.16, Dempster to Seaforth, 25 October 1788 from Dunnichen

36 *The Scots Magazine,* vol.1 p.619

37 The Second Viscount Palmerston's diary for 23 December 1788. See Brian Connell, *Portrait of a Whig Peer,,* p.191

38 UT, Vol 16, Dempster to Seaforth, 25 January 1789 from Knightsbridge

39 NAS, Dempster to Graham of Fintry, 4 February 1789 from Knightsbridge

40 NAS, Dempster to Graham of Fintry, 17 January 1789 from Knightsbridge

41 Hansard, 1789, p.1137–1140 and p.1309 for Navy Estimates in next paragraph.

42 *The Scots Magazine,* June 1789, p.274 –5

43 NAS, Dempster to Graham of Fintry, 22 April 1789 from Knightsbridge

44 William Wilberforce (1759–1833). Supported by Thomas Clarkson and the Society of Friends, his campaign against the slave trade was not won until 1807. He had become an evangelical Christian whilst on tour in Europe between 1784–85 and continued to press for the complete abolition of slavery throughout his parliamentary career.

45 GD Letter '95', 24 March 1807: 'The Irish Bill, the slave trade (and) the Scots judicature' were the three hidden rocks.

46 Hansard, 1789, p.77-8

47 Hansard, 1789, p.208–9

48 NAS, Dempster to Graham of Fintry, 7 November 1789 from Dunnichen

49 NAS, Dempster to Graham of Fintry, 29 June 1789 from Knightsbridge

50 Stockdale, *Debates,* 22 June 1789 record the Bill (as quoted by Dunlop p.114 and FN 2) but GD Letter '60', 2 May 1792, puts the episode in the 'last year he was in Parliament' (1790)

51 See p.31 of his *Discourse,* Knightsbridge, 16th June 1789

52 UT, Vol.16, Dempster to Seaforth, 25 May 1789 from Knightsbridge

53 John Robinson, MP for Westmorland and Harwich (whose parliamentary papers are mentioned elsewhere in these notes).

54 UT, Vol.16, Dempster to Seaforth, 2 March 1788

55 UT, Vol.16, Dempster to Seaforth, 3 July 1788 from Dunnichen

56 UT, Vol.16, Dempster to Seaforth, 25 May 1789 from Knightsbridge

57 UT, Vol.16, Dempster to Seaforth (-) July 1789

58 Bodleian Library, Bland Burges18, ffs. 55–6, 153 and 160

59 NAS, Dempster to Graham of Fintry, 20 July 1789 from Knightsbridge

60 Stockdale, 17. 227–8, 316; quoted by E H-G. Parliament was not dissolved (and Dempster therefore remained an MP) until 10 June 1790.

61 Captain John's wife, Jean, had been at Margate on the Kent coast where little George had 'uniformly mended' during a two-week stay.

62 NAS, Dempster to Graham of Fintry, 20 July 1789 from Knightsbridge.

63 PS to GD Letter '56', 3 August 1789 from Buxton

64 Dempster stated that the 'mechanised' cutting of timber would cut costs and

encourage the use of home-grown trees and a sawmill might cost as much as £1,000: 'In France and Switzerland I have seen some sawmills . . . and one in Holland . . . (do) the business of twenty pairs of sawyers . . . and proved a source of immense fortune to the hereditary proprietors'. *Discourse,* p.65–66

65 James Fergusson, p.198.

66 NLS, LC.2606(2), Dempster to the Duke of Clarence 13 July 1789. The inscription read: 'This Treatise, touching the building of new maritime towns, and fishing stations, is most humbly presented, by George Dempster, to his Royal Highness the Duke of Clarence, as a means of manning those navies, which his Royal Highness is born and bred to command'.

67 UT, Vol.16, Dempster to Seaforth, 27 September 1789 from Dunnichen

68 UT, Vol.16, Dempster to Seaforth, 27 September 1789 from Dunnichen

69 NAS, Dempster to Graham of Fintry, 16 August 1790

70 Argyll III, p.498 and quoted by Dunlop, p.103

71 UT, Vol.16, Dempster to Seaforth, 17 February 1790 from Dunnichen

72 UT, Vol.16, Dempster to Seaforth, 16 July 1789 from Knightsbridge. The Royal Address was not presented immediately. Pitt said 'the season was too far advanced, but if (Dempster) would give up the rest for this year, he would consent to the Address. I snap't you may be sure at such good an offer'.

73 UT, Vol. 16, Dempster to Seaforth, 10 October 1789 from Dunnichen. The routes put forward were: Ullapool – Dingwall, Ullapool – Dornoch, Ullapool – Portmahomack, Inverness – Loch Ewe, Inverness – Loch Torridon, Inverness – Loch Carron, Loch Lowie *(sic)* – Dornoch, and Helmsdale – Loch Laxford.

74 UT, Vol.16, Dempster to Seaforth,17 February 1790 from Dunnichen

75 NAS, Dempster to Graham of Fintry, 8 June 1790 from Dunnichen

76 NAS, Dempster to Graham of Fintry, 26 July 1790 from Dunnichen

77 Brian Connell, *Portrait of a Whig Peer,* pp. 231 and.372. Lady Sutherland took Palmerston to the Paris art world, the theatre, and dinner with Mme de Stael and Lady Hamilton during 1791 and later arranged for him to have a glimpse of Louis and Antoinette at the Tuileries.

78 Leveson-Gower's *Despatches,* 1885

79 Other sources refer to Treihard as the mad chairman of the church affairs committee.

80 *The Roll of Eminent Burgesses of Dundee 1513–1886,* John Leng, 1887, p.221

81 *Scotland and the French Revolution,* Henry W. Meikle, p.44

82 GD Letter '65', 26 March 1793, from Dunnichen, when he recalled the event in the summer of 1790. The record does not show whether any of the guests at Dunnichen that summer encountered the infestation of rats that led Dempster to take Graham's advice on a suitable rat catcher – see NAS, Dempster to Fintry, 29 September 1790.

83 GD Letter '57', 14 October 1791 from Skibo

84 In her clear summary of Dempster's parliamentary career, Edith, Lady Haden-Guest gives these last words to Sir Nathaniel Wraxall (1751–1831) who was a first class observer and vivid describer, particularly of lesser political figures of his day.

85 The description differs somewhat from the portrait medallion by James Tassie (1788) in the Scottish National Portrait Gallery.

86 *'Honest George'* Bicentennial article by James Fergusson in *The Scots Magazine,* December 1932

87 A letter from William Pulteney to Sir John Sinclair quoted by James Fergusson p.203

88 GD Letter '20', 31 January 1774 from London

89 NAS, Dempster to Graham of Fintry, 11 December 1790 from Dunnichen
90 GD Letter '64', 9 September 1792 from Skibo

Chapter 12 (pp. 212–230)

1 GD Letter '67', 2 August 1793 from Dunnichen. Lochfiethie is also spelt Loch Fiethie.
2 Sinclair's *History of Public Revenue*,1789–90
3 James Fergusson, p.312
4 Broadie *The Scottish Enlightenment*, An Anthology pp.558–9
5 The Rev Mr. George Rainy (1734–1810) had been ordained by the Presbytery of Tain in Creich and Kincardine on 8 May 1766.
6 OSA Parish of Creich, p.343; first published in 1793
7 EUL Dempster to Thorkelin, 25 April 1791 from Dunnichen
8 GD Letter '60', 2 May 1792 from Dunnichen
9 GD Letter '59', 10 March 1792 from Dunnichen
10 GD Letter '67', 2 August 1793 from Dunnichen
11 GD Letter '64', 9 September 1792 from Skibo
12 EUL Dempster to Thorkelin, 25 April 1791 from Dunnichen. Thorkelin's circumstances were to deteriorate for a variety of reasons. His finances caused much worry. He lost his home and possessions when Admiral Nelson, having sunk most of the Danish fleet and silenced the shore batteries, shelled Copenhagen in 1801 against the orders of Sir Hyde Parker, his superior.
13 YBL (L423) James Boswell to Dempster, 30 April 1791
14 YBL (C954) Dempster to Boswell, 8 May 1791 from Dunnichen
15 Also in the party had been Miss V. Fergusson, Miss Nell and Mr J. (UT Vol 2 New Year's Day '91)
16 Charlotte Burrington had a house in Bryanston Street in London which, in May 1791 when Charles Fergusson wrote to the Captain, was about to be put in the care of 'an old woman' in preparation of it being advertised to let.
17 Captain George Nicholas Hardinge was the gallant young Captain of HMS *San Fiorenzo* who was killed in the action with *La Piémontaise* off Cape Comorin in 1808.
18 UT, Vol.2, Dempster to Captain John Dempster in Lisbon, 1 January 1791 from Dunnichen
19 UT, Vol.2, Dempster to Captain John Dempster, 20 March 1791 from Dunnichen. Dempster had withdrawn £40 from the Captain's account with Websters and, under his wife's direction, a garment was being made (not with 'bought cloth') that would withstand 'endless wear'. An account was promised of the condition of the horses which, if they were to be sold, would be better done in London.
20 UT, Vol.2, Dempster to Captain John Dempster, 31 May 1791
21 Miss Allan Fergusson (1769–94) was another of Jean (Fergusson) Dempster's sisters. The party left for Edinburgh on Thursday 24 May 1791.
22 UT, Vol.2, Charles Fergusson to Captain John Dempster, 21 May 1791 from Dulwich
23 UT, Vol.2, Sir John Sinclair to Charles Fergusson 12 May 1791
24 UT, Vol.2, Sir Adam Fergusson to Captain John Dempster 14 May 1791
25 UT, Vol.2, Dempster to Captain John Dempster, 31 May 1791 from Dunnichen
26 Either Dempster had forgotten that the total cost of the two estates had been £19,000 (£11,500 plus £7,500, the Captain's 'own cash') or he expected to be able to achieve the higher price of £20,000.

27 William Ramsay had succeeded to the baronetcy and to the estate of Banff in 1790 when Sir George, his brother and the 6th bart, lost his life in a duel with Captain James Macrae of Holmans. He married the same year and fathered three sons – James, George and William.

28 UT, Vol.2, Dempster to Captain John Dempster, 9 June 1791 from Dunnichen

29 GD Letter '57', 14 October 1791 from Skibo

30 UT, Vol.17, John Fraser to Dempster, 18 June 1791. Ever diligent on Dempster's behalf, Fraser had discounted the possibility of advertising for a drover to visit Sutherland in an Edinburgh newspaper but he was to write to a Mr Mackinnon to see if 'he could recommend a drover of credit to come amongst us'. 'Not a penny' had yet been made by the tenants. By this time Dempster was aware that Fraser was applying for the post of factor with Lady Sutherland; he wishes him 'all success'.

31 The Blairs were members of the banking family that had been one of Gray of Skibo's creditors.

32 Henry Grey Graham, *Scottish Men of Letters* p.202

33 Christian Dalrymple (1765–1838), Lord Hailes's daughter and heir apparently transformed the library into something akin to a family shrine.

34 UT, Vol.2, Dempster to Captain John Dempster, (undated but probably June 1791)

35 UT, Vol.2, Dempster to Captain John Dempster, 8 July 1791 from Dunnichen

36 UT, Vol.2, Dempster to Jean Hamilton Dempster (undated)

37 GD Letter '58', 2 November 1791 from Dunnichen

38 UT, Vol.2, Dempster to Captain John Dempster, 9 July 1791 from Dunnichen

39 UT, Vol.2, Copy of letter dated 25 October 1791 at Kilkerran from George Fergusson Esq. He was acting as advocate for Sir William Ramsay. The legal opinion had been passed on to Dempster.

40 Variously recorded as Spengoodall, Spainzidell, Spinziedale and Spainidaile. The last of these names appears on Blaeu's 1654 map of the area. A plan of the estate at the time of its purchase shows 'Spinzadle'. None of these generally Norse names had any connection with cotton spinning.

41 GD Letter '57', 14 October 1791 from Skibo

42 *East Indiamen* by Sir Evan Cotton, p.33

43 Writing to Graham of Fintry, Dempster explained that 'as we were now prosperous (he) hoped they (the other partners) would suffer me to retire at par. Since that Capt. Dempster wishes to be a partner in my room, I have written to Mr MacVicar to mention this to the other partners'. (NAS, 23 July 1791 from Dunnichen)

44 OSA for Creich, p.350

45 George Macintosh (1739–1807) had been born in Ross-shire and was a well-known 'Highland patriot'. He had started work as a clerk in the Glasgow Tanwork Company in which Robert Bogle (to be a shareholder in the Balnoe Company) had an investment. Subsequently he managed the Glasgow Cudbear Works for the Glassford family, one of the major partnership groupings in the Glasgow Tobacco Trade, sharing the responsibility with Adam Grant, a dyer in Glasgow. The capital for this dye works (cudbear being a crimson dye) had been provided by several well-known families, again including George Bogle, the father of Robert Bogle. George Macintosh would never adopt the spelling of his name with a 'k', regarding it as a Saxon innovation. His son Charles invented the waterproof clothing that bears his name and was an eminent chemical 'engineer' of his day. See Anthony J. Cooke, in *Textile History, 26(1)*, pp. 89–94, 1995 – *Cotton and the Scottish Highland Clearances – the Development of*

Spinningdale 1791–1806 and *Biographical Memoir of the late Charles Macintosh FRS* by his son George Macintosh, 1847

46 UT, Vol.2, David Dale to Dempster, 21 December 1791 from Glasgow
47 NAS, Ospisdale MSS, Dempster writing from Glasgow to an unknown correspondent
48 NAS, Ospisdale MSS, Macintosh to Dugald Gilchrist, 2 April 1792
49 UT, Vol.2, Dempster to Captain John Dempster, 11 December 1791 from Dunnichen. It contains the first reference to the Balnoe Co formed to develop a mill at Spinningdale.
50 NAS, Dempster to Graham of Fintry, 30 December 1791 from Dunnichen
51 NAS, Ospisdale MSS, Macintosh to Dugald Gilchrist, 2 April 1792 from Glasgow refers to 'the plan was concerted when I was last at Skibo last harvest and on Mr Dempster *and the Captain coming here thereafter* – matters were more fully finished'.
52 NAS, Ospisdale MSS, Dempster to Dugald Gilchrist (undated) late 1791
53 GD Letter '58', 2 November 1791 from Dunnichen
54 UT, Vol.2, Macintosh to Dempster, December 1791 from Glasgow
55 T.M.Devine, *The Tobacco Lords: A Study of the Tobacco Merchants of Glasgow and their Trading Activities c.1740–1790*, Edinburgh, 1975, and Anthony J.Cooke
56 OSA for Creich parish, p.352
57 NAS, Ospisdale MSS, Macintosh to Gilchrist, 2 April 1792 from Glasgow
58 Ospisdale MSS, Macintosh to Gilchrist, 2 April 1792 from Glasgow
59 UT, Vol.2. Captain John Dempster to Dempster, 6 April 1792
60 In addition to Wemyss Orrok and James Halliburton (chief and 2nd mate respectively), the crew included five midshipmen (including young Charles Fergusson and John Dalrymple), Louis Pepineux, Captain John's French cook and a full complement of seamen, gunners, carpenters, coopers, caulkers, a butcher and a poulterer, surgeon, purser et al. (British Library L/MAR/B/59 (C)
61 The passenger list shows Mrs Helena (sic) Burrington, Miss Helena (sic) Burrington her daughter, and Miss Ann Burrington. Others included Mrs Julia King, the Misses Mary and Jane Richardson, Mr William Law and Mr Evan Marsh White (writers), and Mr John Orrok. In all there were 28 men, seven ladies, at least one infant boy and three female black servants aboard. (British Library L/MAR/B/59 (C)
62 Henry S.Dickey – according to Hardy's *Register of Ships in the service of the EIC*
63 UT, Vol.2, Captain John Dempster to Dempster,12 April 1792
64 NAS, Ospisdale MSS, Macintosh to Gilchrist, 2 April 1792 from Glasgow
65 James Boag signed his letters 'James Boog' (Jim Bell, Dornoch)
66 NAS, Ospisdale MSS, Macintosh to Gilchrist, 2 April 1792 from Glasgow
67 UT, Vol.17, John Fraser to Dempster, 24 May 1792 from Rosehall
68 GD Letter '59' to Sir Adam Fergusson, 10 March 1792
69 WWM, Dempster to Burke, 10 March 1792 from Dunnichen
70 Dempster was not referring to any writings of his own, rather to the printed set of House of Commons *Journals* of which many MPs would have had copies.
71 GD Letter '61', 15 May 1791 to Sir Adam Fergusson from Dunnichen
72 GD Letter '63', 3 July 1791 to Sir Adam Fergusson from Dunnichen
73 UT, Vol.2, Dempster to Mrs Jean Hamilton Dempster, 2 July 1792 from Dunnichen
74 UT, Vol.2, Dempster to Mrs Jean Hamilton Dempster, 12 June 1792 from Dunnichen
75 GD Letter '62', 19 June 1792 to Sir Adam Fergusson from Dunnichen
76 UT, Vol.3, Dempster to Captain John, 6 June 1794 from Dunnichen

77 NAS, PRO 11/1610/502 & PRO 12/209/1818 – Dempster's will entered at Edinburgh 6 March 1818
78 UT, Vol.2, Dempster to Mrs Jean Hamilton Dempster, 12 June 1792 from Dunnichen. The OSA gives the name as Mr Alex Morison (Vol.8, p.383)
79 GD Letter '63', 3 July 1792 from Dunnichen
80 NAS, Dempster to Graham of Fintry, 16 October 1792 from Skibo
81 GD Letter '64', 9 September 1792 from Skibo
82 NAS, Dempster to Graham of Fintry, 24 September 1792 from Skibo
83 Quoted by George Macintosh in his *Biographical Memoir of Charles Macintosh,*p.124
84 UT, Vol.2, Dempster to Jean Hamilton Dempster, 3 December 1792 from Dunnichen
85 GD Letter '62', 19 June 1792 from Dunnichen
86 UT, Vol.2, Dr Black to Dempster, (received) 24 December 1792 at Dunnichen
87 GD Letter '65', 26 March 1793 from Dunnichen.

Chapter 13 (pp. 231–247)

1   GD Letter '67', 2 August 1793 from Dunnichen
2   The subsequent tale about Dunsinnan's hospitality (taken from *Kay's Edinburgh Portraits*) was one of numerous anecdotes about him. These include two puns mentioned by James Fergusson in his *Lowland Lairds*. When the Duchess of Gordon was told what title Nairne had adopted, she said she never knew when he had 'begun sinning'. More subtly, Nairne himself told of a friend who was surprised 'that so good and pious a man should have committed *suicide*' after his carriage ran over a pig – (*sui*, Latin 'of himself'; *suidae*, 'of a pig').
3   Dempster's coachman in 1812 was William McHarre
4   James Fergusson p.333
5   NAS, Dempster to Graham of Fintry, 8 January 1793 from Dunnichen
6   UT, Vol.2, James Anderson to Dempster, 25 January 1793 from Cotfield
7   Rev H.M.B.Reid *The Kirk above Dee Water*, pp.100–1
8   UT, Vol.2, Dempster to Jean Hamilton Dempster, 27 January 1793 from Dunnichen
9   UT, Vol.3, Lord Gower to Dempster, 3 March 1793. Lt.Col. William Wemyss was a cousin of the Countess and nephew of the last Earl of Sutherland. Both the Reay and Sutherland Fencibles were to serve in Ireland.
10 UT, Vol.3, Dempster to Lord Gower, 9 March 1793. Another appointment to the battalion recommended by Dempster was Alexander Sutherland (as Lieutenant), whilst it was left to Major George Sutherland of Rearquar to name a suitable ensign.
11 UT, Vol.17, Captain Kenneth Mackay to Dempster, 11 January 1793 from Torboll
12 The George Gordon mentioned here may have been an inhabitant of Spinningdale who turns up in 1815 as an officer acquaintance of Richard Purvis in India. He died in 1823. See *Soldier of the Raj* by Iain Gordon, pp.154–6
13 PBR, MS101 Dempster to Richardson 4 June 1793 and NAS, RH4/49/2, Dempster to Sinclair 21 January 1800 from Dunnichen. The despatch of a fresh salmon each month during the fishing season lasted well into the 19th century, demonstrating the regard Richardson had for Dempster's initiative about the freeze-packing of fish in 1785.
14 PBR, MS 101, Dempster to Richardson, 4 June 1793 from Dunnichen
15 UT, Vol.3, 24 March 1793, Dempster to Mrs John Hamilton Dempster from Dunnichen

16 UT, Vol.3, 10 June 1793, Dempster to Mrs John Hamilton Dempster from Dunnichen

17 The report about the *Winterton* would appear to have been inaccurate (UT, Vol.3, 15 July 1793, Dempster to Mrs John Hamilton Dempster from Dunnichen). Sir Evan Cotton, quoting Hickey in *East Indiamen* p.133, tells of the loss of the *Winterton* (Captain George Dundas) on her outward bound voyage to the Coast and Bay on 20 August 1792. She was wrecked on the coast of Madagascar and several passengers and crew perished.

18 UT, Vol.3, George Macintosh to Dempster, 30 May 1793 from Glasgow.

19 UT, Vol.3, Dempster to Mrs John Hamilton Dempster, 4 July 1793 from Dunnichen

20 UT, Vol.3, Dempster to Mrs John Hamilton Dempster, 13 August 1793 from Dunnichen

21 NAS, Dempster to Graham of Fintry, 6 June 1792

22 NAS, Dempster to Graham of Fintry, 7 March 1793 from Dunnichen

23 GD Letter '68', 27 September 1793 (postmark) from Dunnichen

24 The *Rose's* journal shows that her homeward voyage from Diamond Harbour on the Hugli River between Calcutta and Saugor began in January 1793. In addition to 37 passengers there was a 'charter party' of 49 returning soldiers. Calling again at Madras but not Cape Town, she reached St Helena in May or June. The return homeward was in the company of '2 men-of-war, 7 Indiamen, 3 Southseamen, 2 French prizes and 1 [other] ship'.

25 British Library L/MAR/B/59 (C)

26 British Library L/MAR/B/59 (C)

27 UT, Vol.3, Captain John Hamilton Dempster to Dempster, 11 October 1793 from London

28 GD Letter '68', 27 September 1793 (postmark) from Dunnichen

29 According to Hickey, William Dance, a great servant of the Company, was 'never finding himself richer, but on the contrary poorer, at the end of a voyage'. The poet Wordsworth's brother, Captain John Wordsworth, made losses of £1,000 on both his first two voyages in command of the *Earl of Abergavenny* before losing his life when the vessel foundered off Portland. (see Sutton, p.83)

30 Richard Purvis, a cadet in his teens bound for Calcutta in 1804 aboard the EIC's *Sir William Bensley*, paid £95 for his passage and the privilege of eating at the Captain's table. Had he been in the third mate's mess his journey would have cost £55. See Iain Gordon's *Soldier of the Raj* p.51

31 The remodelling of East India House in 1799 included construction of a separate sale room of similar design to the General Court room.

32 Elphinstone was the fifth son of Lord Elphinstone who captured the Toulon forts in 1793 and held them until the end of 1794. His success led to other preferment and after being created Viscount Keith in 1814 he commanded the Channel Fleet.

33 UT, Vol.3, Captain John Hamilton Dempster to Dempster, 11 October 1793. William Moffat had been the majority managing owner of the *Ganges* in the 1780s and of the *Rose*. According to Captain John, Moffat's original replacement commander was to have been James Rattray who had captained the *Duke of Atholl* when fire destroyed the vessel in the Madras Roads in April 1783 and who captained the *Phoenix* in 1786. (See Sir Evan Cotton, pp 34 and 135). Captain Gray was to command the *Rose* again before John Hamilton Dempster's friend Wemyss Orrok eventually became the ship's last commander in 1799–1800. Orrok sailed to the Coast and Bay as Captain of the *Phoenix* in 1794 and retired after commanding the *Lord Nelson* between 1804/5.

34 GD Letter '68', 27 September 1793 (postmark) from Dunnichen

35 George Macintosh suspected that Captain John meant 'to settle in London and . . . be connected with Mr Scott and Mr Moffat as Ship's Husbands'. (UT, Vol.3, Macintosh to Dempster on 18 January 1794 from Glasgow)

36 Jean Sutton's *Lords of the East* provides an excellent picture of life in the East India Company at this time.

37 UT, Vol.3, Captain John Hamilton Dempster to Dempster, October 1793 from London (not to be confused with letter dated 11 October 1793)

38 The Arab stallion was named 'Sheik'. It had been 'selected from all the Arabian horses there (in Madras) by a Col.Floyd . . . as having the finest points. He is black, about 14 hands high, no mark of mouth but not a grey hair about him, and in Captain Claverine's opinion about 8 or 9 years old . . . he has already cost me £66.8s.5d'. A month or so later, when Dempster contemplated selling 'Sheik', he was even more precise about what the stallion had cost him: for his passage to Madras, £100; Madras to London, £250; London to Dunnichen, £23; maintenance, £44; a total of £417. (NAS, Dempster to Graham of Fintry, 28 December 1793 and 9 January 1794)

39 UT, Vol, 3, Captain John to Dempster, October 1793

40 GD Letter, '70', 23 December 1793 from Dunnichen

41 GD Letter '71', 9 January 1794 from Skibo. (He may have incorrectly dated this letter since he was writing to Graham of Fintry from Dunnichen on the same day. Dempster had cut his thumb mending his pen and 'as I can hardly read what I have written' the mistake may have been understandable).

42 See Calder, *The Industrial Archaeology of Sutherland* pp.170–1

43 GD Letter '72', 27 November 1794 from Skibo

44 UT, Vol.17, 17 February 1794, Captain Kenneth Mackay to Dempster from Torboll House

45 GD Letter '71', 9 January 1794, from Dunnichen. Fergusson, p.249 reported that 'one of the tubes' still existed at Dunnichen House in 1934.

46 J.R.Hume, *The Industrial Archaeology of New Lanark* and quoted by Calder p.182. James Watt and his son James Junior both wrote memoranda on the history of room heating late in their lives but never mentioned a system developed by Kelly. Watt first constructed devices for heating domestic rooms in 1783–4, installing them in his own house at Heathfield and at Dr William Withering's house. However, Watt's system was based on using a boiler to heat water and the system here described sounds more like a convection system. Watt certainly met Kelly and in 1788 arranged to sell some mill machinery he had bought to David Dale which occasioned Kelly to visit Birmingham. He was described by Dale as 'a very good mechanic'.

47 Miss Dalrymple's *Private Annals*, p.10

48 GD Letter '72', 27 November 1794 from Skibo

49 NAS, Dempster to Graham of Fintry, 21 April 1794 from Dunnichen. It is far from clear who the niece was.

50 NAS, Dempster to Graham of Fintry, 7 May 1794 from Dunnichen

51 NAS, Dempster to Graham of Fintry, 30 June 1794 from Dunnichen

52 In her *Private Annals* Christian Dalrymple records Allan's death on 28 September after Exmouth and Bristol 'had been effectually tried' as cures.

53 UT, Vol.3, Charles Fergusson to Captain John Hamilton Dempster, 27 May 1794 from London

54 UT, Vol 3, Miss Kyd to Captain Dempster, 24 August 1794 from Elie Lodge,

Edinburgh. Colonel Kyd of the Bengal Engineers died in Calcutta in May 1793. A Captain Thomas Kidd listed in Anthony Farrington's *Catalogue* may, or may not, have been a relative or friend of Captain Orrok.

55 In July Fintry had a hand in Dempster again securing the services of the excise cutter. This time the Hamilton Dempsters were to sail along the Moray Firth to Peterhead with Betsy, Sir Adam's niece, who had come back to Skibo with Rosie after seeing Charlotte Burrington off at Portsmouth . There they met up with 'George and his wife' (probably George and Amitia Heming) and Kitty (another Fergusson niece) who would take Betsy back to Newhailes.

56 GD Letter '72', 27 November 1794 from Skibo

57 The Rev James Roger (1767–1849) was the assistant minister at Monifieth and he held a similar position at Dunnichen in 1803. The knowledge he gained from undertaking the Forfarshire report made him an invaluable source of information for Dempster. In June 1816 he suggested writing Dempster's biography.

58 Rev John Sinclair, *Memoirs*, p.47

59 Rev John Sinclair, *Memoirs*, p.70

60 NAS, Thurso MSS, RH4/49/2, f.253 Dempster to Sinclair 16 May 1793 from Dunnichen

61 Mitchison's *Agricultural Sir John*, p.35

62 Mitchison's *Agricultural Sir John*, Chapter 11

63 Initially Sinclair was appointed President and the *ex-officio* members consisted of the great Officers of State, including the two Archbishops, the Bishops of London and Durham, the speaker of the House, the President of the Royal Society, the Surveyor of Crown Lands, several Dukes, Earls and Lords, with Pulteney among 15 or so commoners. (See Rev John Sinclair, *Memoirs*, p.54)

64 NAS, Thurso MSS, RH4/49/2, f.262 Dempster to Sinclair 24 March 1794 from Dunnichen

65 James Fergusson p.253

66 Rev H.M.B.Reid, *The Kirk above Dee Water*, p.101

67 GD Letter '77', 22 March 1796 from Skibo

68 GD Letter '74', 28 February 1795 from Skibo

69 GD Letter '75', 20 July 1795 from Skibo

70 UT, Vol.3, Alex Colvin to Captain John Dempster, 10th February 1795 from Calcutta.

71 UT, Vol.3, Alex Colvin to Captain John Dempster, 21st December 1795 from Calcutta. The vessel commanded by Captain Gilmour was built by Fairlie & Co. and known as *Bengal Ann* to differentiate her from *Bombay Anna*.

72 GD Letter '75', 20 July 1795 from Skibo

73 Lang refers to values shown in 'Sun' Insurance Co. Fire Policies for the respective mills. See FN 73, p.236

74 NAS, Ospisdale MSS, George Macintosh to Dugald Gilchrist, 1 July 1795

75 NAS, Ospisdale MSS, copy of letter from Gilchrist sent to Macintosh, 2 May 1795

76 NAS, Ospisdale MSS, Dugald Gilchrist to George Macintosh, 6 May 1795

77 NAS, Ospisdale MSS, Macintosh's Minute of the Balnoe Co. partners' meeting in Glasgow on 1 July 1795

78 Stewart, *Curiosities of Glasgow Citizenship*, p.81

79 Elizabeth Beaton, *Sutherland – An Illustrated Architectural Guide*, 1995, p.22

80 NAS, Ospisdale MSS, George Macintosh to Dugald Gilchrist, 31 March 1795

81 UT, Vol.3, Captain Orrok to Captain John Dempster, 29 July 1795 from London
82 Captain Orrok lists the *Rose, Phoenix* and the *Arniston*
83 UT, Vol.3, Captain Orrok to Captain John Dempster, 27 August from London and 10 November 1795 from Portsmouth
84 Rev John Sinclair, *Memoirs*, p.101
85 NAS, Thurso MSS, RH4/49/2, ff.258–262 Dempster to Sinclair, 2 September 1795 from Skibo
86 NAS, Dempster to Graham of Fintry, 24 September 1795 from Skibo. The freeholders of a county met at the Head Court each Michaelmas to make up the voters' rolls and elect an MP.

Chapter 14 (pp. 248–261)

1   The Scottish Development Department described Dunnichen House as 'one of the very best of the smaller mansions in Angus'. A month later, in April 1966, the local planning committee gave permission for the property to be demolished!
2   *Private Annals of My Own Time* p.11 Christian Dalrymple reported that Captain John spent some of the summer in England.
3   GD Letter '75', 20 July 1795 from Skibo
4   GD Letter '77', 22 March 1796 from Skibo
5   James Fergusson p.147
6   GD Letter '76', 14 January 1796 from Skibo
7   UT, Vol.4, Dempster to Captain John, 18 June 1796 from Skibo
8   James Henderson returned to Galloway in 1804, becoming both minister at Balmaghie and factor to James Murray Gordon, later Admiral Gordon. He died around 1838. The eulogy preached at his funeral included reference to his service with Dempster, 'a man who was in many ways a truly great and memorable character, and of no mean reputation in his day, as an enterprising and skilful agriculturalist when the improvement of land was little attended to or understood; a liberal and upright statesman, when politicians were narrow and corrupt; and as a parliamentary orator in an age when the eloquence of Parliament was at its full blaze'. See Rev H.M.B.Reid *The Kirk above Dee Water* Chapter IX
9   GD Letter '81', 26 June 1799 from Dunnichen.
10 UT, Vol.4, Dempster to Captain John, 18 June 1796 from Skibo
11 GD Letter '79', 4 December 1796 from Skibo
12 UT, Vol.4, Dempster to Captain John, 7 September 1796 from Skibo
13 UT, Vol.17, James Anderson to Dempster, 1 March 1796
14 UT, Vol.4, To Dempster from (A.H.G. a land agent in Edinburgh), 6 July 1796
15 UT, Vol.4, Dempster to Captain John, 25 June 1796 from Skibo
16 Ann Graham, the housemaid whose task it was to wake Master George, probably lived with the family. Writing to the Captain, Dempster referred to two women in the household, one of which was his wife.
17 UT, Vol.4, Dempster to Captain John, 25 June 1796 from Skibo
18 UT, Vol.4, Dempster to Captain John, 18 June 1796 from Skibo
19 OSA for Creich (p.341) which the Rev George Rainy had written around 1793
20 UT, Vol.4, The Rev George Rainy to Captain John, 10 November 1796 from Creich
21 Hew Scott, D.D. *Fasti Ecclesiae Scoticanae*, p.82
22 UT, Vol 4, Dempster to Captain John, 18 June 1796 from Skibo

23 Probably the same surveyor employed by Henry Beaufoy in 1789 when the first plan for Ullapool was being developed.

24 UT, Vol 4, Captain John to Dempster [undated] 1796. He thought that an alternative to working the mill with horses might be to burn coal.

25 UT, Vol.4, Captain John to Dempster [undated] 1796

26 GD Letter '79', 4 December 1796 from Skibo. Loch Shin is 22 miles long.

27 UT, Vol.4, *Proposals for working the Coal in Sutherland*, a draft text signed by Hon.Murray Guthrie, Dornoch 7 January 1797 (8 December 1796 crossed out)

28 See Malcolm Bangor-Jones *The Early Story of Brora Coal*, 'The Northern Times' of 30 December 1994 and 6 January 1995

29 GD Letter '79', 4 December 1796 from Skibo.

30 UT, Vol.4, Sir William Forbes (1739–1806) to Dempster, 14 February 1797.

31 It seems likely that Dempster looked further into the value of giving financial rewards (premiums) to his tenants. Details of the silver medals awarded by the Perthshire Agricultural Society were sent to him by an officer of the society in August 1797.

32 Adams and Somerville, *Cargoes of Despair and Hope*, p.157

33 UT, Vol.4 ff.22–23, Notice of Record signed by Captain John Hamilton Dempster

34 Some of the two mens' correspondence between 1782 and 1795 is included in Volume 1 of Robert Southey's biography of Dr Bell. Having gone to India in 1787, he became superintendent of the Madras military orphanage newly founded by the EIC where, due to the shortage of teachers, he developed a system whereby the pupils taught one another, a monitorial system which came to be known as the 'Madras System'. In 1811 he founded the National Society for the Education of the Poor whose schools were to number 12,000. He was buried in Westminster Abbey.

35 UT, Vol.4, Dempster to Captain Mackay of Torboll, 27 November 1797 from Dunnichen

36 See UT, Vol.17, Dempster to Ramsay, 17 May 1798 from Dunnichen 'Captain Dempster has taken the resolution of resuming his former profession . . . indeed, he had resolved before that to accept an offer made to him'.

37 Lord Hailes's daughter by his second wife, Helen Fergusson

38 GD Letter '80', 29 April 1798 from Dunnichen

39 Together with an unknown 'female ward of his wife'

40 UT, Vol.17, Dempster to John Ramsay, 17 May 1798 from Dunnichen

41 Subsequent text makes this plain: 'If you begin as far east as opposite to the House of Sichra (Cyder or today's Cyderhall) you will observe some risings in the sands above the rest where the shells are deeper and better than the rest. Of such risings there are a good many between (unreadable) and Providence and more still further eastward'.

42 Probably West Langwell, the land towards Achnaluachrach.

43 Adding that 'I don't mean the dry shells on the links of Ardnacalk. But those found near the flood mark'. Dempster was persuaded that they were situated 'everywhere about a foot below the sand . . . you'll know them by the sand being higher a little . . . it will be worth your while to take the grieve and a spade with you and explore there some forenoon . . . thrice the quantity ought to be applied as slaik (sic) lime because they are not much pulverised'. (UT Vol.4, Dempster to John Ramsay, 16 July 1798 from Dunnichen)

44 GD Letter '91', 12 November 1804 from Dunnichen

45 UT, Vol.17, Mackay to Dempster, 15 August 1799 from Torboll

46 John Ramsay appears to have left his job as manager at the mill around this time and

may be the Ramsay referred to here. Correspondence at the time, however, often spells the name Ramsey. Calder tells of Mr J. Campbell being the manager in 1800 (see p.176).

47 UT, Vol.17, Mackay to Captain Dempster, 8 May and 6 June 1799 from Torboll
48 UT, Vol.17, Mackay to Dempster, 13 August 1799 from Torboll
49 UT, Vol.17, Mackay to Dempster, 15 August 1799 from Torboll
50 Miss Dalrymple's *Private Annals*, p.12
51 GD Letter '82', 6 July 1799 from Dunnichen
52 GD Letter '84a', 10 August 1799, Sir Adam Fergusson to Dempster
53 GD Letters '85', 14 August 1799 from Dunnichen
54 NAS, Dempster to Graham of Fintry, 20 September 1799 from Dunnichen
55 NAS, Dempster to Graham of Fintry, 7 December 1799 from Dunnichen
56 Bought initially by James Craig and James Muir; Robert Owen was to become a partner. Manufacture re-started in June 1802. Subsequently the business changed hands several times and endured many highs and lows throughout the 19th and 20th centuries, only closing finally in 1989. (See Anthony Cooke, *Stanley – Its History and Development*)
57 NAS, Thurso MSS, RH4/49/2, f.269 Dempster to Sinclair, 21 January 1800
58 NAS, Dempster to Graham of Fintry, 20 September 1799 from Dunnichen
59 Dempster mentions both sums, the former to William Soper Dempster in 1802 and latter to George Macintosh in 1803 where Dempster admits that £8,000 was a 'major loss' not to be compared with that at Spinningdale which was 'triffling' by comparison.
60 Dempster to George Macintosh, 11 October 1803, from a letter in the private collection of the late Dr Iain Boyle.
61 Charles Fergusson lived at Grove House at the junction of Dulwich Common and Lordship Lane. The property was owned by 'The Master, Warden and Fellows of Dulwich College'. In 1791 he was in dispute with the College estate and wished to cut down trees and undergrowth, including two or three willows which grew on the pond bank in front of his house. A tenancy of additional land was also under consideration to spite the possibility of additional houses or offices being built near to Grove House. What was a typical landlord/tenant confrontation had to be sorted out by the estate's surveyor and Fergusson's gardener since he 'was so much engaged in Town as a Man of Business' that he could not spare time to deal with the matter personally. He did, however, suggest that some of 'the Gentlemen of the Colledge (sic)' might pay him the honour of dining with him. (Dulwich College MS. XCVIII, f.130)
62 UT, Vol.4, Captain John to Dempster, 24 September 1799 from Percy Street.
63 The ship index in the British Library, India Office Records, shows construction details, some quite fully, others scantily. Although in the case of the *Earl Talbot* her tonnage is given as 1428 tons, it has been the habit of other commentators to use a figure of 1200 tons for the *Earl Talbot* and other ships with whom she sailed such as *Ganges* (3), *Cirencester* and *Canton*.
64 UT, Vol.4, Dempster to William Soper Dempster, 3 February 1802 from Dunnichen
65 Writing to William Soper Dempster on 10 May 1802, Dempster describes the attractions of the estate at Skibo that his wife and he were to inherit. In saying 'if Harriet never saw the estate and cannot describe it to you' Dempster leaves the matter open.
66 The *Dublin* of 786 tons had undertaken 6 voyages between 1785 and 1797. The last,

under Captain William Smith, had been to the Coast and Bay. (J.Sutton, Appendix 9 and Sir Evan Cotton, p.187)

Chapter 15 (pp. 262–278)

1 GD Letter '88', 30 December 1800 from Dunnichen

2 James Headrick (1759–1841) was an expert writer on agriculture who had assisted Sir John Sinclair in the compilation of the OSA. He became minister of Dunnichen Church in 1807.

3 NAS, Thurso MSS, RH4/49/2, f.264 Dempster to Sinclair, 4 January 1800 from Dunnichen

4 Marine Department records in Bombay confirm this date. Dempster quotes a report that Captain John had reached Bombay on 25 May. An August date was shown in the Cleland Petition.

5 A respondentia loan is one made against a cargo and repayable provided the goods arrive safely.

6 UT, Vol.14, letter from Mr Storie W.S contained a copy of Captain John's financial statement sent round to Philip Dundas in Bombay on the 13 August 1800.

7 A copy of the Petition in December 1812 by the Rev John Cleland of Newton Ardes in Ireland against Mrs Harriet Dempster and the Captain's trustees which started lengthy hearings in the Court of Session, is included in Vol.11 of the Dempster Papers held by the University of Toronto. The respondents, however, did not admit that Captain Dempster 'owed a single sixpence to Mr Cleland'.

8 In this part of India a candy was approximately 784lbs. It had been intended that the cargo should have been wholly of cotton but insufficient was available and the sandalwood filled the gap.

9 GMA, Letter to the Secret Committee of the Court of Directors, London, 15 June 1800 (p373–5) Bombay Castle

10 GMA, Letter to the Court of Directors, London, 29 November 1800 (p.370) Bombay Castle. Captains Robertson, Gray and Lushington of the *Cirencester*, *Ganges* and *Canton* respectively were liable for smaller sums. It had been agreed 'on condition of their entering into bonds to refund the amount with interest at the rate of 9 per cent per annum; in the event of the assistance thus extended to them respectively being disapproved of by Your Honourable Court: to exempt them from all charges on that account'.

11 GMA, Surat Factory Records No.39, Pt III 4 June 1800 (p.494–7)

12 See Sir Evan Cotton, pp.178–9. Philip Dundas had commanded the *Melville Castle* for three voyages between 1787 and 1793. He held the rank of Superintendent in 1800 and was a Member of the Marine Board in Bombay.

13 NLS, MS 5319, ff.157–8 Letter from Dempster to Miss Smith, 5 July 1813, the daughter of Mr William Smith MP for Sudbury and then Norwich who had replaced Lord Suffield on the board of the Fisheries Society in 1789.

14 The will was dated the 15 October 1799. Alexander Guthrie was the eldest son of his great friend James Guthrie of Guthrie & Storey, the Edinburgh solicitors. Other trustees included James Fergusson (Sir Adam's nephew), Sir William Ramsay of Banff and George Blair 'late of Arniston; at present in India'. In the event, neither Fergusson nor Ramsay were able to act.

15 GMA, Letter to the Court of Directors, 15 September 1800 (pp.52–53) Bombay Castle

16 NLS, MS 5319 op.cit

17 Pratas Islands, a rocky group in the South China Sea, midway between Hong Kong and the channel to the north of the Philippines. The Paracel Islands on the other hand are some 250 miles south-east of Hainan Island.

18 GD Letter '89', 18 June 1801 from Dunnichen. Fergusson corrected 'Malaga' to 'Malacca'.

19 GMA, *Bombay Courier* of Saturday 14 February 1801

20 Jean Sutton, *Lords of the East*, p.147. *Intrepid* and *Comet* were commanded by Lieutenants George Roper and William Henry respectively

21 GMA, Supplement to the *Bombay Courier* 15 August 1801

22 GMA, Marine Board Diaries 17 March 1802 p.92

23 GMA, *Bombay Courier* 30 October 1802

24 NLS, MS 5319, ff.157–8 Letter from Dempster to Miss Smith, 5 July 1813.

25 British Library Add MS 38311 f.56 and 68, Lord Liverpool to Dempster, 22 March, 26 March and 16 June 1800. The second Lord Liverpool was Prime Minister between 1812 and 1827.

26 Dempster Heming was the 4th son of Mrs Dempster's brother George who had been at Rugby School and who between 1797–9 had attended St Andrews University, spending his holidays with the Dempsters. He was called to the bar in 1807 and died aged 96 in 1874. In a letter to Sinclair in 1807 Dempster described him as 'so comical a dog that I call him sometimes young Dunning'.

27 GD Letter '86', 27 May 1800 from Dunnichen

28 Mr J.C.Smyth, Sir Alexander Douglas of Dundee and Dr John Adam of Forfar (GD Letter '87', 17 November 1800 from Dunnichen

29 GD Letters '87 and 88', 17 November and 30 December 1800 from Dunnichen

30 NAS, Dempster to Graham of Fintry, 17 March 1801 from Dunnichen

31 UT, Vol.4, Dempster to William Soper, 3 February 1802 from Dunnichen

32 GD Letter '89', 18 June 1801 from Dunnichen

33 British Library OIOC, J/1/10 Haileybury Records, ff.89–92

34 Between 1803 and 1806 Wm. Soper is listed 'at home' in the *East India Register and Directories* by his married name of Soper Dempster. It seems that Soper's return to England had been treated by the Company as sick leave and that he had been expected to return to Bombay in due course.

35 GD Letter '90', 1 January 1804 from Dunnichen

36 NLS, MS 5319 ff.141–2 Dempster to William Smith, 23 July 1801

37 NLS, MS 5319, f.143 Dempster to William Smith, 14 August 1805 from Dunnichen

38 NAS, Dempster to Graham of Fintry, 22 January 1802 from Dunnichen

39 Writing to Sir Adam in 1804 (GD '90') Dempster said 'Before the prospect of her noble succession and during her father and brother's lifetime, Mr Soper had taken a fancy for her and married her, so that he is exempted from all suspicion of fortune hunting'.

40 UT, Vol.4, Dempster to William Soper, 3 February 1802 from Dunnichen

41 NLS, MS 5319, f.158, Dempster to Miss Smith, 5 July 1813.

42 UT, Vol.4, Thomas Gordon to Dempster, 20 April 1802 from Dunnichen

43 UT, Vol.4, Dempster to William Soper, 10 May 1802 from Dunnichen

44 NLS, MS 5319, f.157, Dempster to Miss Smith, 5 July 1813.

45 NAS, Dempster to Graham of Fintry, 13 March 1802 from Dunnichen

46 GD Letter '90', 1 January 1804 from Dunnichen

47 Guthrie reported that Soper's agent, Mr L.W.Walford of Greens & Walford, London Wall, had told him that there was a chance of the couple returning home soon – always assuming his affairs in India permitted it. (UT Vol.4 Guthrie to William Soper, 1 July 1802 from Edinburgh)

48 Rose was the tacksman at Skibo Farm and General Baillie understood that 'a decree of removal had been issued against Mr Rose'. (UT Vol.4, General Baillie to Dempster 12 May 1802 from Peterhead)

49 NAS, Thurso MSS, RH4/49/2, f.272, Dempster to Sinclair, 5 December 1802 from Dunnichen

50 The even and unaltered script of the text included in his letter to Sir John suggests that it was being copied from original notes, perhaps written up by his amanuensis, the Rev James Roger.

51 NAS, Thurso MSS, RH4/49/2, ff.273–277 Dempster to Sinclair, 10 April 1802

52 Robert Owen, *The Life of Robert Owen, by Himself*, p.104

53 Dr Iain T.Boyle, Letter from Dempster to Macintosh, 11 October 1803

54 Dempster greatly treasured the snuff box, adorned as it was with a stone from the quartz family – generally white or bluish-white in colour and translucent, bequeathing it in his will to General Hunter of Burnside whose son had been murdered in India (see Chapter 13).

55 UT, Vol.4, Dempster to William Soper at Surat, Bombay, 1 October 1802 from Dunnichen. Also 'we put on mourning the 30th October' from Miss Dalrymple's *Private Annals* p. 11.

56 James Watt (1736–1819), the Scottish inventor of steam locomotion. He had retired in 1800 to Heathfield House outside Birmingham. His son (also James, 1769–1848) was to fit an engine to the first English steamer to leave port, the *Caledonia*, in 1817.

57 Birmingham City Archives JWP4/27 and JWP/LB3. Dempster to James Watt, 18 January 1803; Sir John Sinclair to James Watt, 21 January 1803, and James Watt to Dempster, 30 January 1803.

58 British Library Add.MS.22901, f.154

59 UT, Vol.4, Dempster to Soper and Harriet 19 December 1802 from Dunnichen

60 Philip Dundas married a daughter of Sir John Wedderburn by whom he had two children. He died at sea in 1807 and his second wife soon after in Bengal.

61 Thomas Gordon had lost his wife in 1787 and would die the next year (1804) in London. He was given 'a grand funeral' on 5 December. His remains were interred in Paddington Burial Ground.

62 UT, Vol.4, Dempster to the Sopers, 21 April 1803 from Dunnichen

63 A memorial in Ashburton Church dates their deaths as 1792 and 1795.

64 See Ishbel Kidd and Peter Gill's *The Feuars of Letham* p.9. Scottish barons had usually delegated the authority they gained from the feudal system introduced during the reigns of David I and William the Lion in the 12th century. A Baron bailiff or 'baron-bailie' stood in for their masters, officiating the courts each barony was required to have. Letham's first Baron Bailie and 'Preses' or Provost was Nichol Ford who held the post until 1811.

65 *The Feuars of Letham*, p.10

66 Letter from Dempster to Macintosh, 14 May 1803 from Dunnichen quoted by George Macintosh in his *Biographical Memoir of Charles Macintosh*, p.125

67 Thomas Telford (1757–1834), the great Scottish civil engineer, had been commissioned by the government in 1801 to report on public works required in Scotland.

68 Letter from Sir William Pulteney to Thomas Telford, 19 November 1803 (Macintosh's *Memoir* p.123)

69 Letters from Thomas Telford to Macintosh, 19 November and 2 December 1803 (Macintosh's *Memoir* p.123)

70 *The Municipal History of the Royal Burgh of Dundee*, p.127. It would seem that the petition was to be sent to Sir David Carnegie, the Forfarshire MP in the absence of Mr David Scott, the Member for Dempster's old constituency.

71 James Fergusson p.290

72 NLS, MS.19894. The hand-written minutes of the society refer to it being called the 'Lunan & Vinney Water Farmer Society' when it met on 4 July 1803. (NLS, MS. 1929)

73 Those minuted as attending the inaugural meeting (in addition to Dempster and 'William Soper-Dempster Esq., of Pulrossie') were James Guthrie of Craigie, Patrick Carnegie of Lower, Charles Gardyne of Middleton, Col. Hunter of Burnside, William Henderson of Lawton, James Mudie of Pitmuis, Charles Gray of Carse, George Chapline of Colliston, Wm Scott of Reswallie, David Dickson of Clocksbriggs, Capt Dickson, Mr Nichol Ford of Dunnichen Mains, Mr Henry Puller of [Lourie], Mr Alexander Dickson of Weems, Mr Thomas Milne of Poole, Mr Thomas Scott Senior and Mr John Scott of [Milldens], Mr John Cranston, Mr Wm Webster of Restenneth, Rev. Thomas Wright of Rescobie, Mr David Langlands of Balmadies, Mr James Scott of Waukmills, Mr David Ford of Gask, Mr Robert Scott of Reswallie, Mr James Weir of Prepock, Mr Thomas Scott of Ligarton, Mr Peter Hutton of Craichy Mill, Mr James Scott of Chapelton, Mr George Ford of East Mains of Dunnichen, Mr David Strachan of Finsbegg, Mr James Brown of Conanside and the Rev James Roger.

74 Charles Roger. *Social Life in Scotland from Early to Recent Times*, vol 2 pp398–404.

75 The hyphenated version of the name Soper Dempster (as with other branches of the family) was not common at the beginning of the 19th century.

76 GD Letter '90', 1 January 1804 from Dunnichen

77 George Soper Dempster (1804–1889)

78 Letter from Dempster to Macintosh, 15 September 1803 from Skibo (Macintosh *Memoir* pp.125–6)

79 GD Letter '90', 1 January 1804 from Dunnichen

80 Dempster to George Macintosh, 11 October 1803 (Boyle Archive). He also reported that the carriage road almost reached Laidmore – 'You may drive a Post Chaise from Muckle Ferry to Invershin'.

81 GD Letter '90', 1 January 1804 from Dunnichen. John Dempster had died on 18 November 1803.

82 Among Fintry's children whom Dempster would have known were: Robert, the eldest son who was assassinated in India in 1799; Thomas, who married the daughter of Admiral Dundas of Dundas Manor; and James who died at Broughty Ferry in 1804. Dempster visited the five surviving daughters in 1816.

83 Bequest No.5 from the Will of George Dempster, and its codicil of 2 May 1812, entered at Edinburgh and London.

84 Thomas Graham (1748–1843) was aide-de-camp to Sir John Moore in the Peninsular War fighting in all the major battles. He was created Lord Lynedoch of Balgowan in 1814.

85 James Fergusson p.295 and Miss Dalrymple's *Private Annals* p.18

86 David Dale was to die at Rosebank, his estate near Cambuslang, on 17 March 1806.

87 The fortune of the 3rd Duke of Bridgwater – Francis Egerton – had come from invest-ments in industry, construction and trade. Up to 1803 any surplus from the Sutherland estate was used to finance Earl Gower's political career and sustain a lifestyle he and Elizabeth had adopted in keeping with the accepted extravagances of the Georgian era. Money was not always in great supply with many tenants unable to pay their rents.

88 Letter from Dempster to Macintosh, 10 May 1804 from Dunnichen (Macintosh *Memoir* p.125)

89 He was created 1st Duke of Sutherland in 1833, six months before he died. Elizabeth, his wife, became Duchess/Countess.

90 UT, Vol.5, Macintosh to Dempster, 11 December 1805 from Glasgow. (This and the subsequent paragraph)

91 Macintosh *Memoir* p. 124

Chapter 16 (pp. 279–297)

1 'Snatching time' from his 'military duty and drunkenness', Dempster wrote to James, son of John Johnstone of Alva, on 19 March 1805 from Dunnichen, adding that he now weighed 18 stone 10lbs. (Boyle Archive)

2 Sir John Sinclair's *Correspondence, Vol. 1* pp.358–9

3 NLS, MS.5319 ff.143–6 Dempster to Wm Smith, 14 August 1805 from Dunnichen

4 GD Letter '91', 12 November 1804 from Dunnichen

5 Wurtzburg's *Raffles of the Eastern Isles* p.21 Oxford in Asia Paperback edition. As Raffles was to tell his cousin, he was not many months in Penang before further promotion was forthcoming and his salary rose to £2,000 a year.

6 *Ganges* (3) left for Penang in April 1805. It seems that at Madras the party transferred to the *Warley* for the last leg to Penang. See *Life of Sir Stamford Raffles* by Demetrius Charles Boulger, 1973 edition pp.7–9 and 15.

7 Abdulla's memoirs were translated by J.T.Thompson. See *Historical & Genealogical Records of the Devenish Families of England and Ireland* by Robert Devenish and Charles McLaughlin, p.287

8 Dr George Williamson's life of Andrew and Nathaniel Plimer, published in 1903, contains an annex (Appendix VII) indicating that Lady Metcalf, without a second 'e', of 8, John Street, Mayfair possessed three portraits, not by Andrew, as had been assumed, but by Nathaniel Plimer. They were listed as *Two ladies and a Gentleman, Members of the family of Dempster of Skibo and Dunnichen, but names unknown*. They had been exhibited at Moncorvo House. In 1933 one or two items from the aforesaid Metcalf collection were put into a Sotheby sale in London by the executors of Lady Mount Stephen who lived at 17, Carlton House Terrace until her death. All three portraits had by then acquired some further identification. However, attribution to Andrew, rather than Nathaniel, continued and the text beneath the illustrations wrongly described Mrs Raffles as Mrs Dempster's sister. Katharine Hawkins Dempster (1830–1911) who had married Sir Theophilus Metcalfe had been the orig-inal collector of the miniatures concerned.

9 UT, Vol. 5, A Mary Campbell, writing to Harriet in February 1805, adjures her not to tell her husband he was 'handsome', for 'men are naturally so vain and it is sinful to feed vanity'. Nothing more is known about her.

10 NAS, Thurso MSS, RH4/49/2, f.278–280 Dempster to Sinclair, 13 February 1805 from Dunnichen

11 Sir John Leslie (1766–1832) invented a differential thermometer, a hygrometer and a photometer and had published *An Experimental Inquiry into Heat* in 1804 to which Dempster referred in his letter to Sinclair and for which he received the Rumford medal of the Royal Society. Dempster described it 'as one of the most valuable works that has come into my hands since Dr Hutton's *Theory of the Earth*' (the Scottish geologist). Although he was apparently a candidate for the Chair of Natural Philosophy (according to Dempster – GD Letter '92') he was appointed to the Chair of Mathematics and only became Professor of Natural Philosophy in 1819.

12 James Fergusson pp.297–298. The letter from Sir Adam Fergusson to Dempster in February 1805 was one of only two in the possession of Sir James in 1931.

13 James Fergusson *Lowland Lairds* p.105

14 Although Lord Breadalbane assumed the governorship of the British Fisheries Society on Pulteney's death, William Smith exercised effective control subsequently as Deputy Governor. His appointment as a Commissioner for Highland Roads and Bridges dated from 1802, (Jean Dunlop p.130). Five directors of the Fisheries Society made up the seven-man commission.

15 NLS, MS.5319 ff.143–148, Dempster to William Smith, 14 August 1805 from Dunnichen

16 Jean Dunlop p.135

17 Later stated as £10,000

18 NLS, MS.5319 ff.143–8, Dempster to William Smith, 14 August 1805 from Dunnichen

19 UT, Vol.5, Telford to Dempster, 9 November 1805 from Salop

20 *The Scots Magazine* gives the date as 24 December and refers to her as 'Mrs' Ann Dempster. It is not known whether she married. The only known correspondence is a letter written from Bath to Captain John ('her dear brother') in UT, Vol.3, 28 October 1795 where she talks of rheumatism being 'her old enemy'.

21 The Rev Samuel Bracebridge Heming was the eldest son of George Heming (1733–1802) and Amitia, the 2nd daughter of Dr Bracebridge who married in Jamaica on 19 September 1769. His father died at Ravenstone in Leicestershire in January 1802 and his mother, Amitia, was living at Wedington in 1810. He inherited the estates at Lindley, Rowden and Fenny Stratford in 1801. He was an Honorary Fellow of Caius College, Cambridge; Rector and Lord of the Manor of Wed(d)ing in Warwickshire and the Manor of Lindley and Drayton. See *History and Antiquities of Leicestershire* by John Nichols.

22 NLS, MS.5319 f.227, Dempster to Samuel Heming, 20 July 1806 from Dunnichen

23 The abandoned mill and adjacent property were bought for £2,000 by Robert Mackid in 1815 with the intention of turning parts of the land into a tannery. A.J. Cooke suggests that Mackid's role as Sheriff-substitute at the trial of Patrick Sellar probably prevented him pursuing this development. (*Cotton and the Highland Clearances* p.93)

24 David Dale died on 17 March and George Macintosh was 'seized of an illness of an inflammatory nature' at Moffat in July 1807 after a journey to England and died there on the 26th in his 68th year.

25 Letter from Dempster to Macintosh, 2 February 1806 (Macintosh *Memoir* p.126–7)

26 NAS,Thurso MSS, RH4/49/2, f.282–3, Dempster to Sinclair 28 February 1806 from Dunnichen. As Mitchison (p.214) says, Dempster had enough good sense without any

specialized knowledge to believe that Macpherson had never found even one word of Ossian in writing.

27 NAS,Thurso MSS, RH4/49/2, f.284–6, Dempster to Sinclair 21 February 1806 from Dunnichen

28 Lord Grenville had assumed office on the death of Pitt and formed the ministry of 'All the Talents'. Stamp Duty was £4 for one acre and only £19 for land over 50 acres

29 Andreas Georg Dempster Thorkelin seems to have become a copyist in his father's office at the State Archives and died 'of drink' in 1826.

30 EUL, Dempster to Thorkelin, 4 April 1806 and 12 August 1807 from Dunnichen

31 NLS, MS.5319 f.227, Dempster to Samuel Heming, 20 July 1806 from Dunnichen

32 UT, Vol.5, Dempster to Soper Dempster 28 July 1806 from Broughty Ferry

33 GD Letter '93', 1 January 1807 from Dunnichen

34 NAS, Thurso MSS, RH4/49/2, f.289, Dempster to Sinclair 30 June 1807 from Dunnichen

35 Dempster actually says 'my old ward and our French companion Charlotte (Burrington)'. Such a description of Charlotte is confusing. One explanation might be that her mother, Colonel George Burrington's first wife about whom nothing is known, had been French.

36 NAS,Thurso MSS, RH4/49/2, f.287–8, Dempster to Sinclair 2 March 1807 from Dunnichen

37 GD Letter '96', 8 August 1807 from Dunnichen

38 Dempster wanted Sinclair to establish whether it was true that the strain discovered by Sir Joseph Banks, the botanist, was available for sale.

39 NAS, Thurso MSS, RH4/49/2, f.298 Dempster to Sinclair 17 July 1807 from Dunnichen

40 At the instigation of Mr Storie (Soper Dempster's lawyer) Lord Henry Petty was able to obtain the support of the President of the Lord Advocates. (UT Vol.7 Storie to Soper Dempster, 17 February 1807 and subsequent copy of the 'Draught of a Bill')

41 UT, Vol.7, Dempster to Soper Dempster, 27 October 1807 from Dunnichen

42 UT, Vol.7, Storie to Soper Dempster, 10 September 1807 from Edinburgh.

43 Richard Barré Dunning was the second son of John, the first Baron Ashburton (1731–1783) who had married Elizabeth, daughter of John Baring of Larkbear in Devonshire in 1780. Their first son, John, died before his father and Richard succeeded as the second Baron Ashburton, marrying Ann Cunningham Lainshaw in 1805. He died without issue at Friar's Hall, Roxburghshire in 1823.

44 In 1817 Lord Ashburton recorded that he had 'given the people (there) more work in ten years than all the former lairds of Rosehall from the beginning of time'. (UT Vol.16, 26 May 1817, Ashburton to Soper Dempster from Edinburgh)

45 UT, Vol.8, Ashburton to Dempster, 17 September 1808.

46 UT, Vol.5, William Dick to Wm Soper Dempster, March 1805. Prince of Wales Island was the EIC's name for what later became Penang.

47 UT, Vol.7, A.M.Guthrie to Soper Dempster 12 April 1807 from Craigie

48 GD Letter '97', 7 March 1808 from Dunnichen

49 NAS,Thurso MSS, RH4/49/2, f.295, Dempster to Sinclair 9 December 1807 from Dunnichen

50 UT, Vol.7, Dempster to Soper Dempster, 12 January 1808. The family would have had the dangers of sea voyages on their mind. Also in January Dempster had been 'much gratified' at hearing of the safe return aboard the *Earl Spencer* of George Heming.

51 Mitchison, p.199 and NAS, Thurso MSS, RH4/49/2, f.306, Dempster to Sinclair 11 January 1808 from Dunnichen

52 NAS,Thurso MSS, RH4/49/2, f.316–317, Dempster to Sinclair 12 February 1808 from Dunnichen

53 Mitchison, p.199

54 An extract from a letter Soper Dempster had written was included in Dempster's letter to Sinclair of 12 February 1808 (f.318)

55 UT, Vol.8, Dempster to William Soper Dempster 23 February 1808 from Dunnichen

56 NAS, Thurso MSS, RH4/49/2, f.247–248, Dempster to Sinclair 21 September 1791 from Skibo

57 'Dempster thought it easy to abolish personal services. It might have been so on a small estate, but on a large and remote one there were complications. Tenants, as Sinclair pointed out in his report on the Northern Counties, were frightened at the idea of the whole rent in money'. See Mitchison, p.27

58 NAS,Thurso MSS, RH4/49/2, f.305, Dempster to Sinclair 29 March 1808 from Dunnichen

59 NAS,Thurso MSS, RH4/49/2, f.311–312, Dempster to Sinclair 18 July 1808 from Dunnichen

60 In a letter to the *Dundee Advertiser* dated February 1808 and addressed indirectly to Sir Alexr.Douglas of Glenbervie, Bart. and Dr John Willison, physicians in Dundee, Dempster refers to *Life Ferry Boats*, of different dimensions (which) would effectually prevent the recurrence of so melancholy an accident' (as had recently happened to a Ferry boat). 'Few would begrudge an extra fare, in order to cross our Ferries without danger or fear'. (Included in Thurso MSS, RH4/49/2)

61 Dempster had also addressed a letter on the subject to Mr P. La Touche in Dublin who had not replied.

62 NAS,Thurso MSS, RH4/49/2, f.310, Sinclair to Dempster (undated but certainly in July 1808). Francis Freeling (1764–1836) successively filled the offices of surveyor, principal and resident surveyor, joint secretary and sole secretary at the Post Office for nearly half a century, being created a baronet in 1828. A Bristolian by birth, he was a postal reformer and book collector. He was elected a fellow of the Society of Antiquaries in 1801. The Duke of Wellington stated in the House of Lords in 1836 that under Freeling's management the Post Office had been administered better than anywhere in the world.

63 An alternative last line was suggested, namely: 'Tho' living – to be buried There'; see NAS, Thurso MSS, RH4/49/2, f.301

64 In 1802 Henry Dundas had been made 1st Viscount Melville and Baron Dunira during the Addington administration. He retired to his family seat after an un-successful attempt had been made to impeach him in 1805 for 'gross malversation and breach of duty' whilst he was treasurer of the navy.

65 Namier and Brooke *History of Parliament* Vol.II p.355

66 GD Letter '88', 30 December 1800 from Dunnichen

67 UT, Vol.8, Dundas to Dempster, 22 February 1808 from Dunira

68 UT, Vol.8, Dundas to Dempster, 23 January 1808 from Melville Castle

69 UT, Vol.8, Dundas to Dempster, 23 October 1808 from Dunira. His son Robert was to respond to a request from Dempster in 1812 for him to intervene on behalf of Dr Ferguson's family. (UT, Vol.10, Melville to Dempster 22 January 1812 from Park Lane) This appeal may have related to the state of Ferguson's financial affairs

following his move from Edinburgh to St Andrews along with his two unmarried daughters.

70   Thomas Douglas, 5th Earl of Selkirk (1771–1820). In 1803 the Highlanders had been despatched to Prince Edward Island and Red River in Manitoba. His 200-page 'Observations on the Present State of the Highlands of Scotland' had in fact been published in 1805.

71   The *Dundee Mercury* was a short-lived publication. Started in 1805 it shut down soon after 1813.

72   Seaforth's letter later that year suggests that Dempster had contemplated using the signature *Jollygrand* instead of *Scoto-Britannicus*, but the latter was 'more apropos to the subject of his discussion'.

73   UT, Vol.8, Dempster to the editor of an unmentioned publication, 24 July 1808 from Dunnichen.

74   Dempster's letter of 5 August 1808 appears on p.8 of *Portrait Gallery of Forfar Nobles*. Balfour was born in 1767 and died in 1829.

75   The Woodfall in question was probably William Woodfall (1746–1803), a reporter on the *Morning Chronicle*, not Henry Samson Woodfall (1739–1805) as the Rev Charles Rogers claimed in *Leaves from My Autobiography* p.25. Henry Woodfall was the editor of *The Public Advertiser*, which published the letters of *Junius*.

76   Probably the factor at Skibo who had left Dempster's service in 1792 to return to the Sutherlands at Dunrobin.

77   Lord Seaforth became Lord Lieutenant of Ross-shire in 1794, retaining the post until his death in 1815. He had been a Lt. Colonel and commandant of the 78th Foot between 1793 and 1796; a Major General in the colonial army in 1802, and was a Lt.General in 1808. (Namier & Brooke)

78   UT, Vol.8, Lord Seaforth to Dempster, 16 November 1808 from Brahan

79   UT, Vol.8, Lord Seaforth to Dempster, 29 December 1808 also from Brahan

80   Thomas Erskine, 1st Baron Erskine (1750–1823), had made a remarkable fortune at the bar over a 20-year period. Usually acting for the plaintiff, he did, however, defend amongst others Keppel and then Carnan (1779), Lord George Gordon (1781) and Paine (1792). MP for Portsmouth before and after being ousted as one of Fox's 'martyrs', he was a favourite of the Prince of Wales who made him his own attorney-general. In 1802 he became Chancellor of the Duchy of Cornwall. After the death of Pitt he became Lord Chancellor in the Grenville administration, holding the post for a little over a year before handing in his seals. On 23 February 1815 he was instituted a Knight of the Thistle by the Prince Regent at Carlton House, wearing the insignia on every possible occasion, although he had rarely, if ever, been in Scotland since he went to sea as a youth of 14.

81   GD Letter '98' and '99', 6 and 18 January 1809 from Dunnichen; and p.317

82   UT, Vol.8, Sir Ilay Campbell to Dempster, 1 February 1809

83   UT, Vol.8, Lord Melville to Dempster, 23 February 1809 from Wimbledon

84   UT, Vol.8, Sir Ilay Campbell to Dempster, 20 April 1809

85   UT, Vol.11, 7 January 1809. He added that 'my friends, its readers, will easily perceive from its title the author means (it) as a companion to the Memoirs of . . . a Parish Clerk'.

86   Dempster admitted that his explanatory notes were 'more voluminous than the poem itself'. Here he referred to 'a motion made in the House of Commons anno 1783 for

granting £10,000 to relieve the wants of the Highlanders whose crops were overtaken by the early frost' and in 1788 when rain had 'soaked up and rotted their potatoes'.

87   He 'never built an Army in the Highlands but Castles in the Air' and encouraged 'his little tenants to build stone instead of mud houses'.

88   Dempster favoured landlords who provided 'long leases exempt from every servitude'

89   Dempster's motion in the House 'for building lighthouses around the Highlands'.

90   'Ulepole, Tobermory & Sleen' – being Ullapool, Tobermory and Lochbay.

91   Dempster had retired before work on the Caledonian Canal started but he was 'disposed to arrogate to himself a small share in its conception'.

92   In addition to the suggestion that Law Court judges should speak Gaelic, he propounded the greater use of circuit judges and local jurisdiction in the community as at Letham. (see subsequent comment)

93   The version quoted comes from James Fergusson, p.320.

94   Dempster explained that the Act had been passed in 1782 to gratify the Americans, and to protect the revenue from smuggling. In a separate letter dated 27 April he referred to his own habit of using snuff rather than tobacco: 'my nose costs me as much now as my mouth used to'.

95   NAS, Thurso MSS, RH4/49/2, f.323, Dempster to Sinclair, 13 April 1809 from Dunnichen

96   Dempster explained that 'it was not the first of (the) amicable disputes' with Sinclair that they had agreed between them should be sent to the *Farmers Magazine*. The piece had been entitled *Blossom the First* since Sinclair had asked to be given 'the earliest of the blossoms of his opinion of his work at the Board of Agriculture.

97   NAS, Thurso MSS, RH4/49/2, f.319–321, Dempster to Sinclair, 3 December 1809 from Skibo

98   It is not clear how long the Dempsters planned to remain at Skibo, but they may have intended to return to Dunnichen in the New Year.

99   What was referred to as the Forfar Beefsteak club appears to have been a regular gathering, with typical 'roast beef' being eaten as part of a national campaign against things French. Writing to Sir Adam in 1811 (James Fergusson p.337) Dempster referred to 'the beef steak Captain Shanks, now Admiral, cooked for us'.

100   James Fergusson p.321, Mrs Rose Dempster to Rev Samuel Heming, 28 June 1809. Rose Dempster's partner for the opening reel was Walter Ogilvy of Clova (1733–1819) who had been admitted advocate only a little after Dempster.

101   NAS, Thurso MSS, RH4/49/2, f.329, Sinclair to Dempster, 1 July 1809 from Edinburgh

102   NAS, Thurso MSS, RH4/49/2, f.328, Dempster to Sinclair, 6 August 1809 from Skibo

103   Writing to Sir Adam Fergusson in 1799, a little before the arrival of George Dempster Junior, at Kilkerran, he had asked his friend to introduce the young man to a Captain Smith of Sevenbridge 'to see what may add 4 or 500L a year to his fortune'. (GD Letter '83', 15 July 1799 from Dunnichen)

104   Such 'puddings' may have been sacks of fulmer oil mixed with dung. St Kilda's simple economy depended heavily on the birds that nested there. Martin Martin had estimated that the 70 or so inhabitants ate about 22,600 birds annually. (see Hamish Haswell-Smith, *The Scottish Islands*, Edinburgh, 1998, p.263)

105   NAS, Thurso MSS, RH4/49/2, f.311, Dempster to Sinclair, 12 August 1809

106 William Smith married Frances Coape in 1781. They had five sons and five daughters.

107 NAS, Thurso MSS, RH4/49/2, ff.330–331, Dempster to Sinclair, 4 November 1809 from Skibo

108 An earlier letter from Lord Ashburton reveals that whenever he could he used 'his boat' to go down the Firth from Invershin to Meikle. (UT Vol.8, Ashburton to William Soper Dempster, 17th September 1808 from Rosehall)

109 Jean Dunlop p.135. William Smith nevertheless had an enviable reputation for defending religious freedom. He took part in almost every debate on religious disabilities between the first attempt to repeal the Test and Corporation Acts in 1787 and the successful Act in 1828. His long speeches attracted such satirical verses as:

> At length, when the candles burn low in their sockets,
> Up gets William Smith with both hands in his pockets,
> On a course of morality fearlessly enters,
> With all the opinions of all the Dissenters.

110 NLS, MS.5319, ff.147–8 Dempster to William Smith, 10 October 1809 from Skibo. The Meikle Ferry, which was run by a James McCraw from Golspie, sank on 16 August 1809. It had been overloaded with people going to the Lammas Fair in Tain. Ninety-nine local people, including Sheriff McCulloch of Dornoch, were drowned, along with an unknown number of strangers. Only twelve were saved. The mail coach continued to use the replacement ferry for many years thereafter, but the disaster hastened the building of a bridge at Bonar. (Gillian Nelson, *Highland Bridges*, p.151)

111 Jean Dunlop, p.148

112 The late construction of the pier and storehouses, the departure of the herring in the Minch and a lack of application by the settlers to fishing contributed to the failure at Lochbay, whilst Tobermory flourished only as the result of the commercial activity the new town attracted. (See Jean Dunlop pp.149–151)

113 UT, Vol.9, William Smith writing to Dempster from Hempriggs.

114 NLS, MS.5319, f.152 Dempster to William Smith, [1 or 4] December 1810 from Dunnichen

115 Jean Dunlop, pp.154–157

116 NLS, MS.5319, f.149 (as above)

117 UT, Vol.9, William Smith to Dempster from Hempriggs (undated but before the end of October 1809). Clapham Common was the Smiths' London home.

118 UT, Vol.9, Sir Charles Ross to Soper Dempster, 26 October 1809 from Balnagown Castle

119 UT, Vol.9, Lord Ashburton to Soper Dempster, 26 November 1809. He hoped that 'Mrs Dempster's health is as well as can be after the recent event, which as the news says has taken place in your family'.

120 Dr Gregory added that 'the only probability of danger in this disease (was) from an increased flow of blood to the head . . . (and as) it would be proper to remove her hysterical symptoms and to promote more copious menstruation' he recommended heavy doses of aperient pills, stomach powder (No.2), bathing of feet and legs, progressively colder showers, moderate exercise, the wearing of flannel shifts, drawers and worsted under stockings, a diet chiefly of milk, bread, rice and well-boiled 'garden stuff' with no fat or roasted, smoked or highly seasoned meat or fish, or rich suet or plum puddings, cheese or 'much butter in any shape'. Moderate quantities of weak tea and coffee were, however, to be allowed along with no more than two small glasses of white wine per day. As an afterthought he warned against such a course of aperient

medicine if she was 'in the family way'. (UT Vol.9 Dr Gregory to Soper Dempster, 22 December 1809)

121 Wm Soper Dempster to Rev Sam Heming 27 May 1810 (See James Fergusson p.323–4)

122 UT, Vol.9, Dr Gregory to Soper Dempster, 12 June 1810 from Edinburgh

Chapter 17 (pp. 298–313)

1   GD Letter '100', 9 January 1810 from Skibo. As James Fergusson says in a footnote on p.323, Louis XVIII was a refugee in England and Charles IV of Spain and his son had been entrapped by the French at Bayonne in 1808.

2   NLS, MS.5319, f.229, Dempster to Rev Samuel Heming, 22 March 1810

3   NLS, MS.5319, f.152, Dempster to Wm.Smith, 1 December 1810 from Dunnichen

4   James Fergusson p.323, William Soper Dempster to Samuel Heming, 27 May 1810

5   Other evidence that Dempster 'was inclined to believe' was that Captain Mathieson of Shinness and two of Captain Mackay of Torboll's children had died of 'this fever'. It was creeping down the coast to within a mile of Skibo. Robert Gunn, 'a great practitioner in my neighbourhood', told Dempster that he was 'worn to a shadow running from house to house to bleed their owners' and that 'he had done more execution with his lancet than with all the arms (he had used) in his thirty years service' (as an old army sergeant).

6   NAS, Thurso MSS, RH4/49/2 ff.338–341 Dempster to Sinclair, 7 April [1810] from Skibo

7   Dr J.C.Smyth, physician extraordinary to George III had been sent down to Winchester by the Committee and had produced a learned treatise on 'purifying hospitals' (according to Dempster's letter).

8   A Charter under the Great Seal in favour of Mrs Harriet Dempster of Skibo had given her possession of the lands and Barony of Skibo in 1803 and the sasines recorded that 'the pursuer, George Dempster,' had been 'served heir of taillie'. (P.3 of Dempster's summons against Gilchrist, UT Vol.10, February 1812)

9   They included such marches as those in the vicinity of Cyderhall and the River Evelix, the upper east corner of Ospisdale woods and Rearquar, Beinn Domhnaill and Loch Buie, Meikle Garvary, Maikle and Invershin, and the Langwell enclave in the Rogart valley where land had been disputed at least as far back as 1768. (Copy of Agreement dated 14 December 1810)

10 See Cynthia Swallow *The Gilchrist Family of Ospisdale*

11 NLS, MS.5319, f.152, Dempster to Wm.Smith, 1 December 1810 from Dunnichen

12 UT, Vol.9, Dempster to William Soper Dempster (and Harriet), 16 July 1810 from Dunnichen

13 James Fergusson p.324 Dempster to Sam Heming, 26 July 1810 from Dunnichen

14 GD Letter '101', 27 July 1810 from Dunnichen

15 James Fergusson p.324, Dempster to Sam Heming, 26 July 1811

16 UT, Vol.9, Dempster to William Soper Dempster, 26 July 1810 from Dunnichen

17 UT, Vol 9, Dempster to Soper Dempster and Harriet, 26 July 1810 from Dunnichen

18 UT, Vol.9, Dr Gregory to William Soper Dempster, 31 July 1810 from Edinburgh. It seems the doctor favoured a journey by sea: 'Mr Storie tells me that the Dundee London smacks are almost as good as those at Leith . . . the accommodation in

them . . . is very good . . . and at this season you may reasonably expect good weather and a quick voyage . . . and probably the same from London round (to) Plymouth'.

19 The tablet erected by her husband in St Andrew's Church, Ashburton, gives the date as 16 October 1810. It was taken down for reasons of safety in the 1980s. The Ashburton Burial Register gives the date of the burial as 22 October.

20 GD Letter '102', 1 January 1811 from Dunnichen

21 The inference was that Charles Boddam was fulfilling his judicial duties in India. He may have returned home in time to be at his father's bedside in 1812 when he (Mr Rawson Hunt Boddam) died at Bath. He probably died soon after. There was a bequest to him in Dempster's will.

22 Rev Charles Rogers, *Social Life in Scotland*, p.402

23 NAS, Thurso MSS, RH4/49/2 ff.357–358, being a part copy of Dempster's letter to Sinclair, 15 September 1810 from Dunnichen

24 NAS, Thurso MSS, RH4/49/2 ff.350–351, Dempster to Sinclair, 30 September 1810 from Dunnichen

25 In 1797, with national bankruptcy looming, Pitt in a single night pushed through a bill suspending payments in gold and made bank-notes legal tender so that none could demand cash for their notes.

26 NAS, Thurso MSS, RH4/49/2 ff.355–356, Dempster to Sinclair, 2 October 1810 from Dunnichen

27 NAS, Thurso MSS, RH4/49/2 f.354, Copy of Sinclair to Dempster's letter dated 7 October 1810 from Edinburgh

28 NAS, Thurso MSS, RH4/49/2 f.379, Dempster to Sinclair, 11 January 1814 from St Andrews

29 UT, Vol.9, Dempster to William Soper Dempster, 31 October 1810 from Dunnichen

30 Antaeus, in Greek mythology, a gigantic wrestler who became stronger whenever he touched the earth. Hercules lifted him from the ground and slew him.

31 The signatures included Hugh McKinsey (Elder), Thomas Logan, James Macpherson, Alexander Barclay, Alex. Gunn, and William Mackay.

32 The Rev Neil Kennedy was assistant to the minister of Urray in Ross-shire and Duncan McGillivray the missionary minister in the parish of Farr in the presbytery of Tongue.

33 UT, Vol.16, Lord Ashburton to William Soper Dempster, 26 May 1817 from Edinburgh and 9 August 1817 from Ocht.

34 UT, Vol. 9, James Guthrie to Soper Dempster, 27 October 1810 from Craigie. There is no evidence that his advice was accepted. Soper Dempster's subsequent life remains a mystery.

35 UT, Vol.9, Mrs Helen Burrington to William Soper Dempster, 18 January 1811 from Gloucester Place

36 George Tierney (1761–1830) MP for Southwark and later Athlone, Bandon Bridge, Appleby and Knaresborough. In 1798 he refused to withdraw an aspersion against Pitt and the two men fought a duel on Putney Heath with Speaker Addington looking on. Neither man's two shots hit the target. Reconciliation led to him being appointed to office as President of the Board of Control in 1806.

37 André Masséna (1758–1817) was the greatest of Napoleon's marshals. He had compelled Wellington to fall back at Torres Vedras.

38 NLS, MS.5319, ff.152–154, Dempster to William Smith, 1 December 1810 from Dunnichen

39   UT, Vol.17, Mackay to Captain Dempster, 6 June 1799, in which he questions whether letters to the Captain should be sent 'to St Andrews or Dunnichen'.

40   Charlotte Hawkins Dempster, *Manners of My Time*, p.14

41   His wife was Robert Graham of Fintry's sister. Also mentioned was the wholly impractical alternative of a visit to Ireland.

42   GD Letter '105', 6 April 1811 from Dunnichen (date corrected by James Fergusson on p.333)

43   GD Letter '102', 1 January 1811 from Dunnichen. A similar version of this verse was sent to Lord Melville on 17 January 1811

44   GD Letter '103', 18 January 1811 from Broughty Ferry

45   UT, Vol.9, Dempster to Master George Dempster, 20 February 1811 from Dunnichen

46   GD Letter '105', 6 April 1811. James Fergusson's explanation of the misdating is given on p.333.

47   Although Dempster remained an Episcopalian all his life, he enjoyed the company of many in the Kirk. His sympathy with other branches of the Christian community was the inevitable result of their pre-eminence in a community (certainly at Letham) where 'there is no one person belonging to our communion (and) it would be money thrown away to build an Episcopal Church', (From his essay to Sir John Sinclair entitled *Blossoms* included in UT, Vol.11)

48   NAS, Thurso MSS, RH4/49/2 ff.361–362, Dempster to Sinclair 14 June 1811 from Dunnichen

49   NAS, Thurso MSS, RH4/49/2 ff.359–360, Dempster to Sinclair, 23 December 1811 from St Andrews

50   UT, Vol.10, Submissions by George Dempster and Dugald Gilchrist to the Court of Session in Edinburgh

51   William Soper Dempster's son did not perpetuate the Soper name by adding it to his own. He was always referred to as George Dempster, the fourth member of the family to be so named since the 17th Century.

52   The *Dunnichen Dune Body Club* was a group of 14 aged tenants on the estate who had met in May 1811, gone to church together (where they heard 'an appropriate sermon') and afterwards celebrated their longevity with a jolly party. They were 'all found in sound health of body and mind. There were amissing six wives, 200 jaw teeth, 50 front teeth, seven eyes, and hairs innumerable'. (James Fergusson's bicentenary article *Honest George* from *The Scots Magazine* in 1933, p.208 and GD Letter '106', 17 September 1811 from Dunnichen)

53   UT, Vol.10, Dempster to William Soper Dempster, 12 June 1812 from St Andrews

54   GD Letter '106', 17 September 1811 from Dunnichen

55   GD Letter '107', 6 January 1812 from St Andrews

56   UT, Vol.10, William Smith to Dempster, 17 March 1812 from London. During the parliament of 1812 he bought Parndon House and its estate in Essex whilst retaining his town house.

57   NAS, Thurso MSS, RH4/49/2 ff.366–368, Dempster to Sinclair, 1 May 1812 from Dunnichen

58   NAS, Thurso MSS, RH4/49/2 f.368, Dempster to Sinclair, 1 May 1812 from Dunnichen

59   UT, Vol.11, Dempster to William Soper Dempster (and enclosure), 17 September 1812 from Dunnichen

60   Graham of Fintry met Burns at Blair Castle in 1788, a year or so after he had been appointed a Commissioner of Excise. Through Fintry's intervention Burns obtained

a commission as an officer of the excise which according to Henry Grey Graham in *Scottish Men of Letters* pp.407–412 'he retained in case of emergency'. Burns complained bitterly that 'I am now a poor rascally gauger (one who gauged casks of spirits), with a salary of £35, condemned to gallop 200 miles every week, to inspect dirty yards and yeasty barrels'. When his sympathies with the French Revolution and his outspoken opinions later combined to threaten him with dismissal, and his family with destitution, he sought Fintry's intervention again 'to save me from that misery which threatens me, and which – with my latest breath – I will say I have not deserved'. The matter nevertheless died of its own accord. In 1793 Burns sent Fintry an inscribed copy of three volumes of his poetry as a token of his gratitude.

61 These Burns quotations were from *The Author's Ernest Cry and Prayer to the Scotch Representatives in the House of Commons* and *The Vision*.

62 Elizabeth Harvey Wood interestingly speculates on how Burns might have come to this conclusion since, when Burns first published this poem in the Kilmarnock edition, he was a young man with little experience outside his own native county of Ayr. This made his knowledge of Dempster's reputation more significant. An assumption might be that he had heard of it through Sir Adam Fergusson at Kilkerran.

63 The petition by Rev John Cleland was against Lord Balgray's Interlocutor. (see UT, Vol.11 for printed law papers)

64 UT, Vol.10, Dempster to William Soper Dempster, 12 June 1812 from St Andrews

65 John Pinkerton appears to have moved from Knightsbridge where he lived between 1784 and 1789. (See Elizabeth Harvey Wood, Vol.1 p.178–210, which provides much of the background to these events). At this time he was living in London with a woman referred to by Thorkelin as 'Mrs Pinky'.

66 *The Literary Correspondence of John Pinkerton* I, p.239 Dempster to Pinkerton, 25 November 1789 (Harvey Wood Vol.1 p.193)

67 His works dealt with old Scottish poetry, numismatology, hagiology, iconography, history, geography, petrology, orthography, verse and drama. (Harvey Wood Vol.1 p.178)

68 *The Literary Correspondence of John Pinkerton*, II, p.403 (Harvey Wood Vol.1 p.196)

69 After lengthy visits to various acquaintances among the Scottish nobility he was back in Edinburgh by November 1813 soliciting Dempster's help to obtain employment in the Register House under Lord Frederick Campbell without success. (Harvey Wood Vol.1 p.199)

70 Rev Charles Rogers, *Leaves from My Autobiography*, p.23

71 GD Letter '99', 18 January 1809 from Dunnichen

72 A Mr R.P.Gillies with whom Pinkerton stayed near Fortrose in the summer of 1813 used this nickname in his correspondence. (Harvey Wood Vol.1 p.198)

73 Rev Charles Rogers, *Leaves from My Autobiography*, p.23 and p.61 of *A century of Scottish Life*

74 UT, Vol.10, Dempster to William Soper Dempster, 24 June 1812 from Broughty Ferry. Lord Duncan, brother-in-law of James Fergusson (Sir Adam's nephew), was a frequent visitor and 'pleasanter guests I never had under my roof. I could have nail'd them to my floor'. (GD Letter '97')

75 UT, Vol.11, Dempster to William Soper Dempster, 17 September 1812 from Dunnichen.

76 UT, Vol.11, Elizabeth, Countess of Sutherland to William Soper Dempster, 5 August 1812 from Dunrobin

77 R.Southey, *Journal of a Tour in Scotland in 1819*, 1929

78 NLS, MS.5319, ff.163–164, Dempster to William Smith, 13 October 1814, contains a reference to Dempster's marble cutter waiting for the number of bridges, and miles of roads Smith's committee 'had been assisting in making'. He had been frustrated by the names of several gentlemen being put forward unbeknown to him. His own accreditation read(s) simply: 'This stone was placed here by George Dempster of Dunnichen in the year 1815'.

Chapter 18 (pp. 314–326)

1 James Fergusson p.340

2 GD Letter '109', 6 February 1813, from Broughty Ferry

3 GD Letter '108', 14 January 1813 from St Andrews

4 PS to GD Letter '108', 14 January 1813 from St Andrews

5 As Dempster said, it was the late Lord John Cavendish who had referred to the need for the colonists to attain their majority and 'Go and be happy'. Nations were only 'brave in proportion as they are free'.

6 NLS, MS.5319, ff.155–9, Dempster to William Smith, 5 April 1813 from Broughty Ferry

7 NLS, MS.5319, ff.157v–158v, Dempster to Miss Smith, July 1813 from St Andrews

8 Among whom were Wilberforce and Thomas Clarkson (1760–1846). The latter had written *A Portraiture of Quakerism* in 1806 and a two-volume *History of the Rise, Progress and Accomplishment of the Abolition of the African Slave Trade by the British Parliament* in 1808.

9 UT, Vol.11, William Smith to Dempster, 27 July 1813 from Parndon. Sir William Jones, a judge of the supreme court in India, had founded the Asiatic Society as a centre for studying religion and law in 1783.

10 NAS, Thurso MSS, RH4/49/2 ff.369–371, Dempster to Sinclair, 18 June 1813 from St Andrews

11 NAS, Thurso MSS, RH4/49/2 f.373, Dempster to Sinclair, 13 April 1813 from Dunnichen

12 Louis Simond 's *Journal of a Tour and Residence in Great Britain during 1810 and 1811*

13 In this reference, made in 1813, Dempster pitched the margin a good deal lower than was in fact the case, but the point was still valid. (See Chapter 10)

14 Sinclair's appointment as Cashier to the Scottish Board of Excise necessitated his leaving the House of Commons and handing on his seat to his son George. Overspending and inadequate attention to his Caithness estates had led to debts amounting to £60,000. The price paid by Horne for Langwell was said by Mitchison to be 'nominal'.

15 UT, Vol.11, 15 July 1813, James Guthrie to William Soper Dempster from Craigie

16 UT, Vol.15, 30 September 1813, Lord Sidmouth to Dempster from Whitehall

17 Dalrymple *Private Annals of My Own Time* p.29

18 GD Letter '109', 6 February 1813 from Broughty Ferry

19 James Fergusson (1765–1838) had been a junior partner with Fergusson and Fairlie in Calcutta until his return to Scotland in 1799 and his subsequent marriage.

20 Dempster to James Fergusson, 28 December 1813 from *Ayrshire Archaeological & National History Society Collections 1947–1949*, Second Series, vol.1.p.150. The Ayrshire journal contains a belated reference to Agnes Augusta Dempster's marriage on p.149.

21 James Fergusson *Lowland Lairds*

22 NAS, Thurso MSS.RH4/49/2 ff.374–375 Sinclair to Dempster, 15 January 1814; also f.376 – a copy of a letter to the editor of the *Dundee Mercury* dated 19 December 1813.

23 Chamber's *Eminent Scotsmen*, London 1875 Vol.1 p.442

24 Part of Dempster's facetious epitaph mentioned by Charles Rogers in *Boswelliana* p.34.

25 The Rev James Roger told the two tales in *A Century of Scottish Life* p.59. The barber was probably Dr Andrew Bell's father.

26 UT, Vol.7 Dempster to Soper Dempster December 1807 from Dunnichen

27 James Fergusson p.325; Dempster and others in correspondence at this time spell the previous minister's name as 'Masson'.

28 The first *Statistical Account* for Dunnichen, p.422 gives the stipend as 'about £70 a year, paid chiefly in oat-meal and barley, besides a glebe of four arable acres, and two acres of grass ground'. It had increased to £90 a year by the time of the dispute.

29 Unfortunately this letter of Dempster's is not available. It was referred to in Rev Dr Hill's letter of 19 November 1814 (NLS, MSS 3450, f106).

30 NLS, MS. 3450, f102–3 Dr John Lee to the Rev Dr Hill, St Andrews 13 October 1814

31 NLS, MS. 3450, f104 from Mr Dallas, Edinburgh 18 November 1814.

32 NLS, MS. 3450, f106 Dr John Lee to the Rev Dr Hill, St Andrews 19 November 1814

33 NLS, MS. 3450, ff134–5 James Headrick to Dr John Lee, St Andrews 22 June 1816

34 James Fergusson p.344 Robert Jamieson may well have been the Letham inhabitant mentioned in Chapter 13.

35 NLS, MS. 5319, ff.163–164, Dempster to William Smith, 13 October 1814 from Dunnichen

36 When Dempster left parliament he was succeeded by Captain George Murray of Pitkaithly. David Scott of Dunninald was elected in April 1796 and followed on his death by Sir David Wedderburn of Ballindean in 1805. Archibald Campbell of Blythswood followed in July 1818.

37 Dempster to Mr Hope, 30 August 1815 from Dunnichen (Boyle Archive)

38 Rogers's *A Century of Scottish Life*, pp.93–95. An account of the Musomanik Society of Anstruther appeared in *Chambers's Edinburgh Journal* in July 1840.

39 Graham *Scottish Men of Letters*, p.121

40 Helen, his remaining sister, was living at Gloucester Place in London and would not die until 1831 aged over 90, and the only other member of the Fergusson family of his generation was Lord Hermand, Sir Adam's brother George.

41 NLS, MS.3615, Dempster to Lord Lynedoch 9 January 1816 from St Andrews

42 Rev Charles Rogers *Leaves from My Autobiography*, pp.23 and 25

43 UT, Vol.16, Dempster from Dunnichen to Soper Dempster at Skibo, 6 January 1817

44 Dempster's executors were James Guthrie, Charles Groomhill, Alexander Watson, William Soper Middleton. They were to receive 'all goods, furniture, plate, coins, and animals' in addition to £100 each.

45 UT, Vol.16, James Guthrie to William Soper Dempster, 23 November 1817 from Craigie

46 UT, Vol.16, Lord Ashburton to William Soper Dempster, 30 July 1817 from Rosehall Laundry

47 The whereabouts of Soper Dempster's son, George, by then 13 years old, are not recorded in the available correspondence. The anonymous writer of his *In Memoriam* written in 1889 claims that his education 'began in his grandfather's study' at Dunnichen and that he never went to a public school.

48   After Lord Ashburton refused the Rev Cameron a £27 increase in his wages, the minister promptly preached a sermon on the text 'Thou shalt not covet thy neighbour's house', proving that, in his opinion, the 'meaning of this text is confined to the bare walls of the house'. Also lost had been 400 volumes in his library and 100 duodecimo copies of *Les Amours Complettes de Voltaire* which had been locked up in a private repository. For a fuller story of this episode, see UT, Vol.16, letters to Soper Dempster dated 26 May, 2 June, 30 July and 17 August 1817.

49   UT, Vol.16, W.L.Brown to Soper Dempster, 21 February 1818 from Aberdeen

50   UT, Vol.16, the Marquis of Stafford to Soper Dempster, 26 February 1818 from Cleveland House

51   UT, Vol.16, Sir Robert Anstruther to Soper Dempster, 11 March 1818

52   Private letter from Malcolm Bangor-Jones to Mrs Prue Stokes dated 12 June1989. Bangor-Jones's research indicates that the sale of the Langwell enclave only realised £5,775 and that George Dempster's expenditure on the Pulrossie estate between 1810 and 1836 broke down as follows: £5,393 on building and repairing the mansion house, farm houses and offices; £2,391 for land enclosures and draining; £1,794 for plantations; £2,212 being the statutory contribution to road and bridgeworks; and £2,283 in respect of legal expenses defending his entailed estate and obtaining the division of Creich commonty.

REFERENCES & BIBLIOGRAPHY
Principal references consulted are listed below.

PRIMARY SOURCES

Manuscripts
Aberdeen University Library
Seton of Mounie Papers, MS.2787/4/2/9 George Dempster 1784
Birmingham City Archives
MS 3219/4/44 and MS 3219/4/118 Dempster and James Watt 1803
Blair Charitable Trust
Atholl MSS, Blair Castle 25/9/1 *Considerations on the Cotton Manufacture*
Atholl MSS, 42.II (5) 24 and 49 (7)3 regarding the Order of the Thistle
Atholl MSS, 65/5/171 Wilhelmina Murray to her husband 1786
Bodleian Library, Oxford
Bland Burges 18, ffs.55–6,153, 160, Dempster to Sir James Bland Burges 1789–90
Bland Burges 47, page 125 Burges to Dempster, December 1790
MS Montagu d.7, fols. 34–37v, Dempster to T. Cadell 1781
British Library
(Oriental & India Office Collections):
L/MAR/B/59 Journal of the *Rose's* three voyages in 1786/88, 1788/90 and 1792/3
L/MAR/B/86 Journal of the *Ganges* 1782/5 voyage
Haileybury Records, J/1/10, ff.89–92
East India Register and Directory 1803–6
(Western MS):
Add MS 22091, f.154 Dempster to George Chalmers 1803
Add MS 29133, f.533 Sulivan to Hastings 1772
Add MS 29143, f.247 Sulivan to Hastings 1779
Add MS 38211, f.181–2; 38212, f.203; 38221, f.227; 38222, ff.30–35 and 36–47; 38306, f.165; 38308, f.111; 38309, f.142 and 38311, ff.55–56, 57–68 (1779, 1781 and 1800), Charles Jenkinson, 1st Earl of Liverpool
Add MS 32923 and 32939, Newcastle Papers 1761
Dulwich College, London S.E.21
MS. XCVIII, f.130 – Charles Fergusson
Dundee Central Library
Account Book of George Dempster (1678–1753) for 1736–1753
Dundee Council Minute Book Vol.10 1756–67 and later volumes
Dundee Old Parochial Register
Edinburgh University Library [EUL]

Laing MSS, La.III.379 Dempster to Grimur Jonsson Thorkelin 1787–1807
Ms.Dc.4.41 Dempster to Alexander Carlyle
La.II.37 Professor Charles Mackie's Class List 1746–53
Glasgow University Library
MSS Gen 1035/165, Dempster to Adam Smith, 1783
Caledonian Mercury No 10083
Huntington Library Collection, San Marino, California [HLC]
Dempster letters to Sir William Pulteney 1761- c.1786 (PU 135–181)
John Johnstone's letters to Sir William Pulteney 1767–1785 (PU 624–667)
Government of Maharashtra, Department of Archives [GMA]
Correspondence between Bombay Castle and the Honourable Court of Directors of the
    East India Company
Jonathan Duncan's Despatches 1799–1802
Political Department and Secret Committee Papers 1800, 1801, 1802 & 1804
General Department Minute Books, Vols.12 and 13, 1800
Marine Board Diaries 1799 to 1804
Surat Factory Diary No.39 Part III, 1800
Bombay Courier 1801–5
The National Archives (Kew)
SP54/48/18 & 97 Dempster to Lord Stormont
The National Archives of Scotland [NAS]
CS 112/69 Inglis and Cartier vs Creditors of Gray of Skibo, February 1788
RS3/441, ff.201v – 207r, Sasine
RH4/119/11/8 Dempster to Robert Graham of Fintry (148 letters)
Gilchrist of Ospisdale MSS GD153, Personal & Estate Correspondence
PRO 11/1610/502 and PRO 12/209/1818 Dempster's Will
Thurso Papers RH4/49/2, ff.217r & v and 237 – 377 Dempster and Sir John Sinclair
National Library of Scotland [NLS]
Melville Papers MS.1030, ff1–4 Dempster to Henry Dundas
Melville Papers MS.1055, ff 169–172 Dempster to Henry Dundas
Milton Papers MS. 16714, f.219 Dempster from St Andrews, September 1760
Adv.MSS 23.1.1. Minutes of the Select Society
S.274 The Geddie and Mackintosh Complaint,
Mc 478 W.T.Johnston, Dempster on Agriculture, Sgann Microforms, Edinburgh 1983
RB. S. 1302 (5), Dempster on the Militia Acts
MS. 59 pp.206–7 Robert Dundas and Baron Norton 1809
MS. 1055, f.169 and 171 The Alexander Gilmour affair
MS. 1929, Minutes of Lunan & Vinney Farming Society
MS. 2619, Fisheries Society
MS. 3112, f.22, Dempster to Boswell
MS. 3450, ff.100–109 and 134–5, The Headrick affair
MS. 3615, f.114 Dempster to Lord Lynedoch 1816
MS. 3873, ff.120–1 Dempster to Charles Jenkinson, 1st Earl of Liverpool
MS. 3942, f.245, Dempster to Wm.Robertson
MS. 5319, Dempster and William & Miss Smith
MS. 10787, p.353 John Davidson of Stewartfield, Sir Alexander Gilmour
MS..11015, ff.62 and 73 Dempster and Sir Gilbert Elliot
MS. 16719, f.185 and 219 Dempster on the Vilant affair
MS. 16736, ff.10–11, 27–30, 38–39 Macpherson, Home and Ferguson
LC 2606 (2) Dempster to HRH the Duke of Clarence

Perth & Kinross Council Archive, A.K.Bell Library [PBR]
B59/34/63–69 and 72–76 Dempster and Civic Leaders in Perth 1780–84
MS101 Bundle 35 James Richardson of Pitfour Papers, 1786, 1791 and 1793
St Andrews University Library
Borrowers' Register 1747–1752 (LY205/2)
St Andrews Town Council Minutes 1760–72 and 1780, (B65/11/6&7)
University of St Andrews Senate Minutes (UY452/8)
Sheffield Archives [WWM]
Wentworth Woodhouse Muniments
'accepted in lieu of Inheritance Tax by HM Government and allocated to Sheffield City Council'
Dempster letters to 2nd Marquis of Rockingham 1766–1782 (Papers R)
WWM R1, 481,701, 927, 1128, 1488, 1506, 2056
WWM R133/3/1, R140/15, R117/4/9
Dempster letters to/from Edmund Burke 1767–92 (Papers P)
WWM Bk P 1, 189, 223, 864, 981, 983, 1263, 1443 and 2636
University of Toronto[UT]
Thomas Fisher Rare Book Library
MS. Coll.126.
The first 19 Vols of George (Soper) Dempster's collection of George Dempster's letters
    between 1785 and 1818 (including drawings and other papers) to and from members of
    the family, friends and associates. The original numbering of volumes has been kept.
Yale University, Beinecke Library [YBL]
Boswell Papers Series 1, 10 letters to Dempster (L 414 to L 423)
Boswell Papers Series II, c.26 letters from Dempster (C 929 to C 954)
Other Collections
Dr Iain Boyle's Private Archive of Dempster's papers (3 letters 1803–1815)
The Maitland Club of Glasgow *The Letters and Journals of Mrs Calderwood of Polton*, The
    Coltness Collections 1842

Journals
Asiatic Annual Register Vol.5 1803
Ayrshire Archaeological & National History Society, *Collections 1947–1949*, Second Series.
    Three Letters of George Dempster pp.147–151
The Bee Magazine, March-May 1792
Caledonian Mercury, April 1786 and October 1791
Derby Mercury, May 1785
Dundee Magazine, 1799
Gentleman's Magazine, 1804 et al.
Glasgow Mercury, 1784
Hibernian Chronicle 1785
Huntington Library Quarterly XVII (1953), pp.37–58 *Franklin and the Pulteney Mission:
    An Episode in the Secret History of the American Revolution*, Frederick B. Tolles,
The London Magazine or Gentleman's Monthly Intelligencer 1778
The Northern Times, December 1994 & January 1995, Brora Coal, M.Bangor-Jones
The Scots Magazine from August 1741
The Scots Magazine December 1932, *Honest George – Dempster of Dunnichen Bicentenary* by
    James Fergusson
The Scots Magazine August 1965, *Honest George* – Colin Gibson
The Scots Magazine, December 1997, *A Museum with a Difference* – Douglas M. Scott

Scottish Historical Review Vol XLI, April 1962, L.W.Sharp *Charles Mackie, the First Professor of History at Edinburgh University*

Textile History, 26(1), pp. 89–94, 1995, *Cotton and the Scottish Highland Clearances - the Development of Spinningdale 1791–1806*, Anthony J.Cooke

Yale University Library Gazette, *A Note on the Franklin-Deane Mission to France*, Vol II April 1928

Published Books & Booklets

ADAM, R.J. *Sutherland Estate Management Papers*, Scottish History Society, 1972 (2 volumes)

ALLARDYCE, Alexander (Editor), *Scotland and Scotsmen in the Eighteenth Century - from the MSS of John Ramsay Esq. of Ochtertyre* Two Volumes, Blackwood, 1888

ANDERSON, James, *An Account of the Present State of the Hebrides and Western Coasts of Scotland* Edinburgh 1785

BRADY, Frank and Frederick POTTLE (Editors), *Boswell in Search of a Wife 1766–1769*, 1957

CARLYLE, Alexander, *Anecdotes and Characters of the Times*, London, 1973 (introduced by James Kinsley)

COLE, Richard C (Editor), *The General Correspondence of James Boswell 1766–1769*. Two volumes. EUP/Yale University Press, 1993 and 1997

CONNELL, Brian, *Portrait of a Whig Peer, the Second Viscount Palmerston (1739–1802)*, Andre Deutsch, 1957

COOKE A. J., (Editor), *Stanley, Its History and Development*, Dundee, 1977

COTTON, Sir Evan (Edited by Sir Charles Fawcett) *East Indiamen – The East India Company's Maritime Service*, The Batchworth Press, 1949

DALRYMPLE, Christian, *Private Annals of My Own Time (1765–1812)* Edinburgh, 1914

DEAS, Ann Izard (Editor), *Correspondence of Mr Ralph Izard of South Carolina from the Year 1774 to 1808*, Charles S.Francis & Co. New York, 1844

DEMPSTER, George, *Reasons for Extending the Militia Acts to the Disarmed Counties of Scotland*, Edinburgh, 1760 (NLS)

DEMPSTER, George, *Discourse to the Society for extending the Fisheries and improving the Sea Coasts of Great Britain*, London, 1789

DEMPSTER, George, *An Account of the Magnetic Mountain of Cannay, in Archaeologia Scotica*, 1792

DEVENISH, Robert J. (and Charles H. McLaughlin), *Historical & Genealogical Records of the Devenish Families of England and Ireland, Chicago*, 1948

FERGUSSON, James, (Editor), *Letters of George Dempster to Sir Adam Fergusson 1756–1813 – with some account of his life*, Macmillan, 1934

GORDON, Iain, *Soldier of the Raj – The Life of Richard Purvis 1789–1868* Leo Cooper 2001

HANSARD, T.C., *The Parliamentary History of England*, London 1813, Vol.15 (1753–65) to Vol.28 (1789–91)

HARDY, Charles, *Register of Ships employed by the East India Company 1760–1810*, London, 1810 (with revisions by Horatio Charles Hardy, his son)

HAWKINS DEMPSTER, Charlotte, Louisa, *The Manners of My Time*, (edited by Alice Knox), Grant Richards, 1920

LANG, Andrew, Munro, *A Life of George Dempster, Scottish M.P. of Dunnichen (1732–1818)*, The Edwin Mellen Press, October 1998

LAPRADE, Dr.William, Thomas (Editor), *Parliamentary Papers of John Robinson 1774–1784*, Royal History Society, 1922

LEVESON-GOWER, George, first Duke of Sutherland (1758–1833) *Despatches*, 1885

MACINTOSH, George, *Biographical Memoir of the late Charles Macintosh FRS*, Glasgow, 1847

MARTIN, Peter, *A Life of James Boswell*, Weidenfeld & Nicolson, London 1999

MURRAY, A.C., *The Five Sons of Bare Betty*, John Murray, London, 1938

NAMIER and BROOKE, *The History of Parliament – The House of Commons 1754–1790*, 3 Vols. HMSO, 1964

PHILIPS, Richard (Editor), *Public Characters of 1809–10*, London, 1810

PHILIPS, C.H., *The East India Company 1784–1834*, Manchester University Press, 1940

POTTLE, Professor Frederick A. (Editor), *Boswell in Holland 1763–1764*, Heineman, 1952

POTTLE, Professor Frederick A. (Editor), *Boswell's London Journal 1762–63*, Yale University Press 1992 edition and Heineman 1950 edition

REID, Rev. H.M.B., *The Kirk above Dee Water*, Castle Douglas 1895

ROGERS, Rev. Charles, *Social Life in Scotland from Early to Recent Times*, 3 vols., 1884

ROGERS, Rev. Charles, *A Century of Scottish Life: Memorials and Recollections of Historical and Remarkable Persons with Illustrations of Caledonian Humour*, Edinburgh, 1871

ROGERS, Rev. Charles, *Leaves from My Autobiography*, London, 1876

SELKIRK, Earl of, *Observations on the Recent State of the Highlands* 2nd Edition, Edinburgh 1806

SINCLAIR, Sir John, Bart., *The Correspondence of the Right Honourable Sir John Sinclair, Bart.*, 2 vols, London, 1831

SINCLAIR, Sir John, Bart., *History of Public Revenue*, 1789–90

SINCLAIR, Rev. John, *Memoirs of the Life & Works of Sir John Sinclair*, 2 vols., 1837

SOPER DEMPSTER, George, *George Dempster of Skibo – In Memoriam*, Privately Printed 1889

SOUTHEY, Robert, *The Life of the Rev. Andrew Bell*, London, 1844, 3 volumes

SPENCER, Alfred (Editor), *Memoirs of William Hickey*, 4 Vols., London 1914 – 1925

SWALLOW, Cynthia, *The Gilchrist Family of Ospisdale*, Dornoch, 1998

WAIN, John. (Editor), *The Journals of James Boswell (1762–1795)*, Mandarin, 1991

WILLIAMSON, Dr. George C., *Andrew & Nathaniel Plimer*, Bell, London 1903

WIMSATT Jnr., Professor, and Professor Frederick A. POTTLE (Editors), *Boswell for the Defence 1769–1774*, Heinemann 1960

WRIGHT, J. (Editor), *Sir Henry Cavendish's Debates of the House of Commons during the thirteenth Parliament of Great Britain* 2 vols, London, 1841

WURTZBURG, C.E., *Raffles of the Eastern Isles*, Hodder and Stoughton, 1954

SECONDARY SOURCES

Unpublished Academic Theses

CALDER, Sinclair B., *The Industrial Archaeology of Sutherland – a Scottish Highland Economy 1700–1900* (2 vols – University of Strathclyde 1972)

FERGUSON, W., *Electoral Law and Procedure in 18th Century Scotland* – Glasgow University Ph.D in 1957

HARVEY WOOD, Elizabeth H. *Letters to an Antiquary – The Literary Correspondence of G.J. Thorkelin (1752–1829)*, Ph.D Thesis 1972, 2 volumes, University of Edinburgh

PARKER, James Gordon, *The Directors of the East India Company*, Ph.D Thesis 1977, University of Edinburgh

THOMAS, P.G.D, *The Debates of the House of Commons 1768–1774*, London University Thesis 1958

STEEL, David I. A., *The Linen Industry of Fife in the later Eighteenth and Nineteen Centuries*, Ph.D Thesis 1975, University of St Andrews

Published Books

ADAM SMITH, Janet, *Life among the Scots*, Collins, 1946

ADAMS, Ian and Meredyth SOMERVILLE, *Cargoes of Despair and Hope*, John Donald, Edinburgh 1993

BALDWIN, John R. (Editor), *Firthlands of Ross and Sutherland*, 1986

BEATON, Elizabeth, *Sutherland – An Illustrated Architectural Guide*, The Rutland Press, 1995

De La BERE, Brigadier Sir Ivan, *The Queen's Orders of Chivalry*, Spring Books, London, 1964

BOULGER, D.C. *The Life of Sir Stamford Raffles* 1897, Charles Knight & Co, Ltd published an edition in 1973

BOASE, Charles, *A Century of Banking in Dundee; being the Annual Balance Sheets of the Dundee Banking Company from 1764–1864*, 1867

BROADIE, Alexander (Editor), *The Scottish Enlightenment* – an anthology, Edinburgh, 1997

CALDER William, *The Estate and Castle of Skibo*, Edinburgh, 1949

CAMPBELL, J.L., *Canna, The Story of a Hebridean Island*, Cannongate Press, 3rd Edition 1994

CANNON, John, *The Fox-North Coalition: Crisis of the Constitution, 1782–4*, Cambridge, 1969

CANT, Ronald Gordon, *The University of St Andrews*, 1992 (and Appendix E)

CHALMERS, Robert (Editor), *A Biographical Dictionary of Eminent Scotsmen*, Blackie and Son, Glasgow, 1853,

CHAMBERS, Robert, *Domestic Annals of Scotland*, 3 vols. Edinburgh 1858–61

CHECKLAND, S.G. *Scottish Banking – A History 1695–1973*, Glasgow 1975

DAVENPORT ADAMS, W.H., *The Story of our Lighthouses and Lightships*, Thomas Nelson, 1891

DEVINE, T.M., *The Tobacco Lords: A Study of the Tobacco Merchants of Glasgow and their Trading Activities c.1740–1790*, Edinburgh, 1975,

DONALDSON, Gordon, *Four Centuries: Edinburgh University Life 1583–1983*, Edinburgh, 1983

DUNLOP, Jean, *The British Fisheries Society 1786–1893*, John Donald, Edinburgh 1978

DURIE, Alastair J., *The Scottish Linen Industry in the 18th Century*, John Donald, 1979

DYER, Michael, *Men of Property and Intelligence*, Scottish Cultural Press 1996

(DUNDEE) *The Municipal History of the Royal Burgh of Dundee*, Dundee 1873,

EMERSON, Roger L., *The Social Composition of Enlightened Scotland:The Select Society of Edinburgh 1754–64* (In Studies on Voltaire in the 18th Century.Vol. 114, 1973)

FURBER, H. (Editor), *Correspondence of Edmund Burke, Cambridge 1965*

FERGUSSON, James, *Lowland Lairds*, Faber and Faber, 1949

FITTON, R.S, *The Arkwrights:Spinners of Fortune*, Manchester, 1989

FORBES, Sir William, *Memoirs of a Banking House*, Wm and Robert Chambers, Edinburgh, 1860

FYFE, A.G, *Scottish Diaries and Memoirs 1746–1843*, Mackay, 1942

GRAHAM, Henry Grey, *Scottish Men of Letters in the Eighteenth Century*, Black, 1901

GRAHAM, Louisa G., *Or and Sable (A Book of the Graemes and Grahams)* Brown, Edinburgh, 1903

GRAY, Malcolm, *The Highland Economy 1750–1850*, Oliver and Boyd, 1957

GRAY, Peter, *Skibo – Its Lairds and History,* Oliphant, Anderson & Ferrier, Edinburgh, 1906

HMSO, *Restenneth and Aberlemno,* Ministry of Public Buildings and Works, 1969

HASWELL-SMITH, Hamish, *The Scottish Islands,* Edinburgh, 1998

HENDERSON, J., *General View of the Agriculture of the County of Sutherland,* London, 1812

JERVISE, Andrew, *Memorials of Angus and the Mearns,* 1861

JAMIESON, John, *Etymological Dictionary of the Scottish Language* (Abridged Edition), 1867

JOHNSTONE, C.L., *History of the Johnstones 1191 – 1909,* W & A.K. Johnston, Edinburgh, 1909

KIDD, Ishbel (and Peter Gill), *The Feuars of Letham,* 1988

KIDD, William & Son. *Dundee Past & Present,* (with map) 1909

KINSLEY, James (Editor), *Alexander Carlyle – Anecdotes and Characters of the Times,* Oxford, 1973

KNOX, John, *A View of the British Empire, more especially Scotland; with some proposals for the Improvement of that Country,* London, 1784

LAMB, A.C. *Dundee, Its Quaint and Historic Buildings,* Dundee, George Petrie, 1895

LAWSON, Philip, *The East India Company – A History,* Longman, 1993

LENG, John, *The Roll of Eminent Burgesses of Dundee 1513–1886,* 1887

LENMAN, Bruce, *Integration etc . . . .Scotland 1746 to 1832,* Edinburgh, Arnold, 1878

LOWSON, Alexander, *Portrait Gallery of Forfar Notables,* Aberdeen, 1893

McBAIN, J.M., *Eminent Arbroathians; being Sketches Historical, Genealogical and Biographical 1175 – 1894,* 1897

MacDONALD, James. On the Agriculture of the County of Sutherland, Aberdeen – from *Transactions of the Highland & Agricultural Society* – Fourth Series, Vol XII, 1880

MACLAREN James (Editor), *The History of Dundee,* 1874

MACLEAN, James N.M, *Reward is Secondary,* Hodder and Stoughton, 1963

MALCOLM, J., *The Parish of Monifieth in Ancient and Modern Times,* Green, Edinburgh 1910

MARSHALL, P.J., *East India Fortunes – The British in Bengal in the 18th Century,* Oxford, 1976

MARSHALL, *The Writings and Speeches of Edmund Burke*

MARTIN, J.H., *Scarborough 1766–1866, A Century of Expansion,* North Yorkshire County Library

MATHIESON William Law, *The Awakening of Scotland: A History from 1747 to1797,* Glasgow, 1910

MEIKLE, Henry.W., *Scotland and the French Revolution,*

MILLER, Hugh., *A Scotch Merchant, from Tales and Sketches,* Edinburgh, 1883

MITCHISON, Rosalind., *Agricultural Sir John – The life of Sir John Sinclair of Ulbster 1754–1835,* Geoffrey Bles, 1962

MORSE, H.B., *Chronicles of the East India Company trading to China 1635–1834,* Harvard University Press,1926

MOSSNER, Professor E.C., *The Life of David Hume,* Clarendon Press, 1980

MURRAY, Norman, *The Scottish Hand Loom Weavers 1790–1850* John Donald, 1978

NAMIER, Sir Lewis, *England in the Age of the American Revolution,* Macmillan, London, 1961

NELSON, Gillian, *Highland Bridges,* Aberdeen University Press, 1990

NICHOLAS, Sir Nicholas Harris, *History of the Orders of Knighthood of the British Empire,* Vol.3, London, 1842

NICHOLS, John, *History and Antiquities of Leicestershire,* Vol.IV, early 19th Century.

NORRIE, W., *Dundee Celebrities of the 19th Century*, 1873

(NSA) *New Statistical Account of Scotland*, 15 vols., Edinburgh, 1845

(OSA) *Old Statistical Account – Parishes of Dunnichen, Creich et al*

OMAND, Donald (Editor), *The Sutherland Book*, Golspie, 1991

OWEN, Robert, *The Life of Robert Owen, by Himself*, London, 1920

PHILLIPSON and MITCHISON (Editors), *Scotland in the Age of Improvement. Essays in Scottish History in the Eighteenth Century*, Edinburgh, 1970

RAIT, Robert S., *The History of the Union Bank of Scotland*, Glasgow, 1930

REID, J.M, *Scotland's Progress – The Survival of a Nation*, London, 1971

RENDALL, Jane, *The Origins of the Scottish Enlightenment*, London, 1978

RICHARDS, Eric and MONICA CLOUGH, *Cromartie: Highland Life 1650–1914*, AUP, 1989

ROBERTSON, John, *The Scottish Enlightenment and the Militia Issue*, John Donald, 1985

ROSS, Charles (Editor), *Correspondence of Charles, First Marquis Cornwallis*, 3 vols, London, 1859

SCHOENBRUN, David, *Triumph in Paris – The Exploits of Benjamin Franklin*, Harper & Row, New York, 1976

SCHOFIELD, *Guide to Scarborough*, 1787

SCOTT, Hew, D.D., *Fasti Ecclesiae Scoticanae*, vol.vii, Oliver and Boyd, Edinburgh, 1928

SCOTT-MONCRIEFF, George, *Edinburgh*, Batsford, 1948

SHAW, Dr.William A, *The Knights of England*, Vols 1–2, Sherratt and Hughes, London, 1906

SIMOND, Louis, *Journal of a Tour and Residence in Great Britain during the years 1810 and 1811*, Two volumes, published in Edinburgh 1817

SMART, Alastair, *The Life and Art of Allan Ramsay*, Routledge & Kegan Paul, 1952

SMITH, Graham, *Something to Declare*, Harrap, 1980

SMITH, W.J (Editor), *Grenville Papers*, Vols 1–4, 1853, Inverness Collection

STEUART, A.F. (Editor), *The Last Journals of Horace Walpole*, 1910

STEVEN WATSON, J., *The Reign of George III, 1760–1815*, Oxford, 1960

STEWART, George, *Curiosities of Glasgow Citizenship*, Glasgow, 1881

SUNTER, Ronald M, *Patronage and Politics in Scotland, 1707–1832*, Edinburgh, 1986

SUTHERLAND, L., *East India Company in Eighteenth Century Politics*, Oxford, 1952

SUTHERLAND, L., (Editor) *The Correspondence of Edmund Burke Vol.II July 1768-June 1774*

SUTTON, Jean, *Lords of the East – The East India Company and its Ships*, Conway Maritime Press, 1981

TAYLOR, W.S, and PRINGLE, J.H. (Editors), *The Correspondence of William Pitt, Earl of Chatham*, 4 vols. London, 1838 – 1840

THOMAS, P.G.D., *The House of Commons in the Eighteenth Century*, Oxford, 1971

THOMSON, James, *The History of Dundee*, Dundee 1874

TREVELYAN, G.M., *History of England*, Longmans, 1926

WALL, Joseph Frazier, *Skibo*, OUP, 1984

WALPOLE, Horace, *The Last Journals of Horace Walpole during the Reign of George III, 1771–1783* (2 Vols), The Bodley Head, 1858

WALPOLE, Horace, *Memoirs of the Reign of King George the Third* 4 vols. London, 1845

WARDEN, Alex. J., *Angus or Forfarshire – The Land and People*, vol. III, Charles Alexander, Dundee

FAMILY TREES

in respect of the descendants of:

Col. George Burrington by his first wife
George Dempster (1677-1753)
Sir James Fergusson, 2nd Baronet of Kilkerran
John Soper
Wm Devenish of Rush Hill/Mount Pleasant, Ireland
Richard Heming

Descendants of Col.George Burrington by his first wife

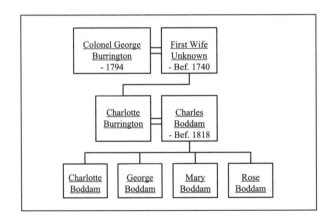

Descendants of George Dempster (1677-1753) to the Mid 1800s

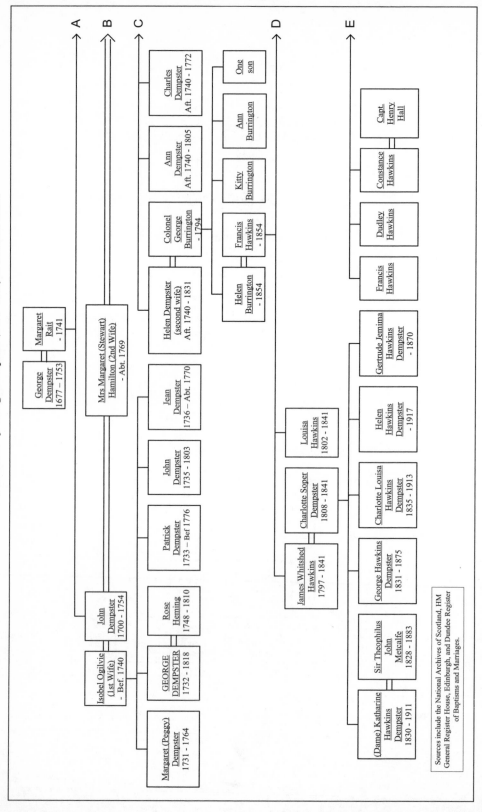

Sources include the National Archives of Scotland, HM General Register House, Edinburgh, and Dundee Register of Baptisms and Marriages.

Descendants of George Dempster (1677-1753) to the Mid 1800s -

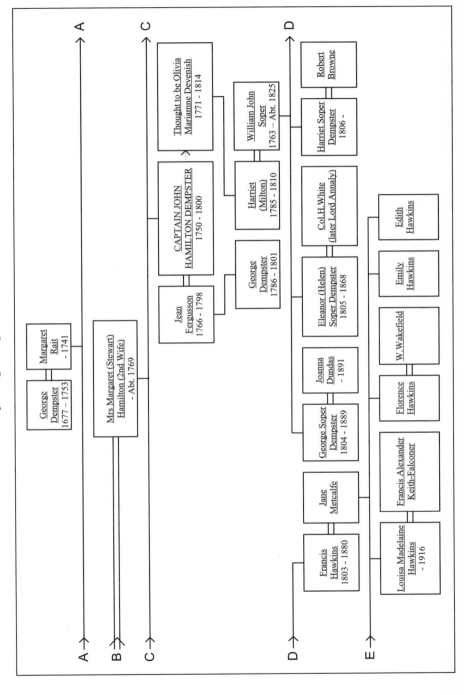

George Dempster
1677 – 1753

Margaret Rait
- 1741

Mrs Margaret (Stewart) Hamilton (2nd Wife)
- Abt. 1769

Thought to be Olivia Marianne Devenish
1771 - 1814

CAPTAIN JOHN HAMILTON DEMPSTER
1750 - 1800

Jean Fergusson
1766 - 1798

William John Soper
1763 – Abt. 1825

Harriet (Milton)
1785 - 1810

George Dempster
1786 - 1801

Robert Browne

Harriet Soper Dempster
1806 -

Col. H. White (later Lord Annaly)

Eleanor (Helen) Soper Dempster
1805 - 1868

Joanna Dundas
- 1891

George Soper Dempster
1804 - 1889

Jane Metcalfe

Francis Hawkins
1803 - 1880

Edith Hawkins

Emily Hawkins

W. Wakefield

Florence Hawkins

Francis Alexander Keith-Falconer

Louisa Madelaine Hawkins
- 1916

A →
B →
C →
D →
E →

A →
C →
D →

Descendants of George Dempster (1677-1753) to the Mid 1800s

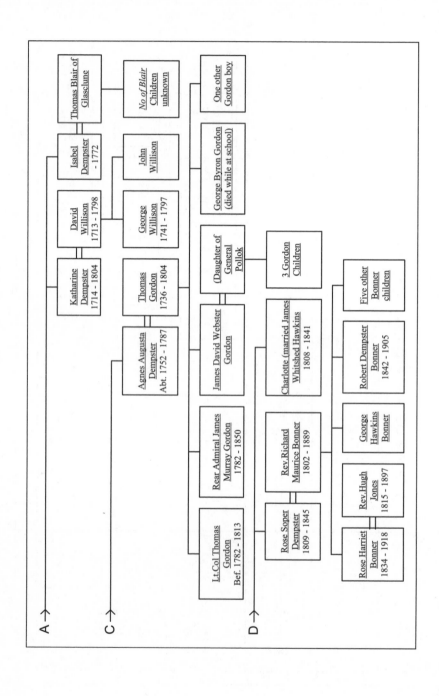

Descendants of Sir James Fergusson, *2nd Baronet of Kilkerran*

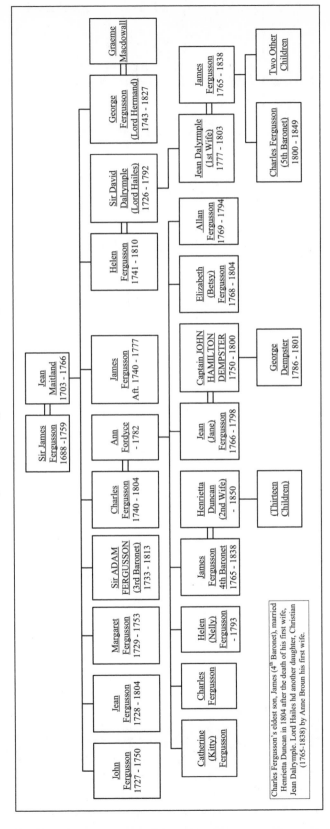

Sir James Fergusson 1688 - 1759 — Jean Maitland 1703 - 1766

Children of Sir James Fergusson and Jean Maitland:

- John Fergusson 1727 - 1750
- Jean Fergusson 1728 - 1804
- Margaret Fergusson 1729 - 1753
- Sir ADAM FERGUSSON (3rd Baronet) 1733 - 1813
- Charles Fergusson 1740 - 1804 — Ann Fordyce - 1782
- James Fergusson Aft. 1740 - 1777
- Helen Fergusson 1741 - 1810 — Sir David Dalrymple (Lord Hailes) 1726 - 1792
- George Fergusson (Lord Hermand) 1743 - 1827 — Graeme Macdowall

Children of Charles Fergusson and Ann Fordyce:

- Catherine (Kitty) Fergusson
- Charles Fergusson
- Helen (Nelly) Fergusson - 1793
- James Fergusson 4th Baronet 1765 - 1838 — Henrietta Duncan (2nd Wife) - 1850
- Jean (Jane) Fergusson 1766 - 1798 — Captain JOHN HAMILTON DEMPSTER 1750 - 1800
- Elizabeth (Betsy) Fergusson 1768 - 1804
- Allan Fergusson 1769 - 1794

Children of James Fergusson and Henrietta Duncan:

- (Thirteen Children)

Children of Jean (Jane) Fergusson and Captain John Hamilton Dempster:

- George Dempster 1786 - 1801

Children of Helen Fergusson and Sir David Dalrymple:

- Jean Dalyrmple (1st Wife) 1777 - 1803 — James Fergusson 1765 - 1838

Children of Jean Dalyrmple and James Fergusson:

- Charles Fergusson (5th Baronet) 1800 - 1849
- Two Other Children

Charles Fergusson's eldest son, James (4th Baronet), married
Henrietta Duncan in 1804 after the death of his first wife,
Jean Dalrymple. Lord Hailes hd another daughter, Christian
(1765-1838) by Anne Broun his first wife.

Descendants of John Soper

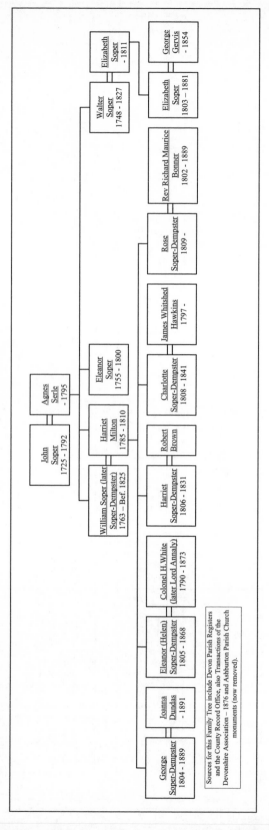

Sources for this Family Tree include Devon Parish Registers and the County Record Office, also Transactions of the Devonshire Association – 1876 and Ashburton Parish Church monuments (now removed).

John Soper 1725 - 1792 — Agnes Serle - 1795

Walter Soper 1748 - 1827 — Elizabeth Soper - 1811

George Gervis - 1854 — Elizabeth Soper 1803 – 1881

Eleanor Soper 1755 - 1800

Rev Richard Maurice Bonner 1802 - 1889 — Rose Soper-Dempster 1809 -

James Whitshed Hawkins 1797 -

Charlotte Soper-Dempster 1808 - 1841

William Soper (later Soper-Dempster) 1763 – Bef. 1825 — Harriet Milton 1785 - 1810

Robert Brown — Harriet Soper-Dempster 1806 - 1831

Colonel H.White (later Lord Annaly) 1790 - 1873 — Eleanor (Helen) Soper-Dempster 1805 - 1868

George Soper-Dempster 1804 - 1889 — Joanna Dundas - 1891

Descendants of Wm Devenish of Rush Hill/Mount Pleasant

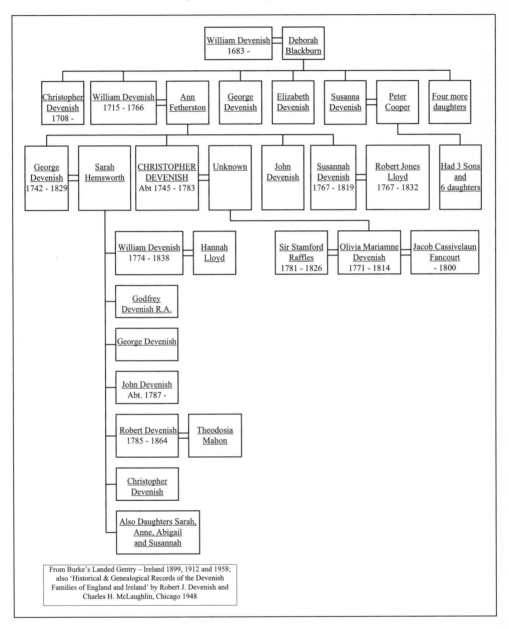

From Burke's Landed Gentry – Ireland 1899, 1912 and 1958; also 'Historical & Genealogical Records of the Devenish Families of England and Ireland' by Robert J. Devenish and Charles H. McLaughlin, Chicago 1948

Descendants of Richard Heming

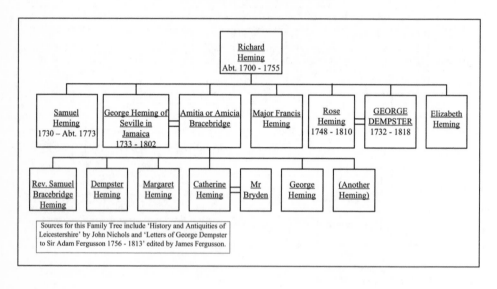

Richard
Heming
Abt. 1700 - 1755

Samuel
Heming
1730 – Abt. 1773

George Heming of
Seville in
Jamaica
1733 - 1802

Amitia or Amicia
Bracebridge

Major Francis
Heming

Rose
Heming
1748 - 1810

GEORGE
DEMPSTER
1732 - 1818

Elizabeth
Heming

Rev. Samuel
Bracebridge
Heming

Dempster
Heming

Margaret
Heming

Catherine
Heming

Mr
Bryden

George
Heming

(Another
Heming)

Sources for this Family Tree include 'History and Antiquities of
Leicestershire' by John Nichols and 'Letters of George Dempster
to Sir Adam Fergusson 1756 - 1813' edited by James Fergusson.

INDEX

Dundas, Henry, 1st Viscount Melville and
    Baron Duneira, 105, 118, 130, 138;
    supports establishment of Fisheries
    Committee, 142; 158, 193, 195, 197, 213,
    223, 254; is appealed to by Dempster, 290;
    292, 351-35, 364-24, 384-64
Joanna, of Arniston, 325
Lawrence, Sir, MP for Edinburgh, 118
Philip, Captain, nephew of Henry and
    brother of Ralph, 264, 268, 269, 272,
    273, 281, 377-12, 379-60
Ralph, Capt., nephew of Henry and brother
    Philip, 243, 264
Robert, son of Henry, later 2nd Viscount
    Melville, 298, 384-69
Thomas, Sir, of Carron Hall, MP for
    Stirlingshire, 131, 183
Thomas, Professor, 25
Dundee, 2, 18-21, 43, 45, 53, 58, 59, 60, 74,
    118, 124, 147, 161; petition from 193; 200;
    Whig Club, 208; 275; '24, 000
    inhabitants', 281;289, 329-16; boats to
    London, 388-18
Dundee Banking Company, 58, 59, 70
Dundee Mercury, 290, 319, 385-71
Dunmore, Robert, tobacco lord, 225
'Dune Body Club', the, 308, 390, 390-52
Dunnichen House and Estate, 7, 9, 11, 17, 19,
    27, 34, 35, 77, 79, 84; 'little farm-house',
    101; 105, 107; 'ever greening', 118; 125,
    131, 163, 173, 185, 191; two 'vendible'
    projects, 192; 193, 194, 204; rich crops,
    206; visitors come and go, 209; 'full of
    occupation, 212; 218; 'enlargement a
    necessity', 220; 12 degrees below freezing,
    223; a ball 'till 4 in the morning', 229; 239;
    decision to rebuild, 240; 'in the hands of
    the undertaker', 241; 255; 'moored' there
    for the rest of the season, 258; restores well
    of St Causnan, 275; 'a cheerful
    appearance', 280; a full house for the New
    Year, 285; 'cooped up' during the winter of
    1808-9, 292; Charlotte Boddam replaces
    Rosie, 301; 'the little property' had
    quadrupled in value, 303; 307; manse
    being repaired 308; library, 323; Dempster
    recommends his heirs to build another
    Dunnichen, 325; 329-4, 366-82, 374-1; a
    stipend paid in cereals, 393-28
Dunning, (see Lord Ashburton)
Dunrobin Castle and estate, 172, 173, 309,
    312, 324, 359-53, 363-56, 385-76
Dunsinnan, Lord (see Nairne)
Dunvegan, Skye, 169, 296
Dysart Burghs, 104

Earl of Abergavenny, East Indiaman, 371-29
Earl Talbot, East Indiaman, 256, 260, 262, 264,
    265, 266, 272, 310, 376-63
Earl Spencer, East Indiaman, 264, 383-50
East India Company
    Charter, 61, 71, 120, 130
    Court of Proprietors, General Court, 5, 6, 62,
        64, 68, 71, 72, 73, 78, 93, 94, 95, 236,
        343-32, 344-59
    Court of Directors, 61, 78, 88, 89; threat to
        solvency, 92; 94, 95, 133, 190, 263, 266,
        268
    Vote-splitting, 64, 66, 68, 71, 72, 337-7
    Commanders' incomes, 123, 236, 237
    Committees, 78, 89, 92, 93, 190
    Employment conditions, 79, 80
    Captains' power and perquisites, 122, 123
    Fleet, the, 122, 123, 355-37
    'John Company', 237
    East India House, Leadenhall Street, 6, 68,
        70, 71, 73, 76, 78, 79, 86, 88, 89, 94;
        meets the Company's hydrographer, 145;
        152, 243, 314, 371-31
East India Judicature Bill, 164
East India Company Relief Bill, 159
Eden, William, (1744–1814), 1st Lord
    Auckland, 131, 352-38
Edgecumbe, Lord, 45
Edinburgh Advertiser, 173, 252
Edinburgh, 29, 30, 31, 33, 34, 35, 38, 51, 58,
    75, 105, 177, 267, 281
    University of, 2, 17, 24-5, 281
Egerton, Francis, 3rd Duke of Bridgwater, 277,
    381-87
Eglinton, Lord, Alexander Montgomery, 132
Elder, Excise captain, 240, 267
Elgin, Lord, 230
Elibank, Patrick, 5th Lord, (see also Wm
    Young), 38, 54, 66, 183
Elliot, Sir Gilbert, 38, 41, 43, 45, 51, 66;
    supports a militia, 105; 333-6, 333-20,
    352-36
Elphinstone, George Keith, (1746–1823) 237,
    371-32
Emigration, 138, 144, 157, 175; from
    Caithness, 288; 290
Enfield, 238
Epictetus, Greek philosopher, 13, 98, 115, 307,
    348-72
Episcopalian (see Dempster as an)
Erith, Kent, 106, 107
Erskine, Andrew, The Hon.'Dash', 3, 50, 54,
    55, 334-30
Erskine, Lady Elizabeth, Andrew Erskine's
    sister, 331-25
Erskine, Professor John, 25
Erskine, Mr D., friend of Fintry, 182
Erskine, Lt.Gen.Sir Henry (Harry), 49, 69,
    338-25
Erskine, Thomas, 1st Baron Erskine, 3, 292,
    321, 385-80
Erskine, Sir William, 103
Eshgrove, Lord, judge, 181
Ethiebeaton, estate of, 18, 85, 329-6, 342-20
Etherington, Mariamne, 280
European Magazine, 210
Exmouth, Devon, 12, 267, 277, 372-52

Falconer, Cosmo, of Rhives, 300
Fall, Robert, merchant, 194

420

Germain, Lord George, afterwards Viscount Sackville, 94, 112, 113, 335-40

Germany and German, 31, 44, 49, 52, 84, 85, 194

Gibraltar, 116

Gilbert of Moravia, 180

Gilchrist, Dugald, of Ospisdale, 173, 182, 186, 227, 244, 250, 300

Gillespie, Captain, 241

Gillespie, William, Glasgow, 225, 245

Gillies, R.P., of Fortrose, 391-72

Gilmour, Sir Alexander, 3rd Baronet of Craigmillar, 131, 132, 352-41

Gilmour, Captain Mungo, 244, 373-71

Glasgow, 58, 59, 137, 148, 162, 222, 244, 368-45

Advertiser and Evening Intelligence, 227

Mercury, 10

merchants, 224

University, 136, 359-61

Gloucester, Duke of (15th century regent) 200

Gloucester Place, 305

Goodall, Walter, clerk to Select Society, 30

Goodwin Sands, 164, 348-71

Gordon Family, (see Dempster Family Tree)
James Murray, Rear Admiral, 232, 374-8,
Thomas, of Balmaghie, 3rd son of William; marries Dempster's sister in Funchal, 115; 126; with George in Ireland, 141; 172, 196, 207, 232; surprises Dempster by standing for parliament, 242; 273, 379-61
Thomas William, Lt. Colonel, 232
William, (died 1785), of Campbelton, 115

Gordon, Lord Adam, C-in-C of the army in Scotland, 207

Gordon, Captain Charles and John, of Pulrossie, 181, 182, 198

Gordon, Lord George, 106, 107, 116; Gordon riots, 117, 125; 385-80

Gordon, George, tenant, 233, 370-12

Gordon, Sir John, 75

Gore, Captain Arthur, 348-71

Gower, Lord and Lady, 86, 158, 172, 173, 175, 182, 186, 194; appointed ambassador to France, 208, 209; 232, 250, 253, 256; double inheritance, 277; 300, 301, 309; Countess sends Dempster her greetings, 314; 324, 359-52, 381-87 and 89

Gower Street, 223

Grafton, 3rd Duke of, 82

Graham, Ann, housemaid at Skibo, 374-16

Graham, Robert, 12th of Fintry, 8, 117, 127, 133, 139, 148, 149; buys shares in Stanley, 151; greatly in debt, 152, 154, 155; 159, 161, 197; rent roll, 182; 185; Dempster tells him he is leaving Parliament, 197; 202, 208, 222; helps Dempster with a destitute widow, 223; 240, 259; dismissed as a Commissioner of Excise, 276; dies, 310; his daughters orphaned, 322, 323; 349-89; his three sons, 380-82; 390-60

Graham, James, Marquis of Graham, 3rd Duke of Montrose, 125, 158

Graham, Lieutenant-General Sir Thomas, of Balgowan, Lord Lynedoch, 276, 310, 323, 380-84

Grant, General James, Elgin and later Sutherland MP, 251

Grant, Isaac, 181

Gratton, Henry, Irish statesman, 141, 354-8

Gray, Alexander, of Overskibo, 346-29

Gray, Captain Alexander, of the *Rose* and *Ganges (3)* 237, 246, 255

Gray, Mrs Janet, née Sutherland, 180, 183, 361-13 and 15

Gray, Miss, 233

Gray, John, first secretary to Northern Lighthouse Board, 161

Gray, Walter, 298

Gray, Captain Walter, 361-22

Gray, William, of Skibo, (husband of Janet), 180, 181

Greenland Whale Fishery Bill, 159

Greenwich, East Indiaman, 348-71

Gregory, Professor David, 23

Gregory, Prof., Dr James; consulted by Soper, 297-300; 302, 306, 307, 387-120

Grenville, George, (1712–1770), 56, 66, 68, 70, 75
Grenville, William Wyndham, (1759–1834), Speaker, later Prime Minister, 201, 383-28

Groomhill, Charles, executor, 393-44

Gunn, Alex., 389-31

Gunn, Robert, 'doctor', 388-5

Guthrie, Alexander, eldest son of James, 377-14
Charles, solicitor, 83
George Dempster, 217, 362-40
James ('Jack') of Craigie, solicitor, 163, 184, 185, 217, 264, 304, 306, 311; his skill as a farmer, 316-317; 323, 362-40 and 42, 377-14, 393-44
Rose, (?one of 'the Misses') 234, 323

Hackney, David, 268

Hadwen, Sidney, 325

Hailes, Lord, Sir David Dalrymple, 11, 30, 35, 86, 145, 173, 196, 220, 228; dies, 230; 314, 342-21, 364-20

Haldane, Captain Robert, (1705–1767), 43, 332-57

Halliburton, James, 246, 369-60

Halliburton, John, 23

Hamilton, James, 81, 341-93

Hamilton, Nanny, 20

Hamilton, Philip of Kilbrachmont, 19, 329-12

Hamilton, Dr Robert, 69

Hardinge, Captain George, 217, 367-17

Hargreaves, James, 351-29

Harley, Alderman George, MP, 93

Harriet, ship, 122, 152

Harrogate, 118, 147

Hartley, David, MP for Hull, 112, 347-58

Harvey, Eliab, 49

Harwich, Essex, 57

McCraw, James, 387-110
McCulloch, Mr, tenant and Sheriff, 363-53, 387-110
Macdonald, Flora, (1725–1790), 282
Macdonald, William, 163
Macdonell, of Barrisdale, 136
McFarlane, Mr, mill owner, 277
McGillivray, Rev Duncan, parish of Farr, 304, 389-32
Macintosh, George, (1739–1807), administrator for Spinningdale, 8, 10, 222; involved 'more from patriotic motives', 223; 224, 225, 226; estimates arrive on his desk, 227; 230, 234; confides in Dugald Gilchrist, 244; 245, 251, 271, 274; tells Dempster outcome of the sale, 277; explains failure, 277, 278; 283, 368-45, 372-35; dies, 382-24
    Charles, (1766–1843), 368-45
McIntosh, John of Swordale, 276
Mackay, the Hon.George, of Skibo, 180, 361-12
Mackay, Captain Kenneth, of Torboll, 8, 233, 239, 255, 257, 258, 269, 388-5
Mackay, Thomas, of Lairg, 187
Mackay, William, 389-31
Mackenzie, Francis Humberstone, (see Lord Seaforth)
Mackenzie, Kenneth, or Coinneach Odhar, seer of Brahan, 203, 204
Mackenzie, Professor Kenneth, 25
Mackenzie, John, of Arcan, 158
Mackenzie, John, Balnoe Co. representative, 225
Mackenzie, John Stewart, 335-50
Mackenzie, William, clerk, 203
Mackid, Robert, purchases Spinningdale, 382-23
Mackie, Professor Charles, 24
Mackie, Robert, merchant, 225
McKinsey, Hugh, 389-31
Mackintosh, Robert, of Auchintully, 73, 74, 75, 76, 339-53
Maclean, Col. Alexander, of Coll, 163, 233
Macleane, Lauchlin, 77, 340-74, 341-80
Macleod, Donald, of Geanies, 194, 203, 208, 227, 253, 364-9
Macleod, Captain, of Herries, 171
Macleod of Macleod, Col. Norman, 175
McNeil, Hector, tacksman on Canna, 172
Macpherson, James, an elder in Creich parish, 389-31
Macpherson, James, poet and forger, 56, 116, 117; Ossian, 116 and 118; 335-60, 348-82 and 83, 349-97, 383-26
Macrae, Captain James, duellist, 368-27
MacTavish, Lachlan, 359-41
MacVicar, David, 202, 208, 259, 368-43
Madeira, Island of, 115, 243
Madras, 114, 120, 122, 158, 163, 197, 222, 234, 341-94, 348-68, 354-32, 371-24, 381-6
'Madras System' of education, 315, 375-34

Maikle or Meakle, 182
Malcolm, Neil, 203
Mallet, David, 54, 335-51
Malt Tax Bill, 118
Manchester Buildings, Westminster, 56
Manchester, 4th Duke of, 104
Manchester Mercury, 147
Marble, 252, 392-78
Margate, Kent, 85, 106, 126, 365-61
Marischall College, 304
Marl, 7, 9, 103, 206, 218, 230
Marquis of Wellesley, East Indiaman, 264, 265
Marshall, Thomas, 151
Marshall, William, 231
Marsham, Charles, MP, 128, 144
Martin, Martin, geographer, 295, 386-104
Martinmas, 11 November, 182, 219
Mason, Dr Thomas, 320, 393-27
Masséna, André, General, 305, 389-37
Mathieson, Captain Donald, of Shinness, 388-5
Matlock, 129
Maule, William, Lord Panmure, 150
Mauritius, 114
Mavors, Mr, 226
Maxwell, Catharine, later Mrs John Fordyce, 331-25
Meikle and the ferry, 187, 295, 296, 312, 387-110
Melville Castle, East Indiaman, 377-12
Melville, Robert, manager at Ullapool, 194, 198
Meriton and Smith, wine merchants, 106, 107
Metcalfe, Dame Katharine, (see Hawkins-Dempster)
Michaelmas, 29 September, 247
Middleton, William Soper, 393-44
Militia for Scotland, (see George Dempster on)
Miller, Hugh, geologist, 211
Miller, Mrs, companion, 305
Milton, Harriet, (see Harriet Soper Dempster)
Minch, the, 170
Minto, Lord, 153
Moffat, William, 122, 163, 237, 246, 256, 371-33
Moira, Lord, Irish landlord, 315
Monboddo, Lord James, 30, 38
Monifieth, town and estates, 16, 46, 241
Montesquieu, Charles-Louis, French philosopher, 38
Montgomerie, Margaret, Boswell's wife, 87, 216
Montrose, town, 41, 124, 193
Moray, Earl of, 158
Morgan, Captain Robert, 122
Morison, Philip, 23
Morres, James, Deacon of the Waulkers, 74
Morrison, Roderick, factor, 198, 365-33
Moscow, 146
Mount Stephen, Lady, 381-8
Mountsinart, Lord, MP, son of Lord Bute, 105
Muir, James, 376-56
Mull of Kintyre, 161
Munro, Sir Hector, Inverness MP, 182

Rose, East Indiaman, 12, 153; sails from Gravesend, 163; second voyage 1789-90, (to Madras and Bengal), 200; third voyage 1792- 93, (to Madras & Bengal), 226; 234, 235; in sight of the mast house, 236; 237, 238, 240, 255, 371-24, 371-33, 374-82

Rose, Hugh, son of Rev Hugh Rose, 172, 186, 227; 'sagacious farmer', 359-54; 362-46, 363-54

Rose, Mr, tacksman, 270, 379-48

Rosehall House, 270, 286; is gutted by fire, 324

Ross-shire, 172, 207, 208, 224, 368-45, 385-77, 389-32

Ross, Benjamin, merchant from Tain, 225, 245

Ross, Sir Charles and Lady Mary, of Balnagown, MP for Ross-shire, 297

Ross, George, of Cromarty, 'improver', 211

Ross, George, of Pitkerrie, 183

Ross, Hugh, 300

Ross, Robert, gardener, 187

Rotherhithe, 164

Rothesay, 150

Rous, Thomas, 64

Roy, Mr James, 186, 362-47

Royal Society of Northern Icelandic Literature, 195

Rugby School, 298, 378-26

Russia and Russian, 107, 146, 168, 213, 328-36

Rutland, Duke and Duchess of, 128

Rymer, Professor Henry, 23

St Albans Tavern Group, 132, 133, 212, 352-45

St Andrew's Church, Tongue, 361-12

St Andrews, town and council, 42, 43, 45, 53, 67, 74; a 'volatile' constituency, 118; 199, 206, 266, 267, 306, 308, 309, 314, 316; 'the *route coach*', 319; 323, 339-36

University, 2, 22-24, 105, 175, 323, 325, 378-26

St Callan's Church, 360-7

St Causnan's well, renamed Camperdown well, 17, 275

St George's Hospital, 223

St Helena, Island of, 232, 234, 235, 246, 341-94, 371-24

St James's Palace, 147

St James's Place, 47

St Kilda 'puddings', 295, 389-104

St Lucia, Island of, 125

St Petersburg, 146

St Salvator's College, (see also St Andrews University), 22

St Stephen's Chapel, (see Parliament at Westminster)

St Vigean's Church, Arbroath, 26, 330-33

Sackville, Lord George, 48

Salt, laws, mines, 137, 143, 145, 202, 205, 353-69

Salt, Mr, of Newton and Fload, 182

Sandeman, William, 151, 231, 356-57

Sandwich, John, 4th Earl of, 89

San Fiorenzo HMS, 367-17

Saratoga, 110

Scalpay, point of, Harris, 161

Scarborough, 128, 129, 144, 269, 321; coaching inns, 351-24

Scott, David, of Dunninald, MP, (1746–1805) 225, 234, 380-70, 393-36

Scott, John, 23

'Scottish Locusts', 48; names, 333-20

Scoto-Britannicus, 290, 292, 385-72

Scott, Sir Walter, novelist and poet, 322

Seaforth, 3rd Earl, 204

Lord, (Baron of Kintail) 8, 158, 167, 174, 194, 198, 199; 'congeniality' 203; 204, 207, 291; 'admires Old Caledonia', 292; 385-77

Select Society, The, 5, 30, 31, 35, 37, 38, 39, 40, 41, 50, 53, 333-6, 342-27

Selkirk, 5th Earl of, 290, 291, 385-70

Session, Court of, 181, 308, 310, 321, 390-50, 377-7

Shaw, John, upholsterer, 19

Shelburne, William, 2nd Earl of, 49, 52, 124, 125; defeated, 127, 341-80

Shell deposits, 35, 186, 192, 256, 257, 375-43

Sheridan, Mrs Frances, mother of Richard, 55, 335-55

Richard Brinsley, dramatist and politician, 167, 195, 331-31, 358-24

Thomas, father of the dramatist, 37, 331-31

Shetland Islands and cattle, 249, 290

Ship-yards, ship-building, 116, 146, 206; Dempster dreams of supplying timber to the Navy, 229; 355-37 and 39, 365-64

Sidmouth, Viscount, 318

Simond, Louis, 354-8

Sinclair, Mrs Ann, 361-22

Sinclair, Sir John, of Ulbster, 8, 169, 173, 212, 213, 217, 241; launch of his Board of Agriculture, 242; 243, 247, 251, 262; in praise of Dempster, 279; 281, 284; appointed Privy Councillor, 303; resigns from the Board but its programmes continue, 317; Dempster 'flabbergasted' at his sale of Langwell, 317; 319, 328-21, 359-41, 392-14

Skene, Provost, 22

Skibo, house and estate, 7, 164, 172, 173, 177, 178; 'wretched life' on the estate, 179; history, 180; appearance, 183; 'the only habitable spot . . . I ever possessed', 184; 185; receives advice about sea shells, 186; 187, 188; 'waste lands', 199; 207; rumour about sale of the two estates, 217, 218; Dunnichen party arrive, 220; 223, 239, 247, 249; gift of trees arrives from Dr Anderson, 250; sale and purchase of parcels of land, 250; 264; George and Rose guests of Soper Dempsters, 275; 'that delightful estate', 284; 286, 288; an enquiry about the Dempsters at the ferry, 291; now 240 tenants on the estate, 295; 'ripe walnuts and luscious peaches', 295; William and